PEARSON CUSTOM
BUSINESS RESOURCES

Compiled by

ACC 312
Cost Management
St. Louis University

Pearson Learning Solutions

New York   Boston   San Francisco
London   Toronto   Sydney   Tokyo   Singapore   Madrid
Mexico City   Munich   Paris   Cape Town   Hong Kong   Montreal

Senior Vice President, Editorial and Marketing: Patrick F. Boles
Editor: Ana Díaz-Caneja
Development Editor: Abbey Lee Briggs
Operations Manager: Eric M. Kenney
Production Manager: Jennifer Berry
Art Director: Renée Sartell
Cover Designer: Renée Sartell

This special edition published in cooperation with Pearson Learning Solutions.

Printed in the United States of America.

Please visit our web site at *www.pearsoncustom.com*.

Attention bookstores: For permission to return any unsold stock, contact us at *pe-uscustomreturns@pearson.com*.

Pearson Learning Solutions, 501 Boylston Street, Suite 900, Boston, MA 02116
A Pearson Education Company
www.pearsoned.com

ISBN 10: 1-256-17575-7
ISBN 13: 978-1-256-17575-9

Editorial Advisory Board

Contents

Decision Making and Relevant Information

From Chapter 11 of *Cost Accounting: A Managerial Emphasis*, 14/e. Charles T. Horngren. Srikant M. Datar. Madhav Rajan.
Copyright © 2012 by Pearson Education. Published by Prentice Hall. All rights reserved.

Decision Making and Relevant Information

How many decisions have you made today?

Maybe you made a big one, such as accepting a job offer. Or maybe your decision was as simple as settling on your plans for the weekend or choosing a restaurant for dinner. Regardless of whether decisions are significant or routine, most people follow a simple, logical process when making them. This process involves gathering information, making predictions, making a choice, acting on the choice, and evaluating results. It also includes deciding what costs and benefits each choice affords. Some costs are irrelevant. For example, once a coffee maker is purchased, its cost is irrelevant when deciding how much money a person saves each time he or she brews coffee at home versus buying it at Starbucks. The cost of the coffee maker was incurred in the past, and the money is spent and can't be recouped. This chapter will explain which costs and benefits are relevant and which are not—and how you should think of them when choosing among alternatives.

Relevant Costs, JetBlue, and Twitter[1]

What does it cost JetBlue to fly a customer on a round-trip flight from New York City to Nantucket? The incremental cost is very small, around $5 for beverages, because the other costs (the plane, pilots, ticket agents, fuel, airport landing fees, and baggage handlers) are fixed. Because most costs are fixed, would it be worthwhile for JetBlue to fill a seat provided it earns at least $5 for that seat? The answer depends on whether the flight is full.

Suppose JetBlue normally charges $330 for this round-trip ticket. If the flight is full, JetBlue would not sell the ticket for anything less than $330, because there are still customers willing to pay this fare for the flight. What if there are empty seats? Selling a ticket for something more than $5 is better than leaving the seat empty and earning nothing.

If a customer uses the Internet to purchase the ticket a month in advance, JetBlue will likely quote $330 because it expects the flight to be full. If, on the Monday before the scheduled Friday departure, JetBlue finds that the plane will not be full, the airline may be willing to lower its prices dramatically in hopes of attracting more customers and earning a profit on the unfilled seats.

---

[1] *Source*: Jones, Charisse. 2009. JetBlue and United give twitter a try to sell airline seats fast. *USA Today*, August 2. www.usatoday.com/travel/flights/2009-08-02-jetblue-united-twitter-airfares_N.htm

Enter Twitter. Like the e-mails that Jet Blue has sent out to customers for years, the widespread messaging service allows JetBlue to quickly connect with customers and fill seats on flights that might otherwise take off less than full. When JetBlue began promoting last-minute fare sales on Twitter in 2009 and Twitter-recipients learned that $330 round-trip tickets from New York City to Nantucket were available for just $18, the flights filled up quickly. JetBlue's Twitter fare sales usually last only eight hours, or until all available seats are sold. To use such a pricing strategy requires a deep understanding of costs in different decision situations.

Just like JetBlue, managers in corporations around the world use a decision process to help them make decisions. Managers at JPMorgan Chase gather information about financial markets, consumer preferences, and economic trends before determining whether to offer new services to customers. Macy's managers examine all the relevant information related to domestic and international clothing manufacturing before selecting vendors. Managers at Porsche gather cost information to decide whether to manufacture a component part or purchase it from a supplier. The decision process may not always be easy, but as Napoleon Bonaparte said, "Nothing is more difficult, and therefore more precious, than to be able to decide."

Information and the Decision Process

Managers usually follow a *decision model* for choosing among different courses of action. A **decision model** is a formal method of making a choice that often involves both quantitative and qualitative analyses. Management accountants analyze and present relevant data to guide managers' decisions.

Consider a strategic decision facing management at Precision Sporting Goods, a manufacturer of golf clubs: Should it reorganize its manufacturing operations to reduce manufacturing labor costs? Precision Sporting Goods has only two alternatives: Do not reorganize or reorganize.

Reorganization will eliminate all manual handling of materials. Current manufacturing labor consists of 20 workers—15 workers operate machines, and 5 workers handle materials. The 5 materials-handling workers have been hired on contracts that

Learning Objective 1

Use the five-step decision-making process to make decisions

. . . the five steps are identify the problem and uncertainties; obtain information; make predictions about the future; make decisions by choosing among alternatives; and implement the decision, evaluate performance, and learn

3

Exhibit 1

Five-Step Decision-Making Process for Precision Sporting Goods

Step 1: Identify the Problem and Uncertainties

Should Precision Sporting Goods reorganize its manufacturing operations to reduce manufacturing labor costs? An important uncertainty is how the reorganization will affect employee morale.

Step 2: Obtain Information

Historical hourly wage rates are $14 per hour. However, a recently negotiated increase in employee benefits of $2 per hour will increase wages to $16 per hour. The reorganization of manufacturing operations is expected to reduce the number of workers from 20 to 15 by eliminating all 5 workers who handle materials. The reorganization is likely to have negative effects on employee morale.

Historical Costs   Other Information

Step 3: Make Predictions About the Future

Managers use information from Step 2 as a basis for predicting future manufacturing labor costs. Under the existing do-not-reorganize alternative, costs are predicted to be $640,000 (20 workers × 2,000 hours per worker per year × $16 per hour), and under the reorganize alternative, costs are predicted to be $480,000 (15 workers × 2,000 hours per worker per year × $16 per hour). Recall, the reorganization is predicted to cost $90,000 per year.

Step 4: Make Decisions by Choosing Among Alternatives

Managers compare the predicted benefits calculated in Step 3 ($640,000 − $480,000 = $160,000—that is, savings from eliminating materials-handling labor costs, 5 workers × 2,000 hours per worker per year × $16 per hour = $160,000) against the cost of the reorganization ($90,000) along with other considerations (such as likely negative effects on employee morale). Management chooses the reorganize alternative because the financial benefits are significant and the effects on employee morale are expected to be temporary and relatively small.

Step 5: Implement the Decision, Evaluate Performance, and Learn

Evaluating performance after the decision is implemented provides critical feedback for managers, and the five-step sequence is then repeated in whole or in part. Managers learn from actual results that the new manufacturing labor costs are $540,000, rather than the predicted $480,000, because of lower-than-expected manufacturing labor productivity. This (now) historical information can help managers make better subsequent predictions that allow for more learning time. Alternatively, managers may improve implementation via employee training and better supervision.

permit layoffs without additional payments. Each worker works 2,000 hours annually. Reorganization is predicted to cost $90,000 each year (mostly for new equipment leases). Production output of 25,000 units as well as the selling price of $250, the direct material cost per unit of $50, manufacturing overhead of $750,000, and marketing costs of $2,000,000 will be unaffected by the reorganization.

Managers use the five-step decision-making process presented in Exhibit 1 and first introduced in chapter entitled, "The Manager and Management Accounting" to make this decision. Study the sequence of steps in this exhibit and note how Step 5 evaluates performance to provide feedback about actions taken in the previous steps. This feedback might affect future predictions, the prediction methods used, the way choices are made, or the implementation of the decision.

Decision Point ▶

What is the five-step process that managers can use to make decisions?

The Concept of Relevance

Much of this chapter focuses on Step 4 in Exhibit 1 and on the concepts of relevant costs and relevant revenues when choosing among alternatives.

Relevant Costs and Relevant Revenues

Relevant costs are *expected future costs*, and **relevant revenues** are *expected future revenues* that differ among the alternative courses of action being considered. Revenues and costs that are *not relevant* are said to be *irrelevant*. It is important to recognize that to be relevant costs and relevant revenues they *must*:

- **Occur in the future**—every decision deals with selecting a course of action based on its expected future results.
- **Differ among the alternative courses of action**—costs and revenues that do not differ will not matter and, hence, will have no bearing on the decision being made.

The question is always, "What difference will an action make?"

Exhibit 2 presents the financial data underlying the choice between the do-not-reorganize and reorganize alternatives for Precision Sporting Goods. There are two ways to analyze the data. The first considers "All revenues and costs," while the second considers only "Relevant revenues and costs."

The first two columns describe the first way and present *all data*. The last two columns describe the second way and present *only relevant costs*—the $640,000 and $480,000 expected future manufacturing labor costs and the $90,000 expected future reorganization costs that differ between the two alternatives. The revenues, direct materials, manufacturing overhead, and marketing items can be ignored because they will remain the same whether or not Precision Sporting Goods reorganizes. They do not differ between the alternatives and, therefore, are irrelevant.

Note, the past (historical) manufacturing hourly wage rate of $14 and total past (historical) manufacturing labor costs of $560,000 (20 workers × 2,000 hours per worker per year × $14 per hour) do not appear in Exhibit 2. *Although they may be a useful basis for making informed predictions of the expected future manufacturing labor costs of $640,000 and $480,000, historical costs themselves are past costs that, therefore, are irrelevant to decision making.* Past costs are also called **sunk costs** because they are unavoidable and cannot be changed no matter what action is taken.

The analysis in Exhibit 2 indicates that reorganizing the manufacturing operations will increase predicted operating income by $70,000 each year. Note that the managers at Precision Sporting Goods reach the same conclusion whether they use all data or include only relevant data in the analysis. By confining the analysis to only the relevant data, managers

---

Exhibit 2   Determining Relevant Revenues and Relevant Costs for Precision Sporting Goods

	All Revenues and Costs		Relevant Revenues and Costs	
	Alternative 1: Do Not Reorganize	**Alternative 2: Reorganize**	**Alternative 1: Do Not Reorganize**	**Alternative 2: Reorganize**
Revenues[a]	$6,250,000	$6,250,000	—	—
Costs:				
Direct materials[b]	1,250,000	1,250,000	—	—
Manufacturing labor	640,000[c]	480,000[d]	$ 640,000[c]	$ 480,000[d]
Manufacturing overhead	750,000	750,000	—	—
Marketing	2,000,000	2,000,000	—	—
Reorganization costs	—	90,000	—	90,000
Total costs	4,640,000	4,570,000	640,000	570,000
Operating income	$1,610,000	$1,680,000	$(640,000)	$(570,000)

               $70,000 Difference $70,000 Difference

[a]25,000 units × $250 per unit = $6,250,000   [c]20 workers × 2,000 hours per worker × $16 per hour = $640,000
[b]25,000 units × $50 per unit = $1,250,000   [d]15 workers × 2,000 hours per worker × $16 per hour = $480,000

Exhibit 3	Key Features of Relevant Information

- Past (historical) costs may be helpful as a basis for making *predictions*. However, past costs themselves are always irrelevant when making *decisions*.
- Different alternatives can be compared by examining differences in expected total future revenues and expected total future costs.
- Not all expected future revenues and expected future costs are relevant. Expected future revenues and expected future costs that do not differ among alternatives are irrelevant and, hence, can be eliminated from the analysis. The key question is always, "What difference will an action make?"
- Appropriate weight must be given to qualitative factors and quantitative nonfinancial factors.

can clear away the clutter of potentially confusing irrelevant data. Focusing on the relevant data is especially helpful when all the information needed to prepare a detailed income statement is unavailable. Understanding which costs are relevant and which are irrelevant helps the decision maker concentrate on obtaining only the pertinent data and is more efficient.

Qualitative and Quantitative Relevant Information

Managers divide the outcomes of decisions into two broad categories: *quantitative* and *qualitative*. **Quantitative factors** are outcomes that are measured in numerical terms. Some quantitative factors are financial; they can be expressed in monetary terms. Examples include the cost of direct materials, direct manufacturing labor, and marketing. Other quantitative factors are nonfinancial; they can be measured numerically, but they are not expressed in monetary terms. Reduction in new product-development time and the percentage of on-time flight arrivals are examples of quantitative nonfinancial factors. **Qualitative factors** are outcomes that are difficult to measure accurately in numerical terms. Employee morale is an example.

Relevant-cost analysis generally emphasizes quantitative factors that can be expressed in financial terms. *But just because qualitative factors and quantitative nonfinancial factors cannot be measured easily in financial terms does not make them unimportant.* In fact, managers must wisely weigh these factors. In the Precision Sporting Goods example, managers carefully considered the negative effect on employee morale of laying-off materials-handling workers, a qualitative factor, before choosing the reorganize alternative. Comparing and trading off nonfinancial and financial considerations is seldom easy.

Exhibit 3 summarizes the key features of relevant information.

An Illustration of Relevance: Choosing Output Levels

The concept of relevance applies to all decision situations. In this and the following several sections of this chapter, we present some of these decision situations. We start by considering decisions that affect output levels such as whether to introduce a new product or to try to sell more units of an existing product.

One-Time-Only Special Orders

One type of decision that affects output levels is accepting or rejecting special orders when there is idle production capacity and the special orders have no long-run implications. We use the term **one-time-only special order** to describe these conditions.

Example 1: Surf Gear manufactures quality beach towels at its highly automated Burlington, North Carolina, plant. The plant has a production capacity of 48,000 towels each month. Current monthly production is 30,000 towels. Retail department stores account for all existing sales. Expected results for the coming month (August) are shown in Exhibit 4. (These amounts are predictions based on past costs.) We assume all costs can be classified as either fixed or variable with respect to a single cost driver (units of output).

As a result of a strike at its existing towel supplier, Azelia, a luxury hotel chain, has offered to buy 5,000 towels from Surf Gear in August at $11 per towel. No subsequent sales to Azelia are anticipated. Fixed manufacturing costs are based on the 48,000-towel production capacity. That is, fixed manufacturing costs relate to the production capacity available and not the actual capacity used. If Surf Gear accepts the special order, it will use existing idle capacity to produce the 5,000 towels, and fixed manufacturing costs will not change. No marketing costs will be necessary for the 5,000-unit one-time-only special order. Accepting this special order is not expected to affect the selling price or the quantity of towels sold to regular customers. Should Surf Gear accept Azelia's offer?

Exhibit 4 presents data for this example on an absorption-costing basis (that is, both variable and fixed manufacturing costs are included in inventoriable costs and cost of goods sold). In this exhibit, the manufacturing cost of $12 per unit and the marketing cost of $7 per unit include both variable and fixed costs. The sum of all costs (variable and fixed) in a particular business function of the value chain, such as manufacturing costs or marketing costs, are called **business function costs**. **Full costs of the product**, in this case $19 per unit, are the sum of all variable and fixed costs in all business functions of the value chain (R&D, design, production, marketing, distribution, and customer service). For Surf Gear, full costs of the product consist of costs in manufacturing and marketing because these are the only business functions. No marketing costs are necessary for the special order, so the manager of Surf Gear will focus

	Home	Insert	Page Layout	Formulas	Data	Review	View
	A			B	C		D
1				Total	Per Unit		
2	Units sold			30,000			
3							
4	Revenues			$600,000	$20.00		
5	Cost of goods sold (manufacturing costs)						
6	Variable manufacturing costs			225,000	7.50[b]		
7	Fixed manufacturing costs			135,000	4.50[c]		
8	Total cost of goods sold			360,000	12.00		
9	Marketing costs						
10	Variable marketing costs			150,000	5.00		
11	Fixed marketing costs			60,000	2.00		
12	Total marketing costs			210,000	7.00		
13	Full costs of the product			570,000	19.00		
14	Operating income			$ 30,000	$ 1.00		
15							
16	[a]Surf Gear incurs no R&D, product-design, distribution, or customer-service costs						
17	[b]Variable manufacturing	Direct material	Variable direct manufacturing	Variable manufacturing			
18	cost per unit	= cost per unit	+ labor cost per unit	+ overhead cost per unit			
19	= $6.00 + $0.50 + $1.00 = $7.50						
20	[c]Fixed manufacturing	Fixed direct manufacturing	Fixed manufacturing				
21	cost per unit	= labor cost per unit	+ overhead cost per unit				
22	= $1.50 + $3.00 = $4.50						

only on manufacturing costs. Based on the manufacturing cost per unit of $12—which is greater than the $11-per-unit price offered by Azelia—the manager might decide to reject the offer.

Exhibit 5 separates manufacturing and marketing costs into their variable- and fixed-cost components and presents data in the format of a contribution income statement. The relevant revenues and costs are the expected future revenues and costs that differ as a result of accepting the special offer—revenues of $55,000 ($11 per unit × 5,000 units) and variable manufacturing costs of $37,500 ($7.50 per unit × 5,000 units). The fixed manufacturing costs and all marketing costs (*including variable marketing costs*) are irrelevant in this case because these costs will not change in total whether the special order is accepted or rejected. Surf Gear would gain an additional $17,500 (relevant revenues, $55,000 – relevant costs, $37,500) in operating income by accepting the special order. In this example, comparing total amounts for 30,000 units versus 35,000 units or focusing only on the relevant amounts in the difference column in Exhibit 5 avoids a misleading implication—the implication that would result from comparing the $11-per-unit selling price against the manufacturing cost per unit of $12 (Exhibit 4), which includes both variable and fixed manufacturing costs.

The assumption of no long-run or strategic implications is crucial to management's analysis of the one-time-only special-order decision. Suppose Surf Gear concludes that the retail department stores (its regular customers) will demand a lower price if it sells towels at $11 apiece to Azelia. In this case, revenues from regular customers will be relevant. Why? Because the future revenues from regular customers will differ depending on whether the special order is accepted or rejected. The relevant-revenue and relevant-cost analysis of the Azelia order would have to be modified to consider both the short-run benefits from accepting the order and the long-run consequences on profitability if prices were lowered to all regular customers.

Exhibit 5

One-Time-Only Special-Order Decision for Surf Gear: Comparative Contribution Income Statements

	A	B	C	D	E	F	G	H
1		Without the Special Order				With the Special Order		Difference: Relevant Amounts
2		30,000				35,000		for the
3		Units to be Sold				Units to be Sold		5,000
4		Per Unit		Total		Total		Units Special Order
5		(1)		(2) = (1) × 30,000		(3)		(4) = (3) – (2)
6	Revenues	$20.00		$600,000		$655,000		$55,000[a]
7	Variable costs:							
8	Manufacturing	7.50		225,000		262,500		37,500[b]
9	Marketing	5.00		150,000		150,000		0[c]
10	Total variable costs	12.50		375,000		412,500		37,500
11	Contribution margin	7.50		225,000		242,500		17,500
12	Fixed costs:							
13	Manufacturing	4.50		135,000		135,000		0[d]
14	Marketing	2.00		60,000		60,000		0[d]
15	Total fixed costs	6.50		195,000		195,000		0
16	Operating income	$ 1.00		$ 30,000		$ 47,500		$17,500
17								
18	[a]5,000 units × $11.00 per unit = $55,000.							
19	[b]5,000 units × $7.50 per unit = $37,500.							
20	[c]No variable marketing costs would be incurred for the 5,000-unit one-time-only special order.							
21	[d]Fixed manufacturing costs and fixed marketing costs would be unaffected by the special order.							

Potential Problems in Relevant-Cost Analysis

Managers should avoid two potential problems in relevant-cost analysis. First, they must watch for incorrect general assumptions, such as all variable costs are relevant and all fixed costs are irrelevant. In the Surf Gear example, the variable marketing cost of $5 per unit is irrelevant because Surf Gear will incur no extra marketing costs by accepting the special order. But fixed manufacturing costs could be relevant. The extra production of 5,000 towels per month does not affect fixed manufacturing costs because we assumed that the relevant range is from 30,000 to 48,000 towels per month. In some cases, however, producing the extra 5,000 towels might increase fixed manufacturing costs. Suppose Surf Gear would need to run three shifts of 16,000 towels per shift to achieve full capacity of 48,000 towels per month. Increasing the monthly production from 30,000 to 35,000 would require a partial third shift because two shifts could produce only 32,000 towels. The extra shift would increase fixed manufacturing costs, thereby making these additional fixed manufacturing costs relevant for this decision.

Second, unit-cost data can potentially mislead decision makers in two ways:

1. **When irrelevant costs are included.** Consider the $4.50 of fixed manufacturing cost per unit (direct manufacturing labor, $1.50 per unit, plus manufacturing overhead, $3.00 per unit) included in the $12-per-unit manufacturing cost in the one-time-only special-order decision (see Exhibits 4 and 5). This $4.50-per-unit cost is irrelevant, given the assumptions in our example, so it should be excluded.

2. **When the same unit costs are used at different output levels.** Generally, managers use total costs rather than unit costs because total costs are easier to work with and reduce the chance for erroneous conclusions. Then, if desired, the total costs can be unitized. In the Surf Gear example, total fixed manufacturing costs remain at $135,000 even if Surf Gear accepts the special order and produces 35,000 towels. Including the fixed manufacturing cost per unit of $4.50 as a cost of the special order would lead to the erroneous conclusion that total fixed manufacturing costs would increase to $157,500 ($4.50 per towel × 35,000 towels).

The best way for managers to avoid these two potential problems is to keep focusing on (1) total revenues and total costs (rather than unit revenue and unit cost) and (2) the relevance concept. Managers should always require all items included in an analysis to be expected total future revenues and expected total future costs that differ among the alternatives.

◄ Decision Point

When is a revenue or cost item relevant for a particular decision and what potential problems should be avoided in relevant cost analysis?

Insourcing-versus-Outsourcing and Make-versus-Buy Decisions

We now apply the concept of relevance to another strategic decision: whether a company should make a component part or buy it from a supplier. We again assume idle capacity.

Outsourcing and Idle Facilities

Outsourcing is purchasing goods and services from outside vendors rather than producing the same goods or providing the same services within the organization, which is **insourcing**. For example, Kodak prefers to manufacture its own film (insourcing) but has IBM do its data processing (outsourcing). Honda relies on outside vendors to supply some component parts but chooses to manufacture other parts internally.

Decisions about whether a producer of goods or services will insource or outsource are also called **make-or-buy decisions**. Surveys of companies indicate that managers consider quality, dependability of suppliers, and costs as the most important factors in the make-or-buy decision. Sometimes, however, qualitative factors dominate management's make-or-buy decision. For example, Dell Computer buys the Pentium chip for its personal computers from Intel because Dell does not have the know-how and technology to make

Learning Objective 3

Explain the opportunity-cost concept and why it is used in decision making

... in all decisions, it is important to consider the contribution to income forgone by choosing a particular alternative and rejecting others the chip itself. In contrast, to maintain the secrecy of its formula, Coca-Cola does not out-source the manufacture of its concentrate.

Example 2: The Soho Company manufactures a two-in-one video system consisting of a DVD player and a digital media receiver (that downloads movies and video from internet sites such as NetFlix). Columns 1 and 2 of the following table show the expected total and per-unit costs for manufacturing the DVD-player of the video system. Soho plans to manufacture the 250,000 units in 2,000 batches of 125 units each. Variable batch-level costs of $625 per batch vary with the number of batches, not the total number of units produced.

	Expected Total Costs of Producing 250,000 Units in 2,000 Batches Next Year (1)	Expected Cost per Unit (2) = (1) ÷ 250,000
Direct materials ($36 per unit × 250,000 units)	$ 9,000,000	$36.00
Direct manufacturing labor ($10 per unit × 250,000 units)	2,500,000	10.00
Variable manufacturing overhead costs of power and utilities ($6 per unit × 250,000 units)	1,500,000	6.00
Mixed (variable and fixed) batch-level manufacturing overhead costs of materials handling and setup [$750,000 + ($625 per batch × 2,000 batches)]	2,000,000	8.00
Fixed manufacturing overhead costs of plant lease, insurance, and administration	3,000,000	12.00
Total manufacturing cost	$18,000,000	$72.00

Broadfield, Inc., a manufacturer of DVD players, offers to sell Soho 250,000 DVD players next year for $64 per unit on Soho's preferred delivery schedule. Assume that financial factors will be the basis of this make-or-buy decision. Should Soho make or buy the DVD player?

Columns 1 and 2 of the preceding table indicate the expected total costs and expected cost per unit of producing 250,000 DVD players next year. The expected manufacturing cost per unit for next year is $72. At first glance, it appears that the company should buy DVD players because the expected $72-per-unit cost of making the DVD player is more than the $64 per unit to buy it. But a make-or-buy decision is rarely obvious. To make a decision, management needs to answer the question, "What is the difference in relevant costs between the alternatives?"

For the moment, suppose (a) the capacity now used to make the DVD players will become idle next year if the DVD players are purchased and (b) the $3,000,000 of fixed manufacturing overhead will continue to be incurred next year regardless of the decision made. Assume the $750,000 in fixed salaries to support materials handling and setup will not be incurred if the manufacture of DVD players is completely shut down.

Exhibit 6 presents the relevant-cost computations. Note that Soho will *save* $1,000,000 by making DVD players rather than buying them from Broadfield. Making DVD players is the preferred alternative.

Note how the key concepts of relevance presented in Exhibit 3 apply here:

- Exhibit 6 compares differences in expected total future revenues and expected total future costs. Past costs are always irrelevant when making decisions.
- Exhibit 6 shows $2,000,000 of future materials-handling and setup costs under the make alternative but not under the buy alternative. Why? Because buying DVD players and not manufacturing them will save $2,000,000 in future variable costs per batch and avoidable fixed costs. The $2,000,000 represents future costs that differ between the alternatives and so is relevant to the make-or-buy decision.

Exhibit 6

Relevant (Incremental)
Items for Make-or-Buy
Decision for DVD
Players at Soho
Company

Relevant Items	Total Relevant Costs		Relevant Cost Per Unit	
	Make	Buy	Make	Buy
Outside purchase of parts ($64 × 250,000 units)		$16,000,000		$64
Direct materials	$ 9,000,000		$36	
Direct manufacturing labor	2,500,000		10	
Variable manufacturing overhead	1,500,000		6	
Mixed (variable and fixed) materials-handling and setup overhead	2,000,000		8	
Total relevant costs[a]	$15,000,000	$16,000,000	$58	$64
Difference in favor of making DVD players	$1,000,000		$4	

[a]The $3,000,000 of plant-lease, plant-insurance, and plant-administration costs could be included under both alternatives. Conceptually, they do not belong in a listing of relevant costs because these costs are irrelevant to the decision. Practically, some managers may want to include them in order to list all costs that will be incurred under each alternative.

- Exhibit 6 excludes the $3,000,000 of plant-lease, insurance, and administration costs under both alternatives. Why? Because these future costs will not differ between the alternatives, so they are irrelevant.

A common term in decision making is *incremental cost*. An **incremental cost** is the additional total cost incurred for an activity. In Exhibit 6, the incremental cost of making DVD players is the additional total cost of $15,000,000 that Soho will incur if it decides to make DVD players. The $3,000,000 of fixed manufacturing overhead is not an incremental cost because Soho will incur these costs whether or not it makes DVD players. Similarly, the incremental cost of buying DVD players from Broadfield is the additional total cost of $16,000,000 that Soho will incur if it decides to buy DVD players. A **differential cost** is the difference in total cost between two alternatives. In Exhibit 6, the differential cost between the make-DVD-players and buy-DVD-players alternatives is $1,000,000 ($16,000,000 − $15,000,000). Note that *incremental cost* and *differential cost* are sometimes used interchangeably in practice. When faced with these terms, always be sure to clarify what they mean.

We define *incremental revenue* and *differential revenue* similarly to incremental cost and differential cost. **Incremental revenue** is the additional total revenue from an activity. **Differential revenue** is the difference in total revenue between two alternatives.

Strategic and Qualitative Factors

Strategic and qualitative factors affect outsourcing decisions. For example, Soho may prefer to manufacture DVD players in-house to retain control over the design, quality, reliability, and delivery schedules of the DVD players it uses in its video-systems. Conversely, despite the cost advantages documented in Exhibit 6, Soho may prefer to outsource, become a leaner organization, and focus on areas of its core competencies—the manufacture and sale of video systems. As an example of focus, advertising companies, such as J. Walter Thompson, only do the creative and planning aspects of advertising (their core competencies), and outsource production activities, such as film, photographs, and illustrations.

Outsourcing is not without risks. As a company's dependence on its suppliers increases, suppliers could increase prices and let quality and delivery performance slip. To minimize these risks, companies generally enter into long-run contracts specifying costs, quality, and delivery schedules with their suppliers. Intelligent managers build close partnerships or alliances with a few key suppliers. Toyota goes so far as to send its own engineers to improve suppliers' processes. Suppliers of companies such as Ford, Hyundai, Panasonic, and Sony have researched and developed innovative products, met demands for increased quantities, maintained quality and on-time delivery, and lowered costs—actions that the companies themselves would not have had the competencies to achieve.

Concepts in Action

Pringles Prints and the Offshoring of Innovation

According to a recent survey, 67% of U.S. companies are engaged in the rapidly-evolving process of "offshoring," which is the outsourcing of business processes and jobs to other countries. Offshoring was initially popular with companies because it yielded immediate labor-cost savings for activities such as software development, call centers, and technical support.

While the practice remains popular today, offshoring has transformed from lowering costs on back-office processes to accessing global talent for innovation. With global markets expanding and domestic talent scarce, companies are now hiring qualified engineers, scientists, inventors, and analysts all over the world for research and development (R&D), new product development (NPD), engineering, and knowledge services.

Innovation Offshoring Services

R&D	NPD	Engineering	Knowledge Services
■ Programming	■ Prototype design	■ Testing	■ Market analysis
■ Code development	■ Product development	■ Reengineering	■ Credit analysis
■ New technologies	■ Systems design	■ Drafting/modeling	■ Data mining
■ New materials/ process research	■ Support services	■ Embedded systems development	■ Forecasting
			■ Risk management

By utilizing offshoring innovation, companies not only continue to reduce labor costs, but cut back-office costs as well. Companies also obtain local market knowledge and access to global best practices in many important areas.

Some companies are leveraging offshore resources by creating global innovation networks. Procter & Gamble (P&G), for instance, established "Connect and Develop," a multi-national effort to create and leverage innovative ideas for product development. When the company wanted to create a new line of Pringles potato chips with pictures and words—trivia questions, animal facts, and jokes—printed on each chip, the company turned to offshore innovation.

Rather than trying to invent the technology required to print images on potato chips in-house, Procter & Gamble created a technology brief that defined the problems it needed to solve, and circulated it throughout the company's global innovation network for possible solutions. As a result, P&G discovered a small bakery in Bologna, Italy, run by a university professor who also manufactured baking equipment. He had invented an ink-jet method for printing edible images on cakes and cookies, which the company quickly adapted for potato chips.

As a result, Pringles Prints were developed in less than a year—as opposed to a more traditional two year process—and immediately led to double-digit product growth.

Sources: Cuoto, Vinay, Mahadeva Mani, Vikas Sehgal, Arie Lewin, Stephan Manning, and Jeff Russell. 2007. *Offshoring 2.0: Contracting knowledge and innovation to expand global capabilities.* Duke University Offshoring Research Network: Durham, NC. Heijmen, Ton, Arie Lewin, Stephan Manning, Nidthida Prem-Ajchariyawong, and Jeff Russell. 2008. *Offshoring reaches the c-suite.* Duke University Offshoring Research Network: Durham, NC. Huston, Larry and Nabil Sakkab. 2006. Connect and develop: Inside Procter & Gamble's new model for innovation. *Harvard Business Review*, March.

Outsourcing decisions invariably have a long-run horizon in which the financial costs and benefits of outsourcing become more uncertain. Almost always, strategic and qualitative factors such as the ones described here become important determinants of the outsourcing decision. Weighing all these factors requires the exercise of considerable management judgment and care.

International Outsourcing

What additional factors would Soho have to consider if the supplier of DVD players was based in Mexico? The most important would be exchange-rate risk. Suppose the Mexican supplier offers to sell Soho 250,000 DVD players for 192,000,000 Pesos. Should Soho make or buy? The answer depends on the exchange rate that Soho expects next year. If Soho forecasts an exchange rate of 12 Pesos per $1, Soho's expected purchase cost equals

$16,000,000 (192,000,000 Pesos/12 Pesos per $) greater than the $15,000,000 relevant costs for making the DVD players in Exhibit 6, so Soho would prefer to make DVD players rather than buy them. If, however, Soho anticipates an exchange rate of 13.50 Pesos per $1, Soho's expected purchase cost equals $14,222,222 (192,000,000 Pesos/13.50 Pesos per $), which is less than the $15,000,000 relevant costs for making the DVD players, so Soho would prefer to buy rather than make the DVD players.

Another option is for Soho to enter into a forward contract to purchase 192,000,000 Pesos. A forward contract allows Soho to contract today to purchase pesos next year at a predetermined, fixed cost, thereby protecting itself against exchange rate risk. If Soho decides to go this route, it would make (buy) DVD players if the cost of the contract is greater (less) than $15,000,000. International outsourcing requires companies to evaluate exchange rate risks and to implement strategies and costs for managing them. The Concepts in Action feature describes *offshoring*—the practice of outsourcing services to lower-cost countries.

Opportunity Costs and Outsourcing

In the simple make-or-buy decision in Exhibit 6, we assumed that the capacity currently used to make DVD players will remain idle if Soho purchases the parts from Broadfield. Often, however, the released capacity can be used for other, profitable purposes. In this case, the choice Soho's managers are faced with is not whether to make or buy; the choice now centers on how best to use available production capacity.

Example 3: Suppose that if Soho decides to buy DVD players for its video systems from Broadfield, then Soho's best use of the capacity that becomes available is to produce 100,000 Digiteks, a portable, stand-alone DVD player. From a manufacturing standpoint, Digiteks are similar to DVD players made for the video system. With help from operating managers, Soho's management accountant estimates the following future revenues and costs if Soho decides to manufacture and sell Digiteks:

Incremental future revenues		$8,000,000
Incremental future costs		
Direct materials	$3,400,000	
Direct manufacturing labor	1,000,000	
Variable overhead (such as power, utilities)	600,000	
Materials-handling and setup overheads	500,000	
Total incremental future costs		5,500,000
Incremental future operating income		$2,500,000

Because of capacity constraints, Soho can make either DVD players for its video-system unit or Digiteks, but not both. Which of the following two alternatives should Soho choose?

1. Make video-system DVD players and do not make Digiteks
2. Buy video-system DVD players and make Digiteks

Exhibit 7, Panel A, summarizes the "total-alternatives" approach—the future costs and revenues for *all* products. Alternative 2, buying video-system DVD players and using the available capacity to make and sell Digiteks, is the preferred alternative. The future incremental costs of buying video-system DVD players from an outside supplier ($16,000,000) exceed the future incremental costs of making video-system DVD players in-house ($15,000,000). Soho can use the capacity freed up by buying video-system DVD players to gain $2,500,000 in operating income (incremental future revenues of $8,000,000 minus total incremental future costs of $5,500,000) by making and selling Digiteks. The *net relevant* costs of buying video-system DVD players and making and selling Digiteks are $16,000,000 – $2,500,000 = $13,500,000.

Exhibit 7	Total-Alternatives Approach and Opportunity-Cost Approach to Make-or-Buy Decisions for Soho Company

	Alternatives for Soho	
Relevant Items	**1. Make Video-System DVD Players and Do Not Make Digitek**	**2. Buy Video-System DVD Players and Make Digitek**
PANEL A Total-Alternatives Approach to Make-or-Buy Decisions		
Total incremental future costs of making/buying video-system DVD players (from Exhibit 6)	$15,000,000	$16,000,000
Deduct excess of future revenues over future costs from Digitek	0	(2,500,000)
Total relevant costs under total-alternatives approach	$15,000,000	$13,500,000
	1. Make Video-System DVD Players	**2. Buy Video-System DVD Players**
PANEL B Opportunity-Cost Approach to Make-or-Buy Decisions		
Total incremental future costs of making/buying video-system DVD players (from Exhibit 6)	$15,000,000	$16,000,000
Opportunity cost: Profit contribution forgone because capacity will not be used to make Digitek, the next-best alternative	2,500,000	0
Total relevant costs under opportunity-cost approach	$17,500,000	$16,000,000

Note that the differences in costs across the columns in Panels A and B are the same: The cost of alternative 3 is $1,500,000 less than the cost of alternative 1, and $2,500,000 less than the cost of alternative 2.

The Opportunity-Cost Approach

Deciding to use a resource in a particular way causes a manager to forgo the opportunity to use the resource in alternative ways. This lost opportunity is a cost that the manager must consider when making a decision. **Opportunity cost** is the contribution to operating income that is forgone by not using a limited resource in its next-best alternative use. For example, the (relevant) cost of going to school for an MBA degree is not only the cost of tuition, books, lodging, and food, but also the income sacrificed (opportunity cost) by not working. Presumably, the estimated future benefits of obtaining an MBA (for example, a higher-paying career) will exceed these costs.

Exhibit 7, Panel B, displays the opportunity-cost approach for analyzing the alternatives faced by Soho. *Note that the alternatives are defined differently in the total alternatives approach (1. Make Video-System DVD Players and Do Not Make Digiteks and 2. Buy Video-System DVD Players and Make Digiteks) and the opportunity cost approach (1. Make Video-System DVD Players and 2. Buy Video-System DVD Players), which does not reference Digiteks. Under the opportunity-cost approach, the cost of each alternative includes (1) the incremental costs and (2) the opportunity cost, the profit forgone from not making Digiteks. This opportunity cost arises because Digitek is excluded from formal consideration in the alternatives.*

Consider alternative 1, making video-system DVD players. What are all the costs of making video-system DVD players? Certainly Soho will incur $15,000,000 of incremental costs to make video-system DVD players, but is this the entire cost? No, because by deciding to use limited manufacturing resources to make video-system DVD players, Soho will give up the opportunity to earn $2,500,000 by not using these resources to make Digiteks. Therefore, the relevant costs of making video-system DVD players are the incremental costs of $15,000,000 plus the opportunity cost of $2,500,000.

Next, consider alternative 2, buy video-system DVD players. The incremental cost of buying video-system DVD players will be $16,000,000. The opportunity cost is zero.

Why? Because by choosing this alternative, Soho will not forgo the profit it can earn from making and selling Digiteks.

Panel B leads management to the same conclusion as Panel A: buying video-system DVD players and making Digiteks is the preferred alternative.

Panels A and B of Exhibit 7 describe two consistent approaches to decision making with capacity constraints. The total-alternatives approach in Panel A includes all future incremental costs and revenues. For example, under alternative 2, the additional future operating income from *using capacity to make and sell Digiteks* ($2,500,000) is subtracted from the future incremental cost of buying video-system DVD players ($16,000,000). The opportunity-cost analysis in Panel B takes the opposite approach. It focuses only on video-system DVD players. *Whenever capacity is not going to be used to make and sell Digiteks* the future forgone operating income is added as an opportunity cost of making video-system DVD players, as in alternative 1. (Note that when Digiteks are made, as in alternative 2, there is no "opportunity cost of not making Digiteks.") Therefore, whereas Panel A *subtracts* $2,500,000 under alternative 2, Panel B *adds* $2,500,000 under alternative 1. *Panel B highlights the idea that when capacity is constrained, the relevant revenues and costs of any alternative equal (1) the incremental future revenues and costs plus (2) the opportunity cost.* However, when more than two alternatives are being considered simultaneously, it is generally easier to use the total-alternatives approach.

Opportunity costs are not recorded in financial accounting systems. Why? Because historical record keeping is limited to transactions involving alternatives that were *actually selected*, rather than alternatives that were rejected. Rejected alternatives do not produce transactions and so they are not recorded. If Soho makes video-system DVD players, it will not make Digiteks, and it will not record any accounting entries for Digiteks. Yet the opportunity cost of making video-system DVD players, which equals the operating income that Soho forgoes by not making Digiteks, is a crucial input into the make-or-buy decision. Consider again Exhibit 7, Panel B. On the basis of only the incremental costs that are systematically recorded in accounting systems, it is less costly for Soho to make rather than buy video-system DVD players. Recognizing the opportunity cost of $2,500,000 leads to a different conclusion: Buying video-system DVD players is preferable.

Suppose Soho has sufficient capacity to make Digiteks even if it makes video-system DVD players. In this case, the opportunity cost of making video-system DVD players is $0 because Soho does not give up the $2,500,000 operating income from making Digiteks even if it chooses to make video-system DVD players. The relevant costs are $15,000,000 (incremental costs of $15,000,000 plus opportunity cost of $0). Under these conditions, Soho would prefer to make video-system DVD players, rather than buy them, and also make Digiteks.

Besides quantitative considerations, the make-or-buy decision should also consider strategic and qualitative factors. If Soho decides to buy video-system DVD players from an outside supplier, it should consider factors such as the supplier's reputation for quality and timely delivery. Soho would also want to consider the strategic consequences of selling Digiteks. For example, will selling Digiteks take Soho's focus away from its video-system business?

Carrying Costs of Inventory

To see another example of an opportunity cost, consider the following data for Soho:

Annual estimated video-system DVD player requirements for next year	250,000 units
Cost per unit when each purchase is equal to 2,500 units	$64.00
Cost per unit when each purchase is equal to or greater than 125,000 units; $64 minus 1% discount	$63.36
Cost of a purchase order	$500

Alternatives under consideration:
   A. Make 100 purchases of 2,500 units each during next year
   B. Make 2 purchases of 125,000 units during the year

Average investment in inventory:

A. (2,500 units × $64.00 per unit) ÷ 2[a] $80,000

B. (125,000 units × $63.36 per unit) ÷ 2[a] $3,960,000

Annual rate of return if cash is invested elsewhere (for example, bonds or stocks) at the same level of risk as investment in inventory   9%

[a] The example assumes that video-system-DVD-player purchases will be used uniformly throughout the year. The average investment in inventory during the year is the cost of the inventory when a purchase is received plus the cost of inventory just before the next purchase is delivered (in our example, zero) divided by 2.

Soho will pay cash for the video-system DVD players it buys. Which purchasing alternative is more economical for Soho?

The following table presents the analysis using the total alternatives approach recognizing that Soho has, on average, $3,960,000 of cash available to invest. If Soho invests only $80,000 in inventory as in alternative A, it will have $3,880,000 ($3,960,000 – $80,000) of cash available to invest elsewhere, which at a 9% rate of return will yield a total return of $349,200. This income is subtracted from the ordering and purchasing costs incurred under alternative A. If Soho invests all $3,960,000 in inventory as in alternative B, it will have $0 ($3,960,000 – $3,960,000) available to invest elsewhere and will earn no return on the cash.

	Alternative A: Make 100 Purchases of 2,500 Units Each During the Year and Invest Any Excess Cash (1)	Alternative B: Make 2 Purchases of 125,000 Units Each During the Year and Invest Any Excess Cash (2)	Difference (3) = (1) – (2)
Annual purchase-order costs (100 purch. orders × $500/purch. order; 2 purch. orders × $500/purch. order)	$ 50,000	$ 1,000	$ 49,000
Annual purchase costs (250,000 units × $64.00/unit; 250,000 units × $63.36/unit)	16,000,000	15,840,000	160,000
Deduct annual rate of return earned by investing cash not tied up in inventory elsewhere at the same level of risk [0.09 × ($3,960,000 – $80,000); 0.09 × ($3,960,000 – $3,960,000)	(349,200)	0	(349,200)
Relevant costs	$15,700,800	$15,841,000	$(140,200)

Consistent with the trends toward holding smaller inventories, purchasing smaller quantities of 2,500 units 100 times a year is preferred to purchasing 125,000 units twice a year by $140,200.

The following table presents the two alternatives using the opportunity cost approach. Each alternative is defined only in terms of the two purchasing choices with no explicit reference to investing the excess cash.

	Alternative A: Make 100 Purchases of 2,500 Units Each During the Year (1)	Alternative B: Make 2 Purchases of 125,000 Units Each During the Year (2)	Difference (3) = (1) – (2)
Annual purchase-order costs (100 purch. orders × $500/purch. order; 2 purch. orders × $500/purch. order)	$ 50,000	$ 1,000	$ 49,000
Annual purchase costs (250,000 units × $64.00/unit; 250,000 units × $63.36/unit)	16,000,000	15,840,000	160,000
Opportunity cost: Annual rate of return that could be earned if investment in inventory were invested elsewhere at the same level of risk (0.09 × $80,000; 0.09 × $3,960,000)	7,200	356,400	(349,200)
Relevant costs	$16,057,200	$16,197,400	$(140,200)

Recall that under the opportunity cost approach, the relevant cost of any alternative is (1) the incremental cost of the alternative plus (2) the opportunity cost of the profit forgone from choosing that alternative. The opportunity cost of holding inventory is the income forgone by tying up money in inventory and not investing it elsewhere. The opportunity cost would not be recorded in the accounting system because, once the money is invested in inventory, there is no money available to invest elsewhere, and hence no return related to this investment to record. On the basis of the costs recorded in the accounting system (purchase-order costs and purchase costs), Soho would erroneously conclude that making two purchases of 125,000 units each is the less costly alternative. Column 3, however, indicates that, as in the total alternatives approach, purchasing smaller quantities of 2,500 units 100 times a year is preferred to purchasing 125,000 units twice during the year by $140,200. Why? Because the lower opportunity cost of holding smaller inventory exceeds the higher purchase and ordering costs. If the opportunity cost of money tied up in inventory were greater than 9% per year, or if other incremental benefits of holding lower inventory were considered—such as lower insurance, materials-handling, storage, obsolescence, and breakage costs—making 100 purchases would be even more economical.

Decision Point

What is an opportunity cost and why should it be included when making decisions?

Product-Mix Decisions with Capacity Constraints

We now examine how the concept of relevance applies to **product-mix decisions**—the decisions made by a company about which products to sell and in what quantities. These decisions usually have only a short-run focus, because they typically arise in the context of capacity constraints that can be relaxed in the long run. In the short run, for example, BMW, the German car manufacturer, continually adapts the mix of its different models of cars (for example, 325i, 525i, and 740i) to fluctuations in selling prices and demand.

To determine product mix, a company maximizes operating income, subject to constraints such as capacity and demand. Throughout this section, we assume that as short-run changes in product mix occur, the only costs that change are costs that are variable with respect to the number of units produced (and sold). Under this assumption, the analysis of individual product contribution margins provides insight into the product mix that maximizes operating income.

Learning Objective 4

Know how to choose which products to produce when there are capacity constraints

. . . select the product with the highest contribution margin per unit of the limiting resource

Example 4: Power Recreation assembles two engines, a snowmobile engine and a boat engine, at its Lexington, Kentucky, plant.

	Snowmobile Engine	Boat Engine
Selling price	$800	$1,000
Variable cost per unit	560	625
Contribution margin per unit	$240	$ 375
Contribution margin percentage ($240 ÷ $800; $375 ÷ $1,000)	30%	37.5%

Assume that only 600 machine-hours are available daily for assembling engines. Additional capacity cannot be obtained in the short run. Power Recreation can sell as many engines as it produces. The constraining resource, then, is machine-hours. It takes two machine-hours to produce one snowmobile engine and five machine-hours to produce one boat engine. What product mix should Power Recreation's managers choose to maximize its operating income?

In terms of contribution margin per unit and contribution margin percentage, boat engines are more profitable than snowmobile engines. The product that Power Recreation should produce and sell, however, is not necessarily the product with the higher individual contribution margin per unit or contribution margin percentage. Managers should choose the product with *the highest contribution margin per unit of the constraining resource (factor)*. That's the resource that restricts or limits the production or sale of products.

	Snowmobile Engine	Boat Engine
Contribution margin per unit	$240	$375
Machine-hours required to produce one unit	2 machine-hours	5 machine-hours
Contribution margin per machine-hour		
$240 per unit ÷ 2 machine-hours/unit	$120/machine-hour	
$375 per unit ÷ 5 machine-hours/unit		$75/machine-hour
Total contribution margin for 600 machine-hours		
$120/machine-hour × 600 machine-hours	$72,000	
$75/machine-hour × 600 machine-hours		$45,000

The number of machine-hours is the constraining resource in this example and snowmobile engines earn more contribution margin per machine-hour ($120/machine-hour) compared to boat engines ($75/machine-hour). Therefore, choosing to produce and sell snowmobile engines maximizes *total* contribution margin ($72,000 versus $45,000 from producing and selling boat engines) and operating income. Other constraints in manufacturing settings can be the availability of direct materials, components, or skilled labor, as well as financial and sales factors. In a retail department store, the constraining resource may be linear feet of display space. Regardless of the specific constraining resource, managers should always focus on maximizing *total* contribution margin by choosing products that give the highest contribution margin per unit of the constraining resource.

In many cases, a manufacturer or retailer has the challenge of trying to maximize total operating income for a variety of products, each with more than one constraining resource. Some constraints may require a manufacturer or retailer to stock minimum quantities of products even if these products are not very profitable. For example, supermarkets must stock less-profitable products because customers will be willing to shop at a supermarket only if it carries a wide range of products that customers desire. To determine the most profitable production schedule and the most profitable product mix, the manufacturer or retailer needs to determine the maximum total contribution margin in the face of many constraints. Optimization techniques, such as linear programming discussed in the appendix to this chapter, help solve these more-complex problems.

Finally, there is the question of managing the bottleneck constraint to increase output and, therefore, contribution margin. Can the available machine-hours for assembling engines be increased beyond 600, for example, by reducing idle time? Can the time needed to assemble each snowmobile engine (two machine-hours) and each boat engine (five machine-hours) be reduced, for example, by reducing setup time and processing time of assembly? Can quality be improved so that constrained capacity is used to produce only good units rather than some good and some defective units? Can some of the assembly operations be outsourced to allow more engines to be built? Implementing any of these options will likely require Power Recreation to incur incremental costs. Power Recreation will implement only those options where the increase in contribution margins exceeds the increase in costs.

> **Decision Point** ▶
>
> When resources are constrained, how should managers choose which of multiple products to produce and sell?

> **Learning Objective 5**
>
> Discuss factors managers must consider when adding or dropping customers or segments
>
> . . . managers should focus on how total costs differ among alternatives and ignore allocated overhead costs

Customer Profitability, Activity-Based Costing, and Relevant Costs

Not only must companies make choices regarding which products and how much of each product to produce, they must often make decisions about adding or dropping a product line or a business segment. Similarly, if the cost object is a customer, companies must make decisions about adding or dropping customers (analogous to a product line) or a branch office (analogous to a business segment). We illustrate relevant-revenue and relevant-cost analysis for these kinds of decisions using customers rather than products as the cost object.

Example 5: Allied West, the West Coast sales office of Allied Furniture, a wholesaler of specialized furniture, supplies furniture to three local retailers: Vogel, Brenner, and Wisk. Exhibit 8 presents expected revenues and costs of Allied West by customer for the upcoming year using its activity-based costing system. Allied West assigns costs to customers based on the activities needed to support each customer. Information on Allied West's costs for different activities at various levels of the cost hierarchy follows:

- Furniture-handling labor costs vary with the number of units of furniture shipped to customers.
- Allied West reserves different areas of the warehouse to stock furniture for different customers. For simplicity, assume that furniture-handling equipment in an area and depreciation costs on the equipment that Allied West has already acquired are identified with individual customers (customer-level costs). Any unused equipment remains idle. The equipment has a one-year useful life and zero disposal value.
- Allied West allocates rent to each customer on the basis of the amount of warehouse space reserved for that customer.
- Marketing costs vary with the number of sales visits made to customers.
- Sales-order costs are batch-level costs that vary with the number of sales orders received from customers; delivery-processing costs are batch-level costs that vary with the number of shipments made.
- Allied West allocates fixed general-administration costs (facility-level costs) to customers on the basis of customer revenues.
- Allied Furniture allocates its fixed corporate-office costs to sales offices on the basis of the square feet area of each sales office. Allied West then allocates these costs to customers on the basis of customer revenues.

In the following sections, we consider several decisions that Allied West's managers face: Should Allied West drop the Wisk account? Should it add a fourth customer, Loral? Should Allied Furniture close down Allied West? Should it open another sales office, Allied South, whose revenues and costs are identical to those of Allied West?

Exhibit 8

Customer Profitability
Analysis for Allied West

| | Customer | | | |
	Vogel	Brenner	Wisk	Total
Revenues	$500,000	$300,000	$400,000	$1,200,000
Cost of goods sold	370,000	220,000	330,000	920,000
Furniture-handling labor	41,000	18,000	33,000	92,000
Furniture-handling equipment cost written off as depreciation	12,000	4,000	9,000	25,000
Rent	14,000	8,000	14,000	36,000
Marketing support	11,000	9,000	10,000	30,000
Sales-order and delivery processing	13,000	7,000	12,000	32,000
General administration	20,000	12,000	16,000	48,000
Allocated corporate-office costs	10,000	6,000	8,000	24,000
Total costs	491,000	284,000	432,000	1,207,000
Operating income	$ 9,000	$ 16,000	$ (32,000)	$ (7,000)

Relevant-Revenue and Relevant-Cost Analysis of Dropping a Customer

Exhibit 8 indicates a loss of $32,000 on the Wisk account. Allied West's managers believe the reason for the loss is that Wisk places low-margin orders with Allied, and has relatively high sales-order, delivery-processing, furniture-handling, and marketing costs. Allied West is considering several possible actions with respect to the Wisk account: reducing its own costs of supporting Wisk by becoming more efficient, cutting back on some of the services it offers Wisk; asking Wisk to place larger, less frequent orders; charging Wisk higher prices; or dropping the Wisk account. The following analysis focuses on the operating-income effect of dropping the Wisk account for the year.

To determine what to do, Allied West's managers must answer the question, what are the relevant revenues and relevant costs? Information about the effect of dropping the Wisk account follows:

- Dropping the Wisk account will save cost of goods sold, furniture-handling labor, marketing support, sales-order, and delivery-processing costs incurred on the account.
- Dropping the Wisk account will leave idle the warehouse space and furniture-handling equipment currently used to supply products to Wisk.
- Dropping the Wisk account will have no effect on fixed general-administration costs or corporate-office costs.

Exhibit 9, column 1, presents the relevant-revenue and relevant-cost analysis using data from the Wisk column in Exhibit 8. Allied West's operating income will be $15,000 lower if it drops the Wisk account—the cost savings from dropping the Wisk account, $385,000, will not be enough to offset the loss of $400,000 in revenues—so Allied West's managers decide to keep the account. Note that there is no opportunity cost of using warehouse space for Wisk because without Wisk, the space and equipment will remain idle.

Depreciation on equipment that Allied West has already acquired is a past cost and therefore irrelevant; rent, general-administration, and corporate-office costs are future costs that will not change if Allied West drops the Wisk account, and hence irrelevant. Overhead costs allocated to the sales office and individual customers are always irrelevant. The only question is, will expected total corporate-office costs decrease as a result of dropping the Wisk account? In our example, they will not, so these costs are irrelevant. *If expected total corporate-office costs* were to decrease by dropping the Wisk account, those savings would be relevant even if *the amount allocated to Allied West did not change.*

	Exhibit 9

Relevant-Revenue and Relevant-Cost Analysis for Dropping the Wisk Account and Adding the Loral Account

	(Incremental Loss in Revenues) and Incremental Savings in Costs from Dropping Wisk Account (1)	Incremental Revenues and (Incremental Costs) from Adding Loral Account (2)
Revenues	$(400,000)	$400,000
Cost of goods sold	330,000	(330,000)
Furniture-handling labor	33,000	(33,000)
Furniture-handling equipment cost written off as depreciation	0	(9,000)
Rent	0	0
Marketing support	10,000	(10,000)
Sales-order and delivery processing	12,000	(12,000)
General administration	0	0
Corporate-office costs	0	0
Total costs	385,000	(394,000)
Effect on operating income (loss)	$ (15,000)	$ 6,000

Now suppose that if Allied West drops the Wisk account, it could lease the extra warehouse space to Sanchez Corporation for $20,000 per year. Then $20,000 would be Allied's opportunity cost of continuing to use the warehouse to service Wisk. Allied West would gain $5,000 by dropping the Wisk account ($20,000 from lease revenue minus lost operating income of $15,000). Before reaching a decision, Allied West's managers must examine whether Wisk can be made more profitable so that supplying products to Wisk earns more than the $20,000 from leasing to Sanchez. The managers must also consider strategic factors such as the effect of the decision on Allied West's reputation for developing stable, long-run business relationships with its customers.

Relevant-Revenue and Relevant-Cost Analysis of Adding a Customer

Suppose that in addition to Vogel, Brenner, and Wisk, Allied West's managers are evaluating the profitability of adding a customer, Loral. There is no other alternative use of the Allied West facility. Loral has a customer profile much like Wisk's. Suppose Allied West's managers predict revenues and costs of doing business with Loral to be the same as the revenues and costs described under the Wisk column of Exhibit 8. In particular, Allied West would have to acquire furniture-handling equipment for the Loral account costing $9,000, with a one-year useful life and zero disposal value. If Loral is added as a customer, warehouse rent costs ($36,000), general-administration costs ($48,000), and *actual total* corporate-office costs will not change. Should Allied West add Loral as a customer?

Exhibit 9, column 2, shows incremental revenues exceed incremental costs by $6,000. The opportunity cost of adding Loral is $0 because there is no alternative use of the Allied West facility. On the basis of this analysis, Allied West's managers would recommend adding Loral as a customer. Rent, general-administration, and corporate-office costs are irrelevant because these costs will not change if Loral is added as a customer. However, the cost of new equipment to support the Loral order (written off as depreciation of $9,000 in Exhibit 9, column 2), is relevant. That's because this cost can be avoided if Allied West decides not to add Loral as a customer. Note the critical distinction here: *Depreciation cost is irrelevant in deciding whether to drop Wisk as a customer because depreciation on equipment that has already been purchased is a past cost, but the cost of purchasing new equipment in the future, that will then be written off as depreciation, is relevant in deciding whether to add Loral as a customer.*

Relevant-Revenue and Relevant-Cost Analysis of Closing or Adding Branch Offices or Segments

Companies periodically confront decisions about closing or adding branch offices or business segments. For example, given Allied West's expected loss of $7,000 (see Exhibit 8), should it be closed for the year? Assume that closing Allied West will have no effect on total corporate-office costs and that there is no alternative use for the Allied West space.

Exhibit 10, column 1, presents the relevant-revenue and relevant-cost analysis using data from the "Total" column in Exhibit 8. The revenue losses of $1,200,000 will exceed the cost savings of $1,158,000, leading to a decrease in operating income of $42,000. Allied West should not be closed. The key reasons are that closing Allied West will not save depreciation cost or actual total corporate-office costs. Depreciation cost is past or sunk because it represents the cost of equipment that Allied West has already purchased. Corporate-office costs allocated to various sales offices will change *but the total amount of these costs will not decline.* The $24,000 no longer allocated to Allied West will be allocated to other sales offices. Therefore, the $24,000 of allocated corporate-office costs is irrelevant, because it does not represent expected cost savings from closing Allied West.

Now suppose Allied Furniture has the opportunity to open another sales office, Allied South, whose revenues and costs would be identical to Allied West's costs, including a cost of $25,000 to acquire furniture-handling equipment with a one-year useful life and zero disposal value. Opening this office will have no effect on total corporate-office costs.

Decision Point

In deciding to add or drop customers or to add or discontinue branch offices or segments, what should managers focus on and how should they take into account allocated overhead costs?

	Exhibit 10	Relevant-Revenue and Relevant-Cost Analysis for Closing Allied West and Opening Allied South

	(Incremental Loss in Revenues) and Incremental Savings in Costs from Closing Allied West (1)	Incremental Revenues and (Incremental Costs) from Opening Allied South (2)
Revenues	$(1,200,000)	$1,200,000
Cost of goods sold	920,000	(920,000)
Furniture-handling labor	92,000	(92,000)
Furniture-handling equipment cost written off as depreciation	0	(25,000)
Rent	36,000	(36,000)
Marketing support	30,000	(30,000)
Sales-order and delivery processing	32,000	(32,000)
General administration	48,000	(48,000)
Corporate-office costs	0	0
Total costs	1,158,000	(1,183,000)
Effect on operating income (loss)	$ (42,000)	$ 17,000

Should Allied Furniture open Allied South? Exhibit 10, column 2, indicates that it should do so because opening Allied South will increase operating income by $17,000. As before, the cost of new equipment to be purchased in the future (and written off as depreciation) is relevant and *allocated* corporate-office costs should be ignored. Total corporate-office costs will not change if Allied South is opened, therefore these costs are irrelevant.

Irrelevance of Past Costs and Equipment-Replacement Decisions

Learning Objective 6

Explain why book value of equipment is irrelevant in equipment-replacement decisions

. . . it is a past cost

At several points in this chapter, when discussing the concept of relevance, we reasoned that past (historical or sunk) costs are irrelevant to decision making. That's because a decision cannot change something that has already happened. We now apply this concept to decisions about replacing equipment. We stress the idea that **book value**—original cost minus accumulated depreciation—of existing equipment is a past cost that is irrelevant.

Example 6: Toledo Company, a manufacturer of aircraft components, is considering replacing a metal-cutting machine with a newer model. The new machine is more efficient than the old machine, but it has a shorter life. Revenues from aircraft parts ($1.1 million per year) will be unaffected by the replacement decision. Here are the data the management accountant prepares for the existing (old) machine and the replacement (new) machine:

	Old Machine	New Machine
Original cost	$1,000,000	$600,000
Useful life	5 years	2 years
Current age	3 years	0 years
Remaining useful life	2 years	2 years
Accumulated depreciation	$600,000	Not acquired yet
Book value	$400,000	Not acquired yet
Current disposal value (in cash)	$40,000	Not acquired yet
Terminal disposal value (in cash 2 years from now)	$0	$0
Annual operating costs (maintenance, energy, repairs, coolants, and so on)	$800,000	$460,000

Toledo Corporation uses straight-line depreciation. To focus on relevance, we ignore the time value of money and income taxes. Should Toledo replace its old machine?

Exhibit 11 presents a cost comparison of the two machines. Consider why each of the four items in Toledo's equipment-replacement decision is relevant or irrelevant:

1. **Book value of old machine, $400,000.** Irrelevant, because it is a past or sunk cost. All past costs are "down the drain." Nothing can change what has already been spent or what has already happened.

2. **Current disposal value of old machine, $40,000.** Relevant, because it is an expected future benefit that will only occur if the machine is replaced.

3. **Loss on disposal, $360,000.** This is the difference between amounts in items 1 and 2. It is a meaningless combination blurring the distinction between the irrelevant book value and the relevant disposal value. Each should be considered separately, as was done in items 1 and 2.

4. **Cost of new machine, $600,000.** Relevant, because it is an expected future cost that will only occur if the machine is purchased.

Exhibit 11 should clarify these four assertions. Column 3 in Exhibit 11 shows that the book value of the old machine does not differ between the alternatives and could be ignored for decision-making purposes. No matter what the timing of the write-off—whether a lump-sum charge in the current year or depreciation charges over the next two years—the total amount is still $400,000 because it is a past (historical) cost. In contrast, the $600,000 cost of the new machine and the current disposal value of $40,000 for the old machine are relevant because they would not arise if Toledo's managers decided not to replace the machine. Note that the operating income from replacing is $120,000 higher for the two years together.

To provide focus, Exhibit 12 concentrates only on relevant items. Note that the same answer—higher operating income as a result of lower costs of $120,000 by replacing the machine—is obtained even though the book value is omitted from the calculations. The only relevant items are the cash operating costs, the disposal value of the old machine, and the cost of the new machine that is represented as depreciation in Exhibit 12.

◀ **Decision Point**

Is book value of existing equipment relevant in equipment replacement decisions?

Exhibit 11

Operating Income Comparison: Replacement of Machine, Relevant, and Irrelevant Items for Toledo Company

| | Two Years Together | | |
	Keep (1)	Replace (2)	Difference (3) = (1) − (2)
Revenues	$2,200,000	$2,200,000	—
Operating costs			
Cash operating costs ($800,000/yr. × 2 years; $460,000/yr. × 2 years)	1,600,000	920,000	$ 680,000
Book value of old machine			
Periodic write-off as depreciation or	400,000	—	—
Lump-sum write-off	—	400,000[a]	
Current disposal value of old machine	—	(40,000)[a]	40,000
New machine cost, written off periodically as depreciation	—	600,000	(600,000)
Total operating costs	2,000,000	1,880,000	120,000
Operating income	$ 200,000	$ 320,000	$(120,000)

[a]In a formal income statement, these two items would be combined as "loss on disposal of machine" of $360,000.

	Two Years Together		
	Keep (1)	Replace (2)	Difference (3) = (1) – (2)
Cash operating costs	$1,600,000	$ 920,000	$680,000
Current disposal value of old machine	—	(40,000)	40,000
New machine, written off periodically as depreciation	—	600,000	(600,000)
Total relevant costs	$1,600,000	$1,480,000	$120,000

Decisions and Performance Evaluation

Consider our equipment-replacement example in light of the five-step sequence in Exhibit 1:

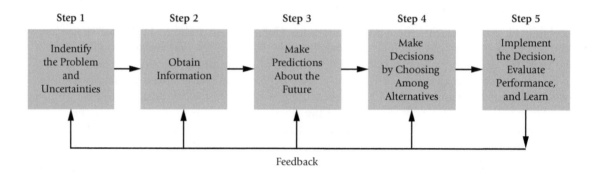

Step 1	Step 2	Step 3	Step 4	Step 5
Indentify the Problem and Uncertainties	Obtain Information	Make Predictions About the Future	Make Decisions by Choosing Among Alternatives	Implement the Decision, Evaluate Performance, and Learn

Feedback

The decision model analysis (Step 4), which is presented in Exhibits 11 and 12, dictates replacing the machine rather than keeping it. In the real world, however, would the manager replace it? An important factor in replacement decisions is the manager's perception of whether the decision model is consistent with how the manager's performance will be judged after the decision is implemented (the performance-evaluation model in Step 5).

From the perspective of their own careers, it is no surprise that managers tend to favor the alternative that makes their performance look better. If the performance-evaluation model conflicts with the decision model, the performance-evaluation model often prevails in influencing managers' decisions. For example, if the promotion or bonus of the manager at Toledo hinges on his or her first year's operating income performance under accrual accounting, the manager's temptation *not* to replace will be overwhelming. Why? Because the accrual accounting model for measuring performance will show a higher first-year operating income if the old machine is kept rather than replaced (as the following table shows):

First-Year Results: Accrual Accounting	Keep	Replace
Revenues	$1,100,000	$1,100,000
Operating costs		
Cash-operating costs	$800,000	$460,000
Depreciation	200,000	300,000
Loss on disposal	—	360,000
Total operating costs	1,000,000	1,120,000
Operating income (loss)	$ 100,000	$ (20,000)

Even though top management's goals encompass the two-year period (consistent with the decision model), the manager will focus on first-year results if his or her evaluation is based on short-run measures such as the first-year's operating income.

Resolving the conflict between the decision model and the performance-evaluation model is frequently a baffling problem in practice. In theory, resolving the difficulty seems obvious: Design models that are consistent. Consider our replacement example. Year-by-year effects on operating income of replacement can be budgeted for the two-year planning horizon. The manager then would be evaluated on the expectation that the first year would be poor and the next year would be much better. Doing this for every decision, however, makes the performance evaluation model very cumbersome. As a result of these practical difficulties, accounting systems rarely track each decision separately. Performance evaluation focuses on responsibility centers for a specific period, not on projects or individual items of equipment over their useful lives. Thus, the impacts of many different decisions are combined in a single performance report and evaluation measure, say operating income. Lower-level managers make decisions to maximize operating income, and top management—through the reporting system—is rarely aware of particular desirable alternatives that were *not* chosen by lower-level managers because of conflicts between the decision and performance-evaluation models.

Consider another conflict between the decision model and the performance-evaluation model. Suppose a manager buys a particular machine only to discover shortly thereafter that a better machine could have been purchased instead. The decision model may suggest replacing the machine that was just bought with the better machine, but will the manager do so? Probably not. Why? Because replacing the machine so soon after its purchase will reflect badly on the manager's capabilities and performance. If the manager's bosses have no knowledge of the better machine, the manager may prefer to keep the recently purchased machine rather than alert them to the better machine.

Decision Point

How can conflicts arise between the decision model used by a manager and the performance-evaluation model used to evaluate that manager?

Problem for Self-Study

Wally Lewis is manager of the engineering development division of Goldcoast Products. Lewis has just received a proposal signed by all 15 of his engineers to replace the workstations with networked personal computers (networked PCs). Lewis is not enthusiastic about the proposal.

Data on workstations and networked PCs are as follows:

	Workstations	Networked PCs
Original cost	$300,000	$135,000
Useful life	5 years	3 years
Current age	2 years	0 years
Remaining useful life	3 years	3 years
Accumulated depreciation	$120,000	Not acquired yet
Current book value	$180,000	Not acquired yet
Current disposal value (in cash)	$95,000	Not acquired yet
Terminal disposal value (in cash 3 years from now)	$0	$0
Annual computer-related cash operating costs	$40,000	$10,000
Annual revenues	$1,000,000	$1,000,000
Annual noncomputer-related operating costs	$880,000	$880,000

Lewis's annual bonus includes a component based on division operating income. He has a promotion possibility next year that would make him a group vice president of Goldcoast Products.

Required

1. Compare the costs of workstations and networked PCs. Consider the cumulative results for the three years together, ignoring the time value of money and income taxes.
2. Why might Lewis be reluctant to purchase the networked PCs?

Solution

1. The following table considers all cost items when comparing future costs of workstations and networked PCs:

	Three Years Together		
All Items	Workstations (1)	Networked PCs (2)	Difference (3) = (1) − (2)
Revenues	$3,000,000	$3,000,000	—
Operating costs			
Noncomputer-related operating costs	2,640,000	2,640,000	—
Computer-related cash operating costs	120,000	30,000	$ 90,000
Workstations' book value			
Periodic write-off as depreciation or	180,000	— ⎫	—
Lump-sum write-off	—	180,000 ⎭	
Current disposal value of workstations	—	(95,000)	95,000
Networked PCs, written off periodically as depreciation	—	135,000	(135,000)
Total operating costs	2,940,000	2,890,000	50,000
Operating income	$ 60,000	$ 110,000	$ (50,000)

Alternatively, the analysis could focus on only those items in the preceding table that differ between the alternatives.

	Three Years Together		
Relevant Items	Workstations	Networked PCs	Difference
Computer-related cash operating costs	$120,000	$ 30,000	$90,000
Current disposal value of workstations	—	(95,000)	95,000
Networked PCs, written off periodically as depreciation	—	135,000	(135,000)
Total relevant costs	$120,000	$ 70,000	$ 50,000

The analysis suggests that it is cost-effective to replace the workstations with the networked PCs.

2. The accrual-accounting operating incomes *for the first year* under the keep workstations versus the buy networked PCs alternatives are as follows:

	Keep Workstations	Buy Networked PCs
Revenues	$1,000,000	$1,000,000
Operating costs		
Noncomputer-related operating costs	$880,000	$880,000
Computer-related cash operating costs	40,000	10,000
Depreciation	60,000	45,000
Loss on disposal of workstations	—	85,000[a]
Total operating costs	980,000	1,020,000
Operating income (loss)	$ 20,000	$ (20,000)

[a] $85,000 = Book value of workstations, $180,000 − Current disposal value, $95,000.

Lewis would be less happy with the expected operating loss of $20,000 if the networked PCs are purchased than he would be with the expected operating income of $20,000 if the workstations are kept. Buying the networked PCs would eliminate the component of his bonus based on operating income. He might also perceive the $20,000 operating loss as reducing his chances of being promoted to a group vice president.

Decision Points

The following question-and-answer format summarizes the chapter's learning objectives. Each decision presents a key question related to a learning objective. The guidelines are the answer to that question.

Decision	Guidelines
1. What is the five-step process that managers can use to make decisions?	The five-step decision-making process is (a) identify the problem and uncertainties, (b) obtain information, (c) make predictions about the future, (d) make decisions by choosing among alternatives, and (e) implement the decision, evaluate performance, and learn.
2. When is a revenue or cost item relevant for a particular decision and what potential problems should be avoided in relevant-cost analysis?	To be relevant for a particular decision, a revenue or cost item must meet two criteria: (a) It must be an expected future revenue or expected future cost, and (b) it must differ among alternative courses of action. The outcomes of alternative actions can be quantitative and qualitative. Quantitative outcomes are measured in numerical terms. Some quantitative outcomes can be expressed in financial terms, others cannot. Qualitative factors, such as employee morale, are difficult to measure accurately in numerical terms. Consideration must be given to relevant quantitative and qualitative factors in making decisions. Two potential problems to avoid in relevant-cost analysis are (a) making incorrect general assumptions—such as all variable costs are relevant and all fixed costs are irrelevant—and (b) losing sight of total amounts, focusing instead on unit amounts.
3. What is an opportunity cost and why should it be included when making decisions?	Opportunity cost is the contribution to income that is forgone by not using a limited resource in its next-best alternative use. Opportunity cost is included in decision making because the relevant cost of any decision is (1) the incremental cost of the decision plus (2) the opportunity cost of the profit forgone from making that decision.
4. When resources are constrained, how should managers choose which of multiple products to produce and sell?	When resources are constrained, managers should select the product that yields the highest contribution margin per unit of the constraining or limiting resource (factor). In this way, total contribution margin will be maximized.
5. In deciding to add or drop customers or to add or discontinue branch offices or segments, what should managers focus on and how should they take into account allocated overhead costs?	When making decisions about adding or dropping customers or adding or discontinuing branch offices and segments, managers should focus on only those costs that will change and any opportunity costs. Managers should ignore allocated overhead costs.
6. Is book value of existing equipment relevant in equipment-replacement decisions?	Book value of existing equipment is a past (historical or sunk) cost and, therefore, is irrelevant in equipment-replacement decisions.
7. How can conflicts arise between the decision model used by a manager and the performance-evaluation model used to evaluate that manager?	Top management faces a persistent challenge: making sure that the performance-evaluation model of lower-level managers is consistent with the decision model. A common inconsistency is to tell these managers to take a multiple-year view in their decision making but then to judge their performance only on the basis of the current year's operating income.

Appendix

Linear Programming

In this chapter's Power Recreation example, suppose both the snowmobile and boat engines must be tested on a very expensive machine before they are shipped to customers. The available machine-hours for testing are limited. Production data are as follows:

Department	Available Daily Capacity in Hours	Use of Capacity in Hours per Unit of Product		Daily Maximum Production in Units	
		Snowmobile Engine	Boat Engine	Snowmobile Engine	Boat Engine
Assembly	600 machine-hours	2.0 machine-hours	5.0 machine-hours	300[a] snow engines	120 boat engines
Testing	120 testing-hours	1.0 machine-hour	0.5 machine-hour	120 snow engines	240 boat engines

[a] For example, 600 machine-hours ÷ 2.0 machine-hours per snowmobile engine = 300, the maximum number of snowmobile engines that the assembly department can make if it works exclusively on snowmobile engines.

Exhibit 13 summarizes these and other relevant data. In addition, as a result of material shortages for boat engines, Power Recreation cannot produce more than 110 boat engines per day. How many engines of each type should Power Recreation produce and sell daily to maximize operating income?

Because there are multiple constraints, a technique called *linear programming* or *LP* can be used to determine the number of each type of engine Power Recreation should produce. LP models typically assume that all costs are either variable or fixed with respect to a single cost driver (units of output). As we shall see, LP models also require certain other linear assumptions to hold. When these assumptions fail, other decision models should be considered.[2]

Steps in Solving an LP Problem

We use the data in Exhibit 13 to illustrate the three steps in solving an LP problem. Throughout this discussion, S equals the number of units of snowmobile engines produced and sold, and B equals the number of units of boat engines produced and sold.

Step 1: Determine the objective function. The **objective function** of a linear program expresses the objective or goal to be maximized (say, operating income) or minimized (say, operating costs). In our example, the objective is to find the combination of snowmobile engines and boat engines that maximizes total contribution margin. Fixed costs remain the same regardless of the product-mix decision and are irrelevant. The linear function expressing the objective for the total contribution margin (TCM) is as follows:

$$TCM = \$240S + \$375B$$

Step 2: Specify the constraints. A **constraint** is a mathematical inequality or equality that must be satisfied by the variables in a mathematical model. The following linear inequalities express the relationships in our example:

Assembly department constraint	$2S + 5B \leq 600$
Testing department constraint	$1S + 0.5B \leq 120$
Materials-shortage constraint for boat engines	$B \leq 110$
Negative production is impossible	$S \geq 0$ and $B \geq 0$

Exhibit 13   Operating Data for Power Recreation

	Department Capacity (per Day) In Product Units		Selling Price	Variable Cost per Unit	Contribution Margin per Unit
	Assembly	Testing			
Only snowmobile engines	300	120	$ 800	$560	$240
Only boat engines	120	240	$1,000	$625	$375

[2] Other decision models are described in J. Moore and L. Weatherford, *Decision Modeling with Microsoft Excel*, 6th ed. (Upper Saddle River, NJ: Prentice Hall, 2001); and S. Nahmias, *Production and Operations Analysis*, 6th ed. (New York: McGraw-Hill/Irwin, 2008).

The three solid lines on the graph in Exhibit 14 show the existing constraints for assembly and testing and the materials-shortage constraint.[3] The feasible or technically possible alternatives are those combinations of quantities of snowmobile engines and boat engines that satisfy all the constraining resources or factors. The shaded "area of feasible solutions" in Exhibit 14 shows the boundaries of those product combinations that are feasible.

Step 3: Compute the optimal solution. **Linear programming (LP)** is an optimization technique used to maximize the *objective function* when there are multiple *constraints*. We present two approaches for finding the optimal solution using LP: trial-and-error approach and graphic approach. These approaches are easy to use in our example because there are only two variables in the objective function and a small number of constraints. Understanding these approaches provides insight into LP. In most real-world LP applications, managers use computer software packages to calculate the optimal solution.[4]

Trial-and-Error Approach

The optimal solution can be found by trial and error, by working with coordinates of the corners of the area of feasible solutions.

First, select any set of corner points and compute the total contribution margin. Five corner points appear in Exhibit 14. It is helpful to use simultaneous equations to obtain the exact coordinates in the graph. To illustrate, the corner point ($S = 75, B = 90$) can be derived by solving the two pertinent constraint inequalities as simultaneous equations:

$$2S + 5B = 600 \quad (1)$$

$$1S + 0.5B = 120 \quad (2)$$

Multiplying (2) by 2: $\quad 2S + B = 240 \quad (3)$

Subtracting (3) from (1): $\quad 4B = 360$

Therefore, $\quad B = 360 \div 4 = 90$

Substituting for B in (2): $1S + 0.5(90) = 120$

$$S = 120 - 45 = 75$$

Given $S = 75$ snowmobile engines and $B = 90$ boat engines, $TCM = (\$240$ per snowmobile engine $\times$ 75 snowmobile engines) + ($\$375$ per boat engine $\times$ 90 boat engines) = $\$51,750$.

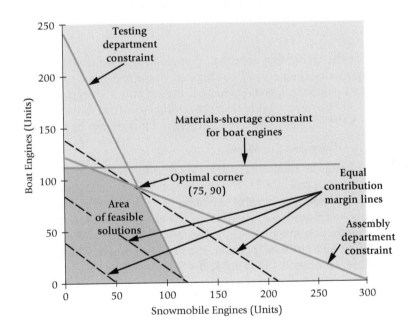

Exhibit 14

Linear Programming: Graphic Solution for Power Recreation

---

[3] As an example of how the lines are plotted in Exhibit 14, use equal signs instead of inequality signs and assume for the assembly department that $B = 0$; then $S = 300$ (600 machine-hours ÷ 2 machine-hours per snowmobile engine). Assume that $S = 0$; then $B = 120$ (600 machine-hours ÷ 5 machine-hours per boat engine). Connect those two points with a straight line.

[4] Standard computer software packages rely on the simplex method. The *simplex method* is an iterative step-by-step procedure for determining the optimal solution to an LP problem. It starts with a specific feasible solution and then tests it by substitution to see whether the result can be improved. These substitutions continue until no further improvement is possible and the optimal solution is obtained.

Second, move from corner point to corner point and compute the total contribution margin at each corner point.

Trial	Corner Point (S, B)	Snowmobile Engines (S)	Boat Engines (B)	Total Contribution Margin
1	(0, 0)	0	0	$240(0) + $375(0) = $0
2	(0, 110)	0	110	$240(0) + $375(110) = $41,250
3	(25,110)	25	110	$240(25) + $375(110) = $47,250
4	(75, 90)	75	90	$240(75) + $375(90) = $51,750[a]
5	(120, 0)	120	0	$240(120) + $375(0) = $28,800

[a] The optimal solution.

The optimal product mix is the mix that yields the highest total contribution: 75 snowmobile engines and 90 boat engines. To understand the solution, consider what happens when moving from the point (25,110) to (75,90). Power Recreation gives up $7,500 [$375 × (110 – 90)] in contribution margin from boat engines while gaining $12,000 [$240 × (75 – 25)] in contribution margin from snowmobile engines. This results in a net increase in contribution margin of $4,500 ($12,000 – $7,500), from $47,250 to $51,750.

Graphic Approach

Consider all possible combinations that will produce the same total contribution margin of, say, $12,000. That is,

$$$240S + $375B = $12,000$$

This set of $12,000 contribution margins is a straight dashed line through [S = 50 ($12,000 ÷ $240); B = 0)] and [S = 0, B = 32 ($12,000 ÷ $375)] in Exhibit 14. Other equal total contribution margins can be represented by lines parallel to this one. In Exhibit 14, we show three dashed lines. Lines drawn farther from the origin represent more sales of both products and higher amounts of equal contribution margins.

The optimal line is the one farthest from the origin but still passing through a point in the area of feasible solutions. This line represents the highest total contribution margin. The optimal solution—the number of snowmobile engines and boat engines that will maximize the objective function, total contribution margin—is the corner point (S = 75, B = 90). This solution will become apparent if you put a straight-edge ruler on the graph and move it outward from the origin and parallel with the $12,000 contribution margin line. Move the ruler as far away from the origin as possible—that is, increase the total contribution margin—without leaving the area of feasible solutions. In general, the optimal solution in a maximization problem lies at the corner where the dashed line intersects an extreme point of the area of feasible solutions. Moving the ruler out any farther puts it outside the area of feasible solutions.

Sensitivity Analysis

What are the implications of uncertainty about the accounting or technical coefficients used in the objective function (such as the contribution margin per unit of snowmobile engines or boat engines) or the constraints (such as the number of machine-hours it takes to make a snowmobile engine or a boat engine)? Consider how a change in the contribution margin of snowmobile engines from $240 to $300 per unit would affect the optimal solution. Assume the contribution margin for boat engines remains unchanged at $375 per unit. The revised objective function will be as follows:

$$TCM = $300S + $375B$$

Using the trial-and-error approach to calculate the total contribution margin for each of the five corner points described in the previous table, the optimal solution is still (S = 75, B = 90). What if the contribution margin of snowmobile engines falls to $160 per unit? The optimal solution remains the same (S = 75, B = 90). Thus, big changes in the contribution margin per unit of snowmobile engines have no effect on the optimal solution in this case. That's because, although the slopes of the equal contribution margin lines in Exhibit 14 change as the contribution margin of snowmobile engines changes from $240 to $300 to $160 per unit, the farthest point at which the equal contribution margin lines intersect the area of feasible solutions is still (S = 75, B = 90).

Terms to Learn

This chapter contains definitions of the following important terms:

book value	decision model	full costs of the product
business function costs	differential cost	incremental cost
constraint	differential revenue	incremental revenue

insourcing

linear programming (LP)

make-or-buy decisions

objective function

one-time-only special order

opportunity cost

outsourcing

product-mix decisions

qualitative factors

quantitative factors

relevant costs

relevant revenues

sunk costs

Assignment Material

Questions

11-1 Outline the five-step sequence in a decision process.

11-2 Define relevant costs. Why are historical costs irrelevant?

11-3 "All future costs are relevant." Do you agree? Why?

11-4 Distinguish between quantitative and qualitative factors in decision making.

11-5 Describe two potential problems that should be avoided in relevant-cost analysis.

11-6 "Variable costs are always relevant, and fixed costs are always irrelevant." Do you agree? Why?

11-7 "A component part should be purchased whenever the purchase price is less than its total manu-facturing cost per unit." Do you agree? Why?

11-8 Define opportunity cost.

11-9 "Managers should always buy inventory in quantities that result in the lowest purchase cost per unit." Do you agree? Why?

11-10 "Management should always maximize sales of the product with the highest contribution margin per unit." Do you agree? Why?

11-11 "A branch office or business segment that shows negative operating income should be shut down." Do you agree? Explain briefly.

11-12 "Cost written off as depreciation on equipment already purchased is always irrelevant." Do you agree? Why?

11-13 "Managers will always choose the alternative that maximizes operating income or minimizes costs in the decision model." Do you agree? Why?

11-14 Describe the three steps in solving a linear programming problem.

11-15 How might the optimal solution of a linear programming problem be determined?

Exercises

11-16 Disposal of assets. Answer the following questions.

1. A company has an inventory of 1,100 assorted parts for a line of missiles that has been discontinued. The inventory cost is $78,000. The parts can be either (a) remachined at total additional costs of $24,500 and then sold for $33,000 or (b) sold as scrap for $6,500. Which action is more profitable? Show your calculations.

2. A truck, costing $101,000 and uninsured, is wrecked its first day in use. It can be either (a) disposed of for $17,500 cash and replaced with a similar truck costing $103,500 or (b) rebuilt for $89,500, and thus be brand-new as far as operating characteristics and looks are concerned. Which action is less costly? Show your calculations.

11-17 Relevant and irrelevant costs. Answer the following questions.

1. DeCesare Computers makes 5,200 units of a circuit board, CB76 at a cost of $280 each. Variable cost per unit is $190 and fixed cost per unit is $90. Peach Electronics offers to supply 5,200 units of CB76 for $260. If DeCesare buys from Peach it will be able to save $10 per unit in fixed costs but continue to incur the remaining $80 per unit. Should DeCesare accept Peach's offer? Explain.

2. LN Manufacturing is deciding whether to keep or replace an old machine. It obtains the following information:

	Old Machine	New Machine
Original cost	$10,700	$9,000
Useful life	10 years	3 years
Current age	7 years	0 years
Remaining useful life	3 years	3 years
Accumulated depreciation	$7,490	Not acquired yet
Book value	$3,210	Not acquired yet
Current disposal value (in cash)	$2,200	Not acquired yet
Terminal disposal value (3 years from now)	$0	$0
Annual cash operating costs	$17,500	$15,500

LN Manufacturing uses straight-line depreciation. Ignore the time value of money and income taxes. Should LN Manufacturing replace the old machine? Explain.

11-18 Multiple choice. (CPA) Choose the best answer.

1. The Woody Company manufactures slippers and sells them at $10 a pair. Variable manufacturing cost is $4.50 a pair, and allocated fixed manufacturing cost is $1.50 a pair. It has enough idle capacity available to accept a one-time-only special order of 20,000 pairs of slippers at $6 a pair. Woody will not incur any marketing costs as a result of the special order. What would the effect on operating income be if the special order could be accepted without affecting normal sales: (a) $0, (b) $30,000 increase, (c) $90,000 increase, or (d) $120,000 increase? Show your calculations.

2. The Reno Company manufactures Part No. 498 for use in its production line. The manufacturing cost per unit for 20,000 units of Part No. 498 is as follows:

Direct materials	$ 6
Direct manufacturing labor	30
Variable manufacturing overhead	12
Fixed manufacturing overhead allocated	16
Total manufacturing cost per unit	$64

The Tray Company has offered to sell 20,000 units of Part No. 498 to Reno for $60 per unit. Reno will make the decision to buy the part from Tray if there is an overall savings of at least $25,000 for Reno. If Reno accepts Tray's offer, $9 per unit of the fixed overhead allocated would be eliminated. Furthermore, Reno has determined that the released facilities could be used to save relevant costs in the manufacture of Part No. 575. For Reno to achieve an overall savings of $25,000, the amount of relevant costs that would have to be saved by using the released facilities in the manufacture of Part No. 575 would be which of the following: (a) $80,000, (b) $85,000, (c) $125,000, or (d) $140,000? Show your calculations.

11-19 Special order, activity-based costing. (CMA, adapted) The Award Plus Company manufactures medals for winners of athletic events and other contests. Its manufacturing plant has the capacity to produce 10,000 medals each month. Current production and sales are 7,500 medals per month. The company normally charges $150 per medal. Cost information for the current activity level is as follows:

Variable costs that vary with number of units produced	
Direct materials	$ 262,500
Direct manufacturing labor	300,000
Variable costs (for setups, materials handling, quality control, and so on) that vary with number of batches, 150 batches × $500 per batch	75,000
Fixed manufacturing costs	275,000
Fixed marketing costs	175,000
Total costs	$1,087,500

Award Plus has just received a special one-time-only order for 2,500 medals at $100 per medal. Accepting the special order would not affect the company's regular business. Award Plus makes medals for its existing customers in batch sizes of 50 medals (150 batches × 50 medals per batch = 7,500 medals). The special order requires Award Plus to make the medals in 25 batches of 100 each.

Required

1. Should Award Plus accept this special order? Show your calculations.
2. Suppose plant capacity were only 9,000 medals instead of 10,000 medals each month. The special order must either be taken in full or be rejected completely. Should Award Plus accept the special order? Show your calculations.
3. As in requirement 1, assume that monthly capacity is 10,000 medals. Award Plus is concerned that if it accepts the special order, its existing customers will immediately demand a price discount of $10 in the month in which the special order is being filled. They would argue that Award Plus's capacity costs are now being spread over more units and that existing customers should get the benefit of these lower costs. Should Award Plus accept the special order under these conditions? Show your calculations.

11-20 Make versus buy, activity-based costing. The Svenson Corporation manufactures cellular modems. It manufactures its own cellular modem circuit boards (CMCB), an important part of the cellular modem. It reports the following cost information about the costs of making CMCBs in 2011 and the expected costs in 2012:

	Current Costs in 2011	Expected Costs in 2012
Variable manufacturing costs		
Direct material cost per CMCB	$ 180	$ 170
Direct manufacturing labor cost per CMCB	50	45
Variable manufacturing cost per batch for setups, materials handling, and quality control	1,600	1,500
Fixed manufacturing cost		
Fixed manufacturing overhead costs that can be avoided if CMCBs are not made	320,000	320,000
Fixed manufacturing overhead costs of plant depreciation, insurance, and administration that cannot be avoided even if CMCBs are not made	800,000	800,000

Svenson manufactured 8,000 CMCBs in 2011 in 40 batches of 200 each. In 2012, Svenson anticipates needing 10,000 CMCBs. The CMCBs would be produced in 80 batches of 125 each.

The Minton Corporation has approached Svenson about supplying CMCBs to Svenson in 2012 at $300 per CMCB on whatever delivery schedule Svenson wants.

Required

1. Calculate the total expected manufacturing cost per unit of making CMCBs in 2012.
2. Suppose the capacity currently used to make CMCBs will become idle if Svenson purchases CMCBs from Minton. On the basis of financial considerations alone, should Svenson make CMCBs or buy them from Minton? Show your calculations.
3. Now suppose that if Svenson purchases CMCBs from Minton, its best alternative use of the capacity currently used for CMCBs is to make and sell special circuit boards (CB3s) to the Essex Corporation. Svenson estimates the following incremental revenues and costs from CB3s:

Total expected incremental future revenues	$2,000,000
Total expected incremental future costs	$2,150,000

On the basis of financial considerations alone, should Svenson make CMCBs or buy them from Minton? Show your calculations.

11-21 Inventory decision, opportunity costs. Lawn World, a manufacturer of lawn mowers, predicts that it will purchase 264,000 spark plugs next year. Lawn World estimates that 22,000 spark plugs will be required each month. A supplier quotes a price of $7 per spark plug. The supplier also offers a special discount option: If all 264,000 spark plugs are purchased at the start of the year, a discount of 2% off the $7 price will be given. Lawn World can invest its cash at 10% per year. It costs Lawn World $260 to place each purchase order.

Required

1. What is the opportunity cost of interest forgone from purchasing all 264,000 units at the start of the year instead of in 12 monthly purchases of 22,000 units per order?
2. Would this opportunity cost be recorded in the accounting system? Why?
3. Should Lawn World purchase 264,000 units at the start of the year or 22,000 units each month? Show your calculations.

11-22 Relevant costs, contribution margin, product emphasis. The Seashore Stand is a take-out food store at a popular beach resort. Susan Sexton, owner of the Seashore Stand, is deciding how much refrigerator space to devote to four different drinks. Pertinent data on these four drinks are as follows:

	Cola	Lemonade	Punch	Natural Orange Juice
Selling price per case	$18.75	$20.50	$27.75	$39.30
Variable cost per case	$13.75	$15.60	$20.70	$30.40
Cases sold per foot of shelf space per day	22	12	6	13

Sexton has a maximum front shelf space of 12 feet to devote to the four drinks. She wants a minimum of 1 foot and a maximum of 6 feet of front shelf space for each drink.

Required

1. Calculate the contribution margin per case of each type of drink.
2. A coworker of Sexton's recommends that she maximize the shelf space devoted to those drinks with the highest contribution margin per case. Evaluate this recommendation.
3. What shelf-space allocation for the four drinks would you recommend for the Seashore Stand? Show your calculations.

11-23 Selection of most profitable product. Body-Builders, Inc., produces two basic types of weight-lifting equipment, Model 9 and Model 14. Pertinent data are as follows:

	A	B	C
		Per Unit	
1		Model 9	Model 14
2		**Model 9**	**Model 14**
3	Selling price	$100.00	$70.00
4	Costs		
5	Direct material	28.00	13.00
6	Direct manufacturing labor	15.00	25.00
7	Variable manufacturing overhead*	25.00	12.50
8	Fixed manufacturing overhead*	10.00	5.00
9	Marketing (all variable)	14.00	10.00
10	Total cost	92.00	65.50
11	Operating income	$ 8.00	$ 4.50
12			
13	*Allocated on the basis of machine-hours		

The weight-lifting craze is such that enough of either Model 9 or Model 14 can be sold to keep the plant operating at full capacity. Both products are processed through the same production departments.

Required Which products should be produced? Briefly explain your answer.

11-24 Which center to close, relevant-cost analysis, opportunity costs. Fair Lakes Hospital Corporation has been operating ambulatory surgery centers in Groveton and Stockdale, two small communities each about an hour away from its main hospital. As a cost control measure the hospital has decided that it needs only one of those two centers permanently, so one must be shut down. The decision regarding which center to close will be made on financial considerations alone. The following information is available:

a. The Groveton center was built 15 years ago at a cost of $5 million on land leased from the City of Groveton at a cost of $40,000 per year. The land and buildings will immediately revert back to the city if the center is closed. The center has annual operating costs of $2.5 million, all of which will be saved if the center is closed. In addition, Fair Lakes allocates $800,000 of common administrative costs to the Groveton center. If the center is closed, these costs would be reallocated to other ambulatory centers. If the center is kept open, Fair Lakes plans to invest $1 million in a fixed income note, which will earn the $40,000 that Fair Lakes needs for the lease payments.

b. The Stockdale center was built 20 years ago at a cost of $4.8 million, of which Fair Lakes and the City of Stockdale each paid half, on land donated by a hospital benefactor. Two years ago, Fair Lakes spent $2 million to renovate the facility. If the center is closed, the property will be sold to developers for $7 million. The operating costs of the center are $3 million per year, all of which will be saved if the center is closed. Fair Lakes allocates $1 million of common administrative costs to the Stockdale center. If the center is closed, these costs would be reallocated to other ambulatory centers.

c. Fair Lakes estimates that the operating costs of whichever center remains open will be $3.5 million per year.

Required The City Council of Stockdale has petitioned Fair Lakes to close the Groveton facility, thus sparing the Stockdale center. The Council argues that otherwise the $2 million spent on recent renovations would be wasted. Do you agree with the Stockdale City Council's arguments and conclusions? In your answer, identify and explain all costs that you consider relevant and all costs that you consider irrelevant for the center-closing decision.

11-25 Closing and opening stores. Sanchez Corporation runs two convenience stores, one in Connecticut and one in Rhode Island. Operating income for each store in 2012 is as follows:

	Connecticut Store	Rhode Island Store
Revenues	$1,070,000	$860,000
Operating costs		
Cost of goods sold	750,000	660,000
Lease rent (renewable each year)	90,000	75,000
Labor costs (paid on an hourly basis)	42,000	42,000
Depreciation of equipment	25,000	22,000
Utilities (electricity, heating)	43,000	46,000
Allocated corporate overhead	50,000	40,000
Total operating costs	1,000,000	885,000
Operating income (loss)	$ 70,000	$ (25,000)

The equipment has a zero disposal value. In a senior management meeting, Maria Lopez, the management accountant at Sanchez Corporation, makes the following comment, "Sanchez can increase its profitability by closing down the Rhode Island store or by adding another store like it."

Required

1. By closing down the Rhode Island store, Sanchez can reduce overall corporate overhead costs by $44,000. Calculate Sanchez's operating income if it closes the Rhode Island store. Is Maria Lopez's statement about the effect of closing the Rhode Island store correct? Explain.
2. Calculate Sanchez's operating income if it keeps the Rhode Island store open and opens another store with revenues and costs identical to the Rhode Island store (including a cost of $22,000 to acquire equipment with a one-year useful life and zero disposal value). Opening this store will increase corporate overhead costs by $4,000. Is Maria Lopez's statement about the effect of adding another store like the Rhode Island store correct? Explain.

11-26 Choosing customers. Broadway Printers operates a printing press with a monthly capacity of 2,000 machine-hours. Broadway has two main customers: Taylor Corporation and Kelly Corporation. Data on each customer for January follows:

	Taylor Corporation	Kelly Corporation	Total
Revenues	$120,000	$80,000	$200,000
Variable costs	42,000	48,000	90,000
Contribution margin	78,000	32,000	110,000
Fixed costs (allocated)	60,000	40,000	100,000
Operating income	$ 18,000	$ (8,000)	$ 10,000
Machine-hours required	1,500 hours	500 hours	2,000 hours

Kelly Corporation indicates that it wants Broadway to do an *additional* $80,000 worth of printing jobs during February. These jobs are identical to the existing business Broadway did for Kelly in January in terms of variable costs and machine-hours required. Broadway anticipates that the business from Taylor Corporation in February will be the same as that in January. Broadway can choose to accept as much of the Taylor and Kelly business for February as its capacity allows. Assume that total machine-hours and fixed costs for February will be the same as in January.

Required

What action should Broadway take to maximize its operating income? Show your calculations.

11-27 Relevance of equipment costs. The Auto Wash Company has just today paid for and installed a special machine for polishing cars at one of its several outlets. It is the first day of the company's fiscal year. The machine costs $20,000. Its annual cash operating costs total $15,000. The machine will have a four-year useful life and a zero terminal disposal value.

After the machine has been used for only one day, a salesperson offers a different machine that promises to do the same job at annual cash operating costs of $9,000. The new machine will cost $24,000 cash, installed. The "old" machine is unique and can be sold outright for only $10,000, minus $2,000 removal cost. The new machine, like the old one, will have a four-year useful life and zero terminal disposal value.

Revenues, all in cash, will be $150,000 annually, and other cash costs will be $110,000 annually, regardless of this decision.

For simplicity, ignore income taxes and the time value of money.

Required

1. a. Prepare a statement of cash receipts and disbursements for each of the four years under each alternative. What is the cumulative difference in cash flow for the four years taken together?

b. Prepare income statements for each of the four years under each alternative. Assume straight-line depreciation. What is the cumulative difference in operating income for the four years taken together?

c. What are the irrelevant items in your presentations in requirements a and b? Why are they irrelevant?

2. Suppose the cost of the "old" machine was $1 million rather than $20,000. Nevertheless, the old machine can be sold outright for only $10,000, minus $2,000 removal cost. Would the net differences in requirements 1a and 1b change? Explain.

3. Is there any conflict between the decision model and the incentives of the manager who has just purchased the "old" machine and is considering replacing it a day later?

11-28 Equipment upgrade versus replacement. (A. Spero, adapted) The TechGuide Company produces and sells 7,500 modular computer desks per year at a selling price of $750 each. Its current production equipment, purchased for $1,800,000 and with a five-year useful life, is only two years old. It has a terminal disposal value of $0 and is depreciated on a straight-line basis. The equipment has a current disposal price of $450,000. However, the emergence of a new molding technology has led TechGuide to consider either upgrading or replacing the production equipment. The following table presents data for the two alternatives:

	A	B	C
		Upgrade	**Replace**
2	One-time equipment costs	$3,000,000	$4,800,000
3	Variable manufacturing cost per desk	$ 150	$ 75
4	Remaining useful life of equipment (years)	3	3
5	Terminal disposal value of equipment	$ 0	$ 0

All equipment costs will continue to be depreciated on a straight-line basis. For simplicity, ignore income taxes and the time value of money.

Required

1. Should TechGuide upgrade its production line or replace it? Show your calculations.

2. Now suppose the one-time equipment cost to replace the production equipment is somewhat negotiable. All other data are as given previously. What is the maximum one-time equipment cost that TechGuide would be willing to pay to replace the old equipment rather than upgrade it?

3. Assume that the capital expenditures to replace and upgrade the production equipment are as given in the original exercise, but that the production and sales quantity is not known. For what production and sales quantity would TechGuide (i) upgrade the equipment or (ii) replace the equipment?

4. Assume that all data are as given in the original exercise. Dan Doria is TechGuide's manager, and his bonus is based on operating income. Because he is likely to relocate after about a year, his current bonus is his primary concern. Which alternative would Doria choose? Explain.

MyAccountingLab

Problems

11-29 Special Order. Louisville Corporation produces baseball bats for kids that it sells for $32 each. At capacity, the company can produce 50,000 bats a year. The costs of producing and selling 50,000 bats are as follows:

	Cost per Bat	Total Costs
Direct materials	$12	$ 600,000
Direct manufacturing labor	3	150,000
Variable manufacturing overhead	1	50,000
Fixed manufacturing overhead	5	250,000
Variable selling expenses	2	100,000
Fixed selling expenses	4	200,000
Total costs	$27	$1,350,000

Required

1. Suppose Louisville is currently producing and selling 40,000 bats. At this level of production and sales, its fixed costs are the same as given in the preceding table. Ripkin Corporation wants to place a one-time special order for 10,000 bats at $25 each. Louisville will incur no variable selling costs for this special order. Should Louisville accept this one-time special order? Show your calculations.

2. Now suppose Louisville is currently producing and selling 50,000 bats. If Louisville accepts Ripkin's offer it will have to sell 10,000 fewer bats to its regular customers. (a) On financial considerations alone, should Louisville accept this one-time special order? Show your calculations. (b) On financial considerations alone, at what price would Louisville be indifferent between accepting the special order and continuing to sell to its regular customers at $32 per bat. (c) What other factors should Louisville consider in deciding whether to accept the one-time special order?

11-30 International outsourcing. Bernie's Bears, Inc., manufactures plush toys in a facility in Cleveland, Ohio. Recently, the company designed a group of collectible resin figurines to go with the plush toy line. Management is trying to decide whether to manufacture the figurines themselves in existing space in the Cleveland facility or to accept an offer from a manufacturing company in Indonesia. Data concerning the decision follows:

Expected annual sales of figurines (in units)	400,000
Average selling price of a figurine	$5
Price quoted by Indonesian company, in Indonesian Rupiah (IDR), for each figurine	27,300 IDR
Current exchange rate	9,100 IDR = $1
Variable manufacturing costs	$2.85 per unit
Incremental annual fixed manufacturing costs associated with the new product line	$200,000
Variable selling and distribution costs[a]	$0.50 per unit
Annual fixed selling and distribution costs[a]	$285,000

[a] Selling and distribution costs are the same regardless of whether the figurines are manufactured in Cleveland or imported.

Required

1. Should Bernie's Bears manufacture the 400,000 figurines in the Cleveland facility or purchase them from the Indonesian supplier? Explain.
2. Bernie's Bears believes that the US dollar may weaken in the coming months against the Indonesian Rupiah and does not want to face any currency risk. Assume that Bernie's Bears can enter into a forward contract today to purchase 27,300 IDRs for $3.40. Should Bernie's Bears manufacture the 400,000 figurines in the Cleveland facility or purchase them from the Indonesian supplier? Explain.
3. What are some of the qualitative factors that Bernie's Bears should consider when deciding whether to outsource the figurine manufacturing to Indonesia?

11-31 Relevant costs, opportunity costs. Larry Miller, the general manager of Basil Software, must decide when to release the new version of Basil's spreadsheet package, Easyspread 2.0. Development of Easyspread 2.0 is complete; however, the diskettes, compact discs, and user manuals have not yet been produced. The product can be shipped starting July 1, 2011.

The major problem is that Basil has overstocked the previous version of its spreadsheet package, Easyspread 1.0. Miller knows that once Easyspread 2.0 is introduced, Basil will not be able to sell any more units of Easyspread 1.0. Rather than just throwing away the inventory of Easyspread 1.0, Miller is wondering if it might be better to continue to sell Easyspread 1.0 for the next three months and introduce Easyspread 2.0 on October 1, 2011, when the inventory of Easyspread 1.0 will be sold out.

The following information is available:

	Easyspread 1.0	Easyspread 2.0
Selling price	$160	$195
Variable cost per unit of diskettes, compact discs, user manuals	25	30
Development cost per unit	70	100
Marketing and administrative cost per unit	35	40
Total cost per unit	130	170
Operating income per unit	$ 30	$ 25

Development cost per unit for each product equals the total costs of developing the software product divided by the anticipated unit sales over the life of the product. Marketing and administrative costs are fixed costs in 2011, incurred to support all marketing and administrative activities of Basil Software. Marketing and administrative costs are allocated to products on the basis of the budgeted revenues of each product. The preceding unit costs assume Easyspread 2.0 will be introduced on October 1, 2011.

Required

1. On the basis of financial considerations alone, should Miller introduce Easyspread 2.0 on July 1, 2011, or wait until October 1, 2011? Show your calculations, clearly identifying relevant and irrelevant revenues and costs.
2. What other factors might Larry Miller consider in making a decision?

11-32 Opportunity costs. (H. Schaefer) The Wild Boar Corporation is working at full production capacity producing 13,000 units of a unique product, Rosebo. Manufacturing cost per unit for Rosebo is as follows:

Direct materials	$ 5
Direct manufacturing labor	1
Manufacturing overhead	7
Total manufacturing cost	$13

Manufacturing overhead cost per unit is based on variable cost per unit of $4 and fixed costs of $39,000 (at full capacity of 13,000 units). Marketing cost per unit, all variable, is $2, and the selling price is $26.

A customer, the Miami Company, has asked Wild Boar to produce 3,500 units of Orangebo, a modification of Rosebo. Orangebo would require the same manufacturing processes as Rosebo. Miami has offered to pay Wild Boar $20 for a unit of Orangebo and share half of the marketing cost per unit.

Required

1. What is the opportunity cost to Wild Boar of producing the 3,500 units of Orangebo? (Assume that no overtime is worked.)
2. The Buckeye Corporation has offered to produce 3,500 units of Rosebo for Wolverine so that Wild Boar may accept the Miami offer. That is, if Wild Boar accepts the Buckeye offer, Wild Boar would manufacture 9,500 units of Rosebo and 3,500 units of Orangebo and purchase 3,500 units of Rosebo from Buckeye. Buckeye would charge Wild Boar $18 per unit to manufacture Rosebo. On the basis of financial considerations alone, should Wild Boar accept the Buckeye offer? Show your calculations.
3. Suppose Wild Boar had been working at less than full capacity, producing 9,500 units of Rosebo at the time the Miami offer was made. Calculate the minimum price Wild Boar should accept for Orangebo under these conditions. (Ignore the previous $20 selling price.)

11-33 Product mix, special order. (N. Melumad, adapted) Pendleton Engineering makes cutting tools for metalworking operations. It makes two types of tools: R3, a regular cutting tool, and HP6, a high-precision cutting tool. R3 is manufactured on a regular machine, but HP6 must be manufactured on both the regular machine and a high-precision machine. The following information is available.

	R3	HP6
Selling price	$ 100	$ 150
Variable manufacturing cost per unit	$ 60	$ 100
Variable marketing cost per unit	$ 15	$ 35
Budgeted total fixed overhead costs	$350,000	$550,000
Hours required to produce one unit on the regular machine	1.0	0.5

Additional information includes the following:

a. Pendleton faces a capacity constraint on the regular machine of 50,000 hours per year.
b. The capacity of the high-precision machine is not a constraint.
c. Of the $550,000 budgeted fixed overhead costs of HP6, $300,000 are lease payments for the high-precision machine. This cost is charged entirely to HP6 because Pendleton uses the machine exclusively to produce HP6. The lease agreement for the high-precision machine can be canceled at any time without penalties.
d. All other overhead costs are fixed and cannot be changed.

Required

1. What product mix—that is, how many units of R3 and HP6—will maximize Pendleton's operating income? Show your calculations.
2. Suppose Pendleton can increase the annual capacity of its regular machines by 15,000 machine-hours at a cost of $150,000. Should Pendleton increase the capacity of the regular machines by 15,000 machine-hours? By how much will Pendleton's operating income increase? Show your calculations.
3. Suppose that the capacity of the regular machines has been increased to 65,000 hours. Pendleton has been approached by Carter Corporation to supply 20,000 units of another cutting tool, S3, for $120 per unit. Pendleton must either accept the order for all 20,000 units or reject it totally. S3 is exactly like R3 except that its variable manufacturing cost is $70 per unit. (It takes one hour to produce one unit of S3 on the regular machine, and variable marketing cost equals $15 per unit.) What product mix should Pendleton choose to maximize operating income? Show your calculations.

11-34 Dropping a product line, selling more units. The Northern Division of Grossman Corporation makes and sells tables and beds. The following estimated revenue and cost information from the division's activity-based costing system is available for 2011.

	4,000 Tables	5,000 Beds	Total
Revenues ($125 × 4,000; $200 × 5,000)	$500,000	$1,000,000	$1,500,000
Variable direct materials and direct manufacturing labor costs			
($75 × 4,000; $105 × 5,000)	300,000	525,000	825,000
Depreciation on equipment used exclusively by each product line	42,000	58,000	100,000
Marketing and distribution costs			
$40,000 (fixed) + ($750 per shipment × 40 shipments)	70,000		
$60,000 (fixed) + ($750 per shipment × 100 shipments)		135,000 }	205,000
Fixed general-administration costs of the division allocated to			
product lines on the basis of revenue	110,000	220,000	330,000
Corporate-office costs allocated to product lines on the basis			
of revenues	50,000	100,000	150,000
Total costs	572,000	1,038,000	1,610,000
Operating income (loss)	$ (72,000)	$ (38,000)	$ (110,000)

Additional information includes the following:

a. On January 1, 2011, the equipment has a book value of $100,000, a one-year useful life, and zero disposal value. Any equipment not used will remain idle.

b. Fixed marketing and distribution costs of a product line can be avoided if the line is discontinued.

c. Fixed general-administration costs of the division and corporate-office costs will not change if sales of individual product lines are increased or decreased or if product lines are added or dropped.

Required

1. On the basis of financial considerations alone, should the Northern Division discontinue the tables product line for the year, assuming the released facilities remain idle? Show your calculations.

2. What would be the effect on the Northern Division's operating income if it were to sell 4,000 more tables? Assume that to do so the division would have to acquire additional equipment costing $42,000 with a one-year useful life and zero terminal disposal value. Assume further that the fixed marketing and distribution costs would not change but that the number of shipments would double. Show your calculations.

3. Given the Northern Division's expected operating loss of $110,000, should Grossman Corporation shut it down for the year? Assume that shutting down the Northern Division will have no effect on corporate-office costs but will lead to savings of all general-administration costs of the division. Show your calculations.

4. Suppose Grossman Corporation has the opportunity to open another division, the Southern Division, whose revenues and costs are expected to be identical to the Northern Division's revenues and costs (including a cost of $100,000 to acquire equipment with a one-year useful life and zero terminal disposal value). Opening the new division will have no effect on corporate-office costs. Should Grossman open the Southern Division? Show your calculations.

11-35 Make or buy, unknown level of volume. (A. Atkinson) Oxford Engineering manufactures small engines. The engines are sold to manufacturers who install them in such products as lawn mowers. The company currently manufactures all the parts used in these engines but is considering a proposal from an external supplier who wishes to supply the starter assemblies used in these engines.

The starter assemblies are currently manufactured in Division 3 of Oxford Engineering. The costs relating to the starter assemblies for the past 12 months were as follows:

Direct materials	$200,000
Direct manufacturing labor	150,000
Manufacturing overhead	400,000
Total	$750,000

Over the past year, Division 3 manufactured 150,000 starter assemblies. The average cost for each starter assembly is $5 ($750,000 ÷ 150,000).

Further analysis of manufacturing overhead revealed the following information. Of the total manufacturing overhead, only 25% is considered variable. Of the fixed portion, $150,000 is an allocation of general overhead that will remain unchanged for the company as a whole if production of the starter assemblies is discontinued. A further $100,000 of the fixed overhead is avoidable if production of the starter assemblies is discontinued. The balance of the current fixed overhead, $50,000, is the division manager's salary. If production of the starter assemblies is discontinued, the manager of Division 3 will be transferred to Division 2 at the same salary. This move will allow the company to save the $40,000 salary that would otherwise be paid to attract an outsider to this position.

Required

1. Tidnish Electronics, a reliable supplier, has offered to supply starter-assembly units at $4 per unit. Because this price is less than the current average cost of $5 per unit, the vice president of manufacturing is eager to accept this offer. On the basis of financial considerations alone, should the outside offer be accepted? Show your calculations. (*Hint:* Production output in the coming year may be different from production output in the past year.)

2. How, if at all, would your response to requirement 1 change if the company could use the vacated plant space for storage and, in so doing, avoid $50,000 of outside storage charges currently incurred? Why is this information relevant or irrelevant?

11-36 Make versus buy, activity-based costing, opportunity costs. The Weaver Company produces gas grills. This year's expected production is 20,000 units. Currently, Weaver makes the side burners for its grills. Each grill includes two side burners. Weaver's management accountant reports the following costs for making the 40,000 burners:

	Cost per Unit	Costs for 40,000 Units
Direct materials	$5.00	$200,000
Direct manufacturing labor	2.50	100,000
Variable manufacturing overhead	1.25	50,000
Inspection, setup, materials handling		4,000
Machine rent		8,000
Allocated fixed costs of plant administration, taxes, and insurance		50,000
Total costs		$412,000

Weaver has received an offer from an outside vendor to supply any number of burners Weaver requires at $9.25 per burner. The following additional information is available:

a. Inspection, setup, and materials-handling costs vary with the number of batches in which the burners are produced. Weaver produces burners in batch sizes of 1,000 units. Weaver will produce the 40,000 units in 40 batches.

b. Weaver rents the machine used to make the burners. If Weaver buys all of its burners from the outside vendor, it does not need to pay rent on this machine.

Required

1. Assume that if Weaver purchases the burners from the outside vendor, the facility where the burners are currently made will remain idle. On the basis of financial considerations alone, should Weaver accept the outside vendor's offer at the anticipated volume of 40,000 burners? Show your calculations.

2. For this question, assume that if the burners are purchased outside, the facilities where the burners are currently made will be used to upgrade the grills by adding a rotisserie attachment. (Note: Each grill contains two burners and one rotisserie attachment.) As a consequence, the selling price of grills will be raised by $30. The variable cost per unit of the upgrade would be $24, and additional tooling costs of $100,000 per year would be incurred. On the basis of financial considerations alone, should Weaver make or buy the burners, assuming that 20,000 grills are produced (and sold)? Show your calculations.

3. The sales manager at Weaver is concerned that the estimate of 20,000 grills may be high and believes that only 16,000 grills will be sold. Production will be cut back, freeing up work space. This space can be used to add the rotisserie attachments whether Weaver buys the burners or makes them in-house. At this lower output, Weaver will produce the burners in 32 batches of 1,000 units each. On the basis of financial considerations alone, should Weaver purchase the burners from the outside vendor? Show your calculations.

11-37 Multiple choice, comprehensive problem on relevant costs. The following are the Class Company's unit costs of manufacturing and marketing a high-style pen at an output level of 20,000 units per month:

Manufacturing cost	
Direct materials	$1.00
Direct manufacturing labor	1.20
Variable manufacturing overhead cost	0.80
Fixed manufacturing overhead cost	0.50
Marketing cost	
Variable	1.50
Fixed	0.90

Required

The following situations refer only to the preceding data; there is *no connection* between the situations. Unless stated otherwise, assume a regular selling price of $6 per unit. Choose the best answer to each question. Show your calculations.

1. For an inventory of 10,000 units of the high-style pen presented in the balance sheet, the appropriate unit cost to use is (a) $3.00, (b) $3.50, (c) $5.00, (d) $2.20, or (e) $5.90.

2. The pen is usually produced and sold at the rate of 240,000 units per year (an average of 20,000 per month). The selling price is $6 per unit, which yields total annual revenues of $1,440,000. Total costs are $1,416,000, and operating income is $24,000, or $0.10 per unit. Market research estimates that unit sales could be increased by 10% if prices were cut to $5.80. Assuming the implied cost-behavior patterns continue, this action, if taken, would

   a. decrease operating income by $7,200.

   b. decrease operating income by $0.20 per unit ($48,000) but increase operating income by 10% of revenues ($144,000), for a net increase of $96,000.

   c. decrease fixed cost per unit by 10%, or $0.14, per unit, and thus decrease operating income by $0.06 ($0.20 – $0.14) per unit.

   d. increase unit sales to 264,000 units, which at the $5.80 price would give total revenues of $1,531,200 and lead to costs of $5.90 per unit for 264,000 units, which would equal $1,557,600, and result in an operating loss of $26,400.

   e. None of these

3. A contract with the government for 5,000 units of the pens calls for the reimbursement of all manufacturing costs plus a fixed fee of $1,000. No variable marketing costs are incurred on the government contract. You are asked to compare the following two alternatives:

Sales Each Month to	Alternative A	Alternative B
Regular customers	15,000 units	15,000 units
Government	0 units	5,000 units

Operating income under alternative B is greater than that under alternative A by (a) $1,000, (b) $2,500, (c) $3,500, (d) $300, or (e) none of these.

4. Assume the same data with respect to the government contract as in requirement 3 except that the two alternatives to be compared are as follows:

Sales Each Month to	Alternative A	Alternative B
Regular customers	20,000 units	15,000 units
Government	0 units	5,000 units

Operating income under alternative B relative to that under alternative A is (a) $4,000 less, (b) $3,000 greater, (c) $6,500 less, (d) $500 greater, or (e) none of these.

5. The company wants to enter a foreign market in which price competition is keen. The company seeks a one-time-only special order for 10,000 units on a minimum-unit-price basis. It expects that shipping costs for this order will amount to only $0.75 per unit, but the fixed costs of obtaining the contract will be $4,000. The company incurs no variable marketing costs other than shipping costs. Domestic business will be unaffected. The selling price to break even is (a) $3.50, (b) $4.15, (c) $4.25, (d) $3.00, or (e) $5.00.

6. The company has an inventory of 1,000 units of pens that must be sold immediately at reduced prices. Otherwise, the inventory will become worthless. The unit cost that is relevant for establishing the minimum selling price is (a) $4.50, (b) $4.00, (c) $3.00, (d) $5.90, or (e) $1.50.

7. A proposal is received from an outside supplier who will make and ship the high-style pens directly to the Class Company's customers as sales orders are forwarded from Class's sales staff. Class's fixed marketing costs will be unaffected, but its variable marketing costs will be slashed by 20%. Class's plant will be idle, but its fixed manufacturing overhead will continue at 50% of present levels. How much per unit would the company be able to pay the supplier without decreasing operating income? (a) $4.75, (b) $3.95, (c) $2.95, (d) $5.35, or (e) none of these.

11-38 Closing down divisions. Belmont Corporation has four operating divisions. The budgeted revenues and expenses for each division for 2011 follows:

	Division			
	A	**B**	**C**	**D**
Sales	$630,000	$ 632,000	$960,000	$1,240,000
Cost of goods sold	550,000	620,000	765,000	925,000
Selling, general, and administrative expenses	120,000	135,000	144,000	210,000
Operating income/loss	$ (40,000)	$(123,000)	$ 51,000	$ 105,000

Further analysis of costs reveals the following percentages of variable costs in each division:

Cost of goods sold	90%	80%	90%	85%
Selling, general, and administrative expenses	50%	50%	60%	60%

Closing down any division would result in savings of 40% of the fixed costs of that division.

Top management is very concerned about the unprofitable divisions (A and B) and is considering closing them for the year.

Required

1. Calculate the increase or decrease in operating income if Belmont closes division A.
2. Calculate the increase or decrease in operating income if Belmont closes division B.
3. What other factors should the top management of Belmont consider before making a decision?

11-39 Product mix, constrained resource. Westford Company produces three products, A110, B382, and C657. Unit data for the three products follows:

	Product		
	A110	**B382**	**C657**
Selling price	$84	$56	70
Variable costs			
Direct materials	24	15	9
Labor and other costs	28	27	40
Quantity of Bistide per unit	8 lb.	5 lb.	3 lb.

All three products use the same direct material, Bistide. The demand for the products far exceeds the direct materials available to produce the products. Bistide costs $3 per pound and a maximum of 5,000 pounds is available each month. Westford must produce a minimum of 200 units of each product.

Required

1. How many units of product A110, B382, and C657 should Westford produce?
2. What is the maximum amount Westford would be willing to pay for another 1,000 pounds of Bistide?

11-40 Optimal product mix. (CMA adapted) Della Simpson, Inc., sells two popular brands of cookies: Della's Delight and Bonny's Bourbon. Della's Delight goes through the Mixing and Baking departments, and Bonny's Bourbon, a filled cookie, goes through the Mixing, Filling, and Baking departments.

Michael Shirra, vice president for sales, believes that at the current price, Della Simpson can sell all of its daily production of Della's Delight and Bonny's Bourbon. Both cookies are made in batches of 3,000. In each department, the time required per batch and the total time available each day are as follows:

	Home	Insert	Page Layout	Formulas	Data	Review
	A		B	C	D	
1			**Department Minutes**			
2			**Mixing**	**Filling**	**Baking**	
3	Della's Delight		30	0	10	
4	Bonny's Bourbon		15	15	15	
5	Total available per day		660	270	300	

Revenue and cost data for each type of cookie are as follows:

	Home	Insert	Page Layout	Formulas	Data
	A		B	C	
7			**Della's**	**Bonny's**	
8			**Delight**	**Bourbon**	
9	Revenue per batch		$ 475	$ 375	
10	Variable cost per batch		175	125	
11	Contribution margin per batch		$ 300	$ 250	
12	Monthly fixed costs				
13	(allocated to each product)		$18,650	$22,350	

Required

1. Using *D* to represent the batches of Della's Delight and *B* to represent the batches of Bonny's Bourbon made and sold each day, formulate Shirra's decision as an LP model.
2. Compute the optimal number of batches of each type of cookie that Della Simpson, Inc., should make and sell each day to maximize operating income.

11-41 Dropping a customer, activity-based costing, ethics. Jack Arnoldson is the management accountant for Valley Restaurant Supply (VRS). Bob Gardner, the VRS sales manager, and Jack are meeting to discuss the profitability of one of the customers, Franco's Pizza. Jack hands Bob the following analysis of Franco's activity during the last quarter, taken from Valley's activity-based costing system:

Sales	$15,600
Cost of goods sold (all variable)	9,350
Order processing (25 orders processed at $200 per order)	5,000
Delivery (2,500 miles driven at $0.50 per mile)	1,250
Rush orders (3 rush orders at $110 per rush order)	330
Sales calls (3 sales calls at $100 per call)	300
Profits	($ 630)

Bob looks at the report and remarks, "I'm glad to see all my hard work is paying off with Franco's. Sales have gone up 10% over the previous quarter!"

Jack replies, "Increased sales are great, but I'm worried about Franco's margin, Bob. We were show-ing a profit with Franco's at the lower sales level, but now we're showing a loss. Gross margin percentage this quarter was 40%, down five percentage points from the prior quarter. I'm afraid that corporate will push hard to drop them as a customer if things don't turn around."

"That's crazy," Bob responds. "A lot of that overhead for things like order processing, deliveries, and sales calls would just be allocated to other customers if we dropped Franco's. This report makes it look like we're losing money on Franco's when we're not. In any case, I am sure you can do something to make its profitability look closer to what we think it is. No one doubts that Franco is a very good customer."

Required

1. Assume that Bob is partly correct in his assessment of the report. Upon further investigation, it is deter-mined that 10% of the order processing costs and 20% of the delivery costs would not be avoidable if VRS were to drop Franco's. Would VRS benefit from dropping Franco's? Show your calculations.
2. Bob's bonus is based on meeting sales targets. Based on the preceding information regarding gross margin percentage, what might Bob have done last quarter to meet his target and receive his bonus? How might VRS revise its bonus system to address this?
3. Should Jack rework the numbers? How should he respond to Bob's comments about making Franco look more profitable?

Collaborative Learning Problem

11-42 Equipment replacement decisions and performance evaluation. Bob Moody manages the Knoxville plant of George Manufacturing. He has been approached by a representative of Darda Engineering regarding the possible replacement of a large piece of manufacturing equipment that George uses in its process with a more efficient model. While the representative made some compelling arguments in favor of replacing the 3-year old equipment, Moody is hesitant. Moody is hoping to be promoted next year to manager of the larger Chicago plant, and he knows that the accrual-basis net operating income of the Knoxville plant will be evaluated closely as part of the promotion decision. The following information is available concerning the equipment replacement decision:

- The historic cost of the old machine is $300,000. It has a current book value of $120,000, two remaining years of useful life, and a market value of $72,000. Annual depreciation expense is $60,000. It is expected to have a salvage value of $0 at the end of its useful life.

- The new equipment will cost $180,000. It will have a two-year useful life and a $0 salvage value. George uses straight-line depreciation on all equipment.

- The new equipment will reduce electricity costs by $35,000 per year, and will reduce direct manufac-turing labor costs by $30,000 per year.

For simplicity, ignore income taxes and the time value of money.

Required

1. Assume that Moody's priority is to receive the promotion, and he makes the equipment replacement decision based on next year's accrual-based net operating income. Which alternative would he choose? Show your calculations.
2. What are the relevant factors in the decision? Which alternative is in the best interest of the company over the next two years? Show your calculations.
3. At what cost of the new equipment would Moody be willing to purchase it? Explain.

Pricing Decisions and Cost Management

From Chapter 12 of *Cost Accounting: A Managerial Emphasis*, 14/e. Charles T. Horngren. Srikant M. Datar. Madhav Rajan.

Pricing Decisions and Cost Management

Most companies make a tremendous effort to analyze their costs and prices.

They know if the price is too high, customers will look elsewhere, too low, and the firm won't be able to cover the cost of making the product. Some companies, however, understand that it is possible to charge a low price to stimulate demand and meet customer needs while relentlessly managing costs to earn a profit. Tata Motors is one such company.

Target Pricing and Tata Motors' $2,500 Car[1]

Despite India's rapid economic growth and growing market for consumer goods, transportation options in the world's most populous country remain limited. Historically, Indians relied on public transportation, bicycles, and motorcycles to get around. Less than 1% owned cars, with most foreign models ill-suited to India's unique traffic conditions. Most cars had unnecessary product features and were priced too high for the vast majority of Indians.

But Ratan Tata, chairman of India's Tata Motors, saw India's dearth of cars as an opportunity. In 2003, after seeing a family riding dangerously on a two-wheel scooter, Mr. Tata set a challenge for his company to build a 'people's car' for the Indian market with three requirements: It should (1) adhere to existing regulatory requirements, (2) achieve certain performance targets for fuel efficiency and acceleration, and (3) cost only $2,500, about the price of the optional DVD player in a new Lexus sport utility vehicle sold in the United States.

The task was daunting: $2,500 was about half the price of the cheapest Indian car. One of Tata's suppliers said, "It's basically throwing out everything the auto industry has thought about cost structures in the past and taking a clean sheet of paper and asking, 'What's possible?'" Mr. Tata and his managers responded with what some analysts have described as "Gandhian engineering"

---

[1] *Sources*: Giridharadas, Anand. 2008. Four wheels for the masses: The $2,500 car. *New York Times*, January 8. http://www.nytimes.com/2008/01/08/business/worldbusiness/08indiacar.html Kripalani, Manjeet. 2008. Inside the Tata Nano Factory. *BusinessWeek*, May 9. http://www.businessweek.com/print/innovate/content/may2008/id2008059_312111.htm

principles: deep frugality with a willingness to challenge conventional wisdom.

At a fundamental level, Tata Motors' engineers created a new category of car by doing more with less. Extracting costs from traditional car development, Tata eschewed traditional long-term supplier relationships, and instead forced suppliers to compete for its business using Internet-based auctions. Engineering innovations led to a hollowed-out steering-wheel shaft, a smaller diameter drive shaft, a trunk with space for a briefcase, one windshield wiper instead of two, and a rear-mounted engine not much more powerful than a high-end riding lawnmower. Moreover, Tata's car has no radio, no power steering, no power windows, and no air conditioning—features standard on most vehicles.

Ajit Solanki/AP Wide World Photos

But when Tata Motors introduced the "Nano" in 2008, the company had successfully built a $2,500 entry-level car that is fuel efficient, 50 miles to the gallon; reaches 65 miles per hour; and meets all current Indian emission, pollution, and safety standards. While revolutionizing the Indian automotive marketplace, the "Nano" is also changing staid global automakers. Already, the French-Japanese alliance Renault-Nissan and the Indian-Japanese joint venture Maruti Suzuki are trying to make ultra-cheap cars for India, while Ford recently made India the manufacturing hub for all of its low-cost cars.

Just like Ratan Tata, managers at many innovative companies are taking a fresh look at their strategic pricing decisions. This chapter describes how managers evaluate demand at different prices and manage costs across the value chain and over a product's life cycle to achieve profitability.

Major Influences on Pricing Decisions

Consider for a moment how managers at Adidas might price their newest line of sneakers, or how decision makers at Microsoft would determine how much to charge for a monthly subscription of MSN Internet service. How companies price a product or a service ultimately depends on the demand and supply for it. Three influences on demand and supply are customers, competitors, and costs.

Customers, Competitors, and Costs

Customers

Customers influence price through their effect on the demand for a product or service, based on factors such as the features of a product and its quality. As the Tata Motors example illustrates, companies must always examine pricing decisions through the eyes of their customers and then manage costs to earn a profit.

Competitors

No business operates in a vacuum. Companies must always be aware of the actions of their competitors. At one extreme, alternative or substitute products of competitors hurt demand and force a company to lower prices. At the other extreme, a company without a competitor is free to set higher prices. When there are competitors, companies try to learn about competitors' technologies, plant capacities, and operating strategies to estimate competitors' costs—valuable information when setting prices.

Because competition spans international borders, fluctuations in exchange rates between different countries' currencies affect costs and pricing decisions. For example, if the yen weakens against the U.S. dollar, Japanese products become cheaper for American consumers and, consequently, more competitive in U.S. markets.

Costs

Costs influence prices because they affect supply. The lower the cost of producing a product, the greater the quantity of product the company is willing to supply. Generally, as companies increase supply, the cost of producing an additional unit initially declines but eventually increases. Companies supply products as long as the revenue from selling additional units exceeds the cost of producing them. Managers who understand the cost of producing products set prices that make the products attractive to customers while maximizing operating income.

Weighing Customers, Competitors, and Costs

Surveys indicate that companies weigh customers, competitors, and costs differently when making pricing decisions. At one extreme, companies operating in a perfectly competitive market sell very similar commodity-type products, such as wheat, rice, steel, and aluminum. These companies have no control over setting prices and must accept the price determined by a market consisting of many participants. Cost information is only helpful in deciding the quantity of output to produce to maximize operating income.

In less-competitive markets, such as those for cameras, televisions, and cellular phones, products are differentiated, and all three factors affect prices: The value customers place on a product and the prices charged for competing products affect demand, and the costs of producing and delivering the product influence supply.

As competition lessens even more, the key factor affecting pricing decisions is the customer's willingness to pay based on the value that customers place on the product or service, not costs or competitors. In the extreme, there are monopolies. A monopolist has no competitors and has much more leeway to set high prices. Nevertheless, there are limits. The higher the price a monopolist sets, the lower the demand for the monopolist's product as customers seek substitute products.

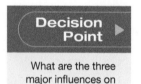

Decision Point

What are the three major influences on pricing decisions?

Costing and Pricing for the Short Run

Short-run pricing decisions typically have a time horizon of less than a year and include decisions such as (a) pricing a *one-time-only special order* with no long-run implications and (b) adjusting product mix and output volume in a competitive market. Long-run pricing decisions have a time horizon of a year or longer and include pricing a product in a market where there is some leeway in setting price.

Consider a short-run pricing decision facing the management team at Astel Computers. Astel manufactures two brands of personal computers (PCs)—Deskpoint, Astel's top-of-the-line product, and Provalue, a less-powerful Pentium chip-based machine. Datatech Corporation has asked Astel to bid on supplying 5,000 Provalue computers over the last three months of 2010. After this three-month period, Datatech is unlikely to place any future sales orders with Astel. Datatech will sell Provalue computers under its own brand name in regions and markets where Astel does not sell Provalue. Whether Astel accepts or rejects this order will not affect Astel's revenues—neither the units sold nor the selling price—from existing sales channels.

Learning Objective 2

Understand how companies make short-run pricing decisions

. . . consider only incremental costs as relevant and price opportunistically to respond to demand and competition

Relevant Costs for Short-Run Pricing Decisions

Before Astel can bid on Datatech's offer, Astel's managers must estimate how much it will cost to supply the 5,000 computers. The relevant costs Astel's managers must focus on include all direct and indirect costs throughout the value chain that will change in total by accepting the one-time-only special order from Datatech. Astel's managers outline the relevant costs as follows:

Direct materials ($460 per computer × 5,000 computers)	$2,300,000
Direct manufacturing labor ($64 per computer × 5,000 computers)	320,000
Fixed costs of additional capacity to manufacture Provalue	250,000
Total costs	$2,870,000*

*No additional costs will be required for R&D, design, marketing, distribution, or customer service.

The relevant cost per computer is $574 ($2,870,000 ÷ 5,000). Therefore, any selling price above $574 will improve Astel's profitability in the short run. What price should Astel's managers bid for the 5,000-computer order?

Strategic and Other Factors in Short-Run Pricing

Based on its market intelligence, Astel believes that competing bids will be between $596 and $610 per computer, so Astel makes a bid of $595 per computer. If it wins this bid, operating income will increase by $105,000 (relevant revenues, $595 × 5,000 = $2,975,000 minus relevant costs, $2,870,000). In light of the extra capacity and strong competition, management's strategy is to bid as high above $574 as possible while remaining lower than competitors' bids.

What if Astel were the only supplier and Datatech could undercut Astel's selling price in Astel's current markets? The relevant cost of the bidding decision would then include the contribution margin lost on sales to existing customers. What if there were many parties eager to bid and win the Datatech contract? In this case, the contribution margin lost on sales to existing customers would be irrelevant to the decision because the existing business would be undercut by Datatech regardless of whether Astel wins the contract.

In contrast to the Astel case, in some short-run situations, a company may experience strong demand for its products or have limited capacity. In these circumstances, a company will strategically increase prices in the short run to as much as the market will bear. We observe high short-run prices in the case of new products or new models of older products, such as microprocessors, computer chips, cellular telephones, and software.

Effect of Time Horizon on Short-Run Pricing Decisions

Two key factors affect short-run pricing.

1. Many costs are irrelevant in short-run pricing decisions. In the Astel example, most of Astel's costs in R&D, design, manufacturing, marketing, distribution, and customer service are irrelevant for the short-run pricing decision, because these costs will not

Decision Point ▶

What do companies consider when making short-run pricing decisions?

change whether Astel wins or does not win the Datatech business. These costs will change in the long run and therefore will be relevant.

2. Short-run pricing is opportunistic. Prices are decreased when demand is weak and competition is strong and increased when demand is strong and competition is weak. As we will see, long-run prices need to be set to earn a reasonable return on investment.

Costing and Pricing for the Long Run

Learning Objective 3

Understand how companies make long-run pricing decisions

Consider all future variable and fixed costs as relevant and earn a target return on investment

Long-run pricing is a strategic decision designed to build long-run relationships with customers based on stable and predictable prices. A stable price reduces the need for continuous monitoring of prices, improves planning, and builds long-run buyer–seller relationships. But to charge a stable price and earn the target long-run return, a company must, over the long run, know and manage its costs of supplying products to customers. As we will see, relevant costs for long-run pricing decisions include *all* future fixed and variable costs.

Calculating Product Costs for Long-Run Pricing Decisions

Let's return to the Astel example. However, this time consider the long-run pricing decision for Provalue.

We start by reviewing data for the year just ended, 2011. Astel has no beginning or ending inventory of Provalue and manufactures and sells 150,000 units during the year. Astel uses activity-based costing (ABC) to calculate the manufacturing cost of Provalue. Astel has three direct manufacturing costs, direct materials, direct manufacturing labor, and direct machining costs, and three manufacturing overhead cost pools, ordering and receiving components, testing and inspection of final products, and rework (correcting and fixing errors and defects), in its accounting system. Astel treats machining costs as a direct cost of Provalue because Provalue is manufactured on machines that only make Provalue.[2]

Astel uses a long-run time horizon to price Provalue. Over this horizon, Astel's managers observe the following:

- Direct material costs vary with number of units of Provalue produced.

- Direct manufacturing labor costs vary with number of direct manufacturing labor-hours used.

- Direct machining costs are fixed costs of leasing 300,000 machine-hours of capacity over multiple years. These costs do not vary with the number of machine-hours used each year. Each unit of Provalue requires 2 machine-hours. In 2011, Astel uses the entire machining capacity to manufacture Provalue (2 machine-hours per unit × 150,000 units = 300,000 machine-hours).

- Ordering and receiving, testing and inspection, and rework costs vary with the quantity of their respective cost drivers. For example, ordering and receiving costs vary with the number of orders. In the long run, staff members responsible for placing orders can be reassigned or laid off if fewer orders need to be placed, or increased if more orders need to be processed.

The following Excel spreadsheet summarizes manufacturing cost information to produce 150,000 units of Provalue in 2011.

---

[2] Recall that Astel makes two types of PCs: Deskpoint and Provalue. If Deskpoint and Provalue had shared the same machines, Astel would have allocated machining costs on the basis of the budgeted machine-hours used to manufacture the two products and would have treated these costs as fixed overhead costs.

	A	B	C	D	E	F	G	H
	Home	Insert		Page Layout	Formulas	Data	Review	View
1				**Manufacturing Cost Information**				
2				**to Produce 150,000 Units of Provalue**				
3	**Cost Category**	**Cost Driver**		**Details of Cost Driver Quantities**			**Total Quantity of Cost Driver**	**Cost per Unit of Cost Driver**
4	(1)	(2)		(3)		(4)	(5) = (3) × (4)	(6)
5	**Direct Manufacturing Costs**							
6	Direct materials	No. of kits	1	kit per unit	150,000	units	150,000	$460
7	Direct manufacturing labor (DML)	DML hours	3.2	DML hours per unit	150,000	units	480,000	$ 20
8	Direct machining (fixed)	Machine-hours					300,000	$ 38
9	**Manufacturing Overhead Costs**							
10	Ordering and receiving	No. of orders	50	orders per component	450	components	22,500	$ 80
11	Testing and inspection	Testing-hours	30	testing-hours per unit	150,000	units	4,500,000	$ 2
12	Rework				8%	defect rate		
13		Rework-hours	2.5	rework-hours per defective unit	12,000[a]	defective units	30,000	$ 40
14								
15	[a]8% defect rate × 150,000 units = 12,000 defective units							

Exhibit 1 indicates that the total cost of manufacturing Provalue in 2011 is $102 million, and the manufacturing cost per unit is $680. Manufacturing, however, is just one business function in the value chain. To set long-run prices, Astel's managers must calculate the *full cost* of producing and selling Provalue.

For each nonmanufacturing business function, Astel's managers trace direct costs to products and allocate indirect costs using cost pools and cost drivers that measure cause-and-effect relationships (supporting calculations not shown). Exhibit 2 summarizes Provalue's 2011 operating income and shows that Astel earned $15 million from Provalue, or $100 per unit sold in 2011.

Alternative Long-Run Pricing Approaches

How should managers at Astel use product cost information to price Provalue in 2012? Two different approaches for pricing decisions are as follows:

1. Market-based
2. Cost-based, which is also called cost-plus

The market-based approach to pricing starts by asking, "Given what our customers want and how our competitors will react to what we do, what price should we charge?" Based on this price, managers control costs to earn a target return on investment. The cost-based approach to pricing starts by asking, "Given what it costs us to make this product, what price should we charge that will recoup our costs and achieve a target return on investment?"

Exhibit 1 Manufacturing Costs of Provalue for 2011 Using Activity-Based Costing

	A	B	C
		Total Manufacturing	
		Costs for	**Manufacturing**
		150,000 Units	**Cost per Unit**
		(1)	**(2) = (1) ÷ 150,000**
5	Direct manufacturing costs		
6	Direct material costs		
7	(150,000 kits × $460 per kit)	$ 69,000,000	$460
8	Direct manufacturing labor costs		
9	(480,000 DML-hours × $20 per hour)	9,600,000	64
10	Direct machining costs		
11	(300,000 machine-hours × $38 per machine-hour)	11,400,000	76
12	Direct manufacturing costs	90,000,000	600
13			
14	Manufacturing overhead costs		
15	Ordering and receiving costs		
16	(22,500 orders × $80 per order)	1,800,000	12
17	Testing and inspection costs		
18	(4,500,000 testing-hours × $2 per hour)	9,000,000	60
19	Rework costs		
20	(30,000 rework-hours × $40 per hour)	1,200,000	8
21	Manufacturing overhead cost	12,000,000	80
22	Total manufacturing costs	$102,000,000	$680

Exhibit 2 Product Profitability of Provalue for 2011 Using Value-Chain Activity-Based Costing

	A	B	C
		Total Amounts	
		for 150,000 Units	**Per Unit**
		(1)	**(2) = (1) ÷ 150,000**
4	Revenues	$150,000,000	$1,000
5	Costs of goods sold[a] (from Exhibit 1)	102,000,000	680
6	Operating costs[b]		
7	R&D costs	5,400,000	36
8	Design cost of product and process	6,000,000	40
9	Marketing costs	15,000,000	100
10	Distribution costs	3,600,000	24
11	Customer-service costs	3,000,000	20
12	Operating costs	33,000,000	220
13	Full cost of the product	135,000,000	900
14	Operating income	$ 15,000,000	$ 100
15			
16	[a]Cost of goods sold = Total manufacturing costs because there is no beginning or ending inventory		
17	of Provalue in 2011		
18	[b]Numbers for operating cost line-items are assumed without supporting calculations		

Companies operating in *competitive* markets (for example, commodities such as steel, oil, and natural gas) use the market-based approach. The items produced or services provided by one company are very similar to items produced or services provided by others. Companies in these markets must accept the prices set by the market.

Companies operating in *less competitive* markets offer products or services that differ from each other (for example, automobiles, computers, management consulting, and legal services), can use either the market-based or cost-based approach as the starting point for pricing decisions. Some companies first look at costs because cost information is more easily available and then consider customers or competitors: the cost-based approach. Others start by considering customers and competitors and then look at costs: the market-based approach. Both approaches consider customers, competitors, and costs. Only their starting points differ. Management must always keep in mind market forces, regardless of which pricing approach it uses. For example, building contractors often bid on a cost-plus basis but then reduce their prices during negotiations to respond to other lower-cost bids.

Companies operating in markets that are *not competitive* favor cost-based approaches. That's because these companies do not need to respond or react to competitors' prices. The margin they add to costs to determine price depends on the value customers place on the product or service.

We consider first the market-based approach.

Decision Point

How do companies make long-run pricing decisions?

Target Costing for Target Pricing

Market-based pricing starts with a target price. A **target price** is the estimated price for a product or service that potential customers are willing to pay. This estimate is based on an understanding of customers' perceived value for a product or service and how competitors will price competing products or services. This understanding of customers and competitors is becoming increasingly important for three reasons:

1. Competition from lower-cost producers is continually restraining prices.
2. Products are on the market for shorter periods of time, leaving less time and opportunity to recover from pricing mistakes, loss of market share, and loss of profitability.
3. Customers are becoming more knowledgeable and incessantly demanding products of higher and higher quality at lower and lower prices.

Learning Objective 4

Price products using the target-costing approach

. . . target costing identifies an estimated price customers are willing to pay and then computes a target cost to earn the desired profit

Understanding Customers' Perceived Value

A company's sales and marketing organization, through close contact and interaction with customers, identifies customer needs and perceptions of product value. Companies such as Apple also conduct market research on features that customers want and the prices they are willing to pay for those features for products such as the iPhone and the Macintosh computer.

Doing Competitor Analysis

To gauge how competitors might react to a prospective price, a company must understand competitors' technologies, products or services, costs, and financial conditions. In general, the more distinctive its product or service, the higher the price a company can charge. Where do companies like Ford Motors or PPG Industries obtain information about their competitors? Usually from former customers, suppliers, and employees of competitors. Another source of information is *reverse engineering*—that is, disassembling and analyzing competitors' products to determine product designs and materials and to become acquainted with the technologies competitors use. At no time should a company resort to illegal or unethical means to obtain information about competitors. For example, a company should never pay off current employees or pose as a supplier or customer in order to obtain competitor information.

Implementing Target Pricing and Target Costing

There are five steps in developing target prices and target costs. We illustrate these steps using our Provalue example.

Step 1: Develop a product that satisfies the needs of potential customers. Customer requirements and competitors' products dictate the product features and design modifications for Provalue for 2012. Astel's market research indicates that customers do not value Provalue's extra features, such as special audio features and designs that accommodate upgrades to make the PC run faster. They want Astel to redesign Provalue into a no-frills but reliable PC and to sell it at a much lower price.

Step 2: Choose a target price. Astel expects its competitors to lower the prices of PCs that compete with Provalue to $850. Astel's management wants to respond aggressively, reducing Provalue's price by 20%, from $1,000 to $800 per unit. At this lower price, Astel's marketing manager forecasts an increase in annual sales from 150,000 to 200,000 units.

Step 3: Derive a target cost per unit by subtracting target operating income per unit from the target price. Target operating income per unit is the operating income that a company aims to earn per unit of a product or service sold. **Target cost per unit** is the estimated long-run cost per unit of a product or service that enables the company to achieve its target operating income per unit when selling at the target price.[3] *Target cost per unit* is the target price minus *target operating income per unit* and is often lower than the existing *full cost of the product.* Target cost per unit is really just that—a target—something the company must commit to achieve.

To attain the target return on the capital invested in the business, Astel's management needs to earn 10% target operating income on target revenues.

Total target revenues	= $800 per unit × 200,000 units = $160,000,000
Total target operating income	= 10% × $160,000,000 = $16,000,000
Target operating income per unit	= $16,000,000 ÷ 200,000 units = $80 per unit
Target cost per unit	= Target price – Target operating income per unit
	= $800 per unit – $80 per unit = $720 per unit
Total current full costs of Provalue	= $135,000,000 (from Exhibit 2)
Current full cost per unit of Provalue	= $135,000,000 ÷ 150,000 units = $900 per unit

Provalue's $720 target cost per unit is $180 below its existing $900 unit cost. Astel must reduce costs in all parts of the value chain—from R&D to customer service—including achieving lower prices on materials and components, while maintaining quality.

Target costs include *all* future costs, variable costs and costs that are fixed in the short run, because in the long run, a company's prices and revenues must recover all its costs if it is to remain in business. Contrast relevant costs for long-run pricing decisions (all variable and fixed costs) with relevant costs for short-run pricing decisions (costs that change in the short run, mostly but not exclusively variable costs).

Step 4: Perform cost analysis. This step analyzes the specific aspects of a product or service to target for cost reduction. Astel's managers focus on the following elements of Provalue:

- The functions performed by and the current costs of different component parts, such as the motherboard, disc drives, and the graphics and video cards.

- The importance that customers place on different product features. For example, Provalue's customers value reliability more than video quality.

- The relationship and tradeoffs across product features and component parts. For example, choosing a simpler mother board enhances reliability but is unable to support the top-of-the-line video card.

---

[3] For a more-detailed discussion of target costing, see S. Ansari, J. Bell, and The CAM-I Target Cost Core Group, *Target Costing: The Next Frontier in Strategic Cost Management* (Martinsville, IN: Mountain Valley Publishing, 2009). For implementation information, see S. Ansari, L. D. Swenson, and J. Bell, "A Template for Implementing Target Costing," *Cost Management* (September–October 2006): 20–27.

Concepts in Action

Extreme Target Pricing and Cost Management at IKEA

Steven Sheppard/AP Wide World Photos

Around the world, IKEA has exploded into a furniture-retailing-industry phenomenon. Known for products named after small Swedish towns, modern design, flat packaging, and do-it-yourself instructions, IKEA has grown from humble beginnings to become the world's largest furniture retailer with 301 stores in 38 countries. How did this happen? Through aggressive target pricing, coupled with relentless cost management. IKEA's prices typically run 30%–50% below its competitors' prices. Moreover, while the prices of other companies' products rise over time, IKEA says it has reduced its retail prices by about 20% over the last four years.

During the conceptualization phase, product developers identify gaps in IKEA's current product portfolio. For example, they might identify the need to create a new flat-screen-television stand. "When we decide about a product, we always start with the consumer need" IKEA Product Developer June Deboehmler said. Second, product developers and their teams survey competitors to determine how much they charge for similar items, if offered, and then select a target price that is 30%–50% less than the competitor's price. With a product and price established, product developers then determine what materials will be used and what manufacturer will do the assembly work—all before the new item is fully designed. For example, a brief describing a new couch's target cost and basic specifications like color and style is submitted for bidding among IKEA's over 1,800 suppliers in more than 50 countries. Suppliers vie to offer the most attractive bid based on price, function, and materials to be used. This value-engineering process promotes volume-based cost efficiencies throughout the design and production process.

Aggressive cost management does not stop there. All IKEA products are designed to be shipped unassembled in flat packages. The company estimates that shipping costs would be at least six times greater if all products were assembled before shipping. To ensure that shipping costs remain low, packaging and shipping technicians work with product developers throughout the product development process. When IKEA recently designed its Lillberg chair, a packaging technician made a small tweak in the angle of the chair's arm. This change allowed more chairs to fit into a single shipping container, which meant a lower cost to the consumer.

What about products that have already been developed? IKEA applies the same cost management techniques to those products, too. For example, one of IKEA's best selling products is the Lack bedside table, which has retailed for the same low price since 1981. How is this possible, you may ask. Since hitting store shelves, more than 100 technical development projects have been performed on the Lack table. Despite the steady increase in the cost of raw materials and wages, IKEA has aggressively sought to reduce product and distribution costs to maintain the Lack table's initial retail price without jeopardizing the company's profit on the product.

As founder Ingvar Kamprad once summarized, "Waste of resources is a mortal sin at IKEA. Expensive solutions are a sign of mediocrity, and an idea without a price tag is never acceptable."

Sources: Baraldi, Enrico and Torkel Strömsten. 2009. Managing product development the IKEA way. Using target costing in inter-organizational networks. Working Paper, December. Margonelli, Lisa. 2002. How IKEA designs its sexy price tags. *Business 2.0*, October. Terdiman, Daniel. 2008. Anatomy of an IKEA product. CNET News.com, April 19.

Step 5: Perform value engineering to achieve target cost. Value engineering is a systematic evaluation of all aspects of the value chain, with the objective of reducing costs and achieving a quality level that satisfies customers. As we describe next, value engineering encompasses improvements in product designs, changes in materials specifications, and modifications in process methods. (See the Concepts in Action feature to learn about IKEA's approach to target pricing and target costing.)

Decision Point

How do companies determine target costs?

Value Engineering, Cost Incurrence, and Locked-In Costs

To implement value engineering, managers distinguish value-added activities and costs from nonvalue-added activities and costs. A **value-added cost** is a cost that, if eliminated, would reduce the actual or perceived value or utility (usefulness) customers experience from using the product or service. Examples are costs of specific product features and attributes desired by customers, such as reliability, adequate memory, preloaded software, clear images, and, in the case of Provalue, prompt customer service.

A **nonvalue-added cost** is a cost that, if eliminated, would not reduce the actual or perceived value or utility (usefulness) customers gain from using the product or service. It is a cost that the customer is unwilling to pay for. Examples of nonvalue-added costs are costs of producing defective products and cost of machine breakdowns. Successful companies keep nonvalue-added costs to a minimum.

Activities and their costs do not always fall neatly into value-added or nonvalue-added categories. Some costs, such as supervision and production control, fall in a gray area because they include mostly value-added but also some nonvalue-added components. Despite these troublesome gray areas, attempts to distinguish value-added from nonvalue-added costs provide a useful overall framework for value engineering.

In the Provalue example, direct materials, direct manufacturing labor, and direct machining costs are value-added costs. Ordering, receiving, testing, and inspection costs fall in the gray area. Rework costs are nonvalue-added costs.

Through value engineering, Astel's managers plan to reduce, and possibly eliminate, nonvalue-added costs and increase the efficiency of value-added activities. They start by distinguishing cost incurrence from locked-in costs. **Cost incurrence** describes when a resource is consumed (or benefit forgone) to meet a specific objective. Costing systems measure cost incurrence. Astel, for example, recognizes direct material costs of Provalue as each unit of Provalue is assembled and sold. But Provalue's direct material cost per unit is *locked in,* or *designed in,* much earlier, when product designers choose Provalue's components. **Locked-in costs,** or **designed-in costs,** are costs that have not yet been incurred but, based on decisions that have already been made, will be incurred in the future.

To manage costs well, a company must identify how design choices lock in costs *before* the costs are incurred. For example, scrap and rework costs incurred during manufacturing are often locked in much earlier by faulty design. Similarly, in the software industry, costly and difficult-to-fix errors that appear during coding and testing are frequently locked in by bad software design and analysis.

Exhibit 3 illustrates the locked-in cost curve and the cost-incurrence curve for Provalue. The bottom curve uses information from Exhibit 2 to plot the cumulative cost per unit incurred across different business functions of the value chain. The top curve plots how cumulative costs are locked in. (The specific numbers underlying this curve are not presented.) Total cumulative cost per unit for both curves is $900. *Observe, however, the wide divergence between when costs are locked in and when they are incurred.* For example, product design decisions lock in more than 86% ($780 ÷ $900) of the unit cost of Provalue (for example, direct materials, ordering, testing, rework, distribution, and customer service), when only about 8% ($76 ÷ $900) of the unit cost is actually incurred!

Value-Chain Analysis and Cross-Functional Teams

A cross-functional value-engineering team consisting of marketing managers, product designers, manufacturing engineers, purchasing managers, suppliers, dealers, and management accountants redesign Provalue to reduce costs while retaining features that customers value. Some of the team's ideas are as follows:

- Use a simpler, more-reliable motherboard without complex features to reduce manufacturing and repair costs.
- Snap-fit rather than solder parts together to decrease direct manufacturing labor-hours and related costs.

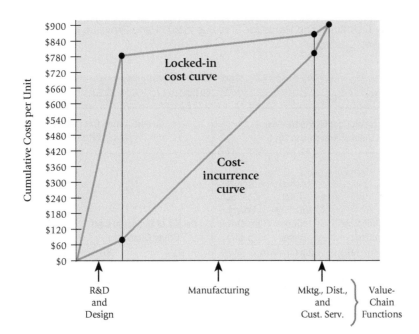

Exhibit 3

Pattern of Cost
Incurrence and
Locked-In Costs for
Provalue

- Use fewer components to decrease ordering, receiving, testing, and inspection costs.
- Make Provalue lighter and smaller to reduce distribution and packaging costs.

Management accountants use their understanding of the value chain to estimate cost savings.

Not all costs are locked in at the design stage. Managers always have opportunities to reduce costs by improving operating efficiency and productivity. *Kaizen,* or *continuous improvement,* seeks to reduce the time it takes to do a task and to eliminate waste during production and delivery of products.

In summary, the key steps in value-engineering are as follows:

1. Understanding customer requirements, value-added and nonvalue-added costs

2. Anticipating how costs are locked in before they are incurred

3. Using cross-functional teams to redesign products and processes to reduce costs while meeting customer needs

Achieving the Target Cost per Unit for Provalue

Exhibit 4 uses an activity-based approach to compare cost-driver quantities and rates for the 150,000 units of Provalue manufactured and sold in 2011 and the 200,000 units of Provalue II budgeted for 2012. Value engineering decreases both value-added costs (by designing Provalue II to reduce direct materials and component costs, direct manufacturing labor-hours, and testing-hours) and nonvalue-added costs (by simplifying Provalue II's design to reduce rework). Value engineering also reduces the machine-hours required to make Provalue II to 1.5 hours per unit. Astel can now use the 300,000 machine-hours of capacity to make 200,000 units of Provalue II (versus 150,000 units for Provalue) reducing machining cost per unit. For simplicity, we assume that value engineering will not reduce the $20 cost per direct manufacturing labor-hour, the $80 cost per order, the $2 cost per testing-hour, or the $40 cost per rework-hour. (The Problem for Self-Study explores how value engineering can also reduce these cost-driver rates.)

Exhibit 5 presents the target manufacturing costs of Provalue II, using cost driver and cost-driver rate data from Exhibit 4. For comparison, Exhibit 5 also shows the actual 2011 manufacturing cost per unit of Provalue from Exhibit 1. Astel's managers expect the new design to reduce total manufacturing cost per unit by $140 (from $680 to $540) and cost per unit in other business functions from $220 (Exhibit 2) to $180 (calculations not shown) at the budgeted sales quantity of 200,000 units. The budgeted full unit cost of Provalue II is $720 ($540 + $180), the target cost per unit. At the end of 2012,

Exhibit 4 Cost-Driver Quantities and Rates for Provalue in 2011 and Provalue II for 2012 Using Activity-Based Costing

Home	Insert		Page Layout		Formulas	Data	Review	View					
A	B	C	D	E	F	G	H	I	J	K	L	M	N

						Manufacturing Cost Information for 150,000 Units of Provalue in 2011				Manufacturing Cost Information for 200,000 Units of Provalue II for 2012			
Cost Category	Cost Driver		Details of Actual Cost Driver Quantities			Actual Total Quantity of Cost Driver	Actual Cost per Unit of Cost Driver (p.437)		Details of Budgeted Cost Driver Quantities			Budgeted Total Quantity of Cost Driver	Budgeted Cost per Unit of Cost Driver (Given)
(1)	(2)		(3)		(4)	(5)=(3)×(4)	(6)		(7)		(8)	(9)=(7)×(8)	(10)
Direct Manufacturing Costs													
Direct materials	No. of kits	1	kit per unit	150,000	units	150,000	$460	1	kit per unit	200,000	units	200,000	$385
Direct manuf. labor (DML)	DML hours	3.2	DML hours per unit	150,000	units	480,000	$ 20	2.65	DML hours per unit	200,000	units	530,000	$ 20
Direct machining (fixed)	Machine-hours					300,000	$ 38					300,000	$ 38
Manufacturing Overhead Costs													
Ordering and receiving	No. of orders	50	orders per component	450	compo-nents	22,500	$ 80	50	orders per compo-nent	425	compo-nents	21,250	$ 80
Testing and inspection	Testing-hours	30	testing-hours per unit	150,000	units	4,500,000	$ 2	15	testing hours per unit	200,000	units	3,000,000	$ 2
Rework					8% defect rate						6.5% defect rate		
	Rework-hours	2.5	rework-hours per defective unit	12,000[a]	defective units	30,000	$ 40	2.5	rework-hours per defective unit	13,000[b]	defective units	32,500	$ 40

[a]8% defect rate × 150,000 units = 12,000 defective units
[b]6.5% defect rate × 200,000 units = 13,000 defective units

Astel's managers will compare actual costs and target costs to gain insight about improvements that can be made in subsequent target-costing efforts.

Unless managed properly, value engineering and target costing can have undesirable effects:

■ Employees may feel frustrated if they fail to attain targets.

■ The cross-functional team may add too many features just to accommodate the different wishes of team members.

■ A product may be in development for a long time as alternative designs are evaluated repeatedly.

■ Organizational conflicts may develop as the burden of cutting costs falls unequally on different business functions in the company's value chain, for example, more on manufacturing than on marketing.

Exhibit 5   Target Manufacturing Costs of Provalue II for 2012

	Home	Insert	Page Layout	Formulas	Data	Review	View			

	A	B	C	D	E	F
1		PROVALUE II				PROVALUE
2		Budgeted		Budgeted		Actual Manufacturing
3		Manufacturing Costs		Manufacturing		Cost per Unit
4		for 200,000 Units		Cost per Unit		(Exhibit 1)
5		(1)		(2) = (1) ÷ 200,000		(3)
6	Direct manufacturing costs					
7	Direct material costs					
8	(200,000 kits × $385 per kit)	$ 77,000,000		$385.00		$460.00
9	Direct manufacturing labor costs					
10	(530,000 DML-hours × $20 per hour)	10,600,000		53.00		64.00
11	Direct machining costs					
12	(300,000 machine-hours × $38 per machine-hour)	11,400,000		57.00		76.00
13	Direct manufacturing costs	99,000,000		495.00		600.00
14	Manufacturing overhead costs					
15	Ordering and receiving costs					
16	(21,250 orders × $80 per order)	1,700,000		8.50		12.00
17	Testing and inspection costs					
18	(3,000,000 testing-hours × $2 per hour)	6,000,000		30.00		60.00
19	Rework costs					
20	(32,500 rework-hours × $40 per hour)	1,300,000		6.50		8.00
21	Manufacturing overhead costs	9,000,000		45.00		80.00
22	Total manufaturing costs	$108,000,000		$540.00		$ 680.00

To avoid these pitfalls, target-costing efforts should always (a) encourage employee participation and celebrate small improvements toward achieving the target, (b) focus on the customer, (c) pay attention to schedules, and (d) set cost-cutting targets for all value-chain functions to encourage a culture of teamwork and cooperation.

◄ **Decision Point**

Why is it important to distinguish cost incurrence from locked-in costs?

Cost-Plus Pricing

Instead of using the market-based approach for long-run pricing decisions, managers sometimes use a cost-based approach. The general formula for setting a cost-based price adds a markup component to the cost base to determine a prospective selling price. Because a markup is added, cost-based pricing is often called cost-plus pricing, with the plus referring to the markup component. Managers use the cost-plus pricing formula as a starting point. The markup component is rarely a rigid number. Instead, it is flexible, depending on the behavior of customers and competitors. The markup component is ultimately determined by the market.[4]

Learning Objective 6

Price products using the cost-plus approach

. . . cost-plus pricing is based on some measure of cost plus a markup

Cost-Plus Target Rate of Return on Investment

We illustrate a cost-plus pricing formula for Provalue II assuming Astel uses a 12% markup on the full unit cost of the product when computing the selling price.

Cost base (full unit cost of Provalue II)	$720.00
Markup component of 12% (0.12 × $720)	86.40
Prospective selling price	$806.40

---

[4] Exceptions are pricing of electricity and natural gas in many countries, where prices are set by the government on the basis of costs plus a return on invested capital. In these situations, products are not subject to competitive forces and cost accounting techniques substitute for markets as the basis for setting prices.

How is the markup percentage of 12% determined? One way is to choose a markup to earn a *target rate of return on investment*. The **target rate of return on investment** is the target annual operating income divided by invested capital. Invested capital can be defined in many ways. In this chapter, we define it as total assets—that is, long-term assets plus current assets. Suppose Astel's (pretax) target rate of return on investment is 18% and Provalue II's capital investment is $96 million. The target annual operating income for Provalue II is as follows:

Invested capital	$96,000,000
Target rate of return on investment	18%
Target annual operating income (0.18 × $96,000,000)	$17,280,000
Target operating income per unit of Provalue II ($17,280,000 ÷ 200,000 units)	$ 86.40

This calculation indicates that Astel needs to earn a target operating income of $86.40 on each unit of Provalue II. The markup ($86.40) expressed as a percentage of the full unit cost of the product ($720) equals 12% ($86.40 ÷ $720).

Do not confuse the 18% target rate of return on investment with the 12% markup percentage.

- The 18% target rate of return on investment expresses Astel's expected annual operating income as a percentage of investment.

- The 12% markup expresses operating income per unit as a percentage of the full product cost per unit.

Astel uses the target rate of return on investment to calculate the markup percentage.

Alternative Cost-Plus Methods

Computing the specific amount of capital invested in a product is seldom easy because it requires difficult and arbitrary allocations of investments in equipment and buildings to individual products. The following table uses alternative cost bases (without supporting calculations) and assumed markup percentages to set prospective selling prices for Provalue II without explicitly calculating invested capital to set prices.

Cost Base	Estimated Cost per Unit (1)	Markup Percentage (2)	Markup Component (3) = (1) × (2)	Prospective Selling Price (4) = (1) + (3)
Variable manufacturing cost	$475.00	65%	$308.75	$783.75
Variable cost of the product	547.00	45	246.15	793.15
Manufacturing cost	540.00	50	270.00	810.00
Full cost of the product	720.00	12	86.40	806.40

The different cost bases and markup percentages give four prospective selling prices that are close to each other. In practice, a company chooses a reliable cost base and markup percentage to recover its costs and earn a target return on investment. For example, consulting companies often choose the full cost of a client engagement as their cost base because it is difficult to distinguish variable costs from fixed costs.

The markup percentages in the preceding table vary a great deal, from a high of 65% on variable manufacturing cost to a low of 12% on full cost of the product. Why the wide variation? When determining a prospective selling price, a cost base such as variable manufacturing cost (that includes fewer costs) requires a higher markup percentage because the price needs to be set to earn a profit margin *and* to recover costs that have been excluded from the base.

Surveys indicate that most managers use the full cost of the product for cost-based pricing decisions—that is, they include both fixed and variable costs when calculating the cost per unit. Managers include fixed cost per unit in the cost base for several reasons:

1. **Full recovery of all costs of the product.** In the long run, the price of a product must exceed the full cost of the product if a company is to remain in business. Using just the variable cost as a base may tempt managers to cut prices as long as prices are

above variable cost and generate a positive contribution margin. As the experience in the airline industry has shown, variable cost pricing may cause companies to lose money because revenues are too low to recover the full cost of the product.

2. **Price stability.** Managers believe that using the full cost of the product as the basis for pricing decisions promotes price stability, because it limits the ability and temptations of salespersons to cut prices. Stable prices facilitate more-accurate forecasting and planning.

3. **Simplicity.** A full-cost formula for pricing does not require a detailed analysis of cost-behavior patterns to separate product costs into fixed and variable components. Variable and fixed cost components are difficult to identify for many costs such as testing, inspection, and setups.

Including fixed cost per unit in the cost base for pricing is not without problems. Allocating fixed costs to products can be arbitrary. Also, calculating fixed cost per unit requires a denominator level that is based on an estimate of capacity or expected units of future sales. Errors in these estimates will cause actual full cost per unit of the product to differ from the estimated amount.

Cost-Plus Pricing and Target Pricing

The selling prices computed under cost-plus pricing are *prospective* prices. Suppose Astel's initial product design results in a $750 full cost for Provalue II. Assuming a 12% markup, Astel sets a prospective price of $840 [$750 + (0.12 × $750)]. In the competitive personal computer market, customer and competitor reactions to this price may force Astel to reduce the markup percentage and lower the price to, say, $800. Astel may then want to redesign Provalue II to reduce the full cost to $720 per unit, as in our example, and achieve a markup close to 12% while keeping the price at $800. The eventual design and cost-plus price must trade-off cost, markup, and customer reactions.

The target-pricing approach reduces the need to go back and forth among prospective cost-plus prices, customer reactions, and design modifications. In contrast to cost-plus pricing, target pricing first determines product characteristics and target price on the basis of customer preferences and expected competitor responses, and then computes a target cost.

Suppliers who provide unique products and services, such as accountants and management consultants, usually use cost-plus pricing. Professional service firms set prices based on hourly cost-plus billing rates of partners, managers, and associates. These prices are, however, lowered in competitive situations. Professional service firms also take a multiple-year client perspective when deciding prices. Certified public accountants, for example, sometimes charge a client a low price initially and a higher price later.

Service companies such as home repair services, automobile repair services, and architectural firms use a cost-plus pricing method called the *time-and-materials method*. Individual jobs are priced based on materials and labor time. The price charged for materials equals the cost of materials plus a markup. The price charged for labor represents the cost of labor plus a markup. That is, the price charged for each direct cost item includes its own markup. The markups are chosen to recover overhead costs and to earn a profit.

Decision Point

How do companies price products using the cost-plus approach?

Life-Cycle Product Budgeting and Costing

Companies sometimes need to consider target prices and target costs over a multiple-year product life cycle. The **product life cycle** spans the time from initial R&D on a product to when customer service and support is no longer offered for that product. For automobile companies such as DaimlerChrysler, Ford, and Nissan, the product life cycle is 12 to 15 years to design, introduce, and sell different car models. For pharmaceutical products, the life cycle at companies such as Pfizer, Merck, and Glaxo Smith Kline may be 15 to 20 years. For banks such as Wachovia and Chase Manhattan Bank, a product such as a newly designed savings account with specific privileges can have a life cycle of 10 to 20 years. Personal computers have a shorter life-cycle of 3 to 5 years, because rapid

Learning Objective **7**

Use life-cycle budgeting and costing when making pricing decisions

. . . accumulate all costs of a product from initial R&D to final customer service for each year of the product's life innovations in the computing power and speed of microprocessors that run the computers make older models obsolete.

In **life-cycle budgeting,** managers estimate the revenues and business function costs across the entire value chain from a product's initial R&D to its final customer service and support. **Life-cycle costing** tracks and accumulates business function costs across the entire value chain from a product's initial R&D to its final customer service and support. Life-cycle budgeting and life-cycle costing span several years.

Life-Cycle Budgeting and Pricing Decisions

Budgeted life-cycle costs provide useful information for strategically evaluating pricing decisions. Consider Insight, Inc., a computer software company, which is developing a new accounting package, "General Ledger." Assume the following budgeted amounts for General Ledger over a six-year product life cycle:

Years 1 and 2

	Total Fixed Costs
R&D costs	$240,000
Design costs	160,000

Years 3 to 6

	Total Fixed Costs	Variable Cost per Package
Production costs	$100,000	$25
Marketing costs	70,000	24
Distribution costs	50,000	16
Customer-service costs	80,000	30

Exhibit 6 presents the six-year life-cycle budget for General Ledger for three alternative selling-price/sales-quantity combinations.

Several features make life-cycle budgeting particularly important:

1. **The development period for R&D and design is long and costly.** When a high percentage of total life-cycle costs are incurred before any production begins and any revenues are received, as in the General Ledger example, the company needs to evaluate revenues and costs over the life-cycle of the product in order to decide whether to begin the costly R&D and design activities.

2. **Many costs are locked in at R&D and design stages, even if R&D and design costs themselves are small.** In our General Ledger example, a poorly designed accounting software package, which is difficult to install and use, would result in higher marketing, distribution, and customer-service costs in several subsequent years. These costs would be even higher if the product failed to meet promised quality-performance levels. A life-cycle revenue-and-cost budget prevents Insight's managers from overlooking these multiple-year relationships among business-function costs. Life-cycle budgeting highlights costs throughout the product's life cycle and, in doing so, facilitates target pricing, target costing, and value engineering at the design stage before costs are locked in. The amounts presented in Exhibit 6 are the outcome of value engineering.

Insight decides to sell the General Ledger package for $480 per package because this price maximizes life-cycle operating income. Insight's managers compare actual costs to life-cycle budgets to obtain feedback and to learn about how to estimate costs better for subsequent products. Exhibit 6 assumes that the selling price per package is the same over the entire life cycle. For strategic reasons, however, Insight may decide to skim the market by charging higher prices to eager customers when General Ledger is first introduced and then lowering prices later as the product matures. In these later stages, Insight may even add new features to differentiate the product to maintain prices and sales. The life-cycle budget must then incorporate the revenues and costs of these strategies.

Exhibit 6	Budgeting Life-Cycle Revenues and Costs for "General Ledger" Software Package of Insight, Inc.[a]

| | Alternative Selling-Price/ Sales-Quantity Combinations | | |
	A	B	C
Selling price per package	$400	$480	$600
Sales quantity in units	5,000	4,000	2,500
Life-cycle revenues			
($400 × 5,000; $480 × 4,000; $600 × 2,500)	$2,000,000	$1,920,000	$1,500,000
Life-cycle costs			
R&D costs	240,000	240,000	240,000
Design costs of product/process	160,000	160,000	160,000
Production costs			
$100,000 + ($25 × 5,000); $100,000 +			
($25 × 4,000); $100,000 + ($25 × 2,500)	225,000	200,000	162,500
Marketing costs			
$70,000 + ($24 × 5,000); $70,000 +			
($24 × 4,000); $70,000 + ($24 × 2,500)	190,000	166,000	130,000
Distribution costs			
$50,000 + ($16 × 5,000); $50,000 +			
($16 × 4,000); $50,000 + ($16 × 2,500)	130,000	114,000	90,000
Customer-service costs			
$80,000 + ($30 × 5,000); $80,000 +			
($30 × 4,000); $80,000 + ($30 × 2,500)	230,000	200,000	155,000
Total life-cycle costs	1,175,000	1,080,000	937,500
Life-cycle operating income	$ 825,000	$ 840,000	$ 562,500

[a]This exhibit does not take into consideration the time value of money when computing life-cycle revenues or life-cycle costs.

Management of environmental costs provides another example of life-cycle costing and value engineering. Environmental laws like the U.S. Clean Air Act and the U.S. Superfund Amendment and Reauthorization Act have introduced tougher environmental standards, imposed stringent cleanup requirements, and introduced severe penalties for polluting the air and contaminating subsurface soil and groundwater. Environmental costs that are incurred over several years of the product's life-cycle are often locked in at the product- and process-design stage. To avoid environmental liabilities, companies in industries such as oil refining, chemical processing, and automobiles practice value engineering; they design products and processes to prevent and reduce pollution over the product's life cycle. For example, laptop computer manufacturers like Hewlett Packard and Apple have introduced costly recycling programs to ensure that chemicals from nickel-cadmium batteries do not leak hazardous chemicals into the soil.

Customer Life-Cycle Costing

A different notion of life-cycle costs is *customer life-cycle costs*. **Customer life-cycle costs** focus on the total costs incurred by a customer to acquire, use, maintain, and dispose of a product or service. Customer life-cycle costs influence the prices a company can charge for its products. For example, Ford can charge a higher price and/or gain market share if its cars require minimal maintenance for 100,000 miles. Similarly, Maytag charges higher prices for appliances that save electricity and have low maintenance costs. Boeing Corporation justifies a higher price for the Boeing 777 because the plane's design allows mechanics easier access to different areas of the plane to perform routine maintenance, reduces the time and cost of maintenance, and significantly decreases the life-cycle cost of owning the plane.

Decision Point

Describe life-cycle budgeting and life-cycle costing and when companies should use these techniques.

Additional Considerations for Pricing Decisions

Learning Objective 8

Describe two pricing practices in which noncost factors are important when setting prices

. . . price discrimination—charging different customers different prices for the same product—and peak-load pricing—charging higher prices when demand approaches capacity limits

In some cases, cost is *not* a major factor in setting prices. We explore some of the ways that market structures and laws and regulations influence price setting outside of cost.

Price Discrimination

Consider the prices airlines charge for a round-trip flight from Boston to San Francisco. A coach-class ticket for a flight with seven-day advance purchase is $450 if the passenger stays in San Francisco over a Saturday night. It is $1,000 if the passenger returns without staying over a Saturday night. Can this price difference be explained by the difference in the cost to the airline of these round-trip flights? No; it costs the same amount to transport the passenger from Boston to San Francisco and back, regardless of whether the passenger stays in San Francisco over a Saturday night. This difference in price is due to *price discrimination.*

Price discrimination is the practice of charging different customers different prices for the same product or service. How does price discrimination work in the airline example? The demand for airline tickets comes from two main sources: business travelers and pleasure travelers. Business travelers must travel to conduct business for their organizations, so their demand for air travel is relatively insensitive to price. Airlines can earn higher operating incomes by charging business travelers higher prices. Insensitivity of demand to price changes is called *demand inelasticity.* Also, business travelers generally go to their destinations, complete their work, and return home without staying over a Saturday night. Pleasure travelers, in contrast, usually don't need to return home during the week, and prefer to spend weekends at their destinations. Because they pay for their tickets themselves, pleasure travelers' demand is price-elastic, lowering prices stimulates demand. Airlines can earn higher operating incomes by charging pleasure travelers lower prices.

How can airlines keep fares high for business travelers while, at the same time, keeping fares low for pleasure travelers? Requiring a Saturday night stay discriminates between the two customer segments. The airlines price-discriminate to take advantage of different sensitivities to prices exhibited by business travelers and pleasure travelers. Prices differ even though there is no difference in cost in serving the two customer segments.

What if economic conditions weaken such that business travelers become more sensitive to price? The airlines may then need to lower the prices they charge to business travelers. Following the events of September 11, 2001, airlines started offering discounted fares on certain routes without requiring a Saturday night stay to stimulate business travel. Business travel picked up and airlines started filling more seats than they otherwise would have. Unfortunately, travel did not pick up enough, and the airline industry as a whole suffered severe losses over the next few years.

Peak-Load Pricing

Decision Point ▶

Describe price discrimination and peak-load pricing.

In addition to price discrimination, other noncost factors such as capacity constraints affect pricing decisions. **Peak-load pricing** is the practice of charging a higher price for the same product or service when the demand for the product or service approaches the physical limit of the capacity to produce that product or service. When demand is high and production capacity is limited, customers are willing to pay more to get the product or service. In contrast, slack or excess capacity leads companies to lower prices in order to stimulate demand and utilize capacity. Peak-load pricing occurs in the telephone, telecommunications, hotel, car rental, and electric-utility industries. During the 2008 Summer Olympics in Beijing, for example, hotels charged very high rates and required multiple-night stays. Airlines charged high fares for flights into and out of many cities in the region for roughly a month around the time of the games. Demand far exceeded capacity and the hospitality industry and airlines employed peak-load pricing to increase their profits.

International Considerations

Another example of factors other than costs affecting prices occurs when the same product is sold in different countries. Consider software, books, and medicines produced in one country and sold globally. The prices charged in each country vary much more than the costs of delivering the product to each country. These price differences arise because of differences in the purchasing power of consumers in different countries (a form of price discrimination) and government restrictions that may limit the prices that can be charged.

Antitrust Laws

Legal considerations also affect pricing decisions. Companies are not always free to charge whatever price they like. For example, under the U.S. Robinson-Patman Act, a manufacturer cannot price-discriminate between two customers if the intent is to lessen or prevent competition for customers. Two key features of price-discrimination laws are as follows:

1. Price discrimination is permissible if differences in prices can be justified by differences in costs.

2. Price discrimination is illegal only if the intent is to lessen or prevent competition.

The price discrimination by airline companies described earlier is legal because their practices do not hinder competition.

**Learning
Objective** 9

Explain the effects of antitrust laws on pricing

. . . antitrust laws attempt to counteract pricing below costs to drive out competitors or fixing prices artificially high to harm consumers

Predatory Pricing

To comply with U.S. antitrust laws, such as the Sherman Act, the Clayton Act, the Federal Trade Commission Act, and the Robinson-Patman Act, pricing must not be predatory.[5] A company engages in **predatory pricing** when it deliberately prices below its costs in an effort to drive competitors out of the market and restrict supply, and then raises prices rather than enlarge demand.[6]

The U.S. Supreme Court established the following conditions to prove that predatory pricing has occurred:

- The predator company charges a price below an appropriate measure of its costs.

- The predator company has a reasonable prospect of recovering in the future, through larger market share or higher prices, the money it lost by pricing below cost.

The Supreme Court has not specified the "appropriate measure of costs."[7]

Most courts in the United States have defined the "appropriate measure of costs" as the short-run marginal or average variable costs.[8] In *Adjustor's Replace-a-Car* v. *Agency Rent-a-Car,* Adjustor's (the plaintiff) claimed that it was forced to withdraw from the Austin and San Antonio, Texas, markets because Agency had engaged in predatory pricing.[9] To prove predatory pricing, Adjustor pointed to "the net loss from operations" in Agency's income statement, calculated after allocating Agency's headquarters overhead. The judge, however, ruled that Agency had not engaged in predatory

---

[5] Discussion of the Sherman Act and the Clayton Act is in A. Barkman and J. Jolley, "Cost Defenses for Antitrust Cases," *Management Accounting* 67 (no. 10): 37–40.

[6] For more details, see W. Viscusi, J. Harrington, and J. Vernon, *Economics of Regulation and Antitrust*, 4th ed. (Cambridge, MA: MIT Press, 2006); and J. L. Goldstein, "Single Firm Predatory Pricing in Antitrust Law: The Rose Acre Recoupment Test and the Search for an Appropriate Judicial Standard," *Columbia Law Review* 91 (1991): 1557–1592.

[7] *Brooke Group* v. *Brown & Williamson Tobacco*, 113 S. Ct. (1993); T. J. Trujillo, "Predatory Pricing Standards Under Recent Supreme Court Decisions and Their Failure to Recognize Strategic Behavior as a Barrier to Entry," *Iowa Journal of Corporation Law* (Summer 1994): 809–831.

[8] An exception is *McGahee* v. *Northern Propane Gas Co.* [858 F, 2d 1487 (1988)], in which the Eleventh Circuit Court held that prices below average total cost constitute evidence of predatory intent. For more discussion, see P. Areeda and D. Turner, "Predatory Pricing and Related Practices under Section 2 of Sherman Act," *Harvard Law Review* 88 (1975): 697–733. For an overview of case law, see W. Viscusi, J. Harrington, and J. Vernon, *Economics of Regulation and Antitrust*, 4th ed. (Cambridge, MA: MIT Press, 2006). See also the "Legal Developments" section of the *Journal of Marketing* for summaries of court cases.

[9] *Adjustor's Replace-a-Car, Inc.* v. *Agency Rent-a-Car*, 735 2d 884 (1984).

pricing because the price it charged for a rental car never dropped below its average variable costs.

The Supreme Court decision in *Brooke Group* v. *Brown & Williamson Tobacco* (*BWT*) increased the difficulty of proving predatory pricing. The Court ruled that pricing below average variable costs is not predatory if the company does not have a reasonable chance of later increasing prices or market share to recover its losses.[10] The defendant, BWT, a cigarette manufacturer, sold brand-name cigarettes and had 12% of the cigarette market. The introduction of generic cigarettes threatened BWT's market share. BWT responded by introducing its own version of generics priced below average variable cost, thereby making it difficult for generic manufacturers to continue in business. The Supreme Court ruled that BWT's action was a competitive response and not predatory pricing. That's because, given BWT's small 12% market share and the existing competition within the industry, it would be unable to later charge a monopoly price to recoup its losses.

Dumping

Closely related to predatory pricing is dumping. Under U.S. laws, **dumping** occurs when a non-U.S. company sells a product in the United States at a price below the market value in the country where it is produced, and this lower price materially injures or threatens to materially injure an industry in the United States. If dumping is proven, an antidumping duty can be imposed under U.S. tariff laws equal to the amount by which the foreign price exceeds the U.S. price. Cases related to dumping have occurred in the cement, computer, lumber, paper, semiconductor, steel, sweater, and tire industries. In September 2009, the U.S. Commerce Department said it would place import duties of 25%–35% on imports of automobile and light-truck tires from China.[11] China challenged the decision to the dispute settlement panel of the World Trade Organization (WTO), an international institution created with the goal of promoting and regulating trade practices among countries.

Collusive Pricing

Decision Point

How do antitrust laws affect pricing?

Another violation of antitrust laws is collusive pricing. **Collusive pricing** occurs when companies in an industry conspire in their pricing and production decisions to achieve a price above the competitive price and so restrain trade. In 2008, for example, LG agreed to pay $400 million and Sharp $120 million for colluding to fix prices of LCD picture tubes in the United States.

---

[10]*Brooke Group* v. *Brown & Williamson Tobacco*, 113 S. Ct. (1993).
[11]Edmund Andrews, "U.S. Adds Tariffs on Chinese Tires," *New York Times* (September 11, 2009).

Problem for Self-Study

Reconsider the Astel Computer example (pp. 436–437). Astel's marketing manager realizes that a further reduction in price is necessary to sell 200,000 units of Provalue II. To maintain a target profitability of $16 million, or $80 per unit, Astel will need to reduce costs of Provalue II by $6 million, or $30 per unit. Astel targets a reduction of $4 million, or $20 per unit, in manufacturing costs, and $2 million, or $10 per unit, in marketing, distribution, and customer-service costs. The cross-functional team assigned to this task proposes the following changes to manufacture a different version of Provalue, called Provalue III:

1. Reduce direct materials and ordering costs by purchasing subassembled components rather than individual components.

2. Reengineer ordering and receiving to reduce ordering and receiving costs per order.

3. Reduce testing time and the labor and power required per hour of testing.

4. Develop new rework procedures to reduce rework costs per hour.

No changes are proposed in direct manufacturing labor cost per unit and in total machining costs.

The following table summarizes the cost-driver quantities and the cost per unit of each cost driver for Provalue III compared with Provalue II.

	Home	Insert		Page Layout		Formulas	Data	Review		View			
	A	B	C	D	E	F	G	H	I	J	K	L	M	N
1				Manufacturing Cost Information						Manufacturing Cost Information				
2				for 200,000 Units of Provalue II for 2012						for 200,000 Units of Provalue III for 2012				
3	Cost Category	Cost Driver		Details of Budgeted Cost Driver Quantities			Budgeted Total Quantity of Cost Driver	Budgeted Cost per Unit of Cost Driver		Details of Budgeted Cost Driver Quantities			Budgeted Total Quantity of Cost Driver	Budgeted Cost per Unit of Cost Driver
4	(1)	(2)		(3)	(4)		(5)=(3)×(4)	(6)		(7)	(8)		(9)=(7)×(8)	(10)
5	Direct materials	No. of kits	1	kit per unit	200,000	units	200,000	$385	1	kit per unit	200,000	units	200,000	$375
6	Direct manuf. labor (DML)	DML hours	2.65	DML hours per unit	200,000	units	530,000	$ 20	2.65	DML hours per unit	200,000	units	530,000	$ 20
7	Direct machining (fixed)	Machine-hours					300,000	$ 38					300,000	$ 38
8	Ordering and receiving	No. of orders	50	orders per component	425	components	21,250	$ 80	50	orders per component	400	components	20,000	$ 60
9	Test and inspection	Testing-hours	15	testing-hours per unit	200,000	units	3,000,000	$ 2	14	testing-hours per unit	200,000	units	2,800,000	$ 1.70
10	Rework				6.5%	defect rate					6.5%	defect rate		
11		Rework-hours	2.5	rework-hours per defective unit	13,000[a]	defective units	32,500	$ 40	2.5	rework-hours per defective unit	13,000[a]	defective units	32,500	$ 32
12														
13	[a]6.5% defect rate × 200,000 units = 13,000 defective units													

Required Will the proposed changes achieve Astel's targeted reduction of $4 million, or $20 per unit, in manufacturing costs for Provalue III? Show your computations.

Solution

Exhibit 7 presents the manufacturing costs for Provalue III based on the proposed changes. Manufacturing costs will decline from $108 million, or $540 per unit (Exhibit 5), to $104 million, or $520 per unit (Exhibit 7), and will achieve the target reduction of $4 million, or $20 per unit.

| Exhibit 7 | Target Manufacturing Costs of Provalue III for 2012 Based on Proposed Changes |

	A	B	C	D
1		**Budgeted**		**Budgeted**
2		**Manufacturing Costs**		**Manufacturing**
3		**for 200,000 Units**		**Cost per Unit**
4		**(1)**		**(2) = (1) ÷ 200,000**
5	Direct manufacturing costs			
6	Direct material costs			
7	(200,000 kits × $375 per kit)	$ 75,000,000		$375.00
8	Direct manufacturing labor costs			
9	(530,000 DML-hours × $20 per hour)	10,600,000		53.00
10	Direct machining costs			
11	(300,000 machine-hours × $38 per machine-hour)	11,400,000		57.00
12	Direct manufacturing costs	97,000,000		485.00
13				
14	Manufacturing overhead costs			
15	Ordering and receiving costs			
16	(20,000 orders × $60 per order)	1,200,000		6.00
17	Testing and inspection costs			
18	(2,800,000 testing-hours × $1.70 per hour)	4,760,000		23.80
19	Rework costs			
20	(32,500 rework-hours × $32 per hour)	1,040,000		5.20
21	Manufacturing overhead costs	7,000,000		35.00
22	Total manufacturing costs	$104,000,000		$520.00

Decision Points

The following question-and-answer format summarizes the chapter's learning objectives. Each decision presents a key question related to a learning objective. The guidelines are the answers to that question.

Decision

Guidelines

1. What are the three major influences on pricing decisions?

Customers, competitors, and costs influence prices through their effects on demand and supply; customers and competitors affect demand, and costs affect supply.

2. What do companies consider when making short-run pricing decisions?

When making short-run pricing decisions companies only consider those (relevant) costs that will change in total as a result of the decision. Pricing is done opportunistically based on demand and competition.

3. How do companies make long-run pricing decisions?

Companies consider all future variable and fixed costs as relevant and use a market-based or a cost-based pricing approach to earn a target return on investment.

4. How do companies determine target costs?

One approach to long-run pricing is to use a target price. Target price is the estimated price that potential customers are willing to pay for a product or service. Target operating income per unit is subtracted from the target price to determine target cost per unit. Target cost per unit is the estimated long-run cost of a product or service that when sold enables the company to achieve target operating income per unit. The challenge for the company is to make the cost improvements necessary through value-engineering methods to achieve the target cost.

5. Why is it important to distinguish cost incurrence from locked-in costs?

Cost incurrence describes when a resource is sacrificed. Locked-in costs are costs that have not yet been incurred but, based on decisions that have already been made, will be incurred in the future. To reduce costs, techniques such as value engineering are most effective *before* costs are locked in.

6. How do companies price products using the cost-plus approach?

The cost-plus approach to pricing adds a markup component to a cost base as the starting point for pricing decisions. Many different costs, such as full cost of the product or manufacturing cost, can serve as the cost base in applying the cost-plus formula. Prices are then modified on the basis of customers' reactions and competitors' responses. Therefore, the size of the "plus" is determined by the marketplace.

7. Describe life-cycle budgeting and life-cycle costing and when companies should use these techniques.

Life-cycle budgeting estimates and life-cycle costing tracks and accumulates the costs (and revenues) attributable to a product from its initial R&D to its final customer service and support. These life-cycle techniques are particularly important when (a) a high percentage of total life-cycle costs are incurred before production begins and revenues are earned over several years, and (b) a high fraction of the life-cycle costs are locked in at the R&D and design stages.

8. Describe price discrimination and peak-load pricing.

Price discrimination is charging some customers a higher price for a given product or service than other customers. Peak-load pricing is charging a higher price for the same product or service when demand approaches physical-capacity limits. Under price discrimination and peak-load pricing, prices differ among market segments and across time periods even though the cost of providing the product or service is approximately the same.

9. How do antitrust laws affect pricing?

To comply with antitrust laws, a company must not engage in predatory pricing, dumping, or collusive pricing, which lessens competition; puts another company at an unfair competitive disadvantage; or harms consumers.

Terms to Learn

The chapter contains definitions of the following important terms:

collusive pricing	locked-in costs	target operating income per unit
cost incurrence	nonvalue-added cost	target price
customer life-cycle costs	peak-load pricing	target rate of return on investment
designed-in costs	predatory pricing	value-added cost
dumping	price discrimination	value engineering
life-cycle budgeting	product life cycle	
life-cycle costing	target cost per unit	

Assignment Material

Questions

MyAccountingLab

12-1 What are the three major influences on pricing decisions?
12-2 "Relevant costs for pricing decisions are full costs of the product." Do you agree? Explain.
12-3 Give two examples of pricing decisions with a short-run focus.
12-4 How is activity-based costing useful for pricing decisions?
12-5 Describe two alternative approaches to long-run pricing decisions.
12-6 What is a target cost per unit?
12-7 Describe value engineering and its role in target costing.
12-8 Give two examples of a value-added cost and two examples of a nonvalue-added cost.
12-9 "It is not important for a company to distinguish between cost incurrence and locked-in costs." Do you agree? Explain.

12-10 What is cost-plus pricing?

12-11 Describe three alternative cost-plus pricing methods.

12-12 Give two examples in which the difference in the costs of two products or services is much smaller than the difference in their prices.

12-13 What is life-cycle budgeting?

12-14 What are three benefits of using a product life-cycle reporting format?

12-15 Define predatory pricing, dumping, and collusive pricing.

MyAccountingLab

Exercises

12-16 Relevant-cost approach to pricing decisions, special order. The following financial data apply to the DVD production plant of the Dill Company for October 2011:

	Budgeted Manufacturing Cost per DVD Pack
Direct materials	$1.60
Direct manufacturing labor	0.90
Variable manufacturing overhead	0.70
Fixed manufacturing overhead	1.00
Total manufacturing cost	$4.20

Variable manufacturing overhead varies with the number of DVD packs produced. Fixed manufacturing overhead of $1 per pack is based on budgeted fixed manufacturing overhead of $150,000 per month and budgeted production of 150,000 packs per month. The Dill Company sells each pack for $5.

Marketing costs have two components:

- Variable marketing costs (sales commissions) of 5% of revenues
- Fixed monthly costs of $65,000

During October 2011, Lyn Randell, a Dill Company salesperson, asked the president for permission to sell 1,000 packs at $4.00 per pack to a customer not in Dill's normal marketing channels. The president refused this special order because the selling price was below the total budgeted manufacturing cost.

Required
1. What would have been the effect on monthly operating income of accepting the special order?
2. Comment on the president's "below manufacturing costs" reasoning for rejecting the special order.
3. What other factors should the president consider before accepting or rejecting the special order?

12-17 Relevant-cost approach to short-run pricing decisions. The San Carlos Company is an electronics business with eight product lines. Income data for one of the products (XT-107) for June 2011 are as follows:

Revenues, 200,000 units at average price of $100 each		$20,000,000
Variable costs		
Direct materials at $35 per unit	$7,000,000	
Direct manufacturing labor at $10 per unit	2,000,000	
Variable manufacturing overhead at $6 per unit	1,200,000	
Sales commissions at 15% of revenues	3,000,000	
Other variable costs at $5 per unit	1,000,000	
Total variable costs		14,200,000
Contribution margin		5,800,000
Fixed costs		5,000,000
Operating income		$ 800,000

Abrams, Inc., an instruments company, has a problem with its preferred supplier of XT-107. This supplier has had a three-week labor strike. Abrams approaches the San Carlos sales representative, Sarah Holtz, about providing 3,000 units of XT-107 at a price of $75 per unit. Holtz informs the XT-107 product manager, Jim McMahon, that she would accept a flat commission of $8,000 rather than the usual 15% of revenues if this special order were accepted. San Carlos has the capacity to produce 300,000 units of XT-107 each month, but demand has not exceeded 200,000 units in any month in the past year.

Required
1. If the 3,000-unit order from Abrams is accepted, how much will operating income increase or decrease? (Assume the same cost structure as in June 2011.)

2. McMahon ponders whether to accept the 3,000-unit special order. He is afraid of the precedent that might be set by cutting the price. He says, "The price is below our full cost of $96 per unit. I think we should quote a full price, or Abrams will expect favored treatment again and again if we continue to do business with it." Do you agree with McMahon? Explain.

12-18 Short-run pricing, capacity constraints. Colorado Mountains Dairy, maker of specialty cheeses, produces a soft cheese from the milk of Holstein cows raised on a special corn-based diet. One kilogram of soft cheese, which has a contribution margin of $10, requires 4 liters of milk. A well-known gourmet restaurant has asked Colorado Mountains to produce 2,600 kilograms of a hard cheese from the same milk of Holstein cows. Knowing that the dairy has sufficient unused capacity, Elise Princiotti, owner of Colorado Mountains, calculates the costs of making one kilogram of the desired hard cheese:

Milk (8 liters × $2.00 per liter)	$16
Variable direct manufacturing labor	5
Variable manufacturing overhead	4
Fixed manufacturing cost allocated	6
Total manufacturing cost	$31

1. Suppose Colorado Mountains can acquire all the Holstein milk that it needs. What is the minimum price per kilogram it should charge for the hard cheese? **Required**

2. Now suppose that the Holstein milk is in short supply. Every kilogram of hard cheese produced by Colorado Mountains will reduce the quantity of soft cheese that it can make and sell. What is the minimum price per kilogram it should charge to produce the hard cheese?

12-19 Value-added, nonvalue-added costs. The Marino Repair Shop repairs and services machine tools. A summary of its costs (by activity) for 2011 is as follows:

a.	Materials and labor for servicing machine tools	$800,000
b.	Rework costs	75,000
c.	Expediting costs caused by work delays	60,000
d.	Materials-handling costs	50,000
e.	Materials-procurement and inspection costs	35,000
f.	Preventive maintenance of equipment	15,000
g.	Breakdown maintenance of equipment	55,000

1. Classify each cost as value-added, nonvalue-added, or in the gray area between. **Required**

2. For any cost classified in the gray area, assume 65% is value-added and 35% is nonvalue-added. How much of the total of all seven costs is value-added and how much is nonvalue-added?

3. Marino is considering the following changes: (a) introducing quality-improvement programs whose net effect will be to reduce rework and expediting costs by 75% and materials and labor costs for servicing machine tools by 5%; (b) working with suppliers to reduce materials-procurement and inspection costs by 20% and materials-handling costs by 25%; and (c) increasing preventive-maintenance costs by 50% to reduce breakdown-maintenance costs by 40%. Calculate the effect of programs (a), (b), and (c) on value-added costs, nonvalue-added costs, and total costs. Comment briefly.

12-20 Target operating income, value-added costs, service company. Calvert Associates prepares architectural drawings to conform to local structural-safety codes. Its income statement for 2012 is as follows:

Revenues	$701,250
Salaries of professional staff (7,500 hours × $52 per hour)	390,000
Travel	15,000
Administrative and support costs	171,600
Total costs	576,600
Operating income	$124,650

Following is the percentage of time spent by professional staff on various activities:

Making calculations and preparing drawings for clients	77%
Checking calculations and drawings	3
Correcting errors found in drawings (not billed to clients)	8
Making changes in response to client requests (billed to clients)	5
Correcting own errors regarding building codes (not billed to clients)	7
Total	100%

Assume administrative and support costs vary with professional-labor costs.

Consider each requirement independently.

Required

1. How much of the total costs in 2012 are value-added, nonvalue-added, or in the gray area between? Explain your answers briefly. What actions can Calvert take to reduce its costs?
2. Suppose Calvert could eliminate all errors so that it did not need to spend any time making corrections and, as a result, could proportionately reduce professional-labor costs. Calculate Calvert's operating income for 2012.
3. Now suppose Calvert could take on as much business as it could complete, but it could not add more professional staff. Assume Calvert could eliminate all errors so that it does not need to spend any time correcting errors. Assume Calvert could use the time saved to increase revenues proportionately. Assume travel costs will remain at $15,000. Calculate Calvert's operating income for 2012.

12-21 Target prices, target costs, activity-based costing. Snappy Tiles is a small distributor of marble tiles. Snappy identifies its three major activities and cost pools as ordering, receiving and storage, and shipping, and it reports the following details for 2011:

Activity	Cost Driver	Quantity of Cost Driver	Cost per Unit of Cost Driver
1. Placing and paying for orders of marble tiles	Number of orders	500	$50 per order
2. Receiving and storage	Loads moved	4,000	$30 per load
3. Shipping of marble tiles to retailers	Number of shipments	1,500	$40 per shipment

For 2011, Snappy buys 250,000 marble tiles at an average cost of $3 per tile and sells them to retailers at an average price of $4 per tile. Assume Snappy has no fixed costs and no inventories.

Required

1. Calculate Snappy's operating income for 2011.
2. For 2012, retailers are demanding a 5% discount off the 2011 price. Snappy's suppliers are only willing to give a 4% discount. Snappy expects to sell the same quantity of marble tiles in 2012 as in 2011. If all other costs and cost-driver information remain the same, calculate Snappy's operating income for 2012.
3. Suppose further that Snappy decides to make changes in its ordering and receiving-and-storing practices. By placing long-run orders with its key suppliers, Snappy expects to reduce the number of orders to 200 and the cost per order to $25 per order. By redesigning the layout of the warehouse and reconfiguring the crates in which the marble tiles are moved, Snappy expects to reduce the number of loads moved to 3,125 and the cost per load moved to $28. Will Snappy achieve its target operating income of $0.30 per tile in 2012? Show your calculations.

12-22 Target costs, effect of product-design changes on product costs. Medical Instruments uses a manufacturing costing system with one direct-cost category (direct materials) and three indirect-cost categories:

a. Setup, production order, and materials-handling costs that vary with the number of batches
b. Manufacturing-operations costs that vary with machine-hours
c. Costs of engineering changes that vary with the number of engineering changes made

In response to competitive pressures at the end of 2010, Medical Instruments used value-engineering techniques to reduce manufacturing costs. Actual information for 2010 and 2011 is as follows:

	2010	2011
Setup, production-order, and materials-handling costs per batch	$ 8,000	$ 7,500
Total manufacturing-operations cost per machine-hour	$ 55	$ 50
Cost per engineering change	$12,000	$10,000

The management of Medical Instruments wants to evaluate whether value engineering has succeeded in reducing the target manufacturing cost per unit of one of its products, HJ6, by 10%.

Actual results for 2010 and 2011 for HJ6 are as follows:

	Actual Results for 2010	Actual Results for 2011
Units of HJ6 produced	3,500	4,000
Direct material cost per unit of HJ6	$ 1,200	$ 1,100
Total number of batches required to produce HJ6	70	80
Total machine-hours required to produce HJ6	21,000	22,000
Number of engineering changes made	14	10

Required

1. Calculate the manufacturing cost per unit of HJ6 in 2010.
2. Calculate the manufacturing cost per unit of HJ6 in 2011.

3. Did Medical Instruments achieve the target manufacturing cost per unit for HJ6 in 2011? Explain.
4. Explain how Medical Instruments reduced the manufacturing cost per unit of HJ6 in 2011.

12-23 Cost-plus target return on investment pricing. John Blodgett is the managing partner of a business that has just finished building a 60-room motel. Blodgett anticipates that he will rent these rooms for 15,000 nights next year (or 15,000 room-nights). All rooms are similar and will rent for the same price. Blodgett estimates the following operating costs for next year:

Variable operating costs	$5 per room-night
Fixed costs	
Salaries and wages	$173,000
Maintenance of building and pool	52,000
Other operating and administration costs	150,000
Total fixed costs	$375,000

The capital invested in the motel is $900,000. The partnership's target return on investment is 25%. Blodgett expects demand for rooms to be uniform throughout the year. He plans to price the rooms at full cost plus a markup on full cost to earn the target return on investment.

1. What price should Blodgett charge for a room-night? What is the markup as a percentage of the full **Required** cost of a room-night?
2. Blodgett's market research indicates that if the price of a room-night determined in requirement 1 is reduced by 10%, the expected number of room-nights Blodgett could rent would increase by 10%. Should Blodgett reduce prices by 10%? Show your calculations.

12-24 Cost-plus, target pricing, working backward. Road Warrior manufactures and sells a model of motorcycle, XR500. In 2011, it reported the following:

Units produced and sold	1,500
Investment	$8,400,000
Markup percentage on full cost	9%
Rate of return on investment	18%
Variable cost per unit	$8,450

1. What was Road Warrior's operating income on XR500 in 2011? What was the full cost per unit? What **Required** was the selling price? What was the percentage markup on variable cost?
2. Road Warrior is considering increasing the annual spending on advertising for the XR500 by $500,000. The company believes that the investment will translate into a 10% increase in unit sales. Should the investment be made? Show your calculations.
3. Refer back to the original data. In 2012, Road Warrior believes that it will only be able to sell 1,400 units at the price calculated in requirement 1. Management has identified $125,000 in fixed cost that can be eliminated. If Road Warrior wants to maintain a 9% markup on full cost, what is the target variable cost per unit?

12-25 Life cycle product costing. Gadzooks, Inc., develops and manufactures toys that it then sells through infomercials. Currently, the company is designing a toy robot that it intends to begin manufacturing and marketing next year. Because of the rapidly changing nature of the toy industry, Gadzooks management projects that the robot will be produced and sold for only three years. At the end of the product's life cycle, Gadzooks plans to sell the rights to the robot to an overseas company for $250,000. Cost information concerning the robot follows:

		Total Fixed Costs over Four Years	Variable Cost per Unit
Year 1	Design costs	$ 650,000	—
Years 2–4	Production costs	$3,560,000	$20 per unit
	Marketing and distribution costs	$2,225,000	$5 per unit

For simplicity, ignore the time value of money.

1. Suppose the managers at Gadzooks price the robot at $50 per unit. How many units do they need to sell **Required** to break even?
2. The managers at Gadzooks are thinking of two alternative pricing strategies.
   a. Sell the robot at $50 each from the outset. At this price they expect to sell 500,000 units over its life-cycle.
   b. Boost the selling price of the robot in year 2 when it first comes out to $70 per unit. At this price they expect to sell 100,000 units in year 2. In years 3 and 4 drop the price to $40 per unit. The managers expect to sell 300,000 units each year in years 3 and 4. Which pricing strategy would you recommend? Explain.

MyAccountingLab **Problems**

12-26 Relevant-cost approach to pricing decisions. Burst, Inc., cans peaches for sale to food distributors. All costs are classified as either manufacturing or marketing. Burst prepares monthly budgets. The March 2012 budgeted absorption-costing income statement is as follows:

Revenues (1,000 crates × $117 a crate)	$117,000
Cost of goods sold	65,000
Gross margin	52,000
Marketing costs	30,000
Operating income	$ 22,000

Gross margin markup percentage: $52,000 ÷ $65,000
= 80% of cost of goods sold (full manufacturing cost)

Monthly costs are classified as fixed or variable (with respect to the number of crates produced for manufacturing costs and with respect to the number of crates sold for marketing costs):

	Fixed	Variable
Manufacturing	$30,000	$35,000
Marketing	13,000	17,000

Burst has the capacity to can 2,000 crates per month. The relevant range in which monthly fixed manufacturing costs will be "fixed" is from 500 to 2,000 crates per month.

Required
1. Calculate the markup percentage based on total variable costs.
2. Assume that a new customer approaches Burst to buy 200 crates at $55 per crate for cash. The customer does not require any marketing effort. Additional manufacturing costs of $3,000 (for special packaging) will be required. Burst believes that this is a one-time-only special order because the customer is discontinuing business in six weeks' time. Burst is reluctant to accept this 200-crate special order because the $55-per-crate price is below the $65-per-crate full manufacturing cost. Do you agree with this reasoning? Explain.
3. Assume that the new customer decides to remain in business. How would this longevity affect your willingness to accept the $55-per-crate offer? Explain.

12-27 Considerations other than cost in pricing decisions. Executive Suites operates a 100-suite hotel in a busy business park. During April, a 30-day month, Executive Suites experienced a 90% occupancy rate from Monday evening through Thursday evening (weeknights), with business travelers making up virtually all of its guests. On Friday through Sunday evenings (weekend nights), however, occupancy dwindled to 20%. Guests on these nights were all leisure travelers. (There were 18 weeknights and 12 weekend nights in April.) Executive Suites charges $68 per night for a suite. Fran Jackson has recently been hired to manage the hotel, and is trying to devise a way to increase the hotel's profitability. The following information relates to Executive Suites' costs:

	Fixed Cost	Variable Cost
Depreciation	$20,000 per month	
Administrative costs	$35,000 per month	
Housekeeping and supplies	$12,000 per month	$25 per room night
Breakfast	$ 5,000 per month	$5 per breakfast served

Executive Suites offers free breakfast to guests. In April, there were an average of 1.0 breakfasts served per room night on weeknights and 2.5 breakfasts served per room night on weekend nights.

Required
1. Calculate the average cost per guest night for April. What was Executive Suites' operating income or loss for the month?
2. Fran Jackson estimates that if Executive Suites increases the nightly rates to $80, weeknight occupancy will only decline to 85%. She also estimates that if the hotel reduces the nightly rate on weekend nights to $50, occupancy on those nights will increase to 50%. Would this be a good move for Executive Suites? Show your calculations.
3. Why would the $30 price difference per night be tolerated by the weeknight guests?
4. A discount travel clearing-house has approached Executive Suites with a proposal to offer last-minute deals on empty rooms on both weeknights and weekend nights. Assuming that there will be an average of two breakfasts served per night per room, what is the minimum price that Executive Suites could accept on the last-minute rooms?

12-28 Cost-plus, target pricing, working backward. The new CEO of Radco Manufacturing has asked for a variety of information about the operations of the firm from last year. The CEO is given the following information, but with some data missing:

Total sales revenue	?
Number of units produced and sold	500,000 units
Selling price	?
Operating income	$195,000
Total investment in assets	$2,000,000
Variable cost per unit	$3.75
Fixed costs for the year	$3,000,000

1. Find (a) total sales revenue, (b) selling price, (c) rate of return on investment, and (d) markup percentage on full cost for this product. **Required**

2. The new CEO has a plan to reduce fixed costs by $200,000 and variable costs by $0.60 per unit while continuing to produce and sell 500,000 units. Using the same markup percentage as in requirement 1, calculate the new selling price.

3. Assume the CEO institutes the changes in requirement 2 including the new selling price. However, the reduction in variable cost has resulted in lower product quality resulting in 10% fewer units being sold compared to before the change. Calculate operating income (loss).

12-29 Target prices, target costs, value engineering, cost incurrence, locked-in costs, activity-based costing. Cutler Electronics makes an MP3 player, CE100, which has 80 components. Cutler sells 7,000 units each month for $70 each. The costs of manufacturing CE100 are $45 per unit, or $315,000 per month. Monthly manufacturing costs are as follows:

Direct material costs	$182,000
Direct manufacturing labor costs	28,000
Machining costs (fixed)	31,500
Testing costs	35,000
Rework costs	14,000
Ordering costs	3,360
Engineering costs (fixed)	21,140
Total manufacturing costs	$315,000

Cutler's management identifies the activity cost pools, the cost driver for each activity, and the cost per unit of the cost driver for each overhead cost pool as follows:

Manufacturing Activity	Description of Activity	Cost Driver	Cost per Unit of Cost Driver
1. Machining costs	Machining components	Machine-hour capacity	$4.50 per machine-hour
2. Testing costs	Testing components and final product (Each unit of CE100 is tested individually.)	Testing-hours	$2 per testing-hour
3. Rework costs	Correcting and fixing errors and defects	Units of CE100 reworked	$20 per unit
4. Ordering costs	Ordering of components	Number of orders	$21 per order
5. Engineering costs	Designing and managing of products and processes	Engineering-hour capacity	$35 per engineering-hour

Cutler's management views direct material costs and direct manufacturing labor costs as variable with respect to the units of CE100 manufactured. Over a long-run horizon, each of the overhead costs described in the preceding table varies, as described, with the chosen cost drivers.

The following additional information describes the existing design:

a. Testing time per unit is 2.5 hours.
b. 10% of the CE100s manufactured are reworked.
c. Cutler places two orders with each component supplier each month. Each component is supplied by a different supplier.
d. It currently takes one hour to manufacture each unit of CE100.

In response to competitive pressures, Cutler must reduce its price to $62 per unit and its costs by $8 per unit. No additional sales are anticipated at this lower price. However, Cutler stands to lose significant sales if it does not reduce its price. Manufacturing has been asked to reduce its costs by $6 per unit. Improvements in manufacturing efficiency are expected to yield a net savings of $1.50 per MP3 player, but that is not enough. The chief engineer has proposed a new modular design that reduces the number of components to 50 and also simplifies testing. The newly designed MP3 player, called "New CE100" will replace CE100.

The expected effects of the new design are as follows:

a. Direct material cost for the New CE100 is expected to be lower by $2.20 per unit.
b. Direct manufacturing labor cost for the New CE100 is expected to be lower by $0.50 per unit.
c. Machining time required to manufacture the New CE100 is expected to be 20% less, but machine-hour capacity will not be reduced.
d. Time required for testing the New CE100 is expected to be lower by 20%.
e. Rework is expected to decline to 4% of New CE100s manufactured.
f. Engineering-hours capacity will remain the same.

Assume that the cost per unit of each cost driver for CE100 continues to apply to New CE100.

Required

1. Calculate Cutler's manufacturing cost per unit of New CE100.
2. Will the new design achieve the per-unit cost-reduction targets that have been set for the manufacturing costs of New CE100? Show your calculations.
3. The problem describes two strategies to reduce costs: (a) improving manufacturing efficiency and (b) modifying product design. Which strategy has more impact on Cutler's costs? Why? Explain briefly.

12-30 Cost-plus, target return on investment pricing. Vend-o-licious makes candy bars for vending machines and sells them to vendors in cases of 30 bars. Although Vend-o-licious makes a variety of candy, the cost differences are insignificant, and the cases all sell for the same price.

Vend-o-licious has a total capital investment of $13,000,000. It expects to produce and sell 500,000 cases of candy next year. Vend-o-licious requires a 10% target return on investment.

Expected costs for next year are as follows:

Variable production costs	$3.50 per case
Variable marketing and distribution costs	$1.50 per case
Fixed production costs	$1,000,000
Fixed marketing and distribution costs	$700,000
Other fixed costs	$500,000

Vend-o-licious prices the cases of candy at full cost plus markup to generate profits equal to the target return on capital.

Required

1. What is the target operating income?
2. What is the selling price Vend-o-licious needs to charge to earn the target operating income? Calculate the markup percentage on full cost.
3. Vend-o-licious's closest competitor has just increased its candy case price to $15, although it sells 36 candy bars per case. Vend-o-licious is considering increasing its selling price to $14 per case. Assuming production and sales decrease by 5%, calculate Vend-o-licious' return on investment. Is increasing the selling price a good idea?

12-31 Cost-plus, time and materials, ethics. R & C Mechanical sells and services plumbing, heating, and air conditioning systems. R & C's cost accounting system tracks two cost categories: direct labor and direct materials. R & C uses a time-and-materials pricing system, with direct labor marked up 100% and direct materials marked up 60% to recover indirect costs of support staff, support materials, and shared equipment and tools, and to earn a profit.

R & C technician Greg Garrison is called to the home of Ashley Briggs on a particularly hot summer day to investigate her broken central air conditioning system. He considers two options: replace the compressor or repair it. The cost information available to Garrison follows:

	Labor	Materials
Repair option	5 hrs.	$100
Replace option	2 hrs.	$200
Labor rate	$30 per hour	

Required

1. If Garrison presents Briggs with the replace or repair options, what price would he quote for each?
2. If the two options were equally effective for the three years that Briggs intends to live in the home, which option would she choose?
3. If Garrison's objective is to maximize profits, which option would he recommend to Briggs? What would be the ethical course of action?

12-32 Cost-plus and market-based pricing. Florida Temps, a large labor contractor, supplies contract labor to building-construction companies. For 2012, Florida Temps has budgeted to supply 84,000 hours of contract labor. Its variable costs are $13 per hour, and its fixed costs are $168,000. Roger Mason, the general manager, has proposed a cost-plus approach for pricing labor at full cost plus 20%.

1. Calculate the price per hour that Florida Temps should charge based on Mason's proposal.
2. The marketing manager supplies the following information on demand levels at different prices:

Price per Hour	Demand (Hours)
$16	124,000
17	104,000
18	84,000
19	74,000
20	61,000

Required

Florida Temps can meet any of these demand levels. Fixed costs will remain unchanged for all the demand levels. On the basis of this additional information, calculate the price per hour that Florida Temps should charge to maximize operating income.
3. Comment on your answers to requirements 1 and 2. Why are they the same or different?

12-33 Cost-plus and market-based pricing. (CMA, adapted) Best Test Laboratories evaluates the reaction of materials to extreme increases in temperature. Much of the company's early growth was attributable to government contracts, but recent growth has come from expansion into commercial markets. Two types of testing at Best Test are Heat Testing (HTT) and Arctic-condition Testing (ACT). Currently, all of the budgeted operating costs are collected in a single overhead pool. All of the estimated testing-hours are also collected in a single pool. One rate per test-hour is used for both types of testing. This hourly rate is marked up by 45% to recover administrative costs and taxes, and to earn a profit.

Rick Shaw, Best Test's controller, believes that there is enough variation in the test procedures and cost structure to establish separate costing rates and billing rates at a 45% mark up. He also believes that the inflexible rate structure currently being used is inadequate in today's competitive environment. After analyzing the company data, he has divided operating costs into the following three cost pools:

Labor and supervision	$ 491,840
Setup and facility costs	402,620
Utilities	368,000
Total budgeted costs for the period	$1,262,460

Rick Shaw budgets 106,000 total test-hours for the coming period. This is also the cost driver for labor and supervision. The budgeted quantity of cost driver for setup and facility costs is 800 setup hours. The budgeted quantity of cost driver for utilities is 10,000 machine-hours.

Rick has estimated that HTT uses 60% of the testing hours, 25% of the setup hours, and half the machine-hours.

1. Find the single rate for operating costs based on test-hours and the hourly billing rate for HTT and ACT.
2. Find the three activity-based rates for operating costs.
3. What will the billing rate for HTT and ACT be based on the activity-based costing structure? State the rates in terms of testing hours. Referring to both requirements 1 and 2, which rates make more sense for Best Test?
4. If Best Test's competition all charge $20 per hour for arctic testing, what can Best Test do to stay competitive?

Required

12-34 Life-cycle costing. New Life Metal Recycling and Salvage has just been given the opportunity to salvage scrap metal and other materials from an old industrial site. The current owners of the site will sign over the site to New Life at no cost. New Life intends to extract scrap metal at the site for 24 months, and then will clean up the site, return the land to useable condition, and sell it to a developer. Projected costs associated with the project follow:

		Fixed	Variable
Months 1–24	Metal extraction and processing	$4,000 per month	$100 per ton
Months 1–27	Rent on temporary buildings	$2,000 per month	—
	Administration	$5,000 per month	—
Months 25–27	Clean-up	$30,000 per month	—
	Land restoration	$475,000 total	—
	Cost of selling land	$150,000 total	—

Ignore time value of money.

1. Assuming that New Life expects to salvage 50,000 tons of metal from the site, what is the total project life cycle cost?
2. Suppose New Life can sell the metal for $150 per ton and wants to earn a profit (before taxes) of $40 per ton. At what price must New Life sell the land at the end of the project to achieve its target profit per ton?
3. Now suppose New Life can only sell the metal for $140 per ton and the land at $100,000 less than what you calculated in requirement 2. If New Life wanted to maintain the same mark-up percentage on total project life-cycle cost as in requirement 2, by how much would it have to reduce its total project life-cycle cost?

12-35 Airline pricing, considerations other than cost in pricing. Air Eagle is about to introduce a daily round-trip flight from New York to Los Angeles and is determining how it should price its round-trip tickets.

The market research group at Air Eagle segments the market into business and pleasure travelers. It provides the following information on the effects of two different prices on the number of seats expected to be sold and the variable cost per ticket, including the commission paid to travel agents:

		Number of Seats Expected to Be Sold	
Price Charged	Variable Cost per Ticket	Business	Pleasure
$ 500	$ 65	200	100
2,100	175	180	20

Pleasure travelers start their travel during one week, spend at least one weekend at their destination, and return the following week or thereafter. Business travelers usually start and complete their travel within the same work week. They do not stay over weekends.

Assume that round-trip fuel costs are fixed costs of $24,000 and that fixed costs allocated to the round-trip flight for airplane-lease costs, ground services, and flight-crew salaries total $188,000.

1. If you could charge different prices to business travelers and pleasure travelers, would you? Show your computations.
2. Explain the key factor (or factors) for your answer in requirement 1.
3. How might Air Eagle implement price discrimination? That is, what plan could the airline formulate so that business travelers and pleasure travelers each pay the price desired by the airline?

12-36 Ethics and pricing. Apex Art has been requested to prepare a bid on 500 pieces of framed artwork for a new hotel. Winning the bid would be a big boost for sales representative Jason Grant, who works entirely on commission. Sonja Gomes, the cost accountant for Apex, prepares the bid based on the following cost information:

Direct costs		
Artwork		$30,000
Framing materials		40,000
Direct manufacturing labor		20,000
Delivery and installation		7,500
Overhead costs		
Production order	2,000	
Setup	4,000	
Materials handling	5,500	
General and administration	12,000	
Total overhead costs		23,500
Full product costs		$121,000

Based on the company policy of pricing at 125% of full cost, Gomes gives Grant a figure of $151,250 to submit for the job. Grant is very concerned. He tells Gomes that at that price, Apex has no chance of winning the job. He confides in her that he spent $500 of company funds to take the hotel's purchasing agent to a basketball playoff game where the purchasing agent disclosed that a bid of $145,000 would win the job. He hadn't planned to tell Gomes because he was confident that the bid she developed would be below that amount. Gomes reasons that the $500 he spent will be wasted if Apex doesn't capitalize on this valuable information. In any case, the company will still make money if it wins the bid at $145,000 because it is higher than the full cost of $121,000.

1. Is the $500 spent on the basketball tickets relevant to the bid decision? Why or why not?
2. Gomes suggests that if Grant is willing to use cheaper materials for the frame, he can achieve a bid of $145,000. The artwork has already been selected and cannot be changed, so the entire amount of reduction in cost will need to come from framing materials. What is the target cost of framing materials that will allow Grant to submit a bid of $145 assuming a target markup of 25% of full cost?
3. Evaluate whether Gomes' suggestion to Grant to use the purchasing agent's tip is unethical. Would it be unethical for Grant to redo the project's design to arrive at a lower bid? What steps should Grant and Gomes take to resolve this situation?

Collaborative Learning Problem

12-37 Value engineering, target pricing, and locked-in costs. Pacific Décor, Inc., designs, manufactures, and sells contemporary wood furniture. Ling Li is a furniture designer for Pacific. Li has spent much of the past month working on the design of a high-end dining room table. The design has been well-received by Jose Alvarez, the product development manager. However, Alvarez wants to make sure that the table can be priced competitively. Amy Hoover, Pacific's cost accountant, presents Alvarez with the following cost data for the expected production of 200 tables:

Design cost	$ 5,000
Direct materials	120,000
Direct manufacturing labor	142,000
Variable manufacturing overhead	64,000
Fixed manufacturing overhead	46,500
Marketing	15,000

1. Alvarez thinks that Pacific can successfully market the table for $2,000. The company's target operating income is 10% of revenue. Calculate the target full cost of producing the 200 tables. Does the cost estimate developed by Hoover meet Pacific's requirements? Is value engineering needed?
2. Alvarez discovers that Li has designed the table two inches wider than the standard size of wood normally used by Pacific. Reducing the table's size by two inches will lower the cost of direct materials by 40%. However, the redesign will require an additional $6,000 of design cost, and the table will be sold for $1,950. Will this design change allow the table to meet its target cost? Are the costs of materials a locked-in cost?
3. Li insists that the two inches are an absolute necessity in terms of the table's design. She believes that spending an additional $7,000 on better marketing will allow Pacific to sell the tables for $2,200. If this is the case, will the table's target cost be achieved without any value engineering?
4. Compare the total operating income on the 200 tables for requirements 2 and 3. What do you recommend Pacific do, based solely on your calculations? Explain briefly.

Strategy, Balanced Scorecard, and Strategic Profitability Analysis

From Chapter 13 of *Cost Accounting: A Managerial Emphasis*, 14/e. Charles T. Horngren. Srikant M. Datar. Madhav Rajan.

Strategy, Balanced Scorecard, and Strategic Profitability Analysis

Olive Garden wants to know.

So do Barnes and Noble, PepsiCo, and L.L.Bean. Even your local car dealer and transit authority are curious. They all want to know how well they are doing and how they score against the measures they strive to meet. The balanced scorecard can help them answer this question by evaluating key performance measures. Many companies have successfully used the balanced scorecard approach. Infosys Technologies, one of India's leading information technology companies, is one of them.

Balanced Scorecard Helps Infosys Transform into a Leading Consultancy[1]

In the early 2000s, Infosys Technologies was a company in transition. The Bangalore-based company was a market leader in information technology outsourcing, but needed to expand to meet increased client demand. Infosys invested in many new areas including business process outsourcing, project management, and management consulting. This put Infosys in direct competition with established consulting firms, such as IBM and Accenture.

Led by CEO Kris Gopalakrishnan, the company developed an integrated management structure that would help align these new, diverse initiatives. Infosys turned to the balanced scorecard to provide a framework the company could use to formulate and monitor its strategy. The balanced scorecard measures corporate performance along four dimensions—financial, customer, internal business process, and learning and growth.

The balanced scorecard immediately played a role in the transformation of Infosys. The executive team used the scorecard to guide discussion during its meetings. The continual process of adaptation, execution, and management that the scorecard fostered helped the team respond to, and even anticipate, its clients' evolving needs. Eventually, use of the scorecard for performance measurement spread to the rest of the organization, with monetary incentives linked to the company's performance along the different dimensions.

Over time, the balanced scorecard became part of the Infosys culture. In recent years, Infosys has begun using the balanced

---

[1] *Source*: Asis Martinez-Jerez, F., Robert S. Kaplan, and Katherine Miller. 2011. Infosys's relationship scorecard: Measuring transformational partnerships. Harvard Business School Case No. 9-109-006. Boston: Harvard Business School Publishing.

scorecard concept to create "relationship scorecards" for many of its largest clients. Using the scorecard framework, Infosys began measuring its performance for key clients not only on project management and client satisfaction, but also on repeat business and anticipating clients' future strategic needs.

The balanced scorecard helped successfully steer the transformation of Infosys from a technology outsourcer to a leading business consultancy. From 1999 to 2007, the company had a compound annual growth rate of 50%, with sales growing from $120 million in 1999 to more than $3 billion in 2007. Infosys was recognized for its achievements by making the *Wired* 40, *BusinessWeek* IT 100, and *BusinessWeek* Most Innovative Companies lists.

This chapter focuses on how management accounting information helps companies such as Infosys, Merck, Verizon, and Volkswagen implement and evaluate their strategies. Strategy drives the operations of a company and guides managers' short-run and long-run decisions. We describe the balanced scorecard approach to implementing strategy and methods to analyze operating income to evaluate the success of a strategy. We also show how management accounting information helps strategic initiatives, such as productivity improvement, reengineering, and downsizing.

Namas Bhojani/Getty Images, Inc.—Bloomberg News

What Is Strategy?

Strategy specifies how an organization matches its own capabilities with the opportunities in the marketplace to accomplish its objectives. In other words, strategy describes how an organization can create value for its customers while differentiating itself from its competitors. For example, Wal-Mart, the retail giant, creates value for its customers by locating stores in suburban and rural areas, and by offering low prices, a wide range of product categories, and few choices within each product category. Consistent with its strategy, Wal-Mart has developed the capability to keep costs down by aggressively negotiating low prices with its suppliers in exchange for high volumes and by maintaining a no-frills, cost-conscious environment.

In formulating its strategy, an organization must first thoroughly understand its industry. Industry analysis focuses on five forces: (1) competitors, (2) potential entrants into the market, (3) equivalent products, (4) bargaining power of customers, and (5) bargaining power of input suppliers.[2] The collective effect of these forces shapes an organization's profit potential. In general, profit potential decreases with greater competition, stronger potential entrants, products that are similar, and more-demanding customers and suppliers. We illustrate these five forces for Chipset, Inc., maker of linear integrated circuit

Learning Objective 1

Recognize which of two generic strategies a company is using

. . . product differentiation or cost leadership

---

[2] M. Porter, *Competitive Strategy* (New York: Free Press, 1980); M. Porter, *Competitive Advantage* (New York: Free Press, 1985); and M. Porter, "What Is Strategy?" *Harvard Business Review* (November–December 1996): 61–78.

devices (LICDs) used in modems and communication networks. Chipset produces a single specialized product, CX1, a standard, high-performance microchip, which can be used in multiple applications. Chipset designed CX1 with extensive input from customers.

1. **Competitors.** The CX1 model faces severe competition with respect to price, timely delivery, and quality. Companies in the industry have high fixed costs, and persistent pressures to reduce selling prices and utilize capacity fully. Price reductions spur growth because it makes LICDs a cost-effective option in new applications such as digital subscriber lines (DSLs).

2. **Potential entrants into the market.** The small profit margins and high capital costs discourage new entrants. Moreover, incumbent companies such as Chipset are further down the learning curve with respect to lowering costs and building close relationships with customers and suppliers.

3. **Equivalent products.** Chipset tailors CX1 to customer needs and lowers prices by continuously improving CX1's design and processes to reduce production costs. This reduces the risk of equivalent products or new technologies replacing CX1.

4. **Bargaining power of customers.** Customers, such as EarthLink and Verizon, negotiate aggressively with Chipset and its competitors to keep prices down because they buy large quantities of product.

5. **Bargaining power of input suppliers.** To produce CX1, Chipset requires high-quality materials (such as silicon wafers, pins for connectivity, and plastic or ceramic packaging) and skilled engineers, technicians, and manufacturing labor. The skill-sets suppliers and employees bring gives them bargaining power to demand higher prices and wages.

In summary, strong competition and the bargaining powers of customers and suppliers put significant pressure on Chipset's selling prices. To respond to these challenges, Chipset must choose one of two basic strategies: *differentiating its product* or *achieving cost leadership*.

Product differentiation is an organization's ability to offer products or services perceived by its customers to be superior and unique relative to the products or services of its competitors. Apple Inc. has successfully differentiated its products in the consumer electronics industry, as have Johnson & Johnson in the pharmaceutical industry and Coca-Cola in the soft drink industry. These companies have achieved differentiation through innovative product R&D, careful development and promotion of their brands, and the rapid push of products to market. Differentiation increases brand loyalty and the willingness of customers to pay higher prices.

Cost leadership is an organization's ability to achieve lower costs relative to competitors through productivity and efficiency improvements, elimination of waste, and tight cost control. Cost leaders in their respective industries include Wal-Mart (consumer retailing), Home Depot and Lowe's (building products), Texas Instruments (consumer electronics), and Emerson Electric (electric motors). These companies provide products and services that are similar to—not differentiated from—their competitors, but at a lower cost to the customer. Lower selling prices, rather than unique products or services, provide a competitive advantage for these cost leaders.

What strategy should Chipset follow? To help it decide, Chipset develops the customer preference map shown in Exhibit 1. The y-axis describes various attributes of the product desired by customers. The x-axis describes how well Chipset and Visilog, a competitor of Chipset that follows a product-differentiation strategy, do along the various attributes desired by customers from 1 (poor) to 5 (very good). The map highlights the trade-offs in any strategy. It shows the advantages CX1 enjoys in terms of price, scalability (the CX1 technology allows Chispet's customer to achieve different performance levels by simply altering the number of CX1 units in their product), and customer service. Visilog's chips, however, are faster and more powerful, and are customized for various applications such as different types of modems and communication networks.

CX1 is somewhat differentiated from competing products. Differentiating CX1 further would be costly, but Chipset may be able to charge a higher price. Conversely, reducing the cost of manufacturing CX1 would allow Chipset to lower price, spur growth, and increase market share. The scalability of CX1 makes it an effective solution for meeting

Exhibit 1

Customer Preference
Map for LICDs

varying customer needs. Also, Chipset's current engineering staff is more skilled at making product and process improvements than at creatively designing new products and technologies. Chipset decides to follow a cost-leadership strategy.

To achieve its cost-leadership strategy, Chipset must improve its own internal capabilities. It must enhance quality and reengineer processes to downsize and eliminate excess capacity. At the same time, Chipset's management team does not want to make cuts in personnel that would hurt company morale and hinder future growth.

Decision Point

What are two generic strategies a company can use?

Building Internal Capabilities: Quality Improvement and Reengineering at Chipset

To improve product quality—that is, to reduce defect rates and improve yields in its manufacturing process—Chipset must maintain process parameters within tight ranges based on real-time data about manufacturing-process parameters, such as temperature and pressure. Chipset must also train its workers in quality-management techniques to help them identify the root causes of defects and ways to prevent them and empower them to take actions to improve quality.

A second element of Chipset's strategy is reengineering its order-delivery process. Some of Chipset's customers have complained about the lengthening time span between ordering products and receiving them. **Reengineering** is the fundamental rethinking and redesign of business processes to achieve improvements in critical measures of performance, such as cost, quality, service, speed, and customer satisfaction.[3] To illustrate reengineering, consider the order-delivery system at Chipset in 2010. When Chipset received an order from a customer, a copy was sent to manufacturing, where a production scheduler began planning the manufacturing of the ordered products. Frequently, a considerable amount of time elapsed before production began on the ordered product. After manufacturing was complete, CX1 chips moved to the shipping department, which matched the quantities of CX1 to be shipped against customer orders. Often, completed CX1 chips stayed in inventory until a truck became available for shipment. If the quantity to be shipped was less than the number of chips requested by the customer, a special shipment was made for the balance of the chips. Shipping documents moved to the billing department for issuing invoices. Special staff in the accounting department followed up with customers for payments.

The many transfers of CX1 chips and information across departments (sales, manufacturing, shipping, billing, and accounting) to satisfy a customer's order created delays. Furthermore, no single individual was responsible for fulfilling a customer order. To respond to these challenges, Chipset formed a cross-functional team in late 2010 and implemented a reengineered order-delivery process in 2011.

Learning Objective 2

Understand what comprises reengineering

. . . redesigning business processes to improve performance by reducing cost and improving quality

---

[3] See M. Hammer and J. Champy, *Reengineering the Corporation: A Manifesto for Business Revolution* (New York: Harper, 1993); E. Ruhli, C. Treichler, and S. Schmidt, "From Business Reengineering to Management Reengineering—A European Study," *Management International Review* (1995): 361–371; and K. Sandberg, "Reengineering Tries a Comeback—This Time for Growth, Not Just for Cost Savings," *Harvard Management Update* (November 2001).

Under the new system, a customer-relationship manager is responsible for each customer and negotiates long-term contracts specifying quantities and prices. The customer-relationship manager works closely with the customer and with manufacturing to specify delivery schedules for CX1 one month in advance of shipment. The schedule of customer orders and delivery dates is sent electronically to manufacturing. Completed chips are shipped directly from the manufacturing plant to customer sites. Each shipment automatically triggers an electronic invoice and customers electronically transfer funds to Chipset's bank.

Companies, such as AT&T, Banca di America e di Italia, Cigna Insurance, Cisco, PepsiCo, and Siemens Nixdorf, have realized significant benefits by reengineering their processes across design, production, and marketing (just as in the Chipset example). Reengineering has only limited benefits when reengineering efforts focus on only a single activity such as shipping or invoicing rather than the entire order-delivery process. To be successful, reengineering efforts must focus on changing roles and responsibilities, eliminating unnecessary activities and tasks, using information technology, and developing employee skills.

Take another look at Exhibit 1 and note the interrelatedness and consistency in Chipset's strategy. To help meet customer preferences for price, quality, and customer service, Chipset decides on a cost-leadership strategy. And to achieve cost leadership, Chipset builds internal capabilities by reengineering its processes. Chipset's next challenge is to effectively implement its strategy

Decision Point ▶

What is reengineering?

Strategy Implementation and the Balanced Scorecard

Learning Objective 3

Understand the four perspectives of the balanced scorecard

. . . financial, customer, internal business process, and learning and growth

Many organizations, such as Allstate Insurance, Bank of Montreal, BP, and Dow Chemical, have introduced a *balanced scorecard* approach to track progress and manage the implementation of their strategies.

The Balanced Scorecard

The **balanced scorecard** translates an organization's mission and strategy into a set of performance measures that provides the framework for implementing its strategy.[4] The balanced scorecard does not focus solely on achieving short-run financial objectives. It also highlights the nonfinancial objectives that an organization must achieve to meet and sustain its financial objectives. The scorecard measures an organization's performance from four perspectives: (1) financial, the profits and value created for shareholders; (2) customer, the success of the company in its target market; (3) internal business processes, the internal operations that create value for customers; and (4) learning and growth, the people and system capabilities that support operations. A company's strategy influences the measures it uses to track performance in each of these perspectives.

Why is this tool called a balanced scorecard? Because it balances the use of financial and nonfinancial performance measures to evaluate short-run and long-run performance in a single report. The balanced scorecard reduces managers' emphasis on short-run financial performance, such as quarterly earnings, because the key strategic nonfinancial and operational indicators, such as product quality and customer satisfaction, measure changes that a company is making for the long run. The financial benefits of these long-run changes may not show up immediately in short-run earnings; however, strong improvement in nonfinancial measures usually indicates the creation of future economic value. For example, an increase in customer satisfaction, as measured by customer surveys and repeat purchases, signals a strong likelihood of higher sales and income in the future. By balancing the mix of financial and nonfinancial measures, the balanced scorecard

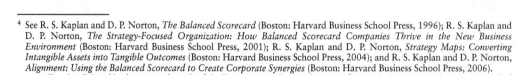

[4] See R. S. Kaplan and D. P. Norton, *The Balanced Scorecard* (Boston: Harvard Business School Press, 1996); R. S. Kaplan and D. P. Norton, *The Strategy-Focused Organization: How Balanced Scorecard Companies Thrive in the New Business Environment* (Boston: Harvard Business School Press, 2001); R. S. Kaplan and D. P. Norton, *Strategy Maps: Converting Intangible Assets into Tangible Outcomes* (Boston: Harvard Business School Press, 2004); and R. S. Kaplan and D. P. Norton, *Alignment: Using the Balanced Scorecard to Create Corporate Synergies* (Boston: Harvard Business School Press, 2006).

For simplicity, this chapter, and much of the literature, emphasizes long-run financial objectives as the primary goal of for-profit companies. For-profit companies interested in long-run financial, environmental, and social objectives adapt the balanced scorecard to implement all three objectives.

broadens management's attention to short-run *and* long-run performance. *Never lose sight of the key point. In for-profit companies, the primary goal of the balanced scorecard is to sustain long-run financial performance. Nonfinancial measures simply serve as leading indicators for the hard-to-measure long-run financial performance.*

Strategy Maps and the Balanced Scorecard

We use the Chipset example to develop strategy maps and the four perspectives of the balanced scorecard. The objectives and measures Chipset's managers choose for each perspective relates to the action plans for furthering Chipset's cost leadership strategy: *improving quality* and *reengineering processes*.

Strategy Maps

A useful first step in designing a balanced scorecard is a *strategy map*. A **strategy map** is a diagram that describes how an organization creates value by connecting strategic objectives in explicit cause-and-effect relationships with each other in the financial, customer, internal business process, and learning and growth perspectives. Exhibit 2 presents Chipset's strategy map. Follow the arrows to see how a strategic objective affects other strategic objectives. For example, empowering the workforce helps align employee and organization goals and improves processes. Employee and organizational alignment also helps improve processes that improve manufacturing quality and productivity, reduce customer delivery time, meet specified delivery dates, and improve post-sales service, all of which increase customer satisfaction. Improving manufacturing quality and productivity

Exhibit 2   Strategy Map for Chipset, Inc., for 2011

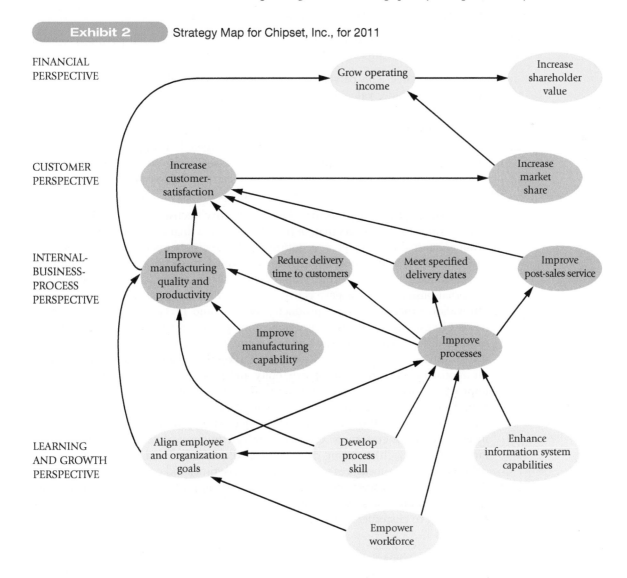

grows operating income and increases customer satisfaction that, in turn, increases market share, operating income, and shareholder value.

Chipset operates in a knowledge-intensive business. To compete successfully, Chipset invests in its employees, implements new technology and process controls, improves quality, and reengineers processes. Doing these activities well enables Chipset to build capabilities and intangible assets, which are not recorded as assets in its financial books. The strategy map helps Chipset evaluate whether these intangible assets are generating financial returns.

Chipset could include many other cause-and-effect relationships in the strategy map in Exhibit 2. But, Chipset, like other companies implementing the balanced scorecard, focuses on only those relationships that it believes to be the most significant.

Chipset uses the strategy map from Exhibit 2 to build the balanced scorecard presented in Exhibit 3. The scorecard highlights the four perspectives of performance: financial, customer, internal business process, and learning and growth. The first column presents the strategic objectives from the strategy map in Exhibit 2. At the beginning of 2011, the company's managers specify the strategic objectives, measures, initiatives (the actions necessary to achieve the objectives), and target performance (the first four columns of Exhibit 3).

Chipset wants to use the balanced scorecard targets to drive the organization to higher levels of performance. Managers therefore set targets at a level of performance that is achievable, yet distinctly better than competitors. Chipset's managers complete the fifth column, reporting actual performance at the end of 2011. This column compares Chipset's performance relative to target.

Four Perspectives of the Balanced Scorecard

We next describe the perspectives in general terms and illustrate each perspective using the measures chosen by Chipset in the context of its strategy.

1. **Financial perspective.** This perspective evaluates the profitability of the strategy and the creation of shareholder value. Because Chipset's key strategic initiatives are cost reduction relative to competitors' costs and sales growth, the financial perspective focuses on how much operating income results from reducing costs and selling more units of CX1.

2. **Customer perspective.** This perspective identifies targeted customer and market segments and measures the company's success in these segments. To monitor its customer objectives, Chipset uses measures such as market share in the communication-networks segment, number of new customers, and customer-satisfaction ratings.

3. **Internal-business-process perspective.** This perspective focuses on internal operations that create value for customers that, in turn, help achieve financial performance. Chipset determines internal-business-process improvement targets after benchmarking against its main competitors using information from published financial statements, prevailing prices, customers, suppliers, former employees, industry experts, and financial analysts. The internal-business-process perspective comprises three subprocesses:
   - **Innovation process:** Creating products, services, and processes that will meet the needs of customers. This is a very important process for companies that follow a product-differentiation strategy and must constantly design and develop innovative new products to remain competitive in the marketplace. Chipset's innovation focuses on improving its manufacturing capability and process controls to lower costs and improve quality. Chipset measures innovation by the number of improvements in manufacturing processes and percentage of processes with advanced controls.
   - **Operations process:** Producing and delivering existing products and services that will meet the needs of customers. Chipset's strategic initiatives are (a) improving manufacturing quality, (b) reducing delivery time to customers, and (c) meeting specified delivery dates so it measures yield, order-delivery time, and on-time deliveries.
   - **Postsales-service process:** Providing service and support to the customer after the sale of a product or service. Chipset monitors how quickly and accurately it is responding to customer-service requests.

Exhibit 3　　　The Balanced Scorecard for Chipset, Inc., for 2011

Strategic Objectives	Measures	Initiatives	Target Performance	Actual Performance
Financial Perspective				
Grow operating income	Operating income from productivity gain	Manage costs and unused capacity	$1,850,000	$1,912,500
	Operating income from growth	Build strong customer relationships	$2,500,000	$2,820,000
Increase shareholder value	Revenue growth		9%	10%[a]
Customer Perspective				
Increase market share	Market share in communication-networks segment	Identify future needs of customers	6%	7%
Increase customer satisfaction	Number of new customers	Identify new target-customer segments	1	1[b]
	Customer-satisfaction ratings	Increase customer focus of sales organization	90% of customers give top two ratings	87% of customers give top two ratings
Internal-Business-Process Perspective				
Improve postsales service	Service response time	Improve customer-service process	Within 4 hours	Within 3 hours
Improve manufacturing quality and productivity	Yield	Identify root causes of problems and improve quality	78%	79.3%
Reduce delivery time to customers	Order-delivery time	Reengineer order-delivery process	30 days	30 days
Meet specified delivery dates	On-time delivery	Reengineer order-delivery process	92%	90%
Improve processes	Number of major improvements in manufacturing and business processes	Organize teams from manufacturing and sales to modify processes	5	5
Improve manufacturing capability	Percentage of processes with advanced controls	Organize R&D/manufacturing teams to implement advanced controls	75%	75%
Learning-and-Growth Perspective				
Align employee and organization goals	Employee-satisfaction ratings	Employee participation and suggestions program to build teamwork	80% of employees give top two ratings	88% of employees give top two ratings
Empower workforce	Percentage of line workers empowered to manage processes	Have supervisors act as coaches rather than decision makers	85%	90%
Develop process skill	Percentage of employees trained in process and quality management	Employee training programs	90%	92%
Enhance information-system capabilities	Percentage of manufacturing processes with real-time feedback	Improve online and offline data gathering	80%	80%

[a](Revenues in 2011 − Revenues in 2010) ÷ Revenues in 2010 = ($25,300,000 − $23,000,000) ÷ $23,000,000 = 10%.
[b]Number of customers increased from seven to eight in 2011.

89

4. **Learning-and-growth perspective.** This perspective identifies the capabilities the organization must excel at to achieve superior internal processes that in turn create value for customers and shareholders. Chipset's learning and growth perspective emphasizes three capabilities: (1) information-system capabilities, measured by the percentage of manufacturing processes with real-time feedback; (2) employee capabilities, measured by the percentage of employees trained in process and quality management; and (3) motivation, measured by employee satisfaction and the percentage of manufacturing and sales employees (line employees) empowered to manage processes.

The arrows in Exhibit 3 indicate the *broad* cause-and-effect linkages: how gains in the learning-and-growth perspective lead to improvements in internal business processes, which lead to higher customer satisfaction and market share, and finally lead to superior financial performance. Note how the scorecard describes elements of Chipset's strategy implementation. Worker training and empowerment improve employee satisfaction and lead to manufacturing and business-process improvements that improve quality and reduce delivery time. The result is increased customer satisfaction and higher market share. These initiatives have been successful from a financial perspective. Chipset has earned significant operating income from its cost leadership strategy, and that strategy has also led to growth.

A major benefit of the balanced scorecard is that it promotes causal thinking. Think of the balanced scorecard as a *linked scorecard* or a *causal scorecard*. Managers must search for empirical evidence (rather than rely on faith alone) to test the validity and strength of the various connections. A causal scorecard enables a company to focus on the key drivers that steer the implementation of the strategy. Without convincing links, the scorecard loses much of its value.

Implementing a Balanced Scorecard

To successfully implement a balanced scorecard requires commitment and leadership from top management. At Chipset, the team building the balanced scorecard (headed by the vice president of strategic planning) conducted interviews with senior managers, probed executives about customers, competitors, and technological developments, and sought proposals for balanced scorecard objectives across the four perspectives. The team then met to discuss the responses and to build a prioritized list of objectives.

In a meeting with all senior managers, the team sought to achieve consensus on the scorecard objectives. Senior management was then divided into four groups, with each group responsible for one of the perspectives. In addition, each group broadened the base of inputs by including representatives from the next-lower levels of management and key functional managers. The groups identified measures for each objective and the sources of information for each measure. The groups then met to finalize scorecard objectives, measures, targets, and the initiatives to achieve the targets. Management accountants played an important role in the design and implementation of the balanced scorecard, particularly in determining measures to represent the realities of the business. This required management accountants to understand the economic environment of the industry, Chipset's customers and competitors, and internal business issues such as human resources, operations, and distribution.

Managers made sure that employees understood the scorecard and the scorecard process. The final balanced scorecard was communicated to all employees. Sharing the scorecard allowed engineers and operating personnel, for example, to understand the reasons for customer satisfaction and dissatisfaction and to make suggestions for improving internal processes directly aimed at satisfying customers and implementing Chipset's strategy. Too often, scorecards are seen by only a select group of managers. By limiting the scorecard's exposure, an organization loses the opportunity for widespread organization engagement and alignment.

Chipset (like Cigna Property, Casualty Insurance, and Wells Fargo) also encourages each department to develop its own scorecard that ties into Chipset's main scorecard described in Exhibit 3. For example, the quality control department's scorecard has measures that its department managers use to improve yield—number of quality circles, statistical process control charts, Pareto diagrams, and root-cause analyses.

Department scorecards help align the actions of each department to implement Chipset's strategy.

Companies frequently use balanced scorecards to evaluate and reward managerial performance and to influence managerial behavior. Using the balanced scorecard for performance evaluation widens the performance management lens and motivates managers to give greater attention to nonfinancial drivers of performance. Surveys indicate, however, that companies continue to assign more weight to the financial perspective (55%) than to the other perspectives—customer (19%), internal business process (12%), and learning and growth (14%). Companies cite several reasons for the relatively smaller weight on nonfinancial measures: difficulty evaluating the relative importance of nonfinancial measures; challenges in measuring and quantifying qualitative, nonfinancial data; and difficulty in compensating managers despite poor financial performance. Many companies, however, are giving greater weight to nonfinancial measures in promotion decisions because they believe that nonfinancial measures (such as customer satisfaction, process improvements, and employee motivation) better assess a manager's potential to succeed at senior levels of management. For the balanced scorecard to be effective, managers must view it as fairly assessing and rewarding all important aspects of a manager's performance and promotion prospects.

Aligning the Balanced Scorecard to Strategy

Different strategies call for different scorecards. Recall Chipset's competitor Visilog, which follows a product-differentiation strategy by designing custom chips for modems and communication networks. Visilog designs its balanced scorecard to fit its strategy. For example, in the financial perspective, Visilog evaluates how much of its operating income comes from charging premium prices for its products. In the customer perspective, Visilog measures the percentage of its revenues from new products and new customers. In the internal-business-process perspective, Visilog measures the number of new products introduced and new product development time. In the learning-and-growth perspective, Visilog measures the development of advanced manufacturing capabilities to produce custom chips. Visilog also uses some of the measures described in Chipset's balanced scorecard in Exhibit 3. For example, revenue growth, customer satisfaction ratings, order-delivery time, on-time delivery, percentage of frontline workers empowered to manage processes, and employee-satisfaction ratings are also important measures under the product-differentiation strategy. The goal is to align the balanced scorecard with company strategy.[5] Exhibit 4 presents some common measures found on company scorecards in the service, retail, and manufacturing sectors.

Features of a Good Balanced Scorecard

A well-designed balanced scorecard has several features:

1. It tells the story of a company's strategy, articulating a sequence of cause-and-effect relationships—the links among the various perspectives that align implementation of the strategy. In for-profit companies, each measure in the scorecard is part of a cause-and-effect chain leading to financial outcomes. Not-for-profit organizations design the cause-and-effect chain to achieve their strategic service objectives—for example, number of people no longer in poverty, or number of children still in school.

2. The balanced scorecard helps to communicate the strategy to all members of the organization by translating the strategy into a coherent and linked set of understandable and measurable operational targets. Guided by the scorecard, managers and employees take actions and make decisions to achieve the company's strategy. Companies that have distinct strategic business units (SBUs)—such as consumer

---

[5] For simplicity, we have presented the balanced scorecard in the context of companies that have followed either a cost-leadership or a product-differentiation strategy. Of course, a company may have some products for which cost leadership is critical and other products for which product differentiation is important. The company will then develop separate scorecards to implement the different product strategies. In still other contexts, product differentiation may be of primary importance, but some cost leadership must also be achieved. The balanced scorecard measures would then be linked in a cause-and-effect way to this strategy.

Exhibit 4

Frequently Cited
Balanced Scorecard
Measures

Financial Perspective
Income measures: Operating income, gross margin percentage
Revenue and cost measures: Revenue growth, revenues from new products, cost reductions in key areas
Income and investment measures: Economic value added (EVA®), return on investment
Customer Perspective
Market share, customer satisfaction, customer-retention percentage, time taken to fulfill customers' requests, number of customer complaints
Internal-Business-Process Perspective
Innovation Process: Operating capabilities, number of new products or services, new-product development times, and number of new patents
Operations Process: Yield, defect rates, time taken to deliver product to customers, percentage of on-time deliveries, average time taken to respond to orders, setup time, manufacturing downtime
Postsales Service Process: Time taken to replace or repair defective products, hours of customer training for using the product
Learning-and-Growth Perspective
Employee measures: Employee education and skill levels, employee-satisfaction ratings, employee turnover rates, percentage of employee suggestions implemented, percentage of compensation based on individual and team incentives
Technology measures: Information system availability, percentage of processes with advanced controls

products and pharmaceuticals at Johnson & Johnson—develop their balanced score-cards at the SBU level. Each SBU has its own unique strategy and implementation goals; building separate scorecards allows each SBU to choose measures that help implement its distinctive strategy.

3. In for-profit companies, the balanced scorecard must motivate managers to take actions that eventually result in improvements in financial performance. Managers sometimes tend to focus too much on innovation, quality, and customer satisfaction as ends in themselves. For example, Xerox spent heavily to increase customer satisfaction without a resulting financial payoff because higher levels of satisfaction did not increase customer loyalty. Some companies use statistical methods, such as regression analysis, to test the anticipated cause-and-effect relationships among nonfinancial measures and financial performance. The data for this analysis can come from either time series data (collected over time) or cross-sectional data (collected, for example, across multiple stores of a retail chain). In the Chipset example, improvements in non-financial factors have, in fact, already led to improvements in financial factors.

4. The balanced scorecard limits the number of measures, identifying only the most crit-ical ones. Chipset's scorecard, for example, has 16 measures, between 3 and 6 meas-ures for each perspective. Limiting the number of measures focuses managers' attention on those that most affect strategy implementation. Using too many meas-ures makes it difficult for managers to process relevant information.

5. The balanced scorecard highlights less-than-optimal trade-offs that managers may make when they fail to consider operational and financial measures together. For example, a company whose strategy is innovation and product differentiation could achieve superior short-run financial performance by reducing spending on R&D. A good balanced scorecard would signal that the short-run financial performance might have been achieved by taking actions that hurt future financial performance because a leading indicator of that performance, R&D spending and R&D output, has declined.

Pitfalls in Implementing a Balanced Scorecard

Pitfalls to avoid in implementing a balanced scorecard include the following:

1. Managers should not assume the cause-and-effect linkages are precise. They are merely hypotheses. Over time, a company must gather evidence of the strength and timing of the linkages among the nonfinancial and financial measures. With experience,

organizations should alter their scorecards to include those nonfinancial strategic objectives and measures that are the best leading indicators (the causes) of financial performance (a lagging indicator or the effect). Understanding that the scorecard evolves over time helps managers avoid unproductively spending time and money trying to design the "perfect" scorecard at the outset. Furthermore, as the business environment and strategy change over time, the measures in the scorecard also need to change.

2. Managers should not seek improvements across all of the measures all of the time. For example, strive for quality and on-time performance but not beyond the point at which further improvement in these objectives is so costly that it is inconsistent with long-run profit maximization. Cost-benefit considerations should always be central when designing a balanced scorecard.

3. Managers should not use only objective measures in the balanced scorecard. Chipset's balanced scorecard includes both objective measures (such as operating income from cost leadership, market share, and manufacturing yield) and subjective measures (such as customer- and employee-satisfaction ratings). When using subjective measures, though, managers must be careful that the benefits of this potentially rich information are not lost by using measures that are inaccurate or that can be easily manipulated.

4. Despite challenges of measurement, top management should not ignore nonfinancial measures when evaluating managers and other employees. Managers tend to focus on the measures used to reward their performance. Excluding nonfinancial measures when evaluating performance will reduce the significance and importance that managers give to nonfinancial measures.

Evaluating the Success of Strategy and Implementation

Decision Point

How can an organization translate its strategy into a set of performance measures?

To evaluate how successful Chipset's strategy and its implementation have been, its management compares the target- and actual-performance columns in the balanced scorecard (Exhibit 3). Chipset met most targets set on the basis of competitor benchmarks in 2011 itself. That's because, in the Chipset context, improvements in the learning and growth perspective quickly ripple through to the financial perspective. Chipset will continue to seek improvements on the targets it did not achieve, but meeting most targets suggests that the strategic initiatives that Chipset identified and measured for learning and growth resulted in improvements in internal business processes, customer measures, and financial performance.

How would Chipset know if it had problems in strategy implementation? If it did not meet its targets on the two perspectives that are more internally focused: learning and growth and internal business processes.

What if Chipset performed well on learning and growth and internal business processes, but customer measures and financial performance in this year and the next did not improve? Chipset's managers would then conclude that Chipset did a good job of implementation (the various internal nonfinancial measures it targeted improved) but that its strategy was faulty (there was no effect on customers or on long-run financial performance and value creation). Management failed to identify the correct causal links. It implemented the wrong strategy well! Management would then reevaluate the strategy and the factors that drive it.

Now what if Chipset performed well on its various nonfinancial measures, and operating income over this year and the next also increased? Chipset's managers might be tempted to declare the strategy a success because operating income increased. Unfortunately, management still cannot conclude with any confidence that Chipset successfully formulated and implemented its strategy. Why? Because operating income can increase simply because entire markets are expanding, not because a company's strategy has been successful. Also, changes in operating income might occur because of factors outside the strategy. For example, a company such as Chipset that has chosen a cost-leadership strategy may find that its operating-income increase actually resulted from, say, some degree of product differentiation. *To evaluate the success of a strategy, managers and management accountants need to link strategy to the sources of operating-income increases.*

For Chipset to conclude that it was successful in implementing its strategy, it must demonstrate that improvements in its financial performance and operating income over time resulted from achieving targeted cost savings and growth in market share. Fortunately, the top two rows of Chipset's balanced scorecard in Exhibit 3 show that operating-income gains from productivity ($1,912,500) and growth ($2,820,000) exceeded targets. The next section of this chapter describes how these numbers were calculated. Because its strategy has been successful, Chipset's management can be more confident that the gains will be sustained in subsequent years.

Chipset's management accountants subdivide changes in operating income into components that can be identified with product differentiation, cost leadership, and growth. Why growth? Because successful product differentiation or cost leadership generally increases market share and helps a company to grow. Subdividing the change in operating income to evaluate the success of a strategy is conceptually similar to variance analysis. One difference, however, is that management accountants compare actual operating performance over two different periods, not actual to budgeted numbers in the same time period as in variance analysis.[6]

Strategic Analysis of Operating Income

The following illustration explains how to subdivide the change in operating income from one period to *any* future period. The individual components describe company performance with regard to product differentiation, cost leadership, and growth.[7] We illustrate the analysis using data from 2010 and 2011 because Chipset implemented key elements of its strategy in late 2010 and early 2011 and expects the financial consequences of these strategies to occur in 2011. Suppose the financial consequences of these strategies had been expected to affect operating income in only 2012. Then we could just as easily have compared 2010 to 2012. If necessary, we could also have compared 2010 to 2011 and 2012 taken together.

Chipset's data for 2010 and 2011 follow:

	2010	2011
1. Units of CX1 produced and sold	1,000,000	1,150,000
2. Selling price	$23	$22
3. Direct materials (square centimeters of silicon wafers)	3,000,000	2,900,000
4. Direct material cost per square centimeter	$1.40	$1.50
5. Manufacturing processing capacity (in square centimeters of silicon wafer)	3,750,000	3,500,000
6. Conversion costs (all manufacturing costs other than direct material costs)	$16,050,000	$15,225,000
7. Conversion cost per unit of capacity (row 6 ÷ row 5)	$4.28	$4.35

Chipset provides the following additional information:

1. Conversion costs (labor and overhead costs) for each year depend on production processing capacity defined in terms of the quantity of square centimeters of silicon wafers that Chipset can process. These costs do not vary with the actual quantity of silicon wafers processed.

2. Chipset incurs no R&D costs. Its marketing, sales, and customer-service costs are small relative to the other costs. Chipset has fewer than 10 customers, each purchasing roughly the same quantities of CX1. Because of the highly technical nature of the product, Chipset uses a cross-functional team for its marketing, sales, and customer-service activities. This cross-functional approach ensures that, although marketing, sales, and customer-service costs are small, the entire Chipset organization, including manufacturing engineers, remains focused on increasing customer satisfaction and

---

[6] Other examples of focusing on actual performance over two periods rather than comparisons of actuals with budgets can be found in J. Hope and R. Fraser, *Beyond Budgeting* (Boston, MA: Harvard Business School Press, 2003).

[7] For other details, see R. Banker, S. Datar, and R. Kaplan, "Productivity Measurement and Management Accounting," *Journal of Accounting, Auditing and Finance* (1989): 528–554; and A. Hayzen and J. Reeve, "Examining the Relationships in Productivity Accounting," *Management Accounting Quarterly* (2000): 32–39.

market share. (The Problem for Self-Study at the end of this chapter describes a situation in which marketing, sales, and customer-service costs are significant.)

3. Chipset's asset structure is very similar in 2010 and 2011.

4. Operating income for each year is as follows:

	2010	2011
Revenues		
($23 per unit × 1,000,000 units; $22 per unit × 1,150,000 units)	$23,000,000	$25,300,000
Costs		
Direct material costs		
($1.40/sq. cm. × 3,000,000 sq. cm.; $1.50/sq. cm. × 2,900,000 sq. cm.)	4,200,000	4,350,000
Conversion costs		
($4.28/sq. cm. × 3,750,000 sq. cm.; $4.35/sq. cm. × 3,500,000 sq. cm.)	16,050,000	15,225,000
Total costs	20,250,000	19,575,000
Operating income	$ 2,750,000	$ 5,725,000
Change in operating income	↑ $2,975,000 F ↑	

The goal of Chipset's managers is to evaluate how much of the $2,975,000 increase in operating income was caused by the successful implementation of the company's cost-leadership strategy. To do this, management accountants start by analyzing three main factors: growth, price recovery, and productivity.

The **growth component** measures the change in operating income attributable solely to the change in the quantity of output sold between 2010 and 2011.

The **price-recovery component** measures the change in operating income attributable solely to changes in Chipset's prices of inputs and outputs between 2010 and 2011. The price-recovery component measures change in output price compared with changes in input prices. A company that has successfully pursued a strategy of product differentiation will be able to increase its output price faster than the increase in its input prices, boosting profit margins and operating income: It will show a large positive price-recovery component.

The **productivity component** measures the change in costs attributable to a change in the quantity of inputs used in 2011 relative to the quantity of inputs that would have been used in 2010 to produce the 2011 output. The productivity component measures the amount by which operating income increases by using inputs efficiently to lower costs. A company that has successfully pursued a strategy of cost leadership will be able to produce a given quantity of output with a lower cost of inputs: It will show a large positive productivity component. Given Chipset's strategy of cost leadership, we expect the increase in operating income to be attributable to the productivity and growth components, not to price recovery. We now examine these three components in detail.

Growth Component of Change in Operating Income

The growth component of the change in operating income measures the increase in revenues minus the increase in costs from selling more units of CX1 in 2011 (1,150,000 units) than in 2010 (1,000,000 units), *assuming nothing else has changed.*

Revenue Effect of Growth

$$\begin{array}{c} \text{Revenue effect} \\ \text{of growth} \end{array} = \left(\begin{array}{c} \text{Actual units of} \\ \text{output sold} \\ \text{in 2011} \end{array} - \begin{array}{c} \text{Actual units of} \\ \text{output sold} \\ \text{in 2010} \end{array} \right) \times \begin{array}{c} \text{Selling} \\ \text{price} \\ \text{in 2010} \end{array}$$

$$= (1,150,000 \text{ units} - 1,000,000 \text{ units}) \times \$23 \text{ per unit}$$

$$= \$3,450,000 \text{ F}$$

This component is favorable (F) because the increase in output sold in 2011 increases operating income. Components that decrease operating income are unfavorable (U).

Note that Chipset uses the 2010 price of CX1 and focuses only on the increase in units sold between 2010 and 2011, because the revenue effect of growth component measures how much revenues would have changed in 2010 if Chipset had sold 1,150,000 units instead of 1,000,000 units.

Cost Effect of Growth

The cost effect of growth measures how much costs would have changed in 2010 if Chipset had produced 1,150,000 units of CX1 instead of 1,000,000 units. To measure the cost effect of growth, Chipset's managers distinguish variable costs such as direct material costs from fixed costs such as conversion costs, because as units produced (and sold) increase, variable costs increase proportionately but fixed costs, generally, do not change.

$$\begin{matrix} \text{Cost effect of} \\ \text{growth for} \\ \text{variable costs} \end{matrix} = \begin{pmatrix} \begin{matrix} \text{Units of input} \\ \text{required to} \\ \text{produce 2011} \\ \text{output in 2010} \end{matrix} - \begin{matrix} \text{Actual units of} \\ \text{input used} \\ \text{to produce} \\ \text{2010 output} \end{matrix} \end{pmatrix} \times \begin{matrix} \text{Input} \\ \text{price} \\ \text{in 2010} \end{matrix}$$

$$\begin{matrix} \text{Cost effect of} \\ \text{growth for} \\ \text{direct materials} \end{matrix} = \left(3,000,000 \text{ sq. cm.} \times \frac{1,150,000 \text{ units}}{1,000,000 \text{ units}} - 3,000,000 \text{ sq. cm.} \right) \times \$1.40 \text{ per sq. cm.}$$

$$= (3,450,000 \text{ sq. cm.} - 3,000,000 \text{ sq. cm.}) \times \$1.40 \text{ per sq. cm.} = \$630,000 \text{ U}$$

The units of input required to produce 2011 output in 2010 can also be calculated as follows:

$$\text{Units of input per unit of output in 2010} = \frac{3,000,000 \text{ sq. cm.}}{1,000,000 \text{ units}} = 3 \text{ sq. cm./unit}$$

Units of input required to produce 2011 output of 1,150,000 units in 2010 = 3 sq. cm. per unit × 1,150,000 units = 3,450,000 sq. cm.

$$\begin{matrix} \text{Cost effect of} \\ \text{growth for} \\ \text{fixed costs} \end{matrix} = \begin{pmatrix} \begin{matrix} \text{Actual units of capacity in} \\ \text{2010 because adequate capacity} \\ \text{exists to produce 2011 output in 2010} \end{matrix} - \begin{matrix} \text{Actual units} \\ \text{of capacity} \\ \text{in 2010} \end{matrix} \end{pmatrix} \times \begin{matrix} \text{Price per} \\ \text{unit of} \\ \text{capacity} \\ \text{in 2010} \end{matrix}$$

$$\begin{matrix} \text{Cost effect of} \\ \text{growth for} \\ \text{conversion costs} \end{matrix} = (3,750,000 \text{ sq. cm.} - 3,750,000 \text{ sq. cm.}) \times \$4.28 \text{ per sq. cm.} = \$0$$

Conversion costs are fixed costs at a given level of capacity. Chipset has manufacturing capacity to process 3,750,000 square centimeters of silicon wafers in 2010 at a cost of $4.28 per square centimeter. To produce 1,150,000 units of output in 2010, Chipset needs to process 3,450,000 square centimeters of direct materials, which is less than the available capacity of 3,750,000 sq. cm. Throughout this chapter, we assume adequate capacity exists in the current year (2010) to produce next year's (2011) output. Under this assumption, the cost effect of growth for capacity-related fixed costs is, by definition, $0. Had 2010 capacity been inadequate to produce 2011 output in 2010, we would need to calculate the additional capacity required to produce 2011 output in 2010. These calculations are beyond the scope of the text.

In summary, the net increase in operating income attributable to growth equals the following:

Revenue effect of growth		$3,450,000 F
Cost effect of growth		
Direct material costs	$630,000 U	
Conversion costs	0	630,000 U
Change in operating income due to growth		$2,820,000 F

Price-Recovery Component of Change in Operating Income

Assuming that the 2010 relationship between inputs and outputs continued in 2011, the price-recovery component of the change in operating income measures solely the effect of price changes on revenues and costs to produce and sell the 1,150,000 units of CX1 in 2011.

Revenue Effect of Price Recovery

$$\begin{array}{c}\text{Revenue effect of}\\\text{price recovery}\end{array} = \left(\begin{array}{c}\text{Selling price}\\\text{in 2011}\end{array} - \begin{array}{c}\text{Selling price}\\\text{in 2010}\end{array}\right) \times \begin{array}{c}\text{Actual units}\\\text{of output}\\\text{sold in 2011}\end{array}$$

$$= (\$22 \text{ per unit} - \$23 \text{ per unit}) \times 1{,}150{,}000 \text{ units}$$

$$= \$1{,}150{,}000 \text{ U}$$

Note that the calculation focuses on revenue changes caused by changes in the selling price of CX1 between 2010 and 2011.

Cost Effect of Price Recovery

Chipset's management accountants calculate the cost effects of price recovery separately for variable costs and for fixed costs, just as they did when calculating the cost effect of growth.

$$\begin{array}{c}\text{Cost effect of}\\\text{price recovery for}\\\text{variable costs}\end{array} = \left(\begin{array}{c}\text{Input price}\\\text{in 2011}\end{array} - \begin{array}{c}\text{Input price}\\\text{in 2010}\end{array}\right) \times \begin{array}{c}\text{Units of input}\\\text{required to}\\\text{produce 2011}\\\text{output in 2010}\end{array}$$

$$\begin{array}{c}\text{Cost effect of}\\\text{price recovery for}\\\text{direct materials}\end{array} = (\$1.50 \text{ per sq.cm.} - \$1.40 \text{ per sq.cm.}) \times 3{,}450{,}000 \text{ sq.} = \$345{,}000 \text{ U}$$

Recall that the direct materials of 3,450,000 square centimeters required to produce 2011 output in 2010 had already been calculated when computing the cost effect of growth.

$$\begin{array}{c}\text{Cost effect of}\\\text{price recovery for}\\\text{fixed costs}\end{array} = \left(\begin{array}{c}\text{Price per}\\\text{unit of}\\\text{capacity}\\\text{in 2011}\end{array} - \begin{array}{c}\text{Price per}\\\text{unit of}\\\text{capacity}\\\text{in 2010}\end{array}\right) \times \begin{array}{c}\text{Actual units of capacity in}\\\text{2010 (because adequate}\\\text{capacity exists to produce}\\\text{2011 output in 2010)}\end{array}$$

Cost effect of price recovery for fixed costs is as follows:

$$\text{Conversion costs: } (\$4.35 \text{ per sq. cm.} - \$4.28 \text{ per sq. cm.}) \times 3{,}750{,}000 \text{ sq. cm.} = \$262{,}500 \text{ U}$$

Note that the detailed analyses of capacities were presented when computing the cost effect of growth.

In summary, the net decrease in operating income attributable to price recovery equals the following:

Revenue effect of price recovery		$1,150,000 U
Cost effect of price recovery		
Direct material costs	$345,000 U	
Conversion costs	262,500 U	607,500 U
Change in operating income due to price recovery		$1,757,500 U

The price-recovery analysis indicates that, even as the prices of its inputs increased, the selling prices of CX1 decreased and Chipset could not pass on input-price increases to its customers.

Productivity Component of Change in Operating Income

The productivity component of the change in operating income uses 2011 input prices to measure how costs have decreased as a result of using fewer inputs, a better mix of inputs, and/or less capacity to produce 2011 output, compared with the inputs and capacity that would have been used to produce this output in 2010.

The productivity-component calculations use 2011 prices and output. That's because the productivity component isolates the change in costs between 2010 and 2011 caused solely by the change in the quantities, mix, and/or capacities of inputs.[8]

$$\begin{array}{l} \text{Cost effect of} \\ \text{productivity for} \\ \text{variable costs} \end{array} = \left(\begin{array}{c} \text{Actual units of} \\ \text{input used} \\ \text{to produce} \\ \text{2011 output} \end{array} - \begin{array}{c} \text{Units of input} \\ \text{required to} \\ \text{produce 2011} \\ \text{output in 2010} \end{array} \right) \times \begin{array}{c} \text{Input} \\ \text{price} \\ \text{in 2011} \end{array}$$

Using the 2011 data given on page 478 and the calculation of units of input required to produce 2011 output in 2010 when discussing the cost effects of growth,

$$\begin{array}{l} \text{Cost effect of} \\ \text{productivity for} \\ \text{direct materials} \end{array} = (2{,}900{,}000 \text{ sq. cm.} - 3{,}450{,}000 \text{ sq. cm.}) \times \$1.50 \text{ per sq. cm}$$

$$= 550{,}000 \text{ sq. cm.} \times \$1.50 \text{ per sq. cm.} = \$825{,}000 \text{ F}$$

Chipset's quality and yield improvements reduced the quantity of direct materials needed to produce output in 2011 relative to 2010.

$$\begin{array}{l} \text{Cost effect of} \\ \text{productivity for} \\ \text{fixed costs} \end{array} = \left(\begin{array}{c} \text{Actual units of} \\ \text{capacity} \\ \text{in 2011} \end{array} - \begin{array}{c} \text{Actual units of capacity in} \\ \text{2010 because adequate} \\ \text{capacity exists to produce} \\ \text{2011 output in 2010} \end{array} \right) \times \begin{array}{c} \text{Price per} \\ \text{unit of} \\ \text{capacity} \\ \text{in 2011} \end{array}$$

To calculate the cost effect of productivity for fixed costs, we use the 2011 data and the analyses of capacity required to produce 2011 output in 2010 when discussing the cost effect of growth.

Cost effects of productivity for fixed costs are

$$\text{Conversion costs: } (3{,}500{,}000 \text{ sq. cm} - 3{,}750{,}000 \text{ sq. cm.}) \times \$4.35 \text{ per sq. cm.} = \$1{,}087{,}500 \text{ F}$$

Chipset's managers decreased manufacturing capacity in 2011 to 3,500,000 square centimeters by selling off old equipment and laying off workers.

In summary, the net increase in operating income attributable to productivity equals,

Cost effect of productivity	
Direct material costs	$ 825,000 F
Conversion costs	1,087,500 F
Change in operating income due to productivity	1,912,500 F

The productivity component indicates that Chipset was able to increase operating income by improving quality and productivity and eliminating capacity to reduce costs. The appendix to this chapter examines partial and total factor productivity changes between 2010 and 2011 and describes how the management accountant can obtain a deeper understanding of Chipset's cost-leadership strategy. Note that the productivity component focuses exclusively on costs, so there is no revenue effect for this component.

Exhibit 5 summarizes the growth, price-recovery, and productivity components of the changes in operating income. Generally, companies that have been successful at cost leadership will show favorable productivity and growth components. Companies that

---

[8] Note that the productivity-component calculation uses actual 2011 input prices, whereas its counterpart, the efficiency variance, uses budgeted prices. (In effect, the budgeted prices correspond to 2010 prices). Year 2011 prices are used in the productivity calculation because Chipset wants its managers to choose input quantities to minimize costs in 2011 based on currently prevailing prices. If 2010 prices had been used in the productivity calculation, managers would choose input quantities based on irrelevant input prices that prevailed a year ago! Why does using budgeted prices not pose a similar problem? Because, unlike 2010 prices that describe what happened a year ago, budgeted prices represent prices that are expected to prevail in the current period. Moreover, budgeted prices can be changed, if necessary, to bring them in line with actual current-period prices.

| Exhibit 5 | Strategic Analysis of Profitability |

	Income Statement Amounts in 2010 (1)	Revenue and Cost Effects of Growth Component in 2011 (2)	Revenue and Cost Effects of Price-Recovery Component in 2011 (3)	Cost Effect of Productivity Component in 2011 (4)	Income Statement Amounts in 2011 (5) = (1) + (2) + (3) + (4)
Revenues	$23,000,000	$3,450,000 F	$1,150,000 U	—	$25,300,000
Costs	20,250,000	630,000 U	607,500 U	$1,912,000 F	19,575,000
Operating income	$ 2,750,000	$2,820,000 F	$1,757,500 U	$1,912,500 F	$ 5,725,000

$2,975,000 F

Change in operating income

have successfully differentiated their products will show favorable price-recovery and growth components. In Chipset's case, consistent with its strategy and its implementation, productivity contributed $1,912,500 to the increase in operating income, and growth contributed $2,820,000. Price-recovery contributed a $1,757,500 decrease in operating income, however, because, even as input prices increased, the selling price of CX1 decreased. Had Chipset been able to differentiate its product and charge a higher price, the price-recovery effects might have been less unfavorable or perhaps even favorable. As a result, Chipset's managers plan to evaluate some modest changes in product features that might help differentiate CX1 somewhat more from competing products.

Further Analysis of Growth, Price-Recovery, and Productivity Components

As in all variance and profit analysis, Chipset's managers want to more closely analyze the change in operating income. Chipset's growth might have been helped, for example, by an increase in industry market size. Therefore, at least part of the increase in operating income may be attributable to favorable economic conditions in the industry rather than to any successful implementation of strategy. Some of the growth might relate to the management decision to decrease selling price, made possible by the productivity gains. In this case, the increase in operating income from cost leadership must include operating income from productivity-related growth in market share in addition to the productivity gain.

We illustrate these ideas, using the Chipset example and the following additional information. *Instructors who do not wish to cover these detailed calculations can go to the next section on "Applying the Five-Step Decision-Making Framework to Strategy" without any loss of continuity.*

- The market growth rate in the industry is 8% in 2011. Of the 150,000 (1,150,000 – 1,000,000) units of increased sales of CX1 between 2010 and 2011, 80,000 (0.08 × 1,000,000) units are due to an increase in industry market size (which Chipset should have benefited from regardless of its productivity gains), and the remaining 70,000 units are due to an increase in market share.

- During 2011, Chipset could have maintained the price of CX1 at the 2010 price of $23 per unit. But management decided to take advantage of the productivity gains to reduce the price of CX1 by $1 to grow market share leading to the 70,000-unit increase in sales.

The effect of the industry-market-size factor on operating income (not any specific strategic action) is as follows:

Change in operating income due to growth in industry market size

$$\$2,820,000 \text{ (Exhibit 5, column 2)} \times \frac{80,000 \text{ units}}{150,000 \text{ units}} = \$1,504,000 \text{ F}$$

99

Concepts in Action

The Growth Versus Profitability Choice at Facebook

Facebook, Inc.

Competitive advantage comes from product differentiation or cost leadership. Successful implementation of these strategies helps a company to be profitable and to grow. Many Internet start-ups pursue a strategy of short-run growth to build a customer base, with the goal of later benefiting from such growth by either charging user fees or sustaining a free service for users supported by advertisers. However, during the 1990s dot-com boom (and subsequent bust), the most spectacular failures occurred in dot-com companies that followed the "get big fast" model but then failed to differentiate their products or reduce their costs.

Today, many social networking companies (Web-based communities that connect friends, colleagues, and groups with shared interests) face this same challenge. At Facebook, the most notable of the social networking sites, users can create personal profiles that allow them to interact with friends through messaging, chat, sharing Web site links, video clips, and more. Additionally, Facebook encourages other companies to build third-party programs, including games and surveys, for its Web site and mobile applications on the iPhone and BlackBerry devices. From 2007 to 2010, Facebook grew from 12 million users to more than 400 million users uploading photos, sharing updates, planning events, and playing games in the Facebook ecosystem.

During this phenomenal growth, the company wrestled with one key question: How could Facebook become profitable? In 2009, experts estimate that Facebook had revenues of $635 million, mostly through advertising and the sale of virtual gifts (as a private company, Facebook does not publicly disclose its financial information). But the company still did not turn a profit. Why not? To keep its global Web site and mobile applications operating, Facebook requires a massive amount of electricity, Internet bandwidth, and storage servers for digital files. In 2009, the company earmarked $100 million to buy 50,000 new servers, along with a new $2 million network storage system per week.

The cost structure of Facebook means that the company must generate tens of millions a month in revenue to sustain its operations over the long term. But how? Facebook has implemented the following popular methods of online revenue generation:

- Additional advertising: To grow its already significant advertising revenue, Facebook recently introduced "Fan Pages" for brands and companies seeking to communicate directly with its users. The company is also working on a tool that will let users share information about their physical whereabouts via the site, which will allow Facebook to sell targeted advertisements for nearby businesses.

- Transactions: Facebook is also testing a feature that would expand Facebook Credits, its transactions platform that allows users to purchase games and gifts, into an Internet-wide "virtual currency," that could be accepted by any Web site integrating the Facebook Connect online identity management platform. Facebook currently gets a 30% cut of all transactions conducted through Facebook Credits.

Despite rampant rumors, Facebook has rejected the idea of charging monthly subscription fees for access to its Web site or for advanced features and premium content.

With increased growth around the world, Facebook anticipates 2010 revenues to exceed $1 billion. Despite the opportunity to become the "world's richest twenty-something," Facebook's 25-year-old CEO Mark Zuckerberg has thus far resisted taking the company public through an initial public offering (IPO). "A lot of companies can go off course because of corporate pressures," says Mr. Zuckerberg. "I don't know what we are going to be building five years from now." With his company's focus on facilitating people's ability to share almost any- and everything with anyone, at any time, via the Internet, mobile phones, and even videogames, Facebook expects to offer users a highly personal and differentiated online experience in the years ahead and expects that this product differentiation will drive its future growth and profitability.

Sources: Vascellaro, Jessica E. 2010. Facebook CEO in no rush to 'friend' wall street. *Wall Street Journal*, March 3. http://online.wsj.com/article/SB100014240527487037873045755075942803630712.html; Eldon, Eric. 2010. Facebook revenues up to $700 million in 2009, on track towards $1.1 billion in 2010. *Inside Facebook*. Blog, March 2. http://www.insidefacebook.com/2010/03/02/facebook-made-up-to-700-million-in-2009-on-track-towards-1-1-billion-in-2010/; Arrington, Michael. 2010. Facebook may be growing too fast. And hitting the capital markets again. *Tech Crunch*. Blog, October 31. http://techcrunch.com/2010/10/31/facebooks-growing-problem/

Lacking a differentiated product, Chipset could have maintained the price of CX1 at $23 per unit even while the prices of its inputs increased.

The effect of product differentiation on operating income is as follows:

Change in prices of inputs (cost effect of price recovery)	607,500 U
Change in operating income due to product differentiation	$607,500 U

To exercise cost and price leadership, Chipset made the strategic decision to cut the price of CX1 by $1. This decision resulted in an increase in market share and 70,000 units of additional sales.

The effect of cost leadership on operating income is as follows:

Productivity component	$1,912,500 F
Effect of strategic decision to reduce price ($1/unit $\times$ 1,150,000 units)	1,150,000 U
Growth in market share due to productivity improvement and strategic decision to reduce prices	
$2,820,000 (Exhibit 5, column 2) $\times$ $\dfrac{70,000 \text{ units}}{150,000 \text{ units}}$	1,316,000 F
Change in operating income due to cost leadership	$2,078,500 F

A summary of the change in operating income between 2010 and 2011 follows.

Change due to industry market size	$1,504,000 F
Change due to product differentiation	607,500 U
Change due to cost leadership	2,078,500 F
Change in operating income	$2,975,000 F

Consistent with its cost-leadership strategy, the productivity gains of $1,912,500 in 2011 were a big part of the increase in operating income from 2010 to 2011. Chipset took advantage of these productivity gains to decrease price by $1 per unit at a cost of $1,150,000 to gain $1,316,000 in operating income by selling 70,000 additional units. The Problem for Self-Study describes the analysis of the growth, price-recovery, and productivity components for a company following a product-differentiation strategy. The Concepts in Action feature describes the unique challenges that dot-com companies face in choosing a profitable strategy.

Under different assumptions about the change in selling price, the analysis will attribute different amounts to the different strategies.

Decision Point

How can a company analyze changes in operating income to evaluate the success of its strategy?

Applying the Five-Step Decision-Making Framework to Strategy

We next briefly describe how the five-step decision-making framework is also useful in making decisions about strategy.

1. *Identify the problem and uncertainties.* Chipset's strategy choice depends on resolving two uncertainties—whether Chipset can add value to its customers that its competitors cannot emulate, and whether Chipset can develop the necessary internal capabilities to add this value.

2. *Obtain information.* Chipset's managers develop customer preference maps to identify various product attributes desired by customers and the competitive advantage or disadvantage it has on each attribute relative to competitors. The managers also gather data on Chipset's internal capabilities. How good is Chipset in designing and developing innovative new products? How good are its process and marketing capabilities?

3. *Make predictions about the future.* Chipset's managers conclude that they will not be able to develop innovative new products in a cost-effective way. They believe that Chipset's strength lies in improving quality, reengineering processes, reducing costs, and delivering products faster to customers.

4. *Make decisions by choosing among alternatives.* Chipset's management decides to follow a cost leadership rather than a product differentiation strategy. It decides to introduce a balanced scorecard to align and measure its quality improvement and process reengineering efforts.

5. *Implement the decision, evaluate performance, and learn.* On its balanced scorecard, Chipset's managers compare actual and targeted performance and evaluate possible cause-and-effect relationships. They learn, for example, that increasing the percentage of processes with advanced controls improves yield. As a result, just as they had anticipated, productivity and growth initiatives result in increases in operating income in 2011. The one change Chipset's managers plan for 2012 is to make modest changes in product features that might help differentiate CX1 somewhat from competing products. In this way, feedback and learning help in the development of future strategies and implementation plans.

Downsizing and the Management of Processing Capacity

Learning Objective 5

Identify unused capacity

... capacity available minus capacity used for engineered costs but difficult to determine for discretionary costs

and how to manage it

... downsize to reduce capacity

As we saw in our discussion of the productivity component, fixed costs are tied to capacity. Unlike variable costs, fixed costs do not change automatically with changes in activity level (for example, fixed conversion costs do not change with changes in the quantity of silicon wafers started into production). How then can managers reduce capacity-based fixed costs? By measuring and managing unused capacity. **Unused capacity** is the amount of productive capacity available over and above the productive capacity employed to meet consumer demand in the current period. To understand unused capacity, it is necessary to distinguish *engineered costs* from *discretionary costs*.

Engineered and Discretionary Costs

Engineered costs result from a cause-and-effect relationship between the cost driver—output—and the (direct or indirect) resources used to produce that output. Engineered costs have a detailed, physically observable, and repetitive relationship with output. In the Chipset example, direct material costs are *direct engineered costs*. Conversion costs are an example of *indirect engineered costs*. Consider 2011. The output of 1,150,000 units of CX1 and the efficiency with which inputs are converted into outputs result in 2,900,000 square centimeters of silicon wafers being started into production. Manufacturing-conversion-cost resources used equal $12,615,000 ($4.35 per sq. cm. × 2,900,000 sq. cm.), but actual conversion costs ($15,225,000) are higher because Chipset has manufacturing capacity to process 3,500,000 square centimeters of silicon wafer ($4.35 per sq. cm. × 3,500,000 sq. cm. = $15,225,000). Although these costs are fixed in the short run, over the long run there is a cause-and-effect relationship between output and manufacturing capacity required (and conversion costs needed). In the long run, Chipset will try to match its capacity to its needs.

Discretionary costs have two important features: (1) They arise from periodic (usually annual) decisions regarding the maximum amount to be incurred, and (2) they have no measurable cause-and-effect relationship between output and resources used. There is often a delay between when a resource is acquired and when it is used. Examples of discretionary costs include advertising, executive training, R&D, and corporate-staff department costs such as legal, human resources, and public relations. Unlike engineered costs, the relationship between discretionary costs and output is a blackbox because it is nonrepetitive and nonroutine. A noteworthy aspect of discretionary costs is that managers are seldom confident that the "correct" amounts are being spent. The founder of Lever Brothers, an international consumer-products company, once noted, "Half the money I spend on advertising is wasted; the trouble is, I don't know which half!"[9]

Identifying Unused Capacity for Engineered and Discretionary Overhead Costs

Identifying unused capacity is very different for engineered costs compared to discretionary costs. Consider engineered conversion costs.

At the start of 2011, Chipset had capacity to process 3,750,000 square centimeters of silicon wafers. Quality and productivity improvements made during 2011 enabled Chipset to produce 1,150,000 units of CX1 by processing 2,900,000 square centimeters of silicon wafers. Unused manufacturing capacity is 850,000 (3,750,000 – 2,900,000) square centimeters of silicon-wafer processing capacity at the beginning of 2011. At the 2011 conversion cost of \$4.35 per square centimeter,

$$\text{Cost of unused capacity} = \text{Cost of capacity at the beginning of the year} - \text{Manufacturing resources used during the year}$$

$$= (3{,}750{,}000 \text{ sq. cm.} \times \$4.35 \text{ per sq. cm.}) - (2{,}900{,}000 \text{ sq. cm.} \times \$4.35 \text{ per sq. cm.})$$

$$= \$16{,}312{,}500 - \$12{,}615{,}000 = \$3{,}697{,}500$$

The absence of a cause-and-effect relationship makes identifying unused capacity for discretionary costs difficult. For example, management cannot determine the R&D resources used for the actual output produced. And without a measure of capacity used, it is not possible to compute unused capacity.

Managing Unused Capacity

What actions can Chipset management take when it identifies unused capacity? In general, it has two alternatives: eliminate unused capacity, or grow output to utilize the unused capacity.

In recent years, many companies have *downsized* in an attempt to eliminate unused capacity. **Downsizing** (also called **rightsizing**) is an integrated approach of configuring processes, products, and people to match costs to the activities that need to be performed to operate effectively and efficiently in the present and future. Companies such as AT&T, Delta Airlines, Ford Motor Company, and IBM have downsized to focus on their core businesses and have instituted organization changes to increase efficiency, reduce costs, and improve quality. However, downsizing often means eliminating jobs, which can adversely affect employee morale and the culture of a company.

Consider Chipset's alternatives with respect to its unused manufacturing capacity. Because it needed to process 2,900,000 square centimeters of silicon wafers in 2011, it could have reduced capacity to 3,000,000 square centimeters (Chipset can add or reduce manufacturing capacity in increments of 250,000 sq. cm.), resulting in cost savings of \$3,262,500 [(3,750,000 sq. cm. – 3,000,000 sq. cm.) × \$4.35 per sq. cm.]. Chipset's strategy, however, is not just to reduce costs but also to grow its business. So early in 2011, Chipset reduces its manufacturing capacity by only 250,000 square centimeters—from 3,750,000 square centimeters to 3,500,000 square centimeters—saving

---

[9] Managers also describe some costs as infrastructure costs—costs that arise from having property, plant, and equipment and a functioning organization. Examples are depreciation, long-run lease rental, and the acquisition of long-run technical capabilities. These costs are generally fixed costs because they are committed to and acquired before they are used. Infrastructure costs can be engineered or discretionary. For instance, manufacturing-overhead cost incurred at Chipset to acquire manufacturing capacity is an infrastructure cost that is an example of an engineered cost. In the long run, there is a cause-and-effect relationship between output and manufacturing-overhead costs needed to produce that output. R&D cost incurred to acquire technical capability is an infrastructure cost that is an example of a discretionary cost. There is no measurable cause-and-effect relationship between output and R&D cost incurred.

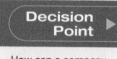

Decision Point ▶

How can a company identify and manage unused capacity?

$1,087,500 ($4.35 per sq. cm. × 250,000 sq. cm.). It retains some extra capacity for future growth. By avoiding greater reductions in capacity, it also maintains the morale of its skilled and capable workforce. The success of this strategy will depend on Chipset achieving the future growth it has projected.

Because identifying unused capacity for discretionary costs, such as R&D costs, is difficult, downsizing or otherwise managing this unused capacity is also difficult. Management must exercise considerable judgment in deciding the level of R&D costs that would generate the needed product and process improvements. Unlike engineered costs, there is no clear-cut way to know whether management is spending too much (or too little) on R&D.

Problem for Self-Study

Following a strategy of product differentiation, Westwood Corporation makes a high-end kitchen range hood, KE8. Westwood's data for 2010 and 2011 follow:

	2010	2011
1. Units of KE8 produced and sold	40,000	42,000
2. Selling price	$100	$110
3. Direct materials (square feet)	120,000	123,000
4. Direct material cost per square foot	$10	$11
5. Manufacturing capacity for KE8	50,000 units	50,000 units
6. Conversion costs	$1,000,000	$1,100,000
7. Conversion cost per unit of capacity (row 6 ÷ row 5)	$20	$22
8. Selling and customer-service capacity	30 customers	29 customers
9. Selling and customer-service costs	$720,000	$725,000
10. Cost per customer of selling and customer-service capacity (row 9 ÷ row 8)	$24,000	$25,000

In 2011, Westwood produced no defective units and reduced direct material usage per unit of KE8. Conversion costs in each year are tied to manufacturing capacity. Selling and customer service costs are related to the number of customers that the selling and service functions are designed to support. Westwood has 23 customers (wholesalers) in 2010 and 25 customers in 2011.

Required

1. Describe briefly the elements you would include in Westwood's balanced scorecard.
2. Calculate the growth, price-recovery, and productivity components that explain the change in operating income from 2010 to 2011.
3. Suppose during 2011, the market size for high-end kitchen range hoods grew 3% in terms of number of units and all increases in market share (that is, increases in the number of units sold greater than 3%) are due to Westwood's product-differentiation strategy. Calculate how much of the change in operating income from 2010 to 2011 is due to the industry-market-size factor, cost leadership, and product differentiation.
4. How successful has Westwood been in implementing its strategy? Explain.

Solution

1. The balanced scorecard should describe Westwood's product-differentiation strategy. Elements that should be included in its balanced scorecard are as follows:
   - **Financial perspective.** Increase in operating income from higher margins on KE8 and from growth
   - **Customer perspective.** Customer satisfaction and market share in the high-end market
   - **Internal business process perspective.** New product features, development time for new products, improvements in manufacturing processes, manufacturing quality, order-delivery time, and on-time delivery
   - **Learning-and-growth perspective.** Percentage of employees trained in process and quality management and employee satisfaction ratings

2. Operating income for each year is as follows:

	2010	2011
Revenues		
($100 per unit × 40,000 units; $110 per unit × 42,000 units)	$4,000,000	$4,620,000
Costs		
Direct material costs		
($10 per sq. ft. × 120,000 sq. ft.; $11 per sq. ft. × 123,000 sq. ft.)	1,200,000	1,353,000
Conversion costs		
($20 per unit × 50,000 units; $22 per unit × 50,000 units)	1,000,000	1,100,000
Selling and customer-service cost		
($24,000 per customer × 30 customers;		
$25,000 per customer × 29 customers)	720,000	725,000
Total costs	2,920,000	3,178,000
Operating income	$1,080,000	$1,442,000
Change in operating income		$362,000 F

Growth Component of Operating Income Change

$$\text{Revenue effect of growth} = \left(\begin{array}{c}\text{Actual units of output sold in 2011} - \text{Actual units of output sold in 2010}\end{array}\right) \times \begin{array}{c}\text{Selling price in 2010}\end{array}$$

$$= (42{,}000 \text{ units} - 40{,}000 \text{ units}) \times \$100 \text{ per unit} = \$200{,}000 \text{ F}$$

$$\text{Cost effect of growth for variable costs} = \left(\begin{array}{c}\text{Units of input required to produce 2011 output in 2010} - \text{Actual units of input used to produce 2010 output}\end{array}\right) \times \begin{array}{c}\text{Input price in 2010}\end{array}$$

$$\text{Cost effect of growth for direct materials} = \left(120{,}000 \text{ sq. ft.} \times \frac{42{,}000 \text{ units}}{40{,}000 \text{ units}} - 120{,}000 \text{ sq. ft.}\right) \times \$10 \text{ per sq. ft.}$$

$$= (126{,}000 \text{ sq. ft.} - 120{,}000 \text{ sq. ft.}) \times \$10 \text{ per sq. ft.} = \$60{,}000 \text{ U}$$

$$\text{Cost effect of growth for fixed costs} = \left(\begin{array}{c}\text{Actual units of capacity in 2010, because adequate capacity exists to produce 2011 output in 2010} - \text{Actual units of capacity in 2010}\end{array}\right) \times \begin{array}{c}\text{Price per unit of capacity in 2010}\end{array}$$

Cost effects of growth for fixed costs are as follows:

$$\text{Conversion costs: } (50{,}000 \text{ units} - 50{,}000 \text{ units}) \times \$20 \text{ per unit} = \$0$$

$$\text{Selling and customer-service costs: } (30 \text{ customers} - 30 \text{ customers}) \times \$24{,}000 \text{ per customer} = \$0$$

In summary, the net increase in operating income attributable to growth equals the following:

Revenue effect of growth		$200,000 F
Cost effect of growth		
Direct material costs	$60,000 U	
Conversion costs	0	
Selling and customer-service costs	0	60,000 U
Change in operating income due to growth		$140,000 F

Price-Recovery Component of Operating-Income Change

$$\begin{array}{c}\text{Revenue effect of}\\\text{price recovery}\end{array} = \left(\begin{array}{c}\text{Selling price}\\\text{in 2011}\end{array} - \begin{array}{c}\text{Selling price}\\\text{in 2010}\end{array}\right) \times \begin{array}{c}\text{Actual units}\\\text{of output}\\\text{sold in 2011}\end{array}$$

$$= (\$110 \text{ per unit} - \$100 \text{ per unit}) \times 42{,}000 \text{ units} = \$420{,}000 \text{ F}$$

$$\begin{array}{c}\text{Cost effect of}\\\text{price recovery}\\\text{for variable costs}\end{array} = \left(\begin{array}{c}\text{Input}\\\text{price}\\\text{in 2011}\end{array} - \begin{array}{c}\text{Input}\\\text{price}\\\text{in 2010}\end{array}\right) \times \begin{array}{c}\text{Units of input}\\\text{required to produce}\\\text{2011 output in 2010}\end{array}$$

Direct material costs: ($11 per sq. ft. − $10 per sq. ft.) × 126,000 sq. ft. = $126,000 U

$$\begin{array}{c}\text{Cost effect of}\\\text{price recovery}\\\text{for fixed costs}\end{array} = \left(\begin{array}{c}\text{Price per}\\\text{unit of}\\\text{capacity}\\\text{in 2011}\end{array} - \begin{array}{c}\text{Price per}\\\text{unit of}\\\text{capacity}\\\text{in 2010}\end{array}\right) \times \begin{array}{c}\text{Actual units of capacity in}\\\text{2010, because adequate capacity}\\\text{exists to produce 2011 output in 2010}\end{array}$$

Cost effects of price recovery for fixed costs are as follows:

Conversion costs: ($22 per unit − 20 per unit) × 50,000 units = $100,000 U

Selling and cust.-service costs: ($25,000 per cust. − $24,000 per cust.) × 30 customers = $30,000 U

In summary, the net increase in operating income attributable to price recovery equals the following:

Revenue effect of price recovery		$420,000 F
Cost effect of price recovery		
Direct material costs	$126,000 U	
Conversion costs	100,000 U	
Selling and customer-service costs	30,000 U	256,000 U
Change in operating income due to price recovery		$164,000 F

Productivity Component of Operating-Income Change

$$\begin{array}{c}\text{Cost effect of}\\\text{productivity for}\\\text{variable costs}\end{array} = \left(\begin{array}{c}\text{Actual units of}\\\text{input used to produce}\\\text{2011 output}\end{array} - \begin{array}{c}\text{Units of input}\\\text{required to produce}\\\text{2011 output in 2010}\end{array}\right) \times \begin{array}{c}\text{Input}\\\text{price in}\\\text{2011}\end{array}$$

$$\begin{array}{c}\text{Cost effect of}\\\text{productivity for}\\\text{direct materials}\end{array} = (123{,}000 \text{ sq. ft.} - 126{,}000 \text{ sq. ft.}) \times \$11 \text{ per sq. ft.} = \$33{,}000 \text{ F}$$

$$\begin{array}{c}\text{Cost effect of}\\\text{productivity for}\\\text{fixed costs}\end{array} = \left(\begin{array}{c}\text{Actual units}\\\text{of capacity}\\\text{in 2011}\end{array} - \begin{array}{c}\text{Actual units of capacity in}\\\text{2010, because adequate}\\\text{capacity exists to produce}\\\text{2011 output in 2010}\end{array}\right) \times \begin{array}{c}\text{Price per}\\\text{unit of}\\\text{capacity}\\\text{in 2011}\end{array}$$

Cost effects of productivity for fixed costs are as follows:

Conversion costs: (50,000 units − 50,000 units) × $22 per unit = $0

Selling and customer-service costs: (29 customers − 30 customers) × $25,000/customer = $25,000 F

In summary, the net increase in operating income attributable to productivity equals the following:

Cost effect of productivity:	
Direct material costs	$33,000 F
Conversion costs	0
Selling and customer-service costs	25,000 F
Change in operating income due to productivity	$58,000 F

A summary of the change in operating income between 2010 and 2011 follows:

	Income Statement Amounts in 2010 (1)	Revenue and Cost Effects of Growth Component in 2011 (2)	Revenue and Cost Effects of Price-Recovery Component in 2011 (3)	Cost Effect of Productivity Component in 2011 (4)	Income Statement Amounts in 2011 (5) = (1) + (2) + (3) + (4)
Revenue	$4,000,000	$200,000 F	$420,000 F	—	$4,620,000
Costs	2,920,000	60,000 U	256,000 U	$58,000 F	3,178,000
Operating income	$1,080,000	$140,000 F	$164,000 F	$58,000 F	$1,442,000
			362,000 F		

Change in operating income

3. **Effect of the Industry-Market-Size Factor on Operating Income**

   Of the increase in sales from 40,000 to 42,000 units, 3%, or 1,200 units (0.03 × 40,000), is due to growth in market size, and 800 units (2,000 − 1,200) are due to an increase in market share. The change in Westwood's operating income from the industry-market-size factor rather than specific strategic actions is as follows:

   $$\$140{,}000 \text{ (column 2 of preceding table)} \times \frac{1{,}200 \text{ units}}{2{,}000 \text{ units}} \quad \$84{,}000 \text{ F}$$

Effect of Product Differentiation on Operating Income

Increase in the selling price of KE8 (revenue effect of the price-recovery component)	$420,000 F
Increase in prices of inputs (cost effect of the price-recovery component)	256,000 U
Growth in market share due to product differentiation	
$140,000 (column 2 of preceding table) × $\dfrac{800 \text{ units}}{2{,}000 \text{ units}}$	56,000 F
Change in operating income due to product differentiation	$220,000 F

Effect of Cost Leadership on Operating Income

Productivity component	$ 58,000 F

A summary of the net increase in operating income from 2010 to 2011 follows:

Change due to the industry-market-size factor	$ 84,000 F
Change due to product differentiation	220,000 F
Change due to cost leadership	58,000 F
Change in operating income	$362,000 F

4. The analysis of operating income indicates that a significant amount of the increase in operating income resulted from Westwood's successful implementation of its product-differentiation strategy. The company was able to continue to charge a premium price for KE8 while increasing market share. Westwood was also able to earn additional operating income from improving its productivity.

Decision Points

The following question-and-answer format summarizes the chapter's learning objectives. Each decision presents a key question related to a learning objective. The guidelines are the answer to that question.

Decision	Guidelines
1. What are two generic strategies a company can use?	Two generic strategies are product differentiation and cost leadership. Product differentiation is offering products and services that are perceived by customers as being superior and unique. Cost leadership is achieving low costs relative to competitors. A company chooses its strategy based on an understanding of customer preferences and its own internal capabilities, while differentiating itself from its competitors.
2. What is reengineering?	Reengineering is the rethinking of business processes, such as the order-delivery process, to improve critical performance measures such as cost, quality, and customer satisfaction.
3. How can an organization translate its strategy into a set of performance measures?	An organization can develop a balanced scorecard that provides the framework for a strategic measurement and management system. The balanced scorecard measures performance from four perspectives: (1) financial, (2) customer, (3) internal business processes, and (4) learning and growth. To build their balanced scorecards, organizations often create strategy maps to represent the cause-and-effect relationships across various strategic objectives.
4. How can a company analyze changes in operating income to evaluate the success of its strategy?	To evaluate the success of its strategy, a company can subdivide the change in operating income into growth, price-recovery, and productivity components. The growth component measures the change in revenues and costs from selling more or less units, assuming nothing else has changed. The price-recovery component measures changes in revenues and costs solely as a result of changes in the prices of outputs and inputs. The productivity component measures the decrease in costs from using fewer inputs, a better mix of inputs, and reducing capacity. If a company is successful in implementing its strategy, changes in components of operating income align closely with strategy.
5. How can a company identify and manage unused capacity?	A company must first distinguish engineered costs from discretionary costs. Engineered costs result from a cause-and-effect relationship between output and the resources needed to produce that output. Discretionary costs arise from periodic (usually annual) management decisions regarding the amount of cost to be incurred. Discretionary costs are not tied to a cause-and-effect relationship between inputs and outputs. Identifying unused capacity is easier for engineered costs and more difficult for discretionary costs. Downsizing is an approach to managing unused capacity that matches costs to the activities that need to be performed to operate effectively.

Appendix

Productivity Measurement

Productivity measures the relationship between actual inputs used (both quantities and costs) and actual outputs produced. The lower the inputs for a given quantity of outputs or the higher the outputs for a given quantity of inputs, the higher the productivity. Measuring productivity improvements over time highlights the specific input-output relationships that contribute to cost leadership.

Partial Productivity Measures

Partial productivity, the most frequently used productivity measure, compares the quantity of output produced with the quantity of an individual input used. In its most common form, partial productivity is expressed as a ratio:

$$\text{Partial productivity} = \frac{\text{Quantity of output produced}}{\text{Quantity of input used}}$$

The higher the ratio, the greater the productivity.

Consider direct materials productivity at Chipset in 2011.

$$\frac{\text{Direct materials}}{\text{partial productivity}} = \frac{\text{Quantity of CX1 units produced during 2011}}{\text{Quantity of direct materials used to produce CX1 in 2011}}$$

$$= \frac{1,150,000 \text{ units of CX1}}{2,900,000 \text{ sq. cm. of direct materials}}$$

$$= 0.397 \text{ units of CX1 per sq. cm. of direct materials}$$

Note direct materials partial productivity ignores Chipset's other input, manufacturing conversion capacity. Partial-productivity measures become more meaningful when comparisons are made that examine productivity changes over time, either across different facilities or relative to a benchmark. Exhibit 6 presents partial-productivity measures for Chipset's inputs for 2011 and the comparable 2010 inputs that would have been used to produce 2011 output, using information from the productivity-component calculations on page 482. These measures compare actual inputs used in 2011 to produce 1,150,000 units of CX1 with inputs that would have been used in 2011 had the input–output relationship from 2010 continued in 2011.

Evaluating Changes in Partial Productivities

Note how the partial-productivity measures differ for variable-cost and fixed-cost components. For variable-cost elements, such as direct materials, productivity improvements measure the reduction in input resources used to produce output (3,450,000 square centimeters of silicon wafers to 2,900,000 square centimeters). For fixed-cost elements such as manufacturing conversion capacity, partial productivity measures the reduction in overall capacity from 2010 to 2011 (3,750,000 square centimeters of silicon wafers to 3,500,000 square centimeters) regardless of the amount of capacity actually used in each period.

An advantage of partial-productivity measures is that they focus on a single input. As a result, they are simple to calculate and easily understood by operations personnel. Managers and operators examine these numbers and try to understand the reasons for the productivity changes—such as, better training of workers, lower labor turnover, better incentives, improved methods, or substitution of materials for labor. Isolating the relevant factors helps Chipset implement and sustain these practices in the future.

For all their advantages, partial-productivity measures also have serious drawbacks. Because partial productivity focuses on only one input at a time rather than on all inputs simultaneously, managers cannot evaluate the effect on overall productivity, if (say) manufacturing-conversion-capacity partial productivity increases while direct materials partial productivity decreases. Total factor productivity (TFP), or total productivity, is a measure of productivity that considers all inputs simultaneously.

Exhibit 6   Comparing Chipset's Partial Productivities in 2010 and 2011

Input (1)	Partial Productivity in 2011 (2)	Comparable Partial Productivity Based on 2010 Input–Output Relationships (3)	Percentage Change from 2010 to 2011 (4)
Direct materials	$\frac{1,150,000}{2,900,000} = 0.397$	$\frac{1,150,000}{3,450,000} = 0.333$	$\frac{0.397 - 0.333}{0.333} = 19.2\%$
Manufacturing conversion capacity	$\frac{1,150,000}{3,500,000} = 0.329$	$\frac{1,150,000}{3,750,000} = 0.307$	$\frac{0.329 - 0.307}{0.307} = 7.2\%$

Total Factor Productivity

Total factor productivity (TFP) is the ratio of the quantity of output produced to the costs of all inputs used based on current-period prices.

$$\text{Total factor productivity} = \frac{\text{Quantity of output produced}}{\text{Costs of all inputs used}}$$

TFP considers all inputs simultaneously and the trade-offs across inputs based on current input prices. Do not think of all productivity measures as physical measures lacking financial content—how many units of output are produced per unit of input. TFP is intricately tied to minimizing total cost—a financial objective.

Calculating and Comparing Total Factor Productivity

We first calculate Chipset's TFP in 2011, using 2011 prices and 1,150,000 units of output produced (based on information from the first part of the productivity-component calculations).

$$\frac{\text{Total factor productivity}}{\text{for 2011 using 2011 prices}} = \frac{\text{Quantity of output produced in 2011}}{\text{Costs of inputs used in 2011 based on 2011 prices}}$$

$$= \frac{1,150,000}{(2,900,000 \times \$1.50) + (3,500,000 \times \$4.35)}$$

$$= \frac{1,150,000}{\$19,575,000}$$

$$= 0.058748 \text{ units of output per dollar of input cost}$$

By itself, the 2011 TFP of 0.058748 units of CX1 per dollar of input costs is not particularly helpful. We need something to compare the 2011 TFP against. One alternative is to compare TFPs of other similar companies in 2011. However, finding similar companies and obtaining accurate comparable data are often difficult. Companies, therefore, usually compare their own TFPs over time. In the Chipset example, we use as a benchmark TFP calculated using the inputs that Chipset would have used in 2010 to produce 1,150,000 units of CX1 at 2011 prices (that is, we use the costs calculated from the second part of the productivity-component calculations). Why do we use 2011 prices? Because using the current year's prices in both calculations controls for input-price differences and focuses the analysis on adjustments the manager made in quantities of inputs in response to changes in prices.

$$\frac{\text{Benchmark}}{\text{TFP}} = \frac{\text{Quantity of output produced in 2011}}{\begin{array}{c}\text{Costs of inputs at 2011 prices that would have been used in 2010}\\\text{to produce 2011 output}\end{array}}$$

$$= \frac{1,150,000}{(3,450,000 \times \$1.50) + (3,750,000 \times \$4.35)}$$

$$= \frac{1,150,000}{\$21,487,500}$$

$$= 0.053519 \text{ units of output per dollar of input cost}$$

Using 2011 prices, TFP increased 9.8% [(058748 – 0.053519) ÷ 0.053519 = 0.098, or 9.8%] from 2010 to 2011. Note that the 9.8% increase in TFP also equals the $1,912,500 gain (Exhibit 5, column 4) divided by the $19,575,000 of actual costs incurred in 2011 (Exhibit 5, column 5). Total factor productivity increased because Chipset produced more output per dollar of input cost in 2011 relative to 2010, measured in both years using 2011 prices. The gain in TFP occurs because Chipset increases the partial productivities of individual inputs and, consistent with its strategy, combines inputs to lower costs. Note that increases in TFP cannot be due to differences in input prices because we used 2011 prices to evaluate both the inputs that Chipset would have used in 2010 to produce 1,150,000 units of CX1 and the inputs actually used in 2011.

Using Partial and Total Factor Productivity Measures

A major advantage of TFP is that it measures the combined productivity of all inputs used to produce output and explicitly considers gains from using fewer physical inputs as well as substitution among inputs. Managers can analyze these numbers to understand the reasons for changes in TFP—for example, better human resource management practices, higher quality of materials, or improved manufacturing methods.

Although TFP measures are comprehensive, operations personnel find financial TFP measures more difficult to understand and less useful than physical partial-productivity measures. For example, companies that are more labor intensive than Chipset use manufacturing-labor partial-productivity measures. However, if productivity-based bonuses depend on gains in manufacturing-labor partial productivity alone, workers have incentives to substitute materials (and capital) for labor. This substitution improves their own productivity measure, while possibly decreasing the overall productivity of the company as measured by TFP. To overcome these incentive problems, some companies—for example, TRW, Eaton, and Whirlpool—explicitly adjust bonuses based on manufacturing-labor partial productivity for the effects of other factors such as investments in new equipment and higher levels of scrap. That is, they combine partial productivity with TFP-like measures.

Many companies such as Behlen Manufacturing, a steel fabricator, and Dell Computers use both partial productivity and total factor productivity to evaluate performance. *Partial productivity and TFP measures work best together because the strengths of one offset the weaknesses of the other.*

Terms to Learn

This chapter contains definitions of the following important terms:

balanced scorecard
cost leadership
discretionary costs
downsizing
engineered costs
growth component

partial productivity
price-recovery component
product differentiation
productivity
productivity component

reengineering
rightsizing
strategy map
total factor productivity (TFP)
unused capacity

Assignment Material

Questions

13-1 Define strategy.
13-2 Describe the five key forces to consider when analyzing an industry.
13-3 Describe two generic strategies.
13-4 What is a customer preference map and why is it useful?
13-5 What is reengineering?
13-6 What are four key perspectives in the balanced scorecard?
13-7 What is a strategy map?
13-8 Describe three features of a good balanced scorecard.
13-9 What are three important pitfalls to avoid when implementing a balanced scorecard?
13-10 Describe three key components in doing a strategic analysis of operating income.
13-11 Why might an analyst incorporate the industry-market-size factor and the interrelationships among the growth, price-recovery, and productivity components into a strategic analysis of operating income?
13-12 How does an engineered cost differ from a discretionary cost?
13-13 What is downsizing?
13-14 What is a partial-productivity measure?
13-15 "We are already measuring total factor productivity. Measuring partial productivities would be of no value." Do you agree? Comment briefly.

Exercises

13-16 **Balanced scorecard.** Ridgecrest Corporation manufactures corrugated cardboard boxes. It competes and plans to grow by selling high-quality boxes at a low price and by delivering them to customers quickly after receiving customers' orders. There are many other manufacturers who produce similar boxes. Ridgecrest believes that continuously improving its manufacturing processes and having satisfied employees are critical to implementing its strategy in 2012.

1. Is Ridgecrest's 2012 strategy one of product differentiation or cost leadership? Explain briefly.
2. Kearney Corporation, a competitor of Ridgecrest, manufactures corrugated boxes with more designs and color combinations than Ridgecrest at a higher price. Kearney's boxes are of high quality but require more time to produce and so have longer delivery times. Draw a simple customer preference map as in Exhibit 1 for Ridgecrest and Kearney using the attributes of price, delivery time, quality, and design.

3. Draw a strategy map as in Exhibit 2 with two strategic objectives you would expect to see under each balanced scorecard perspective.
4. For each strategic objective indicate a measure you would expect to see in Ridgecrest's balanced scorecard for 2012.

13-17 Analysis of growth, price-recovery, and productivity components (continuation of 13-16). An analysis of Ridgecrest's operating-income changes between 2011 and 2012 shows the following:

Operating income for 2011	$1,850,000
Add growth component	85,000
Deduct price-recovery component	(72,000)
Add productivity component	150,000
Operating income for 2011	$2,013,000

The industry market size for corrugated cardboard boxes did not grow in 2012, input prices did not change, and Ridgecrest reduced the prices of its boxes.

Required
1. Was Ridgecrest's gain in operating income in 2012 consistent with the strategy you identified in requirement 1 of Exercise 13-16?
2. Explain the productivity component. In general, does it represent savings in only variable costs, only fixed costs, or both variable and fixed costs?

13-18 Strategy, balanced scorecard, merchandising operation. Roberto & Sons buys T-shirts in bulk, applies its own trendsetting silk-screen designs, and then sells the T-shirts to a number of retailers. Roberto wants to be known for its trendsetting designs, and it wants every teenager to be seen in a distinctive Roberto T-shirt. Roberto presents the following data for its first two years of operations, 2010 and 2011.

		2010	2011
1	Number of T-shirts purchased	200,000	250,000
2	Number of T-shirts discarded	2,000	3,300
3	Number of T-shirts sold (row 1 – row 2)	198,000	246,700
4	Average selling price	$25.00	$26.00
5	Average cost per T-shirt	$10.00	$8.50
6	Administrative capacity (number of customers)	4,000	3,750
7	Administrative costs	$1,200,000	$1,162,500
8	Administrative cost per customer (row 8 ÷ row 7)	$300	$310

Administrative costs depend on the number of customers that Roberto has created capacity to support, not on the actual number of customers served. Roberto had 3,600 customers in 2010 and 3,500 customers in 2011.

Required
1. Is Roberto 's strategy one of product differentiation or cost leadership? Explain briefly.
2. Describe briefly the key measures Roberto should include in its balanced scorecard and the reasons it should do so.

13-19 Strategic analysis of operating income (continuation of 13-18). Refer to Exercise 13-18.

Required
1. Calculate Roberto's operating income in both 2010 and 2011.
2. Calculate the growth, price-recovery, and productivity components that explain the change in operating income from 2010 to 2011.
3. Comment on your answers in requirement 2. What does each of these components indicate?

13-20 Analysis of growth, price-recovery, and productivity components (continuation of 13-19). Refer to Exercise 13-19. Suppose that the market for silk-screened T-shirts grew by 10% during 2011. All increases in sales greater than 10% are the result of Roberto's strategic actions.

Required
Calculate the change in operating income from 2010 to 2011 due to growth in market size, product differentiation, and cost leadership. How successful has Roberto been in implementing its strategy? Explain.

13-21 Identifying and managing unused capacity (continuation of 13-18). Refer to Exercise 13-18.

Required
1. Calculate the amount and cost of unused administrative capacity at the beginning of 2011, based on the actual number of customers Roberto served in 2011.
2. Suppose Roberto can only add or reduce administrative capacity in increments of 250 customers. What is the maximum amount of costs that Roberto can save in 2011 by downsizing administrative capacity?
3. What factors, other than cost, should Roberto consider before it downsizes administrative capacity?

13-22 Strategy, balanced scorecard. Stanmore Corporation makes a special-purpose machine, D4H, used in the textile industry. Stanmore has designed the D4H machine for 2011 to be distinct from its competitors. It has been generally regarded as a superior machine. Stanmore presents the following data for 2010 and 2011.

	2010	2011
1. Units of D4H produced and sold	200	210
2. Selling price	$40,000	$42,000
3. Direct materials (kilograms)	300,000	310,000
4. Direct material cost per kilogram	$8	$8.50
5. Manufacturing capacity in units of D4H	250	250
6. Total conversion costs	$2,000,000	$2,025,000
7. Conversion cost per unit of capacity (row 6 ÷ row 5)	$8,000	$8,100
8. Selling and customer-service capacity	100 customers	95 customers
9. Total selling and customer-service costs	$1,000,000	$940,500
10. Selling and customer-service capacity cost per customer (row 9 ÷ row 8)	$10,000	$9,900

Stanmore produces no defective machines, but it wants to reduce direct materials usage per D4H machine in 2011. Conversion costs in each year depend on production capacity defined in terms of D4H units that can be produced, not the actual units produced. Selling and customer-service costs depend on the number of customers that Stanmore can support, not the actual number of customers it serves. Stanmore has 75 customers in 2010 and 80 customers in 2011.

Required

1. Is Stanmore's strategy one of product differentiation or cost leadership? Explain briefly.
2. Describe briefly key measures that you would include in Stanmore's balanced scorecard and the reasons for doing so.

13-23 Strategic analysis of operating income (continuation of 13-22). Refer to Exercise 13-22.

Required

1. Calculate the operating income of Stanmore Corporation in 2010 and 2011.
2. Calculate the growth, price-recovery, and productivity components that explain the change in operating income from 2010 to 2011.
3. Comment on your answer in requirement 2. What do these components indicate?

13-24 Analysis of growth, price-recovery, and productivity components (continuation of 13-23). Suppose that during 2011, the market for Stanmore's special-purpose machines grew by 3%. All increases in market share (that is, sales increases greater than 3%) are the result of Stanmore's strategic actions.

Required

Calculate how much of the change in operating income from 2010 to 2011 is due to the industry-market-size factor, product differentiation, and cost leadership. How successful has Stanmore been in implementing its strategy? Explain.

13-25 Identifying and managing unused capacity (continuation of 13-22). Refer to Exercise 13-22.

Required

1. Calculate the amount and cost of (a) unused manufacturing capacity and (b) unused selling and customer-service capacity at the beginning of 2011 based on actual production and actual number of customers served in 2011.
2. Suppose Stanmore can add or reduce its manufacturing capacity in increments of 30 units. What is the maximum amount of costs that Stanmore could save in 2011 by downsizing manufacturing capacity?
3. Stanmore, in fact, does not eliminate any of its unused manufacturing capacity. Why might Stanmore not downsize?

13-26 Strategy, balanced scorecard, service company. Westlake Corporation is a small information-systems consulting firm that specializes in helping companies implement standard sales-management software. The market for Westlake's services is very competitive. To compete successfully, Westlake must deliver quality service at a low cost. Westlake presents the following data for 2010 and 2011.

	2010	2011
1. Number of jobs billed	60	70
2. Selling price per job	$50,000	$48,000
3. Software-implementation labor-hours	30,000	32,000
4. Cost per software-implementation labor-hour	$60	$63
5. Software-implementation support capacity (number of jobs it can do)	90	90
6. Total cost of software-implementation support	$360,000	$369,000
7. Software-implementation support-capacity cost per job (row 6 ÷ row 5)	$4,000	$4,100

Software-implementation labor-hour costs are variable costs. Software-implementation support costs for each year depend on the software-implementation support capacity Westlake chooses to maintain each year (that is the number of jobs it can do each year). It does not vary with the actual number of jobs done that year.

Required

1. Is Westlake Corporation's strategy one of product differentiation or cost leadership? Explain briefly.
2. Describe key measures you would include in Westlake's balanced scorecard and your reasons for doing so.

13-27 Strategic analysis of operating income (continuation of 13-26). Refer to Exercise 13-26.

Required

1. Calculate the operating income of Westlake Corporation in 2010 and 2011.
2. Calculate the growth, price-recovery, and productivity components that explain the change in operating income from 2010 to 2011.
3. Comment on your answer in requirement 2. What do these components indicate?

13-28 Analysis of growth, price-recovery, and productivity components (continuation of 13-27). Suppose that during 2011 the market for implementing sales-management software increases by 5%. Assume that any decrease in selling price and any increase in market share more than 5% are the result of strategic choices by Westlake's management to implement its strategy.

Required

Calculate how much of the change in operating income from 2010 to 2011 is due to the industry-market-size factor, product differentiation, and cost leadership. How successful has Westlake been in implementing its strategy? Explain.

13-29 Identifying and managing unused capacity (continuation of 13-26). Refer to Exercise 13-26.

Required

1. Calculate the amount and cost of unused software-implementation support capacity at the beginning of 2011, based on the number of jobs actually done in 2011.
2. Suppose Westlake can add or reduce its software-implementation support capacity in increments of 15 units. What is the maximum amount of costs that Westlake could save in 2011 by downsizing software-implementation support capacity?
3. Westlake, in fact, does not eliminate any of its unused software-implementation support capacity. Why might Westlake not downsize?

MyAccountingLab

Problems

13-30 Balanced scorecard and strategy. Music Master Company manufactures an MP3 player called the Mini. The company sells the player to discount stores throughout the country. This player is significantly less expensive than similar products sold by Music Master's competitors, but the Mini offers just four gigabytes of space, compared with eight offered by competitor Vantage Manufacturing. Furthermore, the Mini has experienced production problems that have resulted in significant rework costs. Vantage's model has an excellent reputation for quality, but is considerably more expensive.

Required

1. Draw a simple customer preference map for Music Master and Vantage using the attributes of price, quality, and storage capacity. Use the format of Exhibit 1.
2. Is Music Master's current strategy that of product differentiation or cost leadership?
3. Music Master would like to improve quality and decrease costs by improving processes and training workers to reduce rework. Music Master's managers believe the increased quality will increase sales. Draw a strategy map as in Exhibit 2 describing the cause-and-effect relationships among the strategic objectives you would expect to see in Music Master's balanced scorecard.
4. For each strategic objective suggest a measure you would recommend in Music Master's balanced scorecard.

13-31 Strategic analysis of operating income (continuation of 13-30). Refer to Problem 13-30. As a result of the actions taken, quality has significantly improved in 2011 while rework and unit costs of the Mini have decreased. Music Master has reduced manufacturing capacity because capacity is no longer needed to support rework. Music Master has also lowered the Mini's selling price to gain market share and unit sales have increased. Information about the current period (2011) and last period (2010) follows:

	2010	2011
1. Units of Mini produced and sold	8,000	9,000
2. Selling price	$45	$43
3. Ounces of direct materials used	32,000	33,000
4. Direct material cost per ounce	$3.50	$3.50
5. Manufacturing capacity in units	12,000	11,000
6. Total conversion costs	$156,000	$143,000
7. Conversion cost per unit of capacity (row 6 ÷ row 5)	$13	$13
8. Selling and customer-service capacity	90 customers	90 customers
9. Total selling and customer-service costs	$45,000	$49,500
10. Selling and customer-service capacity cost per customer (row 9 ÷ row 8)	$500	$550

Conversion costs in each year depend on production capacity defined in terms of units of Mini that can be produced, not the actual units produced. Selling and customer-service costs depend on the number of customers that Music Master can support, not the actual number of customers it serves. Music Master has 70 customers in 2010 and 80 customers in 2011.

1. Calculate operating income of Music Master Company for 2010 and 2011.
2. Calculate the growth, price-recovery, and productivity components that explain the change in operating income from 2010 to 2011.
3. Comment on your answer in requirement 2. What do these components indicate?

Required

13-32 Analysis of growth, price-recovery, and productivity components (continuation of 13-31). Suppose that during 2011, the market for MP3 players grew 3%. All decreases in the selling price of the Mini and increases in market share (that is, sales increases greater than 3%) are the result of Music Master's strategic actions.

Calculate how much of the change in operating income from 2010 to 2011 is due to the industry-market-size factor, product differentiation, and cost leadership. How does this relate to Music Master's strategy and its success in implementation? Explain.

Required

13-33 Identifying and managing unused capacity (continuation of 13-31) Refer to the information for Music Master Company in 13-31.

1. Calculate the amount and cost of (a) unused manufacturing capacity and (b) unused selling and customer-service capacity at the beginning of 2011 based on actual production and actual number of customers served in 2011.
2. Suppose Music Master can add or reduce its selling and customer-service capacity in increments of five customers. What is the maximum amount of costs that Music Master could save in 2011 by downsizing selling and customer-service capacity?
3. Music Master, in fact, does not eliminate any of its unused selling and customer-service capacity. Why might Music Master not downsize?

Required

13-34 Balanced scorecard. Following is a random-order listing of perspectives, strategic objectives, and performance measures for the balanced scorecard.

Perspectives	Performance Measures
Internal business process	Percentage of defective-product units
Customer	Return on assets
Learning and growth	Number of patents
Financial	Employee turnover rate
Strategic Objectives	Net income
Acquire new customers	Customer profitability
Increase shareholder value	Percentage of processes with real-time feedback
Retain customers	Return on sales
Improve manufacturing quality	Average job-related training-hours per employee
Develop profitable customers	Return on equity
Increase proprietary products	Percentage of on-time deliveries by suppliers
Increase information-system capabilities	Product cost per unit
Enhance employee skills	Profit per salesperson
On-time delivery by suppliers	Percentage of error-free invoices
Increase profit generated by each salesperson	Customer cost per unit
Introduce new products	Earnings per share
Minimize invoice-error rate	Number of new customers
	Percentage of customers retained

For each perspective, select those strategic objectives from the list that best relate to it. For each strategic objective, select the most appropriate performance measure(s) from the list.

Required

13-35 Balanced scorecard. (R. Kaplan, adapted) Caltex, Inc., refines gasoline and sells it through its own Caltex Gas Stations. On the basis of market research, Caltex determines that 60% of the overall gasoline market consists of "service-oriented customers," medium- to high-income individuals who are willing to pay a higher price for gas if the gas stations can provide excellent customer service, such as a clean facility, a convenience store, friendly employees, a quick turnaround, the ability to pay by credit card, and high-octane premium gasoline. The remaining 40% of the overall market are "price shoppers" who look to buy the cheapest gasoline available. Caltex's strategy is to focus on the 60% of service-oriented customers. Caltex's balanced scorecard for 2011 follows. For brevity, the initiatives taken under each objective are omitted.

Objectives	Measures	Target Performance	Actual Performance
Financial Perspective			
Increase shareholder value	Operating-income changes from price recovery	$90,000,000	$95,000,000
	Operating-income changes from growth	$65,000,000	$67,000,000
Customer Perspective			
Increase market share	Market share of overall gasoline market	10%	9.8%
Internal-Business-Process Perspective			
Improve gasoline quality	Quality index	94 points	95 points
Improve refinery performance	Refinery-reliability index (%)	91%	91%
Ensure gasoline availability	Product-availability index (%)	99%	100%
Learning-and-Growth Perspective			
Increase refinery process capability	Percentage of refinery processes with advanced controls	88%	90%

Required

1. Was Caltex successful in implementing its strategy in 2011? Explain your answer.
2. Would you have included some measure of employee satisfaction and employee training in the learning-and-growth perspective? Are these objectives critical to Caltex for implementing its strategy? Why or why not? Explain briefly.
3. Explain how Caltex did not achieve its target market share in the total gasoline market but still exceeded its financial targets. Is "market share of overall gasoline market" the correct measure of market share? Explain briefly.
4. Is there a cause-and-effect linkage between improvements in the measures in the internal business-process perspective and the measure in the customer perspective? That is, would you add other measures to the internal-business-process perspective or the customer perspective? Why or why not? Explain briefly.
5. Do you agree with Caltex's decision not to include measures of changes in operating income from productivity improvements under the financial perspective of the balanced scorecard? Explain briefly.

13-36 Balanced scorecard. Lee Corporation manufactures various types of color laser printers in a highly automated facility with high fixed costs. The market for laser printers is competitive. The various color laser printers on the market are comparable in terms of features and price. Lee believes that satisfying customers with products of high quality at low costs is key to achieving its target profitability. For 2011, Lee plans to achieve higher quality and lower costs by improving yields and reducing defects in its manufacturing operations. Lee will train workers and encourage and empower them to take the necessary actions. Currently, a significant amount of Lee's capacity is used to produce products that are defective and cannot be sold. Lee expects that higher yields will reduce the capacity that Lee needs to manufacture products. Lee does not anticipate that improving manufacturing will automatically lead to lower costs because Lee has high fixed costs. To reduce fixed costs per unit, Lee could lay off employees and sell equipment, or it could use the capacity to produce and sell more of its current products or improved models of its current products.

Lee's balanced scorecard (initiatives omitted) for the just-completed fiscal year 2011 follows:

Objectives	Measures	Target Performance	Actual Performance
Financial Perspective			
Increase shareholder value	Operating-income changes from productivity improvements	$1,000,000	$400,000
	Operating-income changes from growth	$1,500,000	$600,000
Customer Perspective			
Increase market share	Market share in color laser printers	5%	4.6%
Internal-Business-Process Perspective			
Improve manufacturing quality	Yield	82%	85%
Reduce delivery time to customers	Order-delivery time	25 days	22 days
Learning-and-Growth Perspective			
Develop process skills	Percentage of employees trained in process and quality management	90%	92%
Enhance information-system capabilities	Percentage of manufacturing processes with real-time feedback	85%	87%

Required

1. Was Lee successful in implementing its strategy in 2011? Explain.
2. Is Lee's balanced scorecard useful in helping the company understand why it did not reach its target market share in 2011? If it is, explain why. If it is not, explain what other measures you might want to add under the customer perspective and why.
3. Would you have included some measure of employee satisfaction in the learning-and-growth perspective and new-product development in the internal-business-process perspective? That is, do you think employee satisfaction and development of new products are critical for Lee to implement its strategy? Why or why not? Explain briefly.
4. What problems, if any, do you see in Lee improving quality and significantly downsizing to eliminate unused capacity?

13-37 Partial productivity measurement. Gerhart Company manufactures wallets from fabric. In 2011, Gerhart made 2,520,000 wallets using 2,000,000 yards of fabric. In 2011, Gerhart has capacity to make 3,307,500 wallets and incurs a cost of $9,922,500 for this capacity. In 2012, Gerhart plans to make 2,646,000 wallets, make fabric use more efficient, and reduce capacity.

Suppose that in 2012 Gerhart makes 2,646,000 wallets, uses 1,764,000 yards of fabric, and reduces capacity to 2,700,000 wallets, incurring a cost of $8,370,000 for this capacity.

Required

1. Calculate the partial-productivity ratios for materials and conversion (capacity costs) for 2012, and compare them to a benchmark for 2011 calculated based on 2012 output.
2. How can Gerhart Company use the information from the partial-productivity calculations?

13-38 Total factor productivity (continuation of 13-37). Refer to the data for Problem 13-37. Assume the fabric costs $3.70 per yard in 2012 and $3.85 per yard in 2011.

Required

1. Compute Gerhart Company's total factor productivity (TFP) for 2012.
2. Compare TFP for 2012 with a benchmark TFP for 2011 inputs based on 2012 prices and output.
3. What additional information does TFP provide that partial productivity measures do not?

Collaborative Learning Problem

13-39 Strategic analysis of operating income. Halsey Company sells women's clothing. Halsey's strategy is to offer a wide selection of clothes and excellent customer service and to charge a premium price. Halsey presents the following data for 2010 and 2011. For simplicity, assume that each customer purchases one piece of clothing.

	2010	2011
1. Pieces of clothing purchased and sold	40,000	40,000
2. Average selling price	$60	$59
3. Average cost per piece of clothing	$40	$41
4. Selling and customer-service capacity	51,000 customers	43,000 customers
5. Selling and customer-service costs	$357,000	$296,700
6. Selling and customer-service capacity cost per customer (row 5 ÷ row 4)	$7 per customer	$6.90 per customer
7. Purchasing and administrative capacity	980 designs	850 designs
8. Purchasing and administrative costs	$245,000	$204,000
9. Purchasing and administrative capacity cost per distinct design (row 8 ÷ row 7)	$250 per design	$240 per design

Total selling and customer-service costs depend on the number of customers that Halsey has created capacity to support, not the actual number of customers that Halsey serves. Total purchasing and administrative costs depend on purchasing and administrative capacity that Halsey has created (defined in terms of the number of distinct clothing designs that Halsey can purchase and administer). Purchasing and administrative costs do not depend on the actual number of distinct clothing designs purchased. Halsey purchased 930 distinct designs in 2010 and 820 distinct designs in 2011.

At the start of 2010, Halsey planned to increase operating income by 10% over operating income in 2011.

Required

1. Is Halsey's strategy one of product differentiation or cost leadership? Explain.
2. Calculate Halsey's operating income in 2010 and 2011.
3. Calculate the growth, price-recovery, and productivity components of changes in operating income between 2010 and 2011.
4. Does the strategic analysis of operating income indicate Halsey was successful in implementing its strategy in 2011? Explain.

Cost Allocation, Customer-Profitability Analysis, and Sales-Variance Analysis

From Chapter 14 of *Cost Accounting: A Managerial Emphasis*, 14/e. Charles T. Horngren. Srikant M. Datar. Madhav Rajan.

Cost Allocation, Customer-Profitability Analysis, and Sales-Variance Analysis

Companies desperately want to make their customers happy.

But how far should they go to please them, and at what price? At what point are you better off not doing business with some customers at all? The following article explains why it's so important for managers to be able to figure out how profitable each of their customers is.

Minding the Store: Analyzing Customers, Best Buy Decides Not All Are Welcome[1]

As the former CEO of Best Buy, Brad Anderson decided to implement a rather unorthodox approach to retail: to separate his 1.5 million daily customers into "angels" and "devils."

The angels, customers who increase profits by purchasing high-definition televisions, portable electronics, and newly released DVDs without waiting for markdowns or rebates, are favored over the devils, who buy products, apply for rebates, return the purchases, and then buy them back at returned-merchandise discounts. These devils focus their spending on "loss leaders," discounted merchandise designed to encourage store traffic, but then flip the goods at a profit on sites like eBay.com.

Best Buy found that its most desirable customers fell into five distinct groups: upper-income men, suburban mothers, small-business owners, young family men, and technology enthusiasts. Male technology enthusiasts, nicknamed Buzzes, are early adopters, interested in buying and showing off the latest gadgets. Each store analyzes the demographics of its local market, and then focuses on two of these groups. For example, at stores popular with Buzzes, Best Buy sets up videogame areas with leather chairs and game players hooked to mammoth, plasma-screen televisions.

Best Buy also began working on ways to deter customers who drove profits down. It couldn't bar them from its stores. Starting in 2004, however, it began taking steps to put a stop to their most damaging practices by enforcing a restocking fee of 15% of the purchase price on returned merchandise. To discourage customers who return items with the intention of repurchasing them at an "open-box" discount, Best Buy started reselling the returned items

[1] *Sources*: Bustillo, Miguel. 2009. Best Buy confronts newer nemesis. *Wall Street Journal*, March 16; McWilliams, Gary. 2004. Minding the store: Analyzing customers, Best Buy decides not all are welcome. *Wall Street Journal*, November 8.

over the Internet, so the goods didn't reappear in the store where they were originally purchased.

This strategy stimulated growth for several years at Best Buy and helped the company survive the economic downturn while Circuit City, its leading competitor, went bankrupt. But Best Buy's angels and devils strategy now must confront a new competitor, Walmart. With Walmart's focus on consumers seeking no-frills bargains, Best Buy intends to match its new

competitor's prices while leveraging its tech-savvy sales force to help consumers navigate increasingly complicated technology.

To determine which product, customer, program, or department is profitable, organizations must decide how to allocate costs. Best Buy analyzed its operations and chose to allocate costs towards serving its most profitable customers. In this chapter, we provide insight into cost allocation. The emphasis in this chapter is on macro issues in cost allocation: allocation of costs into divisions, plants, and customers.

Purposes of Cost Allocation

Recall that *indirect costs* of a particular cost object are costs that are related to that cost object but cannot be traced to it in an economically feasible (cost-effective) way. These costs often comprise a large percentage of the overall costs assigned to such cost objects as products, customers, and distribution channels. Why do managers allocate indirect costs to these cost objects? Exhibit 1 illustrates four purposes of cost allocation.

Different sets of costs are appropriate for different purposes described in Exhibit 1. Consider costs in different business functions of the value chain illustrated as follows:

Learning Objective 1

Identify four purposes for allocating costs to cost objects

. . . to provide information for decisions, motivate managers, justify costs, and measure income

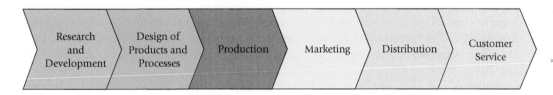

For some decisions related to the economic-decision purpose (for example, long-run product pricing), the costs in all six functions are relevant. For other decisions, particularly short-run economic decisions (for example, make or buy decisions), costs from only one or two functions, such as design and manufacturing, might be relevant.

Purpose	Examples
1. To provide information for economic decisions	To decide whether to add a new airline flight To decide whether to manufacture a component part of a television set or to purchase it from another manufacturer To decide on the selling price for a customized product or service To evaluate the cost of available capacity used to support different products
2. To motivate managers and other employees	To encourage the design of products that are simpler to manufacture or less costly to service To encourage sales representatives to emphasize high-margin products or services
3. To justify costs or compute reimbursement amounts	To cost products at a "fair" price, often required by law and government defense contracts To compute reimbursement for a consulting firm based on a percentage of the cost savings resulting from the implementation of its recommendations
4. To measure income and assets	To cost inventories for reporting to external parties To cost inventories for reporting to tax authorities

For the motivation purpose, costs from more than one but not all business functions are often included to emphasize to decision makers how costs in different functions are related to one another. For example, to estimate product costs, product designers at companies such as Hitachi and Toshiba include costs of production, distribution, and customer service. The goal is to focus designers' attention on how different product-design alternatives affect total costs.

For the cost-reimbursement purpose, a particular contract will often stipulate what costs will be reimbursed. For instance, cost-reimbursement rules for U.S. government contracts explicitly exclude marketing costs.

For the purpose of income and asset measurement for reporting to external parties under GAAP, only manufacturing costs, and in some cases product-design costs, are inventoriable and allocated to products. In the United States, R&D costs in most industries, marketing, distribution, and customer-service costs are period costs that are expensed as they are incurred. Under International Financial Reporting Standards (IFRS), research costs must be expensed as incurred but development costs must be capitalized if a product/process has reached technical feasibility and the firm has the intention and ability to use or sell the future asset.

Criteria to Guide Cost-Allocation Decisions

After identifying the purposes of cost allocation, managers and management accountants must decide how to allocate costs.

Exhibit 2 presents four criteria used to guide cost-allocation decisions. These decisions affect both the number of indirect-cost pools and the cost-allocation base for each indirect-cost pool. We emphasize the superiority of the cause-and-effect and the benefits-received criteria, especially when the purpose of cost allocation is to provide information for economic decisions or to motivate managers and employees.[2] Cause and effect is the primary criterion used in activity-based costing (ABC) applications. ABC systems use the concept of a cost hierarchy to identify the cost drivers that best demonstrate the cause-and-effect relationship between each activity and the costs in the related cost pool. The cost drivers are then chosen as cost-allocation bases.

Fairness and ability-to-bear are less-frequently-used and more problematic criteria than cause-and-effect or benefits-received. Fairness is a difficult criterion on which to

[2] The Federal Accounting Standards Advisory Board (which sets standards for management accounting for U.S. government departments and agencies) recommends the following: "Cost assignments should be performed by: (a) directly tracing costs whenever feasible and economically practicable, (b) assigning costs on a cause-and-effect basis, and (c) allocating costs on a reasonable and consistent basis" (*FASAB*, 1995, p. 12).

Exhibit 2

Criteria for Cost-
Allocation Decisions

1. Cause and Effect. Using this criterion, managers identify the variables that cause resources to be consumed. For example, managers may use hours of testing as the variable when allocating the costs of a quality-testing area to products. Cost allocations based on the cause-and-effect criterion are likely to be the most credible to operating personnel.

2. Benefits Received. Using this criterion, managers identify the beneficiaries of the outputs of the cost object. The costs of the cost object are allocated among the beneficiaries in proportion to the benefits each receives. Consider a corporatewide advertising program that promotes the general image of the corporation rather than any individual product. The costs of this program may be allocated on the basis of division revenues; the higher the revenues, the higher the division's allocated cost of the advertising program. The rationale behind this allocation is that divisions with higher revenues apparently benefited from the advertising more than divisions with lower revenues and, therefore, ought to be allocated more of the advertising costs.

3. Fairness or Equity. This criterion is often cited in government contracts when cost allocations are the basis for establishing a price satisfactory to the government and its suppliers. Cost allocation here is viewed as a "reasonable" or "fair" means of establishing a selling price in the minds of the contracting parties. For most allocation decisions, fairness is a matter of judgment rather than an operational criterion.

4. Ability to Bear. This criterion advocates allocating costs in proportion to the cost object's ability to bear costs allocated to it. An example is the allocation of corporate executive salaries on the basis of division operating income. The presumption is that the more-profitable divisions have a greater ability to absorb corporate headquarters' costs.

obtain agreement. What one party views as fair, another party may view as unfair.[3] For example, a university may view allocating a share of general administrative costs to government contracts as fair because general administrative costs are incurred to support all activities of the university. The government may view the allocation of such costs as unfair because the general administrative costs would have been incurred by the university regardless of whether the government contract existed. Perhaps the fairest way to resolve this issue is to understand, as well as possible, the cause-and-effect relationship between the government contract activity and general administrative costs. In other words, fairness is more a matter of judgment than an easily implementable choice criterion.

To get a sense of the issues that arise when using the ability-to-bear criterion, consider a product that consumes a large amount of indirect costs and currently sells for a price below its direct costs. This product has no ability to bear any of the indirect costs it uses. However, if the indirect costs it consumes are allocated to other products, these other products are subsidizing the product that is losing money. An integrated airline, for example, might allocate fewer costs to its activities in a highly contested market such as freight transportation, thereby subsidizing it via passenger transport. Some airports cross-subsidize costs associated with serving airline passengers through sales of duty-free goods. Such practices provide a distorted view of relative product and service profitability, and have the potential to invite both regulatory scrutiny as well as competitors attempting to undercut artificially higher-priced services.

Most importantly, companies must weigh the costs and benefits when designing and implementing their cost allocations. Companies incur costs not only in collecting data but also in taking the time to educate managers about cost allocations. In general, the more complex the cost allocations, the higher these education costs.

The costs of designing and implementing complex cost allocations are highly visible. Unfortunately, the benefits from using well-designed cost allocations, such as enabling managers to make better-informed sourcing decisions, pricing decisions, cost-control decisions, and so on, are difficult to measure. Nevertheless, when making cost allocations, managers should consider the benefits as well as the costs. As costs of collecting and processing information decrease, companies are building more-detailed cost allocations.

Decision Point

What criteria should managers use to guide cost-allocation decisions?

---

[3] Kaplow and Shavell, in a review of the legal literature, note that "notions of fairness are many and varied. They are analyzed and rationalized by different writers in different way, and they also typically depend upon the circumstances under consideration. Accordingly, it is not possible to identify and consensus view on these notions..." See L. Kaplow and S. Shavell, "Fairness Versus Welfare," *Harvard Law Review* (February 2001); and L. Kaplow and S. Shavell, *Fairness Versus Welfare* (Boston: Harvard University Press, 2002).

Cost Allocation Decisions

In this section, we focus on the first purpose of cost allocation: to provide information for economic decisions, such as pricing, by measuring the full costs of delivering products based on an ABC system.

ABC systems define indirect-cost pools for different activities and use cost drivers as allocation bases to assign costs of indirect-cost pools to products (the second stage of cost allocation). In this section, we focus on the first stage of cost allocation, the assignment of costs to indirect-cost pools.

We will use Consumer Appliances, Inc. (CAI), to illustrate how costs incurred in different parts of a company can be assigned, and then reassigned, for costing products, services, customers, or contracts. CAI has two divisions; each has its own manufacturing plant. The refrigerator division has a plant in Minneapolis, and the clothes dryer division has a plant in St. Paul. CAI's headquarters is in a separate location in Minneapolis. Each division manufactures and sells multiple products that differ in size and complexity.

CAI's management team collects costs at the following levels:

- **Corporate costs**—There are three major categories of corporate costs:
  1. **Treasury costs**—$900,000 of costs incurred for financing the construction of new assembly equipment in the two divisions. The cost of new assembly equipment is $5,200,000 in the refrigerator division and $3,800,000 in the clothes dryer division.
  2. **Human resource management costs**—recruitment and ongoing employee training and development, $1,600,000.
  3. **Corporate administration costs**—executive salaries, rent, and general administration costs, $5,400,000.

- **Division costs**—Each division has two direct-cost categories (direct materials and direct manufacturing labor) and seven indirect-cost pools—one cost pool each for the five activities (design, setup, manufacturing, distribution, and administration), one cost pool to accumulate facility costs, and one cost pool for the allocated corporate treasury costs. Exhibit 3 presents data for six of the division indirect-cost pools and cost-allocation bases. (In a later section, we describe how corporate treasury

Exhibit 3 Division Indirect-Cost Pools and Cost-Allocation Bases, CAI, for Refrigerator Division (R) and Clothes Dryer Division (CD)

Division Indirect-Cost Pools	Example of Costs		Total Indirect Costs	Cost Hierarchy Category	Cost-Allocation Base	Cause-and-Effect Relationship That Motivates Management's Choice of Allocation Base
Design	Design engineering salaries	(R) (CD)	$6,000,000 4,250,000	Product sustaining	Parts times cubic feet	Complex products (more parts and larger size) require greater design resources.
Setup of machines	Setup labor and equipment cost	(R) (CD)	$3,000,000 2,400,000	Batch level	Setup-hours	Overhead costs of the setup activity increase as setup-hours increase.
Manufacturing operations	Plant and equipment, energy	(R) (CD)	$25,000,000 18,750,000	Output unit level	Machine-hours	Manufacturing-operations overhead costs support machines and, hence, increase with machine usage.
Distribution	Shipping labor and equipment	(R) (CD)	$8,000,000 5,500,000	Output unit level	Cubic feet	Distribution-overhead costs increase with cubic feet of product shipped.
Administration	Division executive salaries	(R) (CD)	$1,000,000 800,000	Facility sustaining	Revenues	Weak relationship between division executive salaries and revenues, but justified by CAI on a benefits-received basis.
Facility	Annual building and space costs	(R) (CD)	$4,500,000 3,500,000	All	Square feet	Facility costs increase with square feet of space.

costs are allocated to each division to create the seventh division indirect-cost pool.) CAI identifies the cost hierarchy category for each cost pool: output-unit level, batch level, product sustaining level, and facility-sustaining level.

Exhibit 4 presents an overview diagram of the allocation of corporate and division indirect costs to products of the refrigerator division. Note: The clothes dryer division has its own seven indirect-cost pools used to allocate costs to products. These cost pools and cost-allocation bases parallel the indirect-cost pools and allocation bases for the refrigerator division.

Look first at the middle row of the exhibit, where you see "Division Indirect-Cost Pools," and scan the lower half.

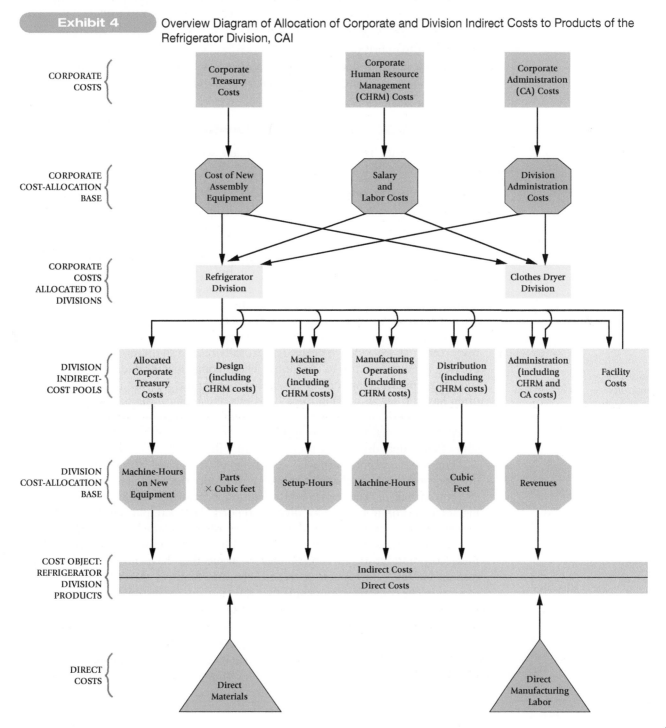

Exhibit 4 Overview Diagram of Allocation of Corporate and Division Indirect Costs to Products of the Refrigerator Division, CAI

In the lower half of Exhibit 4 is the cost pool called Facility Costs (far right, middle row), which accumulates all annual costs of buildings and furnishings (such as depreciation) incurred in the division. The arrows in Exhibit 4 indicate that CAI allocates facility costs to the five activity-cost pools. Recall from Exhibit 3 that CAI uses square feet area required for various activities (design, setup, manufacturing, distribution, and administration) to allocate these facility costs. These activity-cost pools then include the costs of the building and facilities needed to perform the various activities.

The costs in the six remaining indirect-cost pools (that is, after costs of the facility cost pool have been allocated to other cost pools) are allocated to products on the basis of cost drivers described in Exhibit 3. These cost drivers are chosen as the cost-allocation bases because there is a cause-and-effect relationship between the cost drivers and the costs in the indirect-cost pool. A cost rate per unit is calculated for each cost-allocation base. Indirect costs are allocated to products on the basis of the total quantity of the cost allocation base for each activity used by the product.

Next focus on the upper half of Exhibit 4: how corporate costs are allocated to divisions and then to indirect-cost pools.

Before getting into the details of the allocations, let's first consider some broader choices that CAI faces regarding the allocation of corporate costs.

Allocating Corporate Costs to Divisions and Products

CAI's management team has several choices to make when accumulating and allocating corporate costs to divisions.

1. Which corporate-cost categories should CAI allocate as indirect costs of the divisions? Should CAI allocate all corporate costs or only some of them?
   - Some companies allocate all corporate costs to divisions because corporate costs are incurred to support division activities. Allocating all corporate costs motivates division managers to examine how corporate costs are planned and controlled. Also, companies that want to calculate the full cost of products must allocate all corporate costs to indirect-cost pools of divisions.
   - Other companies do not allocate corporate costs to divisions because these costs are not controllable by division managers.
   - Still other companies allocate only those corporate costs, such as corporate human resources, that are widely perceived as causally related to division activities or that provide explicit benefits to divisions. These companies exclude corporate costs such as corporate donations to charitable foundations because division managers often have no say in making these decisions and because the benefits to the divisions are less evident or too remote. If a company decides not to allocate some or all corporate costs, this results in total company profitability being less than the sum of individual division or product profitabilities.

     For some decision purposes, allocating some but not all corporate costs to divisions may be the preferred alternative. Consider the performance evaluation of division managers. The controllability notion is frequently used to justify excluding some corporate costs from division reports. For example, salaries of the top management at corporate headquarters are often excluded from responsibility accounting reports of division managers. Although divisions tend to benefit from these corporate costs, division managers argue they have no say in ("are not responsible for") how much of these corporate resources they use or how much they cost. The contrary argument is that full allocation is justified because the divisions receive benefits from all corporate costs.

2. When allocating corporate costs to divisions, should CAI allocate only costs that vary with division activity or should the company assign fixed costs as well? Companies allocate both variable and fixed costs to divisions and then to products, because the resulting product costs are useful for making long-run strategic decisions, such as which products to sell and at what price. To make good long-run decisions, managers

need to know the cost of all resources (whether variable or fixed) required to produce products. Why? Because in the long run, firms can manage the levels of virtually all of their costs; very few costs are truly fixed. Moreover, to survive and prosper in the long run, firms must ensure that the prices charged for products exceed the total resources consumed to produce them, regardless of whether these costs are variable or fixed in the short run.

Companies that allocate corporate costs to divisions must carefully identify relevant costs for specific decisions. Suppose a division is profitable before any corporate costs are allocated but "unprofitable" after allocation of corporate costs. Should the division be closed down? The relevant corporate costs in this case are not the allocated corporate costs but those corporate costs that will be saved if the division is closed. If division profits exceed the relevant corporate costs, the division should not be closed.

3. If CAI allocates corporate costs to divisions, how many cost pools should it use? One extreme is to aggregate all corporate costs into a single cost pool. The other extreme is to have numerous individual corporate cost pools. A major consideration is to construct **homogeneous cost pools** so that all of the costs in the cost pool have the same or a similar cause-and-effect or benefits-received relationship with the cost-allocation base.

For example, when allocating corporate costs to divisions, CAI can combine corporate administration costs and corporate human-resource-management costs into a single cost pool if both cost categories have the same or similar cause-and-effect relationship with the same cost-allocation base (such as the number of employees in each division). If, however, each cost category has a cause-and-effect relationship with a different cost-allocation base (for example, number of employees in each division affects corporate human-resource-management costs, whereas revenues of each division affect corporate administration costs), CAI will prefer to maintain separate cost pools for each of these costs. Determining homogeneous cost pools requires judgment and should be revisited on a regular basis.

The benefit of using a multiple cost-pool system must be balanced against the costs of implementing it. Advances in information-gathering technology make it more likely that multiple cost-pool systems will pass the cost-benefit test.

Implementing Corporate Cost Allocations

After much discussion and debate, CAI's management team chooses to allocate all corporate costs to divisions. We now illustrate the allocation of corporate costs to divisions in CAI's ABC system.

The demands for corporate resources by the refrigerator division and the clothes dryer division depend on the demands that each division's products place on these resources. The top half of Exhibit 4 graphically represents the allocations.

1. CAI allocates treasury costs to each division on the basis of the cost of new assembly equipment installed in each division (the cost driver of treasury costs). It allocates the $900,000 of treasury costs as follows (using information from p. 506):

$$\text{Refrigerator Division: } \$900,000 \times \frac{\$5,200,000}{\$5,200,000 + \$3,800,000} = \$520,000$$

$$\text{Clothes Dryer Division: } \$900,000 \times \frac{\$3,800,000}{\$5,200,000 + \$3,800,000} = \$380,000$$

Each division then creates a *separate cost pool* consisting of the allocated corporate treasury costs and reallocates these costs to products on the basis of machine-hours used on the new equipment. Treasury costs are an output unit-level cost because they represent resources used on activities performed on each individual unit of a product.

2. CAI's analysis indicates that the demand for corporate human resource management (CHRM) costs for recruitment and training varies with total salary and labor costs in

each division. Suppose salary and labor costs are \$44,000,000 in the refrigerator division and \$36,000,000 in the clothes dryer division. Then CHRM costs are allocated to the divisions as follows:

$$\text{Refrigerator Division: } \$1,600,000 \times \frac{\$44,000,000}{\$44,000,000 + \$36,000,000} = \$880,000$$

$$\text{Clothes Dryer Division: } \$1,600,000 \times \frac{\$36,000,000}{\$44,000,000 + \$36,000,000} = \$720,000$$

Each division reallocates the CHRM costs allocated to it to the indirect-cost pools—design, machine setup, manufacturing operations, distribution, and division administration (the allocated-corporate-treasury cost pool and the facility costs pool have no salary and labor costs, so no CHRM costs are allocated to them)—on the basis of total salary and labor costs of each indirect-cost pool. CHRM costs that are added to division indirect-cost pools are then allocated to products using the cost driver for the respective cost pool. Therefore, CHRM costs are product-sustaining costs (for the portion of CHRM costs allocated to the design cost pool), batch-level costs (for the portion of CHRM costs allocated to the machine-setup cost pool), output unit-level costs (for the portions of CHRM costs allocated to the manufacturing-operations and distribution cost pools), and facility-sustaining costs (for the portion of CHRM costs allocated to the division-administration cost pool).

3. CAI allocates corporate administration costs to each division on the basis of division-administration costs (Exhibit 3 shows the amounts of division-administration costs) because corporate administration's main role is to support division administration.

$$\text{Refrigerator Division: } \$5,400,000 \times \frac{\$1,000,000}{\$1,000,000 + \$800,000} = \$3,000,000$$

$$\text{Clothes Dryer Division: } \$5,400,000 \times \frac{\$800,000}{\$1,000,000 + \$800,000} = \$2,400,000$$

Each division adds the allocated corporate-administration costs to the division-administration cost pool. The costs in this cost pool are facility-sustaining costs and do not have a cause-and-effect relationship with individual products produced and sold by each division. CAI's policy, however, is to allocate all costs to products so that CAI's division managers become aware of all costs incurred at CAI in their pricing and other decisions. It allocates the division-administration costs (including allocated corporate-administration costs) to products on the basis of product revenues (a benefits-received criterion).

The issues discussed in this section regarding divisions and products apply nearly identically to customers, as we shall show next.

Learning Objective 4

Discuss why a company's revenues and costs can differ across customers

. . . revenues can differ because of differences in the quantity purchased and the price discounts given, while costs can differ because different customers place different demands on a company's resources

Customer-Profitability Analysis

Customer-profitability analysis is the reporting and assessment of revenues earned from customers and the costs incurred to earn those revenues. An analysis of customer differences in revenues and costs can provide insight into why differences exist in the operating income earned from different customers. Managers use this information to ensure that customers making large contributions to the operating income of a company receive a high level of attention from the company.

Consider Spring Distribution Company, which sells bottled water. It has two distribution channels: (1) a wholesale distribution channel, in which the wholesaler sells to supermarkets, drugstores, and other stores, and (2) a retail distribution channel for a small number of business customers. We focus mainly on customer-profitability analysis in Spring's retail distribution channel. The list selling price in this channel is \$14.40 per case

(24 bottles). The full cost to Spring is $12 per case. If every case is sold at list price in this distribution channel, Spring would earn a gross margin of $2.40 per case.

Customer-Revenue Analysis

Consider revenues from 4 of Spring's 10 retail customers in June 2012:

	A	B	C	D	E
		Home Insert Page Layout Formulas Data Review View			
1		**CUSTOMER**			
2		**A**	**B**	**G**	**J**
3	Cases sold	42,000	33,000	2,900	2,500
4	List selling price	$ 14.40	$ 14.40	$ 14.40	$ 14.40
5	Price discount	$ 0.96	$ 0.24	$ 1.20	$ 0.00
6	Invoice price	$ 13.44	$ 14.16	$ 13.20	$ 14.40
7	Revenues (Row 3 × Row 6)	$564,480	$467,280	$38,280	$36,000

Two variables explain revenue differences across these four customers: (1) the number of cases they purchased and (2) the magnitude of price discounting. A **price discount** is the reduction in selling price below list selling price to encourage customers to purchase more. Companies that record only the final invoice price in their information system cannot readily track the magnitude of their price discounting.[4]

Price discounts are a function of multiple factors, including the volume of product purchased (higher-volume customers receive higher discounts) and the desire to sell to a customer who might help promote sales to other customers. Discounts could also be because of poor negotiating by a salesperson or the unwanted effect of an incentive plan based only on revenues. At no time should price discounts run afoul of the law by way of price discrimination, predatory pricing, or collusive pricing.

Tracking price discounts by customer and by salesperson helps improve customer profitability. For example, Spring Distribution may decide to strictly enforce its volume-based price discounting policy. It may also require its salespeople to obtain approval for giving large discounts to customers who do not normally qualify for such discounts. In addition, the company could track the future sales of customers who its salespeople have given sizable price discounts to because of their "high growth potential." For example, Spring should track future sales to customer G to see if the $1.20-per-case discount translates into higher future sales.

Customer revenues are one element of customer profitability. The other element that is equally important to understand is the cost of acquiring, serving, and retaining customers. We study this topic next.

Customer-Cost Analysis

A **customer-cost hierarchy** categorizes costs related to customers into different cost pools on the basis of different types of cost drivers, or cost-allocation bases, or different degrees of difficulty in determining cause-and-effect or benefits-received relationships. Spring's ABC system focuses on customers rather than products. It has one direct cost, the cost of bottled water, and multiple indirect-cost pools. Spring identifies five categories of indirect costs in its customer-cost hierarchy:

1. **Customer output unit-level costs**—costs of activities to sell each unit (case) to a customer. An example is product-handling costs of each case sold.

---

[4] Further analysis of customer revenues could distinguish gross revenues from net revenues. This approach highlights differences across customers in sales returns. Additional discussion of ways to analyze revenue differences across customers is in R. S. Kaplan and R. Cooper, *Cost and Effect* (Boston, MA: Harvard Business School Press, 1998, Chapter 10); and G. Cokins, *Activity-Based Cost Management: An Executive's Guide* (New York: John Wiley & Sons, 2001, Chapter 3).

2. **Customer batch-level costs**—costs of activities related to a group of units (cases) sold to a customer. Examples are costs incurred to process orders or to make deliveries.

3. **Customer-sustaining costs**—costs of activities to support individual customers, regardless of the number of units or batches of product delivered to the customer. Examples are costs of visits to customers or costs of displays at customer sites.

4. **Distribution-channel costs**—costs of activities related to a particular distribution channel rather than to each unit of product, each batch of product, or specific customers. An example is the salary of the manager of Spring's retail distribution channel.

5. **Corporate-sustaining costs**—costs of activities that cannot be traced to individual customers or distribution channels. Examples are top-management and general-administration costs.

Spring has one additional cost hierarchy category, distribution-channel costs, for the costs it incurs to support its wholesale and retail distribution channels.

Customer-Level Costs

Spring is particularly interested in analyzing *customer-level indirect costs*—costs incurred in the first three categories of the customer-cost hierarchy: customer output-unit-level costs, customer batch-level costs, and customer-sustaining costs. Spring wants to work with customers to reduce these costs. It believes customer actions will have less impact on distribution-channel and corporate-sustaining costs. The following table shows five activities (in addition to cost of goods sold) that Spring identifies as resulting in customer-level costs. The table indicates the cost drivers and cost-driver rates for each activity, as well as the cost-hierarchy category for each activity.

	G	H	I	J
	Home	Insert	Page Layout Formulas Data Review View	
1	**Activity Area**	**Cost Driver and Rate**		**Cost-Hierarchy Category**
2	Product handling	$0.50	per case sold	Customer output-unit-level costs
3	Order taking	$ 100	per purchase order	Customer batch-level costs
4	Delivery vehicles	$ 2	per delivery mile traveled	Customer batch-level costs
5	Rush deliveries	$ 300	per expedited delivery	Customer batch-level costs
6	Visits to customers	$ 80	per sales visit	Customer-sustaining costs

Information on the quantity of cost drivers used by each of four customers is as follows:

	A	B	C	D	E
	Home Insert Page Layout Formulas Data Review				
10			**CUSTOMER**		
11		**A**	**B**	**G**	**J**
12	Number of purchase orders	30	25	15	10
13	Number of deliveries	60	30	20	15
14	Miles traveled per delivery	5	12	20	6
15	Number of rush deliveries	1	0	2	0
16	Number of visits to customers	6	5	4	3

Exhibit 5 shows a customer-profitability analysis for the four retail customers using information on customer revenues previously presented and customer-level costs from the ABC system.

Spring Distribution can use the information in Exhibit 5 to work with customers to reduce the quantity of activities needed to support them. Consider a comparison of customer G and customer A. Customer G purchases only 7% of the cases that customer A purchases (2,900 versus 42,000). Yet, compared with customer A, customer G uses one-half as many purchase orders, two-thirds as many visits to customers, one-third as many deliveries, and twice as many rush deliveries. By implementing charges for each of these services, Spring might be able to induce customer G to make fewer but larger purchase orders, and require fewer customer visits, deliveries, and rush deliveries while looking to increase sales in the future.

Consider Owens and Minor, a distributor of medical supplies to hospitals. It strategically prices each of its services separately. For example, if a hospital wants a rush delivery or special packaging, Owens and Minor charges the hospital an additional price for each particular service. How have Owens and Minor's customers reacted? Hospitals that value these services continue to demand and pay for them while hospitals that do not value these services stop asking for them, saving Owens and Minor some costs. Owens and Minor's pricing strategy influences customer behavior in a way that increases its revenues or decreases its costs.

The ABC system also highlights a second opportunity for cost reduction. Spring can seek to reduce the costs of each activity. For example, improving the efficiency of the ordering process (such as by having customers order electronically) can reduce costs even if customers place the same number of orders.

Exhibit 6 shows a monthly operating income statement for Spring Distribution. The customer-level operating income of customers A and B in Exhibit 5 are shown in columns 8 and 9 of Exhibit 6. The format of Exhibit 6 is based on Spring's cost hierarchy. All costs incurred to serve customers are not included in customer-level costs and therefore are not allocated to customers in Exhibit 6. For example, distribution-channel costs such as the salary of the manager of the retail distribution channel are not included in customer-level costs and are not allocated to customers. Instead, these costs are identified as costs of the retail channel as a whole, because Spring's management believes that changes in customer behavior will not affect distribution-channel costs. These costs will be affected only by decisions pertaining to the whole channel, such as a decision to discontinue retail distribution. Another reason Spring does not allocate distribution-channel costs to customers is motivation. Spring's managers contend that

Exhibit 5	Customer-Profitability Analysis for Four Retail Channel Customers of Spring Distribution for June 2012

	Home	Insert	Page Layout	Formulas	Data	Review	View			
	A						B	C	D	E
1							CUSTOMER			
2							A	B	G	J
3	Revenues at list price: $14.40 × 42,000; 33,000; 2,900; 2,500						$604,800	$475,200	$41,760	$36,000
4	Price discount: $0.96 x 42,000; $0.24 × 33,000; $1.20 × 2,900; $0 × 2,500						40,320	7,920	3,480	0
5	Revenues (at actual price)						564,480	467,280	38,280	36,000
6	Cost of goods sold: $12 × 42,000; 33,000; 2,900; 2,500						504,000	396,000	34,800	30,000
7	Gross margin						60,480	71,280	3,480	6,000
8	Customer-level operating costs									
9	Product handling $0.50 × 42,000; 33,000; 2,900; 2,500						21,000	16,500	1,450	1,250
10	Order taking $100 × 30; 25; 15; 10						3,000	2,500	1,500	1,000
11	Delivery vehicles $2 × (5 × 60); (12 × 30); (20 × 20); (6 × 15)						600	720	800	180
12	Rush deliveries $300 × 1; 0; 2; 0						300	0	600	0
13	Visits to customers $80 × 6; 5; 4; 3						480	400	320	240
14	Total customer-level operating costs						25,380	20,120	4,670	2,670
15	Customer-level operating income						$ 35,100	$ 51,160	$(1,190)	$ 3,330

| Exhibit 6 | Income Statement of Spring Distribution for June 2012 |

| | Home | Insert | Page Layout | Formulas | Data | Review | View |

	A	B	C	D	E	F	G	H	I	J	K	L	M
1					CUSTOMER DISTRIBUTION CHANNELS								
2			Wholesale Customers						Retail Customers				
3		Total	Total	A1	A2	A3	▪		Total	A[a]	B[a]	C	▪
4		(1) = (2) + (7)	(2)	(3)	(4)	(5)	(6)		(7)	(8)	(9)	(10)	(11)
5	Revenues (at actual prices)	$12,138,120	$10,107,720	$1,946,000	$1,476,000	▪	▪		$2,030,400	$564,480	$467,280	▪	▪
6	Customer-level costs	11,633,760	9,737,280	1,868,000	1,416,000	▪	▪		1,896,480	529,380[b]	416,120[b]	▪	▪
7	Customer-level operating income	504,360	370,440	$ 78,000	$ 60,000	▪	▪		133,920	$ 35,100	$ 51,160	▪	▪
8	Distribution-channel costs	160,500	102,500						58,000				
9	Distribution-channel-level operating income	343,860	$ 267,940						$ 75,920				
10	Corporate-sustaining costs	263,000											
11	Operating income	$ 80,860											
12													
13	[a]Full details are presented in Exhibit 14-5.												
14	[b]Cost of goods sold + Total customer-level operating costs from Exhibit 14-5.												

Decision Point ▶

How can a company's revenues and costs differ across customers?

salespersons responsible for managing individual customer accounts would lose motivation if their bonuses were affected by the allocation to customers of distribution-channel costs over which they had minimal influence.

Next, consider corporate-sustaining costs such as top-management and general-administration costs. Spring's managers have concluded that there is no cause-and-effect or benefits-received relationship between any cost-allocation base and corporate-sustaining costs. Consequently, allocation of corporate-sustaining costs serves no useful purpose in decision making, performance evaluation, or motivation. For example, suppose Spring allocated the $263,000 of corporate-sustaining costs to its distribution channels: $173,000 to the wholesale channel and $90,000 to the retail channel. Using information from Exhibit 6, the retail channel would then show a loss of $14,080 ($75,920 – $90,000).

If this same situation persisted in subsequent months, should Spring shut down the retail distribution channel? No, because if retail distribution were discontinued, corporate-sustaining costs would be unaffected. Allocating corporate-sustaining costs to distribution channels could give the misleading impression that the potential cost savings from discontinuing a distribution channel would be greater than the likely amount.

Some managers and management accountants advocate fully allocating all costs to customers and distribution channels so that (1) the sum of operating incomes of all customers in a distribution channel (segment) equals the operating income of the distribution channel and (2) the sum of the distribution-channel operating incomes equals company-wide operating income. These managers and management accountants argue that customers and products must eventually be profitable on a full-cost basis. In the previous example, CAI allocated all corporate and division-level costs to its refrigerator and clothes dryer products. For some decisions, such as pricing, allocating all costs ensures that long-run prices are set at a level to cover the cost of all resources used to produce and sell products. Nevertheless, the value of the hierarchical format in Exhibit 6 is that it distinguishes among various degrees of objectivity when allocating costs, and it dovetails with the different levels at which decisions are made and performance is evaluated. The issue of when and what costs to allocate is another example of the "different costs for different purposes" theme emphasized throughout this text.

Learning Objective 5

Identify the importance of customer-profitability profiles

. . . highlight that a small percentage of customers contributes a large percentage of operating income.

Customer-Profitability Profiles

Customer-profitability profiles provide a useful tool for managers. Exhibit 7 ranks Spring's 10 retail customers based on customer-level operating income. (Four of these customers are analyzed in Exhibit 5.)

Column 4, computed by adding the individual amounts in column 1, shows the cumulative customer-level operating income. For example, customer C has a cumulative

Exhibit 7 Customer-Profitability Analysis for Retail Channel Customers: Spring Distribution, June 2012

	Home	Insert	Page Layout	Formulas	Data	Review	View	
	A	B	C	D	E	F
1	**Customers Ranked on Customer-Level Operating Income**					
2						**Cumulative**
3						**Customer-Level**
4						**Operating Income**
5				**Customer-Level**	**Cumulative**	**as a % of Total**
6	**Retail**	**Customer-Level**	**Customer**	**Operating Income**	**Customer-Level**	**Customer-Level**
7	**Customer**	**Operating Income**	**Revenue**	**Divided by Revenue**	**Operating Income**	**Operating Income**
8	**Code**	**(1)**	**(2)**	**(3) = (1) ÷ (2)**	**(4)**	**(5) = (4) ÷ $133,920**
9	B	$ 51,160	$ 467,280	10.9%	$ 51,160	38%
10	A	35,100	564,480	6.2%	86,260	64%
11	C	27,070	295,640	9.2%	113,330	85%
12	D	20,580	277,000	7.4%	133,910	100%
13	F	12,504	143,500	8.7%	146,414	109%
14	J	3,330	41,000	8.1%	149,744	112%
15	E	176	123,000	0.1%	149,920	112%
16	G	−1,190	38,280	−3.1%	148,730	111%
17	H	−5,690	38,220	−14.9%	143,040	107%
18	I	−9,120	42,000	−21.7%	133,920	100%
19		$133,920	$2,030,400			
20						

income of $113,330 in column 4. This $113,330 is the sum of $51,160 for customer B, $35,100 for customer A, and $27,070 for customer C.

Column 5 shows what percentage the $113,330 *cumulative* total for customers B, A, and C is of the total customer-level operating income of $133,920 earned in the retail distribution channel from all 10 customers. The three most profitable customers contribute 85% of total customer-level operating income. These customers deserve the highest service and priority. Companies try to keep their best customers happy in a number of ways: special phone numbers and upgrade privileges for elite-level frequent flyers, free usage of luxury hotel suites and big credit limits for high-rollers at casinos, and so on. In many companies, it is common for a small number of customers to contribute a high percentage of operating income. Microsoft uses the phrase "not all revenue dollars are endowed equally in profitability" to stress this point.

Column 3 shows the profitability per dollar of revenue by customer. This measure of customer profitability indicates that, although customer A contributes the second-highest operating income, the profitability per dollar of revenue is lower because of high price discounts. Spring's goal is to increase profit margins for customer A by decreasing the price discounts or saving customer-level costs while maintaining or increasing sales. Customer J has a higher profit margin but has lower total sales. Spring's challenge with customer J is to maintain margins while increasing sales.

Presenting Profitability Analysis

There are two common ways of presenting the results of customer-profitability analysis. Managers often find the bar chart presentation in Exhibit 8, Panel A, to be an intuitive way to visualize customer profitability. The highly profitable customers clearly stand out. Moreover, the number of "unprofitable" customers and the magnitude of their losses are apparent. A popular alternative way to express customer profitability is

Exhibit 8

Panel A: Bar Chart of Customer-Level Operating Income for Spring Distribution's Retail Channel Customers in June 2012

Panel B: The Whale Curve of Cumulative Profitability for Spring Distribution's Retail Channel Customers in June 2012

Customer-Level Operating Income

Retail Channel Customers

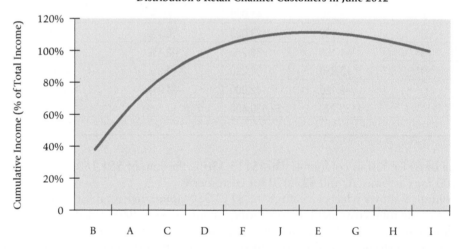

by plotting the contents of column 5 of Exhibit 7. This chart is called the **whale curve** since it is backward bending at the point where customers start to become unprofitable, and thus resembles a humpback whale.[5]

Spring's managers must explore ways to make unprofitable customers profitable. Exhibits 5 to 8 emphasize short-run customer profitability. Other factors managers should consider in deciding how to allocate resources among customers include the following:

- **Likelihood of customer retention.** The more likely a customer will continue to do business with a company, the more valuable the customer. Customers differ in their loyalty and their willingness to frequently "shop their business."

- **Potential for sales growth.** The higher the likely growth of the customer's industry and the customer's sales, the more valuable the customer. Customers to whom a company can cross-sell other products are more desirable.

- **Long-run customer profitability.** This factor will be influenced by the first two factors specified and the cost of customer-support staff and special services required to retain customer accounts.

---

[5] In practice, the curve of the chart can be quite steep. The whale curve for cumulative profitability usually reveals that the most profitable 20% of customers generate between 150% and 300% of total profits, the middle 70% of customers break even, and the least profitable 10% of customers lose from 50% to 200% of total profits (see Robert Kaplan and V.G. Narayanan, Measuring and Managing Customer Profitability, Journal of Cost Management, Sept/Oct 2001, pp. 1–11).

- **Increases in overall demand from having well-known customers.** Customers with established reputations help generate sales from other customers through product endorsements.

- **Ability to learn from customers.** Customers who provide ideas about new products or ways to improve existing products are especially valuable.

Managers should be cautious when deciding to discontinue customers. In Exhibit 7, the current unprofitability of customer G, for example, may provide misleading signals about G's profitability in the long-run. Moreover, as in any ABC-based system, the costs assigned to customer G are not all variable. In the short run, it may well have been efficient for Spring to use its spare capacity to serve G on a contribution-margin basis. Discontinuing customer G will not eliminate all the costs assigned to that customer, and will leave the firm worse off than before.

Of course, particular customers might be chronically unprofitable and hold limited future prospects. Or they might fall outside a firm's target market or require unsustainably high levels of service relative to the firm's strategies and capabilities. In such cases, organizations are becoming increasingly aggressive in severing customer relationships. For example, ING Direct, the largest direct lender and fastest growing financial services organization in the United States, asks 10,000 "high maintenance" customers to close their accounts each month.[6] The Concepts in Action feature on the next page provides an example of a company that is struggling with the question of how to manage its resources and profitability without affecting the satisfaction of its customers.

Using the Five-Step Decision-Making Process to Manage Customer Profitability

The different types of customer analyses that we have just covered provide companies with key information to guide the allocation of resources across customers. Use the five-step decision-making process to think about how managers use these analyses to make customer-management decisions.

1. *Identify the problem and uncertainties.* The problem is how to manage and allocate resources across customers.

2. *Obtain information.* Managers identify past revenues generated by each customer and customer-level costs incurred in the past to support each customer.

3. *Make predictions about the future.* Managers estimate the revenues they expect from each customer and the customer-level costs they will incur in the future. In making these predictions, managers consider the effects that future price discounts will have on revenues, the effect that pricing for different services (such as rush deliveries) will have on the demand for these services by customers, and ways to reduce the cost of providing services. For example, Deluxe, Corp., a leading check printer, initiated process reductions to rein in its cost to serve customers by opening an electronic channel to shift customers from paper to automated ordering.

4. *Make decisions by choosing among alternatives.* Managers use the customer-profitability profiles to identify the small set of customers who deserve the highest service and priority. They also identify ways to make less-profitable customers (such as Spring's customer G) more profitable. Banks, for example, often impose minimum balance requirements on customers. Distribution firms may require minimum order quantities or levy a surcharge for smaller or customized orders. In making resource-allocation decisions, managers also consider long-term effects, such as the potential for future sales growth and the opportunity to leverage a particular customer account to make sales to other customers.

5. *Implement the decision, evaluate performance, and learn.* After the decision is implemented, managers compare actual results to predicted outcomes to evaluate the decision they made, its implementation, and ways in which they might improve profitability.

Decision Point

How do customer-profitability profiles help managers?

---

[6] See, for example, "The New Math of Customer Relationships" at http://hbswk.hbs.edu/item/5884.html.

Concepts in Action

iPhone "Apps" Challenge Customer Profitability at AT&T

Rich Schulz/AP Wide World Photos

AT&T is the second largest wireless provider in the United States. The company provides mobile telephone and data access to more than 85 million individuals, businesses, and government agencies. AT&T uses cost accounting to price its various wireless service plans and calculate overall profitability for its customers, including more than 10 million owners of Apple's iPhone. AT&T is the exclusive wireless provider for the popular iPhone smart phone.

Traditionally, the cost of serving different wireless customers varied. Most business customers, for example, required reliable service during business hours and large amounts of data bandwidth for e-mail and Internet access. In contrast, many individuals use their wireless devices extensively on nights and weekends and use features such as text messages and music ringtones. Accordingly, wireless providers considered the costs for these services when developing pricing plans and calculating customer profitability. Therefore, individuals using their phone service sparingly could select a less-expensive plan with fewer minutes, for use mostly at night and on weekends, whereas more-demanding individuals and lucrative business customers chose plans with more telephone minutes, large amounts of wireless data bandwidth, and guaranteed reliability . . . for a higher price.

When AT&T began selling the iPhone in mid-2007, cost accountants projected the profitability for its new customers, and new plans were designed accordingly. Similar to traditional wireless plans, iPhone buyers were offered subscription options with different amounts of telephone minutes at different price points. For example, 450 telephone minutes cost $59.99, while 1,350 minutes were $99.99. However, to showcase the iPhone's wireless and Internet capabilities, Apple insisted that AT&T offer only one data package, an unlimited plan.

While the unlimited data package proved initially lucrative, technology developments added significant costs to AT&T. When Apple introduced the iPhone 3G in 2008, the third-generation data capabilities encouraged software developers to build new programs for the iPhone platform. Within two years, nearly 140,000 applications, ranging from Pandora's mobile music player to Mint's on-the-go budgeting program, were downloaded more than 3 billion times by iPhone users. Each of the applications, however, uses a lot of data bandwidth.

Recall that AT&T does not charge iPhone subscribers for marginal bandwidth use. As a result, subscribers who download and use many iPhone applications quickly became unprofitable for the company. With each 100MB of bandwidth costing AT&T $1, the company is currently considering cost-reducing options, such as limiting data access and changing its all-you-can-eat data subscription plan, but it is very concerned about alienating its customers.

iPhone application usage has also created a bigger cost problem for the company. With data bandwidth on the AT&T wireless network increasing by 5,000% between 2006 and 2009, the company's network is showing signs of strain and poor performance. To act on these concerns, AT&T will spend $18–19 billion making improvements to its data network in 2010, and more in the years to come. As a result, AT&T will need to balance customer satisfaction with ensuring that its iPhone customers remain profitable for the carrier.

Sources: AT&T Inc. and Apple Inc. 2007. AT&T and Apple announce simple, affordable service plans for iPhone. AT&T Inc. and Apple Inc. Press Release, June 26. http://www.apple.com/pr/library/2007/06/26plans.html; Fazard, Roben. 2010. AT&T's iPhone mess. *Business Week*, February 3; Sheth, Niraj. 2010. AT&T, boosted and stressed by iPhone, lays out network plans. *Wall Street Journal*, January 29; Sheth, Niraj. 2010. For wireless carriers, iPad signals further loss of clout. *Wall Street Journal*, January 28.

Sales Variances

The customer-profitability analysis in the previous section focused on the actual profitability of individual customers within a distribution channel (retail, for example) and their effect on Spring Distribution's profitability for June 2012. At a more-strategic level, however, recall that Spring operates in two different markets: wholesale and retail. The operating margins in the retail market are much higher than the operating margins in the wholesale market. In June 2012, Spring had budgeted to sell 80% of its cases to wholesalers and 20% to retailers. It sold more cases in total than it had budgeted, but its actual sales mix (in cases) was 84% to wholesalers and 16% to retailers. Regardless of the profitability of sales to individual customers within each of the retail and wholesale channels, Spring's actual operating income, relative to the master budget, is likely to be positively affected by the higher sales of cases and negatively affected by the shift in mix away from the more-profitable retail customers. Sales-quantity and sales-mix variances can identify the effect of each of these factors on Spring's profitability. Companies such as Cisco, GE, and Hewlett-Packard perform similar analyses because they sell their products through multiple distribution channels like the Internet, over the telephone, and retail stores.

Spring classifies all customer-level costs as variable costs and distribution-channel and corporate-sustaining costs as fixed costs. To simplify the sales-variances analysis and calculations, we assume that all of the variable costs are variable with respect to units (cases) sold. (This means that average batch sizes remain the same as the total cases sold vary.) Without this assumption, the analysis would become more complex and would have to be done using the ABC-variance analysis approach. The basic insights, however, would not change.

Budgeted and actual operating data for June 2012 are as follows:

Budget Data for June 2012

	Selling Price (1)	Variable Cost per Unit (2)	Contribution Margin per Unit (3) = (1) − (2)	Sales Volume in Units (4)	Sales Mix (Based on Units) (5)	Contribution Margin (6) = (3) × (4)
Wholesale channel	$13.37	$12.88	$0.49	712,000	80%[a]	$348,880
Retail channel	14.10	13.12	0.98	178,000	20%	174,440
Total				890,000	100%	$523,320

[a] Percentage of unit sales to wholesale channel = 712,000 units ÷ 890,000 total unit = 80%.

Actual Results for June 2012

	Selling Price (1)	Variable Cost per Unit (2)	Contribution Margin per Unit (3) = (1) − (2)	Sales Volume in Units (4)	Sales Mix (Based on Units) (5)	Contribution Margin (6) = (3) × (4)
Wholesale channel	$13.37	$12.88	$0.49	756,000	84%[a]	$370,440
Retail channel	14.10	13.17	0.93	144,000	16%	133,920
Total				900,000	100%	$504,360

[a] Percentage of unit sales to wholesale channel = 756,000 units ÷ 900,000 total unit = 84%.

The budgeted and actual fixed distribution-channel costs and corporate-sustaining costs are $160,500 and $263,000, respectively (see Exhibit 6).

Recall that the levels of detail included the static-budget variance (level 1), the flexible-budget variance (level 2), and the sales-volume variance (level 2). The sales-quantity and sales-mix variances are level 3 variances that subdivide the sales-volume variance.[7]

Learning Objective **6**

Subdivide the sales-volume variance into the sales-mix variance

. . . the variance arises because actual sales mix differs from budgeted sales mix

and the sales-quantity variance

. . . this variance arises because actual total unit sales differ from budgeted total unit sales

---

[7] The presentation of the variances in this chapter and the appendix draws on teaching notes prepared by J. K. Harris.

Static-Budget Variance

The *static-budget variance* is the difference between an actual result and the corresponding budgeted amount in the static budget. Our analysis focuses on the difference between actual and budgeted contribution margins (column 6 in the preceding tables). The total static-budget variance is $18,960 U (actual contribution margin of $504,360 – budgeted contribution margin of $523,320). Exhibit 9 (columns 1 and 3) uses the columnar format to show detailed calculations of the static-budget variance. Managers can gain more insight about the static-budget variance by subdividing it into the flexible-budget variance and the sales-volume variance.

Flexible-Budget Variance and Sales-Volume Variance

The *flexible-budget variance* is the difference between an actual result and the corresponding flexible-budget amount based on actual output level in the budget period. The flexible budget contribution margin is equal to budgeted contribution margin per unit times actual units sold of each product. Exhibit 9, column 2, shows the flexible-budget calculations. The flexible budget measures the contribution margin that Spring would have budgeted for the actual quantities of cases sold. The flexible-budget variance is the difference between columns 1 and 2 in Exhibit 9. The only difference between columns 1 and 2 is that actual units sold of each product is multiplied by actual contribution margin per unit in column 1 and budgeted contribution margin per unit in column 2. The $7,200 U flexible-budget variance arises because actual contribution margin on retail sales of $0.93 per case is lower than the budgeted amount of $0.98 per case. Spring's management is aware that this difference of $0.05 per case resulted from excessive price discounts, and it has put in place action plans to reduce discounts in the future.

The *sales-volume variance* is the difference between a flexible-budget amount and the corresponding static-budget amount. In Exhibit 9, the sales-volume variance shows the effect on budgeted contribution margin of the difference between actual quantity of units sold and budgeted quantity of units sold. The sales-volume variance of $11,760 U is the difference between columns 2 and 3 in Exhibit 9. In this case, it is unfavorable overall because while wholesale unit sales were higher than budgeted, retail sales, which are expected to be twice as profitable on a per unit basis, were below budget. Spring's

Exhibit 9   Flexible-Budget and Sales-Volume Variance Analysis of Spring Distribution for June 2012

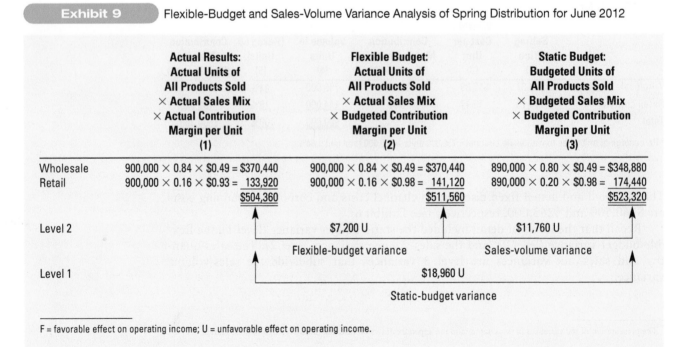

	Actual Results: Actual Units of All Products Sold × Actual Sales Mix × Actual Contribution Margin per Unit (1)	Flexible Budget: Actual Units of All Products Sold × Actual Sales Mix × Budgeted Contribution Margin per Unit (2)	Static Budget: Budgeted Units of All Products Sold × Budgeted Sales Mix × Budgeted Contribution Margin per Unit (3)
Wholesale	900,000 × 0.84 × $0.49 = $370,440	900,000 × 0.84 × $0.49 = $370,440	890,000 × 0.80 × $0.49 = $348,880
Retail	900,000 × 0.16 × $0.93 = 133,920	900,000 × 0.16 × $0.98 = 141,120	890,000 × 0.20 × $0.98 = 174,440
	$504,360	$511,560	$523,320
Level 2		$7,200 U	$11,760 U
		Flexible-budget variance	Sales-volume variance
Level 1		$18,960 U	
		Static-budget variance	

F = favorable effect on operating income; U = unfavorable effect on operating income.

managers can gain substantial insight into the sales-volume variance by subdividing it into the sales-mix variance and the sales-quantity variance.

Sales-Mix Variance

The **sales-mix variance** is the difference between (1) budgeted contribution margin for the *actual sales mix* and (2) budgeted contribution margin for the *budgeted sales mix*. The formula and computations are as follows:

	Actual Units of All Products Sold	×	$\left(\begin{array}{c}\text{Actual} \\ \text{Sales - Mix} \\ \text{Percentage}\end{array} - \begin{array}{c}\text{Budgeted} \\ \text{Sales - Mix} \\ \text{Percentage}\end{array}\right)$	×	Budgeted Contribution Margin per Unit	=	Sales-Mix Variance
Wholesale	900,000 units	×	(0.84 − 0.80)	×	$0.49 per unit	=	$17,640 F
Retail	900,000 units	×	(0.16 − 0.20)	×	$0.98 per unit	=	35,280 U
Total sales-mix variance							$17,640 U

A favorable sales-mix variance arises for the wholesale channel because the 84% actual sales-mix percentage exceeds the 80% budgeted sales-mix percentage. In contrast, the retail channel has an unfavorable variance because the 16% actual sales-mix percentage is less than the 20% budgeted sales-mix percentage. The sales-mix variance is unfavorable because actual sales mix shifted toward the less-profitable wholesale channel relative to budgeted sales mix.

The concept underlying the sales-mix variance is best explained in terms of composite units. A **composite unit** is a hypothetical unit with weights based on the mix of individual units. Given the budgeted sales for June 2012, the composite unit consists of 0.80 units of sales to the wholesale channel and 0.20 units of sales to the retail channel. Therefore, the budgeted contribution margin per composite unit for the budgeted sales mix is as follows:

$$(0.80) \times (\$0.49) + (0.20) \times (\$0.98) = \$0.5880.[8]$$

Similarly, for the actual sales mix, the composite unit consists of 0.84 units of sales to the wholesale channel and 0.16 units of sales to the retail channel. The budgeted contribution margin per composite unit for the actual sales mix is therefore as follows:

$$(0.84) \times (\$0.49) + (0.16) \times (\$0.98) = \$0.5684.$$

The impact of the shift in sales mix is now evident. Spring obtains a lower budgeted contribution margin per composite unit of $0.0196 ($0.5880 − $0.5684). For the 900,000 units actually sold, this decrease translates to a $17,640 U sales-mix variance ($0.0196 per unit × 900,000 units).

Managers should probe why the $17,640 U sales-mix variance occurred in June 2012. Is the shift in sales mix because, as the analysis in the previous section showed, profitable retail customers proved to be more difficult to find? Is it because of a competitor in the retail channel providing better service at a lower price? Or is it because the initial sales-volume estimates were made without adequate analysis of the potential market?

Exhibit 10 uses the columnar format to calculate the sales-mix variance and the sales-quantity variances.

Sales-Quantity Variance

The **sales-quantity variance** is the difference between (1) budgeted contribution margin based on *actual units sold of all products* at the budgeted mix and (2) contribution margin in the static budget (which is based on *budgeted units of all products to*

---

[8] Budgeted contribution margin per composite unit can be computed in another way by dividing total budgeted contribution margin of $523,320 by total budgeted units of 890,000: $523,320 ÷ 890,000 units = $0.5880 per unit.

Exhibit 10 Sales-Mix and Sales-Quantity Variance Analysis of Spring Distribution for June 2012

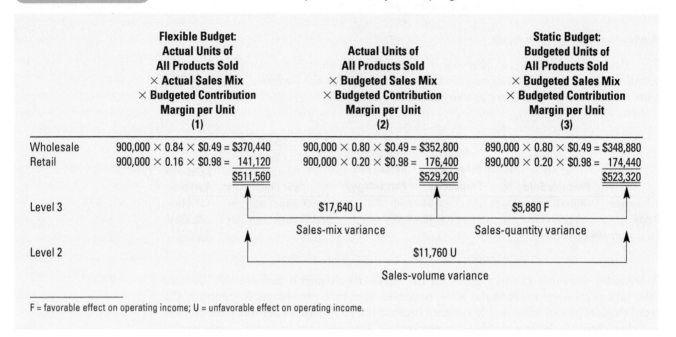

	Flexible Budget: Actual Units of All Products Sold × Actual Sales Mix × Budgeted Contribution Margin per Unit (1)	Actual Units of All Products Sold × Budgeted Sales Mix × Budgeted Contribution Margin per Unit (2)	Static Budget: Budgeted Units of All Products Sold × Budgeted Sales Mix × Budgeted Contribution Margin per Unit (3)
Wholesale	900,000 × 0.84 × $0.49 = $370,440	900,000 × 0.80 × $0.49 = $352,800	890,000 × 0.80 × $0.49 = $348,880
Retail	900,000 × 0.16 × $0.98 = 141,120	900,000 × 0.20 × $0.98 = 176,400	890,000 × 0.20 × $0.98 = 174,440
	$511,560	$529,200	$523,320

Level 3 — $17,640 U — Sales-mix variance | $5,880 F — Sales-quantity variance

Level 2 — $11,760 U — Sales-volume variance

F = favorable effect on operating income; U = unfavorable effect on operating income.

be sold at budgeted mix). The formula and computations are as follows:

			Budgeted Sales-Mix Percentages		Budgeted Contribution Margin per Unit		Sales-Quantity Variance
Wholesale	(900,000 units − 890,000 units)	×	0.80	×	$0.49 per unit	=	$3,920 F
Retail	(900,000 units − 890,000 units)	×	0.20	×	$0.98 per unit	=	1,960 F
Total sales-quantity variance							$5,880 F

This variance is favorable when actual units of all products sold exceed budgeted units of all products sold. Spring sold 10,000 more cases than were budgeted, resulting in a $5,880 F sales-quantity variance (also equal to budgeted contribution margin per composite unit for the budgeted sales mix times additional cases sold, $0.5880 × 10,000). Managers would want to probe the reasons for the increase in sales. Did higher sales come as a result of a competitor's distribution problems? Better customer service? Or growth in the overall market? Additional insight into the causes of the sales-quantity variance can be gained by analyzing changes in Spring's share of the total industry market and in the size of that market. The sales-quantity variance can be decomposed into market-share and market-size variances.[9]

Exhibit 11 presents an overview of the sales-mix and sales-quantity variances for the Spring example. The sales-mix variance and sales-quantity variance can also be calculated in a multiproduct company, in which each individual product has a different contribution margin per unit. The Problem for Self-Study takes you through such a setting, and also demonstrates the link between these sales variances and the market-share and market-size variances studied earlier. The appendix to this chapter describes mix and quantity variances for production inputs.

Decision Point ►

What are the two components of the sales-volume variance?

[9] Recall that the market-share and market-size variances were computed for Webb Company, which sold a single product (jackets) using a single distribution channel. The calculation of these variances is virtually unaffected when multiple distribution channels exist, as in the Spring example. The only change required is to replace the phrase "Budgeted Contribution Margin per Unit" in the market-share and market-size variance formulas with "Budgeted Contribution Margin per Composite Unit for Budgeted Sales Mix" (which equals $0.5880 in the Spring example). For additional details and an illustration, see the Problem for Self-Study for this chapter.

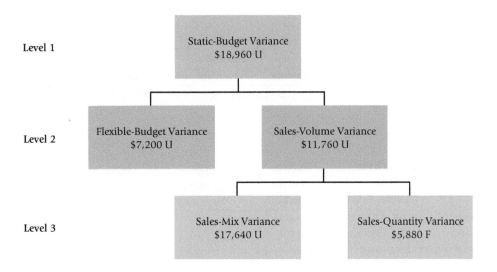

Exhibit 11

Overview of Variances
for Spring Distribution
for June 2012

F = favorable effect on operating income; U = unfavorable effect on operating income

Problem for Self-Study

The Payne Company manufactures two types of vinyl flooring. Budgeted and actual operating data for 2012 are as follows:

	Static Budget			Actual Results		
	Commercial	Residential	Total	Commercial	Residential	Total
Unit sales in rolls	20,000	60,000	80,000	25,200	58,800	84,000
Contribution margin	$10,000,000	$24,000,000	$34,000,000	$11,970,000	$24,696,000	$36,666,000

In late 2011, a marketing research firm estimated industry volume for commercial and residential vinyl flooring for 2012 at 800,000 rolls. Actual industry volume for 2012 was 700,000 rolls.

1. Compute the sales-mix variance and the sales-quantity variance by type of vinyl flooring and in total. (Compute all variances in terms of contribution margins.)
2. Compute the market-share variance and the market-size variance.
3. What insights do the variances calculated in requirements 1 and 2 provide about Payne Company's performance in 2012?

Required

Solution

1. Actual sales-mix percentage:

$$\text{Commercial} = 25,200 \div 84,000 = 0.30, \text{ or } 30\%$$

$$\text{Residential} = 58,800 \div 84,000 = 0.70, \text{ or } 70\%$$

Budgeted sales-mix percentage:

$$\text{Commercial} = 20,000 \div 80,000 = 0.25, \text{ or } 25\%$$

$$\text{Residential} = 60,000 \div 80,000 = 0.75, \text{ or } 75\%$$

Budgeted contribution margin per unit:

$$\text{Commercial} = \$10,000,000 \div 20,000 \text{ units} = \$500 \text{ per unit}$$

$$\text{Residential} = \$24,000,000 \div 60,000 \text{ units} = \$400 \text{ per unit}$$

	Actual Units of All Products Sold	×	$\begin{pmatrix} \text{Actual} \\ \text{Sales-Mix} & - & \text{Budgeted} \\ \text{Sales-Mix} \\ \text{Percentage} & & \text{Percentage} \end{pmatrix}$	×	Budgeted Contribution Margin per Unit	=	Sales-Mix Variance
Commercial	84,000 units	×	(0.30 − 0.25)	×	$500 per unit	=	$2,100,000 F
Residential	84,000 units	×	(0.70 − 0.75)	×	$400 per unit	=	1,680,000 U
Total sales-mix variance							$ 420,000 F

	$\begin{pmatrix} \text{Actual Units} \\ \text{of All} & - & \text{Budgeted} \\ \text{Units of All} \\ \text{Products Sold} & & \text{Products Sold} \end{pmatrix}$	×	Budgeted Sales-Mix Percentage	×	Budgeted Contribution Margin per Unit	=	Sales-Quantity Variance
Commercial	(84,000 units − 80,000 units)	×	0.25	×	$500 per unit	=	$ 500,000 F
Residential	(84,000 units − 80,000 units)	×	0.75	×	$400 per unit	=	1,200,000 F
Total sales-quantity variance							$1,700,000 F

2. Actual market share = 84,000 ÷ 700,000 = 0.12, or 12%
   Budgeted market share = 80,000 ÷ 800,000 units = 0.10, or 10%

   Budgeted contribution margin
   per composite unit   = $34,000,000 ÷ 80,000 units = $425 per unit
   of budgeted mix

Budgeted contribution margin per composite unit of budgeted mix can also be calculated as follows:

   Commercial: $500 per unit × 0.25   = $125
   Residential: $400 per unit × 0.75   = 300
   Budgeted contribution margin per composite unit = $425

$$\begin{aligned} \text{Market-share variance} &= \begin{array}{c}\text{Actual} \\ \text{market size} \\ \text{in units}\end{array} \times \begin{pmatrix} \text{Actual} \\ \text{market} & - & \text{Budgeted} \\ \text{market} \\ \text{share} & & \text{share} \end{pmatrix} \times \begin{array}{c}\text{Budgeted} \\ \text{contribution margin} \\ \text{per composite unit} \\ \text{for budgeted mix}\end{array} \end{aligned}$$

   = 700,000 units × (0.12 − 0.10) × $425 per unit

   = $5,950,000 F

$$\begin{aligned} \text{Market-size variance} &= \begin{pmatrix} \text{Actual} \\ \text{market size} & - & \text{Budgeted} \\ \text{market size} \\ \text{in units} & & \text{in units} \end{pmatrix} \times \begin{array}{c}\text{Budgeted} \\ \text{market} \\ \text{share}\end{array} \times \begin{array}{c}\text{Budgeted} \\ \text{contribution margin} \\ \text{per composite unit} \\ \text{for budgeted mix}\end{array} \end{aligned}$$

   = (700,000 units − 800,000 units) × 0.10 × $425 per unit

   = $4,250,000 U

Note that the algebraic sum of the market-share variance and the market-size variance is equal to the sales-quantity variance: $5,950,000 F + $4,250,000 U = $1,700,000 F.

3. Both the total sales-mix variance and the total sales-quantity variance are favorable. The favorable sales-mix variance occurred because the actual mix comprised more of the higher-margin commercial vinyl flooring. The favorable total sales-quantity variance occurred because the actual total quantity of rolls sold exceeded the budgeted amount.

The company's large favorable market-share variance is due to a 12% actual market share compared with a 10% budgeted market share. The market-size variance is unfavorable because the actual market size was 100,000 rolls less than the budgeted market size. Payne's performance in 2012 appears to be very good. Although overall market size declined, the company sold more units than budgeted and gained market share.

Decision Points

The following question-and-answer format summarizes the chapter's learning objectives. Each decision presents a key question related to a learning objective. The guidelines are the answer to that question.

Decision	Guidelines
1. What are four purposes for allocating costs to cost objects?	Four purposes of cost allocation are (a) to provide information for economic decisions, (b) to motivate managers and other employees, (c) to justify costs or compute reimbursement amounts, and (d) to measure income and assets for reporting to external parties. Different cost allocations are appropriate for different purposes.
2. What criteria should managers use to guide cost-allocation decisions?	Managers should use the cause-and-effect and the benefits-received criteria to guide most cost-allocation decisions. Other criteria are fairness or equity and ability to bear.
3. What are two key decisions managers must make when collecting costs in indirect-cost pools?	Two key decisions related to indirect-cost pools are the number of indirect-cost pools to form and the individual cost items to be included in each cost pool to make homogeneous cost pools.
4. How can a company's revenues and costs differ across customers?	Revenues can differ because of differences in the quantity purchased and price discounts given from the list selling price.
	Costs can differ as different customers place different demands on a company's resources in terms of processing purchase orders, making deliveries, and customer support.
5. How do customer-profitability profiles help managers?	Companies should be aware of and devote sufficient resources to maintaining and expanding relationships with customers who contribute significantly to profitability. Customer-profitability profiles often highlight that a small percentage of customers contributes a large percentage of operating income.
6. What are the two components of the sales-volume variance?	The two components of sales-volume variance are (a) the difference between actual sales mix and budgeted sales mix (the sales-mix variance) and (b) the difference between actual unit sales and budgeted unit sales (the sales-quantity variance).

Appendix

Mix and Yield Variances for Substitutable Inputs

The framework for calculating the sales-mix variance and the sales-quantity variance can also be used to analyze production-input variances in cases in which managers have some leeway in combining and substituting inputs. For example, Del Monte can combine material inputs (such as pineapples, cherries, and grapes) in varying proportions for its cans of fruit cocktail. Within limits, these individual fruits are *substitutable inputs* in making the fruit cocktail.

We illustrate how the efficiency variance can be subdivided into variances that highlight the financial impact of input mix and input yield when inputs are substitutable. Consider Delpino Corporation, which makes tomato ketchup. Our example focuses on direct material inputs and substitution among three of these inputs. The same approach can also be used to examine substitutable direct manufacturing labor inputs.

To produce ketchup of a specified consistency, color, and taste, Delpino mixes three types of tomatoes grown in different regions: Latin American tomatoes (Latoms), California tomatoes (Caltoms), and Florida tomatoes

(Flotoms). Delpino's production standards require 1.60 tons of tomatoes to produce 1 ton of ketchup; 50% of the tomatoes are budgeted to be Latoms, 30% Caltoms, and 20% Flotoms. The direct material inputs budgeted to produce 1 ton of ketchup are as follows:

0.80 (50% of 1.6) ton of Latoms at $70 per ton	$ 56.00
0.48 (30% of 1.6) ton of Caltoms at $80 per ton	38.40
0.32 (20% of 1.6) ton of Flotoms at $90 per ton	28.80
Total budgeted cost of 1.6 tons of tomatoes	$123.20

Budgeted average cost per ton of tomatoes is $123.20 ÷ 1.60 tons = $77 per ton.

Because Delpino uses fresh tomatoes to make ketchup, no inventories of tomatoes are kept. Purchases are made as needed, so all price variances relate to tomatoes purchased and used. Actual results for June 2012 show that a total of 6,500 tons of tomatoes were used to produce 4,000 tons of ketchup:

3,250 tons of Latoms at actual cost of $70 per ton	$227,500
2,275 tons of Caltoms at actual cost of $82 per ton	186,550
975 tons of Flotoms at actual cost of $96 per ton	93,600
6,500 tons of tomatoes	507,650
Budgeted cost of 4,000 tons of ketchup at $123.20 per ton	492,800
Flexible-budget variance for direct materials	$ 14,850 U

Given the standard ratio of 1.60 tons of tomatoes to 1 ton of ketchup, 6,400 tons of tomatoes should be used to produce 4,000 tons of ketchup. At standard mix, quantities of each type of tomato required are as follows:

Latoms:	0.50 × 6,400 = 3,200 tons
Caltoms:	0.30 × 6,400 = 1,920 tons
Flotoms:	0.20 × 6,400 = 1,280 tons

Direct Materials Price and Efficiency Variances

Exhibit 12 presents in columnar format the analysis of the flexible-budget variance for direct materials. The materials price and efficiency variances are calculated separately for each input material and then added together. The variance analysis prompts Delpino to investigate the unfavorable price and efficiency variances. Why did it pay more for tomatoes and use greater quantities than it had budgeted? Were actual market prices of tomatoes higher, in general, or could the purchasing department have negotiated lower prices? Did the inefficiencies result from inferior tomatoes or from problems in processing?

Exhibit 12 Direct Materials Price and Efficiency Variances for the Delpino Corporation June 2012

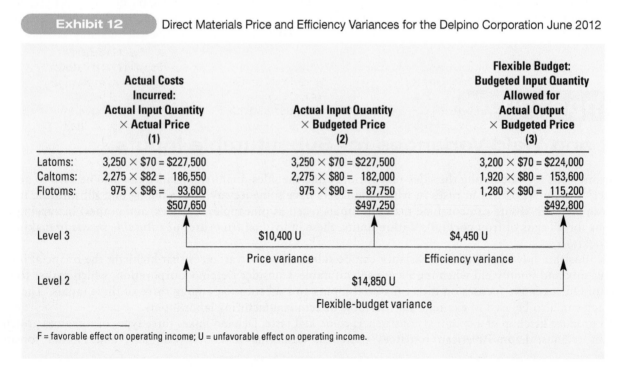

F = favorable effect on operating income; U = unfavorable effect on operating income.

Direct Materials Mix and Direct Materials Yield Variances

Managers sometimes have discretion to substitute one material for another. The manager of Delpino's ketchup plant has some leeway in combining Latoms, Caltoms, and Flotoms without affecting the ketchup's quality. We will assume that to maintain quality, mix percentages of each type of tomato can only vary up to 5% from standard mix. For example, the percentage of Caltoms in the mix can vary between 25% and 35% (30% ± 5%). When inputs are substitutable, direct materials efficiency improvement relative to budgeted costs can come from two sources: (1) using a cheaper mix to produce a given quantity of output, measured by the direct materials mix variance, and (2) using less input to achieve a given quantity of output, measured by the direct materials yield variance.

Holding actual total quantity of all direct materials inputs used constant, the total **direct materials mix variance** is the difference between (1) budgeted cost for actual mix of actual total quantity of direct materials used and (2) budgeted cost of budgeted mix of actual total quantity of direct materials used. Holding budgeted input mix constant, the **direct materials yield variance** is the difference between (1) budgeted cost of direct materials based on actual total quantity of direct materials used and (2) flexible-budget cost of direct materials based on budgeted total quantity of direct materials allowed for actual output produced. Exhibit 13 presents the direct materials mix and yield variances for the Delpino Corporation.

Direct Materials Mix Variance

The total direct materials mix variance is the sum of the direct materials mix variances for each input:

$$\begin{array}{c}\text{Direct} \\ \text{materials} \\ \text{mix variance} \\ \text{for each input}\end{array} = \begin{array}{c}\text{Actual total} \\ \text{quantity of all} \\ \text{direct materials} \\ \text{inputs used}\end{array} \times \left(\begin{array}{c}\text{Actual} \\ \text{direct materials} \\ \text{input mix} \\ \text{percentage}\end{array} - \begin{array}{c}\text{Budgeted} \\ \text{direct materials} \\ \text{input mix} \\ \text{percentage}\end{array}\right) \times \begin{array}{c}\text{Budgeted} \\ \text{price of} \\ \text{direct materials} \\ \text{input}\end{array}$$

The direct materials mix variances are as follows:

Latoms: 6,500 tons × (0.50 − 0.50) × $70 per ton = 6,500 × 0.00 × $70 = $ 0

Caltoms: 6,500 tons × (0.35 − 0.30) × $80 per ton = 6,500 × 0.05 × $80 =   26,000 U

Flotoms: 6,500 tons × (0.15 − 0.20) × $90 per ton = 6,500 × −0.05 × $90 = 29,250 F

Total direct materials mix variance $ 3,250 F

The total direct materials mix variance is favorable because relative to the budgeted mix, Delpino substitutes 5% of the cheaper Caltoms for 5% of the more-expensive Flotoms.

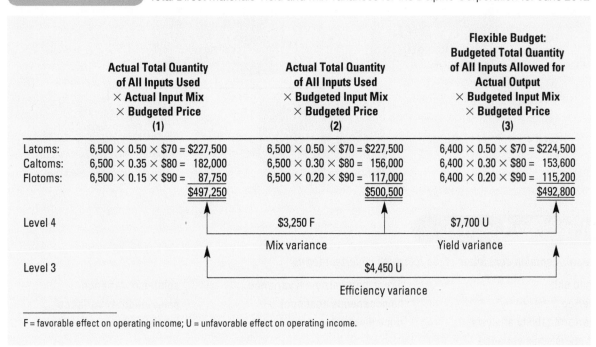

Exhibit 13	Total Direct Materials Yield and Mix Variances for the Delpino Corporation for June 2012

	Actual Total Quantity of All Inputs Used × Actual Input Mix × Budgeted Price (1)	Actual Total Quantity of All Inputs Used × Budgeted Input Mix × Budgeted Price (2)	Flexible Budget: Budgeted Total Quantity of All Inputs Allowed for Actual Output × Budgeted Input Mix × Budgeted Price (3)
Latoms:	6,500 × 0.50 × $70 = $227,500	6,500 × 0.50 × $70 = $227,500	6,400 × 0.50 × $70 = $224,500
Caltoms:	6,500 × 0.35 × $80 = 182,000	6,500 × 0.30 × $80 = 156,000	6,400 × 0.30 × $80 = 153,600
Flotoms:	6,500 × 0.15 × $90 = 87,750	6,500 × 0.20 × $90 = 117,000	6,400 × 0.20 × $90 = 115,200
	$497,250	$500,500	$492,800

Level 4 $3,250 F $7,700 U

                             Mix variance   Yield variance

Level 3 $4,450 U

                             Efficiency variance

F = favorable effect on operating income; U = unfavorable effect on operating income.

Direct Materials Yield Variance

The direct materials yield variance is the sum of the direct materials yield variances for each input:

$$
\begin{pmatrix} \text{Direct} \\ \text{materials} \\ \text{yield variance} \\ \text{for each input} \end{pmatrix} = \begin{pmatrix} \text{Actual total} & \text{Budgeted total} \\ \text{quantity of} & \text{quantity of all} \\ \text{all direct} & - \text{ direct materials} \\ \text{materials} & \text{inputs allowed} \\ \text{inputs used} & \text{for actual output} \end{pmatrix} \times \begin{pmatrix} \text{Budgeted} \\ \text{direct materials} \\ \text{input mix} \\ \text{percentage} \end{pmatrix} \times \begin{pmatrix} \text{Budgeted} \\ \text{price of} \\ \text{direct materials} \\ \text{input} \end{pmatrix}
$$

The direct materials yield variances are as follows:

Latoms:	$(6,500 - 6,400)$ tons $\times 0.50 \times \$70$ per ton $= 100 \times 0.50 \times \$70 =$	\$3,500 U
Caltoms:	$(6,500 - 6,400)$ tons $\times 0.30 \times \$80$ per ton $= 100 \times 0.30 \times \$80 =$	2,400 U
Flotoms:	$(6,500 - 6,400)$ tons $\times 0.20 \times \$90$ per ton $= 100 \times 0.20 \times \$90 =$	1,800 U
Total direct materials yield variance		\$7,700 U

The total direct materials yield variance is unfavorable because Delpino used 6,500 tons of tomatoes rather than the 6,400 tons that it should have used to produce 4,000 tons of ketchup. Holding the budgeted mix and budgeted prices of tomatoes constant, the budgeted cost per ton of tomatoes in the budgeted mix is \$77 per ton. The unfavorable yield variance represents the budgeted cost of using 100 more tons of tomatoes, $(6,500 - 6,400)$ tons $\times \$77$ per ton $= \$7,700$ U. Delpino would want to investigate reasons for this unfavorable yield variance. For example, did the substitution of the cheaper Caltoms for Flotoms that resulted in the favorable mix variance also cause the unfavorable yield variance?

The direct materials variances computed in Exhibits 12 and 13 can be summarized as follows:

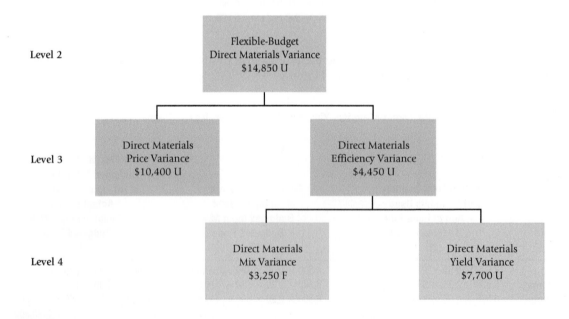

Level 2 — Flexible-Budget Direct Materials Variance $14,850 U

Level 3 — Direct Materials Price Variance $10,400 U / Direct Materials Efficiency Variance $4,450 U

Level 4 — Direct Materials Mix Variance $3,250 F / Direct Materials Yield Variance $7,700 U

Terms to Learn

This chapter contains definitions of the following important terms:

composite unit	direct materials yield variance	sales-mix variance
customer-cost hierarchy	homogeneous cost pool	sales-quantity variance
customer-profitability analysis	price discount	whale curve
direct materials mix variance		

Assignment Material

Questions

14-1 "I am going to focus on the customers of my business and leave cost-allocation issues to my accountant." Do you agree with this comment by a division president? Why?

14-2 A given cost may be allocated for one or more purposes. List four purposes.

14-3 What criteria might be used to guide cost-allocation decisions? Which are the dominant criteria?

14-4 "A company should not allocate all of its corporate costs to its divisions." Do you agree? Explain.

14-5 "Once a company allocates corporate costs to divisions, these costs should not be reallocated to the indirect-cost pools of the division." Do you agree? Explain.

14-6 Why is customer-profitability analysis a vitally important topic to managers?

14-7 How can the extent of price discounting be tracked on a customer-by-customer basis?

14-8 "A customer-profitability profile highlights those customers who should be dropped to improve profitability." Do you agree? Explain.

14-9 Give examples of three different levels of costs in a customer-cost hierarchy.

14-10 What information does the whale curve provide?

14-11 Show how managers can gain insight into the causes of a sales-volume variance by subdividing the components of this variance.

14-12 How can the concept of a composite unit be used to explain why an unfavorable total sales-mix variance of contribution margin occurs?

14-13 Explain why a favorable sales-quantity variance occurs.

14-14 How can the sales-quantity variance be decomposed further?

14-15 Explain how the direct materials mix and yield variances provide additional information about the direct materials efficiency variance.

Exercises

14-16 Cost allocation in hospitals, alternative allocation criteria. Dave Meltzer vacationed at Lake Tahoe last winter. Unfortunately, he broke his ankle while skiing and spent two days at the Sierra University Hospital. Meltzer's insurance company received a $4,800 bill for his two-day stay. One item that caught Meltzer's attention was an $11.52 charge for a roll of cotton. Meltzer is a salesman for Johnson & Johnson and knows that the cost to the hospital of the roll of cotton is in the $2.20 to $3.00 range. He asked for a breakdown of the $11.52 charge. The accounting office of the hospital sent him the following information:

a.	Invoiced cost of cotton roll	$ 2.40
b.	Cost of processing of paperwork for purchase	0.60
c.	Supplies-room management fee	0.70
d.	Operating-room and patient-room handling costs	1.60
e.	Administrative hospital costs	1.10
f.	University teaching-related costs	0.60
g.	Malpractice insurance costs	1.20
h.	Cost of treating uninsured patients	2.72
i.	Profit component	0.60
	Total	$11.52

Meltzer believes the overhead charge is obscene. He comments, "There was nothing I could do about it. When they come in and dab your stitches, it's not as if you can say, 'Keep your cotton roll. I brought my own.'"

Required

1. Compute the overhead rate Sierra University Hospital charged on the cotton roll.
2. What criteria might Sierra use to justify allocation of the overhead items **b–i** in the preceding list? Examine each item separately and use the allocation criteria listed in Exhibit 2 in your answer.
3. What should Meltzer do about the $11.52 charge for the cotton roll?

14-17 Cost allocation and decision making. Greenbold Manufacturing has four divisions named after its locations: Arizona, Colorado, Delaware, and Florida. Corporate headquarters is in Minnesota. Greenbold corporate headquarters incurs $5,600,000 per period, which is an indirect cost of the divisions. Corporate headquarters currently allocates this cost to the divisions based on the revenues of each division. The CEO has asked each division manager to suggest an allocation base for the indirect headquarters costs from among revenues, segment margin, direct costs, and number of employees. The following is relevant information about each division:

	Arizona	Colorado	Delaware	Florida
Revenues	$7,800,000	$8,500,000	$6,200,000	$5,500,000
Direct costs	5,300,000	4,100,000	4,300,000	4,600,000
Segment margin	$2,500,000	$4,400,000	$1,900,000	$ 900,000
Number of employees	2,000	4,000	1,500	500

Required

1. Allocate the indirect headquarters costs of Greenbold Manufacturing to each of the four divisions using revenues, direct costs, segment margin, and number of employees as the allocation bases. Calculate operating margins for each division after allocating headquarters costs.
2. Which allocation base do you think the manager of the Florida division would prefer? Explain.
3. What factors would you consider in deciding which allocation base Greenbold should use?
4. Suppose the Greenbold CEO decides to use direct costs as the allocation base. Should the Florida division be closed? Why or why not?

14-18 Cost allocation to divisions. Rembrandt Hotel & Casino is situated on beautiful Lake Tahoe in Nevada. The complex includes a 300-room hotel, a casino, and a restaurant. As Rembrandt's new controller, you are asked to recommend the basis to be used for allocating fixed overhead costs to the three divisions in 2012. You are presented with the following income statement information for 2011:

	Hotel	Restaurant	Casino
Revenues	$16,425,000	$5,256,000	$12,340,000
Direct costs	9,819,260	3,749,172	4,248,768
Segment margin	$ 6,605,740	$1,506,828	$ 8,091,232

You are also given the following data on the three divisions:

	Hotel	Restaurant	Casino
Floor space (square feet)	80,000	16,000	64,000
Number of employees	200	50	250

You are told that you may choose to allocate indirect costs based on one of the following: direct costs, floor space, or the number of employees. Total fixed overhead costs for 2011 was $14,550,000.

Required

1. Calculate division margins in percentage terms prior to allocating fixed overhead costs.
2. Allocate indirect costs to the three divisions using each of the three allocation bases suggested. For each allocation base, calculate division operating margins after allocations in dollars and as a percentage of revenues.
3. Discuss the results. How would you decide how to allocate indirect costs to the divisions? Why?
4. Would you recommend closing any of the three divisions (and possibly reallocating resources to other divisions) as a result of your analysis? If so, which division would you close and why?

14-19 Cost allocation to divisions. Lenzig Corporation has three divisions: pulp, paper, and fibers. Lenzig's new controller, Ari Bardem, is reviewing the allocation of fixed corporate-overhead costs to the three divisions. He is presented with the following information for each division for 2012:

	A	B	C	D
		Pulp	Paper	Fibers
1				
2	Revenues	$8,500,000	$17,500,000	$24,000,000
3	Direct manufacturing costs	4,100,000	8,600,000	11,300,000
4	Division administrative costs	2,000,000	1,800,000	3,200,000
5	Division margin	$2,400,000	$ 7,100,000	$ 9,500,000
6				
7	Number of employees	350	250	400
8	Floor space (square feet)	35,000	24,000	66,000

Until now, Lenzig Corporation has allocated fixed corporate-overhead costs to the divisions on the basis of division margins. Bardem asks for a list of costs that comprise fixed corporate overhead and suggests the following new allocation bases:

	F	G	H
1	**Fixed Corporate Overhead Costs**		**Suggested Allocation Bases**
2	Human resource management	$1,800,000	Number of employees
3	Facility	2,700,000	Floor space (square feet)
4	Corporate Administration	4,500,000	Division administrative costs
5	Total	$9,000,000	

Required

1. Allocate 2012 fixed corporate-overhead costs to the three divisions using division margin as the allocation base. What is each division's operating margin percentage (division margin minus allocated fixed corporate-overhead costs as a percentage of revenues)?
2. Allocate 2012 fixed costs using the allocation bases suggested by Bardem. What is each division's operating margin percentage under the new allocation scheme?
3. Compare and discuss the results of requirements 1 and 2. If division performance is linked to operating margin percentage, which division would be most receptive to the new allocation scheme? Which division would be the least receptive? Why?
4. Which allocation scheme should Lenzig Corporation use? Why? How might Bardem overcome any objections that may arise from the divisions?

14-20 Customer profitability, customer-cost hierarchy. Orsack Electronics has only two retail and two wholesale customers. Information relating to each customer for 2012 follows (in thousands):

	A	B	C	D	E
1		**Wholesale Customers**		**Retail Customers**	
2		**North America Wholesaler**	**South America Wholesaler**	**Big Sam Stereo**	**World Market**
3	Revenues at list price	$435,000	$550,000	$150,000	$115,000
4	Discounts from list prices	30,000	44,000	7,200	520
5	Cost of goods sold	330,000	475,000	123,000	84,000
6	Delivery costs	475	690	220	130
7	Order processing costs	750	1,020	175	120
8	Costs of sales visits	5,400	2,500	2,500	1,400

Orsack's annual distribution-channel costs are $34 million for wholesale customers and $5 million for retail customers. Its annual corporate-sustaining costs, such as salary for top management and general-administration costs, are $61 million. There is no cause-and-effect or benefits-received relationship between any cost-allocation base and corporate-sustaining costs. That is, corporate-sustaining costs could be saved only if Orsack Electronics were to completely shut down.

Required

1. Calculate customer-level operating income using the format in Exhibit 5.
2. Prepare a customer-cost hierarchy report, using the format in Exhibit 6.
3. Orsack's management decides to allocate all corporate-sustaining costs to distribution channels: $48 million to the wholesale channel and $13 million to the retail channel. As a result, distribution channel costs are now $82 million ($34 million + $48 million) for the wholesale channel and $18 million ($5 million + $13 million) for the retail channel. Calculate the distribution-channel-level operating income. On the basis of these calculations, what actions, if any, should Orsack's managers take? Explain.

14-21 Customer profitability, service company. Instant Service (IS) repairs printers and photocopiers for five multisite companies in a tristate area. IS's costs consist of the cost of technicians and equipment that are directly traceable to the customer site and a pool of office overhead. Until recently, IS estimated customer profitability by allocating the office overhead to each customer based on share of revenues. For 2012, IS reported the following results:

	A	B	C	D	E	F	G
1		Avery	Okie	Wizard	Grainger	Duran	Total
2	Revenues	$260,000	$200,000	$322,000	$122,000	$212,000	$1,116,000
3	Technician and equipment cost	182,000	175,000	225,000	107,000	178,000	867,000
4	Office overhead allocated	31,859	24,507	39,457	14,949	25,978	136,750
5	Operating income	$ 46,141	$ 493	$ 57,543	$ 51	$ 8,022	$ 112,250

Tina Sherman, IS's new controller, notes that office overhead is more than 10% of total costs, so she spends a couple of weeks analyzing the consumption of office overhead resources by customers. She collects the following information:

	I	J	K
1	Activity Area	Cost Driver Rate	
2	Service call handling	$75	per service call
3	Parts ordering	$80	per Web-base parts order
4	Billing and collection	$50	per bill (or reminder)
5	Customer database maintenance	$10	per service call

	A	B	C	D	E	F
8		Avery	Okie	Wizard	Grainger	Duran
9	Number of service calls	150	240	40	120	180
10	Number of Web-based parts orders	120	210	60	150	150
11	Number of bills (or reminders)	30	90	90	60	120

Required

1. Compute customer-level operating income using the new information that Sherman has gathered.
2. Prepare exhibits for IS similar to Exhibits 7 and 8. Comment on the results.
3. What options should IS consider, with regard to individual customers, in light of the new data and analysis of office overhead?

14-22 Customer profitability, distribution. Figure Four is a distributor of pharmaceutical products. Its ABC system has five activities:

Activity Area	Cost Driver Rate in 2012
1. Order processing	$40 per order
2. Line-item ordering	$3 per line item
3. Store deliveries	$50 per store delivery
4. Carton deliveries	$1 per carton
5. Shelf-stocking	$16 per stocking-hour

Rick Flair, the controller of Figure Four, wants to use this ABC system to examine individual customer profitability within each distribution market. He focuses first on the Ma and Pa single-store distribution market. Two customers are used to exemplify the insights available with the ABC approach. Data pertaining to these two customers in August 2012 are as follows:

	Charleston Pharmacy	Chapel Hill Pharmacy
Total orders	13	10
Average line items per order	9	18
Total store deliveries	7	10
Average cartons shipped per store delivery	22	20
Average hours of shelf-stocking per store delivery	0	0.5
Average revenue per delivery	$2,400	$1,800
Average cost of goods sold per delivery	$2,100	$1,650

1. Use the ABC information to compute the operating income of each customer in August 2012. Comment on the results and what, if anything, Flair should do. **Required**
2. Flair ranks the individual customers in the Ma and Pa single-store distribution market on the basis of monthly operating income. The cumulative operating income of the top 20% of customers is $55,680. Figure Four reports operating losses of $21,247 for the bottom 40% of its customers. Make four recommendations that you think Figure Four should consider in light of this new customer-profitability information.

14-23 Variance analysis, multiple products. The Detroit Penguins play in the American Ice Hockey League. The Penguins play in the Downtown Arena (owned and managed by the City of Detroit), which has a capacity of 15,000 seats (5,000 lower-tier seats and 10,000 upper-tier seats). The Downtown Arena charges the Penguins a per-ticket charge for use of its facility. All tickets are sold by the Reservation Network, which charges the Penguins a reservation fee per ticket. The Penguins' budgeted contribution margin for each type of ticket in 2012 is computed as follows:

	Lower-Tier Tickets	Upper-Tier Tickets
Selling price	$35	$14
Downtown Arena fee	10	6
Reservation Network fee	5	3
Contribution margin per ticket	$20	$ 5

The budgeted and actual average attendance figures per game in the 2012 season are as follows:

	Budgeted Seats Sold	Actual Seats Sold
Lower tier	4,000	3,300
Upper tier	6,000	7,700
Total	10,000	11,000

There was no difference between the budgeted and actual contribution margin for lower-tier or upper-tier seats.

The manager of the Penguins was delighted that actual attendance was 10% above budgeted attendance per game, especially given the depressed state of the local economy in the past six months.

1. Compute the sales-volume variance for each type of ticket and in total for the Detroit Penguins in 2012. **Required**
(Calculate all variances in terms of contribution margins.)
2. Compute the sales-quantity and sales-mix variances for each type of ticket and in total in 2012.
3. Present a summary of the variances in requirements 1 and 2. Comment on the results.

14-24 Variance analysis, working backward. The Jinwa Corporation sells two brands of wine glasses: Plain and Chic. Jinwa provides the following information for sales in the month of June 2011:

Static-budget total contribution margin	$11,000
Budgeted units to be sold of all glasses	2,000 units
Budgeted contribution margin per unit of Plain	$4 per unit
Budgeted contribution margin per unit of Chic	$10 per unit
Total sales-quantity variance	$2,200 U
Actual sales-mix percentage of Plain	60%

All variances are to be computed in contribution-margin terms.

Required

1. Calculate the sales-quantity variances for each product for June 2011.
2. Calculate the individual-product and total sales-mix variances for June 2011. Calculate the individual-product and total sales-volume variances for June 2011.
3. Briefly describe the conclusions you can draw from the variances.

14-25 Variance analysis, multiple products. Soda-King manufactures and sells three soft drinks: Kola, Limor, and Orlem. Budgeted and actual results for 2011 are as follows:

	Budget for 2011			Actual for 2011		
Product	Selling Price	Variable Cost per Carton	Cartons Sold	Selling Price	Variable Cost per Carton	Cartons Sold
Kola	$8.00	$5.00	480,000	$8.20	$5.50	467,500
Limor	$6.00	$3.80	720,000	$5.75	$3.75	852,500
Orlem	$7.50	$5.50	1,200,000	$7.80	$5.60	1,430,000

Required

1. Compute the total sales-volume variance, the total sales-mix variance, and the total sales-quantity variance. (Calculate all variances in terms of contribution margin.) Show results for each product in your computations.
2. What inferences can you draw from the variances computed in requirement 1?

14-26 Market-share and market-size variances (continuation of 14-25). Soda-King prepared the budget for 2011 assuming a 12% market share based on total sales in the western region of the United States. The total soft drinks market was estimated to reach sales of 20 million cartons in the region. However, actual total sales volume in the western region was 27.5 million cartons.

Required Calculate the market-share and market-size variances for Soda-King in 2011. (Calculate all variances in terms of contribution margin.) Comment on the results.

MyAccountingLab

Problems

14-27 Allocation of corporate costs to divisions. Dusty Rhodes, controller of Richfield Oil Company, is preparing a presentation to senior executives about the performance of its four divisions. Summary data (dollar amounts in millions) related to the four divisions for the most recent year are as follows:

	A	Oil & Gas Upstream	Oil & Gas Downstream	Chemical Products	Copper Mining	Total
1				DIVISIONS		
3	Revenues	$ 8,000	$16,000	$4,800	$3,200	$32,000
4	Operating Costs	3,000	15,000	3,800	3,500	25,300
5	Operating Income	$ 5,000	$ 1,000	$1,000	$ (300)	$ 6,700
6						
7	Identifiable assets	$14,000	$ 6,000	$3,000	$2,000	$25,000
8	Number of employees	9,000	12,000	6,000	3,000	30,000

Under the existing accounting system, costs incurred at corporate headquarters are collected in a single cost pool ($3,228 million in the most recent year) and allocated to each division on the basis of its actual revenues. The top managers in each division share in a division-income bonus pool. Division income is defined as operating income less allocated corporate costs.

Rhodes has analyzed the components of corporate costs and proposes that corporate costs be collected in four cost pools. The components of corporate costs for the most recent year (dollar amounts in millions) and Rhodes' suggested cost pools and allocation bases are as follows:

	Home	Insert	Page Layout	Formulas	Data	Review	View	
	A		B	C	D		E	F
11	**Corporate Cost Category**		**Amount**	**Suggested Cost Pool**	**Suggested Allocation Base**			
12	Interest on debt		$2,000	Cost Pool 1	Identifiable assets			
13	Corporate salaries		150	Cost Pool 2				
14	Accounting and control		110	Cost Pool 2				
15	General marketing		200	Cost Pool 2	Division revenues			
16	Legal		140	Cost Pool 2				
17	Research and development		200	Cost Pool 2				
18	Public affairs		203	Cost Pool 3	Positive operating income*			
19	Personnel and payroll		225	Cost Pool 4	Number of employees			
20	Total		$3,228					
21								
22	*Since public affairs cost includes the cost of public relations staff, lobbyists, and donations to							
23	environmental charities, Rhodes proposes that this cost be allocated using operating income (if positive)							
24	of divisions, with only divisions with positive operating income included in the allocation base.							

Required

1. Discuss two reasons why Richfield Oil should allocate corporate costs to each division.
2. Calculate the operating income of each division when all corporate costs are allocated based on revenues of each division.
3. Calculate the operating income of each division when all corporate costs are allocated using the four cost pools.
4. How do you think the new proposal will be received by the division managers? What are the strengths and weaknesses of Rhodes' proposal relative to the existing single-cost-pool method?

14-28 Cost allocation to divisions. Forber Bakery makes baked goods for grocery stores, and has three divisions: bread, cake, and doughnuts. Each division is run and evaluated separately, but the main headquarters incurs costs that are indirect costs for the divisions. Costs incurred in the main headquarters are as follows:

Human resources (HR) costs	$1,900,000
Accounting department costs	1,400,000
Rent and depreciation	1,200,000
Other	600,000
Total costs	$5,100,000

The Forber upper management currently allocates this cost to the divisions equally. One of the division managers has done some research on activity-based costing and proposes the use of different allocation bases for the different indirect costs—number of employees for HR costs, total revenues for accounting department costs, square feet of space for rent and depreciation costs, and equal allocation among the divisions of "other" costs. Information about the three divisions follows:

	Bread	Cake	Doughnuts
Total revenues	$20,900,000	$4,500,000	$13,400,000
Direct costs	14,500,000	3,200,000	7,250,000
Segment margin	$ 6,400,000	$1,300,000	$ 6,150,000
Number of employees	400	100	300
Square feet of space	10,000	4,000	6,000

Required

1. Allocate the indirect costs of Forber to each division equally. Calculate division operating income after allocation of headquarter costs.

2. Allocate headquarter costs to the individual divisions using the proposed allocation bases. Calculate the division operating income after allocation. Comment on the allocation bases used to allocate headquarter costs.

3. Which division manager do you think suggested this new allocation. Explain briefly. Which allocation do you think is "better?"

14-29 Customer profitability. Ring Delights is a new company that manufactures custom jewelry. Ring Delights currently has six customers referenced by customer number: 01, 02, 03, 04, 05, and 06. Besides the costs of making the jewelry, the company has the following activities:

1. **Customer orders.** The salespeople, designers, and jewelry makers spend time with the customer. The cost driver rate is $40 per hour spent with a customer.

2. **Customer fittings.** Before the jewelry piece is completed the customer may come in to make sure it looks right and fits properly. Cost driver rate is $25 per hour.

3. **Rush orders.** Some customers want their jewelry quickly. The cost driver rate is $100 per rush order.

4. **Number of customer return visits.** Customers may return jewelry up to 30 days after the pickup of the jewelry to have something refitted or repaired at no charge. The cost driver rate is $30 per return visit.

Information about the six customers follows. Some customers purchased multiple items. The cost of the jewelry is 70% of the selling price.

Customer number	01	02	03	04	05	06
Sales revenue	$600	$4,200	$300	$2,500	$4,900	$700
Cost of item(s)	$420	$2,940	$210	$1,750	$3,430	$490
Hours spent on customer order	2	7	1	5	20	3
Hours on fittings	1	2	0	0	4	1
Number of rush orders	0	0	1	1	3	0
Number of returns visits	0	1	0	1	5	1

Required

1. Calculate the customer-level operating income for each customer. Rank the customers in order of most to least profitable and prepare a customer-profitability analysis, as in Exhibit 7.

2. Are any customers unprofitable? What is causing this? What should Ring Delights do with respect to these customers?

14-30 Customer profitability, distribution. Spring Distribution has decided to analyze the profitability of five new customers. It buys bottled water at $12 per case and sells to retail customers at a list price of $14.40 per case. Data pertaining to the five customers are as follows:

	Customer				
	P	Q	R	S	T
Cases sold	2,080	8,750	60,800	31,800	3,900
List selling price	$14.40	$14.40	$14.40	$14.40	$14.40
Actual selling price	$14.40	$14.16	$13.20	$13.92	$12.96
Number of purchase orders	15	25	30	25	30
Number of customer visits	2	3	6	2	3
Number of deliveries	10	30	60	40	20
Miles traveled per delivery	14	4	3	8	40
Number of expedited deliveries	0	0	0	0	1

Its five activities and their cost drivers are as follows:

Activity	Cost Driver Rate
Order taking	$100 per purchase order
Customer visits	$80 per customer visit
Deliveries	$2 per delivery mile traveled
Product handling	$0.50 per case sold
Expedited deliveries	$300 per expedited delivery

Required

1. Compute the customer-level operating income of each of the five retail customers now being examined (P, Q, R, S, and T). Comment on the results.

2. What insights are gained by reporting both the list selling price and the actual selling price for each customer?

3. What factors should Spring Distribution consider in deciding whether to drop one or more of the five customers?

14-31 Customer profitability in a manufacturing firm. Bizzan Manufacturing makes a component called P14-31. This component is manufactured only when ordered by a customer, so Bizzan keeps no inventory of P14-31. The list price is $100 per unit, but customers who place "large" orders receive a 10% discount on price. Currently, the salespeople decide whether an order is large enough to qualify for the discount. When the product is finished, it is packed in cases of 10. When a customer order is not a multiple of 10, Bizzan uses a full case to pack the partial amount left over (e.g., if customer C orders 25 units, three cases will be required). Customers pick up the order so Bizzan incurs costs of holding the product in the warehouse until customer pick up. The customers are manufacturing firms; if the component needs to be exchanged or repaired, customers can come back within 10 days for free exchange or repair.

The full cost of manufacturing a unit of P14-31 is $80. In addition, Bizzan incurs customer-level costs. Customer-level cost-driver rates are as follows:

Order taking	$390 per order
Product handling	$10 per case
Warehousing (holding finished product)	$55 per day
Rush order processing	$540 per rush order
Exchange and repair costs	$45 per unit

Information about Bizzan's five biggest customers follows:

	A	B	C	D	E
Number of units purchased	6,000	2,500	1,300	4,200	7,800
Discounts given	10%	0	10%	0	10% on half the units
Number of orders	10	12	52	18	12
Number of cases	600	250	120	420	780
Days in warehouse (total for all orders)	14	18	0	12	140
Number of rush orders	0	3	0	0	6
Number of units exchanged/repaired	0	25	4	25	80

The salesperson gave customer C a price discount because, although customer C ordered only 1,300 units in total, 52 orders (one per week) were placed. The salesperson wanted to reward customer C for repeat business. All customers except E ordered units in the same order size. Customer E's order quantity varied, so E got a discount part of the time but not all the time.

1. Calculate the customer-level operating income for these five customers. Use the format in Exhibit 5. Prepare a customer-profitability analysis by ranking the customers from most to least profitable, as in Exhibit 7

2. Discuss the results of your customer-profitability analysis. Does Bizzan have unprofitable customers? Is there anything Bizzan should do differently with its five customers?

Required

14-32 Variance analysis, sales-mix and sales-quantity variances. Chicago Infonautics, Inc., produces handheld Windows CE™-compatible organizers. Chicago Infonautics markets three different handheld models: PalmPro is a souped-up version for the executive on the go, PalmCE is a consumer-oriented version, and PalmKid is a stripped-down version for the young adult market. You are Chicago Infonautics' senior vice president of marketing. The CEO has discovered that the total contribution margin came in lower than budgeted, and it is your responsibility to explain to him why actual results are different from the budget. Budgeted and actual operating data for the company's third quarter of 2012 are as follows:

Budgeted Operating Data, Third Quarter 2012

	Selling Price	Variable Cost per Unit	Contribution Margin per Unit	Sales Volume in Units
PalmPro	$374	$185	$189	13,580
PalmCE	272	96	176	35,890
PalmKid	144	66	78	47,530
				97,000

Actual Operating Data, Third Quarter 2012

	Selling Price	Variable Cost per Unit	Contribution Margin per Unit	Sales Volume in Units
PalmPro	$365	$175	$190	10,120
PalmCE	288	94	194	32,200
PalmKid	110	75	35	49,680
				92,000

Required

1. Compute the actual and budgeted contribution margins in dollars for each product and in total for the third quarter of 2012.
2. Calculate the actual and budgeted sales mixes for the three products for the third quarter of 2012.
3. Calculate total sales-volume, sales-mix, and sales-quantity variances for the third quarter of 2012. (Calculate all variances in terms of contribution margins.)
4. Given that your CEO is known to have temper tantrums, you want to be well prepared for this meeting. In order to prepare, write a paragraph or two comparing actual results to budgeted amounts.

14-33 Market-share and market-size variances (continuation of 14-32). Chicago Infonautics' senior vice president of marketing prepared his budget at the beginning of the third quarter assuming a 25% market share based on total sales. The total handheld-organizer market was estimated by Foolinstead Research to reach sales of 388,000 units worldwide in the third quarter. However, actual sales in the third quarter were 400,000 units.

Required

1. Calculate the market-share and market-size variances for Chicago Infonautics in the third quarter of 2012 (calculate all variances in terms of contribution margins).
2. Explain what happened based on the market-share and market-size variances.
3. Calculate the actual market size, in units, that would have led to no market-size variance (again using budgeted contribution margin per unit). Use this market-size figure to calculate the actual market share that would have led to a zero market-share variance.

14-34 Variance analysis, multiple products. The Split Banana, Inc., operates a chain of Italian gelato stores. Although the Split Banana charges customers the same price for all flavors, production costs vary, depending on the type of ingredients. Budgeted and actual operating data of its three Washington, DC, stores for August 2011 are as follows:

Budget for August 2011

	Selling Price per Pint	Variable Cost per Pint	Contribution Margin per Pints	Sales Volume in Pints
Mint chocolate chip	$9.00	$4.80	$4.20	25,000
Vanilla	9.00	3.20	5.80	35,000
Rum Raisin	9.00	5.00	4.00	5,000
Peach	9.00	5.40	3.60	15,000
Coffee	9.00	3.90	5.10	20,000
				100,000

Actual for August 2011

	Selling Price per Pint	Variable Cost per Pound	Contribution Margin per Pound	Sales Volume in Pounds
Mint chocolate chip	$9.00	$4.60	$4.40	30,800
Vanilla	9.00	3.25	5.75	27,500
Rum Raisin	9.00	5.15	3.85	8,800
Peach	9.00	5.40	3.60	14,300
Coffee	9.00	4.00	5.00	28,600
				110,000

The Split Banana focuses on contribution margin in its variance analysis.

Required

1. Compute the total sales-volume variance for August 2011.
2. Compute the total sales-mix variance for August 2011.
3. Compute the total sales-quantity variance for August 2011.
4. Comment on your results in requirements 1, 2, and 3.

14-35 Direct materials efficiency, mix, and yield variances. Nature's Best Nuts produces specialty nut products for the gourmet and natural foods market. Its most popular product is Zesty Zingers, a mixture of roasted nuts that are seasoned with a secret spice mixture, and sold in one-pound tins. The direct materials used in Zesty Zingers are almonds, cashews, pistachios, and seasoning. For each batch of 100 tins, the budgeted quantities and budgeted prices of direct materials are as follows:

	Quantity for One Batch	Price of Input
Almonds	180 cups	$1 per cup
Cashews	300 cups	$2 per cup
Pistachios	90 cups	$3 per cup
Seasoning	30 cups	$6 per cup

Changing the standard mix of direct material quantities slightly does not significantly affect the overall end product, particularly for the nuts. In addition, not all nuts added to production end up in the finished product, as some are rejected during inspection.

In the current period, Nature's Best made 2,500 tins of Zesty Zingers in 25 batches with the following actual quantity, cost and mix of inputs:

	Actual Quantity	Actual Cost	Actual Mix
Almonds	5,280 cups	$ 5,280	33%
Cashews	7,520 cups	15,040	47%
Pistachios	2,720 cups	8,160	17%
Seasoning	480 cups	2,880	3%
Total actual	16,000 cups	$31,360	100%

Required

1. What is the budgeted cost of direct materials for the 2,500 tins?
2. Calculate the total direct materials efficiency variance.
3. Why is the total direct materials price variance zero?
4. Calculate the total direct materials mix and yield variances. What are these variances telling you about the 2,500 tins produced this period? Are the variances large enough to investigate?

14-36 Direct labor variances: price, efficiency, mix, and yield. Trevor Joseph employs two workers in his guitar-making business. The first worker, George, has been making guitars for 20 years and is paid $30 per hour. The second worker, Earl, is less experienced, and is paid $20 per hour. One guitar requires, on average, 10 hours of labor. The budgeted direct labor quantities and prices for one guitar are as follows:

	Quantity	Price per Hour of Labor	Cost for One Guitar
George	6 hours	$30 per hour	$180
Earl	4 hours	$20 per hour	80

That is, each guitar is budgeted to require 10 hours of direct labor, comprised of 60% of George's labor and 40% of Earl's, although sometimes Earl works more hours on a particular guitar and George less, or vice versa, with no obvious change in the quality or function of the guitar.

During the month of August, Joseph manufactures 25 guitars. Actual direct labor costs are as follows:

George (145 hours)	$4,350
Earl (108 hours)	2,160
Total actual direct labor cost	$6,510

Required

1. What is the budgeted cost of direct labor for 25 guitars?
2. Calculate the total direct labor price and efficiency variances.
3. For the 25 guitars, what is the total actual amount of direct labor used? What is the actual direct labor input mix percentage? What is the budgeted amount of George's and Earl's labor that should have been used for the 25 guitars?
4. Calculate the total direct labor mix and yield variances. How do these numbers relate to the total direct labor efficiency variance? What do these variances tell you?

14-37 Purposes of cost allocation. Sarah Reynolds recently started a job as an administrative assistant in the cost accounting department of Mize Manufacturing. New to the area of cost accounting, Sarah is puzzled by the fact that one of Mize's manufactured products, SR460, seem to have a different cost, depending on who asks for it. When the marketing department requested the cost of SR460 in order to determine pricing for the new catalog, Sarah was told to report one amount, but when a request came in the very next day from the financial reporting department, the cost of SR460, she was told the cost was very different. Sarah runs a report using Mize's cost accounting system, which produces the following cost elements for one unit of SR460:

Direct materials	$28.50
Direct manufacturing labor	16.35
Variable manufacturing overhead	8.76
Allocated fixed manufacturing overhead	32.84
Research and development costs specific to SR460[a]	6.20
Marketing costs[a]	5.95
Sales commissions[a]	11.40
Allocated administrative costs of production department	5.38
Allocated administrative costs of corporate headquarters	18.60
Customer service costs[a]	3.05
Distribution costs[a]	8.80

[a]These costs are specific to SR460, but would not be eliminated if SR460 were purchased from an outside supplier.

Required

1. Explain to Sarah why the cost given to the marketing and financial reporting departments would be different.
2. Calculate the cost of one unit of SR460 to determine the following:
   a. The selling price of SR460
   b. The cost of inventory for financial reporting
   c. Whether to continue manufacturing SR460, or to purchase it from an outside source (Assume that SR460 is used as a component in one of Mize's other products.)
   d. The ability of Mize's production manager to control costs

14-38 Customer-cost hierarchy, customer profitability. Denise Nelson operates Interiors by Denise, an interior design consulting and window treatment fabrication business. Her business is made up of two different distribution channels, a consulting business in which Denise serves two architecture firms (Attractive Abodes and Better Buildings), and a commercial window treatment business in which Denise designs and constructs window treatments for three commercial clients (Cheery Curtains, Delightful Drapes, and Elegant Extras). Denise would like to evaluate the profitability of her two architecture firm clients and three commercial window treatment clients, as well as evaluate the profitability of each of the two divisions, and the business as a whole. Information about her most recent quarter follow:

Gross revenue from Attractive Abodes (AA)	$58,500
Gross revenue from Better Buildings (BB)	47,200
Gross revenue from Cheery Curtains (CC)	89,345
Gross revenue from Delightful Drapes (DD)	36,960
Gross revenue from Elegant Extras (EE)	18,300
Costs specific to AA	36,750
Costs specific to BB	29,300
Costs specific to CC	54,645
Costs specific to DD	28,930
Costs specific to EE	14,260
Overhead costs[a]	85,100

[a]Denise has determined that 25% of her overhead costs relate directly to her architectural business, 40% relate directly to her window treatment business, and the remainder is general in nature.

Denise gave a 10% discount to Attractive Abodes in order to lure it away from a competitor, and gave a 5% discount to Elegant Extras for advance payment in cash.

Required

1. Prepare a customer-cost hierarchy report for Interiors by Denise, using the format in Exhibit 6.
2. Prepare a customer-profitability analysis for the five customers, using the format in Exhibit 7.
3. Comment on the results of the preceding reports. What recommendations would you give Denise?

Collaborative Learning Problem

14-39 Customer profitability and ethics. Snark Corporation manufactures a product called the snark, which it sells to merchandising firms such as Snark Republic (SR), Snarks-R-Us (SRU), Neiman Snark-us (NS), Snark Buy (SB), Snark-Mart (SM), and Wal-Snark (WS). The list price of a snark is $50, and the full manufacturing costs are $35. Salespeople receive a commission on sales, but the commission is based on number of orders taken, not on sales revenue generated or number of units sold. Salespeople receive a commission of $25 per order (in addition to regular salary).

Snark Corporation makes products based on anticipated demand. Snark Corporation carries an inventory of snarks so rush orders do not result in any extra manufacturing costs over and above the $35 per snark. Snark Corporation ships finished product to the customer at no additional charge to the customer for either regular or expedited delivery. Snark incurs significantly higher costs for expedited deliveries than for regular deliveries. Customers occasionally return shipments to Snark, and these returns are subtracted from gross revenue. The customers are not charged a restocking fee for returns

Budgeted (expected) customer-level cost driver rates are as follows:

Order taking (excluding sales commission)	$30 per order
Product handling	$2 per unit
Delivery	$0.50 per mile driven
Expedited (rush) delivery	$325 per shipment
Restocking	$100 per returned shipment
Visits to customers	$150 per customer

Because salespeople are paid $25 per order, they often break up large orders into multiple smaller orders. This practice reduces the actual order taking cost by $16 per smaller order (from $30 per order to $14 per order) because the smaller orders are all written at the same time. This lower cost rate is not included in budgeted rates because salespeople create smaller orders without telling management or the accounting department. All other actual costs are the same as budgeted costs.

Information about Snark's clients follows:

	SR	SRU	NS	SB	SM	WS
Total number of units purchased	250	550	320	130	450	1,200
Number of actual orders	3	15	3	4	5	15
Number of written orders	6	15*	8	7	20	30
Total number of miles driven to deliver all products	420	620	470	280	806	900
Total number of units returned	20	35	0	0	40	60
Number of returned shipments	2	1	0	0	2	6
Number of expedited deliveries	0	6	0	0	2	5

*Because SRU places 15 separate orders, its order costs are $30 per order. All other orders are multiple smaller orders and so have actual order costs of $14 each.

Required

1. Classify each of the customer-level operating costs as a customer output-unit-level, customer batch-level, or customer-sustaining cost.
2. Using the preceding information, calculate the expected customer-level operating income for the six customers of Snark Corporation. Use the number of written orders at $30 each to calculate expected order costs.
3. Recalculate the customer-level operating income using the number of written orders but at their actual $14 cost per order instead of $30 (except for SRU, whose actual cost is $30 per order). How will Snark Corporation evaluate customer-level operating cost performance this period?
4. Recalculate the customer-level operating income if salespeople had not broken up actual orders into multiple smaller orders. Don't forget to also adjust sales commissions.
5. How is the behavior of the salespeople affecting the profit of Snark Corporation? Is their behavior ethical? What could Snark Corporation do to change the behavior of the salespeople?

Cost Allocation: Joint Products and Byproducts

From Chapter 16 of *Cost Accounting: A Managerial Emphasis*, 14/e. Charles T. Horngren. Srikant M. Datar. Madhav Rajan.

Cost Allocation: Joint Products and Byproducts

▶ Learning Objectives

1. Identify the splitoff point in a joint-cost situation and distinguish joint products from byproducts

2. Explain why joint costs are allocated to individual products

3. Allocate joint costs using four methods

4. Explain when the sales value at splitoff method is preferred when allocating joint costs

5. Explain why joint costs are irrelevant in a sell-or-process-further decision

6. Account for byproducts using two methods

Many companies, such as petroleum refiners, produce and sell two or more products simultaneously.

Similarly, some companies, such as health care providers, sell or provide multiple services. The question is, "How should these companies allocate costs to 'joint' products and services?" Knowing how to allocate joint product costs isn't something that only companies need to understand. It's something that farmers have to deal with, too, especially when it comes to the lucrative production of corn to make billions of gallons of ethanol fuel.

Joint Cost Allocation and the Production of Ethanol Fuel[1]

The increased global demand for oil has driven prices higher and forced countries to look for environmentally-sustainable alternatives. In the United States, the largest source of alternative fuel comes from corn-based ethanol. In 2009, the U.S. produced 10.75 billion gallons of ethanol, or 55% of the world's production, up from 1.7 billion gallons per year in 2001.

Producing ethanol requires a significant amount of corn. In 2011, the U.S. Department of Agriculture predicts that more than one-third of U.S. domestic corn production will be used to create ethanol fuel. But not all of that corn winds up in the ethanol that gets blended into gasoline and sold at service station.

Most biotechnology operations, such as making ethanol, produce two or more products. While distilling corn into ethanol, cell mass from the process—such as antibiotic and yeast fermentations—separates from the liquid and becomes a separate product, which is often sold as animal feed. This separation point, where outputs become distinctly identifiable, is called the splitoff point. Similarly, the residues from corn processing plants create secondary products including distillers' dried grains and gluten.

Accountants refer to these secondary products as byproducts. Ethanol byproducts like animal feed and gluten are accounted for by deducting the income from selling these products from the cost of ethanol fuel, the major product. With ethanol production costing

---

[1] *Sources:* Hacking, Andrew. 1987. *Economic aspects of biotechnology.* Cambridge, United Kingdom: Cambridge University Press; Leber, Jessica. 2010. Economics improve for first commercial cellulosic ethanol plants. *New York Times,* February 16; *USDA Agricultural Predictions to 2019.* 2010. Washington, DC: Government Printing Office; PBS. 2006. Glut of ethanol byproducts coming. *The Environmental Report,* Spring; *Entrepreneur.* 2007. Edible ethanol byproduct is source of novel foods. August.

around $2 per gallon and byproducts selling for a few cents per pound, most of the costs of production are allocated to the ethanol fuel itself, the main product. Since manufacturers would otherwise have to pay to dispose of their ethanol byproducts, most just try to "break even" on byproduct revenue.

In the coming years, however, this may change. With ethanol production growing, corn-based animal feed byproducts are becoming more plentiful. Some ethanol manufacturers are working together to create a market for ethanol feed, which is cheaper and higher in protein than plain corn. This allows ranchers' animals to gain weight faster and at a lower cost per pound. Additionally, scientists are trying to create an edible byproduct from distillers' dry grains, which could become a low-calorie, low-carbohydrate substitute in foods like breads and pastas.

Accounting concerns similar to those in the ethanol example also arise when traditional energy companies like ExxonMobil simultaneously produce crude oil, natural gas, and raw liquefied petroleum gas (LPS) from petroleum, in a single process. This chapter examines methods for allocating costs to joint products. We also examine how cost numbers appropriate for one purpose, such as external reporting, may not be appropriate for other purposes, such as decisions about the further processing of joint products.

Jim West\Alamy Images

Joint-Cost Basics

Joint costs are the costs of a production process that yields multiple products simultaneously. Consider the distillation of coal, which yields coke, natural gas, and other products. The costs of this distillation are joint costs. The **splitoff point** is the juncture in a joint production process when two or more products become separately identifiable. An example is the point at which coal becomes coke, natural gas, and other products. **Separable costs** are all costs—manufacturing, marketing, distribution, and so on—incurred beyond the splitoff point that are assignable to each of the specific products identified at the splitoff point. At or beyond the splitoff point, decisions relating to the sale or further processing of each identifiable product can be made independently of decisions about the other products.

Industries abound in which a production process simultaneously yields two or more products, either at the splitoff point or after further processing. Exhibit 1 presents examples of joint-cost situations in diverse industries. In each of these examples, no individual product can be produced without the accompanying products appearing, although in some cases the proportions can be varied. The focus of joint costing is on allocating costs to individual products at the splitoff point.

The outputs of a joint production process can be classified into two general categories: outputs with a positive sales value and outputs with a zero sales value.[2] For

Learning Objective 1

Identify the splitoff point in a joint-cost situation

. . . the point at which two or more products become separately identifiable

and distinguish joint products

. . . products with high sales values

from byproducts

. . . products with low sales values

[2] Some outputs of a joint production process have "negative" revenue when their disposal costs (such as the costs of handling nonsalable toxic substances that require special disposal procedures) are considered. These disposal costs should be added to the joint production costs that are allocated to joint or main products.

Industry	Separable Products at the Splitoff Point
Agriculture and	
Food Processing Industries	
Cocoa beans	Cocoa butter, cocoa powder, cocoa drink mix, tanning cream
Lambs	Lamb cuts, tripe, hides, bones, fat
Hogs	Bacon, ham, spare ribs, pork roast
Raw milk	Cream, liquid skim
Lumber	Lumber of varying grades and shapes
Turkeys	Breast, wings, thighs, drumsticks, digest, feather meal, and poultry meal
Extractive Industries	
Coal	Coke, gas, benzol, tar, ammonia
Copper ore	Copper, silver, lead, zinc
Petroleum	Crude oil, natural gas
Salt	Hydrogen, chlorine, caustic soda
Chemical Industries	
Raw LPG (liquefied petroleum gas)	Butane, ethane, propane
Crude oil	Gasoline, kerosene, benzene, naphtha
Semiconductor Industry	
Fabrication of silicon-wafer chips	Memory chips of different quality (as to capacity), speed, life expectancy, and temperature tolerance

example, offshore processing of hydrocarbons yields oil and natural gas, which have positive sales value, and it also yields water, which has zero sales value and is recycled back into the ocean. The term **product** describes any output that has a positive total sales value (or an output that enables a company to avoid incurring costs, such as an intermediate chemical product used as input in another process). The total sales value can be high or low.

When a joint production process yields one product with a high total sales value, compared with total sales values of other products of the process, that product is called a **main product**. When a joint production process yields two or more products with high total sales values compared with the total sales values of other products, if any, those products are called **joint products**. The products of a joint production process that have low total sales values compared with the total sales value of the main product or of joint products are called **byproducts**.

Consider some examples. If timber (logs) is processed into standard lumber and wood chips, standard lumber is a main product and wood chips are the byproduct, because standard lumber has a high total sales value compared with wood chips. If, however, logs are processed into fine-grade lumber, standard lumber, and wood chips, fine-grade lumber and standard lumber are joint products, and wood chips are the byproduct. That's because both fine-grade lumber and standard lumber have high total sales values when compared with wood chips.

Distinctions among main products, joint products, and byproducts are not so definite in practice. For example, some companies may classify kerosene obtained when refining crude oil as a byproduct because they believe kerosene has a low total sales value relative to the total sales values of gasoline and other products. Other companies may classify kerosene as a joint product because they believe kerosene has a high total sales value relative to the total sales values of gasoline and other products. Moreover, the classification of products—main, joint, or byproduct—can change over time, especially for products such as lower-grade semiconductor chips, whose market prices may increase or decrease by 30% or more in a year. When prices of lower-grade chips are high, they are considered joint products together with higher-grade chips; when prices of lower-grade chips fall considerably, they are considered byproducts. In practice, it is important to understand how a specific company chooses to classify its products.

Decision Point ▶

What do the terms
joint cost and splitoff
point mean, and
how do joint
products differ from
byproducts?

Allocating Joint Costs

Before a manager is able to allocate joint costs, she must first look at the context for doing so. There are several contexts in which joint costs are required to be allocated to individual products or services. These include the following:

Learning Objective 2

Explain why joint costs are allocated to individual products

. . . to calculate cost of goods sold and inventory, and for reimbursements under cost-plus contracts and other types of claims

- Computation of inventoriable costs and cost of goods sold. Absorption costing is required for financial accounting and tax reporting purposes. This necessitates the allocation of joint manufacturing or processing costs to products for calculating ending inventory values.

- Computation of inventoriable costs and cost of goods sold for internal reporting purposes. Many firms use internal accounting data based on joint cost allocations for the purpose of analyzing divisional profitability and in order to evaluate division managers' performance.

- Cost reimbursement for companies that have a few, but not all, of their products or services reimbursed under cost-plus contracts with, say, a government agency. In this case, stringent rules typically specify the manner in which joint costs are assigned to the products or services covered by the cost-plus agreement. That said, fraud in defense contracting, which is often done via cost-plus contracts, remains one of the most active areas of false claim litigation under the Federal False Claims Act. A common practice is "cross-charging," where a contractor shifts joint costs from "fixed-price" defense contracts to those that are done on a cost-plus basis. Defense contractors have also attempted to secure contracts from private businesses or foreign governments by allocating an improper share of joint costs onto the cost-plus agreements they have with the United States government.[3]

- Rate or price regulation for one or more of the jointly produced products or services. This issue is conceptually related to the previous point, and is of great importance in the extractive and energy industries where output prices are regulated to yield a fixed return on a cost basis that includes joint cost allocations. In telecommunications, for example, it is often the case that a firm with significant market power has some products subject to price regulation (e.g., interconnection) and other activities that are unregulated (such as end-user equipment rentals). In this case, it is critical in allocating joint costs to ensure that costs are not transferred from unregulated services to regulated ones.[4]

Decision Point

Why are joint costs allocated to individual products?

- Insurance-settlement computations for damage claims made on the basis of cost information of jointly produced products. In this case, the joint cost allocations are essential in order to provide a cost-based analysis of the loss in value.

- More generally, any commercial litigation situation in which costs of joint products or services are key inputs requires the allocation of joint costs.

Approaches to Allocating Joint Costs

Two approaches are used to allocate joint costs.

Learning Objective 3

Allocate joint costs using four methods

. . . sales value at splitoff, physical measure, net realizable value (NRV), and constant gross-margin percentage NRV

- **Approach 1.** Allocate joint costs using *market-based* data such as revenues. This chapter illustrates three methods that use this approach:
  1. Sales value at splitoff method
  2. Net realizable value (NRV) method
  3. Constant gross-margin percentage NRV method
- **Approach 2.** Allocate joint costs using *physical measures*, such as the weight, quantity (physical units), or volume of the joint products.

Previously, we used the cause-and-effect and benefits-received criteria for guiding cost-allocation decisions. Joint costs do not have a cause-and-effect relationship with individual products because the production process simultaneously yields multiple products. Using the benefits-received criterion leads to a preference for methods under approach 1 because revenues are, in general, a better indicator of benefits received

---

[3] See, for example, www.dodig.mil/iginformation/IGInformationReleases/3eSettlementPR.pdf
[4] For details, see the International Telecommunication Union's ICT Regulation Toolkit at www.ictregulationtoolkit.org/en/Section.3497.html.

than physical measures. Mining companies, for example, receive more benefits from 1 ton of gold than they do from 10 tons of coal.

In the simplest joint production process, the joint products are sold at the splitoff point without further processing. Example 1 illustrates the two methods that apply in this case: the sales value at splitoff method and the physical-measure method. Then we introduce joint production processes that yield products that require further processing beyond the splitoff point. Example 2 illustrates the NRV method and the constant-gross margin percentage NRV method. To help you focus on key concepts, we use numbers and amounts that are smaller than the numbers that are typically found in practice.

The exhibits in this chapter use the following symbols to distinguish a joint or main product from a byproduct:

Joint Product or Main Product   Byproduct

To compare methods, we report gross-margin percentages for individual products under each method.

Example 1: Farmers' Dairy purchases raw milk from individual farms and processes it until the splitoff point, when two products—cream and liquid skim—emerge. These two products are sold to an independent company, which markets and distributes them to supermarkets and other retail outlets.

In May 2012, Farmers' Dairy processes 110,000 gallons of raw milk. During processing, 10,000 gallons are lost due to evaporation and spillage, yielding 25,000 gallons of cream and 75,000 gallons of liquid skim. Summary data follow:

	Home	Insert	Page Layout	Formulas	Data	Review
	A				B	C
1					Joint Costs	
2	Joint costs (costs of 110,000 gallons raw milk and processing to splitoff point)				$400,000	
3						
4					Cream	Liquid Skim
5	Beginnning inventory (gallons)				0	0
6	Production (gallons)				25,000	75,000
7	Sales (gallons)				20,000	30,000
8	Ending inventory (gallons)				5,000	45,000
9	Selling price per gallon				$ 8	$ 4

Exhibit 2 depicts the basic relationships in this example.

How much of the $400,000 joint costs should be allocated to the cost of goods sold of 20,000 gallons of cream and 30,000 gallons of liquid skim, and how much should be allocated to the ending inventory of 5,000 gallons of cream and 45,000 gallons of liquid skim? We begin by illustrating the two methods that use the properties of the products at the splitoff point, the sales value at splitoff method and the physical-measure method.

Sales Value at Splitoff Method

The **sales value at splitoff method** allocates joint costs to joint products produced during the accounting period on the basis of the relative total sales value at the splitoff point. Using this method for Example 1, Exhibit 3, Panel A, shows how joint costs

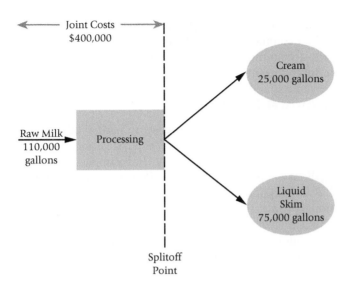

Exhibit 2

Example 1: Overview of
Farmers' Dairy

are allocated to individual products to calculate cost per gallon of cream and liquid skim for valuing ending inventory. This method uses the sales value of the *entire production of the accounting period* (25,000 gallons of cream and 75,000 gallons of liquid skim), not just the quantity sold (20,000 gallons of cream and 30,000 gallons of liquid skim). The reason this method does not rely solely on the quantity sold is that the joint costs were incurred on all units produced, not just the portion sold during the current period. Exhibit 3, Panel B, presents the product-line income statement using the sales value at splitoff method. Note that the gross-margin percentage for each product is 20%, because the sales value at splitoff method allocates joint costs to each product in proportion to the sales value of total production (cream: $160,000 ÷ $200,000 = 80%; liquid skim: $240,000 ÷ $300,000 = 80%). Therefore, the gross-margin percentage for each product manufactured in May 2012 is the same: 20%.[5]

Note how the sales value at splitoff method follows the benefits-received criterion of cost allocation: Costs are allocated to products in proportion to their revenue-generating

Exhibit 3   Joint-Cost Allocation and Product-Line Income Statement Using Sales Value at Splitoff Method: Farmers' Dairy for May 2012

	A	B	C	D
		Cream	Liquid Skim	Total
1	PANEL A: Allocation of Joint Costs Using Sales Value at Splitoff Method			
2	Sales value of total production at splitoff point			
3	(25,000 gallons × $8 per gallon; 75,000 gallons × $4 per gallon)	$200,000	$300,000	$500,000
4	Weighting ($200,000 ÷ $500,000; $300,000 ÷ 500,000)	0.40	0.60	
5	Joint costs allocated (0.40 × $400,000; 0.60 × $400,000)	$160,000	$240,000	$400,000
6	Joint production cost per gallon			
7	($160,000 ÷ 25,000 gallons; $240,000 ÷ 75,000 gallons)	$ 6.40	$ 3.20	
8				
9	PANEL B: Product-Line Income Statement Using Sales Value at Splitoff Method for May 2012	Cream	Liquid Skim	Total
10	Revenues (20,000 gallons × $8 per gallon; 30,000 gallons × $4 per gallon)	$160,000	$120,000	$280,000
11	Cost of goods sold (joint costs)			
12	Production costs (0.40 × $400,000; 0.60 × $400,000)	160,000	240,000	400,000
13	Deduct ending inventory (5,000 gallons × $6.40 per gallon; 45,000 gallons × $3.20 per gallon)	32,000	144,000	176,000
14	Cost of goods sold (joint costs)	128,000	96,000	224,000
15	Gross margin	$ 32,000	$ 24,000	$ 56,000
16	Gross margin percentage ($32,000 ÷ $160,000; $24,000 ÷ $120,000; $56,000 ÷ $280,000)	20%	20%	20%

[5] Suppose Farmers' Dairy has beginning inventory of cream and liquid milk in May 2012 and when this inventory is sold, Farmers' earns a gross margin different from 20%. Then the gross-margin percentage for cream and liquid skim will not be the same. The relative gross-margin percentages will depend on how much of the sales of each product came from beginning inventory and how much came from current-period production.

power (their expected revenues). The cost-allocation base (total sales value at splitoff) is expressed in terms of a common denominator (the amount of revenues) that is systematically recorded in the accounting system. To use this method, selling prices must exist for all products at the splitoff point.

Physical-Measure Method

The **physical-measure method** allocates joint costs to joint products produced during the accounting period on the basis of a *comparable* physical measure, such as the relative weight, quantity, or volume at the splitoff point. In Example 1, the $400,000 joint costs produced 25,000 gallons of cream and 75,000 gallons of liquid skim. Using the number of gallons produced as the physical measure, Exhibit 4, Panel A, shows how joint costs are allocated to individual products to calculate the cost per gallon of cream and liquid skim.

Because the physical-measure method allocates joint costs on the basis of the number of gallons, cost per gallon is the same for both products. Exhibit 4, Panel B, presents the product-line income statement using the physical-measure method. The gross-margin percentages are 50% for cream and 0% for liquid skim.

Under the benefits-received criterion, the physical-measure method is much less desirable than the sales value at splitoff method, because the physical measure of the individual products may have no relationship to their respective revenue-generating abilities. Consider a gold mine that extracts ore containing gold, silver, and lead. Use of a common physical measure (tons) would result in almost all costs being allocated to lead, the product that weighs the most but has the lowest revenue-generating power. In the case of metals, the method of cost allocation is inconsistent with the main reason that the mining company is incurring mining costs—to earn revenues from gold and silver, not lead. When a company uses the physical-measure method in a product-line income statement, products that have a high sales value per ton, like gold and silver, would show a large "profit," and products that have a low sales value per ton, like lead, would show sizable losses.

Obtaining comparable physical measures for all products is not always straightforward. Consider the joint costs of producing oil and natural gas; oil is a liquid and gas is a vapor. To use a physical measure, the oil and gas need to be converted to the energy equivalent for oil and gas, British thermal units (BTUs). Using some physical measures to allocate joint costs may require assistance from technical personnel outside of accounting.

Determining which products of a joint process to include in a physical-measure computation can greatly affect the allocations to those products. Outputs with no sales value

Exhibit 4   Joint-Cost Allocation and Product-Line Income Statement Using Physical-Measure Method: Farmers' Dairy for May 2012

	A	B	C	D
		Cream	Liquid Skim	Total
1	**PANEL A: Allocation of Joint Costs Using Physical-Measure Method**	Cream	Liquid Skim	Total
2	Physical measure of total production (gallons)	25,000	75,000	100,000
3	Weighting (25,000 gallons ÷ 100,000 gallons; 75,000 gallons ÷ 100,000 gallons)	0.25	0.75	
4	Joint costs allocated (0.25 × $400,000; 0.75 × $400,000)	$100,000	$300,000	$400,000
5	Joint production cost per gallon ($100,000 ÷ 25,000 gallons; $300,000 ÷ 75,000 gallons)	$ 4.00	$ 4.00	
6				
7	**PANEL B: Product-Line Income Statement Using Physical-Measure Method for May 2012**	Cream	Liquid Skim	Total
8	Revenues (20,000 gallons × $8 per gallon; 30,000 gallons × $4 per gallon)	$160,000	$120,000	$280,000
9	Cost of goods sold (joint costs)			
10	Production costs (0.25 × $400,000; 0.75 × $400,000)	100,000	300,000	400,000
11	Deduct ending inventory (5,000 gallons × $4 per gallon; 45,000 gallons × $4 per gallon)	20,000	180,000	200,000
12	Cost of goods sold (joint costs)	80,000	120,000	200,000
13	Gross margin	$ 80,000	$ 0	$ 80,000
14	Gross margin percentage ($80,000 ÷ $160,000; $0 ÷ $120,000; $80,000 ÷ $280,000)	50%	0%	28.6%

(such as dirt in gold mining) are always excluded. Although many more tons of dirt than gold are produced, costs are not incurred to produce outputs that have zero sales value. Byproducts are also often excluded from the denominator used in the physical-measure method because of their low sales values relative to the joint products or the main product. The general guideline for the physical-measure method is to include only the joint-product outputs in the weighting computations.

Net Realizable Value Method

In many cases, products are processed beyond the splitoff point to bring them to a marketable form or to increase their value above their selling price at the splitoff point. For example, when crude oil is refined, the gasoline, kerosene, benzene, and naphtha must be processed further before they can be sold. To illustrate, let's extend the Farmers' Dairy example.

> Example 2: Assume the same data as in Example 1 except that both cream and liquid skim can be processed further:
>
> ■ Cream → Buttercream: 25,000 gallons of cream are further processed to yield 20,000 gallons of buttercream at additional processing costs of $280,000. Buttercream, which sells for $25 per gallon, is used in the manufacture of butter-based products.
>
> ■ Liquid Skim → Condensed Milk: 75,000 gallons of liquid skim are further processed to yield 50,000 gallons of condensed milk at additional processing costs of $520,000. Condensed milk sells for $22 per gallon.
>
> ■ Sales during May 2012 are 12,000 gallons of buttercream and 45,000 gallons of condensed milk.

Exhibit 5, Panel A, depicts how (a) raw milk is converted into cream and liquid skim in the joint production process, and (b) how cream is separately processed into buttercream and liquid skim is separately processed into condensed milk. Panel B shows the data for Example 2.

The **net realizable value (NRV) method** allocates joint costs to joint products produced during the accounting period on the basis of their relative NRV—final sales value minus separable costs. The NRV method is typically used in preference to the sales value at splitoff method only when selling prices for one or more products at splitoff do not exist. Using this method for Example 2, Exhibit 6, Panel A, shows how joint costs are allocated to individual products to calculate cost per gallon of buttercream and condensed milk.

Exhibit 6, Panel B presents the product-line income statement using the NRV method. Gross-margin percentages are 22.0% for buttercream and 26.4% for condensed milk.

The NRV method is often implemented using simplifying assumptions. For example, even when selling prices of joint products vary frequently, companies implement the

---

PANEL A: Graphical Presentation of Process for Example 2

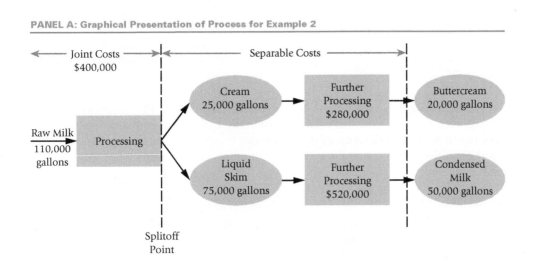

Exhibit 5

Example 2: Overview of Farmers' Dairy

Exhibit 5 Example 2: Overview of Farmers' Dairy (*continued*)

PANEL B: Data for Example 2

| Home | Insert | Page Layout | Formulas | Data | Review | View |

	A	B	C	D	E
1		**Joint Costs**		**Buttercream**	**Condensed Milk**
2	Joint costs (costs of 110,000 gallons raw milk and processing to splitoff point)	$400,000			
3	Separable cost of processing 25,000 gallons cream into 20,000 gallons buttercream			$280,000	
4	Separable cost of processing 75,000 gallons liquid skim into 50,000 gallons condensed milk				$520,000
5					
6		**Cream**	**Liquid Skim**	**Buttercream**	**Condensed Milk**
7	Beginning inventory (gallons)	0	0	0	0
8	Production (gallons)	25,000	75,000	20,000	50,000
9	Transfer for further processing (gallons)	25,000	75,000		
10	Sales (gallons)			12,000	45,000
11	Ending inventory (gallons)	0	0	8,000	5,000
12	Selling price per gallon	$ 8	$ 4	$ 25	$ 22

Exhibit 6 Joint-Cost Allocation and Product-Line Income Statement Using NRV Method: Farmers' Dairy for May 2012

| Home | Insert | Page Layout | Formulas | Data | Review | View |

	A	B	C	D
1	**PANEL A: Allocation of Joint Costs Using Net Realizable Value Method**	**Buttercream**	**Condensed Milk**	**Total**
2	Final sales value of total production during accounting period			
3	(20,000 gallons × $25 per gallon; 50,000 gallons × $22 per gallon)	$500,000	$1,100,000	$1,600,000
4	Deduct separable costs	280,000	520,000	800,000
5	Net realizable value at splitoff point	$220,000	$ 580,000	$ 800,000
6	Weighting ($220,000 ÷ $800,000; $580,000 ÷ $800,000)	0.275	0.725	
7	Joint costs allocated (0.275 × $400,000; 0.725 × $400,000)	$110,000	$ 290,000	$ 400,000
8	Production cost per gallon			
9	([$110,000 + $280,000] ÷ 20,000 gallons; [$290,000 + $520,000] ÷ 50,000 gallons)	$ 19.50	$ 16.20	
10				
11	**PANEL B: Product-Line Income Statement Using Net Realizable Value Method for May 2012**	**Buttercream**	**Condensed Milk**	**Total**
12	Revenues (12,000 gallons × $25 per gallon; 45,000 gallons × $22 per gallon)	$300,000	$ 990,000	$1,290,000
13	Cost of goods sold			
14	Joint costs (0.275 × $400,000; 0.725 × $400,000)	110,000	290,000	400,000
15	Separable costs	280,000	520,000	800,000
16	Production costs	390,000	810,000	1,200,000
17	Deduct ending inventory (8,000 gallons × $19.50 per gallon; 5,000 gallons × $16.20 per gallon)	156,000	81,000	237,000
18	Cost of goods sold	234,000	729,000	963,000
19	Gross margin	$ 66,000	$ 261,000	$ 327,000
20	Gross margin percentage ($66,000 ÷ $300,000; $261,000 ÷ $990,000; $327,000 ÷ $1,290,000)	22.0%	26.4%	25.3%

NRV method using a given set of selling prices throughout the accounting period. Similarly, even though companies may occasionally change the number or sequence of processing steps beyond the splitoff point in order to adjust to variations in input quality or local conditions, they assume a specific constant set of such steps when implementing the NRV method.

Constant Gross-Margin Percentage NRV Method

The **constant gross-margin percentage NRV method** allocates joint costs to joint products produced during the accounting period in such a way that each individual product achieves an identical gross-margin percentage. The method works backward in that the overall gross margin is computed first. Then, for each product, this gross-margin percentage and any separable costs are deducted from the final sales value of production in order to back into the joint cost allocation for that product. The method can be broken down into three discrete steps. Exhibit 7, Panel A, shows these steps for allocating the $400,000 joint costs between buttercream and condensed milk in the Farmers' Dairy example. As we describe each step, refer to Exhibit 7, Panel A, for an illustration of the step.

Step 1: Compute overall gross margin percentage. The overall gross-margin percentage for all joint products together is calculated first. This is based on the final sales value of *total production* during the accounting period, not the *total revenues* of the period. Note, Exhibit 7, Panel A, uses $1,600,000, the final expected sales value of the entire output of buttercream and condensed milk, not the $1,290,000 in actual sales revenue for the month of May.

Step 2: Compute total production costs for each product. The gross margin (in dollars) for each product is computed by multiplying the overall gross-margin percentage by the product's final sales value of total production. The difference between the final sales value of total production and the gross margin then yields the total production costs that the product must bear.

Step 3: Compute allocated joint costs. As the final step, the separable costs for each product are deducted from the total production costs that the product must bear to obtain the joint-cost allocation for that product.

Exhibit 7, Panel B, presents the product-line income statement for the constant gross-margin percentage NRV method.

Exhibit 7 Joint-Cost Allocation and Product-Line Income Statement Using Constant Gross-Margin Percentage NRV Method: Farmers' Dairy for May 2012

	A	B	C	D
	Home Insert Page Layout Formulas Data Review View			
1	PANEL A: Allocation of Joint Costs Using Constant Gross-Margin Percentage NRV Method			
2	Step 1			
3	Final sales value of total production during accounting period: (20,000 gallons × $25 per gallon) + (50,000 gallons × $22 per gallon)	$1,600,000		
4	Deduct joint and separable costs ($400,000 + $280,000 + $520,000)	1,200,000		
5	Gross margin	$ 400,000		
6	Gross margin percentage ($400,000 ÷ $1,600,000)	25%		
7		Buttercream	Condensed Milk	Total
8	Step 2			
9	Final sales value of total production during accounting period: (20,000 gallons × $25 per gallon; 50,000 gallons × $22 per gallon)	$ 500,000	$1,100,000	$1,600,000
10	Deduct gross margin, using overall gross-margin percentage (25% × $500,000; 25% × $1,100,000)	125,000	275,000	400,000
11	Total production costs	375,000	825,000	1,200,000
12	Step 3			
13	Deduct separable costs	280,000	520,000	800,000
14	Joint costs allocated	$ 95,000	$ 305,000	$ 400,000
15				
16	PANEL B: Product-Line Income Statement Using Constant Gross-Margin Percentage NRV Method for May 2012	Buttercream	Condensed Milk	Total
17	Revenues (12,000 gallons × $25 per gallon; 45,000 gallons × $22 per gallon)	$ 300,000	$ 990,000	$1,290,000
18	Cost of goods sold			
19	Joint costs (from Panel A)	95,000	305,000	400,000
20	Separable costs	280,000	520,000	800,000
21	Production costs	375,000	825,000	1,200,000
22	Deduct ending inventory			
23	(8,000 gallons × $18.75 per gallon[a]; 5,000 gallons × $16.50 per gallon[b])	150,000	82,500	232,500
24	Cost of goods sold	225,000	742,500	967,500
25	Gross margin	$ 75,000	$ 247,500	$ 322,500
26	Gross margin percentage ($75,000 ÷ 300,000; $247,500 ÷ $990,000; $322,500 ÷ $1,290,000)	25%	25%	25%
27				
28	[a]Total production costs of buttercream ÷ Total production of buttercream = $375,000 ÷ 20,000 gallons = $18.75 per gallon.			
29	[b]Total production costs of condensed milk ÷ Total production of condensed milk = $825,000 ÷ 50,000 gallons = $16.50 per gallon.			

The constant gross-margin percentage NRV method is the only method of allocating joint costs under which products may receive negative allocations. This may be required in order to bring the gross-margin percentages of relatively unprofitable products up to the overall average. The constant gross-margin percentage NRV method also differs from the other two market-based joint-cost-allocation methods described earlier in another fundamental way. Neither the sales value at splitoff method nor the NRV method takes account of profits earned either before or after the splitoff point when allocating the joint costs. In contrast, the constant gross-margin percentage NRV method allocates both joint costs and profits: Gross margin is allocated to the joint products in order to determine the joint-cost allocations so that the resulting gross-margin percentage for each product is the same.

Choosing an Allocation Method

Which method of allocating joint costs should be used? The sales value at splitoff method is preferable when selling-price data exist at splitoff (even if further processing is done). Reasons for using the sales value at splitoff method include the following:

1. **Measurement of the value of the joint products at the splitoff point.** Sales value at splitoff is the best measure of the benefits received as a result of joint processing relative to all other methods of allocating joint costs. It is a meaningful basis for allocating joint costs because generating revenues is the reason why a company incurs joint costs in the first place. It is also sometimes possible to vary the physical mix of final output and thereby produce more or less market value by incurring more joint costs. In such cases, there is a clear causal link between total cost and total output value, thereby further validating the use of the sales value at splitoff method.[6]

2. **No anticipation of subsequent management decisions.** The sales value at splitoff method does not require information on the processing steps after splitoff if there is further processing. In contrast, the NRV and constant gross-margin percentage NRV methods require information on (a) the specific sequence of further processing decisions, (b) the separable costs of further processing, and (c) the point at which individual products will be sold.

3. **Availability of a common basis to allocate joint costs to products.** The sales value at splitoff method (as well as other market-based methods) has a common basis to allocate joint costs to products, which is revenue. In contrast, the physical-measure at splitoff method may lack an easily identifiable common basis to allocate joint costs to individual products.

4. **Simplicity.** The sales value at splitoff method is simple. In contrast, the NRV and constant gross-margin percentage NRV methods can be complex for processing operations having multiple products and multiple splitoff points. This complexity increases when management makes frequent changes in the specific sequence of post-splitoff processing decisions or in the point at which individual products are sold.

When selling prices of all products at the splitoff point are unavailable, the NRV method is commonly used because it attempts to approximate sales value at splitoff by subtracting from selling prices separable costs incurred after the splitoff point. The NRV method assumes that all the markup or profit margin is attributable to the joint process and none of the markup is attributable to the separable costs. Profit, however, is attributable to all phases of production and marketing, not just the joint process. More of the profit may be attributable to the joint process if the separable process is relatively routine, whereas more of the profit may be attributable to the separable process if the separable process uses a special patented technology. Despite its complexities, the NRV method is used when selling prices at splitoff are not available as it provides a better measure of benefits received compared with the constant gross-margin percentage NRV method or the physical-measure method.

[6] In the semiconductor industry, for example, the use of cleaner facilities, higher quality silicon wafers, and more sophisticated equipment (all of which require higher joint costs) shifts the distribution of output to higher-quality memory devices with more market value. For details, see J. F. Gatti and D. J. Grinnell, "Joint Cost Allocations: Measuring and Promoting Productivity and Quality Improvements," *Journal of Cost Management* (2000). The authors also demonstrate that joint cost allocations based on market value are preferable for promoting quality and productivity improvements.

The constant gross-margin percentage NRV method makes the simplifying assumption of treating the joint products as though they comprise a single product. This method calculates the aggregate gross-margin percentage, applies this gross-margin percentage to each product, and views the residual after separable costs are accounted for as the implicit amount of joint costs assigned to each product. An advantage of this method is that it avoids the complexities inherent in the NRV method to measure the benefits received by each of the joint products at the splitoff point. The main issue with the constant gross-margin percentage NRV method is the assumption that all products have the same ratio of cost to sales value. Recall from our discussion of activity-based costing (ABC) that such a situation is very uncommon when companies offer a diverse set of products.

Although there are difficulties in using the physical-measure method—such as lack of congruence with the benefits-received criterion—there are instances when it may be preferred. Consider rate or price regulation. Market-based measures are difficult to use in this context because using selling prices as a basis for setting prices (rates) and at the same time using selling prices to allocate the costs on which prices (rates) are based leads to circular reasoning. To avoid this dilemma, the physical-measure method is useful in rate regulation.

Not Allocating Joint Costs

Some companies choose to not allocate joint costs to products. The usual rationale given by these firms is the complexity of their production or extraction processes and the difficulty of gathering sufficient data for carrying out the allocations correctly. For example, a recent survey of nine sawmills in Norway revealed that none of them allocated joint costs. The study's authors noted that the "interviewed sawmills considered the joint cost problem very interesting, but pointed out that the problem is not easily solved. For example, there is clearly a shortcoming in management systems designed for handling joint cost allocation."[7]

In the absence of joint cost allocation, some firms simply subtract the joint costs directly from total revenues in the management accounts. If substantial inventories exist, then firms that do not allocate joint costs often carry their product inventories at NRV. Industries that use variations of this approach include meatpacking, canning, and mining. Accountants do not ordinarily record inventories at NRV because this practice results in recognizing income on each product at the time production is completed and *before* sales are made. In response, some companies using this no-allocation approach carry their inventories at NRV minus an estimated operating income margin. When any end-of-period inventories are sold in the next period, the cost of goods sold then equals this carrying value. This approach is akin to the "production method" of accounting for byproducts, which we describe in detail later in this chapter.

Decision Point

When is the sales value at splitoff method considered preferable for allocating joint costs to individual products and why?

Irrelevance of Joint Costs for Decision Making

You should already be familiar with the concepts of *relevant revenues*, expected future revenues that differ among alternative courses of action, and *relevant costs*, expected future costs that differ among alternative courses of action. These concepts can be applied to decisions on whether a joint product or main product should be sold at the splitoff point or processed further.

Learning Objective 5

Explain why joint costs are irrelevant in a sell-or-process-further decision

. . . because joint costs are the same whether or not further processing occurs

Sell-or-Process-Further Decisions

Consider Farmers' Dairy's decision to either sell the joint products, cream and liquid skim, at the splitoff point or to further process them into buttercream and condensed milk. The decision to incur additional costs for further processing should be based on the incremental operating income attainable beyond the splitoff point. Example 2 assumed it was profitable for both cream and liquid skim to be further processed into buttercream

---

[7] For further details, see T. Tunes, A. Nyrud, and B. Eikenes, "Cost and Performance Management in the Sawmill Industry," *Scandinavian Forest Economics* (2006).

and condensed milk, respectively. The incremental analysis for the decision to process further is as follows:

Further Processing Cream into Buttercream

Incremental revenues	
($25/gallon × 20,000 gallons) − ($8/gallon × 25,000 gallons)	$300,000
Deduct incremental processing costs	280,000
Increase in operating income from buttercream	$ 20,000

Further Processing Liquid Skim into Condensed Milk

Incremental revenues	
($22/gallon × 50,000 gallons) − ($4/gallon × 75,000 gallons)	$800,000
Deduct incremental processing costs	520,000
Increase in operating income from condensed milk	$280,000

In this example, operating income increases for both products, so the manager decides to process cream into buttercream and liquid skim into condensed milk. *The $400,000 joint costs incurred before the splitoff point are irrelevant in deciding whether to process further.* Why? Because the joint costs of $400,000 are the same whether the products are sold at the splitoff point or processed further.

Incremental costs are the additional costs incurred for an activity, such as further processing. *Do not assume all separable costs in joint-cost allocations are always incremental costs.* Some separable costs may be fixed costs, such as lease costs on buildings where the further processing is done; some separable costs may be sunk costs, such as depreciation on the equipment that converts cream into buttercream; and some separable costs may be allocated costs, such as corporate costs allocated to the condensed milk operations. None of these costs will differ between the alternatives of selling products at the splitoff point or processing further; therefore, they are irrelevant.

Joint-Cost Allocation and Performance Evaluation

The potential conflict between cost concepts used for decision making and cost concepts used for evaluating the performance of managers could also arise in sell-or-process-further decisions. To see how, let us continue with Example 2. Suppose *allocated* fixed corporate and administrative costs of further processing cream into buttercream equal $30,000 and that these costs will be allocated only to buttercream and to the manager's product-line income statement if buttercream is produced. How might this policy affect the decision to process further?

As we have seen, on the basis of incremental revenues and incremental costs, Farmers' operating income will increase by $20,000 if it processes cream into buttercream. However, producing the buttercream also results in an additional charge for allocated fixed costs of $30,000. If the manager is evaluated on a full-cost basis (that is, after allocating all costs), processing cream into buttercream will lower the manager's performance-evaluation measure by $10,000 (incremental operating income, $20,000 − allocated fixed costs, $30,000). Therefore, the manager may be tempted to sell cream at splitoff and not process it into buttercream.

A similar conflict can also arise with respect to production of joint products. Consider again Example 1. Suppose Farmers' Dairy has the option of selling raw milk at a profit of $20,000. From a decision-making standpoint, Farmers' would maximize operating income by processing raw milk into cream and liquid skim because the total revenues from selling both joint products ($500,000, see Exhibit 3) exceed the joint costs ($400,000) by $100,000. (This amount is greater than the $20,000 Farmers' Dairy would make if it sold the raw milk instead of processing it.) Suppose, however, the cream and liquid-skim product lines are managed by different managers, each of whom is evaluated based on a product-line income statement. If the physical-measure method of joint-cost allocation is used and the selling price per gallon of liquid skim falls below $4.00 per gallon, the liquid-skim product line will show a loss (from Exhibit 4, revenues will be less than $120,000, but cost of goods sold will be unchanged at $120,000). The manager of the liquid-skim line will prefer, from his or her performance-evaluation standpoint, to not produce liquid skim but rather to sell the raw milk.

This conflict between decision making and performance evaluation is less severe if Farmers' Dairy uses any of the market-based methods of joint-cost allocations—sales value at splitoff, NRV, or constant gross-margin percentage NRV—because each of these methods allocates costs using revenues, which generally leads to a positive income for each joint product.

Pricing Decisions

Firms should be wary of using the full cost of a joint product (that is, the cost after joint costs are allocated) as the basis for making pricing decisions. Why? Because in many situations, there is no direct cause-and-effect relationship that identifies the resources demanded by each joint product that can then be used as a basis for pricing. In fact, the use of the sales value at splitoff or the net realizable value method to allocate joint costs results in a reverse effect—selling prices of joint products drive joint-cost allocations, rather than cost allocations serving as the basis for the pricing of joint products! Of course, the principles of pricing apply to the joint process taken as a whole. Even if the firm cannot alter the mix of products generated by the joint process, it must ensure that the joint products generate sufficient combined revenue in the long run to cover the joint costs of processing.

◀ Decision Point

Are joint costs relevant in a sell-or-process-further decision?

Accounting for Byproducts

Joint production processes may yield not only joint products and main products but also byproducts. Although byproducts have relatively low total sales values, the presence of byproducts in a joint production process can affect the allocation of joint costs. Let's consider a two-product example consisting of a main product and a byproduct (also see the Concepts in Action feature on the next page).

Learning Objective 6

Account for byproducts using two methods

. . . recognize in financial statements at time of production or at time of sale

> Example 3: The Westlake Corporation processes timber into fine-grade lumber and wood chips that are used as mulch in gardens and lawns. Information about these products follows:
>
> ■ Fine-Grade lumber (the main product)—sells for $6 per board foot (b.f.)
>
> ■ Wood chips (the byproduct)—sells for $1 per cubic foot (c.f.)
>
> Data for July 2012 are as follows:

	Beginning Inventory	Production	Sales	Ending Inventory
Fine-Grade lumber (b.f.)	0	50,000	40,000	10,000
Wood chips (c.f.)	0	4,000	1,200	2,800

Joint manufacturing costs for these products in July 2012 are $250,000, comprising $150,000 for direct materials and $100,000 for conversion costs. Both products are sold at the splitoff point without further processing, as Exhibit 8 shows.

```
        ◀── Joint Costs ──▶|
            $250,000        |                    ╭─────────╮
                            |                   ╱  Fine-Grade ╲
                            |              ┌──▶ │   Lumber     │
                            |              │     ╲ 50,000 board╱
 Timber  ┌──────────────┐   |             │       ╲   feet   ╱
────────▶│  Processing  │───┼─────────────┤        ╰─────────╯
         └──────────────┘   |             │
                            |             │      ◇───────────◇
                            |             └──▶  ╱ Wood Chips  ╲
                            |                   ╲4,000 cubic feet╱
                            |                    ◇───────────◇
                            |
                        Splitoff
                          Point
```

◀ Exhibit 8

Example 3: Overview of Westlake Corporation

Concepts in Action

Byproduct Costing Keeps Wendy's Chili Profitable . . . and on the Menu

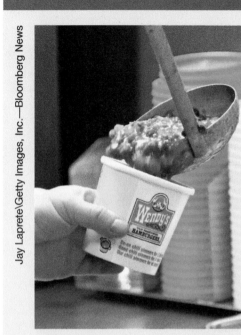

Jay Laprete\Getty Images, Inc.—Bloomberg News

There are many examples in which joint and byproduct costing issues arise, including coal mining, semiconductor manufacturing, and Wendy's chili. You may be asking yourself, "chili from Wendy's?" Yes! The primary ingredient in chili at Wendy's, one of the largest fast-food chains in the United States, is a byproduct of overcooked, unsellable hamburger patties.

The most important product that Wendy's offers its customers is an "old-fashioned" hamburger, which is a hamburger served from the grill in accordance with individual customer orders. Operationally, the only way to serve hamburgers this way is to anticipate customer demand and have a sufficient supply of hamburgers already cooking when the customers arrive at the restaurant. The problem with this approach, however, is the fate of the extra hamburgers that become too well done whenever the cooks overestimate customer demand. Throwing them away would be too costly and wasteful, but serving them as "old-fashioned" hamburgers would likely result in considerable customer dissatisfaction.

For Wendy's, the solution to this dilemma involved finding a product that was unique to the fast-food industry and required ground beef as one of the major ingredients. Thus, Wendy's "rich and meaty" chili became one of its original menu items. For each batch of chili, which is prepared daily in each restaurant, Wendy's needs 48 quarter-pound cooked ground-beef patties along with crushed tomatoes, tomato juice, red beans, and seasoning. Only 10% of the time is it necessary for Wendy's to cook meat specifically for use in making chili.

Several years ago, Wendy's management considered eliminating some of its traditional menu items. Chili, composing only about 5% of total restaurant sales, was targeted for possible elimination, and at $0.99 for an eight-ounce serving, it brought in far less revenue than a product like a single hamburger, which sold for $1.89. When Wendy's compared the cost of making chili to its sale price, however, the product remained on the menu. How? The beef in Wendy's chili recipe was a byproduct of hamburger patties, its main product, which affected the allocation of joint costs.

Excluding ground beef, the costs to produce Wendy's chili are around $0.37 per eight-ounce serving, which includes labor. When Wendy's has to cook meat for its chili, again only 10% of the time, the recipe calls for ground beef that costs around $0.73 per serving. Under those circumstances, the chili costs Wendy's $1.10 to make, and each $.99 serving sells at a $0.11 loss. However, the 90% of the time Wendy's uses precooked ground beef for its chili, most of those costs have already been allocated to hamburgers, the primary product. As a result, each eight-ounce serving of chili Wendy's sells using precooked ground beef is sold at a significant profit. With a lucrative profit margin for each serving sold, customers are likely to find chili on the Wendy's menu for a long time to come.

Source: Brownlee, E. Richard. 2005. Wendy's chili: A costing conundrum. The University of Virginia Darden School of Business Case No. UVA-C-2206. Charlottesville, VA: Darden Business Publishing.

We present two byproduct accounting methods: the production method and the sales method. The production method recognizes byproducts in the financial statements at the time production is completed. The sales method delays recognition of byproducts until the time of sale.[8] Exhibit 9 presents the income statement of Westlake Corporation under both methods.

---

[8] For a discussion of joint cost allocation and byproduct accounting methods, see P. D. Marshall and R. F. Dombrowski, "A Small Business Review of Accounting for Primary Products, Byproducts and Scrap," *The National Public Accountant* (February/March 2003): 10–13.

	Production Method	Sales Method
Revenues		
Main product: Fine-grade lumber (40,000 b.f. × $6 per b.f.)	$240,000	$240,000
Byproduct: Wood chips (1,200 c.f. × $1 per c.f.)	—	1,200
Total revenues	240,000	241,200
Cost of goods sold		
Total manufacturing costs	250,000	250,000
Deduct byproduct revenue (4,000 c.f. × $1 per c.f.)	(4,000)	—
Net manufacturing costs	246,000	250,000
Deduct main-product inventory	(49,200)[a]	(50,000)[b]
Cost of goods sold	196,800	200,000
Gross margin	$ 43,200	$ 41,200
Gross-margin percentage ($43,200 ÷ $240,000; $41,200 ÷ $241,200)	18.00%	17.08%
Inventoriable costs (end of period):		
Main product: Fine-grade lumber	$ 49,200	$ 50,000
Byproduct: Wood chips (2,800 c.f. × $1 per c.f.)[c]	2,800	0

[a](10,000 ÷ 50,000) × net manufacturing cost = (10,000 ÷ 50,000) × $246,000 = $49,200.

[b](10,000 ÷ 50,000) × total manufacturing cost = (10,000 ÷ 50,000) × $250,000 = $50,000.

[c]Recorded at selling prices.

Exhibit 9

Income Statements of Westlake Corporation for July 2012 Using the Production and Sales Methods for Byproduct Accounting

Production Method: Byproducts Recognized at Time Production Is Completed

This method recognizes the byproduct in the financial statements—the 4,000 cubic feet of wood chips—in the month it is produced, July 2012. The NRV from the byproduct produced is offset against the costs of the main product. The following journal entries illustrate the production method:

1. Work in Process — 150,000
   Accounts Payable — 150,000
   To record direct materials purchased and used in production during July.
2. Work in Process — 100,000
   Various accounts such as Wages Payable and Accumulated Depreciation — 100,000
   To record conversion costs in the production process during July; examples include energy, manufacturing supplies, all manufacturing labor, and plant depreciation.
3. Byproduct Inventory—Wood Chips (4,000 c.f. × $1 per c.f.) — 4,000
   Finished Goods—Fine-Grade Lumber ($250,000 − $4,000) — 246,000
   Work in Process ($150,000 + $100,000) — 250,000
   To record cost of goods completed during July.
4a. Cost of Goods Sold [(40,000 b.f. ÷ 50,000 b.f.) × $246,000] — 196,800
   Finished Goods—Fine-Grade Lumber — 196,800
   To record the cost of the main product sold during July.
4b. Cash or Accounts Receivable (40,000 b.f. × $6 per b.f.) — 240,000
   Revenues—Fine-Grade Lumber — 240,000
   To record the sales of the main product during July.
5. Cash or Accounts Receivable (1,200 c.f. × $1 per c.f.) — 1,200
   Byproduct Inventory—Wood Chips — 1,200
   To record the sales of the byproduct during July.

The production method reports the byproduct inventory of wood chips in the balance sheet at its $1 per cubic foot selling price [(4,000 cubic feet − 1,200 cubic feet) × $1 per cubic foot = $2,800].

One variation of this method would be to report byproduct inventory at its NRV reduced by a normal profit margin ($2,800 − 20% × $2,800 = $2,240, assuming a normal profit margin of 20%).[9] When byproduct inventory is sold in a subsequent period, the income statement will match the selling price, $2,800, with the "cost" reported for the byproduct inventory, $2,240, resulting in a byproduct operating income of $560 ($2,800 − $2,240).

Sales Method: Byproducts Recognized at Time of Sale

This method makes no journal entries for byproducts until they are sold. Revenues of the byproduct are reported as a revenue item in the income statement at the time of sale. These revenues are either grouped with other sales, included as other income, or are deducted from cost of goods sold. In the Westlake Corporation example, byproduct revenues in July 2012 are $1,200 (1,200 cubic feet × $1 per cubic foot) because only 1,200 cubic feet of wood chips are sold in July (of the 4,000 cubic feet produced). The journal entries are as follows:

1. and 2.	*Same as for the production method.*		
	Work in Process	150,000	
	Accounts Payable		150,000
	Work in Process	100,000	
	Various accounts such as Wages Payable and Accumulated Depreciation		100,000
3.	Finished Goods—Fine-Grade Lumber	250,000	
	Work in Process		250,000
	To record cost of main product completed during July.		
4a.	Cost of Goods Sold [(40,000 b.f. ÷ 50,000 b.f.) × $250,000]	200,000	
	Finished Goods—Fine-Grade Lumber		200,000
	To record the cost of the main product sold during July.		
4b.	Same as for the production method.		
	Cash or Accounts Receivable (40,000 b.f. × $6 per b.f.)	240,000	
	Revenues—Fine-Grade Lumber		240,000
5.	Cash or Accounts Receivable	1,200	
	Revenues—Wood Chips		1,200
	To record the sales of the byproduct during July.		

Decision Point

What methods can be used to account for byproducts and which of them is preferable?

Which method should a company use? The production method is conceptually correct in that it is consistent with the matching principle. This method recognizes byproduct inventory in the accounting period in which it is produced and simultaneously reduces the cost of manufacturing the main or joint products, thereby better matching the revenues and expenses from selling the main product. However, the sales method is simpler and is often used in practice, primarily on the grounds that the dollar amounts of byproducts are immaterial. Then again, the sales method permits managers to "manage" reported earnings by timing when they sell byproducts. Managers may store byproducts for several periods and give revenues and income a "small boost" by selling byproducts accumulated over several periods when revenues and profits from the main product or joint products are low.

Problem for Self-Study

Inorganic Chemicals (IC) processes salt into various industrial products. In July 2012, IC incurred joint costs of $100,000 to purchase salt and convert it into two products: caustic soda and chlorine. Although there is an active outside market for chlorine, IC processes all 800 tons of chlorine it produces into 500 tons of PVC (polyvinyl chloride), which is

---

[9] One way to make this calculation is to assume all products have the same "normal" profit margin like the constant gross-margin percentage NRV method. Alternatively, the company might allow products to have different profit margins based on an analysis of the margins earned by other companies that sell these products individually.

then sold. There were no beginning or ending inventories of salt, caustic soda, chlorine, or PVC in July. Information for July 2012 production and sales follows:

			Home	Insert	Page Layout	Formulas	Data	Review	View	
		A					B	C	D	
1							Joint Costs		PVC	
2	Joint costs (costs of salt and processing to splitoff point)						$100,000			
3	Separable cost of processing 800 tons chlorine into 500 tons PVC								$20,000	
4										
5							Caustic Soda	Chlorine	PVC	
6	Beginning inventory (tons)						0	0	0	
7	Production (tons)						1,200	800	500	
8	Transfer for further processing (tons)							800		
9	Sales (tons)						1,200		500	
10	Ending inventory (tons)						0	0	0	
11	Selling price per ton in active outside market (for products not actually sold)							$ 75		
12	Selling price per ton for products sold						$ 50		$ 200	

Required

1. Allocate the joint costs of $100,000 between caustic soda and PVC under (a) the sales value at splitoff method and (b) the physical-measure method.
2. Allocate the joint costs of $100,000 between caustic soda and PVC under the NRV method.
3. Under the three allocation methods in requirements 1 and 2, what is the gross-margin percentage of (a) caustic soda and (b) PVC?
4. Lifetime Swimming Pool Products offers to purchase 800 tons of chlorine in August 2012 at $75 per ton. Assume all other production and sales data are the same for August as they were for July. This sale of chlorine to Lifetime would mean that no PVC would be produced by IC in August. How would accepting this offer affect IC's August 2012 operating income?

Solution

The following picture provides a visual illustration of the main facts in this problem.

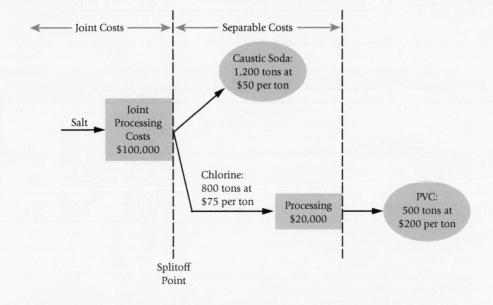

Note that caustic soda is sold as is while chlorine, despite having a market value at split-off, is sold only in processed form as PVC. The goal is to allocate the joint costs of $100,000 to the final products—caustic soda and PVC. However, since PVC exists only in the form of chlorine at the splitoff point, we use chlorine's sales value and physical measure as the basis for allocating joint costs to PVC under the sales value at splitoff and physical measure at splitoff methods. Detailed calculations are shown next.

1a. Sales value at splitoff method

	Home Insert Page Layout Formulas Data Review View			
	A	B	C	D
1	Allocation of Joint Costs Using Sales Value at Splitoff Method	Caustic Soda	PVC / Chlorine	Total
2	Sales value of total production at splitoff point			
3	(1,200 tons × $50 per ton; 800 × $75 per ton)	$60,000	$60,000	$120,000
4	Weighting ($60,000 ÷ $120,000; $60,000 ÷ $120,000)	0.50	0.50	
5	Joint costs allocated (0.50 × $100,000; 0.50 × $100,000)	$50,000	$50,000	$100,000

1b. Physical-measure method

	Home Insert Page Layout Formulas Data Review View			
	A	B	C	D
8	Allocation of Joint Costs Using Physical-Measure Method	Caustic Soda	PVC / Chlorine	Total
9	Physical measure of total production (tons)	1,200	800	2,000
10	Weighting (1,200 tons ÷ 2,000 tons; 800 tons ÷ 2,000 tons)	0.60	0.40	
11	Joint cost allocated (0.60 × $100,000; 0.40 × $100,000)	$60,000	$40,000	$100,000

2. Net realizable value (NRV) method

	Home Insert Page Layout Formulas Data Review View			
	A	B	C	D
14	Allocation of Joint Costs Using Net Realizable Value Method	Caustic Soda	PVC	Total
15	Final sales value of total production during accounting period			
16	(1,200 tons × $50 per ton; 500 tons × $200 per ton)	$60,000	$100,000	$160,000
17	Deduct separable costs to complete and sell	0	20,000	20,000
18	Net realizable value at splitoff point	$60,000	$ 80,000	$140,000
19	Weighting ($60,000 ÷ $140,000; $80,000 ÷ $140,000)	3/7	4/7	
20	Joint costs allocated (3/7 × $100,000; 4/7 × $100,000)	$42,857	$ 57,143	$100,000

3a. Gross-margin percentage of caustic soda

	Home Insert Page Layout Formulas Data Review View			
	A	B	C	D
23	Caustic Soda	Sales Value at Splitoff Point	Physical Measure	NRV
24	Revenues (1,200 tons × $50 per ton)	$60,000	$60,000	$60,000
25	Cost of goods sold (joint costs)	50,000	60,000	42,857
26	Gross margin	$10,000	$ 0	$17,143
27	Gross margin percentage ($10,000 ÷ $60,000; $0 ÷ $60,000; $17,143 ÷ $60,000)	16.67%	0.00%	28.57%

3b. Gross-margin percentage of PVC

	A	B	C	D
		Sales Value at Splitoff Point	Physical Measure	NRV
30	PVC			
31	Revenues (500 tons × $200 per ton)	$100,000	$100,000	$100,000
32	Cost of goods sold			
33	Joint costs	50,000	40,000	57,143
34	Separable costs	20,000	20,000	20,000
35	Cost of goods sold	70,000	60,000	77,143
36	Gross margin	$ 30,000	$ 40,000	$ 22,857
37	Gross margin percentage ($30,000 ÷ $100,000; $40,000 ÷ $100,000; $22,857 ÷ $100,000)	30.00%	40.00%	22.86%

4. Sale of chlorine versus processing into PVC

	A	B
40	Incremental revenue from processing 800 tons of chlorine into 500 tons of PVC	
41	(500 tons × $200 per ton) – (800 tons × $75 per ton)	$40,000
42	Incremental cost of processing 800 tons of chlorine into 500 tons of PVC	20,000
43	Incremental operating income from further processing	$ 20,000

If IC sells 800 tons of chlorine to Lifetime Swimming Pool Products instead of further processing it into PVC, its August 2012 operating income will be reduced by $20,000.

Decision Points

The following question-and-answer format summarizes the chapter's learning objectives. Each decision presents a key question related to a learning objective. The guidelines are the answer to that question.

Decision	Guidelines
1. What do the terms joint cost and splitoff point mean, and how do joint products differ from byproducts?	A joint cost is the cost of a single production process that yields multiple products simultaneously. The splitoff point is the juncture in a joint production process when the products become separately identifiable. Joint products have high total sales values at the splitoff point. A byproduct has a low total sales value at the splitoff point compared with the total sales value of a joint or main product.
2. Why are joint costs allocated to individual products?	The purposes for allocating joint costs to products include inventory costing for financial accounting and internal reporting, cost reimbursement, insurance settlements, rate regulation, and product-cost litigation.
3. What methods can be used to allocate joint costs to individual products?	The methods to allocate joint costs to products are the sales value at splitoff, NRV, constant gross-margin percentage NRV, and physical-measure methods.

4. When is the sales value at splitoff method considered preferable for allocating joint costs to individual products and why?

The sales value at splitoff method is preferable when market prices exist at splitoff because using revenues is consistent with the benefits-received criterion; further, the method does not anticipate subsequent management decisions on further processing, and is simple.

5. Are joint costs relevant in a sell-or-process-further decision?

No, joint costs and how they are allocated are irrelevant in deciding whether to process further because joint costs are the same regardless of whether further processing occurs.

6. What methods can be used to account for byproducts and which of them is preferable?

The production method recognizes byproducts in financial statements at the time of production, whereas the sales method recognizes byproducts in financial statements at the time of sale. The production method is conceptually superior, but the sales method is often used in practice because dollar amounts of byproducts are immaterial.

Terms to Learn

This chapter contains definitions of the following important terms:

byproducts	main product	product
constant gross-margin percentage NRV method	net realizable value (NRV) method	sales value at splitoff method
joint costs	physical-measure method	separable costs
joint products		splitoff point

Assignment Material

MyAccountingLab

Questions

16-1 Give two examples of industries in which joint costs are found. For each example, what are the individual products at the splitoff point?

16-2 What is a joint cost? What is a separable cost?

16-3 Distinguish between a joint product and a byproduct.

16-4 Why might the number of products in a joint-cost situation differ from the number of outputs? Give an example.

16-5 Provide three reasons for allocating joint costs to individual products or services.

16-6 Why does the sales value at splitoff method use the sales value of the total production in the accounting period and not just the revenues from the products sold?

16-7 Describe a situation in which the sales value at splitoff method cannot be used but the NRV method can be used for joint-cost allocation.

16-8 Distinguish between the sales value at splitoff method and the NRV method.

16-9 Give two limitations of the physical-measure method of joint-cost allocation.

16-10 How might a company simplify its use of the NRV method when final selling prices can vary sizably in an accounting period and management frequently changes the point at which it sells individual products?

16-11 Why is the constant gross-margin percentage NRV method sometimes called a "joint-cost-allocation and a profit-allocation" method?

16-12 "Managers must decide whether a product should be sold at splitoff or processed further. The sales value at splitoff method of joint-cost allocation is the best method for generating the information managers need for this decision." Do you agree? Explain.

16-13 "Managers should consider only additional revenues and separable costs when making decisions about selling at splitoff or processing further." Do you agree? Explain.

16-14 Describe two major methods to account for byproducts.

16-15 Why might managers seeking a monthly bonus based on attaining a target operating income prefer the sales method of accounting for byproducts rather than the production method?

MyAccountingLab

Exercises

16-16 **Joint-cost allocation, insurance settlement.** Quality Chicken grows and processes chickens. Each chicken is disassembled into five main parts. Information pertaining to production in July 2012 is as follows:

Parts	Pounds of Product	Wholesale Selling Price per Pound When Production Is Complete
Breasts	100	$0.55
Wings	20	0.20
Thighs	40	0.35
Bones	80	0.10
Feathers	10	0.05

Joint cost of production in July 2012 was $50.

A special shipment of 40 pounds of breasts and 15 pounds of wings has been destroyed in a fire. Quality Chicken's insurance policy provides reimbursement for the cost of the items destroyed. The insurance company permits Quality Chicken to use a joint-cost-allocation method. The splitoff point is assumed to be at the end of the production process.

Required

1. Compute the cost of the special shipment destroyed using the following:
   a. Sales value at splitoff method
   b. Physical-measure method (pounds of finished product)
2. What joint-cost-allocation method would you recommend Quality Chicken use? Explain.

16-17 Joint products and byproducts (continuation of 16-16). Quality Chicken is computing the ending inventory values for its July 31, 2012, balance sheet. Ending inventory amounts on July 31 are 15 pounds of breasts, 4 pounds of wings, 6 pounds of thighs, 5 pounds of bones, and 2 pounds of feathers.

Quality Chicken's management wants to use the sales value at splitoff method. However, management wants you to explore the effect on ending inventory values of classifying one or more products as a byproduct rather than a joint product.

Required

1. Assume Quality Chicken classifies all five products as joint products. What are the ending inventory values of each product on July 31, 2012?
2. Assume Quality Chicken uses the production method of accounting for byproducts. What are the ending inventory values for each joint product on July 31, 2012, assuming breasts and thighs are the joint products and wings, bones, and feathers are byproducts?
3. Comment on differences in the results in requirements 1 and 2.

16-18 Net realizable value method. Convad Company is one of the world's leading corn refiners. It produces two joint products—corn syrup and corn starch—using a common production process. In July 2012, Convad reported the following production and selling-price information:

	A	B	C	D
		Corn Syrup	**Corn Starch**	**Joint Costs**
1				
2	Joint costs (costs of processing corn to splitoff point)			$325,000
3	Separable cost of processing beyond splitoff point	$375,000	$93,750	
4	Beginning inventory (cases)	0	0	
5	Production and Sales (cases)	12,500	6,250	
6	Ending inventory (cases)	0	0	
7	Selling price per case	50	$ 25	

Allocate the $325,000 joint costs using the NRV method.

Required

16-19 Alternative joint-cost-allocation methods, further-process decision. The Wood Spirits Company produces two products—turpentine and methanol (wood alcohol)—by a joint process. Joint costs amount to $120,000 per batch of output. Each batch totals 10,000 gallons: 25% methanol and 75% turpentine. Both products are processed further without gain or loss in volume. Separable processing costs are methanol, $3 per gallon; turpentine, $2 per gallon. Methanol sells for $21 per gallon. Turpentine sells for $14 per gallon.

Required

1. How much of the joint costs per batch will be allocated to turpentine and to methanol, assuming that joint costs are allocated based on the number of gallons at splitoff point?
2. If joint costs are allocated on an NRV basis, how much of the joint costs will be allocated to turpentine and to methanol?
3. Prepare product-line income statements per batch for requirements 1 and 2. Assume no beginning or ending inventories.
4. The company has discovered an additional process by which the methanol (wood alcohol) can be made into a pleasant-tasting alcoholic beverage. The selling price of this beverage would be $60 a gallon. Additional processing would increase separable costs $9 per gallon (in addition to the $3 per gallon separable cost

required to yield methanol). The company would have to pay excise taxes of 20% on the selling price of the beverage. Assuming no other changes in cost, what is the joint cost applicable to the wood alcohol (using the NRV method)? Should the company produce the alcoholic beverage? Show your computations.

16-20 Alternative methods of joint-cost allocation, ending inventories. The Evrett Company operates a simple chemical process to convert a single material into three separate items, referred to here as X, Y, and Z. All three end products are separated simultaneously at a single splitoff point.

Products X and Y are ready for sale immediately upon splitoff without further processing or any other additional costs. Product Z, however, is processed further before being sold. There is no available market price for Z at the splitoff point.

The selling prices quoted here are expected to remain the same in the coming year. During 2012, the selling prices of the items and the total amounts sold were as follows:

- X—75 tons sold for $1,800 per ton
- Y—225 tons sold for $1,300 per ton
- Z—280 tons sold for $800 per ton

The total joint manufacturing costs for the year were $328,000. Evrett spent an additional $120,000 to finish product Z.

There were no beginning inventories of X, Y, or Z. At the end of the year, the following inventories of completed units were on hand: X, 175 tons; Y, 75 tons; Z, 70 tons. There was no beginning or ending work in process.

Required

1. Compute the cost of inventories of X, Y, and Z for balance sheet purposes and the cost of goods sold for income statement purposes as of December 31, 2012, using the following joint cost allocation methods:
   a. NRV method
   b. Constant gross-margin percentage NRV method
2. Compare the gross-margin percentages for X, Y, and Z using the two methods given in requirement 1.

16-21 Joint-cost allocation, process further. Sinclair Oil & Gas, a large energy conglomerate, jointly processes purchased hydrocarbons to generate three nonsaleable intermediate products: ICR8, ING4, and XGE3. These intermediate products are further processed separately to produce crude oil, natural gas liquids (NGL), and natural gas (measured in liquid equivalents). An overview of the process and results for August 2012 are shown here. (Note: The numbers are small to keep the focus on key concepts.)

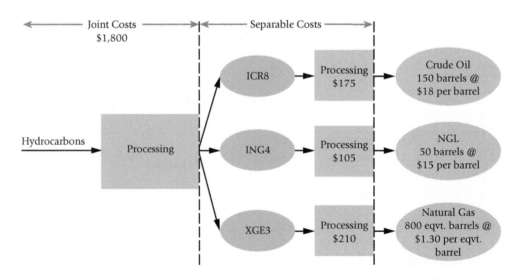

A new federal law has recently been passed that taxes crude oil at 30% of operating income. No new tax is to be paid on natural gas liquid or natural gas. Starting August 2012, Sinclair Oil & Gas must report a separate product-line income statement for crude oil. One challenge facing Sinclair Oil & Gas is how to allocate the joint cost of producing the three separate saleable outputs. Assume no beginning or ending inventory.

Required

1. Allocate the August 2012 joint cost among the three products using the following:
   a. Physical-measure method
   b. NRV method
2. Show the operating income for each product using the methods in requirement 1.
3. Discuss the pros and cons of the two methods to Sinclair Oil & Gas for making decisions about product emphasis (pricing, sell-or-process-further decisions, and so on).
4. Draft a letter to the taxation authorities on behalf of Sinclair Oil & Gas that justifies the joint-cost-allocation method you recommend Sinclair use.

16-22 Joint-cost allocation, sales value, physical measure, NRV methods. Instant Foods produces two types of microwavable products—beef-flavored ramen and shrimp-flavored ramen. The two products share common inputs such as noodle and spices. The production of ramen results in a waste product referred to as stock, which Instant dumps at negligible costs in a local drainage area. In June 2012, the following data were reported for the production and sales of beef-flavored and shrimp-flavored ramen:

			Home	Insert	Page Layout	Formulas	Data	Review

	A	B	C
1		Joint Costs	
2	Joint costs (costs of noodles, spices, and other inputs and processing to splitoff point)	$240,000	
3			
4		Beef Ramen	Shrimp Ramen
5	Beginning inventory (tons)	0	0
6	Production (tons)	10,000	20,000
7	Sales (tons)	10,000	20,000
8	Selling price per ton	$ 10	$ 15

Due to the popularity of its microwavable products, Instant decides to add a new line of products that targets dieters. These new products are produced by adding a special ingredient to dilute the original ramen and are to be sold under the names Special B and Special S, respectively. The following is the monthly data for all the products:

			Home	Insert	Page Layout	Formulas	Data	Review	View

	A	B	C	D	E
11		Joint Costs		Special B	Special S
12	Joint costs (costs of noodles, spices, and other inputs and processing to splitoff point)	$240,000			
13	Separable costs of processing 10,000 tons of Beef Ramen into 12,000 tons of Special B			$48,000	
14	Separable cost of processing 20,000 tons of Shrimp Ramen into 24,000 tons of Special S				$168,000
15					
16		Beef Ramen	Shrimp Ramen	Special B	Special S
17	Beginning inventory (tons)	0	0	0	0
18	Production (tons)	10,000	20,000	12,000	24,000
19	Transfer for further processing (tons)	10,000	20,000		
20	Sales (tons)			12,000	24,000
21	Selling price per ton	$ 10	$ 15	$ 18	$ 25

1. Calculate Instant's gross-margin percentage for Special B and Special S when joint costs are allocated using the following:
   a. Sales value at splitoff method
   b. Physical-measure method
   c. Net realizable value method

2. Recently, Instant discovered that the stock it is dumping can be sold to cattle ranchers at $5 per ton. In a typical month with the production levels shown, 4,000 tons of stock are produced and can be sold by incurring marketing costs of $10,800. Sherrie Dong, a management accountant, points out that treating the stock as a joint product and using the sales value at splitoff method, the stock product would lose about $2,228 each month, so it should not be sold. How did Dong arrive at that final number, and what do you think of her analysis? Should Instant sell the stock?

Required

16-23 Joint cost allocation: sell immediately or process further. Iowa Soy Products (ISP) buys soy beans and processes them into other soy products. Each ton of soy beans that ISP purchases for $300 can be converted for an additional $200 into 500 pounds of soy meal and 100 gallons of soy oil. A pound of soy meal can be sold at splitoff for $1 and soy oil can be sold in bulk for $4 per gallon.

ISP can process the 500 pounds of soy meal into 600 pounds of soy cookies at an additional cost of $300. Each pound of soy cookies can be sold for $2 per pound. The 100 gallons of soy oil can be packaged at a cost of $200 and made into 400 quarts of Soyola. Each quart of Soyola can be sold for $1.25.

Required

1. Allocate the joint cost to the cookies and the Soyola using the following:
   a. Sales value at splitoff method
   b. NRV method
2. Should ISP have processed each of the products further? What effect does the allocation method have on this decision?

16-24 Accounting for a main product and a byproduct. (Cheatham and Green, adapted) Tasty, Inc., is a producer of potato chips. A single production process at Tasty, Inc., yields potato chips as the main product and a byproduct that can also be sold as a snack. Both products are fully processed by the splitoff point, and there are no separable costs.

For September 2012, the cost of operations is $500,000. Production and sales data are as follows:

	Production (in pounds)	Sales (in pounds)	Selling Price per Pound
Main Product:			
Potato Chips	52,000	42,640	$16
Byproduct	8,500	6,500	$10

There were no beginning inventories on September 1, 2012.

1. What is the gross margin for Tasty, Inc., under the production method and the sales method of byproduct accounting?
2. What are the inventory costs reported in the balance sheet on September 30, 2012, for the main product and byproduct under the two methods of byproduct accounting in requirement 1?

16-25 Joint costs and byproducts. (W. Crum adapted) Royston, Inc., is a large food processing company. It processes 150,000 pounds of peanuts in the peanuts department at a cost of $180,000 to yield 12,000 pounds of product A, 65,000 pounds of product B, and 16,000 pounds of product C.

- Product A is processed further in the salting department to yield 12,000 pounds of salted peanuts at a cost of $27,000 and sold for $12 per pound.
- Product B (raw peanuts) is sold without further processing at $3 per pound.
- Product C is considered a byproduct and is processed further in the paste department to yield 16,000 pounds of peanut butter at a cost of $12,000 and sold for $6 per pound.

The company wants to make a gross margin of 10% of revenues on product C and needs to allow 20% of revenues for marketing costs on product C. An overview of operations follows:

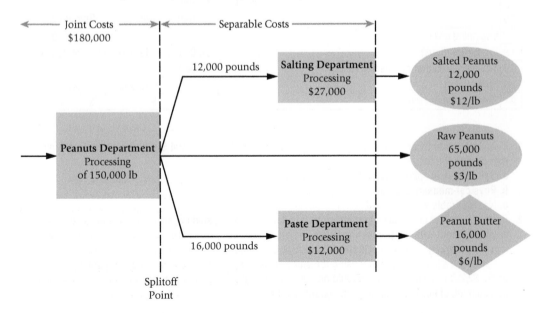

1. Compute unit costs per pound for products A, B, and C, treating C as a byproduct. Use the NRV method for allocating joint costs. Deduct the NRV of the byproduct produced from the joint cost of products A and B.
2. Compute unit costs per pound for products A, B, and C, treating all three as joint products and allocating joint costs by the NRV method.

Problems

16-26 Accounting for a byproduct. Sunny Day Juice Company produces oranges from various organic growers in Florida. The juice is extracted from the oranges and the pulp and peel remain. Sunny Day considers the pulp and peel byproducts of its juice production and can sell them to a local farmer for $2.00 per pound. During the most recent month, Sunny Day purchased 4,000 pounds of oranges and produced 1,500 gallons of juice and 900 pounds of pulp and peel at a joint cost of $7,200. The selling price for a half-gallon of orange juice is $2.50. Sunny Day sold 2,800 half-gallons of juice and 860 pounds of pulp and peel during the most recent month. The company had no beginning inventories.

1. Assuming Sunny Day accounts for the byproduct using the production method, what is the inventoriable cost for each product and Sunny Day's gross margin?
2. Assuming Sunny Day accounts for the byproduct using the sales method, what is the inventoriable cost for each product and Sunny Day's gross margin?
3. Discuss the difference between the two methods of accounting for byproducts.

16-27 Alternative methods of joint-cost allocation, product-mix decisions. The Southern Oil Company buys crude vegetable oil. Refining this oil results in four products at the splitoff point: A, B, C, and D. Product C is fully processed by the splitoff point. Products A, B, and D can individually be further refined into Super A, Super B, and Super D. In the most recent month (December), the output at the splitoff point was as follows:

- Product A, 322,400 gallons
- Product B, 119,600 gallons
- Product C, 52,000 gallons
- Product D, 26,000 gallons

The joint costs of purchasing and processing the crude vegetable oil were $96,000. Southern had no beginning or ending inventories. Sales of product C in December were $24,000. Products A, B, and D were further refined and then sold. Data related to December are as follows:

	Separable Processing Costs to Make Super Products	Revenues
Super A	$249,600	$300,000
Super B	102,400	160,000
Super D	152,000	160,000

Southern had the option of selling products A, B, and D at the splitoff point. This alternative would have yielded the following revenues for the December production:

- Product A, $84,000
- Product B, $72,000
- Product D, $60,000

1. Compute the gross-margin percentage for each product sold in December, using the following methods for allocating the $96,000 joint costs:
   a. Sales value at splitoff
   b. Physical-measure
   c. NRV
2. Could Southern have increased its December operating income by making different decisions about the further processing of products A, B, or D? Show the effect on operating income of any changes you recommend.

16-28 Comparison of alternative joint-cost-allocation methods, further-processing decision, chocolate products. The Chocolate Factory manufactures and distributes chocolate products. It purchases cocoa beans and processes them into two intermediate products: chocolate-powder liquor base and milk-chocolate liquor base. These two intermediate products become separately identifiable at a single splitoff point. Every 1,500 pounds of cocoa beans yields 60 gallons of chocolate-powder liquor base and 90 gallons of milk-chocolate liquor base.

The chocolate-powder liquor base is further processed into chocolate powder. Every 60 gallons of chocolate-powder liquor base yield 600 pounds of chocolate powder. The milk-chocolate liquor base is further processed into milk chocolate. Every 90 gallons of milk-chocolate liquor base yield 1,020 pounds of milk chocolate.

Production and sales data for August 2012 are as follows (assume no beginning inventory):

- Cocoa beans processed, 15,000 pounds
- Costs of processing cocoa beans to splitoff point (including purchase of beans), $30,000

	Production	Sales	Selling Price	Separable Processing Costs
Chocolate powder	6,000 pounds	6,000 pounds	$4 per pound	$12,750
Milk chocolate	10,200 pounds	10,200 pounds	$5 per pound	$26,250

Chocolate Factory fully processes both of its intermediate products into chocolate powder or milk chocolate. There is an active market for these intermediate products. In August 2012, Chocolate Factory could have sold the chocolate-powder liquor base for $21 a gallon and the milk-chocolate liquor base for $26 a gallon.

Required

1. Calculate how the joint costs of $30,000 would be allocated between chocolate powder and milk chocolate under the following methods:
   a. Sales value at splitoff
   b. Physical-measure (gallons)
   c. NRV
   d. Constant gross-margin percentage NRV
2. What are the gross-margin percentages of chocolate powder and milk chocolate under each of the methods in requirement 1?
3. Could Chocolate Factory have increased its operating income by a change in its decision to fully process both of its intermediate products? Show your computations.

16-29 Joint-cost allocation, process further or sell. (CMA, adapted) Sonimad Sawmill, Inc., (SSI) purchases logs from independent timber contractors and processes the logs into three types of lumber products:

- Studs for residential buildings (walls, ceilings)
- Decorative pieces (fireplace mantels, beams for cathedral ceilings)
- Posts used as support braces (mine support braces, braces for exterior fences on ranch properties)

These products are the result of a joint sawmill process that involves removal of bark from the logs, cutting the logs into a workable size (ranging from 8 to 16 feet in length), and then cutting the individual products from the logs.

The joint process results in the following costs of products for a typical month:

Direct materials (rough timber logs)	$ 500,000
Debarking (labor and overhead)	50,000
Sizing (labor and overhead)	200,000
Product cutting (labor and overhead)	250,000
Total joint costs	$1,000,000

Product yields and average sales values on a per-unit basis from the joint process are as follows:

Product	Monthly Output of Materials at Splitoff Point	Fully Processed Selling Price
Studs	75,000 units	$ 8
Decorative pieces	5,000 units	100
Posts	20,000 units	20

The studs are sold as rough-cut lumber after emerging from the sawmill operation without further processing by SSI. Also, the posts require no further processing beyond the splitoff point. The decorative pieces must be planed and further sized after emerging from the sawmill. This additional processing costs $100,000 per month and normally results in a loss of 10% of the units entering the process. Without this planing and sizing process, there is still an active intermediate market for the unfinished decorative pieces in which the selling price averages $60 per unit.

Required

1. Based on the information given for Sonimad Sawmill, allocate the joint processing costs of $1,000,000 to the three products using:
   a. Sales value at splitoff method
   b. Physical-measure method (volume in units)
   c. NRV method
2. Prepare an analysis for Sonimad Sawmill that compares processing the decorative pieces further, as it currently does, with selling them as a rough-cut product immediately at splitoff.

3. Assume Sonimad Sawmill announced that in six months it will sell the unfinished decorative pieces at splitoff due to increasing competitive pressure. Identify at least three types of likely behavior that will be demonstrated by the skilled labor in the planing-and-sizing process as a result of this announcement. Include in your discussion how this behavior could be influenced by management.

16-30 Joint-cost allocation. Elsie Dairy Products Corp. buys one input, full-cream milk, and refines it in a churning process. From each gallon of milk Elsie produces three cups of butter and nine cups of buttermilk. During May 2010, Elsie bought 12,000 gallons of milk for $22,250. Elsie spent another $9,430 on the churning process to separate the milk into butter and buttermilk. Butter could be sold immediately for $2.20 per pound and buttermilk could be sold immediately for $1.20 per quart (note: two cups = one pound; four cups = one quart).

Elsie chooses to process the butter further into spreadable butter by mixing it with canola oil, incurring an additional cost of $1.60 per pound. This process results in two tubs of spreadable butter for each pound of butter processed. Each tub of spreadable butter sells for $2.30.

1. Allocate the $31,680 joint cost to the spreadable butter and the buttermilk using the following:　　**Required**
  a. Physical-measure method (using cups) of joint cost allocation
  b. Sales value at splitoff method of joint cost allocation
  c. NRV method of joint cost allocation
  d. Constant gross margin percentage NRV method of joint cost allocation
2. Each of these measures has advantages and disadvantages; what are they?
3. Some claim that the sales value at split off method is the best method to use. Discuss the logic behind this claim.

16-31 Further processing decision (continuation of 16-30). Elsie has decided that buttermilk may sell better if it was marketed for baking and sold in pints. This would involve additional packaging at an incremental cost of $0.35 per pint. Each pint could be sold for $0.75 (note: one quart = two pints).
  1. If Elsie uses the sales value at splitoff method, what combination of products should Elsie sell to maximize profits?
  2. If Elsie uses the physical-measure method, what combination of products should Elsie sell to maximize profits?
  3. Explain the effect that the different cost allocation methods have on the decision to sell the products at split off or to process them further.

16-32 Joint-cost allocation with a byproduct. Mat Place purchases old tires and recycles them to produce rubber floor mats and car mats. The company washes, shreds, and molds the recycled tires into sheets. The floor and car mats are cut from these sheets. A small amount of rubber shred remains after the mats are cut. The rubber shreds can be sold to use as cover for paths and playgrounds. The company can produce 25 floor mats, 75 car mats, and 40 pounds of rubber shreds from 100 old tires.

In May, Mat Place, which had no beginning inventory, processed 125,000 tires and had joint production costs of $600,000. Mat Place sold 25,000 floor mats, 85,000 car mats, and 43,000 pounds of rubber shreds. The company sells each floor mat for $12 and each car mat for $6. The company treats the rubber shreds as a byproduct that can be sold for $0.70 per pound.

1. Assume that Mat Place allocates the joint costs to floor mats and car mats using the sales value at　　**Required** splitoff method and accounts for the byproduct using the production method. What is the ending inventory cost for each product and gross margin for Mat Place?
2. Assume that Mat Place allocates the joint costs to floor mats and car mats using the sales value at splitoff method and accounts for the byproduct using the sales method. What is the ending inventory cost for each product and gross margin for Mat Place?
3. Discuss the difference between the two methods of accounting for byproducts, focusing on what conditions are necessary to use each method.

16-33 Byproduct-costing journal entries (continuation of 16-32). The Mat Place's accountant needs to record the information about the joint and byproducts in the general journal, but is not sure what the entries should be. The company has hired you as a consultant to help its accountant.

  1. Show journal entries at the time of production and at the time of sale assuming the Mat Place accounts　　**Required** for the byproduct using the production method.
  2. Show journal entries at the time of production and at the time of sale assuming the Mat Place accounts for the byproduct using the sales method.

16-34 Process further or sell, byproduct. (CMA, adapted) Rochester Mining Company (RMC) mines coal, puts it through a one-step crushing process, and loads the bulk raw coal onto river barges for shipment to customers.

RMC's management is currently evaluating the possibility of further processing the raw coal by sizing and cleaning it and selling it to an expanded set of customers at higher prices. The option of building a new sizing and cleaning plant is ruled out as being financially infeasible. Instead, Amy Kimbell, a mining engineer, is asked to explore outside-contracting arrangements for the cleaning and sizing process. Kimbell puts together the following summary:

	A	B	C
	Home Insert Page Layout Formulas Data Review View		
1	Selling price of raw coal	$ 27	per ton
2	Cost of producing raw coal	$ 21	per ton
3	Selling price of sized and cleaned coal	$ 35	per ton
4	Annual raw coal output	9,800,000	tons
5	Percentage of material weight loss in sizing/cleaning coal	10%	
6			
7		**Incremental Costs of Sizing & Cleaning Processes**	
8	Direct labor	$ 820,000	per year
9	Supervisory personnel	$ 225,000	per year
10	Heavy equipment: rental, operating, maintenance costs	$ 15,000	per month
11	Contract sizing and cleaning	$ 3.60	per ton of raw coal
12	Outbound rail freight	$ 210	per 60-ton rail car
13			
14	Percentage of sizing/cleaning waste that can be salvaged for coal fines	75%	
15	Range of costs per ton for preparing coal fine for sale	$2	$4
16	Range of coal fine selling prices (per ton)	$16	$27

Kimbell also learns that 75% of the material loss that occurs in the cleaning and sizing process can be salvaged as coal fines, which can be sold to steel manufacturers for their furnaces. The sale of coal fines is erratic and RMC may need to stockpile it in a protected area for up to one year. The selling price of coal fine ranges from $16 to $27 per ton and costs of preparing coal fines for sale range from $2 to $4 per ton.

Required

1. Prepare an analysis to show whether it is more profitable for RMC to continue selling raw bulk coal or to process it further through sizing and cleaning. (Ignore coal fines in your analysis.)
2. How would your analysis be affected if the cost of producing raw coal could be held down to $17 per ton?
3. Now consider the potential value of the coal fines and prepare an addendum that shows how their value affects the results of your analysis prepared in requirement 1.

16-35 Joint Cost Allocation. Memory Manufacturing Company (MMC) produces memory modules in a two-step process: chip fabrication and module assembly.

In chip fabrication, each batch of raw silicon wafers yields 400 *standard* chips and 600 *deluxe* chips. Chips are classified as standard or deluxe on the basis of their density (the number of memory bits on each chip). Standard chips have 500 memory bits per chip, and deluxe chips have 1,000 memory bits per chip. Joint costs to process each batch are $28,900.

In module assembly, each batch of standard chips is converted into standard memory modules at a separately identified cost of $1,050 and then sold for $14,000. Each batch of deluxe chips is converted into deluxe memory modules at a separately identified cost of $2,450 and then sold for $26,500.

Required

1. Allocate joint costs of each batch to deluxe modules and standard modules using (a) the NRV method, (b) the constant gross-margin percentage NRV method, and (c) the physical-measure method, based on the number of memory bits. Which method should MMC use?
2. MMC can process each batch of 400 standard memory modules to yield 350 DRAM modules at an additional cost of $1,600. The selling price per DRAM module would be $46. Assume MMC uses the physical-measure method. Should MMC sell the standard memory modules or the DRAM modules?

16-36 Joint cost allocation, ending work in process inventories. Tastee Freez, Inc., produces two specialty ice cream mix flavors for soft serve ice cream machines. The two flavors, Extreme Chocolate and Very Strawberry, both start with a vanilla base. The vanilla base can be sold for $2 per gallon. The company did not have any beginning inventories but produced 8,000 gallons of the vanilla base during the most recent month at a cost of $5,200. The 8,000 gallons of base was used to begin production of 5,000 gallons of Extreme Chocolate and 3,000 gallons of Very Strawberry.

At the end of the month, the company had some of its ice cream mix still in process. There were 1,200 gallons of Extreme Chocolate 30% complete and 200 gallons of Very Strawberry 80% complete. Processing costs during the month for Extreme Chocolate and Very Strawberry were $9,152 and $8,880, respectively. The selling prices for Extreme Chocolate and Very Strawberry are $4 and $5, respectively.

1. Allocate the joint costs to Extreme Chocolate and Very Strawberry under the following methods:
   a. Sales value at splitoff
   b. Net realizable value
   c. Constant gross margin percentage NRV
2. Compute the gross margin percentages for Extreme Chocolate and Very Strawberry under each of the methods in requirement 1.

Required

Collaborative Learning Problem

16-37 Joint Cost Allocation, processing further and ethics. Unified Chemical Company has a joint production process that converts Zeta into two chemicals: Alpha and Beta. The company purchases Zeta for $12 per pound and incurs a cost of $30 per pound to process it into Alpha and Beta. For every 10 pounds of Zeta, the company can produce 8 pounds of Alpha and 2 pounds of Beta. The selling price for Alpha and Beta are $76.50 and $144.00, respectively.

Unified Chemical generally processes Alpha and Beta further in separable processes to produce more refined products. Alpha is processed separately into Alphalite at a cost of $25.05 per pound. Beta is processed separately into Betalite at a cost of $112.80 per pound. Alphalite and Betalite sell for $105 and $285 per pound, respectively. In the most recent month, Unified Chemical purchased 15,000 pounds of Zeta. The company had no beginning or ending inventory of Zeta.

1. Allocate the joint costs to Alphalite and Betalite under the following methods:
   a. Sales value at splitoff
   b. Physical measure (pounds)
   c. Net realizable value
   d. Constant gross margin percentage NRV

Required

2. Unified Chemical is considering an opportunity to process Betalite further into a new product called Ultra-Betalite. The separable processing will cost $85 per pound and expects an additional $15 per pound packaging cost for Ultra-Betalite. The expected selling price would be $360 per pound. Should Unified Chemical sell Betalite or Ultra-Betalite? What selling price for Ultra-Betalite would make Unified Chemical indifferent between selling Betalite and Ultra-Betalite?
3. Independent of your answer to requirement (2), suppose Danny Dugard, the assistant controller, has completed an analysis that shows Ultra-Betalite should not be produced. Before presenting his results to top management, he received a visit from Sally Kemper. Sally had been personally responsible for developing Ultra-Betalite and was upset to learn that it would not be manufactured.

   Sally: The company is making a big mistake by passing up this opportunity. Ultra-Betalite will be a big seller and will get us into new markets.
   Danny: But the analysis shows that we would be losing money on every pound of Ultra-Betalite we manufacture.
   Sally: But that is a temporary problem. Eventually the cost of processing will be reduced.
   Danny: Do you have any estimates on the cost reductions you expect?
   Sally: There is no way of knowing that right now. Can't you just fudge the numbers a little to help me get approval to produce Ultra-Betalite. I am confident that cost reductions will follow.

   Comment on the ethical issues in this scenario. What should Danny do?

Spoilage, Rework, and Scrap

Spoilage, Rework, and Scrap

When a product doesn't meet specification but is subsequently repaired and sold, it is called rework.

Firms try to minimize rework, as well as spoilage and scrap, during production. Why? Because higher-than-normal levels of spoilage and scrap can have a significant negative effect on a company's profits. Rework can also cause substantial production delays, as the following article about Boeing shows.

Rework Delays the Boeing Dreamliner by Three Years[1]

In 2007, Boeing was scheduled to introduce its newest airplane, the Dreamliner 787. Engineered to be the most fuel-efficient commercial plane, the Dreamliner received nearly 600 customer orders, making it the fastest selling commercial airplane in history.

By 2010, however, the first Dreamliner still had not rolled off the production line. The design and assembly process was riddled with production snafus, parts shortages, and supply-chain bottlenecks. The Dreamliner was Boeing's first major attempt at giving suppliers and partners far-ranging responsibility for designing and building the wings, fuselage, and other critical components to be shipped to Boeing for final assembly. The approach did not work as planned, with many of the 787's components delivered unfinished, with flaws, and lacking parts.

As a result, the Boeing Dreamliner aircraft required significant rework. The company's engineers had to redesign structural flaws in the airplane's wings, repair cracks in the composite materials used to construct the airplane, and fix faulty software among many other problems. In 2009, one of Boeing's unions calculated that half of its members' time was spent doing rework.

This rework led to costly delays for Boeing. Many of its customers, including Virgin Atlantic and Japan's All Nippon Airways, asked the company to compensate them for keeping less fuel-efficient planes in the air. Other customers cancelled their orders. Australia's Quantas Airways and a Dubai-based aircraft leasing firm each cancelled its

---

[1] *Sources:* Lunsford, J. Lynn. 2009. Dubai firm cancels 16 of Boeing's Dreamliners. *Wall Street Journal*, February 5; Matlack, Carol. 2009. More Boeing 787 woes as Quantas drops order. *BusinessWeek*, June 26; Sanders, Peter. 2009. At Boeing, Dreamliner fix turns up new glitch. *Wall Street Journal*, November 13; West, Karen. 2009. Boeing has much to prove with 787. *MSNBC.com*, December 16; Wilhelm, Steve. 2009. Boeing engineers seek credit for fixing goofs. *Puget Sound Business Journal*, August 17.

orders for 15 airplanes, which cost Boeing at least $4.5 billion. The company also took a $2.5 billion charge in 2009 related to development costs on the Dreamliner program.

Kevin P. Casey\Getty Images, Inc.— Bloomberg News

Like Boeing, companies are increasingly focused on improving the quality of, and reducing defects in, their products, services, and activities. A rate of defects regarded as normal in the past is no longer tolerable. In this chapter, we focus on three types of costs that arise as a result of defects—spoilage, rework, and scrap—and ways to account for them. We also describe how to determine (1) cost of products, (2) cost of goods sold, and (3) inventory values when spoilage, rework, and scrap occur.

Defining Spoilage, Rework and Scrap

While the terms used in this chapter may seem familiar, be sure you understand them in the context of management accounting.

Spoilage is units of production—whether fully or partially completed—that do not meet the specifications required by customers for good units and that are discarded or sold at reduced prices. Some examples of spoilage are defective shirts, jeans, shoes, and carpeting sold as "seconds," or defective aluminum cans sold to aluminum manufacturers for remelting to produce other aluminum products.

Rework is units of production that do not meet the specifications required by customers but that are subsequently repaired and sold as good finished units. For example, defective units of products (such as pagers, computers, and telephones) detected during or after the production process but before units are shipped to customers can sometimes be reworked and sold as good products.

Scrap is residual material that results from manufacturing a product. Examples are short lengths from woodworking operations, edges from plastic molding operations, and frayed cloth and end cuts from suit-making operations. Scrap can sometimes be sold for relatively small amounts. In that sense, scrap is similar to byproducts. The difference is that scrap arises as a residual from the manufacturing process, and is not a product targeted for manufacture or sale by the firm.

Some amounts of spoilage, rework, or scrap are inherent in many production processes. For example, semiconductor manufacturing is so complex and delicate that some spoiled units are commonly produced; usually, the spoiled units cannot be reworked. In the manufacture of high-precision machine tools, spoiled units can be reworked to meet standards, but only at a considerable cost. And in the mining industry, companies process ore that contains varying amounts of valuable metals and rock. Some amount of rock, which is scrap, is inevitable.

Learning Objective 1

Understand the definitions of spoilage,

. . . unacceptable units of production

rework,

. . . unacceptable units of production subsequently repaired

and scrap

. . . leftover material

Decision Point

What are spoilage, rework, and scrap?

Two Types of Spoilage

Accounting for spoilage aims to determine the magnitude of spoilage costs and to distinguish between costs of normal and abnormal spoilage.[2] To manage, control, and reduce spoilage costs, companies need to highlight them, not bury them as an unidentified part of the costs of good units manufactured.

To illustrate normal and abnormal spoilage, consider Mendoza Plastics, which makes casings for the iMac computer using plastic injection molding. In January 2012, Mendoza incurs costs of $615,000 to produce 20,500 units. Of these 20,500 units, 20,000 are good units and 500 are spoiled units. Mendoza has no beginning inventory and no ending inventory that month. Of the 500 spoiled units, 400 units are spoiled because the injection molding machines are unable to manufacture good casings 100% of the time. That is, these units are spoiled even though the machines were run carefully and efficiently. The remaining 100 units are spoiled because of machine breakdowns and operator errors.

Normal Spoilage

Normal spoilage is spoilage inherent in a particular production process. In particular, it arises even when the process is operated in an efficient manner. The costs of normal spoilage are typically included as a component of the costs of good units manufactured, because good units cannot be made without also making some units that are spoiled. There is a tradeoff between the speed of production and the normal spoilage rate. Management makes a conscious decision about how many units to produce per hour with the understanding that, at the rate decided on, a certain level of spoilage is almost unavoidable. For this reason, the cost of normal spoilage is included in the cost of the good units completed. At Mendoza Plastics, the 400 units spoiled because of the limitations of injection molding machines and despite efficient operating conditions are considered normal spoilage. The calculations are as follows:

Manufacturing cost per unit, $615,000 ÷ 20,500 units = $30	
Manufacturing costs of good units alone, $30 per unit × 20,000 units	$600,000
Normal spoilage costs, $30 per unit × 400 units	12,000
Manufacturing costs of good units completed (includes normal spoilage)	$612,000

$$\text{Manufacturing cost per good unit} = \frac{\$612,000}{20,000 \text{ units}} = \$30.60$$

Because normal spoilage is the spoilage related to the good units produced, normal spoilage rates are computed by dividing units of normal spoilage by total *good units completed*, not total *actual units started* in production. At Mendoza Plastics, the normal spoilage rate is therefore computed as 400 ÷ 20,000 = 2%.

Abnormal Spoilage

Abnormal spoilage is spoilage that is not inherent in a particular production process and would not arise under efficient operating conditions. If a firm has 100% good units as its goal, then any spoilage would be considered abnormal. At Mendoza, the 100 units spoiled due to machine breakdowns and operator errors are abnormal spoilage. Abnormal spoilage is usually regarded as avoidable and controllable. Line operators and other plant personnel generally can decrease or eliminate abnormal spoilage by identifying the reasons for machine breakdowns, operator errors, etc., and by taking steps to prevent their recurrence. To highlight the effect of abnormal spoilage costs, companies calculate the units of abnormal spoilage and record the cost in the Loss from Abnormal Spoilage account, which appears as a separate line item in the income statement. At Mendoza, the loss from abnormal spoilage is $3,000 ($30 per unit × 100 units).

Issues about accounting for spoilage arise in both process-costing and job-costing systems. We discuss both instances next, beginning with spoilage in process-costing.

---

[2] The helpful suggestions of Samuel Laimon, University of Saskatchewan, are gratefully acknowledged.

Spoilage in Process Costing Using Weighted-Average and FIFO

How do process-costing systems account for spoiled units? We have already said that units of abnormal spoilage should be counted and recorded separately in a Loss from Abnormal Spoilage account. But what about units of normal spoilage? The correct method is to count these units when computing output units—physical or equivalent—in a process-costing system. The following example and discussion illustrate this approach.

Learning Objective 3

Account for spoilage in process costing using the weighted-average method

. . . spoilage cost based on total costs and equivalent units completed to date

and the first-in, first-out (FIFO) method

. . . spoilage cost based on costs of current period and equivalent units of work done in current period

Count All Spoilage

Example 1: Chipmakers, Inc., manufactures computer chips for television sets. All direct materials are added at the beginning of the production process. To highlight issues that arise with normal spoilage, we assume no beginning inventory and focus only on direct material costs. The following data are available for May 2012.

Home	Insert	Page Layout	Formulas	Data	Review	View	
	A					Physical Units (B)	Direct Materials (C)
2	Work in process, beginning inventory (May 1)					0	
3	Started during May					10,000	
4	Good units completed and transferred out during May					5,000	
5	Units spoiled (all normal spoilage)					1,000	
6	Work in process, ending inventory (May 31)					4,000	
7	Direct material costs added in May						$270,000

Spoilage is detected upon completion of the process and has zero net disposal value.

An **inspection point** is the stage of the production process at which products are examined to determine whether they are acceptable or unacceptable units. Spoilage is typically assumed to occur at the stage of completion where inspection takes place. As a result, the spoiled units in our example are assumed to be 100% complete with respect to direct materials.

Exhibit 1 calculates and assigns cost per unit of direct materials. Overall, Chipmakers generated 10,000 equivalent units of output: 5,000 equivalent units in good units completed (5,000 physical units × 100%), 4,000 units in ending work in process

Exhibit 1

Effect of Recognizing Equivalent Units in Spoilage for Direct Material Costs for Chipmakers, Inc., for May 2012

Home	Insert	Page Layout	Formulas	Data	Review	View	
	A						Approach Counting Spoiled Units When Computing Output in Equivalent Units (B)
2	Costs to account for						$270,000
3	Divide by equivalent units of output						÷ 10,000
4	Cost per equivalent unit of output						$ 27
5	Assignment of costs:						
6	Good units completed (5,000 units × $27 per unit)						$135,000
7	Add normal spoilage (1,000 units × $27 per unit)						27,000
8	Total costs of good units completed and transferred out						162,000
9	Work in process, ending (4,000 units × $27 per unit)						108,000
10	Costs accounted for						$270,000

(4,000 physical units $\times$ 100%), and 1,000 equivalent units in normal spoilage (1,000 physical units $\times$ 100%). Given total direct material costs of $270,000 in May, this yields an equivalent-unit cost of $27. The total cost of good units completed and transferred out, which includes the cost of normal spoilage, is then $162,000 (6,000 equivalent units $\times$ $27), while the ending work in process is assigned a cost of $108,000 (4,000 equivalent units $\times$ $27).

There are two noteworthy features of this approach. First, the 4,000 units in ending work in process are not assigned any of the costs of normal spoilage. This is appropriate because the units have not yet been inspected. While the units in ending work in process undoubtedly include some that will be detected as spoiled when inspected, these units will only be identified when the units are completed in the subsequent accounting period. At that time, costs of normal spoilage will be assigned to the good units completed in that period. Second, the approach used in Exhibit 1 delineates the cost of normal spoilage as $27,000. By highlighting the magnitude of this cost, the approach helps to focus management's attention on the potential economic benefits of reducing spoilage.

Five-Step Procedure for Process Costing with Spoilage

Example 2: Anzio Company manufactures a recycling container in its forming department. Direct materials are added at the beginning of the production process. Conversion costs are added evenly during the production process. Some units of this product are spoiled as a result of defects, which are detectable only upon inspection of finished units. Normally, spoiled units are 10% of the finished output of good units. That is, for every 10 good units produced, there is 1 unit of normal spoilage. Summary data for July 2012 are as follows:

Home Insert Page Layout Formulas Data Review View				
A	B	C	D	E
1	Physical Units (1)	Direct Materials (2)	Conversion Costs (3)	Total Costs (4) = (2) + (3)
2 Work in process, beginning inventory (July 1)	1,500	$12,000	$ 9,000	$ 21,000
3 Degree of completion of beginning work in process		100%	60%	
4 Started during July	8,500			
5 Good units completed and transferred out during July	7,000			
6 Work in process, ending inventory (July 31)	2,000			
7 Degree of completion of ending work in process		100%	50%	
8 Total costs added during July		$76,500	$89,100	$165,600
9 Normal spoilage as a percentage of good units	10%			
10 Degree of completion of normal spoilage		100%	100%	
11 Degree of completion of abnormal spoilage		100%	100%	

The five-step procedure for process costing needs only slight modification to accommodate spoilage.

Step 1: Summarize the Flow of Physical Units of Output. Identify the number of units of both normal and abnormal spoilage.

$$\text{Total Spoilage} = \left(\begin{array}{c} \text{Units in beginning} \\ \text{work-in-process inventory} \end{array} + \begin{array}{c} \text{Units} \\ \text{started} \end{array} \right) - \left(\begin{array}{c} \text{Good units} \\ \text{completed and} + \begin{array}{c} \text{Units in ending} \\ \text{work-in-process inventory} \end{array} \\ \text{transferred out} \end{array} \right)$$

$= (1,500 + 8,500) - (7,000 + 2,000)$

$= 10,000 - 9,000$

$= 1,000 \text{ units}$

Recall that normal spoilage is 10% of good output at Anzio Company. Therefore, normal spoilage = 10% of the 7,000 units of *good* output = 700 units.

$$\text{Abnormal spoilage} = \text{Total spoilage} - \text{Normal spoilage}$$

$$= 1{,}000 \text{ units} - 700 \text{ units}$$

$$= 300 \text{ units}$$

Step 2: Compute Output in Terms of Equivalent Units. Compute equivalent units for spoilage in the same way we compute equivalent units for good units. As illustrated previously, all spoiled units are included in the computation of output units. Because Anzio's inspection point is at the completion of production, the same amount of work will have been done on each spoiled and each completed good unit.

Step 3: Summarize Total Costs to Account For. The total costs to account for are all the costs debited to Work in Process.

Step 4: Compute Cost per Equivalent Unit.

Step 5: Assign Total Costs to Units Completed, to Spoiled Units, and to Units in Ending Work in Process. This step now includes computation of the cost of spoiled units and the cost of good units.

We illustrate these five steps of process costing for the weighted-average and FIFO methods next. *The standard-costing method is illustrated in the appendix to this chapter.*

Weighted-Average Method and Spoilage

Exhibit 2, Panel A, presents Steps 1 and 2 to calculate equivalent units of work done to date and includes calculations of equivalent units of normal and abnormal spoilage. Exhibit 2, Panel B, presents Steps 3, 4, and 5 (together called the production-cost worksheet).

Step 3 summarizes total costs to account for. Step 4 presents cost-per-equivalent-unit calculations using the weighted-average method. Note how, for each cost category, costs of beginning work in process and costs of work done in the current period are totaled and divided by equivalent units of all work done to date to calculate the weighted-average cost per equivalent unit. Step 5 assigns total costs to completed units, normal and abnormal spoiled units, and ending inventory by multiplying the equivalent units calculated in Step 2 by the cost per equivalent unit calculated in Step 4. Also note that the $13,825 costs of normal spoilage are added to the costs of the related good units completed and transferred out.

$$\begin{array}{l} \text{Cost per good unit} \\ \text{completed and transferred} \\ \text{out of the process} \end{array} = \frac{\text{Total costs transferred out (including normal spoilage)}}{\text{Number of good units produced}}$$

$$= \$152{,}075 \div 7{,}000 \text{ good units} = \$21.725 \text{ per good unit}$$

This amount is not equal to $19.75 per good unit, the sum of the $8.85 cost per equivalent unit of direct materials plus the $10.90 cost per equivalent unit of conversion costs. That's because the cost per good unit equals the sum of the direct material and conversion costs per equivalent unit, $19.75, plus a share of normal spoilage, $1.975 ($13,825 ÷ 7,000 good units), for a total of $21.725 per good unit. The $5,925 costs of abnormal spoilage are charged to the Loss from Abnormal Spoilage account and do not appear in the costs of good units.[3]

FIFO Method and Spoilage

Exhibit 3, Panel A, presents Steps 1 and 2 using the FIFO method, which focuses on equivalent units of work done in the current period. Exhibit 3, Panel B, presents Steps 3, 4, and 5. Note how when assigning costs, the FIFO method keeps the costs of

---

[3] The actual costs of spoilage (and rework) are often greater than the costs recorded in the accounting system because the opportunity costs of disruption of the production line, storage, and lost contribution margins are not recorded in accounting systems.

| Exhibit 2 | Weighted-Average Method of Process Costing with Spoilage for Forming Department of the Anzio Company for July 2012 |

PANEL A: Steps 1 and 2—Summarize Output in Physical Units and Compute Equivalent Units

| | Home | Insert | Page Layout | Formulas | Data | Review | View | | | |

	A	B	C	D	E
1			(Step 1)	(Step 2)	
2				Equivalent Units	
3		Flow of Production	Physical Units	Direct Materials	Conversion Costs
4		Work in process, beginning (given)	1,500		
5		Started during current period (given)	8,500		
6		To account for	10,000		
7		Good units completed and transferred out during current period	7,000	7,000	7,000
8		Normal spoilage[a]	700		
9		(700 × 100%; 700 × 100%)		700	700
10		Abnormal spoilage[b]	300		
11		(300 × 100%; 300 × 100%)		300	300
12		Work in process, ending[c] (given)	2,000		
13		(2,000 × 100%; 2,000 × 50%)		2,000	1,000
14		Accounted for	10,000		
15		Equivalent units of work done to date		10,000	9,000
16					
17	[a]Normal spoilage is 10% of good units transferred out: 10% × 7,000 = 700 units. Degree of completion of normal spoilage				
18	in this department: direct materials, 100%; conversion costs, 100%.				
19	[b]Abnormal spoilage = Total spoilage − Normal spoilage = 1,000 − 700 = 300 units. Degree of completion of abnormal spoilage				
20	in this department: direct materials, 100%; conversion costs, 100%.				
21	[c]Degree of completion in this department: direct materials, 100%; conversion costs, 50%.				

PANEL B: Steps 3, 4, and 5—Summarize Total Costs to Account For, Compute Cost per Equivalent Unit, and Assign Total Costs to Units Completed, to Spoiled Units, and to Units in Ending Work Process

			Total Production Costs	Direct Materials	Conversion Costs
23					
24	(Step 3)	Work in process, beginning (given)	$ 21,000	$12,000	$ 9,000
25		Costs added in current period (given)	165,600	76,500	89,100
26		Total costs to account for	$186,600	$88,500	$98,100
27	(Step 4)	Costs incurred to date		$88,500	$98,100
28		Divide by equivalent units of work done to date (Panel A)		÷10,000	÷ 9,000
29		Cost per equivalent unit		$ 8.85	$ 10.90
30	(Step 5)	Assignment of costs:			
31		Good units completed and transferred out (7,000 units)			
32		Costs before adding normal spoilage	$138,250	(7,000[d] × $8.85) +	(7,000[d] × $10.90)
33		Normal spoilage (700 units)	13,825	(700[d] × $8.85) +	(700[d] × $10.90)
34	(A)	Total costs of good units completed and transferred out	152,075		
35	(B)	Abnormal spoilage (300 units)	5,925	(300[d] × $8.85) +	(300[d] × $10.90)
36	(C)	Work in process, ending (2,000 units)	28,600	(2,000[d] × $8.85) +	(1,000[d] × $10.90)
37	(A)+(B)+(C)	Total costs accounted for	$186,600	$88,500 +	$98,100
38					
39	[d]Equivalent units of direct materials and conversion costs calculated in Step 2 in Panel A.				

PANEL A: Steps 1 and 2—Summarize Output in Physical Units and Compute Equivalent Units

Exhibit 3

First-In, First-Out (FIFO) Method of Process Costing with Spoilage for Forming Department of the Anzio Company for July 2012

			(Step 1)	(Step 2)	
				Equivalent Units	
		Flow of Production	**Physical Units**	**Direct Materials**	**Conversion Costs**
4		Work in process, beginning (given)	1,500		
5		Started during current period (given)	8,500		
6		To account for	10,000		
7		Good units completed and transferred out during current period:			
8		From beginning work in process[a]	1,500		
9		[1,500 × (100% −100%); 1,500 × (100% −60%)]		0	600
10		Started and completed	5,500[b]		
11		(5,500 × 100%; 5,500 × 100%)		5,500	5,500
12		Normal spoilage[c]	700		
13		(700 × 100%; 700 × 100%)		700	700
14		Abnormal spoilage[d]	300		
15		(300 × 100%; 300 × 100%)		300	300
16		Work in process, ending[e] (given, p. 648)	2,000		
17		(2,000 × 100%; 2,000 × 50%)		2,000	1,000
18		Accounted for	10,000		
19		Equivalent units of work done in current period		8,500	8,100
20					

[a]Degree of completion in this department: direct materials, 100%; conversion costs, 60%.

[b]7,000 physical units completed and transferred out minus 1,500 physical units completed and transferred out from beginning work-in-process inventory.

[c]Normal spoilage is 10% of good units transferred out: 10% × 7,000 = 700 units. Degree of completion of normal spoilage in this department: direct materials, 100%; conversion costs, 100%.

[d]Abnormal spoilage = Actual spoilage – Normal spoilage = 1,000 – 700 = 300 units. Degree of completion of abnormal spoilage in this department: direct materials, 100%; conversion costs, 100%.

[e]Degree of completion in this department: direct materials, 100%; conversion costs, 50%.

PANEL B: Steps 3, 4, and 5—Summarize Total Costs to Account for, Compute Cost per Equivalent Unit, and Assign Total Costs to Units Completed, to Spoiled Units, and to Units in Ending Work in Process

			Total Production Costs	**Direct Materials**	**Conversion Costs**
31	(Step 3)	Work in process, beginning (given)	$ 21,000	$12,000	$ 9,000
32		Costs added in current period (given)	165,600	76,500	89,100
33		Total costs to account for	$186,600	$88,500	$98,100
34	(Step 4)	Costs added in current period		$76,500	$89,100
35		Divide by equivalent units of work done in current period (Panel A)		÷ 8,500	÷ 8,100
36		Cost per equivalent unit		$ 9.00	$ 11.00
37	(Step 5)	Assignment of costs:			
38		Good units completed and transferred out (7,000 units)			
39		Work in process, beginning (1,500 units)	$ 21,000	$12,000 +	$9,000
40		Costs added to beginning work in process in current period	6,600	(0[f] × $9) +	(600[f] × $11)
41		Total from beginning inventory before normal spoilage	27,600		
42		Started and completed before normal spoilage (5,500 units)	110,000	(5,500[f] × $9) +	(5,500[f] × $11)
43		Normal spoilage (700 units)	14,000	(700[f] × $9) +	(700[f] × $11)
44	(A)	Total costs of good units completed and transferred out	151,600		
45	(B)	Abnormal spoilage (300 units)	6,000	(300[f] × $9) +	(300[f] × $11)
46	(C)	Work in process, ending (2,000 units)	29,000	(2,000[f] × $9) +	(1,000[f] × $11)
47	(A)+(B)+(C)	Total costs accounted for	$186,600	$88,500 +	$98,100
48					
49					
50					

[f]Equivalent units of direct materials and conversion costs calculated in Step 2 in Panel A.

the beginning work in process separate and distinct from the costs of work done in the current period. All spoilage costs are assumed to be related to units completed during this period, using the unit costs of the current period.[4]

Journal Entries

Decision Point ▶

How do the weighted-average and FIFO methods of process costing calculate the costs of good units and spoilage?

The information from Panel B in Exhibits 2 and 3 supports the following journal entries to transfer good units completed to finished goods and to recognize the loss from abnormal spoilage.

	Weighted Average		FIFO	
Finished Goods	152,075		151,600	
Work in Process—Forming		152,075		151,600
To record transfer of good units completed in July.				
Loss from Abnormal Spoilage	5,925		6,000	
Work in Process—Forming		5,925		6,000
To record abnormal spoilage detected in July.				

Inspection Points and Allocating Costs of Normal Spoilage

Learning Objective 4

Account for spoilage at various stages of completion in process costing

. . . spoilage costs vary based on the point at which inspection is carried out

Our Anzio Company example assumes inspection occurs upon completion of the units. Although spoilage is typically detected only at one or more inspection points, it might actually occur at various stages of a production process. The cost of spoiled units is assumed to equal all costs incurred in producing spoiled units up to the point of inspection. When spoiled goods have a disposal value (for example, carpeting sold as "seconds"), the net cost of spoilage is computed by deducting the disposal value from the costs of the spoiled goods that have been accumulated up to the inspection point.

The unit costs of normal and abnormal spoilage are the same when the two are detected at the same inspection point. However, situations may arise when abnormal spoilage is detected at a different point from normal spoilage. Consider shirt manufacturing. Normal spoilage in the form of defective shirts is identified upon inspection at the end of the production process. Now suppose a faulty machine causes many defective shirts to be produced at the halfway point of the production process. These defective shirts are abnormal spoilage and occur at a different point in the production process from normal spoilage. In such cases, the unit cost of abnormal spoilage, which is based on costs incurred up to the halfway point of the production process, differs from the unit cost of normal spoilage, which is based on costs incurred through the end of the production process.

Costs of abnormal spoilage are separately accounted for as losses of the accounting period in which they are detected. However, recall that normal spoilage costs are added to the costs of good units, which raises an additional issue: Should normal spoilage costs be allocated between completed units and ending work-in-process inventory? *The common approach is to presume that normal spoilage occurs at the inspection point in the production cycle and to allocate its cost over all units that have passed that point during the accounting period.*

In the Anzio Company example, spoilage is assumed to occur when units are inspected at the end of the production process, so no costs of normal spoilage are allocated to ending work in process. If the units in ending work in process have passed the inspection point, however, the costs of normal spoilage are allocated to units in ending work in process as well as to completed units. For example, if the inspection point is at the halfway point of production, then any ending work in process that is at least 50% complete would be allocated a full measure of normal spoilage costs, and those spoilage costs would be calculated on the basis of all costs incurred up to the inspection point. If ending work in process is less than 50% complete, however, no normal spoilage costs would be allocated to it.

To better understand these issues, let us now assume that inspection at Anzio Company occurs at various stages in the production process. How does this affect the

---

[4] To simplify calculations under FIFO, spoiled units are accounted for as if they were started in the current period. Although some of the beginning work in process probably did spoil, all spoilage is treated as if it came from current production.

amount of normal and abnormal spoilage? As before, consider the forming department, and recall that direct materials are added at the start of production, while conversion costs are added evenly during the process.

Consider three different cases: Inspection occurs at (1) the 20%, (2) the 55%, or (3) the 100% completion stage. The last option is the one we have analyzed so far (see Exhibit 2). Assume that normal spoilage is 10% of the good units passing inspection. A total of 1,000 units are spoiled in all three cases. Normal spoilage is computed on the basis of the number of *good units* that pass the inspection point *during the current period*. The following data are for July 2012. Note how the number of units of normal and abnormal spoilage changes, depending on when inspection occurs.

Home Insert Page Layout Formulas Data Review View			
	B	C	D
A	Physical Units: Stage of Completion at Which Inspection Occurs		
1			
2 Flow of Production	20%	55%	100%
3 Work in process, beginning[a]	1,500	1,500	1,500
4 Started during July	8,500	8,500	8,500
5 To account for	10,000	10,000	10,000
6 Good units completed and transferred out			
7 (10,000 – 1,000 spoiled – 2,000 ending)	7,000	7,000	7,000
8 Normal spoilage	750[c]	550[d]	700[e]
9 Abnormal spoilage (1,000 – normal spoilage)	250	450	300
10 Work in process, ending[b]	2,000	2,000	2,000
11 Accounted for	10,000	10,000	10,000
12			
13 [a]Degree of completion in this department: direct materials, 100%; conversion costs, 60%.			
14 [b]Degree of completion in this department: direct materials, 100%; conversion costs, 50%.			
15 [c]10% × (8,500 units started – 1,000 units spoiled), because only the units started passed the 20% completion			
16 inspection point in the current period. Beginning work in process is excluded from this calculation because,			
17 being 60% complete at the start of the period, it passed the inspection point in the previous period.			
18 [d]10% × (8,500 units started – 1,000 units spoiled – 2,000 units in ending work in process). Both beginning and			
19 ending work in process are excluded since neither was inspected this period.			
20 [e]10% × 7,000, because 7,000 units are fully completed and inspected in the current period.			

The following diagram shows the flow of physical units for July and illustrates the normal spoilage numbers in the table. Note that 7,000 good units are completed and transferred out—1,500 from beginning work in process and 5,500 started and completed during the period—while 2,000 units are in ending work in process.

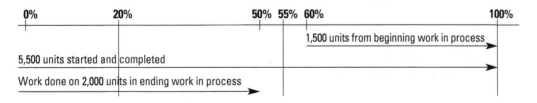

To see the number of units passing each inspection point, consider in the diagram the vertical lines at the 20%, 55%, and 100% inspection points. Note that the vertical line at 20% crosses two horizontal lines—5,500 good units started and completed and 2,000 units in ending work in process—for a total of 7,500 good units. (The 20% vertical line does not cross the line representing work done on the 1,500 good units completed from beginning work in process, because these units are already 60% complete at the start of the period and, hence, are not inspected this period.) Normal spoilage equals 10% of 7,500 = 750 units. On the other hand, the vertical line at the 55% point crosses just the second horizontal line, indicating that only 5,500 good units pass this point. Normal spoilage in this case is 10% of 5,500 = 550 units. At the 100% point, normal spoilage = 10% of 7,000 (1,500 + 5,500) good units = 700 units.

Exhibit 4 shows the computation of equivalent units under the weighted-average method, assuming inspection at the 20% completion stage. The calculations depend on the direct materials and conversion costs incurred to get the units to this inspection point. The spoiled units have a full measure of direct materials and a 20% measure of conversion costs. Calculations of costs per equivalent unit and the assignment of total costs to units completed and to ending work in process are similar to calculations in previous illustrations in this chapter. Because ending work in process has passed the inspection point, these units bear normal spoilage costs, just like the units that have been completed and transferred out. For example, conversion costs for units completed and transferred out include conversion costs for 7,000 good units produced plus 20% × (10% × 5,500) = 110 equivalent units of normal spoilage. *We multiply by 20% to obtain equivalent units of normal spoilage because conversion costs are only 20% complete at the inspection point.* Conversion costs of ending work in process include conversion costs of 50% of 2,000 = 1,000 equivalent good units plus 20% × (10% × 2,000) = 40 equivalent units of normal spoilage. Thus, the equivalent units of normal spoilage accounted for are 110 equivalent units related to units completed and transferred out plus 40 equivalent units related to units in ending work in process, for a total of 150 equivalent units, as shown in Exhibit 4.

Early inspections can help prevent any further direct materials and conversion costs being wasted on units that are already spoiled. For example, if inspection can occur when units are 70% (rather than 100%) complete as to conversion costs and spoilage occurs prior to the 70% point, a company can avoid incurring the final 30% of conversion costs on the spoiled units. The downside to conducting inspections at too early a stage is that spoilage that happens at later stages of the process may go undetected. It is for these reasons that firms often conduct multiple inspections and also empower workers to identify and resolve defects on a timely basis.

Decision Point

How does inspection at various stages of completion affect the amount of normal and abnormal spoilage?

Exhibit 4

Computing Equivalent Units with Spoilage Using Weighted-Average Method of Process Costing with Inspection at 20% of Completion for Forming Department of Anzio Company for July 2012

	A	B	C	D
		(Step 1)	(Step 2)	
			Equivalent Units	
	Flow of Production	Physical Units	Direct Materials	Conversion Costs
4	Work in process, beginning[a]	1,500		
5	Started during current period	8,500		
6	To account for	10,000		
7	Good units completed and transferred out:	7,000	7,000	7,000
8	Normal spoilage	750		
9	(750 × 100%; 750 × 20%)		750	150
10	Abnormal spoilage	250		
11	(250 × 100%; 250 × 20%)		250	50
12	Work in process, ending[b]	2,000		
13	(2,000 × 100%; 2,000 × 50%)		2,000	1,000
14	Accounted for	10,000		
15	Equivalent units of work done to date		10,000	8,200
17	[a]Degree of completion: direct materials, 100%; conversion costs, 60%.			
18	[b]Degree of completion: direct materials, 100%; conversion costs, 50%.			

204

Job Costing and Spoilage

The concepts of normal and abnormal spoilage also apply to job-costing systems. Abnormal spoilage is separately identified so companies can work to eliminate it altogether. Costs of abnormal spoilage are not considered to be inventoriable costs and are written off as costs of the accounting period in which the abnormal spoilage is detected. Normal spoilage costs in job-costing systems—as in process-costing systems—are inventoriable costs, although increasingly companies are tolerating only small amounts of spoilage as normal. When assigning costs, job-costing systems generally distinguish *normal spoilage attributable to a specific job from normal spoilage common to all jobs.*

We describe accounting for spoilage in job costing using the following example.

> Example 3: In the Hull Machine Shop, 5 aircraft parts out of a job lot of 50 aircraft parts are spoiled. Costs assigned prior to the inspection point are $2,000 per part. When the spoilage is detected, the spoiled goods are inventoried at $600 per part, the net disposal value.

Learning **5**
Objective

Account for spoilage in job costing

. . . normal spoilage assigned directly or indirectly to job; abnormal spoilage written off as a loss of the period

Our presentation here and in subsequent sections focuses on how the $2,000 cost per part is accounted for.

Normal Spoilage Attributable to a Specific Job

When normal spoilage occurs because of the specifications of a particular job, that job bears the cost of the spoilage minus the disposal value of the spoilage. The journal entry to recognize disposal value (items in parentheses indicate subsidiary ledger postings) is as follows:

Materials Control (spoiled goods at current net disposal value): 5 units $\times$ $600 per unit	3,000	
Work-in-Process Control (specific job): 5 units $\times$ $600 per unit		3,000

Note, the Work-in-Process Control (specific job) has already been debited (charged) $10,000 for the spoiled parts (5 spoiled parts $\times$ $2,000 per part). The net cost of normal spoilage = $7,000 ($10,000 − $3,000), which is an additional cost of the 45 (50 − 5) good units produced. Therefore, total cost of the 45 good units is $97,000: $90,000 (45 units $\times$ $2,000 per unit) incurred to produce the good units plus the $7,000 net cost of normal spoilage. Cost per good unit is $2,155.56 ($97,000 ÷ 45 good units).

Normal Spoilage Common to All Jobs

In some cases, spoilage may be considered a normal characteristic of the production process. The spoilage inherent in production will, of course, occur when a specific job is being worked on. But the spoilage is not attributable to, and hence is not charged directly to, the specific job. Instead, the spoilage is allocated indirectly to the job as manufacturing overhead because the spoilage is common to all jobs. The journal entry is as follows:

Materials Control (spoiled goods at current disposal value): 5 units $\times$ $600 per unit	3,000	
Manufacturing Overhead Control (normal spoilage): ($10,000 − $3,000)	7,000	
Work-in-Process Control (specific job): 5 units $\times$ $2,000 per unit		10,000

When normal spoilage is common to all jobs, the budgeted manufacturing overhead rate includes a provision for normal spoilage cost. Normal spoilage cost is spread, through overhead allocation, over all jobs rather than allocated to a specific job.[5] For example, if Hull produced 140 good units from all jobs in a given month, the $7,000 of normal spoilage overhead costs would be allocated at the rate of $50 per good unit ($7,000 ÷ 140 good units). Normal spoilage overhead costs allocated to the 45 good units in the job would be $2,250 ($50 $\times$ 45 good units). Total cost of the 45 good units is $92,250: $90,000 (45 units $\times$ $2,000 per unit) incurred to produce the good units plus $2,250 of normal spoilage overhead costs. Cost per good unit is $2,050 ($92,250 ÷ 45 good units).

---

[5] Note that costs already assigned to products are charged back to Manufacturing Overhead Control, which generally accumulates only costs incurred, not both costs incurred and costs already assigned.

Abnormal Spoilage

If the spoilage is abnormal, the net loss is charged to the Loss from Abnormal Spoilage account. Unlike normal spoilage costs, abnormal spoilage costs are not included as a part of the cost of good units produced. Total cost of the 45 good units is $90,000 (45 units × $2,000 per unit). Cost per good unit is $2,000 ($90,000 ÷ 45 good units).

Materials Control (spoiled goods at current disposal value): 5 units × $600 per unit	3,000	
Loss from Abnormal Spoilage ($10,000 − $3,000)	7,000	
Work-in-Process Control (specific job): 5 units × $2,000 per unit		10,000

Even though, for external reporting purposes, abnormal spoilage costs are written off in the accounting period and are not linked to specific jobs or units, companies often identify the particular reasons for abnormal spoilage, and, when appropriate, link abnormal spoilage with specific jobs or units for cost management purposes.

Job Costing and Rework

Rework is units of production that are inspected, determined to be unacceptable, repaired, and sold as acceptable finished goods. We again distinguish (1) normal rework attributable to a specific job, (2) normal rework common to all jobs, and (3) abnormal rework.

    Consider the Hull Machine Shop data in Example 3. Assume the five spoiled parts are reworked. The journal entry for the $10,000 of total costs (the details of these costs are assumed) assigned to the five spoiled units before considering rework costs is as follows:

Work-in-Process Control (specific job)	10,000	
Materials Control		4,000
Wages Payable Control		4,000
Manufacturing Overhead Allocated		2,000

Assume the rework costs equal $3,800 (comprising $800 direct materials, $2,000 direct manufacturing labor, and $1,000 manufacturing overhead).

Normal Rework Attributable to a Specific Job

If the rework is normal but occurs because of the requirements of a specific job, the rework costs are charged to that job. The journal entry is as follows:

Work-in-Process Control (specific job)	3,800	
Materials Control		800
Wages Payable Control		2,000
Manufacturing Overhead Allocated		1,000

Normal Rework Common to All Jobs

When rework is normal and not attributable to a specific job, the costs of rework are charged to manufacturing overhead and are spread, through overhead allocation, over all jobs.

Manufacturing Overhead Control (rework costs)	3,800	
Materials Control		800
Wages Payable Control		2,000
Manufacturing Overhead Allocated		1,000

Abnormal Rework

If the rework is abnormal, it is recorded by charging abnormal rework to a loss account.

Loss from Abnormal Rework	3,800	
Materials Control		800
Wages Payable Control		2,000
Manufacturing Overhead Allocated		1,000

Decision Point ▶

How do job-costing systems account for spoilage?

Learning Objective 6

Account for rework in job costing

. . . normal rework assigned directly or indirectly to job; abnormal rework written off as a loss of the period

Accounting for rework in a process-costing system also requires abnormal rework to be distinguished from normal rework. Process costing accounts for abnormal rework in the same way as job costing. Accounting for normal rework follows the accounting described for normal rework common to all jobs (units) because masses of identical or similar units are being manufactured.

Costing rework focuses managers' attention on the resources wasted on activities that would not have to be undertaken if the product had been made correctly. The cost of rework prompts managers to seek ways to reduce rework, for example, by designing new products or processes, training workers, or investing in new machines. To eliminate rework and to simplify the accounting, some companies set a standard of zero rework. All rework is then treated as abnormal and is written off as a cost of the current period.

Decision Point

How do job-costing systems account for rework?

Accounting for Scrap

Scrap is residual material that results from manufacturing a product; it has low total sales value compared with the total sales value of the product. No distinction is made between normal and abnormal scrap because no cost is assigned to scrap. The only distinction made is between scrap attributable to a specific job and scrap common to all jobs.

There are two aspects of accounting for scrap:

1. Planning and control, including physical tracking
2. Inventory costing, including when and how scrap affects operating income

Learning Objective 7

Account for scrap

. . . reduces cost of job either at time of sale or at time of production

Initial entries to scrap records are commonly expressed in physical terms. In various industries, companies quantify items such as stamped-out metal sheets or edges of molded plastic parts by weighing, counting, or some other measure. Scrap records not only help measure efficiency, but also help keep track of scrap, and so reduce the chances of theft. Companies use scrap records to prepare periodic summaries of the amounts of actual scrap compared with budgeted or standard amounts. Scrap is either sold or disposed of quickly or it is stored for later sale, disposal, or reuse.

Careful tracking of scrap often extends into the accounting records. Many companies maintain a distinct account for scrap costs somewhere in their accounting system. The issues here are similar to the issues regarding the accounting for byproducts:

■ When should the value of scrap be recognized in the accounting records—at the time scrap is produced or at the time scrap is sold?

■ How should revenues from scrap be accounted for?

To illustrate, we extend our Hull example. Assume the manufacture of aircraft parts generates scrap and that the scrap from a job has a net sales value of $900.

Recognizing Scrap at the Time of Its Sale

When the dollar amount of scrap is immaterial, the simplest accounting is to record the physical quantity of scrap returned to the storeroom and to regard scrap sales as a separate line item in the income statement. In this case, the only journal entry is as follows:

Sale of scrap:	Cash or Accounts Receivable	900	
	Scrap Revenues		900

When the dollar amount of scrap is material and the scrap is sold quickly after it is produced, the accounting depends on whether the scrap is attributable to a specific job or is common to all jobs.

Scrap Attributable to a Specific Job

Job-costing systems sometimes trace scrap revenues to the jobs that yielded the scrap. This method is used only when the tracing can be done in an economically feasible way. For example, the Hull Machine Shop and its customers, such as the U.S. Department of Defense, may reach an agreement that provides for charging specific jobs with all rework or spoilage costs and then crediting these jobs with all scrap revenues that arise from the jobs. The journal entry is as follows:

Scrap returned to storeroom:	No journal entry.		
	[Notation of quantity received and related job entered in the inventory record]		
Sale of scrap:	Cash or Accounts Receivable	900	
	Work-in-Process Control		900
	Posting made to specific job cost record.		

Unlike spoilage and rework, there is no cost assigned to the scrap, so no distinction is made between normal and abnormal scrap. All scrap revenues, whatever the amount, are credited to the specific job. Scrap revenues reduce the costs of the job.

Scrap common to all jobs

The journal entry in this case is as follows:

Scrap returned to storeroom:	No journal entry.		
	[Notation of quantity received and related job entered in the inventory record]		
Sale of scrap:	Cash or Accounts Receivable	900	
	Manufacturing Overhead Control		900
	Posting made to subsidiary ledger—"Sales of Scrap" column on department cost record.		

Scrap is not linked with any particular job or product. Instead, all products bear production costs without any credit for scrap revenues except in an indirect manner: Expected scrap revenues are considered when setting the budgeted manufacturing overhead rate. Thus, the budgeted overhead rate is lower than it would be if the overhead budget had not been reduced by expected scrap revenues. This method of accounting for scrap is also used in process costing when the dollar amount of scrap is immaterial, because the scrap in process costing is common to the manufacture of all the identical or similar units produced (and cannot be identified with specific units).

Recognizing Scrap at the Time of Its Production

Our preceding illustrations assume that scrap returned to the storeroom is sold quickly, so it is not assigned an inventory cost figure. Sometimes, as in the case with edges of molded plastic parts, the value of scrap is not immaterial, and the time between storing it and selling or reusing it can be long and unpredictable. In these situations, the company assigns an inventory cost to scrap at a conservative estimate of its net realizable value so that production costs and related scrap revenues are recognized in the same accounting period. Some companies tend to delay sales of scrap until its market price is considered attractive. Volatile price fluctuations are typical for scrap metal. In these cases, it's not easy to determine some "reasonable inventory value."

Scrap Attributable to a Specific Job

The journal entry in the Hull example is as follows:

Scrap returned to storeroom:	Materials Control	900	
	Work-in-Process Control		900

Scrap Common to All Jobs

The journal entry in this case is as follows:

Scrap returned to storeroom:	Materials Control	900	
	Manufacturing Overhead Control		900

Observe that the Materials Control account is debited in place of Cash or Accounts Receivable. When the scrap is sold, the journal entry is as follows:

Sale of scrap:	Cash or Accounts Receivable	900	
	Materials Control		900

Concepts in Action

Managing Waste and Environmental Costs at KB Home

Ed Andrieski\AP Wide World Photos

KB Home is one of the largest home builders in the United States. In recent years, public awareness of environmental issues and interest in environmentally-friendly products and services has led to increased demand for sustainable home construction. KB Home has responded by increasing the sustainability of its homebuilding operations, which includes reducing its waste and environmental costs.

Through its "My Home. My Earth." program, launched in 2007, KB Home has established environmental sustainability as top-priority management issue. It developed core principles to guide its efforts including using "innovation and our process-driven approach to reduce waste and natural resource usage throughout our organization." Much of that focus involves reducing scrap, the residual materials that result from its homebuilding processes. These materials pose additional problems for companies like KB Home, because many federal and state environmental laws dictate that scrap materials be deposed of in an environmentally friendly way; therefore, they add to the cost of generating waste.

To reduce these costs during the homebuilding process, all new homes are built with pre-engineered roof trusses, while 90% also use preconstructed panels. These preconstructed materials are cut offsite for greater precision, which reduces wood waste. Further, these precut materials are made of engineered wood products, which reduce the use of long solid boards that require larger trees to be cut. Beyond scrap reduction, these trusses and panels also eliminate the need for costly job-site rework, or the repair of defective materials during construction.

Similarly, all new homes use oriented strand board, which is made from wood chip rather than plywood. Wood chip is both cheaper and more environmentally sustainable than traditional construction materials. These sustainable practices helped KB Home reduce the cost, exclusive of land, of each home manufactured in 2009 by nearly 39% over the previous year, while increasing profit margins by 13% despite the broader U.S. housing market collapse.

Beyond the construction process, KB Home also includes earth-friendly standard features in all of its homes, at no cost to homebuyers, including energy-efficient windows, recyclable carpets, programmable thermostats, and faucets that reduce water usage. Beyond cutting costs, KB Home's efforts to effectively manage waste and environmental costs have helped the company partially stabilize revenues in a difficult real-estate market. Chief executive Jeffrey Mazger said, "Less than 2% of customers a few years ago were asking about energy-efficient options. Since we introduced 'My Home. My Earth.' in April 2007, it's gone up to 75%." This has helped KB Home differentiate itself within a very competitive market for homebuilders.

Sources: KB Home. 2010. 2009 annual report. Los Angeles: KB Home; KB Home. 2010. 2009 sustainability report. Los Angeles: KB Home; Tischler, Linda. 2008. The green housing boom. *Fast Company*, June 23.

Scrap is sometimes reused as direct material rather than sold as scrap. In this case, Materials Control is debited at its estimated net realizable value and then credited when the scrap is reused. For example, the entries when the scrap is common to all jobs are as follows:

Scrap returned to storeroom:	Materials Control	900	
	Manufacturing Overhead Control		900
Reuse of scrap:	Work-in-Process Control	900	
	Materials Control		900

Accounting for scrap under process costing is similar to accounting under job costing when scrap is common to all jobs. That's because the scrap in process costing is common to the manufacture of masses of identical or similar units.

Managers focus their attention on ways to reduce scrap and to use it more profitably, especially when the cost of scrap is high (see Concepts in Action). For example, General Motors has redesigned its plastic injection molding processes to reduce the scrap plastic that must be broken away from its molded products. General Motors also regrinds and reuses the plastic scrap as direct material, saving substantial input costs.

Decision Point

How is scrap accounted for?

Problem for Self-Study

Burlington Textiles has some spoiled goods that had an assigned cost of $40,000 and zero net disposal value.

Required Prepare a journal entry for each of the following conditions under (a) process costing (department A) and (b) job costing:
1. Abnormal spoilage of $40,000
2. Normal spoilage of $40,000 regarded as common to all operations
3. Normal spoilage of $40,000 regarded as attributable to specifications of a particular job

Solution

	(a) Process Costing			(b) Job Costing		
1.	Loss from Abnormal Spoilage	40,000		Loss from Abnormal Spoilage	40,000	
	Work in Process—Dept. A		40,000	Work-in-Process Control (specific job)		40,000
2.	No entry until units are completed and transferred out. Then the normal spoilage costs are transferred as part of the cost of good units.			Manufacturing Overhead Control	40,000	
				Work-in-Process Control (specific job)		40,000
	Work in Process—Dept. B	40,000				
	Work in Process—Dept. A		40,000			
3.	Not applicable			No entry. Normal spoilage cost remains in Work-in-Process Control (specific job)		

Decision Points

The following question-and-answer format summarizes the chapter's learning objectives. Each decision presents a key question related to a learning objective. The guidelines are the answer to that question.

Decision	Guidelines
1. What are spoilage, rework, and scrap?	Spoilage is units of production that do not meet the specifications required by customers for good units and that are discarded or sold at reduced prices. Spoilage is generally divided into normal spoilage, which is inherent to a particular production process, and abnormal spoilage, which arises because of inefficiency in operations. Rework is unacceptable units that are subsequently repaired and sold as acceptable finished goods. Scrap is residual material that results from manufacturing a product; it has low total sales value compared with the total sales value of the product.
2. What is the distinction between normal and abnormal spoilage?	Normal spoilage is inherent in a particular production process and arises when the process is operated in an efficient manner. Abnormal spoilage on the other hand is not inherent in a particular production process and would not arise under efficient operating conditions. Abnormal spoilage is usually regarded as avoidable and controllable.
3. How do the weighted-average and FIFO methods of process costing calculate the costs of good units and spoilage?	The weighted-average method combines costs in beginning inventory with costs of the current period when determining the costs of good units, which include normal spoilage, and the costs of abnormal spoilage, which are written off as a loss of the accounting period.

The FIFO method keeps separate the costs in beginning inventory from the costs of the current period when determining the costs of good units (which include normal spoilage) and the costs of abnormal spoilage, which are written off as a loss of the accounting period.

4. How does inspection at various stages of completion affect the amount of normal and abnormal spoilage?	The cost of spoiled units is assumed to equal all costs incurred in producing spoiled units up to the point of inspection. Spoilage costs therefore vary based on different inspection points.
5. How do job-costing systems account for spoilage?	Normal spoilage specific to a job is assigned to that job, or when common to all jobs, is allocated as part of manufacturing overhead. Cost of abnormal spoilage is written off as a loss of the accounting period.
6. How do job-costing systems account for rework?	Completed reworked units should be indistinguishable from non-reworked good units. Normal rework specific to a job is assigned to that job, or when common to all jobs, is allocated as part of manufacturing overhead. Cost of abnormal rework is written off as a loss of the accounting period.
7. How is scrap accounted for?	Scrap is recognized in the accounting records either at the time of its sale or at the time of its production. Sale of scrap, if immaterial, is often recognized as other revenue. If not immaterial, sale of scrap or its net realizable value reduces the cost of a specific job or, when common to all jobs, reduces Manufacturing Overhead Control.

Appendix

Standard-Costing Method and Spoilage

The standard-costing method simplifies the computations for normal and abnormal spoilage. To illustrate, we return to the Anzio Company example in the chapter. Suppose Anzio develops the following standard costs per unit for work done in the forming department in July 2012:

Direct materials	$ 8.50
Conversion costs	10.50
Total manufacturing cost	$19.00

Assume the same standard costs per unit also apply to the beginning inventory: 1,500 (1,500 × 100%) equivalent units of direct materials and 900 (1,500 × 60%) equivalent units of conversion costs. Hence, the beginning inventory at standard costs is as follows:

Direct materials, 1,500 units × $8.50 per unit	$12,750
Conversion costs, 900 units × $10.50 per unit	9,450
Total manufacturing costs	$22,200

Exhibit 5, Panel A, presents Steps 1 and 2 for calculating physical and equivalent units. These steps are the same as for the FIFO method described in Exhibit 3. Exhibit 5, Panel B, presents Steps 3, 4, and 5.

The costs to account for in Step 3 are at standard costs and, hence, they differ from the costs to account for under the weighted-average and FIFO methods, which are at actual costs. In Step 4, cost per equivalent unit is simply the standard cost: $8.50 per unit for direct materials and $10.50 per unit for conversion costs. The standard-costing method makes calculating equivalent-unit costs unnecessary, so it simplifies process costing. Step 5 assigns standard costs to units completed (including normal spoilage), to abnormal spoilage, and to ending work-in-process inventory by multiplying the equivalent units calculated in Step 2 by the standard costs per equivalent unit presented in Step 4.

Exhibit 5 Standard-Costing Method of Process Costing with Spoilage for Forming Department of the Anzio Company for July 2012

PANEL A: Steps 1 and 2—Summarize Output in Physical Units and Compute Equivalent Units

	A	B	C	D	E
1			(Step 1)	(Step 2)	
2				Equivalent Units	
3		Flow of Production	Physical Units	Direct Materials	Conversion Costs
4		Work in process, beginning (given)	1,500		
5		Started during current period (given)	8,500		
6		To account for	10,000		
7		Good units completed and transferred out during current period:			
8		From beginning work in process[a]	1,500		
9		[1,500 × (100% − 100%); 1,500 × (100% − 60%)]		0	600
10		Started and completed	5,500[b]		
11		(5,500 × 100%; 5,500 × 100%)		5,500	5,500
12		Normal spoilage[c]	700		
13		(700 × 100%; 700 × 100%)		700	700
14		Abnormal spoilage[d]	300		
15		(300 × 100%; 300 × 100%)		300	300
16		Work in process, ending[e] (given)	2,000		
17		(2,000 × 100%; 2,000 × 50%)		2,000	1,000
18		Accounted for	10,000		
19		Equivalent units of work done in current period		8,500	8,100
20					
21	[a]Degree of completion in this department: direct materials, 100%; conversion costs, 60%.				
22	[b]7,000 physical units completed and transferred out minus 1,500 physical units completed and transferred out from beginning				
23	work-in-process inventory.				
24	[c]Normal spoilage is 10% of good units transferred out: 10% × 7,000 = 700 units. Degree of completion of normal spoilage in this				
25	department: direct materials, 100%; conversion costs, 100%.				
26	[d]Abnormal spoilage = Actual spoilage − Normal spoilage = 1,000 − 700 = 300 units. Degree of completion of abnormal spoilage in this				
27	department: direct materials, 100%; conversion costs, 100%.				
28	[e]Degree of completion in this department: direct materials, 100%; conversion costs, 50%.				

PANEL B: Steps 3, 4, and 5—Summarize Total Costs to Account for, Compute Cost per Equivalent Unit, and Assign Total Costs to Units Completed, to Spoiled Units, and to Units in Ending Work in Process

	A	B	C	D	E
30			Total Production Costs	Direct Materials	Conversion Costs
31	(Step 3)	Work in process, beginning (given)	$ 22,200	(1,500 × $8.50)	(900 × $10.50)
32		Costs added in current period at standard prices	157,300	(8,500 × $8.50)	(8,100 × $10.50)
33		Total costs to account for	$179,500	$85,000	$94,500
34	(Step 4)	Standard costs per equivalent unit (given)	$ 19.00	$ 8.50	$ 10.50
35	(Step 5)	Assignment of costs at standard costs:			
36		Good units completed and transferred out (7,000 units)			
37		Work in process, beginning (1,500 units)	$ 22,200	(1,500 × $8.50) +	(900 × $10.50)
38		Costs added to beginning work in process in current period	6,300	(0[f] × $8.50) +	(600[f] × $10.50)
39		Total from beginning inventory before normal spoilage	28,500		
40		Started and completed before normal spoilage (5,500 units)	104,500	(5,500[f] × $8.50) +	(5,500[f] × $10.50)
41		Normal spoilage (700 units)	13,300	(700[f] × $8.50) +	(700[f] × $10.50)
42	(A)	Total costs of good units completed and transferred out	146,300		
43	(B)	Abnormal spoilage (300 units)	5,700	(300[f] × $8.50) +	(300[f] × $10.50)
44	(C)	Work in process, ending (2,000 units)	27,500	(2,000[f] × $8.50) +	(1,000[f] × $10.50)
45	(A)+(B)+(C)	Total costs accounted for	$179,500	$85,000 +	$94,500
46					
47	[f]Equivalent units of direct materials and conversion costs calculated in Step 2 in Panel A.				

Finally, note that the journal entries corresponding to the amounts calculated in Step 5 are as follows:

Finished Goods	146,300	
Work in Process—Forming		146,300
To record transfer of good units completed in July.		
Loss from Abnormal Spoilage	5,700	
Work in Process—Forming		5,700
To record abnormal spoilage detected in July.		

Terms to Learn

This chapter contains definitions of the following important terms:

abnormal spoilage	normal spoilage	scrap
inspection point	rework	spoilage

Assignment Material

Questions

MyAccountingLab

18-1 Why is there an unmistakable trend in manufacturing to improve quality?

18-2 Distinguish among spoilage, rework, and scrap.

18-3 "Normal spoilage is planned spoilage." Discuss.

18-4 "Costs of abnormal spoilage are losses." Explain.

18-5 "What has been regarded as normal spoilage in the past is not necessarily acceptable as normal spoilage in the present or future." Explain.

18-6 "Units of abnormal spoilage are inferred rather than identified." Explain.

18-7 "In accounting for spoiled units, we are dealing with cost assignment rather than cost incurrence." Explain.

18-8 "Total input includes abnormal as well as normal spoilage and is, therefore, inappropriate as a basis for computing normal spoilage." Do you agree? Explain.

18-9 "The inspection point is the key to the allocation of spoilage costs." Do you agree? Explain.

18-10 "The unit cost of normal spoilage is the same as the unit cost of abnormal spoilage." Do you agree? Explain.

18-11 "In job costing, the costs of normal spoilage that occur while a specific job is being done are charged to the specific job." Do you agree? Explain.

18-12 "The costs of rework are always charged to the specific jobs in which the defects were originally discovered." Do you agree? Explain.

18-13 "Abnormal rework costs should be charged to a loss account, not to manufacturing overhead." Do you agree? Explain.

18-14 When is a company justified in inventorying scrap?

18-15 How do managers use information about scrap?

Exercises

MyAccountingLab

18-16 **Normal and abnormal spoilage in units.** The following data, in physical units, describe a grinding process for January:

Work in process, beginning	19,000
Started during current period	150,000
To account for	169,000
Spoiled units	12,000
Good units completed and transferred out	132,000
Work in process, ending	25,000
Accounted for	169,000

Inspection occurs at the 100% completion stage. Normal spoilage is 5% of the good units passing inspection.

Required

1. Compute the normal and abnormal spoilage in units.
2. Assume that the equivalent-unit cost of a spoiled unit is $10. Compute the amount of potential savings if all spoilage were eliminated, assuming that all other costs would be unaffected. Comment on your answer.

18-17 Weighted-average method, spoilage, equivalent units. (CMA, adapted) Consider the following data for November 2012 from Gray Manufacturing Company, which makes silk pennants and uses a process-costing system. All direct materials are added at the beginning of the process, and conversion costs are added evenly during the process. Spoilage is detected upon inspection at the completion of the process. Spoiled units are disposed of at zero net disposal value. Gray Manufacturing Company uses the weighted-average method of process costing.

	Physical Units (Pennants)	Direct Materials	Conversion Costs
Work in process, November 1[a]	1,000	$ 1,423	$ 1,110
Started in November 2012	?		
Good units completed and transferred out during November 2012	9,000		
Normal spoilage	100		
Abnormal spoilage	50		
Work in process, November 30[b]	2,000		
Total costs added during November 2012		$12,180	$27,750

[a]Degree of completion: direct materials, 100%; conversion costs, 50%.
[b]Degree of completion: direct materials, 100%; conversion costs, 30%.

Required Compute equivalent units for direct materials and conversion costs. Show physical units in the first column of your schedule.

18-18 Weighted-average method, assigning costs (continuation of 18-17).

Required For the data in Exercise 18-17, summarize total costs to account for; calculate the cost per equivalent unit for direct materials and conversion costs; and assign total costs to units completed and transferred out (including normal spoilage), to abnormal spoilage, and to units in ending work in process.

18-19 FIFO method, spoilage, equivalent units. Refer to the information in Exercise 18-17. Suppose Gray Manufacturing Company uses the FIFO method of process costing instead of the weighted-average method.

Required Compute equivalent units for direct materials and conversion costs. Show physical units in the first column of your schedule.

18-20 FIFO method, assigning costs (continuation of 18-19).

Required For the data in Exercise 18-17, use the FIFO method to summarize total costs to account for; calculate the cost per equivalent unit for direct materials and conversion costs; and assign total costs to units completed and transferred out (including normal spoilage), to abnormal spoilage, and to units in ending work in process.

18-21 Weighted-average method, spoilage. Appleton Company makes wooden toys in its forming department, and it uses the weighted-average method of process costing. All direct materials are added at the beginning of the process, and conversion costs are added evenly during the process. Spoiled units are detected upon inspection at the end of the process and are disposed of at zero net disposal value. Summary data for August 2012 are as follows:

				Home	Insert	Page Layout	Formulas	Data	Review	View			
	A										B	C	D
1											Physical Units	Direct Materials	Conversion Costs
2	Work in process, beginning inventory (August 1)										2,000	$17,700	$10,900
3	Degree of completion of beginning work in process											100%	50%
4	Started during August										10,000		
5	Good units completed and transferred out during August										9,000		
6	Work in process, ending inventory (August 31)										1,800		
7	Degree of completion of ending work in process											100%	75%
8	Total costs added during August											$81,300	$93,000
9	Normal spoilage as a percentage of good units										10%		
10	Degree of completion of normal spoilage											100%	100%
11	Degree of completion of abnormal spoilage											100%	100%

1. For each cost category, calculate equivalent units. Show physical units in the first column of your schedule. Required
2. Summarize total costs to account for; calculate cost per equivalent unit for each cost category; and assign total costs to units completed and transferred out (including normal spoilage), to abnormal spoilage, and to units in ending work in process.

18-22 Standard costing method, spoilage, journal entries. Jordan, Inc., is a manufacturer of vents for water heaters. The company uses a process-costing system to account for its work-in-process inventories. When Job 512 was being processed in the machining department, a piece of sheet metal was off center in the bending machine and two vents were spoiled. Because this problem occurs periodically, it is considered normal spoilage and is consequently recorded as an overhead cost. Because this step comes first in the procedure for making the vents, the only costs incurred were $475 for direct materials. Assume the sheet metal cannot be sold, and its cost has been recorded in work-in-process inventory.

Prepare the journal entries to record the spoilage incurred. Required

18-23 Recognition of loss from spoilage. Arokia Electronics manufactures cell phone models in its Walnut Creek plant. Suppose the company provides you with the following information regarding operations for September 2011:

Total cell phones manufactured	8,000
Phones rejected as spoiled units	300
Total manufacturing cost	$320,000

Assume the spoiled units have no disposal value.

1. What is the unit cost of making the 8,000 cell phones? Required
2. What is the total cost of the 300 spoiled units?
3. If the spoilage is considered normal, what is the increase in the unit cost of good phones manufactured as a result of the spoilage?
4. If the spoilage is considered abnormal, prepare the journal entries for the spoilage incurred.

18-24 Weighted-average method, spoilage. Chipcity is a fast-growing manufacturer of computer chips. Direct materials are added at the start of the production process. Conversion costs are added evenly during the process. Some units of this product are spoiled as a result of defects not detectable before inspection of finished goods. Spoiled units are disposed of at zero net disposal value. Chipcity uses the weighted-average method of process costing.

Summary data for September 2011 are as follows:

	A	B	C	D
1		Physical Units (Computer Chips)	Direct Materials	Conversion Costs
2	Work in process, beginning inventory (September 1)	600	$ 96,000	$ 15,300
3	Degree of completion of beginning work in process		100%	30%
4	Started during September	2,550		
5	Good units completed and transferred out during September	2,100		
6	Work in process, ending inventory (September 30)	450		
7	Degree of completion of ending work in process		100%	40%
8	Total costs added during September		$567,000	$230,400
9	Normal spoilage as a percentage of good units	15%		
10	Degree of completion of normal spoilage		100%	100%
11	Degree of completion of abnormal spoilage		100%	100%

1. For each cost category, compute equivalent units. Show physical units in the first column of your schedule. Required
2. Summarize total costs to account for; calculate cost per equivalent unit for each cost category; and assign total costs to units completed and transferred out (including normal spoilage), to abnormal spoilage, and to units in ending work in process.

18-25 FIFO method, spoilage. Refer to the information in Exercise 18-24.

Required Do Exercise 18-24 using the FIFO method of process costing.

18-26 Standard-costing method, spoilage. Refer to the information in Exercise 18-24. Suppose Chipcity determines standard costs of $200 per equivalent unit for direct materials and $75 per equivalent unit for conversion costs for both beginning work in process and work done in the current period.

Required Do Exercise 18-24 using the standard-costing method.

18-27 Spoilage and job costing. (L. Bamber) Barrett Kitchens produces a variety of items in accordance with special job orders from hospitals, plant cafeterias, and university dormitories. An order for 2,100 cases of mixed vegetables costs $9 per case: direct materials, $4; direct manufacturing labor, $3; and manufacturing overhead allocated, $2. The manufacturing overhead rate includes a provision for normal spoilage. Consider each requirement independently.

Required
1. Assume that a laborer dropped 420 cases. Suppose part of the 420 cases could be sold to a nearby prison for $420 cash. Prepare a journal entry to record this event. Calculate and explain briefly the unit cost of the remaining 1,680 cases.
2. Refer to the original data. Tasters at the company reject 420 of the 2,100 cases. The 420 cases are disposed of for $840. Assume that this rejection rate is considered normal. Prepare a journal entry to record this event, and do the following:
   a. Calculate the unit cost if the rejection is attributable to exacting specifications of this particular job.
   b. Calculate the unit cost if the rejection is characteristic of the production process and is not attributable to this specific job.
   c. Are unit costs the same in requirements 2a and 2b? Explain your reasoning briefly.
3. Refer to the original data. Tasters rejected 420 cases that had insufficient salt. The product can be placed in a vat, salt can be added, and the product can be reprocessed into jars. This operation, which is considered normal, will cost $420. Prepare a journal entry to record this event and do the following:
   a. Calculate the unit cost of all the cases if this additional cost was incurred because of the exacting specifications of this particular job.
   b. Calculate the unit cost of all the cases if this additional cost occurs regularly because of difficulty in seasoning.
   c. Are unit costs the same in requirements 3a and 3b? Explain your reasoning briefly.

18-28 Reworked units, costs of rework. White Goods assembles washing machines at its Auburn plant. In February 2012, 60 tumbler units that cost $44 each (from a new supplier who subsequently went bankrupt) were defective and had to be disposed of at zero net disposal value. White Goods was able to rework all 60 washing machines by substituting new tumbler units purchased from one of its existing suppliers. Each replacement tumbler cost $50.

Required
1. What alternative approaches are there to account for the material cost of reworked units?
2. Should White Goods use the $44 tumbler or the $50 tumbler to calculate the cost of materials reworked? Explain.
3. What other costs might White Goods include in its analysis of the total costs of rework due to the tumbler units purchased from the (now) bankrupt supplier?

18-29 Scrap, job costing. The Morgan Company has an extensive job-costing facility that uses a variety of metals. Consider each requirement independently.

Required
1. Job 372 uses a particular metal alloy that is not used for any other job. Assume that scrap is material in amount and sold for $520 quickly after it is produced. Prepare the journal entry.
2. The scrap from Job 372 consists of a metal used by many other jobs. No record is maintained of the scrap generated by individual jobs. Assume that scrap is accounted for at the time of its sale. Scrap totaling $4,400 is sold. Prepare two alternative journal entries that could be used to account for the sale of scrap.
3. Suppose the scrap generated in requirement 2 is returned to the storeroom for future use, and a journal entry is made to record the scrap. A month later, the scrap is reused as direct material on a subsequent job. Prepare the journal entries to record these transactions.

MyAccountingLab

Problems

18-30 Weighted-average method, spoilage. The Boston Company is a food-processing company based in San Francisco. It operates under the weighted-average method of process costing and has two departments: cleaning and packaging. For the cleaning department, conversion costs are added evenly during the process, and direct materials are added at the beginning of the process. Spoiled units are detected upon inspection at the end of the process and are disposed of at zero net disposal value. All completed work is transferred to the packaging department. Summary data for May follow:

	A	B	C	D
1	**The Boston Company: Cleaning Department**	**Physical Units**	**Direct Materials**	**Conversion Costs**
2	Work in process, beginning inventory (May 1)	3,000	$ 4,500	$ 2,700
3	Degree of completion of beginning work in process		100%	60%
4	Started during May	25,000		
5	Good units completed and transferred out during May	20,500		
6	Work in process, ending inventory (May 31)	4,200		
7	Degree of completion of ending work in process		100%	30%
8	Total costs added during May		$46,250	$37,216
9	Normal spoilage as a percentage of good units	10%		
10	Degree of completion of normal spoilage		100%	100%
11	Degree of completion of abnormal spoilage		100%	100%

Required

For the cleaning department, summarize total costs to account for and assign total costs to units completed and transferred out (including normal spoilage), to abnormal spoilage, and to units in ending work in process. Carry unit-cost calculations to four decimal places when necessary. Calculate final totals to the nearest dollar. (Problem 18-32 explores additional facets of this problem.)

18-31 FIFO method, spoilage. Refer to the information in Problem 18-30.

Required

Do Problem 18-30 using the FIFO method of process costing. (Problem 18-33 explores additional facets of this problem.)

18-32 Weighted-average method, packaging department (continuation of 18-30). In Boston Company's packaging department, conversion costs are added evenly during the process, and direct materials are added at the end of the process. Spoiled units are detected upon inspection at the end of the process and are disposed of at zero net disposal value. All completed work is transferred to the next department. The transferred-in costs for May equal the total cost of good units completed and transferred out in May from the cleaning department, which were calculated in Problem 18-30 using the weighted-average method of process costing. Summary data for May follow.

	A	B	C	D	E
1	**The Boston Company: Packaging Department**	**Physical Units**	**Transferred-In Costs**	**Direct Materials**	**Conversion Costs**
2	Work in process, beginning inventory (May 1)	10,500	$39,460	$ 0	$14,700
3	Degree of completion of beginning work in process		100%	0%	70%
4	Started during May	20,500			
5	Good units completed and transferred out during May	22,000			
6	Work in process, ending inventory (May 31)	7,000			
7	Degree of completion of ending work in process		100%	0%	40%
8	Total costs added during May		?	$4,800	$38,900
9	Normal spoilage as a percentage of good units	8%			
10	Degree of completion of normal spoilage			100%	100%
11	Degree of completion of abnormal spoilage			100%	100%

Required

For the packaging department, use the weighted-average method to summarize total costs to account for and assign total costs to units completed and transferred out (including normal spoilage), to abnormal spoilage, and to units in ending work in process.

18-33 FIFO method, packaging department (continuation of 18-31). Refer to the information in Problem 18-32 except for the transferred-in costs for May, which equal the total cost of good units completed and transferred out in May from the cleaning department, which were calculated in Problem 18-31 using the FIFO method of process costing.

Required For the packaging department, use the FIFO method to summarize total costs to account for and assign total costs to units completed and transferred out (including normal spoilage), to abnormal spoilage, and to units in ending work in process.

18-34 Job-costing spoilage and scrap. MetalWorks, Inc., manufactures various metal parts in batches as ordered by customers, and accounts for them using job costing. Job 2346-8, a large job for customer X, incurred $240,000 of direct materials costs and $620,000 of direct labor costs. MetalWorks applies overhead at a rate of 150% of direct labor cost. MetalWorks quoted customer X a fixed price for the job of $2,000,000. The job consisted of 90,000 good units and 10,000 spoiled units with no rework or disposal value. The job also created 200 pounds of scrap which can be sold for $3 per pound.

1. Calculate the gross margin MetalWorks will earn for this job, assuming the scrap sale is treated as material, and
   a. all spoilage is considered abnormal.
   b. normal spoilage is 8% of good units.
   c. normal spoilage is 12% of good units.
2. How would your answer to number 1 differ if the scrap sale is treated as immaterial?

18-35 Spoilage in job costing. Crystal Clear Machine Shop is a manufacturer of motorized carts for vacation resorts.

Peter Cruz, the plant manager of Crystal Clear, obtains the following information for Job #10 in August 2010. A total of 32 units were started, and 7 spoiled units were detected and rejected at final inspection, yielding 25 good units. The spoiled units were considered to be normal spoilage. Costs assigned prior to the inspection point are $1,450 per unit. The current disposal price of the spoiled units is $230 per unit. When the spoilage is detected, the spoiled goods are inventoried at $230 per unit.

Required
1. What is the normal spoilage rate?
2. Prepare the journal entries to record the normal spoilage, assuming the following:
   a. The spoilage is related to a specific job.
   b. The spoilage is common to all jobs.
   c. The spoilage is considered to be abnormal spoilage.

18-36 Rework in job costing, journal entry (continuation of 18-35). Assume that the 7 spoiled units of Whitefish Machine Shop's Job #10 can be reworked for a total cost of $1,700. A total cost of $10,150 associated with these units has already been assigned to Job #10 before the rework.

Required Prepare the journal entries for the rework, assuming the following:

a. The rework is related to a specific job.
b. The rework is common to all jobs.
c. The rework is considered to be abnormal.

18-37 Scrap at time of sale or at time of production, journal entries (continuation of 18-35). Assume that Job #10 of Crystal Clear Machine Shop generates normal scrap with a total sales value of $650 (it is assumed that the scrap returned to the storeroom is sold quickly).

Required Prepare the journal entries for the recognition of scrap, assuming the following:

a. The value of scrap is immaterial and scrap is recognized at the time of sale.
b. The value of scrap is material, is related to a specific job, and is recognized at the time of sale.
c. The value of scrap is material, is common to all jobs, and is recognized at the time of sale.
d. The value of scrap is material, and scrap is recognized as inventory at the time of production and is recorded at its net realizable value.

18-38 Physical units, inspection at various stages of completion. Fantastic Furniture manufactures plastic lawn furniture in a continuous process. The company pours molten plastic into molds and then cools the plastic. Materials are added at the beginning of the process, and conversion is considered uniform through the period. Occasionally, the plastic does not completely fill a mold because of air pockets, and the chair is then considered spoiled. Normal spoilage is 6% of the good units that pass inspection. The following information pertains to March, 2011:

Beginning inventory	1,400 units (100% complete for materials; 20% complete for conversion costs)
Units started	12,000
Units in ending work in process	1,100 (100% complete for materials; 70% complete for conversion costs)

Fantastic Furniture had 1,000 spoiled units in March, 2011.

Required Compute the normal and abnormal spoilage in units, assuming the inspection point is at (a) the 15% stage of completion, (b) the 40% stage of completion, and (c) the 100% stage of completion.

18-39 Weighted-average method, inspection at 80% completion. (A. Atkinson) The Kim Company is a furniture manufacturer with two departments: molding and finishing. The company uses the weighted-average method of process costing. In August, the following data were recorded for the finishing department:

Units of beginning work in process inventory	12,500
Percentage completion of beginning work in process units	25%
Cost of direct materials in beginning work in process	$0
Units started	87,500
Units completed	62,500
Units in ending inventory	25,000
Percentage completion of ending work in process units	95%
Spoiled units	12,500
Total costs added during current period:	
Direct materials	$819,000
Direct manufacturing labor	$794,500
Manufacturing overhead	$770,000
Work in process, beginning:	
Transferred-in costs	$103,625
Conversion costs	$52,500
Cost of units transferred in during current period	$809,375

Conversion costs are added evenly during the process. Direct material costs are added when production is 90% complete. The inspection point is at the 80% stage of production. Normal spoilage is 10% of all good units that pass inspection. Spoiled units are disposed of at zero net disposal value.

Required For August, summarize total costs to account for and assign these costs to units completed and transferred out (including normal spoilage), to abnormal spoilage, and to units in ending work in process.

18-40 Job costing, rework. Riposte Corporation manufactures a computer chip called XD1. Manufacturing costs of one XD1 chip, excluding rework costs, are direct materials, $60; direct manufacturing labor, $12; and manufacturing overhead, $38. At the inspection point, defective units are sent back for rework. Rework costs per XD1 chip are direct materials, $12; direct manufacturing labor, $9; and manufacturing overhead, $15.

In August 2011, Riposte manufactured 1,000 XD1 chips, 80 of which required rework. Of these 80 chips, 50 were considered normal rework common to all jobs and the other 30 were considered abnormal rework.

Required
1. Prepare journal entries to record the accounting for both the normal and abnormal rework.
2. What were the total rework costs of XD1 chips in August 2011?
3. Now assume instead that the normal rework is attributable entirely to job #3879, for 200 units of XD1. In this case, what would be the total and unit cost of the good units produced for that job in August 2011? Prepare journal entries for the manufacture of the 200 units, as well as the normal rework costs.

Collaborative Learning Problem

18-41 Physical units, inspection at various levels of completion, weighted-average process costing report. Lester Company makes metal products and has a forging department. In this department, materials are added at the beginning of the process and conversion takes place uniformly. At the start of November 2011, the forging department had 20,000 units in beginning work in process, which are 100% complete for materials and 40% complete for conversion costs. An additional 100,000 units are started in the department in November, and 30,000 units remain in work in process at the end of the month. These unfinished units are 100% complete for materials and 70% complete for conversion costs.

The forging department had 15,000 spoiled units in November. Normal spoilage is 12% of good units. The department's costs for the month of November are as follows:

	Beginning WIP	Costs Incurred During Period
Direct materials costs	$ 64,000	$ 200,000
Conversion costs	102,500	1,000,000

Required
1. Compute the normal and abnormal spoilage in units for November, assuming the inspection point is at (a) the 30% stage of completion, (b) the 60% stage of completion, and (c) the 100% stage of completion.
2. Refer to your answer in requirement 1. Why are there different amounts of normal and abnormal spoilage at different inspection points?
3. Now assume that the forging department inspects at the 60% stage of completion. Using the weighted-average method, calculate the cost of units transferred out, the cost of abnormal spoilage, and the cost of ending inventory for the forging department in November.

Balanced Scorecard: Quality, Time, and the Theory of Constraints

From Chapter 19 of *Cost Accounting: A Managerial Emphasis*, 14/e. Charles T. Horngren. Srikant M. Datar. Madhav Rajan.

Balanced Scorecard: Quality, Time, and the Theory of Constraints

▶ Learning Objectives

1. Explain the four cost categories in a costs-of-quality program

2. Develop nonfinancial measures and methods to improve quality

3. Combine financial and nonfinancial measures to make decisions and evaluate quality performance

4. Describe customer-response time and explain why delays happen and their costs

5. Explain how to manage bottlenecks

To satisfy ever-increasing customer expectations, managers need to find cost-effective ways to continuously improve the quality of their products and services and shorten response times.

This requires trading off the costs of achieving these improvements and the benefits from higher performance on these dimensions. When companies do not meet customer expectations, the losses can be substantial, as the following article about Toyota Motor Corporation shows.

Toyota Plans Changes After Millions of Defective Cars Are Recalled[1]

Toyota Motor Corporation, the Japanese automaker, built its reputation on manufacturing reliable cars. In 2002, Toyota executives set an ambitious goal to gain 15% of the global auto industry by 2010, meaning it would surpass General Motors as the world's largest carmaker. In the subsequent years, Toyota grew sales by 50% and managed to win bragging rights as the world's biggest car company. But the company's focus on rapid growth appears to have come at a cost to its reputation for quality.

Between November 2009 and January 2010, Toyota was forced to recall 9 million vehicles worldwide because gas pedals began to stick and were causing unwanted acceleration on eight Toyota models. After months of disagreements with government safety officials, the company ultimately recalled 12 models and suspended the production and sales of eight new Toyota and Lexus models, including its popular Camry and Corolla sedans. While most cars were quickly returned to the sales floor, some industry analysts estimated that the loss of revenue to Toyota could have been as much as $500 million each week.

Beyond lost revenue, Toyota's once-vaunted image took a serious hit. As the crisis unfolded, Toyota was slow to take responsibility for manufacturing problems. The company then faced the long and difficult task of restoring its credibility and assuring

---

[1] *Sources*: Kaufman, Wendy. 2010. Can Toyota recover its reputation for quality? Morning Edition, National Public Radio, February 9. http://www.npr.org/templates/story/story.php?storyId=123519027&ps=rs; Linebaugh, Kate and Norihiko Shirouzu. 2010. Toyota heir faces crisis at the wheel. *Wall Street Journal*, January 27. http://online.wsj.com/article/SB10001424052748704094304575029493222357402.html; Maynard, Micheline and Hiroko Tabuchi. 2010. Rapid growth has its perils, Toyota learns. *New York Times*, January 27. http://www.nytimes.com/2010/01/28/business/28toyota.html; Kageyama, Yuri. 2010. Toyota holds quality meeting to help repair reputation; promises quicker complaint response. *Associated Press*, March 29. http://abcnews.go.com/International/wireStory?id=10238266

owners and new-car shoppers that it had fixed the problems.

It established a quality committee led by Akio Toyoda, the company's chief executive; announced plans to add a brake override system to all new models; added four new quality training facilities; and promised faster decisions on future recall situations. "Listening to consumer voices is most important in regaining credibility from our customers," Mr. Toyoda said.

The Toyota example vividly illustrates the importance of quality. But improving quality is hard work. This chapter describes how a balanced scorecard approach helps managers and management accountants improve quality, customer-response time, and throughput.

Steven Senne\AP Wide World Photos

This chapter covers three topics. The first topic addresses quality as a competitive tool, looking at quality from the financial perspective, the customer perspective, the internal business process perspective, and the learning-and-growth perspective before discussing the evaluation of quality performance. The second topic addresses time as a competitive tool and focuses on customer response time, on-time performance, time drivers, and the cost of time. The third topic looks closely at the theory of constraints and throughput-margin analysis, covering the management of bottlenecks and nonfinancial measures of time. The presentation is modular so you can omit a topic or explore it in any order.

Quality as a Competitive Tool

The American Society for Quality defines **quality** as the total features and characteristics of a product or a service made or performed according to specifications to satisfy customers at the time of purchase and during use. Many companies throughout the world—like Cisco Systems and Motorola in the United States and Canada, British Telecom in the United Kingdom, Fujitsu and Honda in Japan, Crysel in Mexico, and Samsung in South Korea—emphasize quality as an important strategic initiative. These companies have found that focusing on the quality of a product or service generally builds expertise in producing it, lowers the costs of providing it, creates higher satisfaction for customers using it, and generates higher future revenues for the company selling it. Several high-profile awards, such as the Malcolm Baldrige National Quality Award in the United States, the Deming Prize in Japan, and the Premio Nacional de Calidad in Mexico, are given to companies that have produced high-quality products and services.

International quality standards have also emerged. ISO 9000, developed by the International Organization for Standardization, is a set of five international standards for quality management adopted by more than 85 countries. ISO 9000 enables companies to effectively document and certify the elements of their production processes that lead to quality. To ensure that their suppliers deliver high-quality products at competitive costs, companies such as DuPont and General Electric require their suppliers to obtain ISO 9000 certification. Documenting evidence of quality through ISO 9000 has become a necessary condition for competing in the global marketplace.

As corporations' responsibilities toward the environment grow, managers are applying the quality management and measurement practices discussed in this chapter to find cost-effective ways to reduce the environmental and economic costs of air pollution, wastewater, oil spills, and hazardous waste disposal. An environmental management standard, ISO 14000, encourages organizations to pursue environmental goals vigorously by developing (1) environmental management systems to reduce environmental costs and (2) environmental auditing and performance-evaluation systems to review and provide feedback on environmental goals. Nowhere has the issue of quality and the environment come together in a bigger way than at the British Petroleum (BP) Deepwater Horizon oil rig in the Gulf of Mexico. An explosion on the oil-drilling platform in April of 2010 resulted in millions of gallons of oil spilling out in the Gulf, causing environmental damage over thousands of square miles and resulting in billions of dollars of clean up costs for BP.

We focus on two basic aspects of quality: design quality and conformance quality. **Design quality** refers to how closely the characteristics of a product or service meet the needs and wants of customers. **Conformance quality** is the performance of a product or service relative to its design and product specifications. Apple Inc. has built a reputation for design quality by developing many innovative products such as the iPod, iPhone, and iPad that have uniquely met customers' music, telephone, entertainment, and business needs. Apple's products have also had excellent conformance quality; the products did what they were supposed to do. In the case of the iPhone 4, however, many customers complained about very weak signal receptions on their phones. The enthusiastic customer response to the iPhone 4 when it was launched in the summer of 2010 indicates good design quality, as customers liked what the iPhone 4 had to offer. The problem with its antenna that caused signals not to be received is a problem of conformance quality, because the phone did not do what it was designed to do. The following diagram illustrates that actual performance can fall short of customer satisfaction because of design-quality failure and because of conformance-quality failure.

We illustrate the issues in managing quality—computing the costs of quality, identifying quality problems, and taking actions to improve quality—using Photon Corporation. While Photon makes many products, we will focus only on Photon's photocopying machines, which earned an operating income of $24 million on revenues of $300 million (from sales of 20,000 copiers) in 2011.

Quality has both financial and nonfinancial components relating to customer satisfaction, improving internal quality processes, reducing defects, and the training and empowering of workers. To provide some structure, we discuss quality from the four perspectives of the balanced scorecard: financial, customer, internal business process, and learning and growth.

The Financial Perspective: Costs of Quality

The financial perspective of Photon's balanced scorecard includes measures such as revenue growth and operating income, financial measures that are impacted by quality. The most direct financial measure of quality, however, is *costs of quality*. **Costs of quality (COQ)**

Learning Objective 1

Explain the four cost categories in a costs-of-quality program

. . . prevention, appraisal, internal failure, and external failure costs are the costs incurred to prevent, or the costs arising as a result of, the production of a low-quality product. Costs of quality are classified into four categories; examples for each category are listed in Exhibit 1.

1. **Prevention costs**—costs incurred to preclude the production of products that do not conform to specifications
2. **Appraisal costs**—costs incurred to detect which of the individual units of products do not conform to specifications
3. **Internal failure costs**—costs incurred on defective products *before* they are shipped to customers
4. **External failure costs**—costs incurred on defective products *after* they have been shipped to customers

The items in Exhibit 1 come from all business functions of the value chain, and they are broader than the internal failure costs of spoilage, rework, and scrap.

An important role for management accountants is preparing COQ reports for managers. Photon determines the COQ of its photocopying machines by adapting the seven-step activity-based costing approach.

Step 1: Identify the Chosen Cost Object. The cost object is the quality of the photocopying machine that Photon made and sold in 2011. Photon's goal is to calculate the total costs of quality of these 20,000 machines.

Step 2: Identify the Direct Costs of Quality of the Product. The photocopying machines have no direct costs of quality because there are no resources such as inspection or repair workers dedicated to managing the quality of the photocopying machines.

Step 3: Select the Activities and Cost-Allocation Bases to Use for Allocating Indirect Costs of Quality to the Product. Column 1 of Exhibit 2, Panel A, classifies the activities that result in prevention, appraisal, and internal and external failure costs of quality at Photon Corporation and the business functions of the value chain in which these costs occur. For example, the quality-inspection activity results in appraisal costs and occurs in the manufacturing function. Photon identifies the total number of inspection-hours (across all products) as the cost-allocation base for the inspection activity. (To avoid details not needed to explain the concepts here, we do not show the total quantities of each cost-allocation base.)

Step 4: Identify the Indirect Costs of Quality Associated with Each Cost-Allocation Base. These are the total costs (variable and fixed) incurred for each of the costs-of-quality activities, such as inspections, across all of Photon's products. (To avoid details not needed to understand the points described here, we do not present these total costs.)

Step 5: Compute the Rate per Unit of Each Cost-Allocation Base. For each activity, total costs (identified in Step 4) are divided by total quantity of the cost-allocation base (calculated in Step 3) to compute the rate per unit of each cost-allocation base. Column 2 of Exhibit 2, Panel A, shows these rates (without supporting calculations).

Prevention Costs	Appraisal Costs	Internal Failure Costs	External Failure Costs
Design engineering	Inspection	Spoilage	Customer support
Process engineering	Online product	Rework	Manufacturing/
Supplier evaluations	manufacturing	Scrap	process
Preventive equipment	and process	Machine repairs	engineering
maintenance	inspection	Manufacturing/	for external
Quality training	Product testing	process	failures
Testing of new		engineering on	Warranty repair
materials		internal failures	costs
			Liability claims

Exhibit 1

Items Pertaining to Costs-of-Quality Reports

Exhibit 2   Analysis of Activity-Based Costs of Quality (COQ) for Photocopying Machines at Photon Corporation

	Home	Insert	Page Layout	Formulas	Data	Review	View	
	A	B	C	D	E	F	G
1	PANEL A: ACCOUNTING COQ REPORT						Percentage of
2		Cost Allocation		Quantity of Cost		Total	Revenues
3	Cost of Quality and Value-Chain Category	Rate[a]		Allocation Base		Costs	(5) = (4) ÷
4	(1)	(2)		(3)		(4) = (2) x (3)	$300,000,000
5	*Prevention costs*						
6	Design engineering (R&D/Design)	$ 80	per hour	40,000	hours	$ 3,200,000	1.1%
7	Process engineering (R&D/Design)	$ 60	per hour	45,000	hours	2,700,000	0.9%
8	Total prevention costs					5,900,000	2.0%
9	*Appraisal costs*						
10	Inspection (Manufacturing)	$ 40	per hour	240,000	hours	9,600,000	3.2%
11	Total appraisal costs					9,600,000	3.2%
12	*Internal failure costs*						
13	Rework (Manufacturing)	$100	per hour	100,000	hours	10,000,000	3.3%
14	Total internal failure costs					10,000,000	3.3%
15	*External failure costs*						
16	Customer support (Marketing)	$ 50	per hour	12,000	hours	600,000	0.2%
17	Transportation (Distribution)	$240	per load	3,000	loads	720,000	0.2%
18	Warranty repair (Customer service)	$110	per hour	120,000	hours	13,200,000	4.4%
19	Total external failure costs					14,520,000	4.8%
20	Total costs of quality					$40,020,000	13.3%
21							
22	[a]Calculations not shown.						
23							
24	PANEL B: OPPORTUNITY COST ANALYSIS						
25						Total Estimated	Percentage
26						Contribution	of Revenues
27	Cost of Quality Category					Margin Lost	(3) = (2) ÷
28	(1)					(2)	$300,000,000
29	*External failure costs*						
30	Estimated forgone contribution margin						
31	and income on lost sales					$12,000,000[b]	4.0%
32	Total external failure costs					$12,000,000	4.0%
33							
34	[b]Calculated as total revenues minus all variable costs (whether output-unit, batch, product-sustaining, or facility-sustaining) on						
35	lost sales in 2011. If poor quality causes Photon to lose sales in subsequent years as well, the opportunity costs will be						
36	even greater.						

Step 6:   Compute the Indirect Costs of Quality Allocated to the Product. The indirect costs of quality of the photocopying machines, shown in Exhibit 2, Panel A, column 4, equal the cost-allocation rate from Step 5 (column 2) multiplied by the total quantity of the cost-allocation base used by the photocopying machines for each activity (column 3). For example, inspection costs for assuring the quality of the photocopying machines are $9,600,000 ($40 per hour × 240,000 inspection-hours).

Step 7:   Compute the Total Costs of Quality by Adding All Direct and Indirect Costs of Quality Assigned to the Product. Photon's total costs of quality in the COQ report for photocopying machines is $40.02 million (Exhibit 2, Panel A, column 4) or 13.3% of current revenues (column 5).

Opportunity costs are not recorded in financial accounting systems. Yet, a very significant component of costs of quality is the opportunity cost of the contribution margin and income forgone from lost sales, lost production, and lower prices resulting from poor design and conformance quality. Photon's market research department estimates that design and conformance quality problems experienced by some customers resulted in lost sales of 2,000 photocopying machines in 2011 and forgone contribution margin and operating income of $12 million (Exhibit 2, Panel B). Total costs of quality, including opportunity costs, equal $52.02 million ($40.02 million recorded in the accounting system and shown in Panel A + $12 million of opportunity costs shown in Panel B), or 17.3% of current revenues. Opportunity costs account for 23.1% ($12 million ÷ $52.02 million) of Photon's total costs of quality.

We turn next to the leading indicators of the costs of quality, the nonfinancial measures of customer satisfaction about the quality of Photon's photocopiers.

Decision Point

What are the four cost categories of a costs-of-quality program?

The Customer Perspective: Nonfinancial Measures of Customer Satisfaction

Similar to Unilever, Federal Express, and TiVo, Photon tracks the following measures of customer satisfaction:

- Market research information on customer preferences for and customer satisfaction with specific product features (to measure design quality)
- Market share
- Percentage of highly satisfied customers
- Number of defective units shipped to customers as a percentage of total units shipped
- Number of customer complaints (Companies estimate that for every customer who actually complains, there are 10–20 others who have had bad experiences with the product or service but did not complain.)
- Percentage of products that fail soon after delivery
- Average delivery delays (difference between the scheduled delivery date and the date requested by the customer)
- On-time delivery rate (percentage of shipments made on or before the scheduled delivery date)

Photon's management monitors whether these numbers improve or deteriorate over time. Higher customer satisfaction should lead to lower costs of quality and higher future revenues from greater customer retention, loyalty, and positive word-of-mouth advertising. Lower customer-satisfaction indicates that costs of quality will likely increase in the future. We next turn to the driver of customer satisfaction, the internal business processes to identify and analyze quality problems and to improve quality.

Learning Objective 2

Develop nonfinancial measures

. . . customer satisfaction measures such as number of customer complaints, internal-business process measures such as percentage of defective and reworked products, and learning and growth measures such as employee empowerment and training

and methods to improve quality

. . . control charts, Pareto diagrams, and cause-and-effect diagrams

The Internal-Business-Process Perspective: Analyzing Quality Problems and Improving Quality

We present three techniques for identifying and analyzing quality problems: control charts, Pareto diagrams, and cause-and-effect diagrams.

Control Charts

Statistical quality control (SQC), also called statistical process control (SPC), is a formal means of distinguishing between random and nonrandom variations in an operating process. Random variations occur, for example, when chance fluctuations in the speed of equipment cause defective products to be produced such as copiers that produce fuzzy and unclear copies or copies that are too light or too dark. Nonrandom variations occur when defective products are produced as a result of a systematic problem such as an incorrect speed setting, a flawed part design, or mishandling of a component part. A **control chart**, an important tool in SQC, is a graph of a series of successive observations of a particular step, procedure, or operation taken at regular intervals of time. Each observation is plotted relative to specified ranges that represent the limits within which observations are expected to fall. Only those observations outside the control limits are ordinarily regarded as nonrandom and worth investigating.

Exhibit 3 presents control charts for the daily defect rates (defective copiers divided by the total number of copiers produced) observed at Photon's three photocopying-machine production lines. Defect rates in the prior 60 days for each production line were assumed to provide a good basis from which to calculate the distribution of daily defect rates. The arithmetic mean (μ, read as mu) and standard deviation (σ, read as sigma, how much an observation deviates from the mean) are the two parameters of the distribution that are used in the control charts in Exhibit 3. On the basis of experience, the company decides that any observation outside the μ ± 2σ range should be investigated.

For production line A, all observations are within the range of μ ± 2σ, so management believes no investigation is necessary. For production line B, the last two observations signal that a much higher percentage of copiers are not performing as they should, indicating that the problem is probably because of a nonrandom, out-of-control occurrence such as an incorrect speed setting or mishandling of a component part. Given the ±2σ rule, both observations would be investigated. Production line C illustrates a process that would not prompt an investigation under the ±2σ rule but that may well be out of control, because the last eight observations show a clear direction, and over the last six days, the percentage of defective copiers are increasing and getting further and further away from the mean. The pattern of observations moving away from the mean could be due, for example, to the tooling on a machine beginning to wear out, resulting in poorly machined parts. As the tooling deteriorates further, the trend in producing defective copiers is likely to persist until the production line is no longer in statistical control. Statistical procedures have been developed using the trend as well as the variation to evaluate whether a process is out of control.

Pareto Diagrams

Observations outside control limits serve as inputs for Pareto diagrams. A **Pareto diagram** is a chart that indicates how frequently each type of defect occurs, ordered from the most frequent to the least frequent. Exhibit 4 presents a Pareto diagram of quality problems for all observations outside the control limits at the final inspection point in 2011. Fuzzy and unclear copies are the most frequently recurring problem. Fuzzy and unclear copies result in high rework costs. Sometimes fuzzy and unclear copies occur at customer sites and result in high warranty and repair costs and low customer satisfaction.

Cause-and-Effect Diagrams

The most frequently recurring and costly problems identified by the Pareto diagram are analyzed using cause-and-effect diagrams. A **cause-and-effect diagram** identifies potential causes of defects using a diagram that resembles the bone structure of a fish (hence, cause-and-effect diagrams are also called *fishbone diagrams*).[2] Exhibit 5 presents the

Exhibit 3   Statistical Quality Control Charts: Daily Defect Rate for Photocopying Machines at Photon Corporation

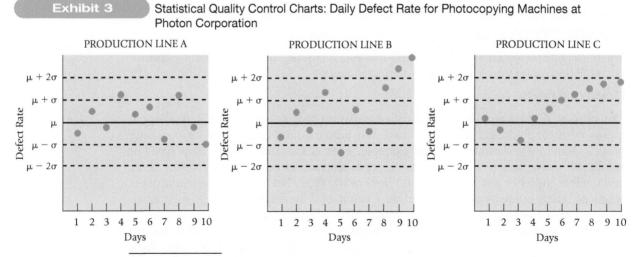

---

[2] See P. Clark, "Getting the Most from Cause-and-Effect Diagrams," *Quality Progress* (June 2000).

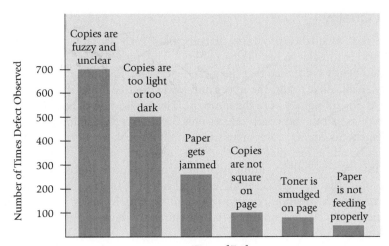

Exhibit 4

Pareto Diagram for Photocopying Machines at Photon Corporation

cause-and-effect diagram describing potential reasons for fuzzy and unclear copies. The "backbone" of the diagram represents the problem being examined. The large "bones" coming off the backbone represent the main categories of potential causes of failure. The exhibit identifies four of these: human factors, methods and design factors, machine-related factors, and materials and components factors. Photon's engineers identify the materials and components factor as an important reason for the fuzzy and unclear copies. Additional arrows or bones are added to provide more-detailed reasons for each higher-level cause. For example, the engineers determine that two potential causes of material and component problems are variation in purchased components and incorrect component specification. They quickly settle on variation in purchased components as the likely cause and focus on the use of multiple suppliers and mishandling of purchased parts as the root causes of variation in purchased components. Further analysis leads them to conclude that mishandling of the steel frame that holds in place various components of the copier such as drums, mirrors, and lenses results in the misalignment of these components, causing fuzzy and unclear copies.

The analysis of quality problems is aided by automated equipment and computers that record the number and types of defects and the operating conditions that existed at the time the defects occurred. Using these inputs, computer programs simultaneously and iteratively prepare control charts, Pareto diagrams, and cause-and-effect diagrams with the goal of continuously reducing the mean defect rate, μ, and the standard deviation, σ.

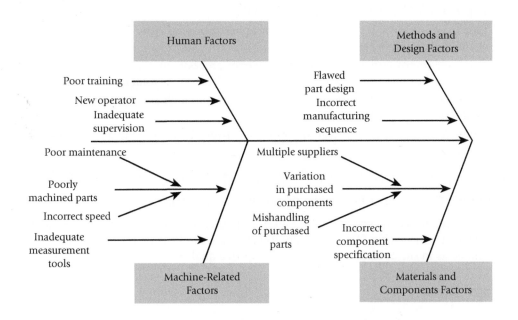

Exhibit 5

Cause-and-Effect Diagram for Fuzzy and Unclear Photocopies at Photon Corporation

Six Sigma Quality

The ultimate goal of quality programs at companies such as Motorola, Honeywell, and General Electric is to achieve Six Sigma quality.[3] This means that the process is so well-understood and tightly controlled that the mean defect rate, μ, and the standard deviation, σ, are both very small. As a result, the upper and lower control limits in Exhibit 3 can be set at a distance of 6σ (six sigma) from the mean (μ). The implication of controlling a process at a Six Sigma level is that the process produces only 3.4 defects per million products produced.

To implement Six Sigma, companies use techniques such as control charts, Pareto diagrams, and cause-and-effect diagrams to define, measure, analyze, improve, and control processes to minimize variability in manufacturing and achieve almost zero defects. Critics of Six Sigma argue that it emphasizes incremental rather than dramatic or disruptive innovation. Nevertheless, companies report substantial benefits from Six Sigma initiatives.

Companies routinely use nonfinancial measures to track the quality improvements they are making.

Nonfinancial Measures of Internal-Business-Process Quality

Photon uses the following measures of internal-business-process quality:

- Percentage of defective products
- Percentage of reworked products
- Number of different types of defects analyzed using control charts, Pareto diagrams, and cause-and-effect diagrams
- Number of design and process changes made to improve design quality or reduce costs of quality

Photon's managers believe that improving these measures will lead to greater customer satisfaction, lower costs of quality, and better financial performance.

The Learning-and-Growth Perspective: Quality Improvements

What are the drivers of internal-business-process quality? Photon believes that recruiting outstanding design engineers, providing more employee training, and lowering employee turnover as a result of greater employee empowerment and satisfaction will reduce the number of defective products and increase customer satisfaction, leading to better financial performance. Photon measures the following factors in the learning-and-growth perspective in the balanced scorecard:

- Experience and qualifications of design engineers
- Employee turnover (ratio of number of employees who leave the company to the average total number of employees)
- Employee empowerment (ratio of the number of processes in which employees have the right to make decisions without consulting supervisors to the total number of processes)
- Employee satisfaction (ratio of employees indicating high satisfaction ratings to the total number of employees surveyed)
- Employee training (percentage of employees trained in different quality-enhancing methods)

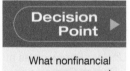

Decision Point ▶

What nonfinancial measures and methods can managers use to improve quality?

Making Decisions and Evaluating Quality Performance

Relevant Costs and Benefits of Quality Improvement

When making decisions and evaluating performance, companies combine financial and nonfinancial information. We use the Photon example to illustrate relevant revenues and relevant costs in the context of decisions to improve quality.

---

[3] Six Sigma is a registered trademark of Motorola Inc.

Recall that Photon's cause-and-effect diagram reveals that the steel frame (or chassis) of the copier is often mishandled as it travels from a supplier's warehouse to Photon's plant. The frame must meet very precise specifications or else copier components (such as drums, mirrors, and lenses) will not fit exactly on the frame. Mishandling frames during transport causes misalignment and results in fuzzy and unclear copies.

A team of engineers offers two solutions: (1) inspect the frames immediately on delivery or (2) redesign and strengthen the frames and their shipping containers to withstand mishandling during transportation. The cost structure for 2012 is expected to be the same as the cost structure for 2011 presented in Exhibit 2.

To evaluate each alternative versus the status quo, management identifies the relevant costs and benefits for each solution by focusing on *how total costs and total revenues will change under each alternative*. Relevant-cost and relevant-revenue analysis ignores allocated amounts.

Photon uses only a one-year time horizon (2012) for the analysis because it plans to introduce a completely new line of copiers at the end of 2012. The new line is so different that the choice of either the inspection or the redesign alternative will have no effect on the sales of copiers in future years.

Exhibit 6 shows the relevant costs and benefits for each alternative.

Learning Objective 3

Combine financial and nonfinancial measures to make decisions and evaluate quality performance

. . . Identify relevant incremental and opportunity costs to evaluate tradeoffs across costs of quality and nonfinancial measures to identify problem areas and to highlight leading indicators of future performance

1. **Estimated incremental costs:** $400,000 for the inspection alternative; $460,000 for the redesign alternative.

2. **Cost savings from less rework, customer support, and repairs:** Exhibit 6, line 10, shows that reducing rework results in savings of $40 per hour. Exhibit 2, Panel A, column 2, line 13, shows total rework cost per hour of $100. Why the difference? Because as it improves quality, Photon will only save the $40 variable cost per rework-hour, not the $60 fixed cost per rework-hour. Exhibit 6, line 10, shows total savings of $960,000 ($40 per hour × 24,000 rework-hours saved) if it inspects the frames and $1,280,000 ($40 per rework-hour × 32,000 rework-hours saved) if it redesigns the frames. Exhibit 6 also shows expected variable-cost savings in customer support, transportation, and warranty repair for the two alternatives.

3. **Increased contribution margin from higher sales as a result of building a reputation for quality and performance (Exhibit 6, line 14):** $1,500,000 for 250 copiers under the inspection alternative and $1,800,000 for 300 copiers under the redesign alternative. Management should always look for opportunities to generate higher revenues, not just cost reductions, from quality improvements.

Exhibit 6 Estimated Effects of Quality-Improvement Actions on Costs of Quality for Photocopying Machines at Photon Corporation

Home	Insert	Page Layout	Formulas	Data	Review	View

	A	B	C	D	E	F	G	H	I	J
1						Relevant Costs and Benefits of				
2				Further Inspecting Incoming Frames				Redesigning Frames		
3	Relevant Items	Relevant Benefit per Unit		Quantity		Total Benefits		Quantity		Total Benefits
4	(1)	(2)		(3)		(4)		(5)		(6)
5	Additional inspection and testing costs					$ (400,000)				
6	Additional process engineering costs									$ (300,000)
7	Additional design engineering costs									(160,000)
8										
9						(2) × (3)				(2) × (5)
10	Savings in rework costs	$ 40	per hour	24,000	hours	$ 960,000		32,000	hours	$1,280,000
11	Savings in customer-support costs	$ 20	per hour	2,000	hours	40,000		2,800	hours	56,000
12	Savings in transportation costs for repair parts	$ 180	per load	500	loads	90,000		700	loads	126,000
13	Savings in warranty repair costs	$ 45	per hour	20,000	hours	900,000		28,000	hours	1,260,000
14	Total contribution margin from additional sales	$6,000	per copier	250	copiers	1,500,000		300	copiers	1,800,000
15										
16	Net cost savings and additional contribution margin					$3,090,000				$4,062,000
17										
18	Difference in favor of redesigning frames (J16) – (F16)						$972,000			

Exhibit 6 shows that both the inspection and the redesign alternatives yield net benefits relative to the status quo. However, the net benefits from the redesign alternative are expected to be $972,000 greater.

Note how making improvements in internal business processes affects the COQ numbers reported in the financial perspective. In our example, redesigning the frame increases prevention costs (design and process engineering), decreases internal failure costs (rework), and decreases external failure costs (customer support and warranty repairs). COQ reports provide more insight about quality improvements when managers compare trends over time. In successful quality programs, companies decrease costs of quality and, in particular, internal and external failure costs, as a percentage of revenues. Many companies, such as Hewlett-Packard, go further and believe they should eliminate all failure costs and have zero defects.

How should Photon use financial and nonfinancial measures to evaluate quality performance? They should utilize both types of measures because financial (COQ) and nonfinancial measures of quality have different advantages.

Advantages of COQ Measures

- Consistent with the attention-directing role of management accounting, COQ measures focus managers' attention on the costs of poor quality.
- Total COQ provides a measure of quality performance for evaluating trade-offs among prevention costs, appraisal costs, internal failure costs, and external failure costs.
- COQ measures assist in problem solving by comparing costs and benefits of different quality-improvement programs and setting priorities for cost reduction.

Advantages of Nonfinancial Measures of Quality

- Nonfinancial measures of quality are often easy to quantify and understand.
- Nonfinancial measures direct attention to physical processes and hence help managers identify the precise problem areas that need improvement.
- Nonfinancial measures, such as number of defects, provide immediate short-run feedback on whether quality-improvement efforts are succeeding.
- Nonfinancial measures such as measures of customer satisfaction and employee satisfaction are useful indicators of long-run performance.

Decision Point

How do managers identify the relevant costs and benefits of quality improvement programs and use financial and nonfinancial measures to evaluate quality?

COQ measures and nonfinancial measures complement each other. Without financial quality measures, companies could be spending more money on improving nonfinancial quality measures than it is worth. Without nonfinancial quality measures, quality problems might not be identified until it is too late. Most organizations use both types of measures to gauge quality performance. McDonald's, for example, evaluates employees and individual franchisees on multiple measures of quality and customer satisfaction. A mystery shopper, an outside party contracted by McDonald's to evaluate restaurant performance, scores individual restaurants on quality, cleanliness, service, and value. A restaurant's performance on these dimensions is evaluated over time and against other restaurants. In its balanced scorecard, Photon evaluates whether improvements in various nonfinancial quality measures eventually lead to improvements in financial measures.

Time as a Competitive Tool

Companies increasingly view time as a driver of strategy.[4] For example, CapitalOne has increased business on its Web site by promising home-loan approval decisions in 30 minutes or less. Companies such as AT&T, General Electric, and Wal-Mart attribute not only higher revenues but also lower costs to doing things faster and on time. They cite, for example, the need to carry less inventory due to their ability to respond rapidly to customer demands.

---

[4] See K. Eisenhardt and S. Brown, "Time Pacing: Competing in Strategic Markets That Won't Stand Still," *Harvard Business Review* (March–April 1998); and T. Willis and A. Jurkus, "Product Development: An Essential Ingredient of Time-Based Competition," *Review of Business* (2001).

Companies need to measure time to manage it properly. In this section, we focus on two *operational measures of time*: *customer-response time*, which reveals how quickly companies respond to customers' demands for their products and services, and *on-time performance*, which indicates how reliably they meet scheduled delivery dates. We also show how companies measure the causes and costs of delays.

Customer-Response Time and On-Time Performance

Customer-response time is how long it takes from the time a customer places an order for a product or service to the time the product or service is delivered to the customer. Fast responses to customers are of strategic importance in industries such as construction, banking, car rental, and fast food. Some companies, such as Airbus, have to pay penalties to compensate their customers (airline companies) for lost revenues and profits (from being unable to operate flights) as a result of delays in delivering aircraft to them.

Exhibit 7 describes the components of customer-response time. *Receipt time* is how long it takes the marketing department to specify to the manufacturing department the exact requirements in the customer's order. **Manufacturing cycle time** (also called **manufacturing lead time**) is how long it takes from the time an order is received by manufacturing to the time a finished good is produced. Manufacturing cycle time is the sum of waiting time and manufacturing time for an order. For example, an aircraft order received by Airbus may need to wait before the equipment required to process it becomes available. *Delivery time* is how long it takes to deliver a completed order to a customer.

Some companies evaluate their response time improvement efforts using a measure called **manufacturing cycle efficiency (MCE)**:

$$\text{MCE} = (\text{Value-added manufacturing time} \div \text{Manufacturing cycle time})$$

Value-added manufacturing activities are activities that customers perceive as adding value or utility to a product. The time actually spent assembling the product is value-added manufacturing time. The rest of manufacturing cycle time, such as the time the product spends waiting for parts or for the next stage in the production process, and being repaired, represents nonvalue-added manufacturing time. Identifying and minimizing the sources of nonvalue-added manufacturing time increases customer responsiveness and reduces costs.

Similar measures apply to service-sector companies. Consider a 40-minute doctor's office visit, of which 9 minutes is spent on administrative tasks such as filling out forms, 20 minutes is spent waiting in the reception area and examination room, and 11 minutes is spent with a nurse or doctor. The service cycle efficiency for this visit equals $11 \div 40$, or 0.275. In other words, only 27.5% of the time in the office added value to the customer. Minimizing nonvalue-added service time in their medical delivery processes has allowed hospitals such as Alle-Kiski Medical Center in Pennsylvania to treat more patients in less time.

Learning Objective 4

Describe customer-response time

. . . time between receipt of customer order and product delivery

and explain why delays happen and their costs

. . . uncertainty about the timing of customer orders and limited capacity lead to lower revenues and higher inventory carrying costs

Exhibit 7

Components of Customer-Response Time

| Customer places order for product | Order received by manufacturing | Machine setup begins for order | Order manufactured: product becomes finished good | Order delivered to customer |

Waiting Time — Manufacturing Time

Receipt Time — Manufacturing Cycle Time — Delivery Time

Customer-Response Time

On-time performance is delivery of a product or service by the time it is scheduled to be delivered. Consider Federal Express, which specifies a price per package and a next-day delivery time of 10:30 A.M. for its overnight courier service. Federal Express measures on-time performance by how often it meets its stated delivery time of 10:30 A.M. On-time performance increases customer satisfaction. For example, commercial airlines gain loyal passengers as a result of consistent on-time service. But there is a trade-off between a customer's desire for shorter customer-response time and better on-time performance. Scheduling longer customer-response times, such as airlines lengthening scheduled arrival times, displeases customers on the one hand but increases customer satisfaction on the other hand by improving on-time performance.

Bottlenecks and Time Drivers

Managing customer-response time and on-time performance requires understanding the causes and costs of delays that occur, for example, at a machine in a manufacturing plant or at a checkout counter in a store.

A **time driver** is any factor that causes a change in the speed of an activity when the factor changes. Two time drivers are as follows:

1. **Uncertainty about when customers will order products or services.** For example, the more randomly Airbus receives orders for its airplanes, the more likely queues will form and delays will occur.

2. **Bottlenecks due to limited capacity.** A **bottleneck** occurs in an operation when the work to be performed approaches or exceeds the capacity available to do it. For example, a bottleneck results and causes delays when products that must be processed at a particular machine arrive while the machine is being used to process other products. Bottlenecks also occur on the Internet, for example, when many users try to operate wireless mobile devices at the same time (see Concepts in Action, p. 684). Many banks, such as Bank of China; grocery stores, such as Krogers; and entertainment parks, such as Disneyland, actively work to reduce queues and delays to better serve their customers.

Consider Falcon Works (FW), which uses one turning machine to convert steel bars into a special gear for planes. FW makes this gear, which is its sole product, only after customers have ordered it. To focus on manufacturing cycle time, we assume FW's receipt time and delivery time are minimal. FW's strategy is to differentiate itself from competitors by offering faster delivery. The company's manager is examining opportunities to sell other products to increase profits without sacrificing the competitive advantage provided by short customer-response times. The manager examines these opportunities using the five-step decision-making process.

Step 1: Identify the problem and uncertainties. FW's manager is considering introducing a second product, a piston for pumps. The primary uncertainty is how the introduction of a second product will affect manufacturing cycle times for gears.

Step 2: Obtain information. The manager gathers data on the number of orders for gears FW has received in the past, the time it takes to manufacture gears, the available capacity, and the average manufacturing cycle time for gears. FW typically receives 30 orders for gears, but it could receive 10, 30, or 50 orders. Each order is for 1,000 units and takes 100 hours of manufacturing time (8 hours of setup time to clean and prepare the machine, and 92 hours of processing time). Annual capacity of the machine is 4,000 hours. If FW receives the 30 orders it expects, the total amount of manufacturing time required on the machine is 3,000 hours (100 hours per order × 30 orders), which is within the available machine capacity of 4,000 hours. Even though capacity utilization is not strained, queues and delays still occur, because uncertainty about when FW's customers place their orders causes an order to be received while the machine is processing an earlier order.

Average waiting time, the average amount of time that an order waits in line before the machine is set up and the order is processed, equals,[5]

$$\frac{\text{Annual average number of orders for gears} \times \left(\begin{array}{c}\text{Manufacturing} \\ \text{time per order} \\ \text{for gears}\end{array}\right)^2}{2 \times \left[\begin{array}{c}\text{Annual machine} \\ \text{capacity}\end{array} - \left(\begin{array}{c}\text{Annual average number} \\ \text{of orders for gears}\end{array} \times \begin{array}{c}\text{Manufacturing} \\ \text{time per order for gears}\end{array}\right)\right]}$$

$$= \frac{30 \times (100)^2}{2 \times [4{,}000 - (30 \times 100)]} = \frac{30 \times 10{,}000}{2 \times (4{,}000 - 3{,}000)} = \frac{300{,}000}{2 \times 1{,}000} = \frac{300{,}000}{2{,}000} = 150 \text{ hours per order (for gears)}$$

Therefore, the average manufacturing cycle time for an order is 250 hours (150 hours of average waiting time + 100 hours of manufacturing time). Note that manufacturing time per order is a squared term in the numerator. It indicates the disproportionately large impact manufacturing time has on waiting time. As the manufacturing time lengthens, there is a much greater chance that the machine will be in use when an order arrives, leading to longer delays. The denominator in this formula is a measure of the unused capacity, or cushion. As the unused capacity becomes smaller, the chance that the machine is processing an earlier order becomes more likely, leading to greater delays.

The formula describes only the *average* waiting time. A particular order might arrive when the machine is free, in which case manufacturing will start immediately. In another situation, FW may receive an order while two other orders are waiting to be processed, which means the delay will be longer than 150 hours.

Step 3: Make predictions about the future. The manager makes the following predictions about pistons: FW expects to receive 10 orders for pistons, each order for 800 units, in the coming year. Each order will take 50 hours of manufacturing time, comprising 3 hours for setup and 47 hours of processing. Expected demand for FW's gears will be unaffected by whether FW introduces pistons.

Average waiting time *before* machine setup begins is expected to be (the formula is an extension of the preceding formula for the single-product case) as follows:

$$\frac{\left[\begin{array}{c}\text{Annual average number} \\ \text{of orders for gears}\end{array} \times \left(\begin{array}{c}\text{Manufacturing} \\ \text{time per order} \\ \text{for gears}\end{array}\right)^2\right] + \left[\begin{array}{c}\text{Annual average number} \\ \text{of orders for pistons}\end{array} \times \left(\begin{array}{c}\text{Manufacturing} \\ \text{time per order} \\ \text{for pistons}\end{array}\right)^2\right]}{2 \times \left[\begin{array}{c}\text{Annual machine} \\ \text{capacity}\end{array} - \left(\begin{array}{c}\text{Annual average number} \\ \text{of orders for gears}\end{array} \times \begin{array}{c}\text{Manufacturing} \\ \text{time per order} \\ \text{for gears}\end{array}\right) - \left(\begin{array}{c}\text{Annual average number} \\ \text{of orders for pistons}\end{array} \times \begin{array}{c}\text{Manufacturing} \\ \text{time per order} \\ \text{for pistons}\end{array}\right)\right]}$$

$$= \frac{[30 \times (100)^2] + [10 \times (50)^2]}{2 \times [4{,}000 - (30 \times 100) - (10 \times 50)]} = \frac{(30 \times 10{,}000) + (10 \times 2{,}500)}{2 \times (4{,}000 - 3{,}000 - 500)}$$

$$= \frac{300{,}000 + 25{,}000}{2 \times 500} = \frac{325{,}000}{1{,}000} = 325 \text{ hours per order (for gears } \textit{and} \text{ pistons)}$$

Introducing pistons will cause average waiting time for an order to more than double, from 150 hours to 325 hours. Waiting time increases because introducing pistons will cause unused capacity to shrink, increasing the probability that new orders will arrive while current orders are being manufactured or waiting to be manufactured. Average waiting time is very sensitive to the shrinking of unused capacity.

If the manager decides to make pistons, average manufacturing cycle time will be 425 hours for a gear order (325 hours of average waiting time + 100 hours of manufacturing time), and 375 hours for a piston order (325 hours of average waiting time + 50 hours

---

[5] The technical assumptions are (a) that customer orders for the product follow a Poisson distribution with a mean equal to the expected number of orders (30 in our example), and (b) that orders are processed on a first-in, first-out (FIFO) basis. The Poisson arrival pattern for customer orders has been found to be reasonable in many real-world settings. The FIFO assumption can be modified. Under the modified assumptions, the basic queuing and delay effects will still occur, but the precise formulas will be different.

Concepts in Action · Overcoming Wireless Data Bottlenecks

Daniel Heighton\Alamy Images

The wired world is quickly going wireless. In 2010, sales of smartphones—such as the Apple iPhone and BlackBerry—in the United States were predicted to be 53 million units. In addition to the smartphone boom, emerging devices including e-book readers and machine-to-machine appliances (the so-called "Internet of things") will add to rapidly growing data traffic.

With every new device that lets users browse the Internet, and every new business that taps into the convenience and speed of the wireless world, the invisible information superhighway gets a little more crowded. Cisco recently forecast that data traffic will grow at a compound rate of 108% from 90,000 terabytes per month in 2009 to 3.6 million terabytes per month by 2014.

This astronomical growth already causes many users to suffer from mobile bottlenecks caused by too many users trying to transfer mobile data at the same time in a given area. These bottlenecks are most harmful to companies buying and selling products and services over the mobile Internet. Without access, Amazon.com Kindle owners cannot download new e-books and mobile brokerage users cannot buy and sell stocks "on the go."

To relieve mobile bottlenecks, wireless providers and other high-tech companies are working on more efficient mobile broadband networks, such as LTE, that make use of complementary technologies to automatically choose the best available wireless network to increase capacity. Technology providers are also deploying Wi-Fi direct, which allows mobile users to freely transfer video, digital music, and photos between mobile devices without choking up valuable bandwidth. Companies and government agencies around the world are also trying to increase the wireless broadband spectrum. In the United States, for example, current holders of spectrum—such as radio stations—are being encouraged to sell their excess capacity to wireless providers in exchange for a share of the profits.

Sources: Edwards, Cliff. 2010. Wi-fi direct seen as way to alleviate network congestion. *BusinessWeek*, January 7. www.businessweek.com/technology/content/jan2010/tc2010017_884186.htm; Morris, John. 2010. CTIA: More spectrum, and other ways to break the wireless data bottleneck. *ZDNet*. "Laptops & Desktops," blog March 24. http://www.zdnet.com/blog/computers/ctia-more-spectrum-and-other-ways-to-break-the-wireless-data-bottleneck/1877; Pyle, George. 2010. Wireless growth leading to bottlenecks. *Buffalo News*, May 9. www.buffalonews.com/2010/05/09/1044893/wireless-growth-leading-to-bottlenecks.html.

of manufacturing time). A gear order will spend 76.5% (325 hours ÷ 425 hours) of its manufacturing cycle time just waiting for manufacturing to start!

Step 4: Make decisions by choosing among alternatives. Given the anticipated effects on manufacturing cycle time of adding pistons, should FW's manager introduce pistons? To help the manager make a decision, the management accountant identifies and analyzes the relevant revenues and relevant costs of adding the piston product and, in particular, the cost of delays on all products. The rest of this section focuses on Step 4. While we do not cover Step 5 in this example, we discuss later in the chapter how the balanced scorecard can be a useful tool to evaluate and learn about time-based performance.

Relevant Revenues and Relevant Costs of Time

To determine the relevant revenues and costs of adding pistons under Step 4, the management accountant prepares the following additional information:

| Product | Annual Average Number of Orders | Average Selling Price per Order If Average Manufacturing Cycle Time per Order Is | | Direct Material Cost per Order | Inventory Carrying Cost per Order per Hour |
		Less Than 300 Hours	More Than 300 Hours		
Gears	30	$22,000	$21,500	$16,000	$1.00
Pistons	10	10,000	9,600	8,000	0.50

Manufacturing cycle times affect both revenues and costs. Revenues are affected because customers are willing to pay a higher price for faster delivery. On the cost side, direct material costs and inventory carrying costs are the only relevant costs of introducing pistons (all other costs are unaffected and hence irrelevant). Inventory carrying costs equal the opportunity costs of investment tied up in inventory and the relevant costs of storage, such as space rental, spoilage, deterioration, and materials handling. Usually, companies calculate inventory carrying costs on a per-unit, per-year basis. To simplify calculations, the management accountant calculates inventory carrying costs on a per-order, per-hour basis. Also, FW acquires direct materials at the time the order is received by manufacturing and, therefore, calculates inventory carrying costs for the duration of the manufacturing cycle time.

Exhibit 8 presents relevant revenues and relevant costs for the "introduce pistons" and "do not introduce pistons" alternatives. Based on the analysis, FW's managers decide not to introduce pistons, even though pistons have a positive contribution margin of $1,600 ($9,600 − $8,000) per order and FW has the capacity to process pistons. If it produces pistons, FW will, on average, use only 3,500 (Gears: 100 hours per order × 30 orders + Pistons: 50 hours per order × 10 orders) of the available 4,000 machine-hours. So why is FW better off not introducing pistons? *Because of the negative effects that producing pistons will have on the existing product, gears.* The following table presents the *costs of time,* the expected loss in revenues and expected increase in carrying costs as a result of delays caused by using machine capacity to manufacture pistons.

| | Effect of Increasing Average Manufacturing Cycle Time | | Expected Loss in Revenues Plus |
| | Expected Loss in Revenues for Gears | Expected Increase in Carrying Costs for All Products | Expected Increase in Carrying Costs of Introducing Pistons |
Product	(1)	(2)	(3) = (1) + (2)
Gears	$15,000[a]	$5,250[b]	$20,250
Pistons	—	1,875[c]	1,875
Total	$15,000	$7,125	$22,125

[a]($22,000 − $21,500) per order × 30 expected orders = $15,000.
[b](425 − 250) hours per order × $1.00 per hour × 30 expected orders = $5,250.
[c](375 − 0) hours per order × $0.50 per hour × 10 expected orders = $1,875.

Introducing pistons causes the average manufacturing cycle time of gears to increase from 250 hours to 425 hours. Longer manufacturing cycle times increases inventory carrying costs of gears and decreases gear revenues (average manufacturing cycle time for gears exceeds 300 hours so the average selling price per order decreases from $22,000 to $21,500). Together

Relevant Items	Alternative 1: Introduce Pistons (1)	Alternative 2: Do Not Introduce Pistons (2)	Difference (3) = (1) − (2)
Expected revenues	741,000[a]	$660,000[b]	$ 81,000
Expected variable costs	560,000[c]	480,000[d]	(80,000)
Expected inventory carrying costs	14,625[e]	7,500[f]	(7,125)
Expected total costs	574,625	487,500	(87,125)
Expected revenues minus expected costs	$166,375	$172,500	$ (6,125)

[a]($21,500 × 30) + ($9,600 × 10) = $741,000; average manufacturing cycle time will be more than 300 hours.

[b]($22,000 × 30) = $660,000; average manufacturing cycle time will be less than 300 hours.

[c]($16,000 × 30) + ($8,000 × 10) = $560,000.

[d]$16,000 × 30 = $480,000.

[e](Average manufacturing cycle time for gears × Unit carrying cost per order for gears × Expected number of orders for gears) + (Average manufacturing cycle time for pistons × Unit carrying cost per order for pistons × Expected number of orders for pistons) = (425 × $1.00 × 30) + (375 × $0.50 × 10) = $12,750 + $1,875 = $14,625.

[f]Average manufacturing cycle time for gears × Unit carrying cost per order for gears × Expected number of orders for gears = 250 × $1.00 × 30 = $7,500.

with the inventory carrying cost of pistons, the expected costs of introducing pistons, $22,125, exceeds the expected contribution margin of $16,000 ($1,600 per order × 10 expected orders) from selling pistons by $6,125 (the difference calculated in Exhibit 8).

Decision Point ▶

What is customer-response time? What are the reasons for and the costs of delays?

This simple example illustrates that when demand uncertainty is high, some unused capacity is desirable.[6] Increasing the capacity of a bottleneck resource reduces manufacturing cycle times and delays. One way to increase capacity is to reduce the time required for setups and processing via more-efficient setups and processing. Another way to increase capacity is to invest in new equipment, such as flexible manufacturing systems that can be programmed to switch quickly from producing one product to producing another. Delays can also be reduced through careful scheduling of orders on machines, such as by batching similar jobs together for processing.

Theory of Constraints and Throughput-Margin Analysis

In this section, we consider products that are made from multiple parts and processed on multiple machines. With multiple parts and machines, dependencies arise among operations—that is, some operations cannot be started until parts from the preceding operation are available. Furthermore, some operations are bottlenecks (have limited capacity), and others are not.

Managing Bottlenecks

Learning Objective 5

Explain how to manage bottlenecks

. . . keep bottlenecks busy and increase their efficiency and capacity by increasing throughput margin

The **theory of constraints** (TOC) describes methods to maximize operating income when faced with some bottleneck and some nonbottleneck operations.[7] The TOC defines three measures as follows:

1. **Throughput margin** equals revenues minus the direct material costs of the goods sold.
2. *Investments* equal the sum of material costs in direct materials, work-in-process, and finished goods inventories; R&D costs; and costs of equipment and buildings.
3. *Operating costs* equal all costs of operations (other than direct materials) incurred to earn throughput margin. Operating costs include salaries and wages, rent, utilities, depreciation, and the like.

The objective of the TOC is to increase throughput margin while decreasing investments and operating costs. *The TOC considers a short-run time horizon and assumes operating costs are fixed.* It focuses on managing bottleneck operations as explained in the following steps:

Step 1:   Recognize that the bottleneck operation determines throughput margin of the entire system.

Step 2:   Identify the bottleneck operation by identifying operations with large quantities of inventory waiting to be worked on.

Step 3:   Keep the bottleneck operation busy and subordinate all nonbottleneck operations to the bottleneck operation. That is, the needs of the bottleneck operation determine the production schedule of the nonbottleneck operations.

Step 3 represents key concepts: To maximize operating income, the manager must maximize contribution margin (in this case, throughput margin) of the constrained or bottleneck resource. The bottleneck machine must always be kept running; it should not be waiting for jobs. To achieve this objective, companies often maintain a small buffer inventory of jobs at the bottleneck machine. The bottleneck machine sets the pace for all nonbottleneck machines. Workers at nonbottleneck machines do not produce more output than can be processed by the bottleneck machine, because producing more

---

[6] Other complexities, such as analyzing a network of machines, priority scheduling, and allowing for uncertainty in processing times, are beyond the scope of this book. In these cases, the basic queuing and delay effects persist, but the precise formulas are more complex.

[7] See E. Goldratt and J. Cox, *The Goal* (New York: North River Press, 1986); E. Goldratt, *The Theory of Constraints* (New York: North River Press, 1990); E. Noreen, D. Smith, and J. Mackey, *The Theory of Constraints and Its Implications for Management Accounting* (New York: North River Press, 1995); and M. Woeppel, *Manufacturers' Guide to Implementing the Theory of Constraints* (Boca Raton, FL: Lewis Publishing, 2000).

nonbottleneck output only creates excess inventory; it does not increase throughput margin.

Step 4: Take actions to increase the efficiency and capacity of the bottleneck operation as long as throughput margin exceeds the incremental costs of increasing efficiency and capacity.

We illustrate Step 4 using data from Cardinal Industries (CI). CI manufactures car doors in two operations: stamping and pressing.

	Stamping	Pressing
Capacity per hour	20 units	15 units
Annual capacity (6,000 hours of capacity available in each operation)		
6,000 hours × 20 units/hour; 6,000 hours × 15 units/hour)	120,000 units	90,000 units
Annual production and sales	90,000 units	90,000 units
Other fixed operating costs (excluding direct materials)	$720,000	$1,080,000
Other fixed operating costs per unit produced		
($720,000 ÷ 90,000 units; $1,080,000 ÷ 90,000 units)	$8 per unit	$12 per unit

Each door sells for $100 and has a direct material cost of $40. Variable costs in other functions of the value chain—design of products and processes, marketing, distribution, and customer service—are negligible. CI's output is constrained by the capacity of 90,000 units in the pressing operation. What can CI do to relieve the bottleneck constraint of the pressing operation?

Desirable actions include the following:

1. **Eliminate idle time at the bottleneck operation (time when the pressing machine is neither being set up to process products nor actually processing products).** CI's manager is evaluating permanently positioning two workers at the pressing operation to unload finished units as soon as one batch of units is processed and to set up the machine to begin processing the next batch. This action will cost $48,000 and bottleneck output will increase by 1,000 doors per year. Should CI incur the additional costs? Yes, because CI's throughput margin will increase by $60,000 [(selling price per door, $100 − direct material cost per door, $40) × 1,000 doors], which is greater than the incremental cost of $48,000. All other costs are irrelevant.

2. **Process only those parts or products that increase throughput margin, not parts or products that will be placed in finished goods or spare parts inventories.** Making products that remain in inventory will not increase throughput margin.

3. **Shift products that do not have to be made on the bottleneck machine to nonbottleneck machines or to outside processing facilities.** Suppose Spartan Corporation, an outside contractor, offers to press 1,500 doors at $15 per door from stamped parts that CI supplies. Spartan's quoted price is greater than CI's own operating costs in the pressing department of $12 per door. Should CI accept the offer? Yes, because pressing is the bottleneck operation. Getting additional doors pressed by Spartan will increase throughput margin by $90,000 [($100 − $40) per door × 1,500 doors], while the relevant cost of increasing capacity will be $22,500 ($15 per door × 1,500 doors). The fact that CI's unit cost is less than Spartan's quoted price is irrelevant.

   Suppose Gemini Industries, another outside contractor, offers to stamp 2,000 doors from direct materials that CI supplies at $6 per door. Gemini's price is lower than CI's operating cost of $8 per door in the stamping department. Should CI accept the offer? No, because other operating costs are fixed costs. CI will not save any costs by subcontracting the stamping operations. Instead, its costs will increase by $12,000 ($6 per door × 2,000 doors) with no increase in throughput margin, which is constrained by pressing capacity.

4. **Reduce setup time and processing time at bottleneck operations (for example, by simplifying the design or reducing the number of parts in the product).** Suppose CI can press 2,500 more doors at a cost of $55,000 a year by reducing setup time at the pressing operation. Should CI incur this cost? Yes, because throughput margin will increase by $150,000 [($100 − $40) per door × 2,500 doors], which is greater than

the incremental costs of $55,000. Will CI find it worthwhile to incur costs to reduce machining time at the nonbottleneck stamping operation? No. Other operating costs will increase, while throughput margin will remain unchanged because bottleneck capacity of the pressing operation will not increase.

5. **Improve the quality of parts or products manufactured at the bottleneck operation.** Poor quality is more costly at a bottleneck operation than at a nonbottleneck operation. The cost of poor quality at a nonbottleneck operation is the cost of materials wasted. If CI produces 1,000 defective doors at the stamping operation, the cost of poor quality is $40,000 (direct material cost per door, $40, × 1,000 doors). No throughput margin is forgone because stamping has unused capacity. Despite the defective production, stamping can produce and transfer 90,000 good-quality doors to the pressing operation. At a bottleneck operation, the cost of poor quality is the cost of materials wasted *plus* the opportunity cost of lost throughput margin. Bottleneck capacity not wasted in producing defective units could be used to generate additional throughput margin. If CI produces 1,000 defective units at the pressing operation, the cost of poor quality is the lost revenue of $100,000, or alternatively stated, direct material costs of $40,000 (direct material cost per door, $40, × 1,000 doors) plus forgone throughput margin of $60,000 [($100 − $40) per door × 1,000 doors].

The high cost of poor quality at the bottleneck operation means that bottleneck time should not be wasted processing units that are defective. That is, parts should be inspected before the bottleneck operation to ensure that only good-quality parts are processed at the bottleneck operation. Furthermore, quality-improvement programs should place special emphasis on minimizing defects at bottleneck machines.

If successful, the actions in Step 4 will increase the capacity of the pressing operation until it eventually exceeds the capacity of the stamping operation. The bottleneck will then shift to the stamping operation. CI would then focus continuous-improvement actions on increasing stamping efficiency and capacity. For example, the contract with Gemini Industries to stamp 2,000 doors at $6 per door from direct material supplied by CI will become attractive because throughput margin will increase by ($100 − $40) per door × 2,000 doors = $120,000, which is greater than the incremental costs of $12,000 ($6 per door × 2,000 doors).

The theory of constraints emphasizes management of bottleneck operations as the key to improving performance of production operations as a whole. It focuses on short-run maximization of throughput margin, revenues minus direct material costs of goods sold. Because TOC regards operating costs as difficult to change in the short run, it does not identify individual activities and drivers of costs. TOC is, therefore, less useful for the long-run management of costs. In contrast, activity-based costing (ABC) systems take a long-run perspective and focus on improving processes by eliminating nonvalue-added activities and reducing the costs of performing value-added activities. ABC systems, therefore, are more useful for long-run pricing, cost control, and capacity management. The short-run TOC emphasis on maximizing throughput margin by managing bottlenecks complements the long-run strategic-cost-management focus of ABC.[8]

Balanced Scorecard and Time-Related Measures

In this section, we focus on the final step of the five-step decision-making process by tracking changes in time-based measures, evaluating and learning whether these changes affect financial performance, and modifying decisions and plans to achieve the company's goals. We use the structure of the balanced scorecard perspectives—financial, customer, internal business processes, and learning and growth—to summarize how financial and nonfinancial measures of time relate to one another, reduce delays, and increase output of bottleneck operations.

Financial measures
 Revenue losses or price discounts attributable to delays
 Carrying cost of inventories
 Throughput margin minus operating costs

---

[8] For an excellent evaluation of TOC, operations management, cost accounting, and the relationship between TOC and activity-based costing, see A. Atkinson, "Cost Accounting, the Theory of Constraints, and Costing," (Issue Paper, CMA Canada, December 2000).

Customer measures

Customer-response time (the time it takes to fulfill a customer order)

On-time performance (delivering a product or service by the scheduled time)

Internal-business-process measures

Average manufacturing time for key products

Manufacturing cycle efficiency for key processes

Idle time at bottleneck operations

Defective units produced at bottleneck operations

Average reduction in setup time and processing time at bottleneck operations

Learning-and-growth measures

Employee satisfaction

Number of employees trained in managing bottleneck operations

To see the cause-and-effect linkages across these balanced scorecard perspectives, consider the example of the Bell Group, a designer and manufacturer of equipment for the jewelry industry. Based on TOC analysis, the company determined that a key financial measure was improving throughput margin by 18% for a specific product line. In the customer perspective, the company set a goal of a two-day turn-around time on all orders for the product. To achieve this goal, the internal-business-process measure was the amount of time a bottleneck machine operated, with a goal of running 22 hours per day, six days a week. Finally, in the learning perspective, the company focused on training new employees to carry out nonbottleneck operations in order to free experienced employees to operate the bottleneck machine. The Bell Group's emphasis on time-related measures in its balanced scorecard has allowed the company to substantially increase manufacturing throughput and slash response times, leading to higher revenues and increased profits.[9]

Decision Point

What are the steps managers can take to manage bottlenecks?

Problem for Self-Study

The Sloan Moving Corporation transports household goods from one city to another within the continental United States. It measures quality of service in terms of (a) time required to transport goods, (b) on-time delivery (within two days of agreed-upon delivery date), and (c) number of lost or damaged items. Sloan is considering investing in a new scheduling-and-tracking system costing $160,000 per year, which should help it improve performance with respect to items (b) and (c). The following information describes Sloan's current performance and the expected performance if the new system is implemented:

	Current Performance	Expected Future Performance
On-time delivery performance	85%	95%
Variable cost per carton lost or damaged	$60	$60
Fixed cost per carton lost or damaged	$40	$40
Number of cartons lost or damaged per year	3,000 cartons	1,000 cartons

Sloan expects each percentage point increase in on-time performance to increase revenue by $20,000 per year. Sloan's contribution margin percentage is 45%.

Required

1. Should Sloan acquire the new system? Show your calculations.
2. Sloan is very confident about the cost savings from fewer lost or damaged cartons as a result of introducing the new system but unsure about the increase in revenues. Calculate the minimum amount of increase in revenues needed to make it worthwhile for Sloan to invest in the new system.

---

[9] Management Roundtable, "The Bell Group Uses the Balanced Scorecard with the Theory of Constraints to Keep Strategic Focus," FastTrack.roundtable.com, fasttrack.roundtable.com/app/content/knowledgesource/item/197 (accessed May 15, 2007).

Solution

1. Additional costs of the new scheduling-and-tracking system are $160,000 per year. Additional annual benefits of the new scheduling-and-tracking system are as follows:

Additional annual revenues from a 10% improvement in on-time performance, from 85% to 95%, $20,000 per 1% × 10 percentage points	$200,000
45% contribution margin from additional annual revenues (0.45 × $200,000)	$ 90,000
Decrease in costs per year from fewer cartons lost or damaged (only variable costs are relevant)[$60 per carton × (3,000 − 1,000) cartons]	120,000
Total additional benefits	$210,000

Because the benefits of $210,000 exceed the costs of $160,000, Sloan should invest in the new system.

2. As long as Sloan earns a contribution margin of $40,000 (to cover incremental costs of $160,000 minus relevant variable-cost savings of $120,000) from additional annual revenues, investing in the new system is beneficial. This contribution margin corresponds to additional revenues of $40,000 ÷ 0.45 = $88,889.

Decision Points

The following question-and-answer format summarizes the chapter's learning objectives. Each decision presents a key question related to a learning objective. The guidelines are the answer to that question.

Decision	Guidelines
1. What are the four cost categories of a costs-of-quality program?	Four cost categories in a costs-of-quality program are prevention costs (costs incurred to preclude the production of products that do not conform to specifications), appraisal costs (costs incurred to detect which of the individual units of products do not conform to specifications), internal failure costs (costs incurred on defective products before they are shipped to customers), and external failure costs (costs incurred on defective products after they are shipped to customers).
2. What nonfinancial measures and methods can managers use to improve quality?	Nonfinancial quality measures managers can use include customer satisfaction measures such as number of customer complaints and percentage of defective units shipped to customers; internal-business process measures such as percentage of defective and reworked products; and learning and growth measures such as percentage of employees trained in and empowered to use quality principles. Three methods to identify quality problems and to improve quality are (a) control charts, to distinguish random from nonrandom variations in an operating process; (b) Pareto diagrams, to indicate how frequently each type of failure occurs; and (c) cause-and-effect diagrams, to identify and respond to potential causes of failure.
3. How do managers identify the relevant costs and benefits of quality improvement programs and use financial and nonfinancial measures to evaluate quality?	The relevant costs of quality improvement programs are the expected incremental costs to implement the program. The relevant benefits are the cost savings and the estimated increase in contribution margin from the higher revenues expected from quality improvements. Financial measures are helpful to evaluate trade-offs among prevention costs, appraisal costs, and failure costs. Nonfinancial measures identify problem areas that need improvement and serve as indicators of future long-run performance.

4. What is customer-response time? What are the reasons for and the costs of delays?

Customer-response time is how long it takes from the time a customer places an order for a product or service to the time the product or service is delivered to the customer. Delays occur because of (a) uncertainty about when customers will order products or services and (b) bottlenecks due to limited capacity. Bottlenecks are operations at which the work to be performed approaches or exceeds available capacity. Costs of delays include lower revenues and increased inventory carrying costs.

5. What are the steps managers can take to manage bottlenecks?

The four steps in managing bottlenecks are (1) recognize that the bottleneck operation determines throughput margin, (2) identify the bottleneck, (3) keep the bottleneck busy and subordinate all nonbottleneck operations to the bottleneck operation, and (4) increase bottleneck efficiency and capacity.

Terms to Learn

This chapter contains definitions of the following important terms:

appraisal costs	design quality	on-time performance
average waiting time	external failure costs	Pareto diagram
bottleneck	internal failure costs	prevention costs
cause-and-effect diagram	manufacturing cycle efficiency (MCE)	quality
conformance quality	manufacturing cycle time	theory of constraints (TOC)
control chart	manufacturing lead time	throughput margin
costs of quality (COQ)		time driver
customer-response time		

Assignment Material

Questions

19-1 Describe two benefits of improving quality.

19-2 How does conformance quality differ from design quality? Explain.

19-3 Name two items classified as prevention costs.

19-4 Distinguish between internal failure costs and external failure costs.

19-5 Describe three methods that companies use to identify quality problems.

19-6 "Companies should focus on financial measures of quality because these are the only measures of quality that can be linked to bottom-line performance." Do you agree? Explain.

19-7 Give two examples of nonfinancial measures of customer satisfaction relating to quality.

19-8 Give two examples of nonfinancial measures of internal-business-process quality.

19-9 Distinguish between customer-response time and manufacturing cycle time.

19-10 "There is no trade-off between customer-response time and on-time performance." Do you agree? Explain.

19-11 Give two reasons why delays occur.

19-12 "Companies should always make and sell all products whose selling prices exceed variable costs." Assuming fixed costs are irrelevant, do you agree? Explain.

19-13 Describe the three main measures used in the theory of constraints.

19-14 Describe the four key steps in managing bottleneck operations.

19-15 Describe three ways to improve the performance of a bottleneck operation.

Exercises

19-16 **Costs of quality.** (CMA, adapted) Costen, Inc., produces cell phone equipment. Jessica Tolmy, Costen's president, decided to devote more resources to the improvement of product quality after learning that her company had been ranked fourth in product quality in a 2009 survey of cell phone users. Costen's quality-improvement program has now been in operation for two years, and the cost report shown here has recently been issued.

	A	B	C	D	E
	Home Insert Page Layout Formulas Data Review View				
1	Semi-Annual COQ Report, Costen, Inc.				
2	(in thousands)				
3		6/30/2010	12/31/2010	6/30/2011	12/31/2011
4	Prevention costs				
5	Machine maintenance	$ 440	$ 440	$ 390	$ 330
6	Supplier training	20	100	50	40
7	Design reviews	50	214	210	200
8	Total prevention costs	510	754	650	570
9	Appraisal costs				
10	Incoming inspections	108	123	90	63
11	Final testing	332	332	293	203
12	Total appraisal costs	440	455	383	266
13	Internal failure costs				
14	Rework	231	202	165	112
15	Scrap	124	116	71	67
16	Total internal failure costs	355	318	236	179
17	External failure costs				
18	Warranty repairs	165	85	72	68
19	Customer returns	570	547	264	188
20	Total external failure costs	735	632	336	256
21	Total quality costs	$2,040	$2,159	$1,605	$1,271
22					
23	Total revenues	$8,240	$9,080	$9,300	$9,020

Required

1. For each period, calculate the ratio of each COQ category to revenues and to total quality costs.
2. Based on the results of requirement 1, would you conclude that Costen's quality program has been successful? Prepare a short report to present your case.
3. Based on the 2009 survey, Jessica Tolmy believed that Costen had to improve product quality. In making her case to Costen management, how might Tolmy have estimated the opportunity cost of not implementing the quality-improvement program?

19-17 Costs of quality analysis. Dream Rider produces car seats for children from newborn to two years old. The company is worried because one of its competitors has recently come under public scrutiny because of product failure. Historically, Dream Rider's only problem with its car seats was stitching in the straps. The problem can usually be detected and repaired during an internal inspection. The cost of the inspection is $4, and the repair cost is $0.75. All 250,000 car seats were inspected last year and 9% were found to have problems with the stitching in the straps during the internal inspection. Another 3% of the 250,000 car seats had problems with the stitching, but the internal inspection did not discover them. Defective units that were sold and shipped to customers needed to be shipped back to Dream Rider and repaired. Shipping costs are $7, and repair costs are $0.75. However, the out-of-pocket costs (shipping and repair) are not the only costs of defects not discovered in the internal inspection. For 20% of the external failures, negative word of mouth will result in a loss of sales, lowering the following year's profits by $300 for each of the 20% of units with external failures.

Required

1. Calculate appraisal cost.
2. Calculate internal failure cost.
3. Calculate out-of-pocket external failure cost.
4. Determine the opportunity cost associated with the external failures.
5. What are the total costs of quality?
6. Dream Rider is concerned with the high up-front cost of inspecting all 250,000 units. It is considering an alternative internal inspection plan that will cost only $1.00 per car seat inspected. During the internal inspection, the alternative technique will detect only 5.0% of the 250,000 car seats that have stitching problems. The other 7.0% will be detected after the car seats are sold and shipped. What are the total costs of quality for the alternative technique?
7. What factors other than cost should Dream Rider consider before changing inspection techniques?

19-18 Costs of quality, ethical considerations. Refer to information in Exercise 19-17 in answering this question. Dream Rider has discovered a more serious problem with the plastic core of its car seats. An accident can cause the plastic in some of the seats to crack and break, resulting in serious injuries to the occupant. It is estimated that this problem will affect about 175 car seats in the next year. This problem could be corrected by using a higher quality of plastic that would increase the cost of every car seat produced by $15. If this problem is not corrected, Dream Rider estimates that out of the 175 accidents, customers will realize that the problem is due to a defect in the seats in only three cases. Dream Rider's legal team has estimated that each of these three accidents would result in a lawsuit that could be settled for about $775,000. All lawsuits settled would include a confidentiality clause, so Dream Rider's reputation would not be affected.

Required

1. Assuming that Dream Rider expects to sell 250,000 car seats next year, what would be the cost of increasing the quality of all 250,000 car seats?
2. What will be the total cost of the lawsuits next year if the problem is not corrected?
3. Suppose Dream Rider has decided not to increase the quality of the plastic because the cost of increasing the quality exceeds the benefits (saving the cost of lawsuits). What do you think of this decision? (Note: Because of the confidentiality clause, the decision will have no effect on Dream Rider's reputation.)
4. Are there any other costs or benefits that Dream Rider should consider?

19-19 Nonfinancial measures of quality and time. Worldwide Cell Phones (WCP) has developed a cell phone that can be used anywhere in the world (even countries like Japan that have a relatively unique cell phone system). WCP has been receiving complaints about the phone. For the past two years, WCP has been test marketing the phones and gathering nonfinancial information related to actual and perceived aspects of the phone's quality. The company expects that, given the lack of competition in this market, increasing the quality of the phone will result in higher sales and thereby higher profits.

Quality data for 2010 and 2011 include the following:

	2010	2011
Cell phones produced and shipped	2,000	10,000
Number of defective units shipped	100	400
Number of customer complaints	150	250
Units reworked before shipping	120	700
Manufacturing cycle time	15 days	16 days
Average customer response time	30 days	28 days

Required

1. For each year, 2010 and 2011, calculate the following:
   a. Percentage of defective units shipped
   b. Customer complaints as a percentage of units shipped
   c. Percentage of units reworked during production
   d. Manufacturing cycle time as a percentage of total time from order to delivery
2. Referring to the information computed in requirement 1, explain whether WCP's quality and timeliness have improved.
3. Why would manufacturing cycle time have increased while customer response time decreased? (It may be useful to first describe what is included in each time measurement—see Exhibit 7.)

19-20 Quality improvement, relevant costs, relevant revenues. SpeedPrint manufactures and sells 18,000 high-technology printing presses each year. The variable and fixed costs of rework and repair are as follows:

	Variable Cost	Fixed Cost	Total Cost
Rework cost per hour	$ 79	$115	$194
Repair costs			
Customer support cost per hour	35	55	90
Transportation cost per load	350	115	465
Warranty repair cost per hour	89	150	239

SpeedPrint's current presses have a quality problem that causes variations in the shade of some colors. Its engineers suggest changing a key component in each press. The new component will cost $70 more than the old one. In the next year, however, SpeedPrint expects that with the new component it will (1) save 14,000 hours of rework, (2) save 850 hours of customer support, (3) move 225 fewer loads, (4) save

8,000 hours of warranty repairs, and (5) sell an additional 140 printing presses, for a total contribution margin of $1,680,000. SpeedPrint believes that even as it improves quality, it will not be able to save any of the fixed costs of rework or repair. SpeedPrint uses a one-year time horizon for this decision because it plans to introduce a new press at the end of the year.

Required

1. Should SpeedPrint change to the new component? Show your calculations.
2. Suppose the estimate of 140 additional printing presses sold is uncertain. What is the minimum number of additional printing presses that SpeedPrint needs to sell to justify adopting the new component?

19-21 Quality improvement, relevant costs, relevant revenues. Flagstar Conference Center and Catering is a conference center and restaurant facility that hosts over 300 national and international events each year attended by 50,000 professionals. Due to increased competition and soaring customer expectations, the company has been forced to revisit its quality standards. In the company's 25 year history, customer demand has never been greater for high quality products and services. Flagstar has the following budgeted fixed and variable costs for 2011:

	Total Conference Center Fixed Cost	Variable Cost per Conference Attendee
Building and facilities	$3,600,000	
Management salaries	$1,400,000	
Customer support and service personnel		$ 55
Food and drink		$100
Conference materials		$ 35
Incidental products and services		$ 15

The company's budgeted operating income is $3,500,000.

After conducting a survey of 3,000 conference attendees, the company has learned that its customers would most like to see the following changes in the quality of the company's products and services: 1) more menu options and faster service, 2) more incidental products and services (wireless access in all meeting rooms, computer stations for internet use, free local calling, etc.), and 3) upscale and cleaner meeting facilities. To satisfy these customer demands, the company would be required to increase fixed costs by 50% per year and increase variable costs by $10 per attendee as follows:

	Additional Variable Cost per Conference Attendee
Customer support and service personnel	$3
Food and drink	$5
Conference materials	$0
Incidental products and services	$2

Flagstar believes that the preceding improvements in product and service quality would increase overall conference attendance by 40%.

Required

1. What is the budgeted revenue per conference attendee?
2. Assuming budgeted revenue per conference attendee is unchanged, should Flagstar implement the proposed changes?
3. Assuming budgeted revenue per conference attendee is unchanged, what is the variable cost per conference attendee at which Flagstar would be indifferent between implementing and not implementing the proposed changes?

19-22 Waiting time, service industry. The registration advisors at a small midwestern university (SMU) help 4,200 students develop each of their class schedules and register for classes each semester. Each advisor works for 10 hours a day during the registration period. SMU currently has 10 advisors. While advising an individual student can take anywhere from 2 to 30 minutes, it takes an average of 12 minutes per student. During the registration period, the 10 advisors see an average of 300 students a day on a first-come, first-served basis.

Required

1. Calculate how long the average student will have to wait in the advisor's office before being advised.

2. The head of the registration advisors would like to increase the number of students seen each day, because at 300 students a day it would take 14 working days to see all of the students. This is a problem because the registration period lasts for only two weeks (10 working days). If the advisors could advise 420 students a day, it would take only two weeks (10 days). However, the head advisor wants to make sure that the waiting time is not excessive. What would be the average waiting time if 420 students were seen each day?

3. SMU wants to know the effect of reducing the average advising time on the average wait time. If SMU can reduce the average advising time to 10 minutes, what would be the average waiting time if 420 students were seen each day?

19-23 Waiting time, cost considerations, customer satisfaction. Refer to the information presented in Exercise 19-22. The head of the registration advisors at SMU has decided that the advisors must finish their advising in two weeks and therefore must advise 420 students a day. However, the average waiting time given a 12-minute advising period will result in student complaints, as will reducing the average advising time to 10 minutes. SMU is considering two alternatives:

A. Hire two more advisors for the two-week (10-working day) advising period. This will increase the available number of advisors to 12 and therefore lower the average waiting time.

B. Increase the number of days that the advisors will work during the two-week registration period to six days a week. If SMU increases the number of days worked to six per week, then the 10 advisors need only see 350 students a day to advise all of the students in two weeks.

1. What would the average wait time be under alternative A and under alternative B?   **Required**
2. If advisors earn $100 per day, which alternative would be cheaper for SMU (assume that if advisors work six days in a given work week, they will be paid time and a half for the sixth day)?
3. From a student satisfaction point of view, which of the two alternatives would be preferred? Why?

19-24 Nonfinancial measures of quality, manufacturing cycle efficiency. (CMA, adapted) Torrance Manufacturing evaluates the performance of its production managers based on a variety of factors, including cost, quality, and cycle time. The following are nonfinancial measures for quality and time for 2010 and 2011 for its only product:

Nonfinancial Quality Measures	2010	2011
Number of returned goods	385	462
Number of defective units reworked	1,122	834
Annual hours spent on quality training per employee	32	36
Number of units delivered on time	12,438	14,990

Annual Totals	2010	2011
Units of finished goods shipped	14,240	16,834
Average total hours worked per employee	2,000	2,000

The following information relates to the average amount of time needed to complete an order:

Time to Complete an Order	2010	2011
Wait time		
From order being placed to start of production	8	6
From start of production to completion	6	7
Inspection time	2	1
Process time	4	4
Move time	2	2

1. Compute the manufacturing cycle efficiency for an order for 2010 and 2011.   **Required**
2. For each year 2010 and 2011, calculate the following:
   a. Percentage of goods returned
   b. Defective units reworked as a percentage of units shipped
   c. Percentage of on-time deliveries
   d. Percentage of hours spent by each employee on quality training
3. Evaluate management's performance on quality and timeliness over the two years.

19-25 Theory of constraints, throughput margin, relevant costs. The Mayfield Corporation manufactures filing cabinets in two operations: machining and finishing. It provides the following information:

	Machining	Finishing
Annual capacity	100,000 units	80,000 units
Annual production	80,000 units	80,000 units
Fixed operating costs (excluding direct materials)	$640,000	$400,000
Fixed operating costs per unit produced ($640,000 ÷ 80,000; $400,000 ÷ 80,000)	$8 per unit	$5 per unit

Each cabinet sells for $72 and has direct material costs of $32 incurred at the start of the machining operation. Mayfield has no other variable costs. Mayfield can sell whatever output it produces. The following requirements refer only to the preceding data. There is no connection between the requirements.

Required

1. Mayfield is considering using some modern jigs and tools in the finishing operation that would increase annual finishing output by 1,000 units. The annual cost of these jigs and tools is $30,000. Should Mayfield acquire these tools? Show your calculations.
2. The production manager of the machining department has submitted a proposal to do faster setups that would increase the annual capacity of the machining department by 10,000 units and would cost $5,000 per year. Should Mayfield implement the change? Show your calculations.
3. An outside contractor offers to do the finishing operation for 12,000 units at $10 per unit, double the $5 per unit that it costs Mayfield to do the finishing in-house. Should Mayfield accept the subcontractor's offer? Show your calculations.
4. The Hunt Corporation offers to machine 4,000 units at $4 per unit, half the $8 per unit that it costs Mayfield to do the machining in-house. Should Mayfield accept Hunt's offer? Show your calculations.

19-26 Theory of constraints, throughput margin, quality. Refer to the information in Exercise 19-25 in answering the following requirements. There is no connection between the requirements.

Required

1. Mayfield produces 2,000 defective units at the machining operation. What is the cost to Mayfield of the defective items produced? Explain your answer briefly.
2. Mayfield produces 2,000 defective units at the finishing operation. What is the cost to Mayfield of the defective items produced? Explain your answer briefly.

MyAccountingLab

Problems

19-27 Quality improvement, relevant costs, and relevant revenues. The Thomas Corporation sells 300,000 V262 valves to the automobile and truck industry. Thomas has a capacity of 110,000 machine-hours and can produce 3 valves per machine-hour. V262's contribution margin per unit is $8. Thomas sells only 300,000 valves because 30,000 valves (10% of the good valves) need to be reworked. It takes one machine-hour to rework 3 valves, so 10,000 hours of capacity are used in the rework process. Thomas's rework costs are $210,000. Rework costs consist of the following:

- Direct materials and direct rework labor (variable costs): $3 per unit
- Fixed costs of equipment, rent, and overhead allocation: $4 per unit

Thomas's process designers have developed a modification that would maintain the speed of the process and ensure 100% quality and no rework. The new process would cost $315,000 per year. The following additional information is available:

- The demand for Thomas's V262 valves is 370,000 per year.
- The Jackson Corporation has asked Thomas to supply 22,000 T971 valves (another product) if Thomas implements the new design. The contribution margin per T971 valve is $10. Thomas can make two T971 valves per machine-hour with 100% quality and no rework.

Required

1. Suppose Thomas's designers implement the new design. Should Thomas accept Jackson's order for 22,000 T971 valves? Show your calculations.
2. Should Thomas implement the new design? Show your calculations.
3. What nonfinancial and qualitative factors should Thomas consider in deciding whether to implement the new design?

19-28 Quality improvement, relevant costs, and relevant revenues. The Tan Corporation uses multicolor molding to make plastic lamps. The molding operation has a capacity of 200,000 units per year. The demand for lamps is very strong. Tan will be able to sell whatever output quantities it can produce at $40 per lamp.

Tan can start only 200,000 units into production in the molding department because of capacity constraints on the molding machines. If a defective unit is produced at the molding operation, it must be scrapped at a net disposal value of zero. Of the 200,000 units started at the molding operation, 30,000 defective units (15%) are produced. The cost of a defective unit, based on total (fixed and variable) manufacturing costs incurred up to the molding operation, equals $25 per unit, as follows:

Direct materials (variable)	$16 per unit
Direct manufacturing labor, setup labor, and materials-handling labor (variable)	3 per unit
Equipment, rent, and other allocated overhead, including inspection and testing costs on scrapped parts (fixed)	6 per unit
Total	$25 per unit

Tan's designers have determined that adding a different type of material to the existing direct materials would result in no defective units being produced, but it would increase the variable costs by $4 per lamp in the molding department.

1. Should Tan use the new material? Show your calculations.
2. What nonfinancial and qualitative factors should Tan consider in making the decision?

Required

19-29 Statistical quality control. Keltrex Cereals produces a wide variety of breakfast products. The company's three best selling breakfast cereals are Double Bran Bits, Honey Wheat Squares, and Sugar King Pops. Each box of a particular type of cereal is required to meet pre-determined weight specifications, so that no single box contains more or less cereal than another. The company measures the mean weight per production run to determine if there are variances over or under the company's specified upper and lower level control limits. A production run that falls outside of the specified control limit does not meet quality standards and is investigated further by management to determine the cause of the variance. The three Keltrex breakfast cereals had the following weight standards and production run data for the month of March:

Quality Standard: Mean Weight per Production Run

Double Bran Bits	Honey Wheat Squares	Sugar King Pops
17.97 ounces	14 ounces	16.02 ounces

Actual Mean Weight per Production Run (Ounces)

Production Run	Double Bran Bits	Honey Wheat Squares	Sugar King Pops
1	18.23	14.11	15.83
2	18.14	14.13	16.11
3	18.22	13.98	16.24
4	18.30	13.89	15.69
5	18.10	13.91	15.95
6	18.05	14.01	15.50
7	17.84	13.94	15.86
8	17.66	13.99	16.23
9	17.60	14.03	16.15
10	17.52	13.97	16.60
Standard Deviation	0.28	0.16	0.21

Required

1. Using the $\pm 2\sigma$ rule, what variance investigation decisions would be made?
2. Present control charts for each of the three breakfast cereals for March. What inferences can you draw from the charts?
3. What are the costs of quality in this example? How could Keltrex employ Six Sigma programs to improve quality?

19-30 Compensation linked with profitability, waiting time, and quality measures. East Coast Healthcare operates two medical groups, one in Philadelphia and one in Baltimore. The semi-annual bonus plan for each medical group's president has three components:

a. Profitability performance. Add 0.75% of operating income.
b. Average patient waiting time. Add $40,000 if the average waiting time for a patient to see a doctor after the scheduled appointment time is less than 10 minutes. If average patient waiting time is more than 10 minutes, add nothing.
c. Patient satisfaction performance. Deduct $40,000 if patient satisfaction (measured using a survey asking patients about their satisfaction with their doctor and their overall satisfaction with East Coast Healthcare) falls below 65 on a scale from 0 (lowest) to 100 (highest). No additional bonus is awarded for satisfaction scores of 65 or more.

Semi-annual data for 2011 for the Philadelphia and Baltimore groups are as follows:

	January–June	July–December
Philadelphia		
Operating income	$11,150,000	$10,500,000
Average waiting time	13 minutes	12 minutes
Patient satisfaction	74	72
Baltimore		
Operating income	$ 9,500,000	$ 5,875,000
Average waiting time	12 minutes	9.5 minutes
Patient satisfaction	59	68

Required

1. Compute the bonuses paid in each half year of 2011 to the Philadelphia and Baltimore medical group presidents.
2. Discuss the validity of the components of the bonus plan as measures of profitability, waiting time performance, and patient satisfaction. Suggest one shortcoming of each measure and how it might be overcome (by redesign of the plan or by another measure).
3. Why do you think East Coast Healthcare includes measures of both operating income and waiting time in its bonus plan for group presidents? Give one example of what might happen if waiting time was dropped as a performance measure.

19-31 Waiting times, manufacturing cycle times. The Seawall Corporation uses an injection molding machine to make a plastic product, Z39, after receiving firm orders from its customers. Seawall estimates that it will receive 50 orders for Z39 during the coming year. Each order of Z39 will take 80 hours of machine time. The annual machine capacity is 5,000 hours.

Required

1. Calculate (a) the average amount of time that an order for Z39 will wait in line before it is processed and (b) the average manufacturing cycle time per order for Z39.
2. Seawall is considering introducing a new product, Y28. The company expects it will receive 25 orders of Y28 in the coming year. Each order of Y28 will take 20 hours of machine time. Assuming the demand for Z39 will not be affected by the introduction of Y28, calculate (a) the average waiting time for an order received and (b) the average manufacturing cycle time per order for each product, if Seawall introduces Y28.

19-32 Waiting times, relevant revenues, and relevant costs (continuation of 19-31). Seawall is still debating whether it should introduce Y28. The following table provides information on selling prices, variable costs, and inventory carrying costs for Z39 and Y28:

Product	Annual Average Number of Orders	Selling Price per Order if Average Manufacturing Cycle Time per Order Is Less Than 320 Hours	Selling Price per Order if Average Manufacturing Cycle Time per Order Is More Than 320 Hours	Variable Cost per Order	Inventory Carrying Cost per Order per Hour
Z39	50	$27,000	$26,500	$15,000	$0.75
Y28	25	8,400	8,000	5,000	0.25

Required

1. Using the average manufacturing cycle times calculated in Problem 19-31, requirement 2, should Seawall manufacture and sell Y28? Show your calculations.
2. Should Seawall manufacture and sell Y28 if the data are changed as follows:

Product	Annual Average Number of Orders	Selling Price per Order if Average Manufacturing Cycle Time per Order Is Less Than 320 Hours	Selling Price per Order if Average Manufacturing Cycle Time per Order Is More Than 320 Hours	Variable Cost per Order	Inventory Carrying Cost per Order per Hour
Z39	50	$27,000	$26,500	$15,000	$0.75
Y28	25	6,400	6,000	5,000	0.25

19-33 Manufacturing cycle times, relevant revenues, and relevant costs. The Brandt Corporation makes wire harnesses for the aircraft industry only upon receiving firm orders form its customers. Brandt has recently purchased a new machine to make two types of wire harnesses, one for Boeing airplanes (B7) and the other for Airbus Industries airplanes (A3). The annual capacity of the new machine is 6,000 hours. The following information is available for next year:

Customer	Annual Average Number of Orders	Manufacturing Time Required	Selling Price per Order if Average Manufacturing Cycle Time per Order Is		Variable Cost per Order	Inventory Carrying Cost per Order per Hour
			Less Than 200 Hours	More Than 200 Hours		
B7	125	40 hours	$15,000	$14,400	$10,000	$0.50
A3	10	50 hours	13,500	12,960	9,000	0.45

Required

1. Calculate the average manufacturing cycle times per order (a) if Brandt manufactures only B7 and (b) if Brandt manufactures both B7 and A3.
2. Even though A3 has a positive contribution margin, Brandt's managers are evaluating whether Brandt should (a) make and sell only B7 or (b) make and sell both B7 and A3. Which alternative will maximize Brandt's operating income? Show your calculations.
3. What other factors should Brandt consider in choosing between the alternatives in requirement 2?

19-34 Theory of constraints, throughput margin, and relevant costs. Nevada Industries manufactures electronic testing equipment. Nevada also installs the equipment at customers' sites and ensures that it functions smoothly. Additional information on the manufacturing and installation departments is as follows (capacities are expressed in terms of the number of units of electronic testing equipment):

	Equipment Manufactured	Equipment Installed
Annual capacity	400 units per year	250 units per year
Equipment manufactured and installed	250 units per year	250 units per year

Nevada manufactures only 250 units per year because the installation department has only enough capacity to install 250 units. The equipment sells for $60,000 per unit (installed) and has direct material costs of $35,000. All costs other than direct material costs are fixed. The following requirements refer only to the preceding data. There is no connection between the requirements.

Required

1. Nevada's engineers have found a way to reduce equipment manufacturing time. The new method would cost an additional $60 per unit and would allow Nevada to manufacture 20 additional units a year. Should Nevada implement the new method? Show your calculations.
2. Nevada's designers have proposed a change in direct materials that would increase direct material costs by $3,000 per unit. This change would enable Nevada to install 280 units of equipment each year. If Nevada makes the change, it will implement the new design on all equipment sold. Should Nevada use the new design? Show your calculations.
3. A new installation technique has been developed that will enable Nevada's engineers to install 7 additional units of equipment a year. The new method will increase installation costs by $45,000 each year. Should Nevada implement the new technique? Show your calculations.
4. Nevada is considering how to motivate workers to improve their productivity (output per hour). One proposal is to evaluate and compensate workers in the manufacturing and installation departments on the basis of their productivities. Do you think the new proposal is a good idea? Explain briefly.

19-35 Theory of constraints, throughput margin, quality, and relevant costs. Aardee Industries manufactures pharmaceutical products in two departments: mixing and tablet making. Additional information on the two departments follows. Each tablet contains 0.5 gram of direct materials.

	Mixing	Tablet Making
Capacity per hour	150 grams	200 tablets
Monthly capacity (2,000 hours available in each department)	300,000 grams	400,000 tablets
Monthly production	200,000 grams	390,000 tablets
Fixed operating costs (excluding direct materials)	$16,000	$39,000
Fixed operating cost per unit ($16,000 ÷ 200,000 grams; $39,000 ÷ 390,000 tablets)	$0.08 per gram	$0.10 per tablet

The mixing department makes 200,000 grams of direct materials mixture (enough to make 400,000 tablets) because the tablet-making department has only enough capacity to process 400,000 tablets. All direct material costs of $156,000 are incurred in the mixing department. The tablet-making department manufactures only 390,000 tablets from the 200,000 grams of mixture processed; 2.5% of the direct materials mixture is lost in the tablet-making process. Each tablet sells for $1. All costs other than direct material costs are fixed costs. The following requirements refer only to the preceding data. There is no connection between the requirements.

Required

1. An outside contractor makes the following offer: If Aardee will supply the contractor with 10,000 grams of mixture, the contractor will manufacture 19,500 tablets for Aardee (allowing for the normal 2.5% loss of the mixture during the tablet-making process) at $0.12 per tablet. Should Aardee accept the contractor's offer? Show your calculations.
2. Another company offers to prepare 20,000 grams of mixture a month from direct materials Aardee supplies. The company will charge $0.07 per gram of mixture. Should Aardee accept the company's offer? Show your calculations.
3. Aardee's engineers have devised a method that would improve quality in the tablet-making department. They estimate that the 10,000 tablets currently being lost would be saved. The modification would cost $7,000 a month. Should Aardee implement the new method? Show your calculations.
4. Suppose that Aardee also loses 10,000 grams of mixture in its mixing department. These losses can be reduced to zero if the company is willing to spend $9,000 per month in quality-improvement methods. Should Aardee adopt the quality-improvement method? Show your calculations.
5. What are the benefits of improving quality in the mixing department compared with improving quality in the tablet-making department?

19-36 Theory of constraints, contribution margin, sensitivity analysis. Fun Time Toys (FTT) produces dolls in two processes: molding and assembly. FTT is currently producing two models: Chatty Chelsey and Talking Tanya. Production in the molding department is limited by the amount of materials available. Production in the assembly department is limited by the amount of trained labor available. The only variable costs are materials in the molding department and labor in the assembly department. Following are the requirements and limitations by doll model and department:

	Molding Materials	Assembly Time	Selling Price
Chatty Chelsey	1.5 pounds per doll	20 minutes per doll	$39 per doll
Talking Tanya	2 pounds per doll	30 minutes per doll	$51 per doll
Materials/Labor Available	30,000 pounds	8,500 hours	
Cost	$12 per pound	$18 per hour	

Required

1. If there were enough demand for either doll, which doll would FTT produce? How many of these dolls would it make and sell?
2. If FTT sells two Chatty Chelseys for each Talking Tanya, how many dolls of each type would it produce and sell? What would be the total contribution margin?
3. If FTT sells two Chatty Chelseys for each Talking Tanya, how much would production and contribution margin increase if the molding department could buy 15 more pounds of materials for $12 per pound?
4. If FTT sells two Chatty Chelseys for each Talking Tanya, how much would production and contribution margin increase if the assembly department could get 10 more labor hours at $18 per hour?

19-37 Quality improvement, Pareto diagram, cause-and-effect diagram. Pauli's Pizza has recently begun collecting data on the quality of its customer order processing and delivery. Pauli's made 1,800 deliveries during the first quarter of 2012. The following quality data pertains to first quarter deliveries:

Type of Quality Failure	Quality Failure Incidents First Quarter 2012
Late delivery	50
Damaged or spoiled product delivered	5
Incorrect order delivered	12
Service complaints by customer of delivery personnel	8
Failure to deliver incidental items with order (drinks, side items, etc.)	18

Required

1. Draw a Pareto diagram of the quality failures experienced by Pauli's Pizza.
2. Give examples of prevention activities that could reduce the failures experienced by Pauli's.
3. Draw a cause-and-effect diagram of possible causes for late deliveries.

19-38 Ethics and quality. Wainwright Corporation manufactures auto parts for two leading Japanese automakers. Nancy Evans is the management accountant for one of Wainwright's largest manufacturing plants. The plant's General Manager, Chris Sheldon, has just returned from a meeting at corporate headquarters where quality expectations were outlined for 2012. Chris calls Nancy into his office to relay the corporate quality objective that total quality costs will not exceed 10% of total revenues by plant under any circumstances. Chris asks Nancy to provide him with a list of options for meeting corporate headquarter's quality objective. The plant's initial budgeted revenues and quality costs for 2012 are as follows:

Revenue	3,400,000
Quality Costs:	
Testing of purchased materials	32,000
Quality control training for production staff	5,000
Warranty repairs	82,000
Quality design engineering	48,000
Customer support	37,000
Materials scrap	12,000
Product inspection	102,000
Engineering redesign of failed parts	21,000
Rework of failed parts	18,000

Prior to receiving the new corporate quality objective, Nancy had collected information for all of the plant's possible options for improving both product quality and costs of quality. She was planning to introduce the idea of reengineering the manufacturing process at a one-time cost of $75,000, which would decrease product inspection costs by approximately 25% per year and was expected to reduce warranty repairs and customer support by an estimated 40% per year. After seeing the new corporate objective, Nancy is reconsidering the reengineering idea.

Nancy returns to her office and crunches the numbers again to look for other alternatives. She concludes that by increasing the cost of quality control training for production staff by $15,000 per year, the company would reduce inspection costs by 10% annually and reduce warranty repairs and customer support costs by 20% per year, as well. She is leaning toward only presenting this latter option to Chris, the general manager, since this is the only option that meets the new corporate quality objective.

Required

1. Calculate the ratio of each costs-of-quality category (prevention, appraisal, internal failure, and external failure) to revenues for 2012. Are the total costs of quality as a percentage of revenues currently less than 10%?
2. Which of the two quality options should Nancy propose to the general manager, Chris Sheldon? Show the two-year outcome for each option: (a) reengineer the manufacturing process for $75,000 and (b) increase quality training expenditure by $15,000 per year.
3. Suppose Nancy decides not to present the reengineering option to Chris. Is Nancy's action unethical? Explain.

Collaborative Learning Problem

19-39 Quality improvement, theory of constraints. The Wellesley Corporation makes printed cloth in two departments: weaving and printing. Currently, all product first moves through the weaving department and then through the printing department before it is sold to retail distributors for $1,250 per roll. Wellesley provides the following information:

	Weaving	Printing
Monthly capacity	10,000 rolls	15,000 rolls
Monthly production	9,500 rolls	8,550 rolls
Direct material cost per roll of cloth processed at each operation	$500	$100
Fixed operating costs	$2,850,000	$427,500

Wellesley can start only 10,000 rolls of cloth in the weaving department because of capacity constraints of the weaving machines. Of the 10,000 rolls of cloth started in the weaving department, 500 (5%) defective rolls are scrapped at zero net disposal value. The good rolls from the weaving department (called gray cloth) are sent to the printing department. Of the 9,500 good rolls started at the printing operation, 950 (10%) defective rolls are scrapped at zero net disposal value. The Wellesley Corporation's total monthly sales of printed cloth equal the printing department's output.

Required

1. The printing department is considering buying 5,000 additional rolls of gray cloth from an outside supplier at $900 per roll, which is much higher than Wellesley's cost to manufacture the roll. The printing department expects that 10% of the rolls obtained from the outside supplier will result in defective products. Should the printing department buy the gray cloth from the outside supplier? Show your calculations.
2. Wellesley's engineers have developed a method that would lower the printing department's rate of defective products to 6% at the printing operation. Implementing the new method would cost $350,000 per month. Should Wellesley implement the change? Show your calculations.
3. The design engineering team has proposed a modification that would lower the weaving department's rate of defective products to 3%. The modification would cost the company $175,000 per month. Should Wellesley implement the change? Show your calculations.

Inventory Management, Just-in-Time, and Simplified Costing Methods

From Chapter 20 of *Cost Accounting: A Managerial Emphasis*, 14/e. Charles T. Horngren. Srikant M. Datar. Madhav Rajan.

Inventory Management, Just-in-Time, and Simplified Costing Methods

Suppose you could receive a large quantity discount for a product that you regularly use, but the discount requires you to buy a year's supply and necessitates a large up-front expenditure.

Would you take the quantity discount? Companies face similar decisions because firms pay a price for tying up money in inventory sitting on their shelves or elsewhere. Money tied up in inventory is a particularly serious problem when times are tough. When faced with these circumstances, companies like Costco work very hard to better manage their inventories.

Costco Aggressively Manages Inventory to Thrive in Tough Times[1]

When consumers reduced their spending in 2008, traditional stalwarts like Circuit City and Linens 'n Things wilted under the weight of their own massive inventories. They could not turn their inventories quickly enough to pay suppliers and were forced to close their doors when cash ran out.

At the same time, Costco continued to thrive! How? By intentionally stocking *fewer* items than its competitors—and employing inventory management practices that successfully reduced costs throughout its operations. While the average grocery store carries around 40,000 items, Costco limits its offerings to about 4,000 products, or 90% less! Limiting the number of products on its shelves reduces Costco's costs of carrying inventory.

Costco also employs a just-in-time inventory management system, which includes sharing data directly with many of its largest suppliers. Companies like Kimberly-Clark calculate re-order points in real time and send new inventory, as needed, to replenish store shelves. Costco also works to redesign product packaging to squeeze more bulky goods onto trucks and shelves, reducing the number of orders Costco needs to place with suppliers.

Occasionally, the company leverages its 75 million square feet of warehouse space to reduce purchasing costs. For example, when Procter & Gamble recently announced a 6% price increase for its paper goods, Costco bought 258 truckloads of paper towels at the old rate and stored them using available capacity in its distribution centers and warehouses.

[1] *Source*: McGregor, Jena. 2008. Costco's artful discounts. *Business Week*, October 20.

These inventory management techniques have allowed Costco to succeed in tough times while others have failed. Costco turns its inventory nearly 12 times a year, far more often than other retailers. With many suppliers agreeing to be paid 30 days after delivery, Costco often sells many of its goods before it even has to pay for them!

Inventory management is important because materials costs often account for more than 40% of total costs of manufacturing companies and more than 70% of total costs in merchandising companies. In this chapter, we describe the components of inventory costs, relevant costs for different inventory-related decisions, and planning and control systems for managing inventory.

Inventory Management in Retail Organizations

Inventory management includes planning, coordinating, and controlling activities related to the flow of inventory into, through, and out of an organization. Consider this breakdown of operations for three major retailers for which cost of goods sold constitutes their largest cost item.

	Kroger	Costco	Wal-Mart
Revenues	100.0%	100.0%	100.0%
Deduct costs:			
Cost of goods sold	76.8%	87.2%	74.7%
Selling and administration costs	21.7%	10.2%	19.5%
Other costs, interest, and taxes	1.4%	1.1%	2.3%
Total costs	99.9%	98.5%	96.5%
Net income	0.1%	1.5%	3.5%

The low percentages of net income to revenues mean that improving the purchase and management of goods for sale can cause dramatic percentage increases in net income.

Costs Associated with Goods for Sale

Managing inventories to increase net income requires companies to effectively manage costs that fall into the following six categories:

1. **Purchasing costs** are the cost of goods acquired from suppliers, including incoming freight costs. These costs usually make up the largest cost category of goods for sale. Discounts for various purchase-order sizes and supplier payment terms affect purchasing costs.

Learning Objective 1

Identify six categories of costs associated with goods for sale

. . . purchasing, ordering, carrying, stockout, quality, and shrinkage

257

2. **Ordering costs** arise in preparing and issuing purchase orders, receiving and inspecting the items included in the orders, and matching invoices received, purchase orders, and delivery records to make payments. Ordering costs include the cost of obtaining purchase approvals, as well as other special processing costs.

3. **Carrying costs** arise while holding an inventory of goods for sale. Carrying costs include the opportunity cost of the investment tied up in inventory and the costs associated with storage, such as space rental, insurance, obsolescence, and spoilage.

4. **Stockout costs** arise when a company runs out of a particular item for which there is customer demand, a *stockout*. The company must act quickly to replenish inventory to meet that demand or suffer the costs of not meeting it. A company may respond to a stockout by expediting an order from a supplier, which can be expensive because of additional ordering costs plus any associated transportation costs. Or the company may lose sales due to the stockout. In this case, the opportunity cost of the stockout includes lost contribution margin on the sale not made plus any contribution margin lost on future sales due to customer ill will.

5. **Costs of quality** result when features and characteristics of a product or service are not in conformance with customer specifications. There are four categories of quality costs (prevention costs, appraisal costs, internal failure costs, and external failure costs).

6. **Shrinkage costs** result from theft by outsiders, embezzlement by employees, misclassifications, and clerical errors. Shrinkage is measured by the difference between (a) the cost of the inventory recorded on the books in the absence of theft and other incidents just mentioned, and (b) the cost of inventory when physically counted. Shrinkage can often be an important measure of management performance. Consider, for example, the grocery business, where operating income percentages hover around 2%. With such small margins, it is easy to see why one of a store manager's prime responsibilities is controlling inventory shrinkage. A $1,000 increase in shrinkage will erase the operating income from sales of $50,000 (2% × $50,000 = $1,000).

Note that not all inventory costs are available in financial accounting systems. For example, opportunity costs are not recorded in these systems and are a significant component in several of these cost categories.

Information-gathering technology increases the reliability and timeliness of inventory information and reduces costs in the six cost categories. For example, barcoding technology allows a scanner to record purchases and sales of individual units. As soon as a unit is scanned, an instantaneous record of inventory movements is created that helps in the management of purchasing, carrying, and stockout costs. In the next several sections, we consider how relevant costs are computed for different inventory-related decisions in merchandising companies.

Economic-Order-Quantity Decision Model

The first decision in managing goods for sale is *how much to order* of a given product. The **economic order quantity (EOQ)** is a decision model that, under a given set of assumptions, calculates the optimal quantity of inventory to order.

- The simplest version of an EOQ model assumes there are only ordering and carrying costs.
- The same quantity is ordered at each reorder point.
- Demand, ordering costs, and carrying costs are known with certainty. The **purchase-order lead time**, the time between placing an order and its delivery, is also known with certainty.
- Purchasing cost per unit is unaffected by the order quantity. This assumption makes purchasing costs irrelevant to determining EOQ, because the purchase price is the same, whatever the order size.

Decision Point

What are the six categories of costs associated with goods for sale?

Learning Objective 2

Balance ordering costs with carrying costs using the economic-order-quantity (EOQ) decision model

. . . choose the inventory quantity per order to minimize these costs

- No stockouts occur. The basis for this assumption is that the costs of stockouts are so high that managers maintain adequate inventory to prevent them.

- In deciding on the size of a purchase order, managers consider costs of quality and shrinkage costs only to the extent that these costs affect ordering or carrying costs.

Given these assumptions, EOQ analysis ignores purchasing costs, stockout costs, costs of quality, and shrinkage costs. EOQ is the order quantity that minimizes the relevant ordering and carrying costs (that is, the ordering and carrying costs affected by the quantity of inventory ordered):

$$\text{Relevant total costs} = \text{Relevant ordering costs} + \text{Relevant carrying costs}$$

We use the following notations:

D = Demand in units for a specified period (one year in this example)

Q = Size of each order (order quantity)

$$\text{Number of purchase orders per period (one year)} = \frac{\text{Demand in units for a period (one year)}}{\text{Size of each order (order quantity)}} = \frac{D}{Q}$$

Average inventory in units = $\dfrac{Q}{2}$, because each time the inventory goes down to 0, an order for Q units is received. The inventory varies from Q to 0 so the average inventory is $\dfrac{0 + Q}{2}$.

P = Relevant ordering cost per purchase order

C = Relevant carrying cost of one unit in stock for the time period used for D (one year)

For any order quantity, Q,

$$\text{Annual relevant ordering costs} = \left(\begin{array}{ccc} \text{Number of} & & \text{Relevant ordering} \\ \text{purchase orders} & \times & \text{cost per} \\ \text{per year} & & \text{purchase order} \end{array} \right) = \left(\frac{D}{Q} \times P \right)$$

$$\text{Annual relevant carrying costs} = \left(\begin{array}{ccc} & & \text{Annual} \\ \text{Average inventory} & \times & \text{relevant carrying} \\ \text{in units} & & \text{cost per unit} \end{array} \right) = \left(\frac{Q}{2} \times C \right)$$

$$\text{Annual relevant total costs} = \begin{array}{c} \text{Annual} \\ \text{relevant ordering} \\ \text{costs} \end{array} + \begin{array}{c} \text{Annual} \\ \text{relevant carrying} \\ \text{costs} \end{array} = \left(\frac{D}{Q} \times P \right) + \left(\frac{Q}{2} \times C \right)$$

The order quantity that minimizes annual relevant total costs is

$$EOQ = \sqrt{\frac{2DP}{C}}$$

The EOQ model is solved using calculus but the key intuition is that relevant total costs are minimized when relevant ordering costs equal relevant carrying costs. If carrying costs are less (greater) than ordering costs, total costs can be reduced by increasing (decreasing) the order quantity. To solve for EOQ, we set

$$\left(\frac{Q}{2} \times C \right) = \left(\frac{D}{Q} \times P \right)$$

Multiplying both sides by $\dfrac{2Q}{C}$, we get $Q^2 = \dfrac{2DP}{C}$

$$Q = \sqrt{\frac{2DP}{C}}$$

The formula indicates that EOQ increases with higher demand and/or higher ordering costs and decreases with higher carrying costs.

Let's consider an example to see how EOQ analysis works. CD World is an independent electronics store that sells blank compact disks. CD World purchases the CDs from

Sontek at $14 a package (each package contains 20 disks). Sontek pays for all incoming freight. No inspection is necessary at CD World because Sontek supplies quality merchandise. CD World's annual demand is 13,000 packages, at a rate of 250 packages per week. CD World requires a 15% annual rate of return on investment. The purchase-order lead time is two weeks. Relevant ordering cost per purchase order is $200.

Relevant carrying cost per package per year is as follows:

Required annual return on investment, 0.15 × $14	$2.10
Relevant costs of insurance, materials handling, breakage, shrinkage, and so on, per year	3.10
Total	$5.20

What is the EOQ of packages of disks?

Substituting D = 13,000 packages per year, P = $200 per order, and C = $5.20 per package per year, in the EOQ formula, we get,

$$EOQ = \sqrt{\frac{2 \times 13{,}000 \times \$200}{\$5.20}} = \sqrt{1{,}000{,}000} = 1{,}000 \text{ packages}$$

Purchasing 1,000 packages per order minimizes total relevant ordering and carrying costs. Therefore, the number of deliveries each period (one year in this example) is as follows:

$$\frac{D}{EOQ} = \frac{13{,}000}{1{,}000} = 13 \text{ deliveries}$$

Recall the annual relevant total costs (RTC) = $\left(\dfrac{D}{Q} \times P\right) + \left(\dfrac{Q}{2} \times C\right)$
For Q = 1,000 units,

$$RTC = \frac{13{,}000 \times \$200}{1{,}000} + \frac{1{,}000 \times \$5.20}{2}$$

$$= \$2{,}600 + \$2{,}600 = \$5{,}200$$

Exhibit 1 graphs the annual relevant total costs of ordering (DP/Q) and carrying inventory $(QC/2)$ under various order sizes (Q), and it illustrates the trade-off between these two types of costs. The larger the order quantity, the lower the annual relevant ordering costs, but the higher the annual relevant carrying costs. *Annual relevant total costs are at a minimum at the EOQ at which the relevant ordering and carrying costs are equal.*

Exhibit 1   Graphic Analysis of Ordering Costs and Carrying Costs for Compact Disks at CD World

When to Order, Assuming Certainty

The second decision in managing goods for sale is *when to order* a given product. The **reorder point** is the quantity level of inventory on hand that triggers a new purchase order. The reorder point is simplest to compute when both demand and purchase-order lead time are known with certainty:

$$\text{Reorder point} = \frac{\text{Number of units sold}}{\text{per time period}} \times \frac{\text{Purchase-order}}{\text{lead time}}$$

In our CD World example, we choose one week as the time period in the reorder-point formula:

Economic order quantity	1,000 packages
Number of units sold per week	250 packages per week (13,000 packages ÷ 52 weeks)
Purchase-order lead time	2 weeks

$$\text{Reorder point} = 250 \text{ packages per week} \times 2 \text{ weeks} = 500 \text{ packages}$$

CD World will order 1,000 packages each time inventory stock falls to 500 packages.[2] The graph in Exhibit 2 shows the behavior of the inventory level of compact disk packages, assuming demand occurs uniformly during each week. If purchase-order lead time is two weeks, a new order will be placed when the inventory level falls to 500 packages, so the 1,000 packages ordered will be received at the precise time that inventory reaches zero.

Safety Stock

We have assumed that demand and purchase-order lead time are known with certainty. Retailers who are uncertain about demand, lead time, or the quantity that suppliers can provide, hold safety stock. **Safety stock** is inventory held at all times regardless of the quantity of inventory ordered using the EOQ model. Safety stock is used as a buffer against unexpected increases in demand, uncertainty about lead time, and unavailability of stock from suppliers. Suppose that in the CD World example, the only uncertainty is about demand. CD World's managers will have some notion (usually based on experience) of the range of weekly demand. CD World's managers expect demand to be 250 packages per week, but they feel that a maximum demand of 400 packages per week

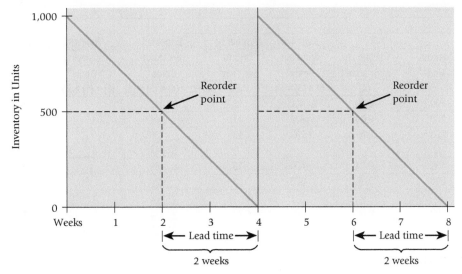

Exhibit 2

Inventory Level of Compact Disks at CD World[a]

[a] This exhibit assumes that demand and purchase-order lead time are certain:
Demand = 250 CD packages per week
Purchase-order lead time = 2 weeks

---

[2] This handy but special formula does not apply when receipt of the order fails to increase inventory to the reorder-point quantity (for example, when lead time is three weeks and the order is a one-week supply). In these cases, orders will overlap.

may occur. If stockout costs are very high, CD World will hold a safety stock of 300 packages and incur higher carrying costs. The 300 packages equal the maximum excess demand of 150 (400 − 250) packages per week times the two weeks of purchase-order lead time. If stockout costs are minimal, CD World will hold no safety stocks and avoid incurring the additional carrying costs.

A frequency distribution based on prior daily or weekly levels of demand forms the basis for computing safety-stock levels. Assume that one of the following levels of demand will occur over the two-week purchase-order lead time at CD World.

Total Demand for 2 Weeks	200 Units	300 Units	400 Units	500 Units	600 Units	700 Units	800 Units
Probability (sums to 1.00)	0.06	0.09	0.20	0.30	0.20	0.09	0.06

We see that 500 units is the most likely level of demand for two weeks because it has the highest probability of occurrence. We see also a 0.35 probability that demand will be 600, 700, or 800 packages (0.20 + 0.09 + 0.06 = 0.35).

If a customer wants to buy compact disks and the store has none in stock, CD World can "rush" them to the customer at an additional cost to CD World of $4 per package. The relevant stockout costs in this case are $4 per package. The optimal safety-stock level is the quantity of safety stock that minimizes the sum of annual relevant stockout and carrying costs. Note that CD World will place 13 orders per year and will incur the same ordering costs whatever level of safety stock it chooses. Therefore, ordering costs are irrelevant for the safety-stock decision. Recall that the relevant carrying cost for CD World is $5.20 per package per year.

Exhibit 3 tabulates annual relevant total stockout and carrying costs when the reorder point is 500 units. Over the two-week purchase-order lead time, stockouts can occur if demand is 600, 700, or 800 units because these levels of demand exceed the 500 units in stock at the time CD World places the purchase orders. Consequently, CD World only evaluates safety stock levels of 0, 100, 200, and 300 units. If safety stock is 0 units, CD World will

Exhibit 3 Computation of Safety Stock for CD World When Reorder Point Is 500 Units

	Home	Insert	Page Layout	Formulas	Data	Review	View		
	A	B	C	D	E	F	G	H	I
1	Safety	Demand							
2	Stock	Levels			Relevant	Number of	Expected	Relevant	Relevant
3	Level	Resulting	Stockout	Probability	Stockout	Orders	Stockout	Carrying	Total
4	in Units	in Stockouts	in Units[a]	of Stockout	Costs[b]	per Year[c]	Costs[d]	Costs[e]	Costs
5	(1)	(2)	(3) = (2) − 500 − (1)	(4)	(5) = (3) × $4	(6)	(7) = (4) × (5) × (6)	(8) = (1) × $5.20	(9) = (7) + (8)
6	0	600	100	0.20	$ 400	13	$1,040		
7		700	200	0.09	800	13	936		
8		800	300	0.06	1,200	13	936		
9							$2,912	$ 0	$2,912
10	100	700	100	0.09	400	13	$ 468		
11		800	200	0.06	800	13	624		
12							$1,092	$ 520	$1,612
13	200	800	100	0.06	400	13	$ 312	$1,040	$1,352
14	300	-	-	-	-	-	$ 0[f]	$1,560	$1,560
15									
16	[a]Demand level resulting in stockouts − Inventory available during lead time (excluding safety stock), 500 units − Safety stock.								
17	[b]Stockout in units × Relevant stockout costs of $4.00 per unit.								
18	[c]Annual demand, 13,000 ÷ 1,000 EOQ = 13 orders per year.								
19	[d]Probability of stockout × Relevant stockout costs × Number of orders per year.								
20	[e]Safety stock × Annual relevant carrying costs of $5.20 per unit (assumes that safety stock is on hand at all times and that there is no overstocking								
21	caused by decreases in expected usage).								
22	[f]At a safety stock level of 300 units, no stockout will occur and, hence, expected stockout costs = $0.								

incur stockout costs if demand is 600, 700, or 800 units but will have no additional carrying costs. At the other extreme, if safety stock is 300 units, CD World will never incur stockout costs but will have higher carrying costs. As Exhibit 3 shows, annual relevant total stockout and carrying costs would be the lowest ($1,352) when a safety stock of 200 packages is maintained. Therefore, 200 units is the optimal safety-stock level. Consider the 200 units of safety stock as extra stock that CD World maintains. For example, CD World's total inventory of compact disks at the time of reordering its EOQ of 1,000 units would be 700 units (the reorder point of 500 units plus safety stock of 200 units).

Decision
Point

What does the EOQ
decision model help
managers do and
how do managers
decide on the level
of safety stocks?

Estimating Inventory-Related Relevant Costs and Their Effects

Just as we did in earlier chapters, we need to determine which costs are relevant when making and evaluating inventory management decisions. We next describe the estimates that need to be made to calculate the annual relevant carrying costs of inventory, stockout costs, and ordering costs.

Learning
Objective 3

Identify the effect of
errors that can arise
when using the EOQ
decision model

. . . errors in predicting
parameters have a
small effect on costs

and ways to reduce
conflicts between the
EOQ model and models
used for performance
evaluation

. . . by making the two
models congruent

Considerations in Obtaining Estimates of Relevant Costs

Relevant inventory carrying costs consist of the *relevant incremental costs* plus the *relevant opportunity cost of capital*.

What are the *relevant incremental costs* of carrying inventory? Only those costs of the purchasing company, such as warehouse rent, warehouse workers' salaries, costs of obsolescence, costs of shrinkage, and costs of breakage, that change with the quantity of inventory held. Salaries paid to clerks, stock keepers, and materials handlers are irrelevant if they are unaffected by changes in inventory levels. Suppose, however, that as inventories increase (decrease), total salary costs increase (decrease) as clerks, stock keepers, and materials handlers are added (transferred to other activities or laid off). In this case, salaries paid are relevant costs of carrying inventory. Similarly, costs of storage space owned that cannot be used for other profitable purposes when inventories decrease are irrelevant. But if the space has other profitable uses, or if total rental cost is tied to the amount of space occupied, storage costs are relevant costs of carrying inventory.

What is the *relevant opportunity cost of capital*? It is the return forgone by investing capital in inventory rather than elsewhere. It is calculated as the required rate of return multiplied by the per-unit costs such as the purchase price of units, incoming freight, and incoming inspection. Opportunity costs are not computed on investments (say, in buildings) if these investments are unaffected by changes in inventory levels.

In the case of stockouts, the relevant incremental cost is the cost of expediting an order from a supplier. The relevant opportunity cost is (1) the lost contribution margin on sales forgone because of the stockout and (2) lost contribution margin on future sales forgone as a result of customer ill will.

Relevant ordering costs are only those ordering costs that change with the number of orders placed (for example, costs of preparing and issuing purchase orders and receiving and inspecting materials).

Cost of a Prediction Error

Predicting relevant costs is difficult and seldom flawless, which raises the question, "What is the cost when actual relevant costs differ from the estimated relevant costs used for decision making?"

Let's revisit the CD World example. Suppose relevant ordering costs per purchase order are $100, while the manager predicts them to be $200 at the time of calculating the order quantity. We can calculate the cost of this "prediction" error using a three-step approach.

Step 1: Compute the Monetary Outcome from the Best Action That Could Be Taken, Given the *Actual* Amount of the Cost Input (Cost per Purchase Order). This is the benchmark, the decision the manager would have made if the manager had known the correct ordering cost against which actual performance can be measured. Using $D = 13{,}000$ packages per year, $P = \$100$, and $C = \$5.20$ per package per year,

$$EOQ = \sqrt{\frac{2DP}{C}}$$

$$= \sqrt{\frac{2 \times 13{,}000 \times \$100}{\$5.20}} = \sqrt{500{,}000}$$

$$= 707 \text{ packages (rounded)}$$

Annual relevant total costs when EOQ = 707 packages are as follows:

$$RTC = \frac{DP}{Q} + \frac{QC}{2}$$

$$= \frac{13{,}000 \times \$100}{707} + \frac{707 \times \$5.20}{2}$$

$$= \$1{,}839 + \$1{,}838 = \$3{,}677$$

Step 2: Compute the Monetary Outcome from the Best Action Based on the Incorrect *Predicted* Amount of the Cost Input (Cost per Purchase Order). In this step, the manager calculates the order quantity based on the prediction (that later proves to be wrong) that the ordering cost is $200. If the relevant ordering cost per purchase order is predicted to be $200, the best action is to purchase 1,000 packages in each order (p. 706). The actual cost of the purchase order turns out to be $100 so the actual annual relevant total costs when $D = 13{,}000$ packages per year, $Q = 1{,}000$ packages, $P = \$100$, and $C = \$5.20$ per package per year are as follows:

$$RTC = \frac{13{,}000 \times \$100}{1{,}000} + \frac{1{,}000 \times \$5.20}{2}$$

$$= \$1{,}300 + \$2{,}600 = \$3{,}900$$

Step 3: Compute the Difference Between the Monetary Outcomes from Step 1 and Step 2.

	Monetary Outcome
Step 1	$3,677
Step 2	3,900
Difference	$ (223)

The cost of the prediction error, $223, is less than 7% of the relevant total costs of $3,677. Note that the annual relevant-total-costs curve in Exhibit 1 is somewhat flat over the range of order quantities from 650 to 1,300 units. *The square root in the EOQ model dampens the effect of errors in predicting parameters because taking square roots results in the incorrect numbers becoming smaller.*

In the next section, we consider a planning-and-control and performance-evaluation issue that frequently arises when managing inventory.

Conflict Between the EOQ Decision Model and Managers' Performance Evaluation

What happens if the order quantity calculated based on the EOQ decision model differs from the order quantity that managers making inventory management decisions would choose to make their own performance look best? For example, because there are no opportunity costs recorded in financial accounting systems, conflicts may arise between the EOQ model's optimal order quantity and the order quantity that purchasing managers (who are evaluated on financial accounting numbers) will regard as optimal. As a result of ignoring some carrying costs (the opportunity costs), managers will be inclined to purchase larger lot sizes of materials than the lot sizes calculated according to the EOQ model. To achieve congruence between the EOQ decision model and managers' performance evaluations, companies such as Wal-Mart design performance-evaluation

Decision Point ▶

What is the effect on costs of errors in predicting parameters of the EOQ model? How can companies reduce the conflict between the EOQ decision model and models used for performance evaluation?

models that charge managers responsible for managing inventory levels with carrying costs that include a required return on investment.

Just-in-Time Purchasing

Just-in-time (JIT) purchasing is the purchase of materials (or goods) so that they are delivered just as needed for production (or sales). Consider JIT purchasing for Hewlett-Packard's (HP's) manufacture of computer printers. HP has long-term agreements with suppliers for the major components of its printers. Each supplier is required to make frequent deliveries of small orders directly to the production floor, based on the production schedule that HP gives its suppliers. Suppliers work hard to keep their commitments because failure to deliver components on time, or to meet agreed-upon quality standards, can cause an HP assembly plant not to meet its own scheduled deliveries for printers.

Learning Objective 4

Describe why companies are using just-in-time purchasing

. . . high carrying costs, low ordering costs, high-quality suppliers, and reliable supply chains

JIT Purchasing and EOQ Model Parameters

Companies moving toward JIT purchasing to reduce their costs of carrying inventories (parameter C in the EOQ model) say that, in the past, carrying costs have actually been much greater than estimated because costs of warehousing, handling, shrinkage, and investment have not been fully identified. At the same time, the cost of placing a purchase order (parameter P in the EOQ model) is decreasing because of the following:

- Companies are establishing long-term purchasing agreements that define price and quality terms over an extended period. Individual purchase orders covered by those agreements require no additional negotiation regarding price or quality.

- Companies are using electronic links to place purchase orders at a cost that is estimated to be a small fraction of the cost of placing orders by telephone or by mail.

- Companies are using purchase-order cards (similar to consumer credit cards such as VISA and MasterCard). As long as purchasing personnel stay within preset total and individual-transaction dollar limits, traditional labor-intensive procurement-approval procedures are not required.

Exhibit 4 tabulates the sensitivity of CD World's EOQ (p. 705) to changes in carrying and ordering costs. Exhibit 4 supports JIT purchasing because, as relevant carrying costs increase and relevant ordering costs per purchase order decrease, EOQ decreases and ordering frequency increases.

Relevant Costs of JIT Purchasing

JIT purchasing is not guided solely by the EOQ model. The EOQ model is designed only to emphasize the trade-off between relevant carrying and ordering costs. However, inventory management also includes purchasing costs, stockout costs, costs of quality, and shrinkage costs. We next present the calculation of relevant costs in a JIT purchasing decision.

Exhibit 4

Sensitivity of EOQ to Variations in Relevant Ordering and Carrying Costs for CD World

	A	B	C	D	E	F	G
		Home Insert Page Layout Formulas Data Review View					
1				Economic Order Quantity in Units			
2				At Different Ordering and Carrying Costs			
3	Annual Demand (D) =	13,000	units				
4							
5	Relevant Carrying Costs			Relevant Ordering Costs per Purchase Order (P)			
6	Per Package per Year (C)			$ 200	$150	$100	$ 30
7	$ 5.20			1,000	866	707	387
8	7.00			862	746	609	334
9	10.00			721	624	510	279
10	15.00			589	510	416	228

Exhibit 5   Annual Relevant Costs of Current Purchasing Policy and JIT Purchasing Policy for CD World

	Home	Insert	Page Layout	Formulas	Data	Review	View				
	A	B	C	D	E	F	G	H	I	J	

	A — Relevant Items (1)	B — Relevant Cost Per Unit (2)	C	D — Quantity Per Year (3)	E — Total Costs (4) = (2) × (3)	F	G — Relevant Cost Per Unit (5)	H	I — Quantity Per Year (6)	J — Total Costs (7) = (5) × (6)
1				Relevant Costs Under						
2			Current Purchasing Policy					JIT Purchasing Policy		
5	Purchasing costs	$14.00	per unit	13,000	$182,000		$14.02	per unit	13,000	$182,260
6	Ordering costs	2.00	per order	13	26		2.00	per order	130	260
7	Opportunity carrying costs	2.10[a]	per unit of average inventory per year	500[b]	1,050		2.10[a]	per unit of average inventory per year	50[c]	105
8	Other carrying costs (insurance, materials handling, and so on)	3.10	per unit of average inventory per year	500[b]	1,550		3.10	per unit of average inventory per year	50[c]	155
9	Stockout costs	4.00	per unit	0	0		4.00	per unit	150	600
10	Total annual relevant costs				$184,626					$183,380
11	Annual difference in favor of JIT purchasing					$1,246				
12										
13	[a]Purchasing cost per unit × 0.15 per year									
14	[b]Order quantity ÷ 2 = 1,000 ÷ 2 = 500 units									
15	[c]Order quantity ÷ 2 = 100 ÷ 2 = 50 units									

CD World has recently established an Internet business-to-business purchase-order link with Sontek. CD World triggers a purchase order for compact disks by a single computer entry. Payments are made electronically for batches of deliveries, rather than for each individual delivery. These changes reduce the ordering cost from $200 to only $2 per purchase order! CD World will use the Internet purchase-order link whether or not it shifts to JIT purchasing. CD World is negotiating to have Sontek deliver 100 packages of disks 130 times per year (5 times every 2 weeks), instead of delivering 1,000 packages 13 times per year, as shown in Exhibit 1. Sontek is willing to make these frequent deliveries, but it would add $0.02 to the price per package. As before, CD World's required rate of return on investment is 15% and the annual relevant carrying cost of insurance, materials handling, shrinkage, breakage, and the like is $3.10 per package per year.

Also assume that CD World incurs no stockout costs under its *current* purchasing policy, because demand and purchase-order lead times during each four-week period are known with certainty. CD World is concerned that lower inventory levels from implementing JIT purchasing will lead to more stockouts, because demand variations and delays in supplying disks are more likely in the short time intervals between orders delivered under JIT purchasing. Sontek has flexible manufacturing processes that enable it to respond rapidly to changing demand patterns. Nevertheless, CD World expects to incur stockout costs on 150 compact disk packages per year under the JIT purchasing policy. When a stockout occurs, CD World must rush-order compact disk packages from another supplier at an additional cost of $4 per package. Should CD World implement the JIT purchasing option of 130 deliveries per year? Exhibit 5 compares CD World's relevant total costs under the current purchasing policy and the JIT policy, and it shows net cost savings of $1,246 per year by shifting to a JIT purchasing policy.

Supplier Evaluation and Relevant Costs of Quality and Timely Deliveries

Companies that implement JIT purchasing choose their suppliers carefully and develop long-term supplier relationships. Some suppliers are better positioned than others to support JIT purchasing. For example, Frito-Lay, a supplier of potato chips and other snack foods, has a corporate strategy that emphasizes service, consistency, freshness, and quality of the delivered products. As a result, the company makes deliveries to retail outlets more frequently than many of its competitors.

Exhibit 6   Annual Relevant Costs of Purchasing from Sontek and Denton

| | | | Home | Insert | Page Layout | Formulas | Data | Review | View | | | |

	A	B	C	D	E	F	G	H	I	J
1					Relevant Cost of Purchasing From					
2			Sontek					Denton		
3	Relevant Items	Relevant Cost Per Unit		Quantity Per Year	Total Costs		Relevant Cost Per Unit		Quantity Per Year	Total Costs
4	(1)	(2)		(3)	(4) = (2) × (3)		(5)		(6)	(7) = (5) × (6)
5	Purchasing costs	$14.02	per unit	13,000	$182,260		$13.80	per unit	13,000	$179,400
6	Ordering costs	2.00	per order	130	260		2.00	per order	130	260
7	Inspection costs	0.05	per unit	0	0		0.05	per unit	13,000	650
8	Opportunity carrying costs	2.10[a]	per unit of average inventory per year	50[b]	105		2.07[a]	per unit of average inventory per year	50[b]	103
9	Other carrying costs (insurance, materials handling, and so on)	3.10	per unit of average inventory per year	50[b]	155		3.00	per unit of average inventory per year	50[b]	150
10	Customer return costs	10.00	per unit returned	0	0		10.00	per unit returned	325[c]	3,250
11	Stockout costs	4.00	per unit	150	600		4.00	per unit	360	1,440
12	Total annual relevant costs				$183,380					$185,253
13	Annual difference in favor of Sontek					$1,873				
14										
15	[a]Purchasing cost per unit × 0.15 per year									
16	[b]Order quantity ÷ 2 = 100 ÷ 2 = 50 units									
17	[c]2.5% of units returned × 13,000 units									

What are the relevant total costs when choosing suppliers? Consider again CD World. Denton Corporation, another supplier of disks, offers to supply all of CD World's compact disk needs at a price of $13.80 per package, less than Sontek's price of $14.02, under the same JIT delivery terms that Sontek offers. Denton proposes an Internet purchase-order link identical to Sontek's link, making CD World's ordering cost $2 per purchase order. CD World's relevant cost of insurance, materials handling, breakage, and the like would be $3.00 per package per year if it purchases from Denton, versus $3.10 if it purchases from Sontek. Should CD World buy from Denton? To answer this, we need to consider the relevant costs of quality and delivery performance.

CD World has used Sontek in the past and knows that Sontek will deliver quality disks on time. In fact, CD World does not even inspect the compact disk packages that Sontek supplies and therefore incurs zero inspection costs. Denton, however, does not enjoy such a sterling reputation for quality. CD World anticipates the following negative aspects of using Denton:

- Inspection cost of $0.05 per package.

- Average stockouts of 360 packages per year requiring rush orders at an additional cost of $4 per package.

- Product returns of 2.5% of all packages sold due to poor compact disk quality. CD World estimates an additional cost of $10 to handle each returned package.

Exhibit 6 shows the relevant total costs of purchasing from Sontek and Denton. Even though Denton is offering a lower price per package, there is a net cost savings of $1,873 per year by purchasing disks from Sontek. Selling Sontek's high-quality compact disks also enhances CD World's reputation and increases customer goodwill, which could lead to higher sales and profitability in the future.

JIT Purchasing, Planning and Control, and Supply-Chain Analysis

The levels of inventories held by retailers are influenced by the demand patterns of their customers and supply relationships with their distributors and manufacturers, the suppliers to their manufacturers, and so on. The *supply chain* describes the flow of goods, services, and information from the initial sources of materials and services to the delivery of products to consumers, regardless of whether those activities occur in the same company or in other companies. Retailers can purchase inventories on a JIT basis only if activities throughout the supply chain are properly planned, coordinated, and controlled.

Procter and Gamble's (P&G's) experience with its Pampers product illustrates the gains from supply-chain coordination. Retailers selling Pampers encountered variability in weekly demand because families purchased disposable diapers randomly. Anticipating even more demand variability and lacking information about available inventory with P&G, retailers' orders to P&G became more variable that, in turn, increased variability of orders at P&G's suppliers, resulting in high levels of inventory at all stages in the supply chain.

How did P&G respond to these problems? By sharing information and planning and coordinating activities throughout the supply chain among retailers, P&G, and P&G's suppliers. Sharing sales information reduced the level of uncertainty that P&G and its suppliers had about retail demand for Pampers and led to (1) fewer stockouts at the retail level, (2) reduced manufacture of Pampers not immediately needed by retailers, (3) fewer manufacturing orders that had to be "rushed" or "expedited," and (4) lower inventories held by each company in the supply chain. The benefits of supply chain coordination at P&G have been so great that retailers such as Wal-Mart have contracted with P&G to manage Wal-Mart's retail inventories on a just-in-time basis. This practice is called *supplier- or vendor-managed inventory*. Supply-chain management, however, has challenges in sharing accurate, timely, and relevant information about sales, inventory, and sales forecasts caused by problems of communication, trust, incompatible information systems, and limited people and financial resources.

Decision Point

Why are companies using just-in-time purchasing?

Inventory Management, MRP and JIT Production

We now turn our attention away from purchasing to managing production inventories in manufacturing companies. Managers at manufacturing companies have developed numerous systems to plan and implement inventory activities within their plants. We consider two widely used types of systems: materials requirements planning (MRP) and just-in-time (JIT) production.

Materials Requirements Planning

Learning Objective 5

Distinguish materials requirements planning (MRP) systems

. . . manufacturing products based on demand forecasts

from just-in-time (JIT) systems for manufacturing

. . . manufacturing products only upon receiving customer orders

Materials requirements planning (MRP) is a "push-through" system that manufactures finished goods for inventory on the basis of demand forecasts. To determine outputs at each stage of production, MRP uses (1) demand forecasts for final products; (2) a bill of materials detailing the materials, components, and subassemblies for each final product; and (3) available inventories of materials, components, and products. Taking into account the lead time required to purchase materials and to manufacture components and finished products, a master production schedule specifies the quantity and timing of each item to be produced. Once production starts as scheduled, the output of each department is pushed through the production line. This "push through" can sometimes result in an accumulation of inventory when workstations receive work they are not yet ready to process.

Maintaining accurate inventory records and costs is critical in an MRP system. For example, after becoming aware of the full costs of carrying finished goods inventory in its MRP system, National Semiconductor contracted with Federal Express to airfreight its microchips from a central location in Singapore to customer sites worldwide, instead of storing products at geographically dispersed warehouses. This change enabled National to move products from plant to customer in 4 days rather than 45 days and to reduce distribution costs from 2.6% to 1.9% of revenues. These benefits subsequently led National to outsource all its shipping activities to Federal Express.

MRP is a push-through approach. We now consider JIT production, a "demand-pull" approach, which is used by companies such as Toyota in the automobile industry, Dell in the computer industry, and Braun in the appliance industry.

JIT Production

Just-in-time (JIT) production, which is also called **lean production**, is a "demand-pull" manufacturing system that manufactures each component in a production line as soon as, and only when, needed by the next step in the production line. In a JIT production line, manufacturing activity at any particular workstation is prompted by the need for that workstation's output at the following workstation. Demand triggers each step of the production process, starting with customer demand for a finished product at the end of the process and working all the way back to the demand for direct materials at the beginning of the process. In this way, demand pulls an order through the production line. The demand-pull feature of JIT production systems achieves close coordination among workstations. It smooths the flow of goods, despite low quantities of inventory. JIT production systems aim to simultaneously (1) meet customer demand in a timely manner (2) with high-quality products and (3) at the lowest possible total cost.

Decision Point

How do materials requirements planning (MRP) systems differ from just-in-time (JIT) production systems?

Features of JIT Production Systems

A JIT production system has these features:

- Production is organized in **manufacturing cells**, groupings of all the different types of equipment used to make a given product. Materials move from one machine to another, and various operations are performed in sequence, minimizing materials-handling costs.

- Workers are hired and trained to be multiskilled and capable of performing a variety of operations and tasks, including minor repairs and routine equipment maintenance.

- Defects are aggressively eliminated. Because of the tight links between workstations in the production line and the minimal inventories at each workstation, defects arising at one workstation quickly affect other workstations in the line. JIT creates an urgency for solving problems immediately and eliminating the root causes of defects as quickly as possible. Low levels of inventories allow workers to trace problems to and solve problems at earlier workstations in the production process, where the problems likely originated.

- *Setup time*, the time required to get equipment, tools, and materials ready to start the production of a component or product, and *manufacturing cycle time*, the time from when an order is received by manufacturing until it becomes a finished good, are reduced. Setup costs correspond to the ordering costs *P* in the EOQ model. Reducing setup time and costs makes production in smaller batches economical, which in turn reduces inventory levels. Reducing manufacturing cycle time enables a company to respond faster to changes in customer demand (see also Concepts in Action).

- Suppliers are selected on the basis of their ability to deliver quality materials in a timely manner. Most companies implementing *JIT production* also implement *JIT purchasing*. JIT plants expect JIT suppliers to make timely deliveries of high-quality goods directly to the production floor.

Learning Objective 6

Identify the features and benefits of a just-in-time production system

. . . for example, organizing work in manufacturing cells, improving quality, and reducing manufacturing lead time to reduce costs and earn higher margins

We next present a relevant-cost analysis for deciding whether to implement a JIT production system.

Financial Benefits of JIT and Relevant Costs

Early advocates saw the benefit of JIT production as lower carrying costs of inventory. But there are other benefits of lower inventories: heightened emphasis on improving quality by eliminating the specific causes of rework, scrap, and waste, and lower manufacturing cycle times. In computing the relevant benefits and costs of reducing inventories in JIT production systems, the cost analyst should take into account all benefits and all costs.

Consider Hudson Corporation, a manufacturer of brass fittings. Hudson is considering implementing a JIT production system. To implement JIT production, Hudson must incur $100,000 in annual tooling costs to reduce setup times. Hudson expects that JIT will reduce average inventory by $500,000 and that relevant costs of insurance, storage, materials handling, and setup will decline by $30,000 per year. The company's required rate of return on inventory investments is 10% per year. Should Hudson implement a JIT production system? On the basis of the information provided, we would be tempted to say "no," because annual relevant total cost savings amount to $80,000 [(10% of $500,000) + $30,000)], which is less than the additional annual tooling costs of $100,000.

Our analysis, however, is incomplete. We have not considered the other benefits of lower inventories in JIT production. Hudson estimates that implementing JIT will improve quality and reduce rework on 500 units each year, resulting in savings of $50 per unit. Also, better quality and faster delivery will allow Hudson to charge $2 more per unit on the 20,000 units that it sells each year.

The annual relevant benefits and costs from implementing JIT equal the following:

Incremental savings in insurance, storage, materials handling, and set up	$ 30,000
Incremental savings in inventory carrying costs (10% × $500,000)	50,000
Incremental savings from reduced rework ($50 per unit × 500 units)	25,000
Additional contribution margin from better quality and faster delivery ($2 per unit × 20,000 units)	40,000
Incremental annual tooling costs	(100,000)
Net incremental benefit	$ 45,000

Therefore, Hudson *should* implement a JIT production system.

JIT in Service Industries

JIT purchasing and production methods can be applied in service industries as well. For example, inventories and supplies, and the associated labor costs to manage them, represent more than a third of the costs in most hospitals. By implementing a JIT purchasing and distribution system, Eisenhower Memorial Hospital in Palm Springs, California, reduced its inventories and supplies by 90% in 18 months. McDonald's has adapted JIT production practices to making hamburgers.[3] Before, McDonald's precooked a batch of hamburgers that were placed under heat lamps to stay warm until ordered. If the hamburgers didn't sell within a specified period of time, they were discarded resulting in high inventory holding costs and spoilage costs. Moreover, the quality of hamburgers deteriorated the longer they sat under the heat lamps. Finally, customers placing a special order for a hamburger (such as a hamburger with no cheese) had to wait for the hamburger to be cooked. Today, the use of new technology (including an innovative bun toaster) and JIT production practices allow McDonald's to cook hamburgers only when they are ordered, significantly reducing inventory holding and spoilage costs. More importantly, JIT has improved customer satisfaction by increasing the quality of hamburgers and reducing the time needed for special orders.

We next turn our attention to planning and control in JIT production systems.

Enterprise Resource Planning (ERP) Systems[4]

The success of a JIT production system hinges on the speed of information flows from customers to manufacturers to suppliers. Information flows are a problem for large companies that have fragmented information systems spread over dozens of unlinked computer systems. Enterprise Resource Planning (ERP) systems improve these information flows. An ERP system is an integrated set of software modules covering accounting, distribution, manufacturing, purchasing, human resources, and other functions. ERP uses a single database to collect and feed data into all software applications, allowing integrated, real-time information sharing and providing visibility to the company's business processes as a whole. For example, using an ERP system, a salesperson can

---

[3] Charles Atkinson, "McDonald's, A Guide to the Benefits of JIT," *Inventory Management Review*, www.inventorymanagementreview.org/2005/11/mcdonalds_a_gui.html (accessed May 2, 2007).

[4] For an excellent discussion, see T. H. Davenport, "Putting the Enterprise into the Enterprise System," *Harvard Business Review*, (July–August 1998); also see A. Cagilo, "Enterprise Resource Planning Systems and Accountants: Towards Hybridization?" *European Accounting Review*, (May 2003).

Concepts in Action | After the Encore: Just-in-Time Live Concert Recordings

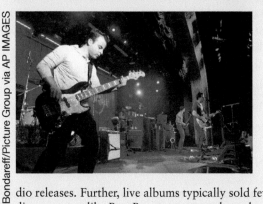

Diane Bondareff/Picture Group via AP IMAGES

Each year, millions of music fans flock to concerts to see artists ranging from Lady Gaga to rock-band O.A.R. Although many of them stop by the merchandise stand to pick up a t-shirt or poster after the show ends, they increasingly have another option: buying a professional recording of the concert they just saw! Just-in-time production, enabled by recent advances in audio and computer technology, now allows fans to relive the live concert experience just a few minutes after the final chord is played.

Live concert recordings have long been hampered by production and distribution difficulties. Traditionally, fans could only hear these recordings via unofficial "bootleg" cassettes or CDs. Occasionally, artists would release official live albums between studio releases. Further, live albums typically sold few copies, and retail outlets that profit from volume-driven merchandise turnover, like Best Buy, were somewhat reluctant to carry them.

Enter instant concert recordings. Organizations such as Adreea, Concert Live, and Live Nation employ microphones, recording and audio mixing hardware and software, and an army of high-speed computers to produce concert recordings during the show. As soon as each song is complete, engineers burn that track onto hundreds of CDs or USB drives. At the end of the show, they have to burn only one last song. Once completed, the CDs or USB drives are packaged and rushed to merchandise stands throughout the venue for instant sale.

There are, of course, some limitations to this technology. With such a quick turnaround time, engineers cannot edit or remaster any aspect of the show. Also, although just-in-time live recordings work successfully in smaller venues, the logistics for arenas, amphitheatres, and stadiums are much more difficult. Despite these concerns, the benefits of this new technology include sound-quality assurance, near-immediate production turnaround, and low finished-goods carrying costs. These recordings can also be distributed through Apple's iTunes platform and artist Web sites, making live recordings more accessible than ever. With such opportunities, it's no wonder that bands like O.A.R. augment their existing CD sales with just-in-time recordings.

Sources: Buskirk, Eliot Van. 2009. Apple unveils 'live music' in iTunes. *Wired.* "Epicenter," blog November 24. www.wired.com/epicenter/2009/11/apple-unveils-live-music-in-itunes/ Chartrand, Sabra. 2004. How to take the concert home. *New York Times,* May 3. www.nytimes.com/2004/05/03/technology/03patent.html *Daily Telegraph.* 2009. Online exclusive: How Concert Live co-founders overcame barriers. February 3. www.telegraph.co.uk/sponsored/business/businesstruth/diary_of_a/4448290/Online-Exclusive-How-Concert-Live-co-founders-overcame-barriers.html Humphries, Stephen. 2003. Get your official 'bootleg' here. *Christian Science Monitor,* November 21. www.csmonitor.com/2003/1121/p16s01-almp.html *Websites:* Live O.A.R. http://liveoar.com/store/first_index.php Aderra. www.aderra.net/ Concert Live. www.concertlive.co.uk/

generate a contract for a customer in Germany, verify the customer's credit limits, and place a production order. The system then uses this same information to schedule manufacturing in, say, Brazil, requisition materials from inventory, order components from suppliers, and schedule shipments. At the same time, it credits sales commissions to the salesperson and records all the costing and financial accounting information.

ERP systems give lower-level managers, workers, customers, and suppliers access to detailed and timely operating information. This benefit, coupled with tight coordination across business functions of the value chain, enables ERP systems to shift manufacturing and distribution plans rapidly in response to changes in supply and demand. Companies believe that an ERP system is essential to support JIT initiatives because of the effect it has on lead times. Using an ERP system, Autodesk, a maker of computer-aided design software, reduced order lead time from two weeks to one day; and Fujitsu reduced lead time from 18 days to 1.5 days.

ERP systems are large and unwieldy. Because of its complexity, suppliers of ERP systems such as SAP and Oracle provide software packages that are standard but that can be customized, although at considerable cost. Without some customization, unique and distinctive features that confer strategic advantage will not be available. The challenge when implementing ERP systems is to strike the proper balance between the lower cost of standardized systems and the strategic benefits that accrue from customization.

Performance Measures and Control in JIT Production

In addition to personal observation, managers use financial and nonfinancial measures to evaluate and control JIT production. We describe these measures and indicate the effect that JIT systems are expected to have on these measures.

1. Financial performance measures, such as inventory turnover ratio (Cost of goods sold ÷ Average inventory), which is expected to increase
2. Nonfinancial performance measures of inventory, quality, and time such as the following:
   - Number of days of inventory on hand, expected to decrease
   - Units produced per hour, expected to increase
   - $\dfrac{\text{Number of units scrapped or requiring rework}}{\text{Total number of units started and completed}}$, expected to decrease
   - Manufacturing cycle time, expected to decrease
   - $\dfrac{\text{Total setup time for machines}}{\text{Total manufacturing time}}$, expected to decrease

Personal observation and nonfinancial performance measures provide the most timely, intuitive, and easy to understand measures of manufacturing performance. Rapid, meaningful feedback is critical because the lack of inventories in a demand-pull system makes it urgent to detect and solve problems quickly. JIT measures can also be incorporated into the four perspectives of the balanced scorecard (financial, customer, internal business process, and learning and growth). The logic is as follows: Multiskilled, and well-trained employees (learning and growth measures) improve internal business processes measured by the preceding inventory, quality, and time measures. As operational performance improves, customer satisfaction also increases because of greater flexibility, responsiveness, and quality resulting in better financial performance from lower purchasing, inventory holding, and quality costs, and higher revenues.

Effect of JIT Systems on Product Costing

Decision Point

What are the features and benefits of a JIT production system?

By reducing materials handling, warehousing, and inspection, JIT systems reduce overhead costs. JIT systems also aid in direct tracing of some costs usually classified as indirect. For example, the use of manufacturing cells makes it cost-effective to trace materials handling and machine operating costs to specific products or product families made in these cells. These costs then become direct costs of those products. Also, the use of multiskilled workers in these cells allows the costs of setup, maintenance, and quality inspection to be traced as direct costs. These changes have prompted some companies using JIT to adopt simplified product costing methods that dovetail with JIT production and that are less costly to operate than traditional costing systems. We examine two of these methods next: backflush costing and lean accounting.

Backflush Costing

Organizing manufacturing in cells, reducing defects and manufacturing cycle time, and ensuring timely delivery of materials enables purchasing, production, and sales to occur in quick succession with minimal inventories. The absence of inventories makes choices about cost-flow assumptions (such as weighted average or first-in, first-out) or inventory-costing methods (such as absorption or variable costing) unimportant: All manufacturing costs of the accounting period flow directly into cost of goods sold. The rapid conversion of direct materials into finished goods that are immediately sold greatly simplifies the costing system.

Simplified Normal or Standard Costing Systems

Learning Objective 7

Describe different ways backflush costing can simplify traditional inventory-costing systems

. . . for example, by not recording journal entries for work in process, purchase of materials, or production of finished goods

Traditional normal or standard-costing systems use **sequential tracking,** which is a costing system in which recording of the journal entries occurs in the same order as actual purchases and progress in production. Costs are tracked sequentially as products pass through each of the following four stages:

A sequential-tracking costing system has four *trigger points*, corresponding to Stages A, B, C, and D. A **trigger point** is a stage in the cycle, from purchase of direct materials and incurring of conversion costs (Stage A) to sale of finished goods (Stage D), at which journal entries are made in the accounting system. The journal entries (with Dr. representing debits and Cr. representing credits) for each stage are displayed below the box for that stage.

An alternative approach to sequential tracking is backflush costing. **Backflush costing** is a costing system that omits recording some of the journal entries relating to the stages from purchase of direct materials to the sale of finished goods. When journal entries for one or more stages are omitted, the journal entries for a subsequent stage use normal or standard costs to work backward to "flush out" the costs in the cycle for which journal entries were *not* made. When inventories are minimal, as in JIT production systems, backflush costing simplifies costing systems without losing much information.

Consider the following data for the month of April for Silicon Valley Computer (SVC), which produces keyboards for personal computers.

- There are no beginning inventories of direct materials and no beginning or ending work-in-process inventories.

- SVC has only one direct manufacturing cost category (direct materials) and one indirect manufacturing cost category (conversion costs). All manufacturing labor costs are included in conversion costs.

- From its bill of materials and an operations list (description of operations to be undergone), SVC determines that the standard direct material cost per keyboard unit is $19 and the standard conversion cost is $12.

- SVC purchases $1,950,000 of direct materials. To focus on the basic concepts, we assume SVC has no direct materials variances. Actual conversion costs equal $1,260,000. SVC produces 100,000 good keyboard units and sells 99,000 units.

- Any underallocated or overallocated conversion costs are written off to cost of goods sold at the end of April.

We use three examples to illustrate backflush costing. *They differ in the number and placement of trigger points.*

Example 1: The three trigger points for journal entries are Purchase of direct materials and incurring of conversion costs (Stage A), Completion of good finished units of product (Stage C), and Sale of finished goods (Stage D).

Note that there is no journal entry for Production resulting in work in process (Stage B) because JIT production has minimal work in process.

SVC records two inventory accounts:

Type	Account Title
Combined materials inventory and materials in work in process	Materials and In-Process Inventory Control
Finished goods	Finished Goods Control

Exhibit 7, Panel A, summarizes the journal entries for Example 1 with three trigger points: Purchase of direct materials and incurring of conversion costs, Completion of good

| Exhibit 7 | Journal Entries and General Ledger Overview for Backflush Costing and Journal Entries for Sequential Tracking with Three Trigger Points: Purchase of Direct Materials and Incurring of Conversion Costs, Completion of Good Finished Units of Product, and Sale of Finished Goods |

PANEL A: Journal Entries

Backflush Costing			Sequential Tracking		

Stage A: Record Purchase of Direct Materials and Incurring of Conversion Costs

1. Record Direct Materials Purchased.

Entry (A1)	Materials and In-Process Inventory Control	1,950,000	Materials Inventory Control	1,950,000	
	Accounts Payable Control		1,950,000	Accounts Payable Control		1,950,000

2. Record Conversion Costs Incurred.

Entry (A2)	Conversion Costs Control	1,260,000	Conversion Costs Control	1,260,000	
	Various accounts (such as Wages		Various accounts (such as Wages		1,260,000
	Payable Control)		1,260,000	Payable Control)	

Stage B: Record Production Resulting in Work in Process.

Entry (B1)	No Entry Recorded		Work-in-Process Control	3,100,000	
			Materials Inventory Control		1,900,000
			Conversion Costs Allocated		1,200,000

Stage C: Record Cost of Good Finished Units Completed.

Entry (C1)	Finished Goods Control	3,100,000	Finished Goods Control	3,100,000	
	Materials and In-Process Inventory Control		1,900,000	Work-in-Process Control		3,100,000
	Conversion Costs Allocated		1,200,000		

Stage D: Record Cost of Finished Goods Sold (and Under- or Overallocated Conversion Costs).

1. Record Cost of Finished Goods Sold.

Entry (D1)	Cost of Goods Sold	3,069,000	Cost of Goods Sold	3,069,000	
	Finished Goods Control		3,069,000	Finished Goods Control		3,069,000

2. Record Underallocated or Overallocated Conversion Costs.

Entry (D2)	Conversion Costs Allocated	1,200,000	Conversion Costs Allocated	1,200,000	
	Cost of Goods Sold	60,000	Cost of Goods Sold	60,000	
	Conversion Costs Control		1,260,000	Conversion Costs Control		1,260,000

PANEL B: General Ledger Overview for Backflush Costing

The coding that appears in parentheses for each entry indicates the stage in the production process that the entry relates to as presented in the text.

finished units of product, and Sale of finished goods (and recognizing under- or overallocated costs). For each stage, the backflush costing entries for SVC are shown on the left. The comparable entries under sequential tracking (costing) are shown on the right.

Consider first the entries for purchase of direct materials and incurring of conversion costs (Stage A). As described earlier, the inventory account under backflush costing combines direct materials and work in process. When materials are purchased, these costs increase (are debited to) Materials and In-Process Inventory Control. Under the sequential tracking approach, the direct materials and work in process accounts are separate, so the purchase of direct materials is debited to Materials Inventory Control. Actual conversion costs are recorded as incurred under backflush costing, just as in sequential tracking, and they increase (are debited to) Conversion Costs Control.

Next consider the entries for production resulting in work in process (Stage B). Recall that 100,000 units were started into production in April and that the standard cost for the units produced is $31 ($19 direct materials + $12 conversion costs) per unit. Under backflush costing, no entry is recorded in Stage B because work-in-process inventory is minimal and all units are quickly converted to finished goods. Under sequential tracking, work-in-process inventory is increased as manufacturing occurs and later decreased as manufacturing is completed and the product becomes a finished good.

The entries to record completion of good finished units of product (Stage C) gives backflush costing its name. Costs have not been recorded sequentially with the flow of product along its production route through work in process and finished goods. Instead, the output trigger point reaches *back* and pulls ("*flushes*") the standard direct material costs from Materials and In-Process Inventory Control and the standard conversion costs for manufacturing the finished goods. Under the sequential tracking approach, Finished Goods Control is debited (increased) and Work-in-Process Control is credited (decreased) as manufacturing is completed and finished goods are produced. The net effect of Stages B and C under sequential tracking is the same as the effect under backflush costing (except for the name of the inventory account).

Finally consider entries to record the sale of finished goods (and under- or overallocated conversion costs) (Stage D). The standard cost of 99,000 units sold in April equals $3,069,000 (99,000 units × $31 per unit). The entries to record the cost of finished goods sold are exactly the same under backflush costing and sequential tracking.

Actual conversion costs may be underallocated or overallocated in an accounting period. Companies that use backflush costing typically have low inventories, so proration of underallocated or overallocated conversion costs between work in process, finished goods, and cost of goods sold is seldom necessary. Many companies write off underallocated or overallocated conversion costs to cost of goods sold only at the end of the fiscal year. Other companies, like SVC, record the write-off monthly. The journal entry to dispose of the difference between actual conversion costs incurred and standard conversion costs allocated is exactly the same under backflush costing and sequential tracking.

The April 30 ending inventory balances under backflush costing are as follows:

Materials and In-Process Inventory Control ($1,950,000 − $1,900,000)	$50,000
Finished Goods Control, 1,000 units × $31/unit ($3,100,000 − $3,069,000)	31,000
Total	$81,000

The April 30 ending inventory balances under sequential tracking would be exactly the same except that the inventory account would be Materials Inventory Control. Exhibit 7, Panel B, provides a general-ledger overview of this version of backflush costing.

The elimination of the typical Work-in-Process Control account reduces the amount of detail in the accounting system. Units on the production line may still be tracked in physical terms, but there is "no assignment of costs" to specific work orders while they are in the production cycle. In fact, there are no work orders or labor-time records in the accounting system.

The three trigger points to make journal entries in Example 1 will lead SVC's backflush costing system to report costs that are similar to the costs reported under sequential tracking when SVC has minimal work-in-process inventory. In Example 1, any inventories of direct materials or finished goods are recognized in SVC's backflush costing system when they first appear (as would be done in a costing system using sequential tracking). International Paper Company uses a method similar to Example 1 in its specialty papers plant.

Accounting for Variances Accounting for variances between actual and standard costs is basically the same under all standard-costing systems. Suppose that in Example 1, SVC had an unfavorable direct materials price variance of $42,000. Then the journal entry would be as follows:

Materials and In-Process Inventory Control	1,950,000	
Direct Materials Price Variance	42,000	
Accounts Payable Control		1,992,000

Direct material costs are often a large proportion of total manufacturing costs, sometimes well over 60%. Consequently, many companies will at least measure the direct materials efficiency variance in total by physically comparing what remains in direct materials inventory against what should remain based on the output of finished goods for the accounting period. In our example, suppose that such a comparison showed an unfavorable materials efficiency variance of $30,000. The journal entry would be as follows:

Direct Materials Efficiency Variance	30,000	
Materials and In-Process Inventory Control		30,000

The underallocated or overallocated conversion costs are split into various overhead variances (spending variance, efficiency variance, and production-volume variance). Each variance is closed to cost of goods sold, if it is immaterial in amount.

Example 2: The two trigger points are Purchase of direct materials and incurring of conversion costs (Stage A) and Sale of finished goods (Stage D).

This example uses the SVC data to illustrate a backflush costing that differs more from sequential tracking than the backflush costing in Example 1. This example and Example 1 have the same first trigger point, purchase of direct materials and incurring of conversion costs. But the second trigger point in Example 2 is the sale, not the completion, of finished goods. *Note that in this example, there is no journal entry for Production resulting in work in progress (Stage B) and Completion of good finished units of product (Stage C) because there are minimal work in process and finished goods inventories.*

In this example, there is only one inventory account: direct materials, whether they are in storerooms, in process, or in finished goods.

Type	Account Title
Combines direct materials inventory and any direct materials in work-in-process and finished goods inventories	Inventory Control

Exhibit 8, Panel A, summarizes the journal entries for Example 2 with two trigger points: Purchase of direct materials and incurring of conversion costs, and Sale of finished goods (and recognizing under- or overallocated costs). As in Example 1, for each stage, the backflush costing entries for SVC are shown on the left. The comparable entries under sequential tracking are shown on the right.

The entries for direct materials purchased and conversion costs incurred (Stage A) are the same as in Example 1, except that the inventory account is called Inventory Control. As in Example 1, no entry is made to record production of work-in-process inventory (Stage B) because work-in-process inventory is minimal. When finished goods are completed (Stage C), no entry is recorded because the completed units are expected to be sold quickly and finished goods inventory is expected to be minimal. As finished goods are sold (Stage D), the cost of goods sold is calculated as 99,000 units sold × $31 per unit = $3,069,000, which is composed of direct material costs (99,000 units × $19 per unit = $1,881,000) and conversion costs allocated (99,000 units × $12 per unit = $1,188,000). This is the same Cost of Goods Sold calculated under sequential tracking as described in Example 1.

Exhibit 8   Journal Entries and General Ledger Overview for Backflush Costing and Journal Entries for Sequential Tracking with Two Trigger Points: Purchase of Direct Materials and Incurring of Conversion Costs and Sale of Finished Goods

PANEL A: Journal Entries

Backflush Costing			Sequential Tracking		

Stage A: Record Purchase of Direct Materials and Incurring of Conversion Costs

1. Record Direct Materials Purchased.

Entry (A1)	Inventory: Control	1,950,000	Materials Inventory Control	1,950,000	
	Accounts Payable Control		1,950,000	Accounts Payable Control		1,950,000

2. Record Conversion Costs Incurred.

Entry (A2)	Conversion Costs Control	1,260,000	Conversion Costs Control	1,260,000	
	Various accounts (such as Wages		Various accounts (such as Wages		1,260,000
	Payable Control)		1,260,000	Payable Control)	

Stage B: Record Production Resulting in Work in Process.

Entry (B1)	No Entry Recorded		Work-in-Process Control	3,100,000	
			Materials Inventory Control		1,900,000
			Conversion Costs Allocated		1,200,000

Stage C: Record Cost of Good Finished Units Completed.

Entry (C1)	No Entry Recorded		Finished Goods Control	3,100,000	
			Work-in-Process Control		3,100,000

Stage D: Record Cost of Finished Goods Sold (and Under- or Overallocated Conversion Costs).

1. Record Cost of Finished Goods Sold.

Entry (D1)	Cost of Goods Sold	3,069,000	Cost of Goods Sold	3,069,000	
	Inventory Control		1,881,000	Finished Goods Control		3,069,000
	Conversion Costs Allocated		1,188,000		

2. Record Underallocated or Overallocated Conversion Costs.

Entry (D2)	Conversion Costs Allocated	1,188,000	Conversion Costs Allocated	1,200,000	
	Cost of Goods Sold	72,000	Cost of Goods Sold	60,000	
	Conversion Costs Control		1,260,000	Conversion Costs Control		1,260,000

PANEL B: General Ledger Overview for Backflush Costing

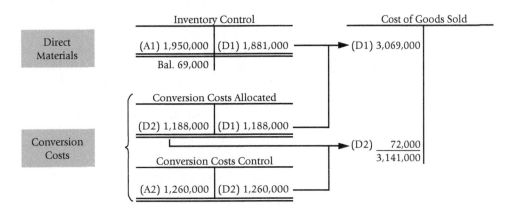

The coding that appears in parentheses for each entry indicates the stage in the production process that the entry relates to as presented in the text.

Under this method of backflush costing, conversion costs are not inventoried because no entries are recorded when finished goods are produced in Stage C. That is, compared with sequential tracking, Example 2 does not assign $12,000 ($12 per unit × 1,000 units) of conversion costs to finished goods inventory produced but not sold. Of the $1,260,000 in conversion costs, $1,188,000 is allocated at standard cost to the units sold. The remaining $72,000 ($1,260,000 − $1,188,000) of conversion costs is underallocated. Entry (D2) presents the journal entry if SVC, like many companies, writes off these underallocated costs monthly as additions to cost of goods sold.

The April 30 ending balance of Inventory Control is $69,000 ($1,950,000 − $1,881,000). This balance represents the $50,000 direct materials still on hand + $19,000 direct materials embodied in the 1,000 good finished units manufactured but not sold during the period. Exhibit 8, Panel B, provides a general-ledger overview of Example 2. The approach described in Example 2 closely approximates the costs computed using sequential tracking when a company holds minimal work-in-process and finished goods inventories.

Toyota's cost accounting system at its Kentucky plant is similar to this example. Two advantages of this system are (1) it removes the incentive for managers to produce for inventory because conversion costs are recorded as period costs instead of inventoriable costs and (2) it focuses managers on sales.

Example 3: The two trigger points are Completion of good finished units of product (Stage C) and Sale of finished goods (Stage D).

This example has two trigger points. In contrast to Example 2, the first trigger point in Example 3 is delayed until Stage C, SVC's completion of good finished units of product. *Note that in this example, there are no journal entries for Purchase of direct materials and incurring of conversion costs (Stage A) and Production resulting in work in process (Stage B) because there are minimal direct materials and work-in-process inventories.*

Exhibit 9, Panel A, summarizes the journal entries for Example 3 with two trigger points: Completion of good finished units of product and Sale of finished goods (and recognizing under- or overallocated costs). As in Examples 1 and 2, for each stage, the backflush costing entries for SVC are shown on the left. The comparable entries under sequential tracking are shown on the right.

No entry is made for direct materials purchases of $1,950,000 (Stage A) because the acquisition of direct materials is not a trigger point in this form of backflush costing. As in Examples 1 and 2, actual conversion costs are recorded as incurred and no entry is made to record production resulting in work-in-process inventory (Stage B). The cost of 100,000 good finished units completed (Stage C) is recorded at standard cost of $31 ($19 direct materials + $12 conversion costs) per unit as in Example 1 except that Accounts Payable Control is credited (instead of Materials and In-Process Inventory Control) because no entry had been made when direct materials were purchased in Stage A. Note that at the end of April, $50,000 of direct materials purchased have not yet been placed into production ($1,950,000 − $1,900,000 = $50,000), nor have the cost of those direct materials been entered into the inventory-costing system. The Example 3 version of backflush costing is suitable for a JIT production system in which both direct materials inventory and work-in-process inventory are minimal. As finished goods are sold (Stage D), the cost of goods sold is calculated as 99,000 units sold × $31 per unit = $3,069,000. This is the same Cost of Goods sold calculated under sequential tracking. Finished Goods Control has a balance of $31,000 under both this form of backflush costing and sequential tracking. The journal entry to dispose of the difference between actual conversion costs incurred and standard conversion costs allocated is the same under backflush costing and sequential tracking. The only difference between this form of backflush costing and sequential tracking is that direct materials inventory of $50,000 (and the corresponding Accounts Payable Control) is not recorded, which is no problem if direct materials inventories are minimal. Exhibit 9, Panel B, provides a general-ledger overview of Example 3.

Exhibit 9 — Journal Entries and General Ledger Overview for Backflush Costing and Journal Entries for Sequential Tracking with Two Trigger Points: Completion of Good Finished Units of Product and Sale of Finished Goods

PANEL A: Journal Entries

	Backflush Costing			Sequential Tracking		

Stage A: Record Purchase of Direct Materials and Incurring of Conversion Costs.

1. Record Direct Materials Purchased.

	Backflush Costing			Sequential Tracking		
Entry (A1)	No Entry Recorded			Materials Inventory Control	1,950,000	
				Accounts Payable Control		1,950,000

2. Record Conversion Costs Incurred.

Entry (A2)	Conversion Costs Control	1,260,000		Conversion Costs Control	1,260,000	
	Various accounts (such as Wages			Various accounts (such as Wages		1,260,000
	Payable Control)		1,260,000	Payable Control)		

Stage B: Record Production Resulting in Work in Process.

Entry (B1)	No Entry Recorded			Work-in-Process Control	3,100,000	
				Materials Inventory Control		1,900,000
				Conversion Costs Allocated		1,200,000

Stage C: Record Cost of Good Finished Units Completed.

Entry (C1)	Finished Goods Control	3,100,000		Finished Goods Control	3,100,000	
	Accounts Payable Control		1,900,000	Work-in-Process Control		3,100,000
	Conversion Costs Allocated		1,200,000			

Stage D: Record Cost of Finished Goods Sold (and Under- or Overallocated Conversion Costs).

1. Record Cost of Finished Goods Sold.

Entry (D1)	Cost of Goods Sold	3,069,000		Cost of Goods Sold	3,069,000	
	Finished Goods Control		3,069,000	Finished Goods Control		3,069,000

2. Record Underallocated or Overallocated Conversion Costs.

Entry (D2)	Conversion Costs Allocated	1,200,000		Conversion Costs Allocated	1,200,000	
	Cost of Goods Sold	60,000		Cost of Goods Sold	60,000	
	Conversion Costs Control		1,260,000	Conversion Costs Control		1,260,000

PANEL B: General Ledger Overview for Backflush Costing

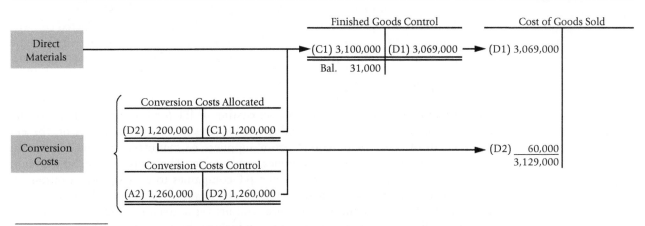

The coding that appears in parentheses for each entry indicates the stage in the production process that the entry relates to as presented in the text.

Extending Example 3, backflush costing systems could use the sale of finished goods as the only trigger point. This version of backflush costing is most suitable for a JIT production system with minimal direct materials, work-in-process, and finished goods inventories. That's because this backflush costing system maintains no inventory accounts.

Special Considerations in Backflush Costing

The accounting procedures illustrated in Examples 1, 2, and 3 do not strictly adhere to generally accepted accounting principles (GAAP). For example, work in process inventory, which is an asset, exists although it is not recognized in the financial accounting system. Advocates of backflush costing, however, cite the generally accepted accounting principle of materiality in support of the various versions of backflush costing. As the three examples illustrate, backflush costing can approximate the costs that would be reported under sequential tracking by varying the number of trigger points and where they are located. If significant amounts of direct materials inventory or finished goods inventory exist, adjusting entries can be incorporated into backflush costing (as explained next).

Suppose there are material differences in operating income and inventories based on a backflush costing system and a conventional standard-costing system. A journal entry can be recorded to adjust the backflush number to satisfy GAAP. For example, the backflush entries in Example 2 would result in expensing all conversion costs to Cost of Goods Sold ($1,188,000 at standard costs + $72,000 write-off of underallocated conversion costs = $1,260,000). But suppose conversion costs were regarded as sufficiently material in amount to be included in Inventory Control. Then entry (D2) in Example 2, closing the Conversion Costs accounts, would change as follows:

Original entry (D2)	Conversion Costs Allocated	1,188,000	
	Cost of Goods Sold	72,000	
	Conversion Costs Control		1,260,000
Revised entry (D2)	Conversion Costs Allocated	1,188,000	
	Inventory Control (1,000 units × $12)	12,000	
	Cost of Goods Sold	60,000	
	Conversion Costs Control		1,260,000

Critics say backflush costing leaves no audit trails—the ability of the accounting system to pinpoint the uses of resources at each step of the production process. However, the absence of sizable amounts of materials inventory, work-in-process inventory, and finished goods inventory means managers can keep track of operations by personal observations, computer monitoring, and nonfinancial measures.

What are the implications of JIT and backflush costing systems for activity-based costing (ABC) systems? Simplifying the production process, as in a JIT system, makes more of the costs direct and reduces the extent of overhead cost allocations. Simple ABC systems are often adequate for companies implementing JIT. These simple ABC systems work well with backflush costing. Costs from ABC systems yield more-accurate budgeted conversion cost per unit for different products in the backflush costing system. The activity-based cost information is also useful for product costing, decision making, and cost management.

Lean Accounting

Another approach for simplified product costing in JIT (or lean production) systems is *lean accounting*. Successful JIT production requires companies to focus on the entire value chain of business functions (from suppliers to manufacturing to customers) in order to reduce inventories, lead times, and waste. The emphasis on improvements throughout the value chain has led some JIT companies to develop organization structures and costing systems that focus on **value streams**, which are all the value-added activities needed to design, manufacture, and deliver a given product or product line to customers. For example, a value stream can include the activities needed to develop and engineer products, advertise and market those products, process orders, purchase and receive materials, manufacture and ship orders, bill customers, and collect payments. The focus on value streams is aided by the use of manufacturing cells in JIT systems that group together the operations needed to make a given product or product line.

Decision Point

How does backflush costing simplify traditional inventory costing?

Learning Objective 8

Understand the principles of lean accounting

. . . focus on costing value streams rather than products, and limit arbitrary allocations

Lean accounting is a costing method that supports creating value for customers by costing the value streams, as distinguished from individual products or departments, thereby eliminating waste in the accounting process.[5] If multiple, related products are made in a single value stream, product costs for the individual products are not computed. Actual costs are directly traced to the value stream and standard costs and variances are not computed. Tracing direct costs to value streams is simple because companies using lean accounting dedicate resources to individual value streams.

Consider the following product costs for Allston Company that makes two models of designer purses in one manufacturing cell and two models of designer wallets in another manufacturing cell.

	Purses		Wallets	
	Model A	**Model B**	**Model C**	**Model D**
Revenues	$600,000	$700,000	$800,000	$550,000
Direct materials	340,000	400,000	410,000	270,000
Direct manufacturing labor	70,000	78,000	105,000	82,000
Manufacturing overhead costs (e.g., equipment lease, supervision, and unused facility costs)	112,000	130,000	128,000	103,000
Rework costs	15,000	17,000	14,000	10,000
Design costs	20,000	21,000	24,000	18,000
Marketing and sales costs	30,000	33,000	40,000	28,000
Total costs	587,000	679,000	721,000	511,000
Operating income	$ 13,000	$ 21,000	$ 79,000	$ 39,000
Direct materials purchased	$350,000	$420,000	$430,000	$285,000
Unused facility costs	$ 22,000	$ 38,000	$ 18,000	$ 15,000

Using lean accounting principles, Allston calculates value-stream operating costs and operating income for purses and wallets, not individual models, as follows:

	Purses	Wallets
Revenues ($600,000 + $700,000; $800,000 + $550,000)	$1,300,000	$1,350,000
Direct material purchases ($350,000 + $420,000; $430,000 + $285,000)	770,000	715,000
Direct manufacturing labor (70,000 + $78,000; $105,000 + $82,000)	148,000	187,000
Manufacturing overhead (after deducting unused facility costs) ($112,000 – $22,000) + ($130,000 – $38,000); ($128,000 – $18,000) + $103,000 – $15,000)	182,000	198,000
Design costs ($20,000 + $21,000; $24,000 + $18,000)	41,000	42,000
Marketing and sales costs ($30,000 + $33,000; $40,000 + $28,000)	63,000	68,000
Total value stream operating costs	1,204,000	1,210,000
Value stream operating income	$ 96,000	$ 140,000

Allston Company, like many lean accounting systems, expenses the costs of all purchased materials in the period in which they are bought to signal that direct material and work-in-process inventory need to be reduced. In our example, the cost of direct material purchases under lean accounting exceeds the cost of direct materials used in the operating income statement.

Facility costs (such as depreciation, property taxes, and leases) are allocated to value streams based on the square footage used by each value stream to encourage managers to use less space for holding and moving inventory. Note that unused facility costs are subtracted when calculating manufacturing overhead costs of value streams. These costs are instead treated as plant or business unit expenses. Excluding unused facility costs from value stream costs means that only those costs that add value are included in value-stream costs.

---

[5] See B. Baggaley, "Costing by Value Stream," *Journal of Cost Management* (May–June 2003).

Moreover, increasing the visibility of unused capacity costs creates incentives to reduce these costs or to find alternative uses for capacity. Allston Company excludes rework costs when calculating value-stream costs and operating income because these costs are nonvalue-added costs. Companies also exclude from value stream costs common costs such as corporate or support department costs that cannot reasonably be assigned to value streams.

The analysis indicates that while total cost for purses is $1,266,000 ($587,000 + $679,000), the value stream cost using lean accounting is $1,204,000 (95.1% of $1,266,000), indicating significant opportunities for improving profitability by reducing unused facility and rework costs, and by purchasing direct materials only as needed for production. Wallets portray a different picture. Total cost for wallets is $1,232,000 ($721,000 + $511,000) while the value-stream cost using lean accounting is $1,210,000 (98.2% of $1,232,000). The wallets value stream has low unused facility and rework costs and is more efficient.

Lean accounting is much simpler than traditional product costing. Why? Because calculating actual product costs by value streams requires less overhead allocation. Compared to traditional product costing methods, the focus on value streams and costs is consistent with the emphasis of JIT and lean production on improvements in the value chain from suppliers to customers. Moreover, the practices that lean accounting encourages (such as reducing direct material and work-in-process inventories, improving quality, using less space, and eliminating unused capacity) reflect the goals of JIT production.

A potential limitation of lean accounting is that it does not compute costs for individual products. Critics charge that this limits its usefulness for decision making. Proponents of lean accounting argue that the lack of individual product costs is not a problem because most decisions are made at the product line level rather than the individual product level, and that pricing decisions are based on the value created for the customer (market prices) and not product costs.

Another criticism is that lean accounting excludes certain support costs and unused capacity costs. As a result, the decisions based on only value stream costs will look profitable because they do not consider all costs. Supporters argue that lean accounting overcomes this problem by adding a larger markup on value stream costs to compensate for some of these excluded costs. Moreover, in a competitive market, prices will eventually settle at a level that represents a reasonable markup above value stream costs because customers will be unwilling to pay for nonvalue-added costs. The goal must therefore be to eliminate nonvalue-added costs. A final criticism is that lean accounting, like backflush costing, does not correctly account for inventories under generally accepted accounting principles (GAAP). However, proponents are quick to point out that in lean accounting environments, work in process and finished goods inventories are immaterial from an accounting perspective.

Decision Point ▶

How is lean accounting different from traditional costing systems?

Problems for Self-Study

Problem 1

Lee Company has a Singapore plant that manufactures MP3 players. One component is an XT chip. Expected demand is for 5,200 of these chips in March 2011. Lee estimates the ordering cost per purchase order to be $250. The monthly carrying cost for one unit of XT in stock is $5.

Required
1. Compute the EOQ for the XT chip.
2. Compute the number of deliveries of XT in March 2011.

Solution

$$EOQ = \sqrt{\frac{2 \times 5{,}200 \times \$250}{\$5}}$$

$$= 721 \text{ chips (rounded)}$$

$$\text{Number of deliveries} = \frac{5{,}200}{721}$$

$$= 8 \text{ (rounded)}$$

Problem 2

Littlefield Company uses a backflush costing system with three trigger points:

- Purchase of direct materials
- Completion of good finished units of product
- Sale of finished goods

There are no beginning inventories. Information for April 2011 is as follows:

Direct materials purchased	$880,000	Conversion costs allocated	$ 400,000
Direct materials used	$850,000	Costs transferred to finished goods	$1,250,000
Conversion costs incurred	$422,000	Cost of goods sold	$1,190,000

1. Prepare journal entries for April (without disposing of underallocated or overallo- **Required**
   cated conversion costs). Assume there are no direct materials variances.
2. Under an ideal JIT production system, how would the amounts in your journal
   entries differ from the journal entries in requirement 1?

Solution

1. Journal entries for April are as follows:

Entry (A1)	Materials and In-Process Inventory Control	880,000	
	Accounts Payable Control		880,000
	(direct materials purchased)		
Entry (A2)	Conversion Costs Control	422,000	
	Various accounts (such as Wages Payable Control)		422,000
	(conversion costs incurred)		
Entry (C1)	Finished Goods Control	1,250,000	
	Materials and In-Process Inventory Control		850,000
	Conversion Costs Allocated		400,000
	(standard cost of finished goods completed)		
Entry (D1)	Cost of Goods Sold	1,190,000	
	Finished Goods Control		1,190,000
	(standard costs of finished goods sold)		

2. Under an ideal JIT production system, if the manufacturing lead time per unit is very
   short, there would be zero inventories at the end of each day. Entry (C1) would be
   $1,190,000 finished goods production [to match finished goods sold in entry (D1)], not
   $1,250,000. If the marketing department could only sell goods costing $1,190,000, the
   JIT production system would call for direct materials purchases and conversion costs of
   lower than $880,000 and $422,000, respectively, in entries (A1) and (A2).

Decision Points

*The following question-and-answer format summarizes the chapter's learning objectives. Each decision presents a
key question related to a learning objective. The guidelines are the answer to that question.*

Decision

Guidelines

1. What are the six categories
   of costs associated with
   goods for sale?

The six categories are purchasing costs (costs of goods acquired from suppliers),
ordering costs (costs of preparing a purchase order and receiving goods), carrying costs (costs of holding inventory of goods for sale), stockout costs (costs
arising when a customer demands a unit of product and that unit is not on
hand), costs of quality (prevention, appraisal, internal failure, and external failure costs), and shrinkage costs (the costs resulting from theft by outsiders,
embezzlement by employees, misclassifications, and clerical errors).

2. What does the EOQ decision model help managers do and how do managers decide on the level of safety stocks?

The economic-order-quantity (EOQ) decision model helps managers to calculate the optimal quantity of inventory to order by balancing ordering costs and carrying costs. The larger the order quantity, the higher the annual carrying costs and the lower the annual ordering costs. The EOQ model includes costs recorded in the financial accounting system as well as opportunity costs not recorded in the financial accounting system. Managers choose a level of safety stocks to minimize stock out costs and carrying costs of holding more inventory.

3. What is the effect on costs of errors in predicting parameters of the EOQ model? How can companies reduce the conflict between the EOQ decision model and models used for performance evaluation?

The cost of prediction errors when using the EOQ model is small. To reduce the conflict between the EOQ decision model and the performance evaluation model, companies should include the opportunity cost of investment when evaluating managers. The opportunity cost of investment tied up in inventory is a key input in the EOQ decision model that is often ignored in the performance-evaluation model.

4. Why are companies using just-in-time purchasing?

Just-in-time (JIT) purchasing is making purchases in small order quantities just as needed for production (or sales). JIT purchasing is a response to high carrying costs and low ordering costs. JIT purchasing increases the focus of companies and suppliers on quality and timely deliveries. Companies coordinate their activities and reduce inventories throughout the supply chain, from the initial sources of materials and services to the delivery of products to consumers.

5. How do materials requirements planning (MRP) systems differ from just-in-time (JIT) production systems?

Materials requirements planning (MRP) systems use a "push-through" approach that manufactures finished goods for inventory on the basis of demand forecasts. Just-in-time (JIT) production systems use a "demand-pull" approach in which goods are manufactured only to satisfy customer orders.

6. What are the features and benefits of a JIT production system?

JIT production systems (a) organize production in manufacturing cells, (b) hire and train multiskilled workers, (c) emphasize total quality management, (d) reduce manufacturing lead time and setup time, and (e) build strong supplier relationships. The benefits of JIT production include lower costs and higher margins from better flow of information, higher quality, and faster delivery.

7. How does backflush costing simplify traditional inventory costing?

Traditional inventory-costing systems use sequential tracking, in which recording of the journal entries occurs in the same order as actual purchases and progress in production. Most backflush costing systems do not record journal entries for the work-in-process stage of production. Some backflush costing systems also do not record entries for either the purchase of direct materials or the completion of finished goods.

8. How is lean accounting different from traditional costing systems?

Lean accounting costs value streams rather than products. Nonvalue-added costs, unused capacity costs and costs that cannot be easily traced to value streams are not allocated but instead expensed.

Terms to Learn

This chapter contains definitions of the following important terms:

backflush costing	lean production	reorder point
carrying costs	manufacturing cells	safety stock
economic order quantity (EOQ)	materials requirements planning (MRP)	sequential tracking
inventory management		shrinkage costs
just-in-time (JIT) production	ordering costs	stockout costs
just-in-time (JIT) purchasing	purchase-order lead time	trigger point
lean accounting	purchasing costs	value streams

Assignment Material

Questions

20-1 Why do better decisions regarding the purchasing and managing of goods for sale frequently cause dramatic percentage increases in net income?

20-2 Name six cost categories that are important in managing goods for sale in a retail company.

20-3 What assumptions are made when using the simplest version of the economic-order-quantity (EOQ) decision model?

20-4 Give examples of costs included in annual carrying costs of inventory when using the EOQ decision model.

20-5 Give three examples of opportunity costs that typically are not recorded in accounting systems, although they are relevant when using the EOQ model in the presence of demand uncertainty.

20-6 What are the steps in computing the cost of a prediction error when using the EOQ decision model?

20-7 Why might goal-congruence issues arise when an EOQ model is used to guide decisions on how much to order?

20-8 Describe JIT purchasing and its benefits.

20-9 What are three factors causing reductions in the cost to place purchase orders for materials?

20-10 "You should always choose the supplier who offers the lowest price per unit." Do you agree? Explain.

20-11 What is supply-chain analysis, and how can it benefit manufacturers and retailers?

20-12 What are the main features of JIT production?

20-13 Distinguish inventory-costing systems using sequential tracking from those using backflush costing.

20-14 Describe three different versions of backflush costing.

20-15 Discuss the differences between lean accounting and traditional cost accounting.

Exercises

20-16 Economic order quantity for retailer. Fan Base (FB) operates a megastore featuring sports merchandise. It uses an EOQ decision model to make inventory decisions. It is now considering inventory decisions for its Los Angeles Galaxy soccer jerseys product line. This is a highly popular item. Data for 2011 are as follows:

Expected annual demand for Galaxy jerseys	10,000
Ordering cost per purchase order	$200
Carrying cost per year	$7 per jersey

Each jersey costs FB $40 and sells for $80. The $7 carrying cost per jersey per year comprises the required return on investment of $4.80 (12% × $40 purchase price) plus $2.20 in relevant insurance, handling, and theft-related costs. The purchasing lead time is 7 days. FB is open 365 days a year.

Required

1. Calculate the EOQ.
2. Calculate the number of orders that will be placed each year.
3. Calculate the reorder point.

20-17 Economic order quantity, effect of parameter changes (continuation of 20-16). Athletic Textiles (AT) manufactures the Galaxy jerseys that Fan Base (FB) sells to its customers. AT has recently installed computer software that enables its customers to conduct "one-stop" purchasing using state-of-the-art Web site technology. FB's ordering cost per purchase order will be $30 using this new technology.

Required

1. Calculate the EOQ for the Galaxy jerseys using the revised ordering cost of $30 per purchase order. Assume all other data from Exercise 20-16 are the same. Comment on the result.
2. Suppose AT proposes to "assist" FB. AT will allow FB customers to order directly from the AT Web site. AT would ship directly to these customers. AT would pay $10 to FB for every Galaxy jersey purchased by one of FB's customers. Comment qualitatively on how this offer would affect inventory management at FB. What factors should FB consider in deciding whether to accept AT's proposal?

20-18 EOQ for a retailer. The Denim World sells fabrics to a wide range of industrial and consumer users. One of the products it carries is denim cloth, used in the manufacture of jeans and carrying bags. The supplier for the denim cloth pays all incoming freight. No incoming inspection of the denim is necessary because the supplier has a track record of delivering high-quality merchandise. The purchasing officer of the Denim World has collected the following information:

Annual demand for denim cloth	26,400 yards
Ordering cost per purchase order	$165
Carrying cost per year	20% of purchase costs
Safety-stock requirements	None
Cost of denim cloth	$9 per yard

The purchasing lead time is 2 weeks. The Denim World is open 250 days a year (50 weeks for 5 days a week).

Required

1. Calculate the EOQ for denim cloth.
2. Calculate the number of orders that will be placed each year.
3. Calculate the reorder point for denim cloth.

20-19 EOQ for manufacturer. Lakeland Company produces lawn mowers and purchases 18,000 units of a rotor blade part each year at a cost of $60 per unit. Lakeland requires a 15% annual rate of return on investment. In addition, the relevant carrying cost (for insurance, materials handling, breakage, and so on) is $6 per unit per year. The relevant ordering cost per purchase order is $150.

Required

1. Calculate Lakeland's EOQ for the rotor blade part.
2. Calculate Lakeland's annual relevant ordering costs for the EOQ calculated in requirement 1.
3. Calculate Lakeland's annual relevant carrying costs for the EOQ calculated in requirement 1.
4. Assume that demand is uniform throughout the year and known with certainty so that there is no need for safety stocks. The purchase-order lead time is half a month. Calculate Lakeland's reorder point for the rotor blade part.

20-20 Sensitivity of EOQ to changes in relevant ordering and carrying costs, cost of prediction error. Alpha Company's annual demand for its only product, XT-590, is 10,000 units. Alpha is currently analyzing possible combinations of relevant carrying cost per unit per year and relevant ordering cost per purchase order, depending on the company's choice of supplier and average levels of inventory. This table presents three possible combinations of carrying and ordering costs.

Relevant Carrying Cost per Unit per Year	Relevant Ordering Cost per Purchase Order
$10	$400
$20	$200
$40	$100

Required

1. For each of the relevant ordering and carrying-cost alternatives, determine (a) EOQ and (b) annual relevant total costs.
2. How does your answer to requirement 1 give insight into the impact of changes in relevant ordering and carrying costs on EOQ and annual relevant total costs? Explain briefly.
3. Suppose the relevant carrying cost per unit per year was $20 and the relevant ordering cost per purchase order was $200. Suppose further that Alpha calculates EOQ after incorrectly estimating relevant carrying cost per unit per year to be $10 and relevant ordering cost per purchase order to be $400. Calculate the actual annual relevant total costs of Alpha's EOQ decision. Compare this cost to the annual relevant total costs that Alpha would have incurred if it had correctly estimated the relevant carrying cost per unit per year of $20 and the relevant ordering cost per purchase order of $200 that you have already calculated in requirement 1. Calculate and comment on the cost of the prediction error.

20-21 Inventory management and the balanced scorecard. Devin Sports Cars (DSC) has implemented a balanced scorecard to measure and support its just-in-time production system. In the learning and growth category, DSC measures the percentage of employees who are cross-trained to perform a wide variety of production tasks. Internal business process measures are inventory turns and on-time delivery. The customer perspective is measured using a customer satisfaction measure and financial performance using operating income. DSC estimates that if it can increase the percentage of cross-trained employees by 5%, the resulting increase in labor productivity will reduce inventory-related costs by $100,000 per year and shorten delivery times by 10%. The 10% reduction in delivery times, in turn, is expected to increase customer satisfaction by 5%, and each 1% increase in customer satisfaction is expected to increase revenues by 2% due to higher prices.

Required

1. Assume that budgeted revenues in the coming year are $5,000,000. Ignoring the costs of training, what is the expected increase in operating income in the coming year if the number of cross-trained employees is increased by 5%?
2. What is the most DSC would be willing to pay to increase the percentage of cross-trained employees if it is only interested in maximizing operating income in the coming year?
3. What factors other than short-term profits should DSC consider when assessing the benefits from employee cross-training?

20-22 JIT production, relevant benefits, relevant costs. The Champion Hardware Company manufactures specialty brass door handles at its Lynchburg plant. Champion is considering implementing a JIT production system. The following are the estimated costs and benefits of JIT production:

a. Annual additional tooling costs would be $100,000.
b. Average inventory would decline by 80% from the current level of $1,000,000.

c. Insurance, space, materials-handling, and setup costs, which currently total $300,000 annually, would decline by 25%.

d. The emphasis on quality inherent in JIT production would reduce rework costs by 30%. Champion currently incurs $200,000 in annual rework costs.

e. Improved product quality under JIT production would enable Champion to raise the price of its product by $4 per unit. Champion sells 40,000 units each year.

Champion's required rate of return on inventory investment is 15% per year.

Required

1. Calculate the net benefit or cost to Champion if it adopts JIT production at the Lynchburg plant.
2. What nonfinancial and qualitative factors should Champion consider when making the decision to adopt JIT production?
3. Suppose Champion implements JIT production at its Lynchburg plant. Give examples of performance measures Champion could use to evaluate and control JIT production. What would be the benefit of Champion implementing an enterprise resource planning (ERP) system?

20-23 Backflush costing and JIT production. Road Warrior Corporation assembles handheld computers that have scaled-down capabilities of laptop computers. Each handheld computer takes six hours to assemble. Road Warrior uses a JIT production system and a backflush costing system with three trigger points:

- Purchase of direct materials and incurring of conversion costs
- Completion of good finished units of product
- Sale of finished goods

There are no beginning inventories of materials or finished goods and no beginning or ending work-in-process inventories. The following data are for August 2011:

Direct materials purchased	$2,754,000	Conversion costs incurred	$723,600
Direct materials used	$2,733,600	Conversion costs allocated	$750,400

Road Warrior records direct materials purchased and conversion costs incurred at actual costs. It has no direct materials variances. When finished goods are sold, the backflush costing system "pulls through" standard direct material cost ($102 per unit) and standard conversion cost ($28 per unit). Road Warrior produced 26,800 finished units in August 2011 and sold 26,400 units. The actual direct material cost per unit in August 2011 was $102, and the actual conversion cost per unit was $27.

Required

1. Prepare summary journal entries for August 2011 (without disposing of under- or overallocated conversion costs).
2. Post the entries in requirement 1 to T-accounts for applicable Materials and In-Process Inventory Control, Finished Goods Control, Conversion Costs Control, Conversion Costs Allocated, and Cost of Goods Sold.
3. Under an ideal JIT production system, how would the amounts in your journal entries differ from those in requirement 1?

20-24 Backflush costing, two trigger points, materials purchase and sale (continuation of 20-23). Assume the same facts as in Exercise 20-23, except that Road Warrior now uses a backflush costing system with the following two trigger points:

- Purchase of direct materials and incurring of conversion costs
- Sale of finished goods

The Inventory Control account will include direct materials purchased but not yet in production, materials in work in process, and materials in finished goods but not sold. No conversion costs are inventoried. Any under- or overallocated conversion costs are written off monthly to Cost of Goods Sold.

Required

1. Prepare summary journal entries for August, including the disposition of under- or overallocated conversion costs.
2. Post the entries in requirement 1 to T-accounts for Inventory Control, Conversion Costs Control, Conversion Costs Allocated, and Cost of Goods Sold.

20-25 Backflush costing, two trigger points, completion of production and sale (continuation of 20-23). Assume the same facts as in Exercise 20-23, except now Road Warrior uses only two trigger points, Completion of good finished units of product and Sale of finished goods. Any under- or overallocated conversion costs are written off monthly to Cost of Goods Sold.

Required

1. Prepare summary journal entries for August, including the disposition of under- or overallocated conversion costs.
2. Post the entries in requirement 1 to T-accounts for Finished Goods Control, Conversion Costs Control, Conversion Costs Allocated, and Cost of Goods Sold.

Problems

20-26 Effect of different order quantities on ordering costs and carrying costs, EOQ. Soothing Meadow, a retailer of bed and bath linen, sells 380,000 packages of Mona Lisa designer sheets each year. Soothing Meadow incurs an ordering cost of $57 per purchase order placed with Mona Lisa Enterprises and an annual carrying cost of $12.00 per package. Liv Carrol, purchasing manager at Soothing Meadow, seeks your help: She wants to understand how ordering and carrying costs vary with order quantity.

	Scenario				
	1	2	3	4	5
Annual demand (packages)	380,000	380,000	380,000	380,000	380,000
Cost per purchase order	$ 57	$ 57	$ 57	$ 57	$ 57
Carrying cost per package per year	$ 12.00	$ 12.00	$ 12.00	$ 12.00	$ 12.00
Quantity (packages) per purchase order	760	1,000	1,900	3,800	4,750
Number of purchase orders per year					
Annual relevant ordering costs					
Annual relevant carrying costs					
Annual relevant total costs of ordering and carrying inventory					

Required

1. Complete the table for Liv Carrol. What is the EOQ? Comment on your results.
2. Mona Lisa is about to introduce a Web-based ordering system for its customers. Liv Carrol estimates that Soothing Meadow's ordering costs will reduce to $30 per purchase order. Calculate the new EOQ and the new annual relevant costs of ordering and carrying inventory.
3. Liv Carrol estimates that Soothing Meadow will incur a cost of $2,150 to train its two purchasing assistants to use the new Mona Lisa system. Will Soothing Meadow recoup its training costs within the first year of adoption?

20-27 EOQ, uncertainty, safety stock, reorder point. Chadwick Shoe Co. produces and sells an excellent quality walking shoe. After production, the shoes are distributed to 20 warehouses around the country. Each warehouse services approximately 100 stores in its region. Chadwick uses an EOQ model to determine the number of pairs of shoes to order for each warehouse from the factory. Annual demand for Warehouse OR2 is approximately 120,000 pairs of shoes. The ordering cost is $250 per order. The annual carrying cost of a pair of shoes is $2.40 per pair.

Required

1. Use the EOQ model to determine the optimal number of pairs of shoes per order.
2. Assume each month consists of approximately 4 weeks. If it takes 1 week to receive an order, at what point should warehouse OR2 reorder shoes?
3. Although OR2's average weekly demand is 2,500 pairs of shoes (120,000 ÷ 12 months ÷ 4 weeks), demand each week may vary with the following probability distribution:

Total demand for 1 week	2,000 pairs	2,250 pairs	2,500 pairs	2,750 pairs	3,000 pairs
Probability (sums to 1.00)	0.04	0.20	0.52	0.20	0.04

If a store wants shoes and OR2 has none in stock, OR2 can "rush" them to the store at an additional cost of $2 per pair. How much safety stock should Warehouse OR2 hold? How will this affect the reorder point and reorder quantity?

20-28 MRP, EOQ, and JIT. Global Tunes Corp. produces J-Pods, music players that can download thousands of songs. Global Tunes forecasts that demand in 2011 will be 48,000 J-Pods. The variable production cost of each J-Pod is $54. Due to the large $10,000 cost per setup, Global Tunes plans to produce J-Pods once a month in batches of 4,000 each. The carrying cost of a unit in inventory is $17 per year.

Required

1. Using an MRP system, what is the annual cost of producing and carrying J-Pods in inventory? (Assume that, on average, half of the units produced in a month are in inventory.)
2. A new manager at Global Tunes has suggested that the company use the EOQ model to determine the optimal batch size to produce. (To use the EOQ model, Global Tunes needs to treat the setup cost in the same way it would treat ordering cost in a traditional EOQ model.) Determine the optimal batch size and number of batches. Round up the number of batches to the nearest whole number. What would be the annual cost of producing and carrying J-Pods in inventory if it uses the optimal batch size? Compare this cost to the cost calculated in requirement 1. Comment briefly.
3. Global Tunes is also considering switching from an MRP system to a JIT system. This will result in producing J-Pods in batch sizes of 600 J-Pods and will reduce obsolescence, improve quality, and result in a higher selling price. The frequency of production batches will force Global Tunes to reduce setup

time and will result in a reduction in setup cost. The new setup cost will be $500 per setup. What is the annual cost of producing and carrying J-Pods in inventory under the JIT system?

4. Compare the models analyzed in the previous parts of the problem. What are the advantages and disadvantages of each?

20-29 Effect of management evaluation criteria on EOQ model. Computers 4 U purchases one model of computer at a wholesale cost of $200 per unit and resells it to end consumers. The annual demand for the company's product is 500,000 units. Ordering costs are $800 per order and carrying costs are $50 per computer, including $20 in the opportunity cost of holding inventory.

Required

1. Compute the optimal order quantity using the EOQ model.
2. Compute a) the number of orders per year and b) the annual relevant total cost of ordering and carrying inventory.
3. Assume that when evaluating the manager, the company excludes the opportunity cost of carrying inventory. If the manager makes the EOQ decision excluding the opportunity cost of carrying inventory, the relevant carrying cost would be $30 not $50. How would this affect the EOQ amount and the actual annual relevant cost of ordering and carrying inventory?
4. What is the cost impact on the company of excluding the opportunity cost of carrying inventory when making EOQ decisions? Why do you think the company currently excludes the opportunity costs of carrying inventory when evaluating the manager's performance? What could the company do to encourage the manager to make decisions more congruent with the goal of reducing total inventory costs?

20-30 JIT purchasing, relevant benefits, relevant costs. (CMA, adapted) The Margro Corporation is an automotive supplier that uses automatic turning machines to manufacture precision parts from steel bars. Margro's inventory of raw steel averages $600,000. John Oates, president of Margro, and Helen Gorman, Margro's controller, are concerned about the costs of carrying inventory. The steel supplier is willing to supply steel in smaller lots at no additional charge. Gorman identifies the following effects of adopting a JIT inventory program to virtually eliminate steel inventory:

- Without scheduling any overtime, lost sales due to stockouts would increase by 35,000 units per year. However, by incurring overtime premiums of $40,000 per year, the increase in lost sales could be reduced to 20,000 units per year. This would be the maximum amount of overtime that would be feasible for Margro.
- Two warehouses currently used for steel bar storage would no longer be needed. Margro rents one warehouse from another company under a cancelable leasing arrangement at an annual cost of $60,000. The other warehouse is owned by Margro and contains 12,000 square feet. Three-fourths of the space in the owned warehouse could be rented for $1.50 per square foot per year. Insurance and property tax costs totaling $14,000 per year would be eliminated.

Margro's required rate of return on investment is 20% per year. Margro's budgeted income statement for the year ending December 31, 2011 (in thousands) is as follows:

Revenues (900,000 units)		$10,800
Cost of goods sold		
Variable costs	$4,050	
Fixed costs	1,450	
Total costs of goods sold		5,500
Gross margin		5,300
Marketing and distribution costs		
Variable costs	$ 900	
Fixed costs	1,500	
Total marketing and distribution costs		2,400
Operating income		$ 2,900

Required

1. Calculate the estimated dollar savings (loss) for the Margro Corporation that would result in 2011 from the adoption of JIT purchasing.
2. Identify and explain other factors that Margro should consider before deciding whether to adopt JIT purchasing.

20-31 Supply chain effects on total relevant inventory cost. Cow Spot Computer Co. outsources the production of motherboards for its computers. It is currently deciding which of two suppliers to use: Maji or Induk. Due to differences in the product failure rates across the two companies, 5% of motherboards purchased from Maji will be inspected and 25% of motherboards purchased from Induk will be inspected. The following data refers to costs associated with Maji and Induk.

	Maji	Induk
Number of orders per year	50	50
Annual motherboards demanded	10,000	10,000
Price per motherboard	$93	$90
Ordering cost per order	$10	$8
Inspection cost per unit	$5	$5
Average inventory level	100 units	100 units
Expected number of stockouts	100	300
Stockout cost (cost of rush order) per stockout	$5	$8
Units returned by customers for replacing motherboards	50	500
Cost of replacing each motherboard	$25	$25
Required annual return on investment	10%	10%
Other carrying cost per unit per year	$2.50	$2.50

Required

1. What is the relevant cost of purchasing from Maji and Induk?
2. What factors other than cost should Cow Spot consider?

20-32 Backflush costing and JIT production. The Rippel Corporation manufactures electrical meters. For August, there were no beginning inventories of direct materials and no beginning or ending work in process. Rippel uses a JIT production system and backflush costing with three trigger points for making entries in the accounting system:

- Purchase of direct materials and incurring of conversion costs
- Completion of good finished units of product
- Sale of finished goods

Rippel's August standard cost per meter is direct material, $26, and conversion cost, $19. Rippel has no direct materials variances. The following data apply to August manufacturing:

Direct materials purchased	$546,000	Number of finished units manufactured	20,000
Conversion costs incurred	$399,000	Number of finished units sold	19,000

Required

1. Prepare summary journal entries for August (without disposing of under- or overallocated conversion costs). Assume no direct materials variances.
2. Post the entries in requirement 1 to T-accounts for Materials and In-Process Inventory Control, Finished Goods Control, Conversion Costs Control, Conversion Costs Allocated, and Cost of Goods Sold.

20-33 Backflush, two trigger points, materials purchase and sale (continuation of 20-32). Assume that the second trigger point for Rippel Corporation is the sale—rather than the completion—of finished goods. Also, the inventory account is confined solely to direct materials, whether these materials are in a storeroom, in work in process, or in finished goods. No conversion costs are inventoried. They are allocated to the units sold at standard costs. Any under- or overallocated conversion costs are written off monthly to Cost of Goods Sold.

Required

1. Prepare summary journal entries for August, including the disposition of under- or overallocated conversion costs. Assume no direct materials variances.
2. Post the entries in requirement 1 to T-accounts for Inventory Control, Conversion Costs Control, Conversion Costs Allocated, and Cost of Goods Sold.

20-34 Backflush, two trigger points, completion of production and sale (continuation of 20-32). Assume the same facts as in Problem 20-32 except now there are only two trigger points: Completion of good finished units of product and Sale of finished goods.

Required

1. Prepare summary journal entries for August, including the disposition of under- or overallocated conversion costs. Assume no direct materials variances.
2. Post the entries in requirement 1 to T-accounts for Finished Goods Control, Conversion Costs Control, Conversion Costs Allocated, and Cost of Goods Sold.

20-35 Lean Accounting. Flexible Security Devices (FSD) has introduced a just-in-time production process and is considering the adoption of lean accounting principles to support its new production philosophy. The company has two product lines: Mechanical Devices and Electronic Devices. Two individual products are made in each line. Product-line manufacturing overhead costs are traced directly to product lines, and then allocated to the two individual products in each line. The company's traditional cost accounting system allocates all plant-level facility costs and some corporate overhead costs to individual products. The latest accounting report using traditional cost accounting methods included the following information (in thousands of dollars).

	Mechanical Devices		Electronic Devices	
	Product A	Product B	Product C	Product D
Sales	$700	$500	$900	$450
Direct material (based on quantity used)	200	100	250	75
Direct manufacturing labor	150	75	200	60
Manufacturing overhead (equipment lease, supervision, production control)	90	120	200	95
Allocated plant-level facility costs	50	40	80	30
Design and marketing costs	95	50	105	42
Allocated corporate overhead costs	15	10	20	8
Operating income	$100	$105	$ 45	$140

FSD has determined that each of the two product lines represents a distinct value stream. It has also determined that out of the $200,000 ($50,000 + $40,000 + $80,000 + $30,000) plant-level facility costs, product A occupies 22% of the plant's square footage, product B occupies 18%, product C occupies 36%, and product D occupies 14%. The remaining 10% of square footage is not being used. Finally, FSD has decided that direct material should be expensed in the period it is purchased, rather than when the material is used. According to purchasing records, direct material purchase costs during the period were as follows:

	Mechanical Devices		Electronic Devices	
	Product A	Product B	Product C	Product D
Direct material (purchases)	$210	$120	$250	$90

1. What are the cost objects in FSD's lean accounting system? **Required**
2. Compute operating income for the cost objects identified in requirement 1 using lean accounting principles. Why does operating income differ from the operating income computed using traditional cost accounting methods? Comment on your results.

Collaborative Learning Problem

20-36 JIT production, relevant benefits, relevant costs, ethics. Parson Container Corporation is considering implementing a JIT production system. The new system would reduce current average inventory levels of $2,000,000 by 75%, but would require a much greater dependency on the company's core suppliers for on-time deliveries and high quality inputs. The company's operations manager, Jim Ingram, is opposed to the idea of a new JIT system. He is concerned that the new system will be too costly to manage; will result in too many stockouts; and will lead to the layoff of his employees, several of whom are currently managing inventory. He believes that these layoffs will affect the morale of his entire production department. The plant controller, Sue Winston is in favor of the new system, due to the likely cost savings. Jim wants Sue to rework the numbers because he is concerned that top management will give more weight to financial factors and not give due consideration to nonfinancial factors such as employee morale. In addition to the reduction in inventory described previously, Sue has gathered the following information for the upcoming year regarding the JIT system:

■ Annual insurance and warehousing costs for inventory would be reduced by 60% of current budgeted level of $350,000.
■ Payroll expenses for current inventory management staff would be reduced by 15% of the budgeted total of $600,000.
■ Additional annual costs for JIT system implementation and management, including personnel costs, would equal $220,000.
■ The additional number of stockouts under the new JIT system is estimated to be 5% of the total number of shipments annually. 10,000 shipments are budgeted for the upcoming year. Each stockout would result in an average additional cost of $250.
■ Parson's required rate of return on inventory investment is 10% per year.

1. From a financial perspective should Parson adopt the new JIT system? **Required**
2. Should Sue Winston rework the numbers?
3. How should she manage Jim Ingram's concerns?

Capital Budgeting and Cost Analysis

From Chapter 21 of *Cost Accounting: A Managerial Emphasis*, 14/e. Charles T. Horngren. Srikant M. Datar. Madhav Rajan.

Capital Budgeting and Cost Analysis

A firm's accountants play an important role when it comes to deciding the major expenditures, or investments, a company should make.

Accountants, along with top executives, have to figure out how and when to best allocate the firm's financial resources among alternative opportunities to create future value for the company. Because it's hard to know what the future holds and what projects will ultimately cost, this can be a challenging task, one that companies like Target constantly confront. To meet this challenge, Target has developed a special group to make project-related capital budgeting decisions. This chapter explains the different methods managers use to get the "biggest bang" for the firm's "buck" in terms of the projects they undertake.

Target's Capital Budgeting Hits the Bull's-Eye[1]

In 2010, Target Corporation, one of the largest retailers in the United States, will spend more than $2 billion on opening new stores, remodeling and expanding existing stores, and investing in information technology and distribution infrastructure.

With intense competition from Wal-Mart, which focuses on low-prices, Target's strategy is to consider the shopping experience as a whole. With the slogan, "Expect more. Pay less." the company is focused on creating a shopping experience that appeals to the profile of its core customer: a college-educated woman with children at home who is more affluent than the typical Wal-Mart customer. This shopping experience is created by emphasizing store décor that gives just the right shopping ambiance.

As a result, investments in the shopping experience are critical to Target. To manage these complex capital investments, Target has a Capital Expenditure Committee (CEC), composed of a team of top executives, that reviews and approves all capital project requests in excess of $100,000. Project proposals that are reviewed by the CEC vary widely and include remodeling, relocating, rebuilding, and closing an existing store to build a new store.

Target's CEC considers several factors in determining whether to accept or reject a project. An overarching objective is to meet the corporate goals of adding a certain number of stores each year (for

---

[1] *Sources:* David Ding and Saul Yeaton. 2008. Target Corporation. University of Virginia Darden School of Business No. UV1057, Charlottesville, VA: Darden Business Publishing; Target Corporation. 2010. 2009 annual report. Minneapolis, MN: Target Corporation.

2010, 13 stores) while maintaining a positive brand image. Projects also need to meet a variety of financial objectives, starting with providing a suitable return as measured by discounted cash flow metrics net present value (NPV) and internal rate of return (IRR). Other financial considerations include projected profit and earnings per share impacts, total investment size, impact on sales of other nearby Target stores, and sensitivity of the NPV and IRR to sales variations, like the recent global economic recession.

Managers at companies such as Target, Honda, Sony, and Gap face challenging investment decisions. In this chapter, we introduce several capital budgeting methods used to evaluate long-term investment projects. These methods help managers choose the projects that will contribute the most value to their organizations.

Charles Krupa\AP Wide World Photos

Stages of Capital Budgeting

Capital budgeting is the process of making long-run planning decisions for investments in projects. In much of accounting, income is calculated on a period-by-period basis. In choosing investments, however, managers make a selection from among a group of multiple projects, each of which may span several periods. Exhibit 1 illustrates these two different, yet intersecting, dimensions of cost analysis: (1) horizontally across, as the *project dimension*, and (2) vertically upward, as the *accounting-period dimension*. Each project is represented as a horizontal rectangle starting and ending at different times and stretching over time spans longer than one year. The vertical rectangle for the 2012 accounting period, for example, represents the dimensions of income determination and routine annual planning and control that cuts across all projects that are ongoing that year.

Capital budgeting analyzes each project by considering all the lifespan cash flows from its initial investment through its termination and is analogous to life-cycle budgeting and costing. For example, when Honda considers a new line of automobiles, it begins by estimating all potential revenues from the new line as well as any costs that will be incurred along its life cycle, which may be as long as 10 years. Only after examining the potential costs and benefits across all of the business functions in the value chain, from research and development (R&D) to customer service, across the entire lifespan of the new-car project, does Honda decide whether the new model is a wise investment.

Capital budgeting is both a decision-making and a control tool. Like the five-step decision process that we have emphasized throughout this book, there are five stages to the capital budgeting process:

Stage 1: Identify Projects *Identify potential capital investments that agree with the organization's strategy.* For example, when the Microsoft Office group sought a strategy of product differentiation, it listed possible upgrades and changes from its present offering. Alternatively, a strategy of cost leadership could be promoted by projects that improve productivity and efficiency. In the case of a manufacturer of computer hardware such as Dell, this includes the outsourcing of certain components to lower-cost contract

Learning Objective 1

Understand the five stages of capital budgeting for a project

. . . identify projects; obtain information; make predictions; make decisions; and implement the decision, evaluate performance, and learn

295

Exhibit 1

The Project and Time
Dimensions of Capital
Budgeting

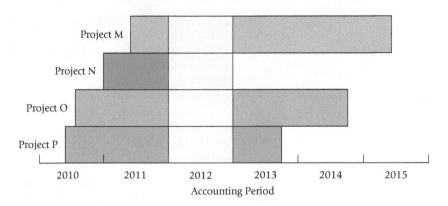

manufacturing facilities located overseas. Identifying which types of capital projects to invest in is largely the responsibility of senior line managers.

Stage 2: Obtain Information *Gather information from all parts of the value chain to evaluate alternative projects.* Returning to the new car example at Honda, in this stage, marketing is queried for potential revenue numbers, plant managers are asked about assembly times, and suppliers are consulted about prices and the availability of key components. Some projects may even be rejected at this stage. For example, suppose Honda learns that the car simply cannot be built using existing plants. It may then opt to cancel the project altogether.

Stage 3: Make Predictions *Forecast all potential cash flows attributable to the alternative projects.* Capital investment projects generally involve substantial initial outlays, which are recouped over time through annual cash inflows and the disposal values from the termination of the project. As a result, they require the firm to make forecasts of cash flows several years into the future. BMW, for example, estimates yearly cash flows and sets its investment budgets accordingly using a 12-year planning horizon. Because of the greater uncertainty associated with these predictions, firms typically analyze a wide range of alternate scenarios. In the case of BMW, the marketing group is asked to estimate a band of possible sales figures within a 90% confidence interval.

Stage 4: Make Decisions by Choosing Among Alternatives *Determine which investment yields the greatest benefit and the least cost to the organization.* Using the quantitative information obtained in stage 3, the firm uses any one of several capital budgeting methodologies to determine which project best meets organizational goals. While capital budgeting calculations are typically limited to financial information, managers use their judgment and intuition to factor in qualitative information and strategic considerations as well. For example, even if a proposed new line of cars meets its financial targets on a standalone basis, Honda might decide not to pursue it further if it feels that the new model will lessen Honda's perceived quality among consumers and affect the value of the firm's brand.

Stage 5: Implement the Decision, Evaluate Performance, and Learn Given the complexities of capital investment decisions and the long time horizons they span, this stage can be separated into two phases:

■ *Obtain funding and make the investments selected in stage 4.* Sources of funding include internally generated cash flow as well as equity and debt securities sold in capital markets. Making capital investments is often an arduous task, laden with the purchase of many different goods and services. If Honda opts to build a new car, it must order steel, aluminum, paint, and so on. If some of the planned supplies are unavailable, managers must revisit and determine the economic feasibility of substituting the missing material with alternative inputs.

■ *Track realized cash flows, compare against estimated numbers, and revise plans if necessary.* As the cash outflows and inflows begin to accumulate, managers can verify whether the predictions made in stage 3 agree with the actual flows of cash from the project. When the BMW group initially released the new Mini, its realized sales were substantially higher than the original demand estimates. BMW responded by manufacturing more cars to meet the higher demand. It also decided to expand the Mini line to include convertibles and the larger Clubman model.

To illustrate capital budgeting, consider Top-Spin tennis racquets. Top-Spin was one of the first major tennis-racquet producers to introduce graphite in its racquets. This allowed Top-Spin to produce some of the lightest and stiffest racquets in the market. However, new carbon-fiber impregnated racquets are even lighter and stiffer than their graphite counterparts. Top-Spin has always been an innovator in the tennis-racquet industry, and wants to stay that way, so in stage 1, it identifies the carbon fiber racquet project. In the information gathering stage (stage 2), the company learns that it could feasibly begin using carbon-fiber in its racquets as early as 2011 if it replaces one of its graphite forming machines with a carbon-fiber weaving machine. After collecting additional data, Top-Spin begins to forecast future cash flows if it invests in the new machine (stage 3). Top-Spin estimates that it can purchase a carbon-fiber weaving machine with a useful life of five years for a net after-tax initial investment of $379,100, which is calculated as follows:

Cost of new machine	$390,000
Investment in working capital	9,000
Cash flow from disposing of existing machine (after-tax)	(19,900)
Net initial investment for new machine	$379,100

Working capital refers to the difference between current assets and current liabilities. New projects often necessitate additional investments in current assets such as inventories and receivables. In the case of Top-Spin, the purchase of the new machine is accompanied by an outlay of $9,000 for supplies and spare parts inventory. At the end of the project, the $9,000 in supplies and spare parts inventory is liquidated, resulting in a cash inflow. However, the machine itself is believed to have no terminal disposal value after five years.

Managers estimate that by introducing carbon-fiber impregnated racquets, operating cash inflows (cash revenues minus cash operating costs) will increase by $100,000 (after tax) in the first four years and $91,000 in year 5. To simplify the analysis, suppose that all cash flows occur at the end of each year. Note that cash flow at the end of the fifth year also increases by $100,000, $91,000 in operating cash inflows and $9,000 in working capital. Management next calculates the costs and benefits of the proposed project (stage 4). This chapter discusses four capital budgeting methods to analyze financial information:

Decision Point

What are the five stages of capital budgeting?

1. Net present value (NPV)

2. Internal rate of return (IRR)

3. Payback

4. Accrual accounting rate of return (AARR)

Both the net present value (NPV) and internal rate of return (IRR) methods use *discounted cash flows*, which we discuss in the following section.

Discounted Cash Flow

Discounted cash flow (DCF) methods measure all expected future cash inflows and outflows of a project discounted back to the present point in time. The key feature of DCF methods is the **time value of money**, which means that a dollar (or any other monetary unit) received today is worth more than a dollar received at any future time. The reason is that $1 received today can be invested at, say, 10% per year so that it grows to $1.10 at the end of one year. The time value of money is the opportunity cost (the return of $0.10 forgone per year) from not having the money today. In this example, $1 received one year from now is worth $1 ÷ 1.10 = $0.9091 today. Similarly, $100 received one year from now will be weighted by 0.9091 to yield a discounted cash flow of $90.91, which is today's value of that $100 next year. In this way, discounted cash flow methods explicitly weigh cash flows by the time value of money. Note that DCF focuses exclusively on cash inflows and outflows rather than on operating income as determined by accrual accounting.

The compound interest tables and formulas used in DCF analysis are in the Appendix. If you are unfamiliar with compound interest, do not proceed until you have studied the Appendix, as the tables in the Appendix will be used frequently in this chapter.

Learning Objective 2

Use and evaluate the two main discounted cash flow (DCF) methods: the net present value (NPV) method and the internal rate-of-return (IRR) method

. . . to explicitly consider all project cash flows and the time value of money

The two DCF methods we describe are the net present value (NPV) method and the internal rate-of-return (IRR) method. Both DCF methods use what is called the **required rate of return (RRR)**, the minimum acceptable annual rate of return on an investment. The RRR is internally set, usually by upper management, and typically reflects the return that an organization could expect to receive elsewhere for an investment of comparable risk. The RRR is also called the **discount rate, hurdle rate, cost of capital,** or **opportunity cost of capital.** Suppose the CFO at Top-Spin has set the required rate of return for the firm's investments at 8% per year.

Net Present Value Method

The **net present value (NPV) method** calculates the expected monetary gain or loss from a project by discounting all expected future cash inflows and outflows back to the present point in time using the required rate of return. To use the NPV method, apply the following three steps:

Step 1: Draw a Sketch of Relevant Cash Inflows and Outflows. The right side of Exhibit 2 shows arrows that depict the cash flows of the new carbon-fiber machine. The sketch helps the decision maker visualize and organize the data in a systematic way. *Note that parentheses denote relevant cash outflows throughout all exhibits in this chapter.* Exhibit 2 includes the outflow for the acquisition of the new machine at the start of year 1 (also referred to as end of year 0), and the inflows over the subsequent five years. The NPV method specifies cash flows regardless of the source of the cash flows, such as from operations, purchase or sale of equipment, or investment in or recovery of working capital. However, accrual-accounting concepts such as sales made on credit or noncash expenses are not included since the focus is on *cash* inflows and outflows.

Exhibit 2 Net Present Value Method: Top-Spin's Carbon-Fiber Machine

	A	B	C	D	E	F	G	H	I
1			Net initial investment	$379,100					
2			Useful life	5 years					
3			Annual cash inflow	$100,000					
4			Required rate of return	8%					
5									
6		Present Value	Present Value of	Sketch of Relevant Cash Flows at End of Each Year					
7		of Cash Flow	$1 Discounted at 8%	0	1	2	3	4	5
8	Approach 1: Discounting Each Year's Cash Flow Separately[a]								
9	Net initial investment	$(379,100)	1.000	$(379,100)					
10		92,600	0.926		$100,000				
11		85,700	0.857			$100,000			
12	Annual cash inflow	79,400	0.794				$100,000		
13		73,500	0.735					$100,000	
14		68,100	0.681						$100,000
15	NPV if new machine purchased	$ 20,200							
16									
17	Approach 2: Using Annuity Table[b]								
18	Net initial investment	$(379,100)	1.000	$(379,100)					
19					$100,000	$100,000	$100,000	$100,000	$100,000
20									
21	Annual cash inflow	399,300	3.993						
22	NPV if new machine purchased	$ 20,200							
23									
24	Note: Parentheses denote relevant cash outflows throughout all exhibits in Chapter 21.								
25	[a] Present values from Table 2, Appendix. For example, $0.857 = 1 \div (1.08)^2$.								
26	[b] Annuity present value from Table 4, Appendix. The annuity value of 3.993 is the sum of the individual discount rates 0.926 + 0.857 + 0.794 + 0.735 + 0.681.								

Step 2: Discount the Cash Flows Using the Correct Compound Interest Table from Appendix and Sum Them. In the Top-Spin example, we can discount each year's cash flow separately using Table 2, or we can compute the present value of an annuity, a series of equal cash flows at equal time intervals, using Table 4. (Both tables are in the Appendix.) If we use Table 2, we find the discount factors for periods 1–5 under the 8% column. Approach 1 in Exhibit 2 uses the five discount factors. To obtain the present value amount, multiply each discount factor by the corresponding amount represented by the arrow on the right in Exhibit 2 ($- \$379,100 \times 1.000$; $\$100,000 \times 0.926$; and so on to $\$100,000 \times 0.681$). Because the investment in the new machine produces an annuity, we may also use Table 4. Under Approach 2, we find that the annuity factor for five periods under the 8% column is 3.993, which is the sum of the five discount factors used in Approach 1. We multiply the uniform annual cash inflow by this factor to obtain the present value of the inflows ($\$399,300 = \$100,000 \times 3.993$). Subtracting the initial investment then reveals the NPV of the project as $20,200 ($\$20,200 = \$399,300 - \$379,100$).

Step 3: Make the Project Decision on the Basis of the Calculated NPV. If NPV is zero or positive, financial considerations suggest that the project should be accepted; its expected rate of return equals or exceeds the required rate of return. If NPV is negative, the project should be rejected; its expected rate of return is below the required rate of return.

Exhibit 2 calculates an NPV of $20,200 at the required rate of return of 8% per year. The project is acceptable based on financial information. The cash flows from the project are adequate (1) to recover the net initial investment in the project and (2) to earn a return greater than 8% per year on the investment tied up in the project over its useful life.

Managers must also weigh nonfinancial factors such as the effect that purchasing the machine will have on Top-Spin's brand. This is a nonfinancial factor because the financial benefits that accrue from Top-Spin's brand are very difficult to estimate. Nevertheless, managers must consider brand effects before reaching a final decision. Suppose, for example, that the NPV of the carbon-fiber machine is negative. Management may still decide to buy the machine if it maintains Top-Spin's technological image and helps sell other Top-Spin products.

Pause here. Do not proceed until you understand what you see in Exhibit 2. Compare Approach 1 with Approach 2 in Exhibit 2 to see how Table 4 in the Appendix merely aggregates the present value factors of Table 2. That is, the fundamental table is Table 2. Table 4 simply reduces calculations when there is an annuity.

Internal Rate-of-Return Method

The **internal rate-of-return (IRR) method** calculates the discount rate at which an investment's present value of all expected cash inflows equals the present value of its expected cash outflows. That is, the IRR is the discount rate that makes NPV = $0. Exhibit 3 presents the cash flows and shows the calculation of NPV using a 10% annual discount rate for Top-Spin's carbon-fiber project. At a 10% discount rate, the NPV of the project is $0. Therefore, IRR is 10% per year.

How do managers determine the discount rate that yields NPV = $0? In most cases, managers or analysts solving capital budgeting problems use a calculator or computer program to provide the internal rate of return. The following trial-and-error approach can also provide the answer.

Step 1: Use a discount rate and calculate the project's NPV.

Step 2: If the calculated NPV is less than zero, use a lower discount rate. (A *lower* discount rate will *increase* NPV. Remember that we are trying to find a discount rate for which NPV = $0.) If NPV is greater than zero, use a higher discount rate to lower NPV. Keep adjusting the discount rate until NPV = $0. In the Top-Spin example, a discount rate of 8% yields an NPV of + $20,200 (see Exhibit 2). A discount rate of 12% yields an NPV of − $18,600 (3.605, the present value annuity factor from Table 4, × $100,000 minus $379,100). Therefore, the discount rate that makes NPV = $0 must lie between 8% and 12%. We use 10% and get NPV = $0. Hence, the IRR is 10% per year.

Exhibit 3 Internal Rate-of-Return Method: Top-Spin's Carbon-Fiber Machine[a]

	A	B	C	D	E	F	G	H	I
	Home Insert Page Layout Formulas Data Review View								
1			Net initial investment	$379,100					
2			Useful life	5 years					
3			Annual cash inflow	$100,000					
4			Annual discount rate	10%					
5									
6		Present Value	Present Value of	Sketch of Relevant Cash Flows at End of Each Year					
7		of Cash Flow	$1 Discounted at 10%	0	1	2	3	4	5
8	**Approach 1: Discounting Each Year's Cash Flow Separately[b]**								
9	Net initial investment	$(379,100)	1.000	$(379,100)					
10		90,900	0.909		$100,000				
11		82,600	0.826			$100,000			
12	Annual cash inflow	75,100	0.751				$100,000		
13		68,300	0.683					$100,000	
14		62,100	0.621						$100,000
15	NPV if new machine purchased[c]	$ 0							
16	(the zero difference proves that								
17	the internal rate of return is 10%)								
18									
19	**Approach 2: Using Annuity Table**								
20	Net initial investment	$(379,100)	1.000	$(379,100)					
21					$100,000	$100,000	$100,000	$100,000	$100,000
22									
23	Annual cash inflow	379,100	3.791[d]						
24	NPV if new machine purchased	$ 0							
25									
26	Note: Parentheses denote relevant cash outflows throughout all exhibits in this chapter.								
27	[a]The internal rate of return is computed by methods.								
28	[b]Present values from Table 2, Appendix.								
29	[c]Sum is $(100) due to rounding. We round to $0.								
30	[d]Annuity present value from Table 4, Appendix. The annuity table value of 3.791 is the sum of the individual discount rates								
31	0.909 + 0.826 + 0.751 + 0.683 + 0.621, subject to rounding.								

The step-by-step computations of internal rate of return are easier when the cash inflows are constant, as in our Top-Spin example. Information from Exhibit 3 can be expressed as follows:

$$\$379,100 = \text{Present value of annuity of \$100,000 at } X\% \text{ per year for five years}$$

Or, what factor F in Table 4 (in the Appendix) will satisfy this equation?

$$\$379,100 = \$100,000F$$

$$F = \$379,100 \div \$100,000 = 3.791$$

On the five-period line of Table 4, find the percentage column that is closest to 3.791. It is exactly 10%. If the factor (F) falls between the factors in two columns, straight-line interpolation is used to approximate IRR. This interpolation is illustrated in the Problem for Self-Study.

A project is accepted only if IRR equals or exceeds required rate of return (RRR). In the Top-Spin example, the carbon-fiber machine has an IRR of 10%, which is greater than the RRR of 8%. On the basis of financial factors, Top-Spin should invest in the new machine. In general, the NPV and IRR decision rules result in consistent project acceptance or rejection decisions. If IRR exceeds RRR, then the project has a positive NPV (favoring acceptance). If IRR equals RRR, NPV = $0, so project acceptance and rejection yield the same value. If IRR is less than RRR, NPV is negative (favoring rejection). Obviously, managers prefer projects with higher IRRs to projects with lower IRRs, if all other things are equal. The IRR of 10% means the cash inflows from the project are adequate to (1) recover the net initial investment in the project and (2) earn a return of exactly 10% on the investment tied up in the project over its useful life.

Comparison of Net Present Value and Internal Rate-of-Return Methods

The NPV method is generally regarded as the preferred method for project selection decisions. The reason is that choosing projects using the NPV criterion leads to shareholder value maximization. At an intuitive level, this occurs because the NPV measure for a project captures the value, in today's dollars, of the surplus the project generates for the firm's shareholders, over and above the required rate of return.[2] Next, we highlight some of the limitations of the IRR method relative to the NPV technique.

One advantage of the NPV method is that it expresses computations in dollars, not in percentages. Therefore, we can sum NPVs of individual projects to calculate an NPV of a combination or portfolio of projects. In contrast, IRRs of individual projects cannot be added or averaged to represent the IRR of a combination of projects.

A second advantage is that the NPV of a project can always be computed and expressed as a unique number. From the sign and magnitude of this number, the firm can then make an accurate assessment of the financial consequences of accepting or rejecting the project. Under the IRR method, it is possible that more than one IRR may exist for a given project. In other words, there may be multiple discount rates that equate the NPV of a set of cash flows to zero. This is especially true when the signs of the cash flows switch over time; that is, when there are outflows, followed by inflows, followed by additional outflows and so forth. In such cases, it is difficult to know which of the IRR estimates should be compared to the firm's required rate of return.

A third advantage of the NPV method is that it can be used when the RRR varies over the life of a project. Suppose Top-Spin's management sets an RRR of 9% per year in years 1 and 2 and 12% per year in years 3, 4, and 5. Total present value of the cash inflows can be calculated as $378,100 (computations not shown). It is not possible to use the IRR method in this case. That's because different RRRs in different years mean there is no single RRR that the IRR (a single figure) can be compared against to decide if the project should be accepted or rejected.

Finally, there are specific settings in which the IRR method is prone to indicating erroneous decisions, such as when comparing mutually exclusive projects with unequal lives or unequal levels of initial investment. The reason is that the IRR method implicitly assumes that project cash flows can be reinvested at the *project's* rate of return. The NPV method, in contrast, accurately assumes that project cash flows can only be reinvested at the *company's* required rate of return.

Despite its limitations, surveys report widespread use of the IRR method.[3] Why? Probably because managers find the percentage return computed under the IRR method easy to understand and compare. Moreover, in most instances where a single project is being evaluated, their decisions would likely be unaffected by using IRR or NPV.

Sensitivity Analysis

To present the basics of the NPV and IRR methods, we have assumed that the expected values of cash flows will occur *for certain*. In reality, there is substantial uncertainty associated with the prediction of future cash flows. To examine how a result will change if the predicted financial outcomes are not achieved or if an underlying assumption changes, managers use *sensitivity analysis*.

A common way to apply sensitivity analysis in capital budgeting decisions is to vary each of the inputs to the NPV calculation by a certain percentage and assess the effect of the change on the project's NPV. Sensitivity analysis can take on other forms as well. Suppose the manager at Top-Spin believes forecasted cash flows are difficult to predict.

---

[2] More detailed explanations of the preeminence of the NPV criterion can be found in corporate finance texts.
[3] In a recent survey, John Graham and Campbell Harvey found that 75.7% of CFOs always or almost always used IRR for capital budgeting decisions, while a slightly smaller number, 74.9%, always or almost always used the NPV criterion.

Exhibit 4

Net Present Value
Calculations for Top-
Spin's Carbon-Fiber
Machine Under
Different Assumptions
of Annual Cash Flows
and Required Rates
of Return[a]

	A	B	C	D	E	F
1	**Required**	**Annual Cash Flows**				
2	**Rate of Return**	**$ 80,000**	**$ 90,000**	**$100,000**	**$110,000**	**$120,000**
3	6%	$(42,140)	$ (20)	$ 42,100	$ 84,220	$126,340
4	8%	$(59,660)	$(19,730)	$ 20,200	$ 60,130	$100,060
5	10%	$(75,820)	$(37,910)	$ 0	$ 37,910	$ 75,820
6						
7	[a]All calculated amounts assume the project's useful life is five years.					

She asks, "What are the minimum annual cash inflows that make the investment in a new carbon-fiber machine acceptable—that is, what inflows lead to an NPV = $0?" For the data in Exhibit 2, let A = Annual cash flow and let NPV = $0. Net initial investment is $379,100, and the present value factor at the 8% required annual rate of return for a five-year annuity of $1 is 3.993. Then,

$$NPV = \$0$$

$$3.993A - \$379{,}100 = \$0$$

$$3.993A = \$379{,}100$$

$$A = \$94{,}941$$

At the discount rate of 8% per year, the annual (after tax) cash inflows can decrease to $94,941 (a decline of $100,000 − $94,941 = $5,059) before the NPV falls to $0. If the manager believes she can attain annual cash inflows of at least $94,941, she can justify investing in the carbon-fiber machine on financial grounds.

Exhibit 4 shows that variations in the annual cash inflows or RRR significantly affect the NPV of the carbon-fiber machine project. NPVs can also vary with different useful lives of a project. Sensitivity analysis helps managers to focus on decisions that are most sensitive to different assumptions and to worry less about decisions that are not so sensitive.

Decision Point ▶

What are the two
primary discounted
cash flow (DCF)
methods for project
evaluation?

Payback Method

We now consider the third method for analyzing the financial aspects of projects. The **payback method** measures the time it will take to recoup, in the form of expected future cash flows, the net initial investment in a project. As in NPV and IRR, payback does not distinguish among the sources of cash flows, such as from operations, purchase or sale of equipment, or investment or recovery of working capital. Payback is simpler to calculate when a project has uniform cash flows, as opposed to nonuniform cash flows. We consider the former case first.

Learning Objective 3

Use and evaluate the
payback and
discounted payback
methods

. . . to calculate the time
it takes to recoup the
investment

Uniform Cash Flows

In the Top-Spin example, the carbon-fiber machine costs $379,100, has a five-year expected useful life, and generates $100,000 *uniform* cash flow each year. Calculation of the payback period is as follows:

$$\text{Payback period} = \frac{\text{Net initial investment}}{\text{Uniform increase in annual future cash flows}}$$

$$= \frac{\$379{,}100}{\$100{,}000} = 3.8 \text{ years}^4$$

---

[4] Cash inflows from the new carbon-fiber machine occur uniformly *throughout* the year, but for simplicity in calculating NPV and IRR, we assume they occur at the *end* of each year. A literal interpretation of this assumption would imply a payback of four years because Top-Spin will only recover its investment when cash inflows occur at the end of year 4. The calculations shown in the chapter, however, better approximate Top-Spin's payback on the basis of uniform cash flows throughout the year.

The payback method highlights liquidity, a factor that often plays a role in capital budgeting decisions, particularly when the investments are large. Managers prefer projects with shorter payback periods (projects that are more liquid) to projects with longer payback periods, if all other things are equal. Projects with shorter payback periods give an organization more flexibility because funds for other projects become available sooner. Also, managers are less confident about cash flow predictions that stretch far into the future, again favoring shorter payback periods.

Unlike the NPV and IRR methods where management selected a RRR, under the payback method, management chooses a cutoff period for a project. Projects with a payback period that is less than the cutoff period are considered acceptable, and those with a payback period that is longer than the cutoff period are rejected. Japanese companies favor the payback method over other methods and use cutoff periods ranging from three to five years depending on the risks involved with the project. In general, modern risk management calls for using shorter cutoff periods for riskier projects. If Top-Spin's cutoff period under the payback method is three years, it will reject the new machine.

The payback method is easy to understand. As in DCF methods, the payback method is not affected by accrual accounting conventions such as depreciation. Payback is a useful measure when (1) preliminary screening of many proposals is necessary, (2) interest rates are high, and (3) the expected cash flows in later years of a project are highly uncertain. Under these conditions, companies give much more weight to cash flows in early periods of a capital budgeting project and to recovering the investments they have made, thereby making the payback criterion especially relevant.

Two weaknesses of the payback method are that (1) it fails to explicitly incorporate the time value of money and (2) it does not consider a project's cash flows after the payback period. Consider an alternative to the $379,100 carbon-fiber machine. Another carbon-fiber machine, with a three-year useful life and no terminal disposal value, requires only a $300,000 net initial investment and will also result in cash inflows of $100,000 per year. First, compare the payback periods:

$$\text{Machine 1} = \frac{\$379,100}{\$100,000} = 3.8 \text{ years}$$

$$\text{Machine 2} = \frac{\$300,000}{\$100,000} = 3.0 \text{ years}$$

The payback criterion favors machine 2, with the shorter payback. If the cutoff period were three years, machine 1 would fail to meet the payback criterion.

Consider next the NPV of the two investment options using Top-Spin's 8% required rate of return for the carbon-fiber machine investment. At a discount rate of 8%, the NPV of machine 2 is −$42,300 (2.577, the present value annuity factor for three years at 8% per year from Table 4, times $100,000 = $257,700 minus net initial investment of $300,000). Machine 1, as we know, has a positive NPV of $20,200 (from Exhibit 2). The NPV criterion suggests Top-Spin should acquire machine 1. Machine 2, with a negative NPV, would fail to meet the NPV criterion.

The payback method gives a different answer from the NPV method in this example because the payback method ignores cash flows after the payback period and ignores the time value of money. Another problem with the payback method is that choosing too short a cutoff period for project acceptance may promote the selection of only short-lived projects. An organization will tend to reject long-run, positive-NPV projects. Despite these differences, companies find it useful to look at both NPV and payback when making capital investment decisions.

Nonuniform Cash Flows

When cash flows are not uniform, the payback computation takes a cumulative form: The cash flows over successive years are accumulated until the amount of net initial investment is recovered. Assume that Venture Law Group is considering the purchase of videoconferencing equipment for $150,000. The equipment is expected to provide a total cash savings of $340,000 over the next five years, due to reduced travel costs and more effective use of associates' time. The cash savings occur uniformly throughout each year, but are not uniform across years.

Year	Cash Savings	Cumulative Cash Savings	Net Initial Investment Unrecovered at End of Year
0	—	—	$150,000
1	$50,000	$ 50,000	100,000
2	55,000	105,000	45,000
3	60,000	165,000	—
4	85,000	165,000	—
5	90,000	340,000	—

It is clear from the chart that payback occurs during the third year. Straight-line interpolation within the third year reveals that the final $45,000 needed to recover the $150,000 investment (that is, $150,000 − $105,000 recovered by the end of year 2) will be achieved three-quarters of the way through year 3 (in which $60,000 of cash savings occur):

$$\text{Payback period} = 2 \text{ years} + \left(\frac{\$45,000}{\$60,000} \times 1 \text{ year} \right) = 2.75 \text{ years}$$

It is relatively simple to adjust the payback method to incorporate the time value of money by using a similar cumulative approach. The **discounted payback method** calculates the amount of time required for the discounted expected future cash flows to recoup the net initial investment in a project. For the videoconferencing example, we can modify the preceding chart by discounting the cash flows at the 8% required rate of return.

Year (1)	Cash Savings (2)	Present Value of $1 Discounted at 8% (3)	Discounted Cash Savings (4) = (2) × (3)	Cumulative Discounted Cash Savings (5)	Net Initial Investment Unrecovered at End of Year (6)
0	—	1.000	—	—	$150,000
1	$50,000	0.926	$46,300	$ 46,300	103,700
2	55,000	0.857	47,135	93,435	56,565
3	60,000	0.794	47,640	141,075	8,925
4	85,000	0.735	62,475	203,550	—
5	90,000	0.681	61,290	264,840	—

The fourth column represents the present values of the future cash savings. It is evident from the chart that discounted payback occurs between years 3 and 4. At the end of the third year, $8,925 of the initial investment is still unrecovered. Comparing this to the $62,475 in present value of savings achieved in the fourth year, straight-line interpolation then reveals that the discounted payback period is exactly one-seventh of the way into the fourth year:

$$\text{Discounted payback period} = 3 \text{ years} + \left(\frac{\$8,925}{\$62,475} \times 1 \text{ year} \right) = 3.14 \text{ years}$$

While discounted payback does incorporate the time value of money, it is still subject to the other criticism of the payback method—cash flows beyond the discounted payback period are ignored, resulting in a bias toward shorter-term projects. Companies such as Hewlett-Packard value the discounted payback method (HP refers to it as "breakeven time") because they view longer-term cash flows as inherently unpredictable in high-growth industries.

Finally, the videoconferencing example has a single cash outflow of $150,000 in year 0. When a project has multiple cash outflows occurring at different points in time, these outflows are first aggregated to obtain a total cash-outflow figure for the project. For computing the payback period, the cash flows are simply added, with no adjustment for the time value of money. For calculating the discounted payback period, the present values of the outflows are added instead.

Decision Point ▶

What are the payback and discounted payback methods? What are their main weaknesses?

Accrual Accounting Rate-of-Return Method

We now consider a fourth method for analyzing the financial aspects of capital budgeting projects. The **accrual accounting rate of return (AARR) method** divides the average annual (accrual accounting) income of a project by a measure of the investment in it. We illustrate AARR for the Top-Spin example using the project's net initial investment as the amount in the denominator:

Learning Objective 4

Use and evaluate the accrual accounting rate-of-return (AARR) method

. . . after-tax operating income divided by investment

$$\text{Accrual accounting rate of return} = \frac{\text{Increase in expected average annual after-tax operating income}}{\text{Net initial investment}}$$

If Top-Spin purchases the new carbon-fiber machine, its net initial investment is $379,100. The increase in expected average annual after-tax operating cash inflows is $98,200. This amount is the expected after-tax total operating cash inflows of $491,000 ($100,000 for four years and $91,000 in year 5), divided by the time horizon of five years. Suppose that the new machine results in additional depreciation deductions of $70,000 per year ($78,000 in annual depreciation for the new machine, relative to $8,000 per year on the existing machine).[5] The increase in expected average annual after-tax income is therefore $28,200 (the difference between the cash flow increase of $98,200 and the depreciation increase of $70,000). The AARR on net initial investment is computed as follows:

$$AARR = \frac{\$98,200 - \$70,000}{\$379,100} = \frac{\$28,200 \text{ per year}}{\$379,100} = 0.074, \text{ or } 7.4\% \text{ per year}$$

The 7.4% figure for AARR indicates the average rate at which a dollar of investment generates after-tax operating income. The new carbon-fiber machine has a low AARR for two reasons: (1) the use of net initial investment as the denominator, and (2) the use of income as the numerator, which necessitates deducting depreciation charges from the annual operating cash flows. To mitigate the first issue, many companies calculate AARR using an average level of investment. This alternative procedure recognizes that the book value of the investment declines over time. In its simplest form, average investment for Top-Spin is calculated as the arithmetic mean of the net initial investment of $379,100 and the net terminal cash flow of $9,000 (terminal disposal value of machine of $0, plus the terminal recovery of working capital of $9,000):

$$\text{Average investment over five years} = \frac{\text{Net initial investment} + \text{Net terminal cash flow}}{2}$$
$$= \frac{\$379,100 + \$9,000}{2} = \$194,050$$

The AARR on average investment is then calculated as follows:

$$AARR = \frac{\$28,200}{\$194,050} = 0.145, \text{ or } 14.5\% \text{ per year}$$

Our point here is that companies vary in how they calculate AARR. There is no uniformly preferred approach. Be sure you understand how AARR is defined in each individual situation. Projects whose AARR exceeds a specified hurdle required rate of return are regarded as acceptable (the higher the AARR, the better the project is considered to be).

The AARR method is similar to the IRR method in that both methods calculate a rate-of-return percentage. The AARR method calculates return using operating-income numbers after considering accruals and taxes, whereas the IRR method calculates return on the basis of after-tax cash flows and the time value of money. Because cash flows and time value of money are central to capital budgeting decisions, the IRR method is regarded as better than the AARR method.

AARR computations are easy to understand, and they use numbers reported in the financial statements. AARR gives managers an idea of how the accounting numbers they will report in the future will be affected if a project is accepted. Unlike the payback method,

---

[5] We provide further details on these numbers in the next section.

What are the strengths and weaknesses of the accrual accounting rate-of-return (AARR) method for evaluating long-term projects?

which ignores cash flows after the payback period, the AARR method considers income earned *throughout* a project's expected useful life. Unlike the NPV method, the AARR method uses accrual accounting income numbers, it does not track cash flows, and it ignores the time value of money. Critics cite these arguments as drawbacks of the AARR method.

Overall, keep in mind that companies frequently use multiple methods for evaluating capital investment decisions. When different methods lead to different rankings of projects, finance theory suggests that more weight be given to the NPV method because the assumptions made by the NPV method are most consistent with making decisions that maximize company value.

Relevant Cash Flows in Discounted Cash Flow Analysis

Learning Objective 5

Identify relevant cash inflows and outflows for capital budgeting decisions

. . . the differences in expected future cash flows resulting from the investment

So far, we have examined methods for evaluating long-term projects in settings where the expected future cash flows of interest were assumed to be known. One of the biggest challenges in capital budgeting, particularly DCF analysis, however, is determining which cash flows are relevant in making an investment selection. Relevant cash flows are the differences in expected future cash flows as a result of making the investment. In the Top-Spin example, the relevant cash flows are the differences in expected future cash flows between continuing to use the old technology and updating its technology with the purchase of a new machine. *When reading this section, focus on identifying expected future cash flows and the differences in expected future cash flows.*

To illustrate relevant cash flow analysis, consider a more complex version of the Top-Spin example with these additional assumptions:

- Top-Spin is a profitable company. The income tax rate is 40% of operating income each year.

- The before-tax additional operating cash inflows from the carbon-fiber machine are $120,000 in years 1 through 4 and $105,000 in year 5.

- For tax purposes, Top-Spin uses the straight-line depreciation method and assumes no terminal disposal value.

- Gains or losses on the sale of depreciable assets are taxed at the same rate as ordinary income.

- The tax effects of cash inflows and outflows occur at the same time that the cash inflows and outflows occur.

- Top-Spin uses an 8% required rate of return for discounting after-tax cash flows.

Summary data for the machines follow:

	Old Graphite Machine	New Carbon-Fiber Machine
Purchase price	—	$390,000
Current book value	$40,000	—
Current disposal value	6,500	Not applicable
Terminal disposal value five years from now	0	0
Annual depreciation	8,000[a]	78,000[b]
Working capital required	6,000	15,000

[a]$40,000 ÷ 5 years = $8,000 annual depreciation.
[b]$390,000 ÷ 5 years = $78,000 annual depreciation.

Relevant After-Tax Flows

We use the concepts of differential cost and differential revenue introduced in Chapter 11. We compare (1) the after-tax cash outflows as a result of replacing the old machine with (2) the additional after-tax cash inflows generated from using the new machine rather than the old machine.

As Benjamin Franklin said, "Two things in life are certain: death and taxes." Income taxes are a fact of life for most corporations and individuals. It is important first to understand how income taxes affect cash flows in each year. Exhibit 5 shows how investing in the new machine will affect Top-Spin's cash flow from operations and its income taxes in year 1. Recall that Top-Spin will generate $120,000 in before-tax additional operating cash inflows by investing in the new machine, but it will record additional depreciation of $70,000 ($78,000 − $8,000) for tax purposes.

Panel A shows that the year 1 cash flow from operations, net of income taxes, equals $100,000, using two methods based on the income statement. The first method focuses on cash items only, the $120,000 operating cash inflows minus income taxes of $20,000. The second method starts with the $30,000 increase in net income (calculated after subtracting the $70,000 additional depreciation deductions for income tax purposes) and adds back that $70,000, because depreciation is an operating cost that reduces net income but is a noncash item itself.

Panel B of Exhibit 5 describes a third method that we will use frequently to compute cash flow from operations, net of income taxes. The easiest way to interpret the third method is to think of the government as a 40% (equal to the tax rate) partner in Top-Spin. Each time Top-Spin obtains operating cash inflows, C, its income is higher by C, so it will pay 40% of the operating cash inflows ($0.40C$) in taxes. This results in additional after-tax cash operating flows of $C − 0.40C$, which in this example is $120,000 − (0.40 \times \$120,000) = \$72,000$, or $\$120,000 \times (1 − 0.40) = \$72,000$.

To achieve the higher operating cash inflows, C, Top-Spin incurs higher depreciation charges, D, from investing in the new machine. Depreciation costs do not directly affect cash flows because depreciation is a noncash cost, but higher depreciation cost *lowers* Top-Spin's taxable income by D, saving income tax cash outflows of $0.40D$, which in this example is $0.40 \times \$70,000 = \$28,000$.

Letting t = tax rate, cash flow from operations, net of income taxes, in this example equals the operating cash inflows, C, minus the tax payments on these inflows, $t \times C$, plus the tax savings on depreciation deductions, $t \times D$: $\$120,000 − (0.40 \times \$120,000) + (0.40 \times \$70,000) = \$120,000 − \$48,000 + \$28,000 = \$100,000$.

By the same logic, each time Top-Spin has a gain on the sale of assets, G, it will show tax outflows, $t \times G$; and each time Top-Spin has a loss on the sale of assets, L, it will show tax benefits or savings of $t \times L$.

PANEL A: Two Methods Based on the Income Statement

C	Operating cash inflows from investment in machine	$120,000
D	Additional depreciation deduction	70,000
OI	Increase in operating income	50,000
T	Income taxes (Income tax rate $t \times OI$) =	
	40% × $50,000	20,000
NI	Increase in net income	$ 30,000
	Increase in cash flow from operations, net of income taxes	
	Method 1: $C − T$ = $120,000 − $20,000 = $100,000 or	
	Method 2: $NI + D$ = $30,000 + $70,000 = $100,000	

PANEL B: Item-by-Item Method

	Effect of cash operating flows	
C	Operating cash inflows from investment in machine	$120,000
$t \times C$	Deduct income tax cash outflow at 40%	48,000
$\left.\begin{array}{l} C − (t \times C) \\ = (1 − t) \times C \end{array}\right\}$	After-tax cash flow from operations (excluding the depreciation effect)	72,000
	Effect of depreciation	
D	Additional depreciation deduction, $70,000	
$t \times D$	Income tax cash savings from additional depreciation deduction at 40% × $70,000	28,000
$\begin{array}{l}(1 − t) \times C + (t \times D) \\ = C − (t \times C) + (t \times D)\end{array}$	Cash flow from operations, net of income taxes	$100,000

Exhibit 5

Effect on Cash Flow from Operations, Net of Income Taxes, in Year 1 for Top-Spin's Investment in the New Carbon-Fiber Machine

Categories of Cash Flows

A capital investment project typically has three categories of cash flows: (1) net initial investment in the project, which includes the acquisition of assets and any associated additions to working capital, minus the after-tax cash flow from the disposal of existing assets; (2) after-tax cash flow from operations (including income tax cash savings from annual depreciation deductions); and (3) after-tax cash flow from terminal disposal of an asset and recovery of working capital. We use the Top-Spin example to discuss these three categories.

As you work through the cash flows in each category, refer to Exhibit 6. This exhibit sketches the relevant cash flows for Top-Spin's decision to purchase the new machine as described in items 1 through 3 here. Note that the total relevant cash flows for each year equal the relevant cash flows used in Exhibits 2 and 3 to illustrate the NPV and IRR methods.

1. **Net Initial Investment.** Three components of net-initial-investment cash flows are (a) cash outflow to purchase the machine, (b) cash outflow for working capital, and (c) after-tax cash inflow from current disposal of the old machine.

   1a. *Initial machine investment.* These outflows, made for purchasing plant and equipment, occur at the beginning of the project's life and include cash outflows for transporting and installing the equipment. In the Top-Spin example, the $390,000 cost (including transportation and installation) of the carbon-fiber machine is an outflow in year 0. These cash flows are relevant to the capital budgeting decision because they will be incurred only if Top-Spin decides to purchase the new machine.

   1b. *Initial working-capital investment.* Initial investments in plant and equipment are usually accompanied by additional investments in working capital. These additional investments take the form of current assets, such as accounts receivable and inventories, minus current liabilities, such as accounts payable. Working-capital investments are similar to plant and equipment investments in that they require cash. The magnitude of the investment generally increases as a function of the level of additional sales generated by the project. However, the exact relationship varies based on the nature of the project and the operating cycle of the industry.

Exhibit 6   Relevant Cash Inflows and Outflows for Top-Spin's Carbon-Fiber Machine

			Sketch of Relevant Cash Flows at End of Year					
	A	B	C	D	E	F	G	H
1								
2			0	1	2	3	4	5
3	1a.	Initial machine investment	$(390,000)					
4	1b.	Initial working-capital investment	(9,000)					
5	1c.	After-tax cash flow from current disposal						
6		of old machine	19,900					
7	Net initial investment		(379,100)					
8	2a.	Annual after-tax cash flow from operations						
9		(excluding the depreciation effect)		$ 72,000	$ 72,000	$ 72,000	$ 72,000	$ 63,000
10	2b.	Income tax cash savings from annual						
11		depreciation deductions		28,000	28,000	28,000	28,000	28,000
12	3a.	After-tax cash flow from terminal disposal						
13		of machine						0
14	3b.	After-tax cash flow from recovery of						
15		working capital						9,000
16	Total relevant cash flows,							
17	as shown in Exhibits 21-2 and 21-3		$(379,100)	$ 100,000	$100,000	$100,000	$100,000	$100,000
18								

For a given dollar of sales, a maker of heavy equipment, for example, would require more working capital support than Top-Spin, which in turn has to invest more in working capital than a retail grocery store.

The Top-Spin example assumes a $9,000 additional investment in working capital (for supplies and spare-parts inventory) if the new machine is acquired. The additional working-capital investment is the difference between working capital required to operate the new machine ($15,000) and working capital required to operate the old machine ($6,000). The $9,000 additional investment in working capital is a cash outflow in year 0 and is returned, that is, becomes a cash inflow, at the end of year 5.

1c. *After-tax cash flow from current disposal of old machine.* Any cash received from disposal of the old machine is a relevant cash inflow (in year 0). That's because it is an expected future cash flow that differs between the alternatives of investing and not investing in the new machine. Top-Spin will dispose of the old machine for $6,500 only if it invests in the new carbon-fiber machine. The book value (which is original cost minus accumulated depreciation) of the old equipment is generally irrelevant to the decision since it is a past, or sunk, cost. However, when tax considerations are included, book value does play a role. The reason is that the book value determines the gain or loss on sale of the machine and, therefore, the taxes paid (or saved) on the transaction.

Consider the tax consequences of disposing of the old machine. We first have to compute the gain or loss on disposal:

Current disposal value of old machine (given)	$ 6,500
Deduct current book value of old machine (given)	40,000
Loss on disposal of machine	$(33,500)

Any loss on the sale of assets lowers taxable income and results in tax savings. The after-tax cash flow from disposal of the old machine is as follows:

Current disposal value of old machine	$ 6,500
Tax savings on loss (0.40 × $33,500)	13,400
After-tax cash inflow from current disposal of old machine	$19,900

The sum of items **1a, 1b,** and **1c** appears in Exhibit 6 as the year 0 net initial investment for the new carbon-fiber machine equal to $379,100 (initial machine investment, $390,000, plus additional working-capital investment, $9,000, minus after-tax cash inflow from current disposal of the old machine, $19,900).[6]

2. **Cash Flow from Operations.** This category includes the difference between each year's cash flow from operations under the two alternatives. Organizations make capital investments to generate future cash inflows. These inflows may result from savings in operating costs, or, as for Top-Spin, from producing and selling additional goods. Annual cash flow from operations can be net outflows in some years. Chevron makes periodic upgrades to its oil extraction equipment, and in years of upgrades, cash flow from operations tends to be negative for the site being upgraded, although in the long-run such upgrades are NPV positive. Always focus on cash flow from operations, not on revenues and expenses under accrual accounting.

Top-Spin's additional operating cash inflows—$120,000 in each of the first four years and $105,000 in the fifth year—are relevant because they are expected future cash flows that will differ between the alternatives of investing and not investing in the new machine. The after-tax effects of these cash flows follow.

2a. *Annual after-tax cash flow from operations (excluding the depreciation effect).* The 40% tax rate reduces the benefit of the $120,000 additional operating cash

---

[6] To illustrate the case when there is a gain on disposal, suppose that the old machine could be sold now for $50,000 instead. Then, the firm would record a gain on disposal of $10,000 ($50,000 less the book value of $40,000), resulting in additional tax payments of $4,000 (0.40 tax rate × $10,000 gain). The after-tax cash inflow from current disposal would therefore equal $46,000 (the disposal value of $50,000, less the tax payment of $4,000).

inflows for years 1 through 4 with the new carbon-fiber machine. After-tax cash flow (excluding the depreciation effect) is as follows:

Annual cash flow from operations with new machine	$120,000
Deduct income tax payments (0.40 × $120,000)	48,000
Annual after-tax cash flow from operations	$ 72,000

For year 5, the after-tax cash flow (excluding the depreciation effect) is as follows:

Annual cash flow from operations with new machine	$105,000
Deduct income tax payments (0.40 × $105,000)	42,000
Annual after-tax cash flow from operations	$ 63,000

Exhibit 6, item **2a,** shows the $72,000 amounts for each of the years 1 through 4 and $63,000 for year 5.

To reinforce the idea about focusing on cash flows, consider the following additional fact about the Top-Spin example. Suppose the total plant overhead costs will not change whether the new machine is purchased or the old machine is kept. The production plant's overhead costs are allocated to individual machines— Top-Spin has several—on the basis of the labor costs for operating each machine. Because the new carbon-fiber machine would have lower labor costs, overhead costs allocated to it would be $30,000 less than the amount allocated to the machine it would replace. How should Top-Spin incorporate the decrease in allocated overhead costs of $30,000 in the relevant cash flow analysis?

To answer that question, we need to ask, "Do *total* overhead costs decrease at Top-Spin's production plant as a result of acquiring the new machine?" In our example, they do not. Total overhead costs of the production plant remain the same whether or not the new machine is acquired. *Only the overhead costs allocated to individual machines change.* The overhead costs allocated to the new machine are $30,000 less than the amount allocated to the machine it would replace. This $30,000 difference in overhead would be allocated to *other* machines in the department. That is, no cash flow savings in total overhead would occur. Therefore, the $30,000 should not be included as part of annual cash savings from operations.

Next consider the effects of depreciation. *The depreciation line item is itself irrelevant in DCF analysis.* That's because it's a noncash allocation of costs, whereas DCF is based on inflows and outflows of *cash*. In DCF methods, the initial cost of equipment is regarded as a *lump-sum* outflow of cash in year 0. Deducting depreciation expenses from operating cash inflows would result in counting the lump-sum amount twice. *However, depreciation results in income tax cash savings. These tax savings are a relevant cash flow.*

2b. *Income tax cash savings from annual depreciation deductions.* Tax deductions for depreciation, in effect, partially offset the cost of acquiring the new carbon-fiber machine. By purchasing the new machine, Top-Spin is able to deduct $78,000 in depreciation each year, relative to the $8,000 depreciation on the old graphite machine. The additional annual depreciation deduction of $70,000 results in incremental income tax cash savings of $70,000 × 0.4, or $28,000 annually. Exhibit 6, item **2b,** shows these $28,000 amounts for years 1 through 5.[7]

For economic-policy reasons, usually to encourage (or in some cases, discourage) investments, tax laws specify which depreciation methods and which depreciable lives are permitted. Suppose the government permitted accelerated depreciation to be used, allowing for higher depreciation deductions in earlier years. If allowable, should Top-Spin use accelerated depreciation? Yes, because there is a general rule in tax planning for profitable companies such as Top-Spin: When there is a legal choice, take the depreciation (or any other deduction) sooner rather than later. Doing so causes the (cash) income tax savings to occur earlier, which increases the project's NPV.

---

[7] If Top-Spin were a nonprofit foundation not subject to income taxes, cash flow from operations would equal $120,000 in years 1 through 4 and $105,000 in year 5. The revenues would not be reduced by 40%, nor would there be income tax cash savings from the depreciation deduction.

3. **Terminal Disposal of Investment.** The disposal of the new investment generally increases cash inflow when the project terminates. Errors in forecasting terminal disposal value are seldom critical for long-duration projects, because the present value of amounts to be received in the distant future is usually small. Two components of the terminal disposal value of an investment are (a) after-tax cash flow from terminal disposal of machines and (b) after-tax cash flow from recovery of working capital.

3a. *After-tax cash flow from terminal disposal of machines.* At the end of the useful life of the project, the machine's terminal disposal value may be $0 or an amount considerably less than the net initial investment. The relevant cash inflow is the difference in expected after-tax cash inflow from terminal disposal at the end of five years under the two alternatives of purchasing the new machine or keeping the old machine.

   Although the old machine has a positive terminal disposal value today (year 0), in year 5, it will have a zero terminal value. As such, both the existing and the new machines have zero after-tax cash inflow from terminal disposal in year 5. Hence, the difference in after-tax cash inflow from terminal disposal is also $0.

   In this example, there are no tax effects at the terminal point because both the existing and new machine have disposal values that equal their book values at the time of disposal (in each case, this value is $0). What if either the existing or the new machine had a terminal value that differed from its book value at the time of disposal? In that case, the approach for computing the terminal inflow is identical to that for calculating the after-tax cash flow from current disposal illustrated earlier in part 1c.

3b. *After-tax cash flow from terminal recovery of working-capital investment.* The initial investment in working capital is usually fully recouped when the project is terminated. At that time, inventories and accounts receivable necessary to support the project are no longer needed. Top-Spin receives cash equal to the book value of its working capital. Thus, there is no gain or loss on working capital and, hence, no tax consequences. The relevant cash inflow is the difference in the expected working capital recovered under the two alternatives. At the end of year 5, Top-Spin recovers $15,000 cash from working capital if it invests in the new carbon-fiber machine versus $6,000 if it continues to use the old machine. The relevant cash inflow at the end of year 5 if Top-Spin invests in the new machine is thus $9,000 ($15,000 − $6,000).

   Some capital investment projects *reduce* working capital. Assume that a computer-integrated manufacturing (CIM) project with a seven-year life will reduce inventories and, hence, working capital by $20 million from, say, $50 million to $30 million. This reduction will be represented as a $20 million cash *inflow* for the project in year 0. At the end of seven years, the recovery of working capital will show a relevant incremental cash *outflow* of $20 million. That's because, at the end of year 7, the company recovers only $30 million of working capital under CIM, rather than the $50 million of working capital it would have recovered had it not implemented CIM.

Exhibit 6 shows items **3a** and **3b** in the "year 5" column. The relevant cash flows in Exhibit 6 serve as inputs for the four capital budgeting methods described earlier in the chapter.

Project Management and Performance Evaluation

We have so far looked at ways to identify relevant cash flows and appropriate techniques for analyzing them. The final stage (stage 5) of capital budgeting begins with implementing the decision, or managing the project.[8] This includes management control of the investment activity itself, as well as management control of the project as a whole.

Capital budgeting projects, such as purchasing a carbon-fiber machine or video-conferencing equipment, are easier to implement than projects involving building shopping

Decision Point

What are the relevant cash inflows and outflows for capital budgeting decisions? How should accrual accounting concepts be considered?

Learning Objective 6

Understand issues involved in implementing capital budgeting decisions and evaluating managerial performance

. . . the importance of post-investment audits and the correct choice of performance measures

---

[8] In this section, we do not consider the different options for financing a project (refer to a text on corporate finance for details).

malls or manufacturing plants. The building projects are more complex, so monitoring and controlling the investment schedules and budgets are critical to successfully completing the investment activity. This leads to the second dimension of stage 5 in the capital budgeting process: evaluate performance and learn.

Post-Investment Audits

A post-investment audit provides management with feedback about the performance of a project, so management can compare actual results to the costs and benefits expected at the time the project was selected. Suppose actual outcomes (such as additional operating cash flows from the new carbon-fiber machine in the Top-Spin example) are much lower than expected. Management must then investigate to determine if this result occurred because the original estimates were overly optimistic or because of implementation problems. Either of these explanations is a concern.

Optimistic estimates may result in the acceptance of a project that should have been rejected. To discourage optimistic estimates, companies such as DuPont maintain records comparing actual results to the estimates made by individual managers when seeking approval for capital investments. Post-investment audits punish inaccurate estimates, and therefore discourage unrealistic forecasts. This prevents managers from overstating project cash inflows and accepting projects that should never have been undertaken. Implementation problems, such as weak project management, poor quality control, or inadequate marketing are also a concern. Post-investment audits help to alert senior management to these problems so that they can be quickly corrected.

However, post-investment audits require thoughtfulness and care. They should be done only after project outcomes have stabilized because performing audits too early may yield misleading feedback. Obtaining actual results to compare against estimates is often not easy. For example, additional revenues from the new carbon-fiber technology may not be comparable to the estimated revenues because in any particular season, the rise or decline of a tennis star can greatly affect the popularity of the sport and the subsequent demand for racquets. A better evaluation would look at the average revenues across a couple of seasons.

Performance Evaluation

As the preceding discussion suggests, ideally one should evaluate managers on a project-by-project basis and look at how well managers achieve the amounts and timing of forecasted cash flows. In practice, however, managers are often evaluated based on aggregate information, especially when multiple projects are underway at any point in time. It is important then to ensure that the method of evaluation does not conflict with the use of the NPV method for making capital budgeting decisions. For example, suppose that Top-Spin uses the accrual accounting rate of return generated in each period to assess managerial performance. We know from the NPV method that the manager of the racquet production plant should purchase the carbon-fiber machine because it has a positive NPV of $20,200. Despite that, the project may be rejected if the AARR of 7.4% on the net initial investment is lower than the minimum accounting rate of return the manager is required to achieve.

There is an inconsistency between using the NPV method as best for capital budgeting decisions and then using a different method to evaluate performance. This inconsistency means managers are tempted to make capital budgeting decisions on the basis of the method by which they are being evaluated. Such temptations become more pronounced if managers are frequently transferred (or promoted), or if their bonuses are affected by the level of year-to-year accrual income.

Other conflicts between decision making and performance evaluation persist even if a company uses similar measures for both purposes. If the AARR on the carbon-fiber machine exceeds the minimum required AARR but is below the current AARR of the production plant, the manager may still be tempted to reject purchase of the carbon-fiber machine because the lower AARR of the carbon-fiber machine will reduce the AARR of the entire plant and hurt the manager's reported performance. Or, consider an example where the cash inflows from the carbon-fiber machine occur mostly in the later years of the project. Then, even if the AARR on the project exceeds the current AARR of the plant

Decision Point ▶

What conflicts can arise between using DCF methods for capital budgeting decisions and accrual accounting for performance evaluation? How can these conflicts be reduced?

(as well as the minimum required return), the manager may still reject the purchase since it will have a negative effect on the realized accrual accounting rate of return for the first few years.

Strategic Considerations in Capital Budgeting

Learning Objective 7

Identify strategic considerations in capital budgeting decisions

. . . critical investments whose benefits are uncertain or difficult to estimate

A company's strategy is the source of its strategic capital budgeting decisions. Strategic decisions by United Airlines, Westin Hotels, Federal Express, and Pizza Hut to expand in Europe and Asia required capital investments to be made in several countries (see also Concepts in Action feature). The strategic decision by Barnes & Noble to support book sales over the Internet required capital investments creating barnesandnoble.com and an Internet infrastructure. News Corp.'s decision to enlarge its online presence resulted in a large investment to purchase MySpace, and additional supporting investments to integrate MySpace with the firm's pre-existing assets. Pfizer's decision to develop its cholesterol-reducing drug Lipitor led to major investments in R&D and marketing. Toyota's decision to offer a line of hybrids across both its Toyota and Lexus platforms required start-up investments to form a hybrid division and ongoing investments to fund the division's continuing research efforts.

Capital investment decisions that are strategic in nature require managers to consider a broad range of factors that may be difficult to estimate. Consider some of the difficulties of justifying investments made by companies such as Mitsubishi, Sony, and Audi in computer-integrated manufacturing (CIM) technology. In CIM, computers give instructions that quickly and automatically set up and run equipment to manufacture many different products. Quantifying these benefits requires some notion of how quickly consumer-demand will change in the future. CIM technology also increases worker knowledge of, and experience with automation; however, the benefit of this knowledge and experience is difficult to measure. Managers must develop judgment and intuition to make these decisions.

Investment in Research and Development

Companies such as GlaxoSmithKline, in the pharmaceutical industry, and Intel, in the semiconductor industry, regard research and development (R&D) projects as important strategic investments. The distant payoffs from R&D investments, however, are more uncertain than other investments such as new equipment. On the positive side, R&D investments are often staged: As time unfolds, companies can increase or decrease the resources committed to a project based on how successful it has been up to that point. This option feature of R&D investments, called real options, is an important aspect of R&D investments and increases the NPV of these investments, because a company can limit its losses when things are going badly and take advantage of new opportunities when things are going well.

Customer Value and Capital Budgeting

Finally, note that the framework described in this chapter to evaluate investment projects can also be used to make strategic decisions regarding which customers to invest in. Consider Potato Supreme, which makes potato products for sale to retail outlets. It is currently analyzing two of its customers: Shine Stores and Always Open. Potato Supreme predicts the following cash flow from operations, net of income taxes (in thousands), from each customer account for the next five years:

	2011	2012	2013	2014	2015
Shine Stores	$1,450	$1,305	$1,175	$1,058	$ 950
Always Open	690	1,160	1,900	2,950	4,160

Which customer is more valuable to Potato Supreme? Looking at only the current period, 2011, Shine Stores provides more than double the cash flow compared to Always Open ($1,450 versus $690). A different picture emerges, however, when looking over the entire

Concepts in Action   International Capital Budgeting at Disney

Yoshikazu Tsuno/AFP/Getty Images/Newscom

The Walt Disney Company, one of the world's leading entertainment producers, had more than $36 billion in 2009 revenue through movies, television networks, branded products, and theme parks and resorts. Within its theme park business, Disney spends around $1 billion annually in capital investments for new theme parks, rides and attractions, and other park construction and improvements. This money is divided between its domestic properties and international parks in Paris, Hong Kong, and Tokyo.

Years ago, Disney developed a robust capital budgeting approval process. Project approval relied heavily on projected returns on capital investment as measured by net present value (NPV) and internal rate of return (IRR) calculations. While this worked well for Disney's investments in its domestic theme park business, the company experienced challenges when it considered building the DisneySea theme park near Tokyo, Japan.

While capital budgeting in the United States relies on discounted cash flow analysis, Japanese firms frequently use the average accounting return (AAR) method instead. AAR is analogous to an accrual accounting rate of return (AARR) measure based on average investment. However, it focuses on the first few years of a project (five years, in the case of DisneySea) and ignores terminal values.

Disney discovered that the difference in capital budgeting techniques between U.S. and Japanese firms reflected the difference in corporate governance in the two countries. The use of NPV and IRR in the United States underlined the perspective of shareholder-value maximization. On the other hand, the preference for the simple accounting-based measure in Japan reflected the importance of achieving complete consensus among all parties affected by the investment decision.

When the DisneySea project was evaluated, it was found to have a positive NPV, but a negative AAR. To account for the differences in philosophies and capital budgeting techniques, managers at Disney introduced a third calculation method called average cash flow return (ACFR). This hybrid method measured the average cash flow over the first five years, with the asset assumed to be sold for book value at the end of that period as a fraction of the initial investment in the project. The resulting ratio was found to exceed the return on Japanese government bonds, and hence to yield a positive return for DisneySea. As a result, the DisneySea theme park was constructed next to Tokyo Disneyland and has since become a profitable addition to Disney's Japanese operations.

Sources: Misawa, Mitsuru. 2006. Tokyo Disneyland and the DisneySea Park: Corporate governance and differences in capital budgeting concepts and methods between American and Japanese companies. University of Hong Kong No. HKU568, Hong Kong: University of Hong Kong Asia Case Research Center; and The Walt Disney Company. 2010. 2009 annual report. Burbank, CA: The Walt Disney Company.

five-year horizon. Potato Supreme anticipates Always Open's orders to increase; meanwhile, it expects Shine Stores' orders to decline. Using Potato Supreme's 10% RRR, the NPV of the Always Open customer is $7,610, compared to $4,591 for Shine Stores (computations not shown). Note how NPV captures in its estimate of customer value the future growth of Always Open. Potato Supreme uses this information to allocate more resources and salespersons to service the Always Open account. Potato Supreme can also use NPV calculations to examine the effects of alternative ways of increasing customer loyalty and retention, such as introducing frequent-purchaser cards.

A comparison of year-to-year changes in customer NPV estimates highlights whether managers have been successful in maintaining long-run profitable relationships with their customers. Suppose the NPV of Potato Supreme's customer base declines 15% in one year. Management can then examine the reasons for the decline, such as aggressive pricing by competitors, and devise new-product development and marketing strategies for the future.

Capital One, a financial-services company, uses NPV to estimate the value of different credit-card customers. Cellular telephone companies such as Cellular One and Verizon Wireless attempt to sign up customers for multiple years of service. The objective is to prevent "customer churn," customers switching frequently from one company to another. The higher the probability of customer churn, the lower the NPV of the customer.

Decision Point ▶

What strategic considerations arise in the capital budgeting process?

Problem for Self-Study

Part A

Returning to the Top-Spin carbon-fiber machine project, assume that Top-Spin is a *nonprofit organization* and that the expected additional operating cash inflows are $130,000 in years 1 through 4 and $121,000 in year 5. Using data from page 750, the net initial investment is $392,500 (new machine, $390,000 plus additional working capital, $9,000 minus terminal disposal value of old machine, $6,500). All other facts are unchanged: a five-year useful life, no terminal disposal value, and an 8% RRR. Year 5 cash inflows are $130,000, which includes a $9,000 recovery of working capital.

Calculate the following:
1. Net present value
2. Internal rate of return
3. Payback
4. Accrual accounting rate of return on net initial investment

Required

Solution

1. $NPV = (\$130,000 \times 3.993) - \$392,500$
   $= \$519,090 - \$392,500 = \$126,590$

2. There are several approaches to computing IRR. One is to use a calculator with an IRR function. This approach gives an IRR of 19.6%. Another approach is to use Table 4 in the Appendix:

$$\$392,500 = \$130,000F$$

$$F = \frac{\$392,500}{\$130,000} = 3.019$$

On the five-period line of Table 4, the column closest to 3.019 is 20%. To obtain a more-accurate number, use straight-line interpolation:

	Present Value Factors	
18%	3.127	3.127
IRR	—	3.019
20%	2.,991	—
Difference	0.136	0.108

$$IRR = 18\% + \frac{0.108}{0.136}(2\%) = 19.6\% \text{ per year}$$

3. Payback period $= \dfrac{\text{Net initial investment}}{\text{Uniform increase in annual future cash flows}}$

   $= \$392,500 \div \$130,000 = 3.0 \text{ years}$

4. $AARR = \dfrac{\text{Increase in expected average annual operating income}}{\text{Net initial investment}}$

   $\text{Increase in expected average annual operating cash inflows} = [(\$130,000 \times 4) + \$121,000] \div 5 \text{ years}$

   $= \$641,000 \div 5 = \$128,200$

   $\text{Increase in annual depreciation} = \$70,000 \ (\$78,000 - \$8,000, \text{ see p. 000})$

   $\text{Increase in expected average annual operating income} = \$128,200 - \$70,000 = \$58,200$

   $AARR = \dfrac{\$58,200}{\$392,500} = 14.8\% \text{ per year}$

Part B

Assume that Top-Spin is subject to income tax at a 40% rate. All other information from Part A is unchanged. Compute the NPV of the new carbon-fiber machine project.

Solution

To save space, Exhibit 7 shows the calculations using a format slightly different from the format used in this chapter. Item **2a** is where the new $130,000 cash flow assumption affects the NPV analysis (compared to Exhibit 6). All other amounts in Exhibit 7 are identical to the corresponding amounts in Exhibit 6. For years 1 through 4, after-tax cash flow (excluding the depreciation effect) is as follows:

Annual cash flow from operations with new machine	$130,000
Deduct income tax payments (0.40 × $130,000)	52,000
Annual after-tax cash flow from operations	$ 78,000

For year 5, after-tax cash flow (excluding the depreciation effect) is as follows:

Annual cash flow from operations with new machine	$121,000
Deduct income tax payments (0.40 × $121,000)	48,400
Annual after-tax cash flow from operations	$ 72,600

NPV in Exhibit 7 is $46,610. As computed in Part A, NPV when there are no income taxes is $126,590. The difference in these two NPVs illustrates the impact of income taxes in capital budgeting analysis.

Exhibit 7   Net Present Value Method Incorporating Income Taxes: Top-Spin's Carbon-Fiber Machine with Revised Annual Cash Flow from Operations

	Home	Insert	Page Layout	Formulas	Data	Review	View					
	A	B		C	D	E	F	G	H	I	J	
1				Present	Present Value of							
2				Value of	$1 Discounted at		Sketch of Relevant Cash Flows at End of Year					
3				Cash Flow	8%	0	1	2	3	4	5	
4	1a.	Initial machine investment		$(390,000)	← 1.000 ←	$(390,000)						
5												
6	1b.	Initial working-capital investment		(9,000)	← 1.000 ←	$ (9,000)						
7	1c.	After-tax cash flow from current										
8		disposal of old machine		19,900	← 1.000 ←	$ 19,900						
9		Net initial investment		(379,100)								
10	2a.	Annual after-tax cash flow from										
11		operations (excluding the depreciation effect)										
12		Year 1		72,228	← 0.926 ←		$78,000					
13		Year 2		66,846	← 0.857 ←			$78,000				
14		Year 3		61,932	← 0.794 ←				$78,000			
15		Year 4		57,330	← 0.735 ←					$78,000		
16		Year 5		49,441	← 0.681 ←						$72,600	
17	2b.	Income tax cash savings from annual										
18		depreciation deductions										
19		Year 1		25,928	← 0.926 ←		$28,000					
20		Year 2		23,996	← 0.857 ←			$28,000				
21		Year 3		22,232	← 0.794 ←				$28,000			
22		Year 4		20,580	← 0.735 ←					$28,000		
23		Year 5		19,068	← 0.681 ←						$28,000	
24	3.	After-tax cash flow from										
25		a. Terminal disposal of machine		0	← 0.681 ←						$ 0	
26		b. Recovery of working capital		6,129	← 0.681 ←						$ 9,000	
27		NPV if new machine purchased		$ 46,610								
28												

Decision Points

The following question-and-answer format summarizes the chapter's learning objectives. Each decision presents a key question related to a learning objective. The guidelines are the answer to that question.

Decision	Guidelines
1. What are the five stages of capital budgeting?	Capital budgeting is long-run planning for proposed investment projects. The five stages of capital budgeting are as follows: 1) Identify projects: Identify potential capital investments that agree with the organization's strategy; 2) Obtain information: Gather information from all parts of the value chain to evaluate alternative projects; 3) Make predictions: Forecast all potential cash flows attributable to the alternative projects; 4) Make decisions by choosing among alternatives: Determine which investment yields the greatest benefit and the least cost to the organization; and 5) Implement the decision, evaluate performance, and learn: Obtain funding and make the investments selected in stage 4; track realized cash flows, compare against estimated numbers, and revise plans if necessary.
2. What are the two primary discounted cash flow (DCF) methods for project evaluation?	The two main DCF methods are the net present value (NPV) method and the internal rate-of-return (IRR) method. The NPV method calculates the expected net monetary gain or loss from a project by discounting to the present all expected future cash inflows and outflows, using the required rate of return. A project is acceptable in financial terms if it has a positive NPV. The IRR method computes the rate of return (also called the discount rate) at which the present value of expected cash inflows from a project equals the present value of expected cash outflows from the project. A project is acceptable in financial terms if its IRR exceeds the required rate of return. DCF is the best approach to capital budgeting. It explicitly includes all project cash flows and recognizes the time value of money. The NPV method is the preferred DCF method.
3. What are the payback and discounted payback methods? What are their main weaknesses?	The payback method measures the time it will take to recoup, in the form of cash inflows, the total cash amount invested in a project. The payback method neglects the time value of money and ignores cash flows beyond the payback period. The discounted payback method measures the time taken for the present value of cash inflows to equal the present value of outflows. It adjusts for the time value of money but overlooks cash flows after the discounted payback period.
4. What are the strengths and weaknesses of the accrual accounting rate-of-return (AARR) method for evaluating long-term projects?	The accrual accounting rate of return (AARR) divides an accrual accounting measure of average annual income from a project by an accrual accounting measure of its investment. AARR gives managers an idea of the effect of accepting a project on their future reported accounting profitability. However, AARR uses accrual accounting income numbers, does not track cash flows, and ignores the time value of money.
5. What are the relevant cash inflows and outflows for capital budgeting decisions? How should accrual accounting concepts be considered?	Relevant cash inflows and outflows in DCF analysis are the differences in expected future cash flows as a result of making the investment. Only cash inflows and outflows matter; accrual accounting concepts are irrelevant for DCF methods. For example, the income taxes saved as a result of depreciation deductions are relevant because they decrease cash outflows, but the depreciation itself is a noncash item.
6. What conflicts can arise between using DCF methods for capital budgeting decisions and accrual accounting for performance evaluation? How can these conflicts be reduced?	Using accrual accounting to evaluate the performance of a manager may create conflicts with using DCF methods for capital budgeting. Frequently, the decision made using a DCF method will not report good "operating income" results in the project's early years under accrual accounting. For this reason, managers are tempted to not use DCF methods even though the decisions based on them would be in the best interests of the company as a whole over the long run. This conflict can be reduced by evaluating managers on a project-by-project basis and by looking at their ability to achieve the amounts and timing of forecasted cash flows.

7. What strategic considerations arise in the capital budgeting process?

A company's strategy is the source of its strategic capital budgeting decisions. Such decisions require managers to consider a broad range of factors that may be difficult to estimate. Managers must develop judgment and intuition to make these decisions. R&D projects, for example, are important strategic investments, with distant and usually highly uncertain payoffs.

Appendix

Capital Budgeting and Inflation

The Top-Spin example (Exhibits 2 to 6) does not include adjustments for inflation in the relevant revenues and costs. **Inflation** is the decline in the general purchasing power of the monetary unit, such as dollars. An inflation rate of 10% per year means that an item bought for $100 at the beginning of the year will cost $110 at the end of the year.

Why is it important to account for inflation in capital budgeting? Because declines in the general purchasing power of the monetary unit will inflate future cash flows above what they would have been in the absence of inflation. These inflated cash flows will cause the project to look better than it really is unless the analyst recognizes that the inflated cash flows are measured in dollars that have less purchasing power than the dollars that were initially invested. When analyzing inflation, distinguish real rate of return from nominal rate of return:

Real rate of return is the rate of return demanded to cover investment risk if there is no inflation. The real rate is made up of two elements: (a) a risk-free element (that's the pure rate of return on risk-free long-term government bonds when there is no expected inflation) and (b) a business-risk element (that's the risk premium demanded for bearing risk).

Nominal rate of return is the rate of return demanded to cover investment risk and the decline in general purchasing power of the monetary unit as a result of expected inflation. The nominal rate is made up of three elements: (a) a risk-free element when there is no expected inflation, (b) a business-risk element, and (c) an inflation element. Items (a) and (b) make up the real rate of return to cover investment risk. The inflation element is the premium above the real rate. The rates of return earned in the financial markets are nominal rates, because investors want to be compensated both for the investment risks they take and for the expected decline in the general purchasing power, as a result of inflation, of the money they get back.

Assume that the real rate of return for investments in high-risk cellular data-transmission equipment at Network Communications is 20% per year and that the expected inflation rate is 10% per year. Nominal rate of return is as follows:

$$\text{Nominal rate} = (1 + \text{Real rate})(1 + \text{Inflation rate}) - 1$$
$$= (1 + 0.20)(1 + 0.10) - 1$$
$$= (1.20 \times 1.10) - 1 = 1.32 - 1 = 0.32, \text{ or } 32\%$$

Nominal rate of return is related to the real rate of return and the inflation rate:

Real rate of return	0.20
Inflation rate	0.10
Combination (0.20 × 0.10)	0.02
Nominal rate of return	0.32

Note the nominal rate, 0.32, is slightly higher than 0.30, the real rate (0.20) plus the inflation rate (0.10). That's because the nominal rate recognizes that inflation of 10% also decreases the purchasing power of the real rate of return of 20% earned during the year. The combination component represents the additional compensation investors seek for the decrease in the purchasing power of the real return earned during the year because of inflation.[9]

Net Present Value Method and Inflation

When incorporating inflation into the NPV method, the key is *internal consistency*. There are two internally consistent approaches:

1. **Nominal approach**—predicts cash inflows and outflows in nominal monetary units *and* uses a nominal rate as the required rate of return
2. **Real approach**—predicts cash inflows and outflows in real monetary units *and* uses a real rate as the required rate of return

We will limit our discussion to the simpler nominal approach. Consider an investment that is expected to generate sales of 100 units and a net cash inflow of $1,000 ($10 per unit) each year for two years *absent inflation*. Assume cash flows

---

[9] The real rate of return can be expressed in terms of the nominal rate of return as follows:
$$\text{Real rate} = \frac{1 + \text{Nominal rate}}{1 + \text{Inflation rate}} - 1 = \frac{1 + 0.32}{1 + 0.10} - 1 = 0.20, \text{ or } 20\%$$

occur at the end of each year. If inflation of 10% is expected each year, net cash inflows from the sale of each unit would be $11 ($10 × 1.10) in year 1 and $12.10 ($11 × 1.10, or $10 × (1.10)^2) in year 2, resulting in net cash inflows of $1,100 in year 1 and $1,210 in year 2. The net cash inflows of $1,100 and $1,210 are nominal cash inflows because they include the effects of inflation. *Nominal cash flows are the cash flows that are recorded in the accounting system.* The cash inflows of $1,000 each year are real cash flows. The accounting system does not record these cash flows. The nominal approach is easier to understand and apply because it uses nominal cash flows from accounting systems and nominal rates of return from financial markets.

Assume that Network Communications can purchase equipment to make and sell a cellular data-transmission product at a net initial investment of $750,000. It is expected to have a four-year useful life and no terminal disposal value. An annual inflation rate of 10% is expected over this four-year period. Network Communications requires an after-tax nominal rate of return of 32%. The following table presents the predicted amounts of real (that's assuming no inflation) and nominal (that's after considering cumulative inflation) net cash inflows from the equipment over the next four years (excluding the $750,000 investment in the equipment and before any income tax payments):

Year (1)	Before-Tax Cash Inflows in Real Dollars (2)	Cumulative Inflation Rate Factor[a] (3)	Before-Tax Cash Inflows in Nominal Dollars (4) = (2) × (3)
1	$500,000	(1.10)^1 = 1.1000	$550,000
2	600,000	(1.10)^2 = 1.2100	726,000
3	600,000	(1.10)^3 = 1.3310	798,600
4	300,000	(1.10)^4 = 1.4641	439,230

[a]1.10 = 1.00 + 0.10 inflation rate.

We continue to make the simplifying assumption that cash flows occur at the end of each year. The income tax rate is 40%. For tax purposes, the cost of the equipment will be depreciated using the straight-line method.

Exhibit 8 shows the calculation of NPV using cash flows in nominal dollars and using a nominal discount rate. The calculations in Exhibit 8 include the net initial machine investment, annual after-tax cash flows from operations

Exhibit 8 Net Present Value Method Using Nominal Approach to Inflation for Network Communication's New Equipment

	A	B	C	D	E	F	G	H	I	J	K	L
1						Present	Present Value					
2						Value of	Discount Factor[a] at		Sketch of Relevant Cash Flows at End of Each Year			
3						Cash Flow	32%	0	1	2	3	4
4	1.	Net initial investment										
5		Year	Investment Outflows									
6		0	$(750,000)			$(750,000)	← 1.000 ←	$(750,000)				
7	2a.	Annual after-tax cash flow from										
8		operations (excluding the depreciation effect)										
9			Annual		Annual							
10			Before-Tax	Income	After-Tax							
11			Cash Flow	Tax	Cash Flow							
12		Year	from Operations	Outflows	from Operations							
13		(1)	(2)	(3) = 0.40 x (2)	(4) = (2) - (3)							
14		1	$550,000	$220,000	$330,000	250,140	← 0.758 ←		$330,000			
15		2	726,000	290,400	435,600	250,034	← 0.574 ←			$435,600		
16		3	798,600	319,440	479,160	208,435	← 0.435 ←				$479,160	
17		4	439,230	175,692	263,538	86,704	← 0.329 ←					$263,538
18						795,313						
19	2b.	Income tax cash savings from annual										
20		depreciation deductions										
21		Year	Depreciation	Tax Cash Savings								
22		(1)	(2)	(3) = 0.40 x (2)								
23		1	$187,500[b]	$75,000		56,850	← 0.758 ←		$ 75,000			
24		2	187,500	75,000		43,050	← 0.574 ←			$ 75,000		
25		3	187,500	75,000		32,625	← 0.435 ←				$ 75,000	
26		4	187,500	75,000		24,675	← 0.329 ←					$ 75,000
27						157,200						
28	NPV if new equipment purchased					$ 202,513						
29												
30												
31	[a]The nominal discount rate of 32% is made up of the real rate of return of 20% and the inflation rate of 10% [(1 + 0.20) (1 + 1.10)] – 1 = 0.32.										
32	[b]$750,000 ÷ 4 = $187,500										

319

(excluding the depreciation effect), and income tax cash savings from annual depreciation deductions. The NPV is $202,513 and, based on financial considerations alone, Network Communications should purchase the equipment.

Terms to Learn

This chapter contains definitions of the following important terms:

accrual accounting rate of return (AARR) method

capital budgeting

cost of capital

discount rate

discounted cash flow (DCF) methods

discounted payback method

hurdle rate

inflation

internal rate-of-return (IRR) method

net present value (NPV) method

nominal rate of return

opportunity cost of capital

payback method

real rate of return

required rate of return (RRR)

time value of money

Assignment Material

Questions

21-1 "Capital budgeting has the same focus as accrual accounting." Do you agree? Explain.

21-2 List and briefly describe each of the five stages in capital budgeting.

21-3 What is the essence of the discounted cash flow methods?

21-4 "Only quantitative outcomes are relevant in capital budgeting analyses." Do you agree? Explain.

21-5 How can sensitivity analysis be incorporated in DCF analysis?

21-6 What is the payback method? What are its main strengths and weaknesses?

21-7 Describe the accrual accounting rate-of-return method. What are its main strengths and weaknesses?

21-8 "The trouble with discounted cash flow methods is that they ignore depreciation." Do you agree? Explain.

21-9 "Let's be more practical. DCF is not the gospel. Managers should not become so enchanted with DCF that strategic considerations are overlooked." Do you agree? Explain.

21-10 "All overhead costs are relevant in NPV analysis." Do you agree? Explain.

21-11 Bill Watts, president of Western Publications, accepts a capital budgeting project proposed by division X. This is the division in which the president spent his first 10 years with the company. On the same day, the president rejects a capital budgeting project proposal from division Y. The manager of division Y is incensed. She believes that the division Y project has an internal rate of return at least 10 percentage points higher than the division X project. She comments, "What is the point of all our detailed DCF analysis? If Watts is panting over a project, he can arrange to have the proponents of that project massage the numbers so that it looks like a winner." What advice would you give the manager of division Y?

21-12 Distinguish different categories of cash flows to be considered in an equipment-replacement decision by a taxpaying company.

21-13 Describe three ways income taxes can affect the cash inflows or outflows in a motor-vehicle-replacement decision by a taxpaying company.

21-14 How can capital budgeting tools assist in evaluating a manager who is responsible for retaining customers of a cellular telephone company?

21-15 Distinguish the nominal rate of return from the real rate of return.

Exercises

21-16 **Exercises in compound interest, no income taxes.** To be sure that you understand how to use the tables in the Appendix, solve the following exercises. Ignore income tax considerations. The correct answers, rounded to the nearest dollar, appear at the end of this chapter.

Required

1. You have just won $10,000. How much money will you accumulate at the end of 10 years if you invest it at 8% compounded annually? At 10%?

2. Ten years from now, the unpaid principal of the mortgage on your house will be $154,900. How much do you need to invest today at 4% interest compounded annually to accumulate the $154,900 in 10 years?

3. If the unpaid mortgage on your house in 10 years will be $154,900, how much money do you need to invest at the end of each year at 10% to accumulate exactly this amount at the end of the 10th year?

4. You plan to save $7,500 of your earnings at the end of each year for the next 10 years. How much money will you accumulate at the end of the 10th year if you invest your savings compounded at 8% per year?

5. You have just turned 65 and an endowment insurance policy has paid you a lump sum of $250,000. If you invest the sum at 8%, how much money can you withdraw from your account in equal amounts at the end of each year so that at the end of 10 years (age 75) there will be nothing left?

6. You have estimated that for the first 10 years after you retire you will need a cash inflow of $65,000 at the end of each year. How much money do you need to invest at 8% at your retirement age to obtain this annual cash inflow? At 12%?

7. The following table shows two schedules of prospective operating cash inflows, each of which requires the same net initial investment of $10,000 now:

	Annual Cash Inflows	
Year	Plan A	Plan B
1	$ 3,000	$ 1,000
2	5,000	2,000
3	2,000	3,000
4	3,000	4,000
5	2,000	5,000
Total	$15,000	$15,000

The required rate of return is 8% compounded annually. All cash inflows occur at the end of each year. In terms of net present value, which plan is more desirable? Show your computations.

21-17 Capital budgeting methods, no income taxes. Riverbend Company runs hardware stores in a tri-state area. Riverbend's management estimates that if it invests $250,000 in a new computer system, it can save $67,000 in annual cash operating costs. The system has an expected useful life of eight years and no terminal disposal value. The required rate of return is 8%. Ignore income tax issues in your answers. Assume all cash flows occur at year-end except for initial investment amounts.

1. Calculate the following for the new computer system: **Required**
   a. Net present value
   b. Payback period
   c. Discounted payback period
   d. Internal rate of return (using the interpolation method)
   e. Accrual accounting rate of return based on the net initial investment (assume straight-line depreciation)
2. What other factors should Riverbend consider in deciding whether to purchase the new computer system?

21-18 Capital budgeting methods, no income taxes. City Hospital, a non-profit organization, estimates that it can save $28,000 a year in cash operating costs for the next 10 years if it buys a special-purpose eye-testing machine at a cost of $110,000. No terminal disposal value is expected. City Hospital's required rate of return is 14%. Assume all cash flows occur at year-end except for initial investment amounts. City Hospital uses straight-line depreciation.

1. Calculate the following for the special-purpose eye-testing machine: **Required**
   a. Net present value
   b. Payback period
   c. Internal rate of return
   d. Accrual accounting rate of return based on net initial investment
   e. Accrual accounting rate of return based on average investment
2. What other factors should City Hospital consider in deciding whether to purchase the special-purpose eye-testing machine?

21-19 Capital budgeting, income taxes. Assume the same facts as in Exercise 21-18 except that City Hospital is a taxpaying entity. The income tax rate is 30% for all transactions that affect income taxes.

1. Do requirement 1 of Exercise 21-18.   **Required**
2. How would your computations in requirement 1 be affected if the special-purpose machine had a $10,000 terminal disposal value at the end of 10 years? Assume depreciation deductions are based on the $110,000 purchase cost and zero terminal disposal value using the straight-line method. Answer briefly in words without further calculations.

21-20 Capital budgeting with uneven cash flows, no income taxes. Southern Cola is considering the purchase of a special-purpose bottling machine for $23,000. It is expected to have a useful life of four years with no terminal disposal value. The plant manager estimates the following savings in cash operating costs:

Year	Amount
1	$10,000
2	8,000
3	6,000
4	5,000
Total	$29,000

Southern Cola uses a required rate of return of 16% in its capital budgeting decisions. Ignore income taxes in your analysis. Assume all cash flows occur at year-end except for initial investment amounts.

Required Calculate the following for the special-purpose bottling machine:
1. Net present value
2. Payback period
3. Discounted payback period
4. Internal rate of return (using the interpolation method)
5. Accrual accounting rate of return based on net initial investment (Assume straight-line depreciation. Use the average annual savings in cash operating costs when computing the numerator of the accrual accounting rate of return.)

21-21 Comparison of projects, no income taxes. (CMA, adapted) New Bio Corporation is a rapidly growing biotech company that has a required rate of return of 10%. It plans to build a new facility in Santa Clara County. The building will take two years to complete. The building contractor offered New Bio a choice of three payment plans, as follows:

■ **Plan I** Payment of $100,000 at the time of signing the contract and $4,575,000 upon completion of the building. The end of the second year is the completion date.
■ **Plan II** Payment of $1,550,000 at the time of signing the contract and $1,550,000 at the end of each of the two succeeding years.
■ **Plan III** Payment of $200,000 at the time of signing the contract and $1,475,000 at the end of each of the three succeeding years.

Required
1. Using the net present value method, calculate the comparative cost of each of the three payment plans being considered by New Bio.
2. Which payment plan should New Bio choose? Explain.
3. Discuss the financial factors, other than the cost of the plan, and the nonfinancial factors that should be considered in selecting an appropriate payment plan.

21-22 Payback and NPV methods, no income taxes. (CMA, adapted) Andrews Construction is analyzing its capital expenditure proposals for the purchase of equipment in the coming year. The capital budget is limited to $6,000,000 for the year. Lori Bart, staff analyst at Andrews, is preparing an analysis of the three projects under consideration by Corey Andrews, the company's owner.

	Home	Insert	Page Layout	Formulas	Data	Review	View
		A		B	C	D	
1				Project A	Project B	Project C
2	Projected cash outflow					
3	Net initial investment			$3,000,000	$1,500,000	$4,000,000
4						
5	Projected cash inflows					
6	Year 1			$1,000,000	$ 400,000	$2,000,000
7	Year 2			1,000,000	900,000	2,000,000
8	Year 3			1,000,000	800,000	200,000
9	Year 4			1,000,000		100,000
10						
11	Required rate of return			10%	10%	10%

Required
1. Because the company's cash is limited, Andrews thinks the payback method should be used to choose between the capital budgeting projects.
   a. What are the benefits and limitations of using the payback method to choose between projects?

b. Calculate the payback period for each of the three projects. Ignore income taxes. Using the payback method, which projects should Andrews choose?
2. Bart thinks that projects should be selected based on their NPVs. Assume all cash flows occur at the end of the year except for initial investment amounts. Calculate the NPV for each project. Ignore income taxes.
3. Which projects, if any, would you recommend funding? Briefly explain why.

21-23 DCF, accrual accounting rate of return, working capital, evaluation of performance, no income taxes. Century Lab plans to purchase a new centrifuge machine for its New Hampshire facility. The machine costs $137,500 and is expected to have a useful life of eight years, with a terminal disposal value of $37,500. Savings in cash operating costs are expected to be $31,250 per year. However, additional working capital is needed to keep the machine running efficiently. The working capital must continually be replaced, so an investment of $10,000 needs to be maintained at all times, but this investment is fully recoverable (will be "cashed in") at the end of the useful life. Century Lab's required rate of return is 14%. Ignore income taxes in your analysis. Assume all cash flows occur at year-end except for initial investment amounts. Century Lab uses straight-line depreciation for its machines.

1. Calculate net present value.
2. Calculate internal rate of return.
3. Calculate accrual accounting rate of return based on net initial investment.
4. Calculate accrual accounting rate of return based on average investment.
5. You have the authority to make the purchase decision. Why might you be reluctant to base your decision on the DCF methods?

21-24 New equipment purchase, income taxes. Anna's Bakery plans to purchase a new oven for its store. The oven has an estimated useful life of four years. The estimated pretax cash flows for the oven are as shown in the table that follows, with no anticipated change in working capital. Anna's Bakery has a 12% after-tax required rate of return and a 40% income tax rate. Assume depreciation is calculated on a straight-line basis for tax purposes using the initial oven investment and estimated terminal disposal value of the oven. Assume all cash flows occur at year-end except for initial investment amounts.

A	B	C	D	E	F
	Relevant Cash Flows at End of Each Year				
	0	**1**	**2**	**3**	**4**
3 Initial machine investment	$(88,000)				
4 Annual cash flow from operations (excluding the depreciation effect)		$36,000	$36,000	$36,000	$36,000
5 Cash flow from terminal disposal of machine					$ 8,000

1. Calculate (a) net present value, (b) payback period, and (c) internal rate of return.
2. Calculate accrual accounting rate of return based on net initial investment.

21-25 New equipment purchase, income taxes. Innovation, Inc., is considering the purchase of a new industrial electric motor to improve efficiency at its Fremont plant. The motor has an estimated useful life of five years. The estimated pretax cash flows for the motor are shown in the table that follows, with no anticipated change in working capital. Innovation has a 10% after-tax required rate of return and a 35% income tax rate. Assume depreciation is calculated on a straight-line basis for tax purposes. Assume all cash flows occur at year-end except for initial investment amounts.

A	B	C	D	E	F	G
	Relevant Cash Flows at End of Each Year					
	0	**1**	**2**	**3**	**4**	**5**
3 Initial motor investment	$(75,000)					
4 Annual cash flow from operations (excluding the depreciation effect)		$25,000	$25,000	$25,000	$25,000	$25,000
5 Cash flow from terminal disposal of motor						$ 0

Required 1. Calculate (a) net present value, (b) payback period, (c) discounted payback period, and (d) internal rate of return.
2. Compare and contrast the capital budgeting methods in requirement 1.

21-26 Selling a plant, income taxes. (CMA, adapted) The Crossroad Company is an international clothing manufacturer. Its Santa Monica plant will become idle on December 31, 2011. Peter Laney, the corporate controller, has been asked to look at three options regarding the plant.

■ Option 1: The plant, which has been fully depreciated for tax purposes, can be sold immediately for $450,000.
■ Option 2: The plant can be leased to the Austin Corporation, one of Crossroad's suppliers, for four years. Under the lease terms, Austin would pay Crossroad $110,000 rent per year (payable at year-end) and would grant Crossroad a $20,000 annual discount off the normal price of fabric purchased by Crossroad. (Assume that the discount is received at year-end for each of the four years.) Austin would bear all of the plant's ownership costs. Crossroad expects to sell this plant for $75,000 at the end of the four-year lease.
■ Option 3: The plant could be used for four years to make souvenir jackets for the Olympics. Fixed overhead costs (a cash outflow) before any equipment upgrades are estimated to be $10,000 annually for the four-year period. The jackets are expected to sell for $55 each. Variable cost per unit is expected to be $43. The following production and sales of jackets are expected: 2012, 9,000 units; 2013, 13,000 units; 2014, 15,000 units; 2015, 5,000 units. In order to manufacture the jackets, some of the plant equipment would need to be upgraded at an immediate cost of $80,000. The equipment would be depreciated using the straight-line depreciation method and zero terminal disposal value over the four years it would be in use. Because of the equipment upgrades, Crossroad could sell the plant for $135,000 at the end of four years. No change in working capital would be required.

Crossroad treats all cash flows as if they occur at the end of the year, and it uses an after-tax required rate of return of 10%. Crossroad is subject to a 35% tax rate on all income, including capital gains.

Required 1. Calculate net present value of each of the options and determine which option Crossroad should select using the NPV criterion.
2. What nonfinancial factors should Crossroad consider before making its choice?

MyAccountingLab

Problems

21-27 Equipment replacement, no income taxes. Pro Chips is a manufacturer of prototype chips based in Dublin, Ireland. Next year, in 2012, Pro Chips expects to deliver 552 prototype chips at an average price of $80,000. Pro Chips' marketing vice president forecasts growth of 60 prototype chips per year through 2018. That is, demand will be 552 in 2012, 612 in 2013, 672 in 2014, and so on.

The plant cannot produce more than 540 prototype chips annually. To meet future demand, Pro Chips must either modernize the plant or replace it. The old equipment is fully depreciated and can be sold for $3,600,000 if the plant is replaced. If the plant is modernized, the costs to modernize it are to be capitalized and depreciated over the useful life of the updated plant. The old equipment is retained as part of the modernize alternative. The following data on the two options are available:

	Modernize	Replace
Initial investment in 2012	$33,600,000	$58,800,000
Terminal disposal value in 2018	$6,000,000	$14,400,000
Useful life	7 years	7 years
Total annual cash operating costs per prototype chip	$62,000	$56,000

Pro Chips uses straight-line depreciation, assuming zero terminal disposal value. For simplicity, we assume no change in prices or costs in future years. The investment will be made at the beginning of 2012, and all transactions thereafter occur on the last day of the year. Pro Chips' required rate of return is 12%.

There is no difference between the modernize and replace alternatives in terms of required working capital. Pro Chips has a special waiver on income taxes until 2018.

Required 1. Sketch the cash inflows and outflows of the modernize and replace alternatives over the 2012–2018 period.
2. Calculate payback period for the modernize and replace alternatives.
3. Calculate net present value of the modernize and replace alternatives.
4. What factors should Pro Chips consider in choosing between the alternatives?

21-28 Equipment replacement, income taxes (continuation of 21-27). Assume the same facts as in Problem 21-27, except that the plant is located in Austin, Texas. Pro Chips has no special waiver on income taxes. It pays a 30% tax rate on all income. Proceeds from sales of equipment above book value are taxed at the same 30% rate.

1. Sketch the after-tax cash inflows and outflows of the modernize and replace alternatives over the 2012–2018 period. **Required**
2. Calculate net present value of the modernize and replace alternatives.
3. Suppose Pro Chips is planning to build several more plants. It wants to have the most advantageous tax position possible. Pro Chips has been approached by Spain, Malaysia, and Australia to construct plants in their countries. Use the data in Problem 21-27 and this problem to briefly describe in qualitative terms the income tax features that would be advantageous to Pro Chips.

21-29 DCF, sensitivity analysis, no income taxes. (CMA, adapted) Whimsical Corporation is an international manufacturer of fragrances for women. Management at Whimsical is considering expanding the product line to men's fragrances. From the best estimates of the marketing and production managers, annual sales (all for cash) for this new line is 900,000 units at $100 per unit; cash variable cost is $50 per unit; and cash fixed costs is $9,000,000 per year. The investment project requires $120,000,000 of cash outflow and has a project life of seven years.

At the end of the seven-year useful life, there will be no terminal disposal value. Assume all cash flows occur at year-end except for initial investment amounts.

Men's fragrance is a new market for Whimsical, and management is concerned about the reliability of the estimates. The controller has proposed applying sensitivity analysis to selected factors. Ignore income taxes in your computations. Whimsical's required rate of return on this project is 10%.

1. Calculate the net present value of this investment proposal. **Required**
2. Calculate the effect on the net present value of the following two changes in assumptions. (Treat each item independently of the other.)
   a. 20% reduction in the selling price
   b. 20% increase in the variable cost per unit
3. Discuss how management would use the data developed in requirements 1 and 2 in its consideration of the proposed capital investment.

21-30 NPV, IRR, and sensitivity analysis. Crumbly Cookie Company is considering expanding by buying a new (additional) machine that costs $62,000, has zero terminal disposal value, and has a 10-year useful life. It expects the annual increase in cash revenues from the expansion to be $28,000 per year. It expects additional annual cash costs to be $18,000 per year. Its cost of capital is 8%. Ignore taxes.

1. Calculate the net present value and internal rate of return for this investment. **Required**
2. Assume the finance manager of Crumbly Cookie Company is not sure about the cash revenues and costs. The revenues could be anywhere from 10% higher to 10% lower than predicted. Assume cash costs are still $18,000 per year. What are NPV and IRR at the high and low points for revenue?
3. The finance manager thinks that costs will vary with revenues, and if the revenues are 10% higher, the costs will be 7% higher. If the revenues are 10% lower, the costs will be 10% lower. Recalculate the NPV and IRR at the high and low revenue points with this new cost information.
4. The finance manager has decided that the company should earn 2% more than the cost of capital on any project. Recalculate the original NPV in requirement 1 using the new discount rate and evaluate the investment opportunity.
5. Discuss how the changes in assumptions have affected the decision to expand.

21-31 Payback methods, even and uneven cash flows. You have the opportunity to expand your business by purchasing new equipment for $159,000. The equipment has a useful life of nine years. You expect to incur cash fixed costs of $96,000 per year to use this new equipment, and you expect to incur cash variable costs in the amount of 10% of cash revenues. Your cost of capital is 12%.

1. Calculate the payback period and the discounted payback period for this investment, assuming you will generate $140,000 in cash revenues every year. **Required**
2. Assume instead that you expect the following cash revenue stream for this investment:

Year 1	$ 90,000
Year 2	115,000
Year 3	130,000
Year 4	155,000
Year 5	170,000
Year 6	180,000
Year 7	140,000
Year 8	125,000
Year 9	110,000

Based on this estimated revenue stream, what are the payback and discounted payback periods for this investment?

21-32 Replacement of a machine, income taxes, sensitivity. (CMA, adapted) The Smacker Company is a family-owned business that produces fruit jam. The company has a grinding machine that has been in use for three years. On January 1, 2011, Smacker is considering the purchase of a new grinding machine. Smacker has two options: (1) continue using the old machine or (2) sell the old machine and purchase a new machine. The seller of the new machine isn't offering a trade-in. The following information has been obtained:

	Home Insert Page Layout Formulas Data Review View		
	A	B	C
1		**Old Machine**	**New Machine**
2	Initial purchase cost of machines	$150,000	$190,000
3	Useful life from acquisition date (years)	8	5
4	Terminal disposal value at the end of useful life on Dec. 31, 2015, assumed for depreciation purposes	$ 20,000	$ 25,000
5	Expected annual cash operating costs:		
6	Variable cost per can of jam	$ 0.25	$ 0.19
7	Total fixed costs	$ 25,000	$ 24,000
8	Depreciation method for tax purposes	Straight line	Straight line
9	Estimated disposal value of machines:		
10	January 1, 2011	$ 68,000	$190,000
11	December 31, 2015	$ 12,000	$ 22,000
12	Expected cans of jam made and sold each year	475,000	475,000

Smacker is subject to a 36% income tax rate. Assume that any gain or loss on the sale of machines is treated as an ordinary tax item and will affect the taxes paid by Smacker in the year in which it occurs. Smacker's after-tax required rate of return is 14%. Assume all cash flows occur at year-end except for initial investment amounts.

Required

1. You have been asked whether Smacker should buy the new machine. To help in your analysis, calculate the following:
   a. One-time after-tax cash effect of disposing of the old machine on January 1, 2011
   b. Annual recurring after-tax cash operating savings from using the new machine (variable and fixed)
   c. Cash tax savings due to differences in annual depreciation of the old machine and the new machine
   d. Difference in after-tax cash flow from terminal disposal of new machine and old machine
2. Use your calculations in requirement 1 and the net present value method to determine whether Smacker should use the old machine or acquire the new machine.
3. How much more or less would the recurring after-tax cash operating savings of the new machine need to be for Smacker to earn exactly the 14% after-tax required rate of return? Assume that all other data about the investment do not change.

21-33 NPV and AARR, goal-congruence issues. Jack Garrett, a manager of the plate division for the Marble Top Manufacturing company, has the opportunity to expand the division by investing in additional machinery costing $420,000. He would depreciate the equipment using the straight-line method, and expects it to have no residual value. It has a useful life of seven years. The firm mandates a required after-tax rate of return of 14% on investments. Jack estimates annual net cash inflows for this investment of $125,000 before taxes, and an investment in working capital of $2,500. Tax rate is 35%.

Required

1. Calculate the net present value of this investment.
2. Calculate the accrual accounting rate of return on initial investment for this project.
3. Should Jack accept the project? Will Jack accept the project if his bonus depends on achieving an accrual accounting rate of return of 14%? How can this conflict be resolved?

21-34 Recognizing cash flows for capital investment projects. Ludmilla Quagg owns a fitness center and is thinking of replacing the old Fit-O-Matic machine with a brand new Flab-Buster 3000. The old Fit-O-Matic has a historical cost of $50,000 and accumulated depreciation of $46,000, but has a trade-in value of $5,000. It currently costs $1,200 per month in utilities and another $10,000 a year in maintenance to run the Fit-O-Matic. Ludmilla feels that the Fit-O-Matic can be used for another 10 years, after which it would have no salvage value.

The Flab-Buster 3000 would reduce the utilities costs by 30% and cut the maintenance cost in half. The Flab-Buster 3000 costs $98,000, has a 10-year life, and an expected disposal value of $10,000 at the end of its useful life.

Ludmilla charges customers $10 per hour to use the fitness center. Replacing the fitness machine will not affect the price of service or the number of customers she can serve.

Required

1. Ludmilla wants to evaluate the Flab-Buster 3000 project using capital budgeting techniques, but does not know how to begin. To help her, read through the problem and separate the cash flows into four groups: (1) net initial investment cash flows, (2) cash flow savings from operations, (3) cash flows from terminal disposal of investment, and (4) cash flows not relevant to the capital budgeting problem.
2. Assuming a tax rate of 40%, a required rate of return of 8%, and straight-line depreciation over remaining useful life of machines, should Ludmilla buy the Flab-Buster 3000?

21-35 Recognizing cash flows for capital investment projects, NPV. Unbreakable Manufacturing manufactures over 20,000 different products made from metal, including building materials, tools, and furniture parts. The manager of the furniture parts division has proposed that his division expand into bicycle parts as well. The furniture parts division currently generates cash revenues of $5,000,000 and incurs cash costs of $3,550,000, with an investment in assets of $12,050,000. One-fourth of the cash costs are direct labor.

The manager estimates that the expansion of the business will require an investment in working capital of $25,000. Because the company already has a facility, there would be no additional rent or purchase costs for a building, but the project would generate an additional $390,000 in annual cash overhead. Moreover, the manager expects annual materials cash costs for bicycle parts to be $1,300,000, and labor for the bicycle parts to be about the same as the labor cash costs for furniture parts.

The controller of Unbreakable, working with various managers, estimates that the expansion would require the purchase of equipment with a $2,575,000 cost and an expected disposal value of $370,000 at the end of its seven-year useful life. Depreciation would occur on a straight-line basis.

The CFO of Unbreakable determines the firm's cost of capital as 14%. The CFO's salary is $150,000 per year. Adding another division will not change that. The CEO asks for a report on expected revenues for the project, and is told by the marketing department that it might be able to achieve cash revenues of $3,372,500 annually from bicycle parts. Unbreakable Manufacturing has a tax rate of 35%.

Required

1. Separate the cash flows into four groups: (1) net initial investment cash flows, (2) cash flows from operations, (3) cash flows from terminal disposal of investment, and (4) cash flows not relevant to the capital budgeting problem.
2. Calculate the NPV of the expansion project and comment on your analysis.

21-36 NPV, inflation and taxes. Best-Cost Foods is considering replacing all 10 of its old cash registers with new ones. The old registers are fully depreciated and have no disposal value. The new registers cost $749,700 (in total). Because the new registers are more efficient than the old registers, Best-Cost will have annual incremental cash savings from using the new registers in the amount of $160,000 per year. The registers have a seven-year useful life and no terminal disposal value, and are depreciated using the straight-line method. Best-Cost requires an 8% real rate of return.

Required

1. Given the preceding information, what is the net present value of the project? Ignore taxes.
2. Assume the $160,000 cost savings are in current real dollars, and the inflation rate is 5.5%. Recalculate the NPV of the project.
3. Based on your answers to requirements 1 and 2, should Best-Cost buy the new cash registers?
4. Now assume that the company's tax rate is 30%. Calculate the NPV of the project assuming no inflation.
5. Again assuming that the company faces a 30% tax rate, calculate the NPV of the project under an inflation rate of 5.5%.
6. Based on your answers to requirements 4 and 5, should Best-Cost buy the new cash registers?

21-37 Net present value, Internal Rate of Return, Sensitivity Analysis. Sally wants to purchase a Burgers-N-Fries franchise. She can buy one for $500,000. Burgers-N-Fries headquarters provides the following information:

Estimated annual cash revenues	$280,000
Typical annual cash operating expenses	$165,000

Sally will also have to pay Burgers-N-Fries a franchise fee of 10% of her revenues each year. Sally wants to earn at least 10% on the investment because she has to borrow the $500,000 at a cost of 6%. Use a 10-year window, and ignore taxes.

Required

1. Find the NPV and IRR of Sally's investment.
2. Sally is nervous about the revenue estimate provided by Burgers-N-Fries headquarters. Calculate the NPV and IRR under alternative annual revenue estimates of $260,000 and $240,000.
3. Sally estimates that if her revenues are lower, her costs will be lower as well. For each revised level of revenue used in requirement 2, recalculate NPV and IRR with a proportional decrease in annual operating expenses.

4. Suppose Sally also negotiates a lower franchise and has to pay Burgers-N-Fries only 8% of annual revenues. Redo the calculations in requirement 3.
5. Discuss how the sensitivity analysis will affect Sally's decision to buy the franchise.

Collaborative Learning Problem

21-38 NPV, Relevant costs, Income taxes. Phish Corporation is the largest manufacturer and distributor of novelty ice creams across the East Coast. The company's products, because of their perishable nature, require careful packaging and transportation. Phish uses a special material called ICI that insulates the core of its boxes, thereby preserving the quality and freshness of the ice creams.

Patrick Scott, the newly appointed COO, believed that the company could save money by closing the internal Packaging department and outsourcing the manufacture of boxes to an outside vendor. He requested a report outlining Phish Corporation's current costs of manufacturing boxes from the company's controller, Reesa Morris. After conducting some of his own research, he approached a firm that specialized in packaging, Containers Inc., and obtained a quote for the insulated boxes. Containers Inc. quoted a rate of $700,000 for 7,000 boxes annually. The contract would run for five years and if there was a greater demand for boxes the cost would increase proportionately. Patrick compared these numbers to those on the cost report prepared by Reesa. Her analysis of the packaging department's annual costs is as follows:

Direct material (ICI)	$ 80,000
Other direct material	120,000
Direct labor	220,000
Department manager's salary	85,000
Depreciation of machinery	60,000
Department overhead	65,000
Rent	15,000
Allocation of general administrative overhead	70,000

After consulting with Reesa, Patrick gathers the following additional information:

i. The machinery used for production was purchased two years ago for $430,000 and was expected to last for seven years, with a terminal disposal value of $10,000. Its current salvage value is $280,000.

ii. Phish uses 20 tons of ICI each year. Three years ago, Phish purchased 100 tons of ICI for $400,000. ICI has since gone up in value and new purchases would cost $4,500 a ton. If Phish were to discontinue manufacture of boxes, it could dispose of its stock of ICI for a net amount of $3,800 per ton, after handling and transportation expenses.

iii. Phish has no inventory of other direct materials; it purchases them on an as-needed basis.

iv. The rent charge represents an allocation based on the packaging department's share of the building's floor space. Phish is currently renting a secondary warehouse for $27,000; this space would no longer be needed if the contract is signed with Containers Inc.

v. If the manufacture of boxes is outsourced, the packaging department's overhead costs would be avoided. The department manager would be moved to a similar position in another group that the company has been looking to fill with an external hire.

vi. Phish has a marginal tax rate of 40% and an after-tax required rate of return of 10%.

Required

1. Sketch the cash inflows and outflows of the two alternatives over a five-year time period.
2. Using the NPV criterion, which option should Phish Corporation select?
3. What other factors should Phish Corporation consider in choosing between the alternatives?

Answers to Exercises in Compound Interest (Exercise 21-16)

The general approach to these exercises centers on a key question: Which of the four basic tables in the Appendix should be used? No computations should be made until this basic question has been answered with confidence.

1. **From Table 1.** The $10,000 is the present value P of your winnings. Their future value S in 10 years will be as follows:

$$S = P(1 + r)^n$$

The conversion factor, $(1 + r)^n$, is on line 10 of Table 1.

Substituting at 8%: $S = \$10,000(2.159) = \$21,590$

Substituting at 10%: $S = \$10,000(2.594) = \$25,940$

2. **From Table 2.** The $154,900 is a future value. You want the present value of that amount. $P = S \div (1 + r)^n$. The conversion factor, $1 \div (1 + r)^n$, is on line 10 of Table 2. Substituting,

$$P = \$154,900(.676) = \$104,712.40$$

3. **From Table 3.** The $154,900 is a future value. You are seeking the uniform amount (annuity) to set aside annually. Note that $1 invested each year for 10 years at 10% has a future value of $15.937 after 10 years, from line 10 of Table 3.

$$\$154,900 / 15.937 = \$9719.52$$

4. **From Table 3.** You need to find the future value of an annuity of $7,500 per year. Note that $1 invested each year for 10 years at 8% has a future value of $14.487 after 10 years.

$$\$7,500 \ (14.487) = \$108,652.50$$

5. **From Table 4.** When you reach age 65, you will get $250,000, a present value at that time. You need to find the annuity that will exactly exhaust the invested principal in 10 years. To pay yourself $1 each year for 10 years when the interest rate is 6% requires you to have $6.710 today, from line 10 of Table 4.

$$\$250,000 / 6.710 = \$37,257.82$$

6. **From Table 4.** You need to find the present value of an annuity for 10 years at 8% and at 12%:

$$8\%: \$65,000 \ (6.710) = \$436,150.00$$

$$12\%: \$65,000 \ (5.650) = \$367,250.00$$

7. Plan A is preferable. The NPV of plan A exceeds that of plan B by $851.

| | | Plan A | | Plan B | |
Year	PV Factor at 8%	Cash Inflows	PV of Cash Inflows	Cash Inflows	PV of Cash Inflows
0	1.000	$(10,000)	$ (10,000)	$(10,000)	$ (10,000)
1	0.926	3,000	2,778.00	1,000	926.00
2	0.857	5,000	4285.00	2,000	1,714.00
3	0.794	2,000	1,588.00	3,000	2,382.00
4	0.735	3,000	2,205.00	4,000	2,940.00
5	0.681	2,000	1,362.00	5,000	3,405.00
			$2,218.00		$1,367.00

Even though plans A and B have the same total cash inflows over the five years, plan A is preferred because it has greater cash inflows occurring earlier.

Management Control Systems, Transfer Pricing, and Multinational Considerations

From Chapter 22 of *Cost Accounting: A Managerial Emphasis*, 14/e. Charles T. Horngren. Srikant M. Datar. Madhav Rajan.

Management Control Systems, Transfer Pricing, and Multinational Considerations

Transfer pricing is the price one subunit of a company charges for the services it provides another subunit of the same company.

Top management uses transfer prices (1) to focus managers' attention on the performance of their own subunits and (2) to plan and coordinate the actions of different subunits to maximize the company's income as a whole. While transfer pricing is productive, it can also be contentious, because managers of different subunits often have very different preferences about how transfer prices should be set. For example, some managers prefer the prices be based on market prices. Others prefer the prices be based on costs alone. Controversy also arises when multinational corporations seek to reduce their overall income tax burden by charging high transfer prices to units located in countries with high tax rates. Many countries, including the United States, attempt to restrict this practice, as the following article shows.

Symantec Wins $545 million Opinion in Transfer Pricing Dispute with the IRS[1]

Symantec Corp., a large U.S. software company, won a significant court decision in December 2009, potentially saving it $545 million in contested back taxes. The Internal Revenue Service (IRS) had been seeking back taxes it alleged were owed by Veritas Software Corp., a company acquired by Symantec in 2005. The dispute was over the company's formula for "transfer pricing," a complex set of rules determining how companies set prices, fees, and cost-allocation arrangements between their operations in different tax jurisdictions.

At issue were the fees and cost-allocation arrangements between Veritas and its Irish subsidiary. Ireland has emerged as a popular tax haven for U.S. technology companies. Veritas granted rights to Veritas Ireland to conduct research and development on various intangibles (such as computer programs and manufacturing process technologies) related to data storage software and related devices. Under the agreement in effect, Veritas Ireland paid $160 million for this grant of rights from 1999 to 2001. Based on a discounted cash flow analysis, the IRS contended that the true value of the transferred rights was closer to $1.675 billion. As a consequence, it claimed that the transaction artificially increased the income of Veritas Ireland at the

---

[1] *Source*: Chinnis, Cabell et al. 2009. Tax court upends IRS's billion dollar buy-in valuation adjustment in "Veritas." Mondaq Business Briefing, December 17; Letzing, John. 2009. Symantec wins $545M opinion in tax case. *Dow Jones News Service*, December 11.

expense of income in the U.S. parent corporation, consequently lowering the U.S. tax bills during this period.

Veritas, however, maintained that it acted appropriately. The company testified that the $160 million figure was based on royalty rates it had received from seven original equipment manufacturers (OEMs) for rights to incorporate Veritas United States' software and technologies into an operating system, with adjustments made for purposes of comparability. At trial, the United States Tax Court supported this position, and called the IRS's valuation of the intangibles "arbitrary, capricious, and unreasonable." Among other things, the court took issue with the discount and growth rates used in the IRS expert's analysis, and disagreed with his assumption that the transferred intangibles had a perpetual useful life.

Though not all companies face multinational tax concerns, transfer-pricing issues are common to many companies. In these companies, transfer pricing is part of the larger management control system. This chapter develops the links among strategy, organization structure, management control systems, and accounting information. We'll examine the benefits and costs of centralized and decentralized organization structures, and we'll look at the pricing of products or services transferred between subunits of the same company. We emphasize how accounting information, such as costs, budgets, and prices, helps in planning and coordinating actions of subunits.

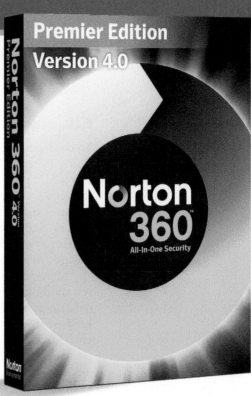

Symantec Corporation

Management Control Systems

A **management control system** is a means of gathering and using information to aid and coordinate the planning and control decisions throughout an organization and to guide the behavior of its managers and other employees. Some companies design their management control system around the concept of the balanced scorecard. For example, ExxonMobil's management control system contains financial and nonfinancial information in each of the four perspectives of the balanced scorecard. Well-designed management control systems use information both from within the company, such as net income and employee satisfaction, and from outside the company, such as stock price and customer satisfaction.

Formal and Informal Systems

Management control systems consist of formal and informal control systems. The formal management control system of a company includes explicit rules, procedures, performance measures, and incentive plans that guide the behavior of its managers and other employees. The formal control system is comprised of several systems, such as the

Learning Objective 1

Describe a management control system

. . . gathers information for planning and control decisions

and its three key properties

. . . aligns with strategy, supports organizational responsibility of managers, and motivates employees management accounting system, which provides information regarding costs, revenues, and income; the human resources systems, which provide information on recruiting, training, absenteeism, and accidents; and the quality systems, which provide information on yield, defective products, and late deliveries to customers.

The informal management control system includes shared values, loyalties, and mutual commitments among members of the organization, company culture, and the unwritten norms about acceptable behavior for managers and other employees. Examples of company slogans that reinforce values and loyalties are "At Ford, Quality Is Job 1," and "At Home Depot, Low Prices Are Just the Beginning."

Effective Management Control

To be effective, management control systems should be closely aligned with the organization's strategies and goals. Two examples of strategies at ExxonMobil are (1) providing innovative products and services to increase market share in key customer segments (by targeting customers who are willing to pay more for faster service, better facilities, and well-stocked convenience stores) and (2) reducing costs and targeting price-sensitive customers. Suppose ExxonMobil decides to pursue the former strategy. The management control system must then reinforce this goal, and ExxonMobil should tie managers' rewards to achieving the targeted measures.

Management control systems should also be designed to support the organizational responsibilities of individual managers. Different levels of management at ExxonMobil need different kinds of information to perform their tasks. For example, top management needs stock-price information to evaluate how much shareholder value the company has created. Stock price, however, is less important for line managers supervising individual refineries. They are more concerned with obtaining information about on-time delivery of gasoline, equipment downtime, product quality, number of days lost to accidents and environmental problems, cost per gallon of gasoline, and employee satisfaction. Similarly, marketing managers are more concerned with information about service at gas stations, customer satisfaction, and market share.

Effective management control systems should also motivate managers and other employees. **Motivation** is the desire to attain a selected goal (the *goal-congruence* aspect) combined with the resulting pursuit of that goal (the *effort* aspect).

Goal congruence exists when individuals and groups work toward achieving the organization's goals—that is, managers working in their own best interest take actions that align with the overall goals of top management. Suppose the goal of ExxonMobil's top management is to maximize operating income. If the management control system evaluates the refinery manager *only* on the basis of costs, the manager may be tempted to make decisions that minimize cost but overlook product quality or timely delivery to retail stations. This oversight is unlikely to maximize operating income of the company as a whole. In this case, the management control system will not achieve goal congruence.

Decision Point

What is a management control system and how should it be designed?

Effort is the extent to which managers strive or endeavor in order to achieve a goal. Effort goes beyond physical exertion, such as a worker producing at a faster rate, to include mental actions as well. For example, effort includes the diligence or acumen with which a manager gathers and analyzes data before authorizing a new investment. It is impossible to directly observe or reward effort. As a result, management control systems motivate employees to exert effort by rewarding them for the achievement of observable goals, such as profit targets or stock returns. This induces managers to exert effort because higher levels of effort increase the likelihood that the goals are achieved. The rewards can be monetary (such as cash, shares of company stock, use of a company car, or membership in a club) or nonmonetary (such as a better title, greater responsibility, or authority over a larger number of employees).

Decentralization

Management control systems must fit an organization's structure. An organization whose structure is decentralized has additional issues to consider for its management control system to be effective.

Decentralization is the freedom for managers at lower levels of the organization to make decisions. **Autonomy** is the degree of freedom to make decisions. The greater the freedom, the greater the autonomy. As we discuss the issues of decentralization and autonomy, we use the term "subunit" to refer to any part of an organization. A subunit may be a large division, such as the refining division of ExxonMobil, or a small group, such as a two-person advertising department of a local clothing chain.

Until the mid-twentieth century, many firms were organized in a centralized, hierarchical fashion. Power was concentrated at the top and there was relatively little freedom for managers at the lower levels to make decisions. Perhaps the most famous example of a highly centralized structure is the Soviet Union, prior to its collapse in the late 1980s. Today, organizations are far more decentralized and many companies have pushed decision-making authority down to subunit managers. Examples of firms with decentralized structures include Nucor, the U.S. steel giant, which allows substantial operational autonomy to the general managers of its plants, and Tesco, Britain's largest retailer, which offers great latitude to its store managers. Of course, no firm is completely decentralized. At Nucor headquarters management still retains responsibility for overall strategic planning, company financing, setting base salary levels and bonus targets, purchase of steel scrap, etc. How much decentralization is optimal? Companies try to choose the degree of decentralization that maximizes benefits over costs. From a practical standpoint, top management can seldom quantify either the benefits or the costs of decentralization. Still, the cost-benefit approach helps management focus on the key issues.

Learning Objective 2

Describe the benefits of decentralization

. . . responsiveness to customers, faster decision making, management development

and the costs of decentralization

. . . loss of control, duplication of activities

Benefits of Decentralization

Supporters of decentralizing decision making and granting responsibilities to managers of subunits advocate the following benefits:

1. **Creates greater responsiveness to needs of a subunit's customers, suppliers, and employees.** Good decisions cannot be made without good information. Compared with top managers, subunit managers are better informed about their customers, competitors, suppliers, and employees, as well as about local factors that affect performance, such as ways to decrease costs, improve quality, and be responsive to customers. Eastman Kodak reports that two advantages of decentralization are an "increase in the company's knowledge of the marketplace and improved service to customers."

2. **Leads to gains from faster decision making by subunit managers.** Decentralization speeds decision making, creating a competitive advantage over centralized organizations. Centralization slows decision making as responsibility for decisions creeps upward through layer after layer of management. Interlake, a manufacturer of materials handling equipment, cites this benefit of decentralization: "We have distributed decision-making powers more broadly to the cutting edge of product and market opportunity." Interlake's materials-handling equipment must often be customized to fit customers' needs. Delegating decision making to the sales force allows Interlake to respond faster to changing customer requirements.

3. **Increases motivation of subunit managers.** Subunit managers are more motivated and committed when they can exercise initiative. Hawei & Hawei, a highly decentralized company, maintains that "Decentralization = Creativity = Productivity."

4. **Assists management development and learning.** Giving managers more responsibility helps develop an experienced pool of management talent to fill higher-level management positions. The company also learns which people are unlikely to be successful top managers. According to Tektronix, an electronics instruments company, "Decentralized units provide a training ground for general managers and a visible field of combat where product champions can fight for their ideas."

5. **Sharpens the focus of subunit managers, broadens the reach of top management.** In a decentralized setting, the manager of a subunit has a concentrated focus. The head of Yahoo Japan, for example, can develop country-specific knowledge and expertise (local advertising trends, cultural norms, payment forms, etc.) and focus attention on maximizing Yahoo's profits in Japan. At the same time, this relieves Yahoo's top

management in Sunnyvale, CA from the burden of controlling day-to-day operating decisions in Japan. The American managers can now spend more time and effort on strategic planning for the entire organization.

Costs of Decentralization

Advocates of more-centralized decision making point to the following costs of decentralizing decision making:

1. **Leads to suboptimal decision making.** This cost arises because top management has given up control over decision making. If the subunit managers do not have the necessary expertise or talent to handle this responsibility, the company, as a whole, is worse off.

   Even if subunit managers are sufficiently skilled, **suboptimal decision making**—also called **incongruent decision making** or **dysfunctional decision making**—occurs when a decision's benefit to one subunit is more than offset by the costs to the organization as a whole. This is most prevalent when the subunits in the company are highly interdependent, such as when the end product of one subunit is used or sold by another subunit. For example, suppose that Nintendo's marketing group receives an order for additional Wii consoles in Australia following the release of some unexpectedly popular new games. A manufacturing manager in Japan who is evaluated on the basis of costs may be unwilling to arrange this rush order since altering production schedules invariably increases manufacturing costs. From Nintendo's viewpoint, however, supplying the consoles may be optimal, both because the Australian customers are willing to pay a premium price and because the current shipment is expected to stimulate orders for other Nintendo games and consoles in the future.

2. **Focuses manager's attention on the subunit rather than the company as a whole.** Individual subunit managers may regard themselves as competing with managers of other subunits in the same company as if they were external rivals. This pushes them to view the relative performance of the subunit as more important than the goals of the company. Consequently, managers may be unwilling to assist when another subunit faces an emergency (as in the Nintendo example) or share important information. In the recent Congressional hearings on the recall of Toyota vehicles, it was revealed that it was common for Toyota's Japan unit to not share information about engineering problems or reported defects between its United States, Asian, and European operations. Toyota has since asserted that this dysfunctional behavior will no longer be tolerated.

3. **Results in duplication of output.** If subunits provide similar products or services, their internal competition could lead to failure in the external markets. The reason is that divisions may find it easier to steal market share from one another, by mimicking each other's successful products, rather than from outside firms. Eventually, this leads to confusion in the minds of customers, and the loss of each division's distinctive strengths. The classic example is General Motors, which has had to wind down its Oldsmobile, Pontiac, and Saturn divisions and is now in bankruptcy reorganization. Similarly, Condé Nast Publishing's initially distinct (and separately run) food magazines, *Bon Appétit* and *Gourmet*, eventually ended up chasing the same readers and advertisers, to the detriment of both. *Gourmet* magazine stopped publication in November 2009.[2]

4. **Results in duplication of activities.** Even if the subunits operate in distinct markets, several individual subunits of the company may undertake the same activity separately. In a highly decentralized company, each subunit may have personnel to carry out staff functions such as human resources or information technology. Centralizing these functions helps to streamline and use fewer resources for these activities, and eliminates wasteful duplication. For example, ABB (Switzerland), a global leader in power and automation technology, is decentralized but has generated significant cost savings of late by centralizing its sourcing decisions across business units for parts, such as pipe pumps and fittings, as well as engineering and erection services. The

---

[2] For an intriguing comparison of the failure of decentralization in these disparate settings, see Jack Shafer's article, "How Condé Nast is Like General Motors: The Magazine Empire as Car Wreck," Slate, October 5, 2009, www.slate.com/id/2231177/.

growing popularity of the "shared service center" model, especially for financial transactions and human resources, is predicated on the 30%–40% savings enabled by the consolidation of such functions, rather than allowing them to be controlled by the subunits.[3]

Comparison of Benefits and Costs

To choose an organization structure that will implement a company's strategy, top managers must compare the benefits and costs of decentralization, often on a function-by-function basis. Surveys of U.S. and European companies report that the decisions made most frequently at the decentralized level are related to product mix and product advertising. In these areas, subunit managers develop their own operating plans and performance reports and make faster decisions based on local information. Decisions related to the type and source of long-term financing and income taxes are made least frequently at the decentralized level. Corporate managers have better information about financing terms in different markets and can obtain the best terms. Centralizing income tax strategies allows the organization to trade off and manage income in a subunit with losses in others. The benefits of decentralization are generally greater when companies face uncertainties in their environments, require detailed local knowledge for performing various jobs, and have few interdependencies among divisions.

Decentralization in Multinational Companies

Multinational companies—companies that operate in multiple countries—are often decentralized because centralized control of a company with subunits around the world is often physically and practically impossible. Also, language, customs, cultures, business practices, rules, laws, and regulations vary significantly across countries. Decentralization enables managers in different countries to make decisions that exploit their knowledge of local business and political conditions and enables them to deal with uncertainties in their individual environments. For example, Philips, a global electronics company headquartered in the Netherlands, delegates marketing and pricing decisions for its television business in the Indian and Singaporean markets to the managers in those countries. Multinational corporations often rotate managers between foreign locations and corporate headquarters. Job rotation combined with decentralization helps develop managers' abilities to operate in the global environment.

There are drawbacks to decentralizing multinational companies. One of the most important is the lack of control and the resulting risks. Barings PLC, a British investment banking firm, went bankrupt and had to be sold when one of its traders in Singapore caused the firm to lose more than £1 billion on unauthorized trades that were not detected until after the trades were made. Similarly, a trader at Sumitomo Corporation racked up $2.6 billion in copper-trading losses because poor controls failed to detect the magnitude of the trader's activities. Multinational corporations that implement decentralized decision making usually design their management control systems to measure and monitor division performance. Information and communications technology helps the flow of information for reporting and control.

Choices About Responsibility Centers

A responsibility center is a segment or subunit of the organization whose manager is accountable for a specified set of activities. To measure the performance of subunits in centralized or decentralized companies, the management control system uses one or a mix of the four types of responsibility centers:

1. *Cost center*—the manager is accountable for costs only.
2. *Revenue center*—the manager is accountable for revenues only.
3. *Profit center*—the manager is accountable for revenues and costs.
4. *Investment center*—the manager is accountable for investments, revenues, and costs.

Centralization or decentralization is not mentioned in the descriptions of these centers because each type of responsibility center can be found in either centralized or decentralized companies.

---

[3] For more on this topic, see http://www.sap.com/solutions/business-suite/erp/pdf/BWP_WP_Shared_Services.pdf.

Decision Point ▶

What are the benefits and costs of decentralization?

A common misconception is that *profit center*—and, in some cases, *investment center*—is a synonym for a decentralized subunit, and *cost center* is a synonym for a centralized subunit. *Profit centers can be coupled with a highly centralized organization, and cost centers can be coupled with a highly decentralized organization.* For example, managers in a division organized as a profit center may have little freedom in making decisions. They may need to obtain approval from corporate headquarters for introducing new products and services, or to make expenditures over some preset limit. When Michael Eisner ran Walt Disney Co., the giant media and entertainment conglomerate, the strategic-planning division applied so much scrutiny to business proposals that managers were reluctant to even pitch new ideas.[4] In other companies, divisions such as Information Technology may be organized as cost centers, but their managers may have great latitude with regard to capital expenditures and the purchase of materials and services. In short, the labels "profit center" and "cost center" are independent of the degree of centralization or decentralization in a company.

Transfer Pricing

Learning Objective 3

Explain transfer prices

. . . price one subunit charges another for product

and four criteria used to evaluate alternative transfer-pricing methods

. . . goal congruence, management effort, subunit performance evaluation, and subunit autonomy

In decentralized organizations, much of the decision-making power resides in its individual subunits. In these cases, the management control system often uses *transfer prices* to coordinate the actions of the subunits and to evaluate their performance.

As you may recall from the opener, a **transfer price** is the price one subunit (department or division) charges for a product or service supplied to another subunit of the same organization. If, for example, a car manufacturer has a separate division that manufactures engines, the transfer price is the price the engine division charges when it transfers engines to the car assembly division. The transfer price creates revenues for the selling subunit (the engine division in our example) and purchase costs for the buying subunit (the assembly division in our example), affecting each subunit's operating income. These operating incomes can be used to evaluate subunits' performances and to motivate their managers. The product or service transferred between subunits of an organization is called an **intermediate product**. This product may either be further worked on by the receiving subunit (as in the engine example) or, if transferred from production to marketing, sold to an external customer.

In one sense, transfer pricing is a curious phenomenon. Activities within an organization are clearly nonmarket in nature; products and services are not bought and sold as they are in open-market transactions. Yet, establishing prices for transfers among subunits of a company has a distinctly market flavor. The rationale for transfer prices is that subunit managers (such as the manager of the engine division), when making decisions, need only focus on how their decisions will affect their subunit's performance without evaluating their impact on company-wide performance. In this sense, transfer prices ease the subunit managers' information-processing and decision-making tasks. In a well-designed transfer-pricing system, a manager focuses on optimizing subunit performance (the performance of the engine division) and in so doing optimizes the performance of the company as a whole.

Criteria for Evaluating Transfer Prices

As in all management control systems, transfer prices should help achieve a company's strategies and goals and fit its organization structure. We describe four criteria to evaluate transfer pricing: (1) Transfer prices should promote goal congruence. (2) They should induce managers to exert a high level of effort. Subunits selling a product or service should be motivated to hold down their costs; subunits buying the product or service should be motivated to acquire and use inputs efficiently. (3) The transfer price should help top management evaluate the performance of individual subunits. (4) If top management favors a high degree of decentralization, transfer prices should preserve a high degree of subunit autonomy in decision making. That is, a subunit manager seeking to maximize the operating income of the subunit should have the freedom to transact with other subunits of the company (on the basis of transfer prices) or to transact with external parties.

---

[4] When Robert Iger replaced Eisner as CEO in 2005, one of his first acts was to disassemble the strategic-planning division, thereby giving more authority to Disney's business units (parks and resorts, consumer products, and media networks).

Calculating Transfer Prices

There are three broad categories of methods for determining transfer prices. They are as follows:

1. **Market-based transfer prices.** Top management may choose to use the price of a similar product or service publicly listed in, say, a trade association Web site. Also, top management may select, for the internal price, the external price that a subunit charges to outside customers.

2. **Cost-based transfer prices.** Top management may choose a transfer price based on the cost of producing the product in question. Examples include variable production cost, variable and fixed production costs, and full cost of the product. Full cost of the product includes all production costs plus costs from other business functions (R&D, design, marketing, distribution, and customer service). The cost used in cost-based transfer prices can be actual cost or budgeted cost. Sometimes, the cost-based transfer price includes a markup or profit margin that represents a return on subunit investment.

3. **Hybrid transfer prices.** Hybrid transfer prices take into account both cost and market information. Top management may administer such prices, for example by specifying a transfer price that is an average of the cost of producing and transporting the product internally and the market price for comparable products. At other times, a hybrid transfer price may take the form where the revenue recognized by the selling unit is different from the cost recognized by the buying unit. The most common form of hybrid prices arise via negotiation—the subunits of a company are asked to negotiate the transfer price between them and to decide whether to buy and sell internally or deal with external parties. The eventual transfer price is then the outcome of a bargaining process between selling and buying subunits. Even though there is no requirement that the chosen transfer price bear any specific relationship to cost or market-price data, information regarding costs and prices plays a critical role in the negotiation process. Negotiated transfer prices are often employed when market prices are volatile and change constantly.

To see how each of the three transfer-pricing methods works and to see the differences among them, we examine transfer pricing at Horizon Petroleum against the four criteria of promoting goal congruence, motivating management effort, evaluating subunit performance, and preserving subunit autonomy (if desired).

An Illustration of Transfer Pricing

Horizon Petroleum has two divisions, each operating as a profit center. The transportation division purchases crude oil in Matamoros, Mexico, and transports it from Matamoros to Houston, Texas. The refining division processes crude oil into gasoline. For simplicity, we assume gasoline is the only salable product the Houston refinery makes and that it takes two barrels of crude oil to yield one barrel of gasoline.

Variable costs in each division are variable with respect to a single cost driver: barrels of crude oil transported by the transportation division, and barrels of gasoline produced by the refining division. The fixed cost per unit is based on the budgeted annual fixed costs and practical capacity of crude oil that can be transported by the transportation division, and the budgeted fixed costs and practical capacity of gasoline that can be produced by the refining division. Horizon Petroleum reports all costs and revenues of its non-U.S. operations in U.S. dollars using the prevailing exchange rate.

- The transportation division has obtained rights to certain oil fields in the Matamoros area. It has a long-term contract to purchase crude oil produced from these fields at $72 per barrel. The division transports the oil to Houston and then "sells" it to the refining division. The pipeline from Matamoros to Houston has the capacity to carry 40,000 barrels of crude oil per day.

- The refining division has been operating at capacity (30,000 barrels of crude oil a day), using oil supplied by Horizon's transportation division (an average of 10,000 barrels per day) and oil bought from another producer and delivered to the Houston refinery (an average of 20,000 barrels per day at $85 per barrel).

- The refining division sells the gasoline it produces to outside parties at $190 per barrel.

Exhibit 1 summarizes Horizon Petroleum's variable and fixed costs per barrel of crude oil in the transportation division and variable and fixed costs per barrel of gasoline in the refining division, the external market prices of buying crude oil, and the external market price of selling gasoline. What's missing in the exhibit is the actual transfer price from the transportation division to the refining division. This transfer price will vary depending on the transfer-pricing method used. Transfer prices from the transportation division to the refining division under each of the three methods are as follows:

1. Market-based transfer price of $85 per barrel of crude oil based on the competitive market price in Houston.

2. Cost-based transfer prices at, say, 105% of full cost, where full cost is the cost of the crude oil purchased in Matamoros plus the transportation division's own variable and fixed costs (from Exhibit 1): $1.05 \times (\$72 + \$1 + \$3) = \$79.80$.

3. Hybrid transfer price of, say, $82 per barrel of crude oil, which is between the market-based and cost-based transfer prices. We describe later in this section the various ways in which hybrid prices can be determined.

Exhibit 2 presents division operating incomes per 100 barrels of crude oil purchased under each transfer-pricing method. Transfer prices create income for the selling division and corresponding costs for the buying division that cancel out when division results are consolidated for the company as a whole. The exhibit assumes all three transfer-pricing methods yield transfer prices that are in a range that does not cause division managers to change the business relationships shown in Exhibit 1. That is, Horizon Petroleum's total operating income from purchasing, transporting, and refining the 100 barrels of crude oil and selling the 50 barrels of gasoline is the same, $1,200, *regardless of the internal transfer prices used.*

$$\begin{matrix} \text{Operating} \\ \text{income} \end{matrix} = \text{Revenues} - \begin{matrix} \text{Cost of crude} \\ \text{oil purchases} \\ \text{in Matamoros} \end{matrix} - \begin{matrix} \text{Transportation} \\ \text{Division} \\ \text{costs} \end{matrix} - \begin{matrix} \text{Refining} \\ \text{Division} \\ \text{costs} \end{matrix}$$

$$= (\$190 \times 50 \text{ barrels of gasoline}) - (\$72 \times 100 \text{ barrels of crude oil})$$

$$- (\$4 \times 100 \text{ barrels of crude oil}) - (\$14 \times 50 \text{ barrels of gasoline})$$

$$= \$9,500 - \$7,200 - \$400 - \$700 = \$1,200$$

Note further that under all three methods, summing the two division operating incomes equals Horizon Petroleum's total operating income of $1,200. By keeping total operating

Exhibit 1   Operating Data for Horizon Petroleum

	Home	Insert	Page Layout	Formulas	Data	Review	View				
	A		B	C	D		E	F	G		H
1											
2					**Transportation Division**						
3	Contract price per barrel of crude oil supplied in Matamoros				Variable cost per barrel of crude oil		$1				
4		=	$72		Fixed cost per barrel of crude oil		3				
5					Full cost per barrel of crude oil		$4				
6											
7											
8					Barrels of crude oil transferred						
9											
10											
11					**Refining Division**						
12	Market price per barrel of crude oil supplied to Houston refinery				Variable cost per barrel of gasoline		$ 8		Market price per barrel of gasoline sold to external parties	=	$190
13		=	$85		Fixed cost per barrel of gasoline		6				
14					Full cost per barrel of gasoline		$14				
15											

Exhibit 2   Division Operating Income of Horizon Petroleum for 100 Barrels of Crude Oil Under Alternative Transfer-Pricing Methods

	Home	Insert	Page Layout	Formulas	Data	Review	View						
	A				B	C	D	E	F	G	H
1		**Production and Sales Data**									
2		Barrels of crude oil transferred = 100									
3		Barrels of gasoline sold = 50									
4											
5					**Internal Transfers at**			**Internal Transfers at**			
6					**Market Price =**			**105% of Full Cost =**		**Hybrid Price =**	
7					**$85 per Barrel**			**$79.80 per Barrel**		**$82 per Barrel**	
8	**Transportation Division**										
9	Revenues, $85, $79.80, $82 × 100 barrels of crude oil				$8,500			$7,980		$8,200	
10	Costs										
11	Crude oil purchase costs, $72 × 100 barrels of crude oil				7,200			7,200		7,200	
12	Division variable costs, $1 × 100 barrels of crude oil				100			100		100	
13	Division fixed costs, $3 × 100 barrels of crude oil				300			300		300	
14	Total division costs				7,600			7,600		7,600	
15	Division operating income				$ 900			$ 380		$ 600	
16											
17	**Refining Division**										
18	Revenues, $190 × 50 barrels of gasoline				$9,500			$9,500		$9,500	
19	Costs										
20	Transferred-in costs, $85, $79.80, $82										
21	× 100 barrels of crude oil				8,500			7,980		8,200	
22	Division variable costs, $8 × 50 barrels of gasoline				400			400		400	
23	Division fixed costs, $6 × 50 barrels of gasoline				300			300		300	
24	Total division costs				9,200			8,680		8,900	
25	Division operating income				$ 300			$ 820		$ 600	
26	Operating income of both divisions together				$1,200			$1,200		$1,200	

income the same, we focus attention on the effects of different transfer-pricing methods on the operating income of each division. Subsequent sections of this chapter show that different transfer-pricing methods can cause managers to take different actions leading to different total operating incomes.

Consider the two methods in the first two columns of Exhibit 2. The operating income of the transportation division is $520 more ($900 – $380) if transfer prices are based on market prices rather than on 105% of full cost. The operating income of the refining division is $520 more ($820 – $300) if transfer prices are based on 105% of full cost rather than market prices. If the transportation division's sole criterion were to maximize its own division operating income, it would favor transfer prices at market prices. In contrast, the refining division would prefer transfer prices at 105% of full cost to maximize its own division operating income. The hybrid transfer price of $82 is between the 105% of full cost and market-based transfer prices. It splits the $1,200 of operating income equally between the divisions, and could arise as a result of negotiations between the transportation and refining division managers.

It's not surprising that subunit managers, especially those whose compensation or promotion directly depends on subunit operating income, take considerable interest in setting transfer prices. To reduce the excessive focus of subunit managers on their own subunits, many companies compensate subunit managers on the basis of both subunit and company-wide operating incomes.

We next examine market-based, cost-based, and hybrid transfer prices in more detail. We show how the choice of transfer-pricing method combined with managers' sourcing decisions can determine the size of the company-wide operating-income pie itself.

◀ **Decision Point**

What are alternative ways of calculating transfer prices, and what criteria should be used to evaluate them?

Market-Based Transfer Prices

Learning Objective 4

Illustrate how market-based transfer prices promote goal congruence in perfectly competitive markets

. . . division managers transacting internally are motivated to take the same actions as if they were transacting externally

Transferring products or services at market prices generally leads to optimal decisions when three conditions are satisfied: (1) The market for the intermediate product is perfectly competitive, (2) interdependencies of subunits are minimal, and (3) there are no additional costs or benefits to the company as a whole from buying or selling in the external market instead of transacting internally.

Perfectly-Competitive-Market Case

A **perfectly competitive market** exists when there is a homogeneous product with buying prices equal to selling prices and no individual buyers or sellers can affect those prices by their own actions. By using market-based transfer prices in perfectly competitive markets, a company can (1) promote goal congruence, (2) motivate management effort, (3) evaluate subunit performance, and (4) preserve subunit autonomy.

Consider Horizon Petroleum again. Assume there is a perfectly competitive market for crude oil in the Houston area. As a result, the transportation division can sell and the refining division can buy as much crude oil as each wants at $85 per barrel. Horizon would prefer its managers to buy or sell crude oil internally. Think about the decisions that Horizon's division managers would make if each had the autonomy to sell or buy crude oil externally. If the transfer price between Horizon's transportation and refining divisions is set below $85, the manager of the transportation division will be motivated to sell all crude oil to external buyers in the Houston area at $85 per barrel. If the transfer price is set above $85, the manager of the refining division will be motivated to purchase all crude oil requirements from external suppliers. Only an $85 transfer price will motivate the transportation division and the refining division to buy and sell internally. That's because neither division profits by buying or selling in the external market.

Suppose Horizon evaluates division managers on the basis of their individual division's operating income. The transportation division will sell, either internally or externally, as much crude oil as it can profitably transport, and the refining division will buy, either internally or externally, as much crude oil as it can profitably refine. An $85-per-barrel transfer price achieves goal congruence—the actions that maximize each division's operating income are also the actions that maximize operating income of Horizon Petroleum as a whole. Furthermore, because the transfer price is not based on costs, it motivates each division manager to exert management effort to maximize his or her own division's operating income. Market prices also serve to evaluate the economic viability and profitability of each division individually. For example, Koch Industries, the second-largest private company in the United States, uses market-based pricing for all internal transfers. As their CFO, Steve Feilmeier, notes, "We believe that the alternative for any given asset should always be considered in order to best optimize the profitability of the asset. If you simply transfer price between two different divisions at cost, then you may be subsidizing your whole operation and not know it." Returning to our Horizon example, suppose that under market-based transfer prices, the refining division consistently shows small or negative profits. Then, Horizon may consider shutting down the refining division and simply transport and sell the oil to other refineries in the Houston area.

Distress Prices

When supply outstrips demand, market prices may drop well below their historical averages. If the drop in prices is expected to be temporary, these low market prices are sometimes called "distress prices." Deciding whether a current market price is a distress price is often difficult. Prior to the worldwide spike in commodity prices in the 2006–2008 period, the market prices of several mineral and agricultural commodities, including nickel, uranium, and wheat, stayed for many years at what people initially believed were temporary distress levels!

Which transfer price should be used for judging performance if distress prices prevail? Some companies use the distress prices themselves, but others use long-run average prices, or "normal" market prices. In the short run, the manager of the selling subunit should supply the product or service at the distress price as long as it exceeds the *incremental costs* of supplying the product or service. If the distress price is used as the transfer price, the selling division will show a loss because the distress price will not exceed the *full cost* of the division. If the long-run average market price is used, forcing the manager to buy internally at a price above the current market price will hurt the buying division's short-run operating income. But the long-run average market price will provide a better measure of the long-run profitability and viability of the supplier division. Of course, if the price remains low in the long run, the company should use the low market price as the transfer price. If this price is lower than the variable and fixed costs that can be saved if manufacturing facilities are shut down, the production facilities of the selling subunit should be sold, and the buying subunit should purchase the product from an external supplier.

Imperfect Competition

If markets are not perfectly competitive, selling prices affect the quantity of product sold. If the selling division sells its product in the external market, the selling division manager would choose a price and quantity combination that would maximize the division's operating income. If the transfer price is set at this selling price, the buying division may find that acquiring the product is too costly and results in a loss. It may decide not to purchase the product. Yet, from the point of view of the company as a whole, it may well be that profits are maximized if the selling division transfers the product to the buying division for further processing and sale. For this reason, when the market for the intermediate good is imperfectly competitive, the transfer price must generally be set below the external market price (but above the selling division's variable cost) in order to induce efficient transfers.[5]

Decision Point

Under what market conditions do market-based transfer prices promote goal congruence?

Cost-Based Transfer Prices

Cost-based transfer prices are helpful when market prices are unavailable, inappropriate, or too costly to obtain, such as when markets are not perfectly competitive, when the product is specialized, or when the internal product is different from the products available externally in terms of quality and customer service.

Learning Objective 5

Understand how to avoid making suboptimal decisions when transfer prices are based on full cost plus a markup

. . . in situations when buying divisions regard the fixed costs and the markup as variable costs

Full-Cost Bases

In practice, many companies use transfer prices based on full cost. To approximate market prices, cost-based transfer prices are sometimes set at full cost plus a margin. These transfer prices, however, can lead to suboptimal decisions. Suppose Horizon Petroleum makes internal transfers at 105% of full cost. Recall that the refining division purchases, on average, 20,000 barrels of crude oil per day from a local Houston supplier, who delivers the crude oil to the refinery at a price of $85 per barrel. To reduce crude oil costs, the refining division has located an independent producer in Matamoros—Gulfmex Corporation—that is willing to sell 20,000 barrels of crude oil per day at $79 per barrel, delivered to Horizon's pipeline in Matamoros. Given Horizon's organization structure, the transportation division would purchase the 20,000 barrels of crude oil in Matamoros from Gulfmex, transport it to Houston, and then sell it to the refining division. The pipeline has unused capacity and can ship the 20,000 barrels per day at its variable cost of $1 per barrel without affecting the shipment of the 10,000 barrels of crude oil per day acquired under its existing long-term contract arrangement. Will Horizon Petroleum incur lower costs by

---

[5] Consider a firm where division S produces the intermediate product. S has a capacity of 15 units and a variable cost per unit of $2. The imperfect competition is reflected in a downward-sloping demand curve for the intermediate product—if S wants to sell Q units, it has to lower the market price to $P = 20 - Q$. The division's profit function is therefore given by $Q \times (20 - Q) - 2Q = 18Q - Q^2$. Simple calculus reveals that it is optimal for S to sell 9 units of the intermediate product at a price of $11, thereby making a profit of $81. Now, suppose that division B in the same firm can take the intermediate product, incur an additional variable cost of $4 and sell it in the external market for $12. Since S has surplus capacity (it only uses 9 of its 15 units of capacity), it is clearly in the firm's interest to have S make additional units and transfer them to B. The firm makes an incremental profit of $12 - $2 - $4 = $6 for each transferred unit. However, if the transfer price for the intermediate product were set equal to the market price of $11, B would reject the transaction since it would lose money on it ($12 - $11 - $4 = - $3 per unit).

To resolve this conflict, the transfer price should be set at a suitable *discount* to the external price in order to induce the buying division to seek internal transfers. In our example, the selling price must be greater than S's variable cost of $2, but less than B's contribution margin of $8. That is, the transfer price has to be discounted relative to the market price ($11) by a minimum of $3. We explore the issue of feasible transfer pricing ranges further in the section on hybrid transfer prices.

purchasing crude oil from Gulfmex in Matamoros or by purchasing crude oil from the Houston supplier? Will the refining division show lower crude oil purchasing costs by acquiring oil from Gulfmex or by acquiring oil from its current Houston supplier?

The following analysis shows that Horizon Petroleum's operating income would be maximized by purchasing oil from Gulfmex. The analysis compares the incremental costs in both divisions under the two alternatives. The analysis assumes the fixed costs of the transportation division will be the same regardless of the alternative chosen. That is, the transportation division cannot save any of its fixed costs if it does not transport Gulfmex's 20,000 barrels of crude oil per day.

- **Alternative 1:** Buy 20,000 barrels from the Houston supplier at $85 per barrel. Total costs to Horizon Petroleum are 20,000 barrels × $85 per barrel = $1,700,000.
- **Alternative 2:** Buy 20,000 barrels in Matamoros at $79 per barrel and transport them to Houston at a variable cost of $1 per barrel. Total costs to Horizon Petroleum are 20,000 barrels × ($79 + $1) per barrel = $1,600,000.

There is a reduction in total costs to Horizon Petroleum of $100,000 ($1,700,000 − $1,600,000) by acquiring oil from Gulfmex.

Suppose the transportation division's transfer price to the refining division is 105% of full cost. The refining division will see its reported division costs increase if the crude oil is purchased from Gulfmex:

$$\text{Transfer price} = 1.05 \times \left(\begin{array}{ccc} \text{Purchase price} & \text{Variable cost per unit} & \text{Fixed cost per unit} \\ \text{from} & + \text{ of Transportation} & + \text{ of Transportation} \\ \text{Gulfmex} & \text{Division} & \text{Division} \end{array} \right)$$

$$= 1.05 \times (\$79 + \$1 + \$3) = 1.05 \times \$83 = \$87.15 \text{ per barrel}$$

- **Alternative 1:** Buy 20,000 barrels from Houston supplier at $85 per barrel. Total costs to refining division are 20,000 barrels × $85 per barrel = $1,700,000.
- **Alternative 2:** Buy 20,000 barrels from the transportation division of Horizon Petroleum that were purchased from Gulfmex. Total costs to refining division are 20,000 barrels × $87.15 per barrel = $1,743,000.

As a profit center, the refining division can maximize its short-run division operating income by purchasing from the Houston supplier at $1,700,000.

The refining division looks at each barrel that it obtains from the transportation division as a variable cost of $87.15 per barrel; if 10 barrels are transferred, it costs the refining division $871.50; if 100 barrels are transferred, it costs $8,715. In fact, the variable cost per barrel is $80 ($79 to purchase the oil from Gulfmex plus $1 to transport it to Houston). The remaining $7.15 ($87.15 − $80) per barrel is the transportation division's fixed cost and markup. *The full cost plus a markup transfer-pricing method causes the refining division to regard the fixed cost (and the 5% markup) of the transportation division as a variable cost and leads to goal incongruence.*

Should Horizon's top management interfere and force the refining division to buy from the transportation division? Top management interference would undercut the philosophy of decentralization, so Horizon's top management would probably view the decision by the refining division to purchase crude oil from external suppliers as an inevitable cost of decentralization and not interfere. Of course, some interference may occasionally be necessary to prevent costly blunders. But recurring interference and constraints would simply transform Horizon from a decentralized company into a centralized company.

What transfer price will promote goal congruence for both the transportation and refining divisions? The minimum transfer price is $80 per barrel. A transfer price below $80 does not provide the transportation division with an incentive to purchase crude oil from Gulfmex in Matamoros because it is below the transportation division's incremental costs. The maximum transfer price is $85 per barrel. A transfer price above $85 will cause the refining division to purchase crude oil from the external market rather than from the transportation division. A transfer price between the minimum and maximum transfer prices of $80 and $85 will promote goal congruence: Each division will increase its own reported operating income while increasing Horizon Petroleum's operating income if the refining division purchases crude oil from Gulfmex in Matamoros.

In the absence of a market-based transfer price, senior management at Horizon Petroleum cannot easily determine the profitability of the investment made in the transportation division and hence whether Horizon should keep or sell the pipeline. Furthermore, if the transfer price had been based on the actual costs of the transportation division, it would provide the division with no incentive to control costs. That's because all cost inefficiencies of the transportation division would get passed along as part of the actual full-cost transfer price. In fact, every additional dollar of cost arising from wastefulness in the transportation division would generate an additional five cents in profit for the division under the "105% of full cost" rule!

Surveys indicate that, despite the limitations, managers generally prefer to use full-cost-based transfer prices. That's because these transfer prices represent relevant costs for long-run decisions, they facilitate external pricing based on variable and fixed costs, and they are the least costly to administer. However, full-cost transfer pricing does raise many issues. How are each subunit's indirect costs allocated to products? Have the correct activities, cost pools, and cost-allocation bases been identified? Should the chosen fixed-cost rates be actual or budgeted? The issues here are similar to the issues that arise in allocating fixed costs. Many companies determine the transfer price based on budgeted rates and practical capacity because it overcomes the problem of inefficiencies in actual costs and costs of unused capacity getting passed along to the buying division.

Variable-Cost Bases

Transferring 20,000 barrels of crude oil from the transportation division to the refining division at the variable cost of $80 per barrel achieves goal congruence, as shown in the preceding section. The refining division would buy from the transportation division because the transportation division's variable cost is less than the $85 price charged by external suppliers. Setting the transfer price equal to the variable cost has other benefits. Knowledge of the variable cost per barrel of crude oil is very helpful to the refining division for many decisions such as short-run pricing decisions. However, at the $80-per-barrel transfer price, the transportation division would record an operating loss, and the refining division would show large profits because it would be charged only for the variable costs of the transportation division. One approach to addressing this problem is to have the refining division make a lump-sum transfer payment to cover fixed costs and generate some operating income for the transportation division while the transportation division continues to make transfers at variable cost. The fixed payment is the price the refining division pays for using the capacity of the transportation division. The income earned by each division can then be used to evaluate the performance of each division and its manager.

Hybrid Transfer Prices

Consider again Horizon Petroleum. As we saw earlier, the transportation division has unused capacity it can use to transport oil from Matamoros to Houston at an incremental cost of $80 per barrel of crude oil. Horizon Petroleum, as a whole, maximizes operating income if the refining division purchases crude oil from the transportation division rather than from the Houston market (incremental cost per barrel of $80 versus price per barrel of $85). Both divisions would be interested in transacting with each other (and the firm achieves goal congruence) if the transfer price is between $80 and $85.

For any internal transaction, there is generally a minimum transfer price the selling division will not go below, based on its cost structure. In the Horizon Petroleum example, the minimum price acceptable to the transportation division is $80. There is also a maximum price the buying division will not wish to exceed, given by the lower of two quantities—the eventual contribution it generates from an internal transaction and the price of purchasing a comparable intermediate product from an outside party. For the

Decision Point

What problems can arise when full cost plus a markup is used as the transfer price?

Learning Objective 6

Describe the range of feasible transfer prices when there is unused capacity

. . . from variable cost to market price of the product transferred refining division, each barrel of gasoline sold to external parties generates $182 in contribution (the $190 price less the $8 variable cost of refining). Since it takes two barrels of crude oil to generate a barrel of gasoline, this is equivalent to a contribution of $91 per barrel of crude. For any price higher than $91, the refining division would lose money for each barrel of crude it takes from the transportation division. On the other hand, the refining division can purchase crude oil on the open market for $85 rather than having it transported internally. The maximum feasible transfer price is thus the lower of $91 and $85, or $85 in this instance. We saw previously that a transfer price between the minimum price ($80) and the maximum ($85) would promote goal congruence. We now describe three different ways in which firms attempt to determine the specific transfer price within these bounds.

Prorating the Difference Between Maximum and Minimum Transfer Prices

One approach that Horizon Petroleum could pursue is to choose a transfer price that splits, on some fair basis, the $5 difference between the $85-per-barrel market-based maximum price the refining division is willing to pay and the $80-per-barrel variable cost-based minimum price the transportation division wants to receive. An easy solution is to split the difference equally, resulting in a transfer price of $82.50. However, this solution ignores the relative costs incurred by the two divisions and might lead to disparate profit margins on the work contributed by each division to the final product. As an alternative approach, Horizon Petroleum could allocate the $5 difference on the basis of the variable costs of the two divisions. Using the data in Exhibit 1, variable costs are as follows:

Transportation division's variable costs to transport 100 barrels of crude oil ($1 × 100)	$100
Refining division's variable costs to refine 100 barrels of crude oil and produce 50 barrels of gasoline ($8 × 50)	400
Total variable costs	$500

Of the $5 difference, the transportation division gets to keep ($100 ÷ $500) × $5.00 = $1.00, and the refining division gets to keep ($400 ÷ $500) × $5.00 = $4.00. That is, the transfer price is $81 per barrel of crude oil ($79 purchase cost + $1 variable cost + $1 that the transportation division gets to keep). In effect, this approach results in a budgeted variable-cost-plus transfer price. The "plus" indicates the setting of a transfer price above variable cost.

To decide on the $1 and $4 allocations of the $5 incremental benefit to total company operating income per barrel, the divisions must share information about their variable costs. In effect, each division does not operate (at least for this transaction) in a totally decentralized manner. Furthermore, each division has an incentive to overstate its variable costs to receive a more-favorable transfer price. In the preceding example, suppose the transportation division claims a cost of $2 per barrel to ship crude oil from Gulfmex to Houston. This increased cost raises the variable cost-based minimum price to $79 + $2 = $81 per barrel; the maximum price remains $85. Of the $4 difference between the minimum and maximum, the transportation division now gets to keep ($200 ÷ ($200 + $400)) × $4.00 = $1.33, resulting in a higher transfer price of $82.33. The refining division similarly benefits from asserting that its variable cost to refine 100 barrels of crude oil is greater than $400. As a consequence, proration methods either require a high degree of trust and information exchange among divisions or include provisions for objective audits of cost information in order to be successful.

Negotiated Pricing

This is the most common hybrid method. Under this approach, top management does not administer a specific split of the eventual profits across the transacting divisions. Rather, the eventual transfer price results from a bargaining process between the selling and buying subunits. In the Horizon Petroleum case, for example, the transportation division and the refining division would be free to negotiate a price that is mutually acceptable to both.

As described earlier, the minimum and maximum feasible transfer prices are $80 and $85, respectively, per barrel of crude oil. Where between $80 and $85 will the transfer price per barrel be set? Under a negotiated transfer price, the answer depends on several things: the bargaining strengths of the two divisions; information the transportation division has about the price minus incremental marketing costs of supplying crude oil to outside refineries; and the information the refining division has about its other available sources of crude oil. Negotiations become particularly sensitive because Horizon Petroleum can now evaluate each division's performance on the basis of division operating income. The price negotiated by the two divisions will, in general, have no specific relationship to either costs or market price. But cost and price information is often the starting point in the negotiation process.

Consider the following situation: Suppose the refining division receives an order to supply specially processed gasoline. The incremental cost to purchase and supply crude oil is still $80 per barrel. However, suppose the refining division will profit from this order only if the transportation division can supply crude oil at a price not exceeding $82 per barrel.[6] In this case, the transfer price that would benefit both divisions must be greater than $80 but less than $82. Negotiations would allow the two divisions to achieve an acceptable transfer price. By contrast, a rule-based transfer price, such as a market-based price of $85 or a 105% of full-cost-based price of $87.15, would result in Horizon passing up a profitable opportunity.

A negotiated transfer price strongly preserves division autonomy. It also has the advantage that each division manager is motivated to put forth effort to increase division operating income. Surveys have found that approximately 15%–20% of firms set transfer prices based on negotiation among divisions. The key reason cited by firms that do not use negotiated prices is the cost of the bargaining process, that is, the time and energy spent by managers haggling over transfer prices.

Dual Pricing

There is seldom a single transfer price that simultaneously meets the criteria of promoting goal congruence, motivating management effort, evaluating subunit performance, and preserving subunit autonomy. As a result, some companies choose **dual pricing**, using two separate transfer-pricing methods to price each transfer from one subunit to another. An example of dual pricing arises when the selling division receives a full-cost-based price and the buying division pays the market price for the internally transferred products. Assume Horizon Petroleum purchases crude oil from Gulfmex in Matamoros at $79 per barrel. One way of recording the journal entry for the transfer between the transportation division and the refining division is as follows:

1. Debit the refining division (the buying division) with the market-based transfer price of $85 per barrel of crude oil.

2. Credit the transportation division (the selling division) with the 105%-of-full-cost transfer price of $87.15 per barrel of crude oil.

3. Debit a corporate cost account for the $2.15 ($87.15 − $85) per barrel difference between the two transfer prices.

The dual-pricing system promotes goal congruence because it makes the refining division no worse off if it purchases the crude oil from the transportation division rather than from the external supplier at $85 per barrel. The transportation division receives a corporate subsidy. In dual pricing, the operating income for Horizon Petroleum as a whole is less than the sum of the operating incomes of the divisions.

Dual pricing is not widely used in practice even though it reduces the goal incongruence associated with a pure cost-based transfer-pricing method. One concern with dual pricing is that it leads to problems in computing the taxable income of subunits located in different tax jurisdictions, such as in our example, where the transportation division is taxed in Mexico while the refining division is taxed in the United States. A second concern is that dual pricing insulates managers from the frictions of the marketplace because costs, not market prices, affect the revenues of the supplying division.

Decision Point

Within a range of feasible transfer prices, what are alternative ways for firms to arrive at the eventual price?

---

[6] For example, suppose a barrel of specially processed gasoline could be sold for $200 but also required a higher variable cost of refining of $36 per barrel. In this setting, the incremental contribution to the refining division is $164 per barrel of gasoline, which implies that it will pay at most $82 for a barrel of crude oil (since two barrels of crude are required for one barrel of gasoline).

A General Guideline for Transfer-Pricing Situations

Learning Objective 7

Apply a general guideline for determining a minimum transfer price

. . . incremental cost plus opportunity cost of supplying division

Exhibit 3 summarizes the properties of market-based, cost-based, and negotiated transfer-pricing methods using the criteria described in this chapter. As the exhibit indicates, it is difficult for a transfer-pricing method to meet all criteria. Market conditions, the goal of the transfer-pricing system, and the criteria of promoting goal congruence, motivating management effort, evaluating subunit performance, and preserving subunit autonomy (if desired) must all be considered simultaneously. The transfer price a company will eventually choose depends on the economic circumstances and the decision at hand. Surveys of company practice indicate that the full-cost-based transfer price is generally the most frequently used transfer-pricing method around the world, followed by market-based transfer price and negotiated transfer price.

Our discussion thus far highlight that, barring settings in which a perfectly competitive market exists for the intermediate product, there is generally a range of possible transfer prices that would induce goal congruence. We now provide a general guideline for determining the minimum price in that range. The following formula is a helpful first step in setting the minimum transfer price in many situations:

$$\text{Minimum transfer price} = \begin{array}{c} \text{Incremental cost} \\ \text{per unit} \\ \text{incurred up} \\ \text{to the point of transfer} \end{array} + \begin{array}{c} \text{Opportunity cost} \\ \text{per unit} \\ \text{to the selling subunit} \end{array}$$

Incremental cost in this context means the additional cost of producing and transferring the product or service. Opportunity cost here is the maximum contribution margin forgone by the selling subunit if the product or service is transferred internally. For example, if the selling subunit is operating at capacity, the opportunity cost of transferring a unit internally rather than selling it externally is equal to the market price minus variable cost. That's because by transferring a unit internally, the subunit forgoes the contribution margin it could have obtained by selling the unit in the external market. We distinguish incremental cost from opportunity cost because financial accounting systems record incremental cost but do not record opportunity cost. The guideline measures a *minimum* transfer price because it represents the selling unit's cost of transferring the product. We illustrate the general guideline in some specific situations using data from Horizon Petroleum.

1. **A perfectly competitive market for the intermediate product exists, and the selling division has no unused capacity.** If the market for crude oil in Houston is perfectly

Exhibit 3

Comparison of Different Transfer-Pricing Methods

Criteria	Market-Based	Cost-Based	Negotiated
Achieves goal congruence	Yes, when markets are competitive	Often, but not always	Yes
Motivates management effort	Yes	Yes, when based on budgeted costs; less incentive to control costs if transfers are based on actual costs	Yes
Useful for evaluating subunit performance	Yes, when markets are competitive	Difficult unless transfer price exceeds full cost and even then is somewhat arbitrary	Yes, but transfer prices are affected by bargaining strengths of the buying and selling divisions
Preserves subunit autonomy	Yes, when markets are competitive	No, because it is rule-based	Yes, because it is based on negotiations between subunits
Other factors	Market may not exist, or markets may be imperfect or in distress	Useful for determining full cost of products and services; easy to implement	Bargaining and negotiations take time and may need to be reviewed repeatedly as conditions change

competitive, the transportation division can sell all the crude oil it transports to the external market at $85 per barrel, and it will have no unused capacity. The transportation division's incremental cost (as shown in Exhibit 1) is $73 per barrel (purchase cost of $72 per barrel plus variable transportation cost of $1 per barrel) for oil purchased under the long-term contract or $80 per barrel (purchase cost of $79 plus variable transportation cost of $1) for oil purchased at current market prices from Gulfmex. The transportation division's opportunity cost per barrel of transferring the oil internally is the contribution margin per barrel forgone by not selling the crude oil in the external market: $12 for oil purchased under the long-term contract (market price, $85, minus variable cost, $73) and $5 for oil purchased from Gulfmex (market price, $85, minus variable cost, $80). In either case,

$$\begin{matrix} \text{Minimum transfer price} \\ \text{per barrel} \end{matrix} = \begin{matrix} \text{Incremental cost} \\ \text{per barrel} \end{matrix} + \begin{matrix} \text{Opportunity cost} \\ \text{per barrel} \end{matrix}$$

$$= \$73 + \$12 = \$85$$

or

$$= \$80 + \$5 = \$85$$

2. **An intermediate market exists that is not perfectly competitive, and the selling division has unused capacity.** In markets that are not perfectly competitive, capacity utilization can only be increased by decreasing prices. Unused capacity exists because decreasing prices is often not worthwhile—it decreases operating income.

   If the transportation division has unused capacity, its opportunity cost of transferring the oil internally is zero because the division does not forgo any external sales or contribution margin from internal transfers. In this case,

$$\begin{matrix} \text{Minimum transfer price} \\ \text{per barrel} \end{matrix} = \begin{matrix} \text{Incremental cost} \\ \text{per barrel} \end{matrix} = \begin{matrix} \text{\$73 per barrel for oil purchased under the} \\ \text{long-term contract or \$80 per barrel for} \\ \text{oil purchased from Gulfmex in Matamoros} \end{matrix}$$

In general, when markets are not perfectly competitive, the potential to influence demand and operating income through prices complicates the measurement of opportunity costs. The transfer price depends on constantly changing levels of supply and demand. There is not just one transfer price. Rather, the transfer prices for various quantities supplied and demanded depend on the incremental costs and opportunity costs of the units transferred.

3. **No market exists for the intermediate product.** This situation would occur for the Horizon Petroleum case if the crude oil transported by the transportation division could be used only by the Houston refinery (due to, say, its high tar content) and would not be wanted by external parties. Here, the opportunity cost of supplying crude oil internally is zero because the inability to sell crude oil externally means no contribution margin is forgone. For the transportation division of Horizon Petroleum, the minimum transfer price under the general guideline is the incremental cost per barrel (either $73 or $80). As in the previous case, any transfer price between the incremental cost and $85 will achieve goal congruence.

Multinational Transfer Pricing and Tax Considerations

Transfer pricing is an important accounting priority for managers around the world. A 2007 Ernst & Young survey of multinational enterprises in 24 countries found that 74% of parent firms and 81% of subsidiary respondents believed that transfer pricing was "absolutely critical" or "very important" to their organizations. The reason is that parent companies identify transfer pricing as the single most important tax issue they face. The sums of money involved are often staggering. Google, for example, has a 90% market share of UK internet searches and earned £1.6 billion in advertising revenues last year in Britain; yet, Google UK reported a pretax loss of £26 million. The reason is that revenues from customers in Britain are transferred to Google's European headquarters in Dublin. By paying the low Irish corporate tax rate of 12.5%, Google saved £450 million in UK taxes in 2009 alone. Transfer prices affect not just income taxes, but

Decision Point

What is the general guideline for determining a minimum transfer price?

Learning Objective 8

Incorporate income tax considerations in multinational transfer pricing

. . . set transfer prices to minimize tax payments to the extent permitted by tax authorities also payroll taxes, customs duties, tariffs, sales taxes, value-added taxes, environment-related taxes, and other government levies. Our aim here is to highlight tax factors, and in particular income taxes, as important considerations in determining transfer prices.

Transfer Pricing for Tax Minimization

Consider the Horizon Petroleum data in Exhibit 2. Assume that the transportation division based in Mexico pays Mexican income taxes at 30% of operating income and that the refining division based in the United States pays income taxes at 20% of operating income. Horizon Petroleum would minimize its total income tax payments with the 105%-of-full-cost transfer-pricing method, as shown in the following table, because this method minimizes income reported in Mexico, where income is taxed at a higher rate than in the United States.

	Operating Income for 100 Barrels of Crude Oil			Income Tax on 100 Barrels of Crude Oil		
Transfer-Pricing Method	Transportation Division (Mexico) (1)	Refining Division (United States) (2)	Total (3) = (1) + (2)	Transportation Division (Mexico) (4) = 0.30 × (1)	Refining Division (United States) (5) = 0.20 × (2)	Total (6) = (4) + (5)
Market price	$900	$300	$1,200	$270	$ 60	$330
105% of full costs	380	820	1,200	114	164	278
Hybrid price	600	600	1,200	180	120	300

Income tax considerations raise additional issues. Tax issues may conflict with other objectives of transfer pricing. Suppose the market for crude oil in Houston is perfectly competitive. In this case, the market-based transfer price achieves goal congruence, provides incentives for management effort, and helps Horizon to evaluate the economic profitability of the transportation division. But it is costly from the perspective of income taxes. To minimize income taxes, Horizon would favor using 105% of full cost for tax reporting. Tax laws in the United States and Mexico, however, constrain this option. In particular, the Mexican tax authorities, aware of Horizon's incentives to minimize income taxes by reducing the income reported in Mexico, would challenge any attempts to shift income to the refining division through an unreasonably low transfer price (see also Concepts in Action).

Section 482 of the U.S. Internal Revenue Code governs taxation of multinational transfer pricing. Section 482 requires that transfer prices between a company and its foreign division or subsidiary, for both tangible and intangible property, equal the price that would be charged by an unrelated third party in a comparable transaction. Regulations related to Section 482 recognize that transfer prices can be market-based or cost-plus-based, where the plus represents margins on comparable transactions.[7]

If the market for crude oil in Houston is perfectly competitive, Horizon would be required to calculate taxes using the market price of $85 for transfers from the transportation division to the refining division. Horizon might successfully argue that the transfer price should be set below the market price because the transportation division incurs no marketing and distribution costs when selling crude oil to the refining division. For example, if marketing and distribution costs equal $2 per barrel, Horizon could set the transfer price at $83 ($85 − $2) per barrel, the selling price net of marketing and distribution costs. Under the U.S. Internal Revenue Code, Horizon could obtain advanced approval of the transfer-pricing arrangements from the tax authorities, called an *advanced pricing agreement* (*APA*). The APA is a binding agreement for a specified number of years. The goal of the APA program is to avoid costly transfer-pricing disputes between taxpayers and tax authorities. In 2007, there were 81 APAs executed, of which 54 were bilateral agreements with other tax treaty countries. Included in this was the completion of the first bilateral APA between the United States and China, involving Wal-Mart Stores.

The current global recession has pushed governments around the world to impose tighter trading rules and more aggressively pursue tax revenues. The number of countries

---

[7] J. Styron, "Transfer Pricing and Tax Planning: Opportunities for US Corporations Operating Abroad," *CPA Journal Online* (November 2007); R. Feinschreiber (Ed.), *Transfer Pricing Handbook*, 3rd ed. (New York: John Wiley & Sons, 2002).

Concepts in Action
Transfer Pricing Dispute Temporarily Stops the Flow of Fiji Water

Lenscap VAlamy Images

Tax authorities and government officials across the globe pay close attention to taxes paid by multinational companies operating within their boundaries. At the heart of the issue are the transfer prices that companies use to transfer products from one country to another. Since 2008, Fiji Water, LLC, a U.S.-based company that markets its famous brand of bottled water in more than a dozen counties, has been engaged in a fierce transfer-pricing dispute with the government of the Fiji Islands, where its water bottling plant is located.

While Fiji Water is produced in the Fiji Islands, all other activities in the company's value chain—importing, distributing, and retailing—occur in the countries where Fiji Water is sold. Over time, the Fiji Islands government became concerned that Fiji Water was engaging in transfer price manipulations, selling the water shipments produced in the Fiji Islands at a very low price to the company headquarters in Los Angeles. It was feared that very little of the wealth generated by Fiji Water, the country's second largest exporter, was coming into the Fiji Islands as foreign reserves from export earnings, which Fiji badly needed to fund its imports. To the Fiji Islands government, Fiji Water was funneling most of its cash to the United States.

As a result of these concerns, the Fiji Islands Revenue and Customs Authority (FIRCA) decided to take action against Fiji Water. FIRCA halted exports in January 2008 at ports in the Fiji Islands by putting 200 containers loaded with Fiji Water bottled under armed guard, and issuing a statement accusing Fiji Water of transfer price manipulations. FIRCA's chief executive, Jitoko Tikolevu, said, "The wholly U.S.-owned Fijian subsidiary sold its water exclusively to its U.S. parent at the declared rate, in Fiji, of $4 a carton. In the U.S., though, the same company then sold it for up to $50 a carton."

Fiji Water immediately filed a lawsuit against FIRCA with the High Court of Fiji. The court issued an interim order, allowing the company to resume shipment of the embargoed containers upon payment of a bond to the court. In the media and subsequent court filings, the company stated that on a global basis it sold each carton of water for $20–28, and it did not make a profit due to "heavy investments in assets, employees, and marketing necessary to aggressively grow a successful branded product."

The dispute between FICRA and Fiji Water remains unresolved in the Fiji Islands court system. In the interim, Fiji Water has maintained its previous transfer price of $4 for water produced at its bottling plant in the Fiji Islands. To pressure the company to change its transfer pricing practices, the Fiji Islands government considered adding a 20-cents-per-litre excise tax on water produced in the country, but the tax was ultimately rejected as too draconian. As this high-profile case demonstrates, transfer pricing formulas and taxation details remain a contentious issue for governments and countries around the globe.

Source: Matau, Robert. 2008. Fiji water explains saga. *Fiji Times*, February 9; McMaster, James and Jan Novak. 2009. Fiji water and corporate social responsibility—Green makeover or 'green-washing'? The University of Western Ontario Richard Ivey School of Business No. 909A08, London, Ontario: Ivey Publishing.

that have imposed transfer pricing regulations has approximately quadrupled from 1995 to 2007, according to a 2008 KPMG report. Officials in China, where foreign businesses enjoyed favorable treatment until last year, recently issued new rules requiring multinationals to submit extensive transfer-pricing documentation. Countries such as India, Canada, Turkey, and Greece have brought greater scrutiny to bear on transfer pricing, focusing in particular on intellectual-property values, costs of back-office functions and losses of any type. In the United States, the Obama administration plans to shrink a "tax gap" the IRS estimates may be as high as $345 billion by restricting or closing several widely used tax loopholes. While the plan does not directly address transfer pricing practice, the IRS has become even more aggressive with enforcement. The agency added 1,200 people to its international staff in 2009, and the 2010 budget called for hiring another 800.

Transfer Prices Designed for Multiple Objectives

To meet multiple transfer-pricing objectives, such as minimizing income taxes, achieving goal congruence, and motivating management effort, a company may choose to keep one set of accounting records for tax reporting and a second set for internal management reporting.

Of course, it is costly to maintain two sets of books and companies such as Case New Holland, a world leader in the agricultural and construction equipment business, also oppose it for conceptual reasons. However, a survey by the AnswerThink Consulting Group of large companies (more than $2 billion in revenues) found that 77% used separate reporting systems to track internal pricing information, compared with about 25% of large companies outside that "best practices" group. Microsoft, for example, believes in "delinking" transfer pricing and employs an internal measurement system (Microsoft Accounting Principles, or MAPs) that uses a separate set of company-designed rules and accounts.[8] A key aspect of management control at Microsoft is the desire to hold local managers accountable for product profitability and to establish appropriate sales and marketing spending levels for every product line. To establish these sales and spending levels, the firm creates a profitability statement for every product in every region, and allocates G&A and R&D costs across sales divisions in ways that aren't necessarily the most tax efficient.

Even if a company does not have such formal separated reporting systems, it can still informally adjust transfer prices to satisfy the tradeoff between tax minimization and incentive provision. Consider a multinational firm that makes semiconductor products that it sells through its sales organization in a higher-tax country. To minimize taxes, the parent sets a high transfer price, thereby lowering the operating income of the foreign sales organization. It would be inappropriate to penalize the country sales manager for this low income since the sales organization has no say in determining the transfer price. As an alternative, the company can evaluate the sales manager on the direct contribution (revenues minus marketing costs) incurred in the country. That is, the transfer price incurred to acquire the semiconductor products is omitted for performance-evaluation purposes. Of course, this is not a perfect solution. By ignoring the cost of acquiring the products, the sales manager is given incentives to overspend on local marketing relative to what would be optimal from the firm's overall perspective. If the dysfunctional effects of this are suitably large, corporate managers must then step in and dictate specific operational decisions and goals for the manager based on the information available to them. More generally, adoption of a tax-compliant transfer pricing policy creates a need for nonfinancial performance indicators at lower management levels in order to better evaluate and reward performance.[9]

Additional Issues in Transfer Pricing

Additional factors that arise in multinational transfer pricing include tariffs and customs duties levied on imports of products into a country. The issues here are similar to income tax considerations; companies will have incentives to lower transfer prices for products imported into a country to reduce tariffs and customs duties charged on those products.

In addition to the motivations for choosing transfer prices already described, multinational transfer prices are sometimes influenced by restrictions that some countries place on dividend- or income-related payments to parties outside their national borders. By increasing the prices of goods or services transferred into divisions in these countries, companies can seek to increase the cash paid out of these countries without violating dividend- or income-related restrictions.

Decision Point ▶

How do income tax considerations affect transfer pricing in multinationals?

Problem for Self-Study

The Pillercat Corporation is a highly decentralized company. Each division manager has full authority for sourcing decisions and selling decisions. The machining division of Pillercat has been the major supplier of the 2,000 crankshafts that the tractor division needs each year.

The tractor division, however, has just announced that it plans to purchase all its crankshafts in the forthcoming year from two external suppliers at $200 per crankshaft.

---

[8] For further details, see I. Springsteel, "Separate but Unequal," *CFO Magazine*, August 1999.

[9] Cools et al. "Management control in the transfer pricing tax compliant multinational enterprise," *Accounting, Organizations and Society*, August 2008 provides an illustrative case study of this issue in the context of a semiconductor product division of a multinational firm.

The machining division of Pillercat recently increased its selling price for the forthcoming year to $220 per unit (from $200 per unit in the current year).

Juan Gomez, manager of the machining division, feels that the 10% price increase is justified. It results from a higher depreciation charge on some new specialized equipment used to manufacture crankshafts and an increase in labor costs. Gomez wants the president of Pillercat Corporation to force the tractor division to buy all its crankshafts from the machining division at the price of $220. The following table summarizes the key data.

	Home Insert Page Layout Formulas Data Review	
	A	B
1	Number of crankshafts purchased by tractor division	2,000
2	External supplier's market price per crankshaft	$ 200
3	Variable cost per crankshaft in machining division	$ 190
4	Fixed cost per crankshaft in machining division	$ 20

Required

1. Compute the advantage or disadvantage in terms of annual operating income to the Pillercat Corporation as a whole if the tractor division buys crankshafts internally from the machining division under each of the following cases:
   a. The machining division has no alternative use for the facilities used to manufacture crankshafts.
   b. The machining division can use the facilities for other production operations, which will result in annual cash operating savings of $29,000.
   c. The machining division has no alternative use for its facilities, and the external supplier drops the price to $185 per crankshaft.
2. As the president of Pillercat, how would you respond to Juan Gomez's request that you force the tractor division to purchase all of its crankshafts from the machining division? Would your response differ according to the three cases described in requirement 1? Explain.

Solution

1. Computations for the tractor division buying crankshafts internally for one year under cases **a, b,** and **c** are as follows:

	Home Insert Page Layout Formulas Data Review View			
	A	B	C	D
1			Case	
2		a	b	c
3	Number of crankshafts purchased by tractor division	2,000	2,000	2,000
4	External supplier's market price per crankshaft	$ 200	$ 200	$ 185
5	Variable cost per crankshaft in machining division	$ 190	$ 190	$ 190
6	Opportunity costs of the machining division supplying crankshafts to the tractor division	-	$ 29,000	-
7				
8	Total purchase costs if buying from an external supplier			
9	(2,000 shafts × $200, $200, $185 per shaft)	$400,000	$400,000	$370,000
10	Incremental cost of buying from the machining division			
11	(2,000 shafts × $190 per shaft)	380,000	380,000	380,000
12	Total opportunity costs of the machining division	-	29,000	-
13	Total relevant costs	380,000	409,000	380,000
14	Annual operating income advantage (disadvantage) to			
15	Pillercat of buying from the machining division	$ 20,000	$ (9,000)	$ (10,000)

The general guideline that was introduced in the chapter as a first step in setting a transfer price can be used to highlight the alternatives:

	Home	Insert	Page Layout	Formulas	Data	Review	View
	A	B	C	D	E	F	G
1	Case	Incremental Cost per Unit Incurred to Point of Transfer	+	Opportunity Cost per Unit to the Supplying Division	=	Transfer Price	External Market Price
2	a	$190	+	$0	=	$190.00	$200
3	b	$190	+	$14.50[a]	=	$204.50	$200
4	c	$190	+	$0	=	$190.00	$185
5							
6	[a]Opportunity cost per unit	=	Total opportunity costs	÷	Number of crankshafts	= $29,000 ÷ 2,000 = $14.50	
7							

Comparing transfer price to external-market price, the tractor division will maximize annual operating income of Pillercat Corporation as a whole by purchasing from the machining division in case a and by purchasing from the external supplier in cases b and c.

2. Pillercat Corporation is a highly decentralized company. If no forced transfer were made, the tractor division would use an external supplier, a decision that would be in the best interest of the company as a whole in cases b and c of requirement 1 but not in case a.

Suppose in case a, the machining division refuses to meet the price of $200. This decision means that the company will be $20,000 worse off in the short run. Should top management interfere and force a transfer at $200? This interference would undercut the philosophy of decentralization. Many top managers would not interfere because they would view the $20,000 as an inevitable cost of a suboptimal decision that can occur under decentralization. But how high must this cost be before the temptation to interfere would be irresistible? $30,000? $40,000?

Any top management interference with lower-level decision making weakens decentralization. Of course, Pillercat's management may occasionally interfere to prevent costly mistakes. But recurring interference and constraints would hurt Pillercat's attempts to operate as a decentralized company.

Decision Points

The following question-and-answer format summarizes the chapter's learning objectives. Each decision presents a key question related to a learning objective. The guidelines are the answer to that question.

Decision	Guidelines
1. What is a management control system and how should it be designed?	A management control system is a means of gathering and using information to aid and coordinate the planning and control decisions throughout the organization and to guide the behavior of managers and other employees. Effective management control systems (a) are closely aligned to the organization's strategy, (b) support the organizational responsibilities of individual managers, and (c) motivate managers and other employees to give effort to achieve the organization's goals.

2. What are the benefits and costs of decentralization?

The benefits of decentralization include (a) greater responsiveness to local needs, (b) gains from faster decision making, (c) increased motivation of subunit managers, (d) greater management development and learning, and (e) sharpened focus of subunit managers. The costs of decentralization include (a) suboptimal decision making, (b) excessive focus on the subunit rather than the company as a whole, (c) increased costs of information gathering, and (d) duplication of activities.

3. What are alternative ways of calculating transfer prices, and what criteria should be used to evaluate them?

A transfer price is the price one subunit charges for a product or service supplied to another subunit of the same organization. Transfer prices can be (a) market-based, (b) cost-based, or (c) hybrid. Different transfer-pricing methods produce different revenues and costs for individual subunits, and hence, different operating incomes for the subunits. Transfer prices seek to (a) promote goal congruence, (b) motivate management effort, (c) help evaluate subunit performance, and (d) preserve subunit autonomy (if desired).

4. Under what market conditions do market-based transfer prices promote goal congruence?

In perfectly competitive markets, there is no unused capacity, and division managers can buy and sell as much of a product or service as they want at the market price. In such settings, using the market price as the transfer price motivates division managers to transact internally and to take exactly the same actions as they would if they were transacting in the external market.

5. What problems can arise when full cost plus a markup is used as the transfer price?

A transfer price based on full cost plus a markup may lead to suboptimal decisions because it leads the buying division to regard the fixed costs and the markup of the selling division as a variable cost. The buying division may then purchase products from an external supplier expecting savings in costs that, in fact, will not occur.

6. Within a range of feasible transfer prices, what are alternative ways for firms to arrive at the eventual price?

When there is unused capacity, the transfer-price range lies between the minimum price at which the selling division is willing to sell (its variable cost per unit) and the maximum price the buying division is willing to pay (the lower of its contribution or price at which the product is available from external suppliers). Methods for arriving at a price in this range include proration (such as splitting the difference equally or on the basis of relative variable costs), negotiation between divisions, and dual pricing.

7. What is the general guideline for determining a minimum transfer price?

The general guideline states that the minimum transfer price equals the incremental cost per unit incurred up to the point of transfer plus the opportunity cost per unit to the selling division resulting from transferring products or services internally.

8. How do income tax considerations affect transfer pricing in multinationals?

Transfer prices can reduce income tax payments by reporting more income in low-tax-rate countries and less income in high-tax-rate countries. However, tax regulations of different countries restrict the transfer prices that companies can use.

Terms to Learn

This chapter contains definitions of the following important terms:

autonomy	goal congruence	motivation
decentralization	incongruent decision making	perfectly competitive market
dual pricing	intermediate product	suboptimal decision making
dysfunctional decision making	management control system	transfer price
effort		

Assignment Material

Questions

MyAccountingLab

22-1 What is a management control system?

22-2 Describe three criteria you would use to evaluate whether a management control system is effective.

22-3 What is the relationship among motivation, goal congruence, and effort?

22-4 Name three benefits and two costs of decentralization.

22-5 "Organizations typically adopt a consistent decentralization or centralization philosophy across all their business functions." Do you agree? Explain.

22-6 "Transfer pricing is confined to profit centers." Do you agree? Explain.

22-7 What are the three methods for determining transfer prices?

22-8 What properties should transfer-pricing systems have?

22-9 "All transfer-pricing methods give the same division operating income." Do you agree? Explain.

22-10 Under what conditions is a market-based transfer price optimal?

22-11 What is one potential limitation of full-cost-based transfer prices?

22-12 Give two reasons why the dual-pricing system of transfer pricing is not widely used.

22-13 "Cost and price information play no role in negotiated transfer prices." Do you agree? Explain.

22-14 "Under the general guideline for transfer pricing, the minimum transfer price will vary depending on whether the supplying division has unused capacity or not." Do you agree? Explain.

22-15 How should managers consider income tax issues when choosing a transfer-pricing method?

MyAccountingLab

Exercises

22-16 Evaluating management control systems, balanced scorecard. Adventure Parks Inc. (API) operates ten theme parks throughout the United States. The company's slogan is "Name Your Adventure," and its mission is to offer an exciting theme park experience to visitors of all ages. API's corporate strategy supports this mission by stressing the importance of sparkling clean surroundings, efficient crowd management and, above all, cheerful employees. Of course, improved shareholder value drives this strategy.

Required

1. Assuming that API uses a balanced scorecard approach (see Chapter 13) to formulating its management control system. List three measures that API might use to evaluate each of the four balanced scorecard perspectives: financial perspective, customer perspective, internal-business-process perspective, and learning-and-growth perspective.
2. How would the management controls related to financial and customer perspectives at API differ between the following three managers: a souvenir shop manager, a park general manager, and the corporation's CEO?

22-17 Cost centers, profit centers, decentralization, transfer prices. Fenster Corporation manufactures windows with wood and metal frames. Fenster has three departments: glass, wood, and metal. The glass department makes the window glass and sends it to either the wood or metal department where the glass is framed. The window is then sold. Upper management sets the production schedules for the three departments and evaluates them on output quantity, cost variances, and product quality.

Required

1. Are the three departments cost centers, revenue centers, or profit centers?
2. Are the three departments centralized or decentralized?
3. Can a centralized department be a profit center? Why or why not?
4. Suppose the upper management of Fenster Corporation decides to let the three departments set their own production schedules, buy and sell products in the external market, and have the wood and metal departments negotiate with the glass department for the glass panes using a transfer price.
   a. Will this change your answers to requirements 1 and 2?
   b. How would you recommend upper management evaluate the three departments if this change is made?

22-18 Benefits and costs of decentralization. Jackson Markets, a chain of traditional supermarkets, is interested in gaining access to the organic and health food retail market by acquiring a regional company in that sector. Jackson intends to operate the newly-acquired stores independently from its supermarkets.

One of the prospects is Health Source, a chain of twenty stores in the mid-Atlantic. Buying for all twenty stores is done by the company's central office. Store managers must follow strict guidelines for all aspects of store management in an attempt to maintain consistency among stores. Store managers are evaluated on the basis of achieving profit goals developed by the central office.

The other prospect is Harvest Moon, a chain of thirty stores in the Northeast. Harvest Moon managers are given significant flexibility in product offerings, allowing them to negotiate purchases with local organic farmers. Store managers are rewarded for exceeding self-developed return on investment goals with company stock options. Some managers have become significant shareholders in the company, and have even decided on their own to open additional store locations to improve market penetration. However, the increased autonomy has led to competition and price cutting among Harvest Moon stores within the same geographic market, resulting in lower margins.

Required

1. Would you describe Health Source as having a centralized or a decentralized structure? Explain.
2. Would you describe Harvest Moon as having a centralized or a decentralized structure? Discuss some of the benefits and costs of that type of structure.

3. Would stores in each chain be considered cost centers, revenue centers, profit centers, or investment centers? How does that tie into the evaluation of store managers?

4. Assume that Jackson chooses to acquire Harvest Moon. What steps can Jackson take to improve goal congruence between store managers and the larger company?

22-19 Multinational transfer pricing, effect of alternative transfer-pricing methods, global income tax minimization. Tech Friendly Computer, Inc., with headquarters'in San Francisco, manufactures and sells a desktop computer. Tech Friendly has three divisions, each of which is located in a different country:

a. China division—manufactures memory devices and keyboards

b. South Korea division—assembles desktop computers using locally manufactured parts, along with memory devices and keyboards from the China division

c. U.S. division—packages and distributes desktop computers

Each division is run as a profit center. The costs for the work done in each division for a single desktop computer are as follows:

China division: Variable cost = 900 yuan

Fixed cost = 1,980 yuan

South Korea division: Variable cost = 350,000 won

Fixed cost = 470,000 won

U.S. division: Variable cost = $125

Fixed cost = $325

- Chinese income tax rate on the China division's operating income: 40%
- South Korean income tax rate on the South Korea division's operating income: 20%
- U.S. income tax rate on the U.S. division's operating income: 30%

Each desktop computer is sold to retail outlets in the United States for $3,800. Assume that the current foreign exchange rates are as follows:

9 yuan = $1 U.S.

1,000 won = $1 U.S.

Both the China and the South Korea divisions sell part of their production under a private label. The China division sells the comparable memory/keyboard package used in each Tech Friendly desktop computer to a Chinese manufacturer for 4,500 yuan. The South Korea division sells the comparable desktop computer to a South Korean distributor for 1,340,000 won.

Required

1. Calculate the after-tax operating income per unit earned by each division under the following transfer-pricing methods: (a) market price, (b) 200% of full cost, and (c) 350% of variable cost. (Income taxes are not included in the computation of the cost-based transfer prices.)

2. Which transfer-pricing method(s) will maximize the after-tax operating income per unit of Tech Friendly Computer?

22-20 Transfer-pricing methods, goal congruence. British Columbia Lumber has a raw lumber division and a finished lumber division. The variable costs are as follows:

- Raw lumber division: $100 per 100 board-feet of raw lumber
- Finished lumber division: $125 per 100 board-feet of finished lumber

Assume that there is no board-feet loss in processing raw lumber into finished lumber. Raw lumber can be sold at $200 per 100 board-feet. Finished lumber can be sold at $275 per 100 board-feet.

Required

1. Should British Columbia Lumber process raw lumber into its finished form? Show your calculations.

2. Assume that internal transfers are made at 110% of variable cost. Will each division maximize its division operating-income contribution by adopting the action that is in the best interest of British Columbia Lumber as a whole? Explain.

3. Assume that internal transfers are made at market prices. Will each division maximize its division operating-income contribution by adopting the action that is in the best interest of British Columbia Lumber as a whole? Explain.

22-21 Effect of alternative transfer-pricing methods on division operating income. (CMA, adapted) Ajax Corporation has two divisions. The mining division makes toldine, which is then transferred to the metals division. The toldine is further processed by the metals division and is sold to customers at a price of $150 per unit. The mining division is currently required by Ajax to transfer its total yearly output of

200,000 units of toldine to the metals division at 110% of full manufacturing cost. Unlimited quantities of toldine can be purchased and sold on the outside market at $90 per unit.

The following table gives the manufacturing cost per unit in the mining and metals divisions for 2012:

	Mining Division	Metals Division
Direct material cost	$12	$ 6
Direct manufacturing labor cost	16	20
Manufacturing overhead cost	32[a]	25[b]
Total manufacturing cost per unit	$60	$51

[a]Manufacturing overhead costs in the mining division are 25% fixed and 75% variable.
[b]Manufacturing overhead costs in the metals division are 60% fixed and 40% variable.

Required

1. Calculate the operating incomes for the mining and metals divisions for the 200,000 units of toldine transferred under the following transfer-pricing methods: (a) market price and (b) 110% of full manufacturing cost.
2. Suppose Ajax rewards each division manager with a bonus, calculated as 1% of division operating income (if positive). What is the amount of bonus that will be paid to each division manager under the transfer-pricing methods in requirement 1? Which transfer-pricing method will each division manager prefer to use?
3. What arguments would Brian Jones, manager of the mining division, make to support the transfer-pricing method that he prefers?

22-22 Transfer pricing, general guideline, goal congruence. (CMA, adapted). Quest Motors, Inc., operates as a decentralized multidivision company. The Vivo division of Quest Motors purchases most of its airbags from the airbag division. The airbag division's incremental cost for manufacturing the airbags is $90 per unit. The airbag division is currently working at 80% of capacity. The current market price of the airbags is $125 per unit.

Required

1. Using the general guideline presented in the chapter, what is the minimum price at which the airbag division would sell airbags to the Vivo division?
2. Suppose that Quest Motors requires that whenever divisions with unused capacity sell products internally, they must do so at the incremental cost. Evaluate this transfer-pricing policy using the criteria of goal congruence, evaluating division performance, motivating management effort, and preserving division autonomy.
3. If the two divisions were to negotiate a transfer price, what is the range of possible transfer prices? Evaluate this negotiated transfer-pricing policy using the criteria of goal congruence, evaluating division performance, motivating management effort, and preserving division autonomy.
4. Instead of allowing negotiation, suppose that Quest specifies a hybrid transfer price that "splits the difference" between the minimum and maximum prices from the divisions' standpoint. What would be the resulting transfer price for airbags?

22-23 Multinational transfer pricing, global tax minimization. The Mornay Company manufactures telecommunications equipment at its plant in Toledo, Ohio. The company has marketing divisions throughout the world. A Mornay marketing division in Vienna, Austria, imports 10,000 units of Product 4A36 from the United States. The following information is available:

U.S. income tax rate on the U.S. division's operating income	35%
Austrian income tax rate on the Austrian division's operating income	40%
Austrian import duty	15%
Variable manufacturing cost per unit of Product 4A36	$ 550
Full manufacturing cost per unit of Product 4A36	$ 800
Selling price (net of marketing and distribution costs) in Austria	$1,150

Suppose the United States and Austrian tax authorities only allow transfer prices that are between the full manufacturing cost per unit of $800 and a market price of $950, based on comparable imports into Austria. The Austrian import duty is charged on the price at which the product is transferred into Austria. Any import duty paid to the Austrian authorities is a deductible expense for calculating Austrian income taxes due.

Required

1. Calculate the after-tax operating income earned by the United States and Austrian divisions from transferring 10,000 units of Product 4A36 (a) at full manufacturing cost per unit and (b) at market price of comparable imports. (Income taxes are not included in the computation of the cost-based transfer prices.)
2. Which transfer price should the Mornay Company select to minimize the total of company import duties and income taxes? Remember that the transfer price must be between the full manufacturing cost per unit of $800 and the market price of $950 of comparable imports into Austria. Explain your reasoning.

22-24 Multinational transfer pricing, goal congruence (continuation of 22-23). Suppose that the U.S. division could sell as many units of Product 4A36 as it makes at $900 per unit in the U.S. market, net of all marketing and distribution costs.

1. From the viewpoint of the Mornay Company as a whole, would after-tax operating income be maximized **Required** if it sold the 10,000 units of Product 4A36 in the United States or in Austria? Show your computations.
2. Suppose division managers act autonomously to maximize their division's after-tax operating income. Will the transfer price calculated in requirement 2 of Exercise 22-23 result in the U.S. division manager taking the actions determined to be optimal in requirement 1 of this exercise? Explain.
3. What is the minimum transfer price that the U.S. division manager would agree to? Does this transfer price result in the Mornay Company as a whole paying more import duty and taxes than the answer to requirement 2 of Exercise 22-23? If so, by how much?

22-25 Transfer-pricing dispute. The Allison-Chambers Corporation, manufacturer of tractors and other heavy farm equipment, is organized along decentralized product lines, with each manufacturing division operating as a separate profit center. Each division manager has been delegated full authority on all decisions involving the sale of that division's output both to outsiders and to other divisions of Allison-Chambers. Division C has in the past always purchased its requirement of a particular tractor-engine component from division A. However, when informed that division A is increasing its selling price to $150, division C's manager decides to purchase the engine component from external suppliers.

Division C can purchase the component for $135 per unit in the open market. Division A insists that, because of the recent installation of some highly specialized equipment and the resulting high depreciation charges, it will not be able to earn an adequate return on its investment unless it raises its price. Division A's manager appeals to top management of Allison-Chambers for support in the dispute with division C and supplies the following operating data:

C's annual purchases of the tractor-engine component	1,000 units
A's variable cost per unit of the tractor-engine component	$120
A's fixed cost per unit of the tractor-engine component	$ 20

1. Assume that there are no alternative uses for internal facilities of division A. Determine whether the com- **Required** pany as a whole will benefit if division C purchases the component from external suppliers for $135 per unit. What should the transfer price for the component be set at so that division managers acting in their own divisions' best interests take actions that are also in the best interest of the company as a whole?
2. Assume that internal facilities of division A would not otherwise be idle. By not producing the 1,000 units for division C, division A's equipment and other facilities would be used for other production operations that would result in annual cash-operating savings of $18,000. Should division C purchase from external suppliers? Show your computations.
3. Assume that there are no alternative uses for division A's internal facilities and that the price from outsiders drops $20. Should division C purchase from external suppliers? What should the transfer price for the component be set at so that division managers acting in their own divisions' best interests take actions that are also in the best interest of the company as a whole?

22-26 Transfer-pricing problem (continuation of 22-25). Refer to Exercise 22-25. Assume that division A can sell the 1,000 units to other customers at $155 per unit, with variable marketing cost of $5 per unit.

Determine whether Allison-Chambers will benefit if division C purchases the 1,000 units from external sup- **Required** pliers at $135 per unit. Show your computations.

Problems

MyAccountingLab

22-27 General guideline, transfer pricing. The Slate Company manufactures and sells television sets. Its assembly division (AD) buys television screens from the screen division (SD) and assembles the TV sets. The SD, which is operating at capacity, incurs an incremental manufacturing cost of $65 per screen. The SD can sell all its output to the outside market at a price of $100 per screen, after incurring a variable marketing and distribution cost of $8 per screen. If the AD purchases screens from outside suppliers at a price of $100 per screen, it will incur a variable purchasing cost of $7 per screen. Slate's division managers can act autonomously to maximize their own division's operating income.

1. What is the minimum transfer price at which the SD manager would be willing to sell screens to the AD? **Required**
2. What is the maximum transfer price at which the AD manager would be willing to purchase screens from the SD?
3. Now suppose that the SD can sell only 70% of its output capacity of 20,000 screens per month on the open market. Capacity cannot be reduced in the short run. The AD can assemble and sell more than 20,000 TV sets per month.
   a. What is the minimum transfer price at which the SD manager would be willing to sell screens to the AD?

b. From the point of view of Slate's management, how much of the SD output should be transferred to the AD?

c. If Slate mandates the SD and AD managers to "split the difference" on the minimum and maximum transfer prices they would be willing to negotiate over, what would be the resulting transfer price? Does this price achieve the outcome desired in requirement 3b?

22-28 Pertinent transfer price. Europa, Inc., has two divisions, A and B, that manufacture expensive bicycles. Division A produces the bicycle frame, and division B assembles the rest of the bicycle onto the frame. There is a market for both the subassembly and the final product. Each division has been designated as a profit center. The transfer price for the subassembly has been set at the long-run average market price. The following data are available for each division:

Selling price for final product	$300
Long-run average selling price for intermediate product	200
Incremental cost per unit for completion in division B	150
Incremental cost per unit in division A	120

The manager of division B has made the following calculation:

Selling price for final product		$300
Transferred-in cost per unit (market)	$200	
Incremental cost per unit for completion	150	350
Contribution (loss) on product		$ (50)

Required

1. Should transfers be made to division B if there is no unused capacity in division A? Is the market price the correct transfer price? Show your computations.
2. Assume that division A's maximum capacity for this product is 1,000 units per month and sales to the intermediate market are now 800 units. Should 200 units be transferred to division B? At what transfer price? Assume that for a variety of reasons, division A will maintain the $200 selling price indefinitely. That is, division A is not considering lowering the price to outsiders even if idle capacity exists.
3. Suppose division A quoted a transfer price of $150 for up to 200 units. What would be the contribution to the company as a whole if a transfer were made? As manager of division B, would you be inclined to buy at $150? Explain.

22-29 Pricing in imperfect markets (continuation of 22-28). Refer to Problem 22-28.

Required

1. Suppose the manager of division A has the option of (a) cutting the external price to $195, with the certainty that sales will rise to 1,000 units or (b) maintaining the external price of $200 for the 800 units and transferring the 200 units to division B at a price that would produce the same operating income for division A. What transfer price would produce the same operating income for division A? Is that price consistent with that recommended by the general guideline in the chapter so that the resulting decision would be desirable for the company as a whole?
2. Suppose that if the selling price for the intermediate product were dropped to $195, sales to external parties could be increased to 900 units. Division B wants to acquire as many as 200 units if the transfer price is acceptable. For simplicity, assume that there is no external market for the final 100 units of division A's capacity.
   a. Using the general guideline, what is (are) the minimum transfer price(s) that should lead to the correct economic decision? Ignore performance-evaluation considerations.
   b. Compare the total contributions under the alternatives to show why the transfer price(s) recommended lead(s) to the optimal economic decision.

22-30 Effect of alternative transfer-pricing methods on division operating income. Crango Products is a cranberry cooperative that operates two divisions, a harvesting division and a processing division. Currently, all of harvesting's output is converted into cranberry juice by the processing division, and the juice is sold to large beverage companies that produce cranberry juice blends. The processing division has a yield of 500 gallons of juice per 1,000 pounds of cranberries. Cost and market price data for the two divisions are as follows:

	Home	Insert	Page Layout	Formulas	Data	Review	View	

	A	B	C	D	E
1	**Harvesting Division**			**Processing Division**	
2	Variable cost per pound of cranberries	$0.10		Variable processing cost per gallon of juice produced	$0.20
3	Fixed cost per pound of cranberries	$0.25		Fixed cost per gallon of juice produced	$0.40
4	Selling price per pound of cranberries in outside market	$0.60		Selling price per gallon of juice	$2.10

1. Compute Crango's operating income from harvesting 400,000 pounds of cranberries during June 2012 and processing them into juice. **Required**
2. Crango rewards its division managers with a bonus equal to 5% of operating income. Compute the bonus earned by each division manager in June 2012 for each of the following transfer pricing methods:
   a. 200% of full cost
   b. Market price
3. Which transfer-pricing method will each division manager prefer? How might Crango resolve any conflicts that may arise on the issue of transfer pricing?

22-31 Goal-congruence problems with cost-plus transfer-pricing methods, dual-pricing system (continuation of 22-30). Assume that Pat Borges, CEO of Crango, had mandated a transfer price equal to 200% of full cost. Now he decides to decentralize some management decisions and sends around a memo that states the following: "Effective immediately, each division of Crango is free to make its own decisions regarding the purchase of direct materials and the sale of finished products."

1. Give an example of a goal-congruence problem that will arise if Crango continues to use a transfer price of 200% of full cost and Borges's decentralization policy is adopted. **Required**
2. Borges feels that a dual transfer-pricing policy will improve goal congruence. He suggests that transfers out of the harvesting division be made at 200% of full cost and transfers into the processing division be made at market price. Compute the operating income of each division under this dual transfer pricing method when 400,000 pounds of cranberries are harvested during June 2012 and processed into juice.
3. Why is the sum of the division operating incomes computed in requirement 2 different from Crango's operating income from harvesting and processing 400,000 pounds of cranberries?
4. Suggest two problems that may arise if Crango implements the dual transfer prices described in requirement 2.

22-32 Multinational transfer pricing, global tax minimization. Industrial Diamonds, Inc., based in Los Angeles, has two divisions:

- South African mining division, which mines a rich diamond vein in South Africa
- U.S. processing division, which polishes raw diamonds for use in industrial cutting tools

The processing division's yield is 50%: It takes 2 pounds of raw diamonds to produce 1 pound of top-quality polished industrial diamonds. Although all of the mining division's output of 8,000 pounds of raw diamonds is sent for processing in the United States, there is also an active market for raw diamonds in South Africa. The foreign exchange rate is 6 ZAR (South African Rand) = $1 U.S. The following information is known about the two divisions:

	Home	Insert	Page Layout	Formulas	Data	Review
	A	B	C	D	F	G
1	South African Mining Division					
2	Variable cost per pound of raw diamonds				600	ZAR
3	Fixed cost per pound of raw diamonds				1,200	ZAR
4	Market price per pound of raw diamonds				3,600	ZAR
5	Tax rate				25%	
6						
7	U.S. Processing Division					
8	Variable cost per pound of polished diamonds				220	U.S. dollars
9	Fixed cost per pound of polished diamonds				850	U.S. dollars
10	Market price per pound of polished diamonds				3,500	U.S. dollars
11	Tax rate				40%	

1. Compute the annual pretax operating income, in U.S. dollars, of each division under the following transfer-pricing methods: (a) 250% of full cost and (b) market price. **Required**
2. Compute the after-tax operating income, in U.S. dollars, for each division under the transfer-pricing methods in requirement 1. (Income taxes are not included in the computation of cost-based transfer price, and Industrial Diamonds does not pay U.S. income tax on income already taxed in South Africa.)
3. If the two division managers are compensated based on after-tax division operating income, which transfer-pricing method will each prefer? Which transfer-pricing method will maximize the total after-tax operating income of Industrial Diamonds?
4. In addition to tax minimization, what other factors might Industrial Diamonds consider in choosing a transfer-pricing method?

22-33 International transfer pricing, taxes, goal congruence. Argone division of Gemini Corporation is located in the United States. Its effective income tax rate is 30%. Another division of Gemini, Calcia, is located in Canada, where the income tax rate is 42%. Calcia manufactures, among other things, an intermediate product for Argone called IP-2007. Calcia operates at capacity and makes 15,000 units of IP-2007 for Argone each period, at a variable cost of $60 per unit. Assume that there are no outside customers for IP-2007. Because the IP-2007 must be shipped from Canada to the United States, it costs Calcia an additional $4 per unit to ship the IP-2007 to Argone. There are no direct fixed costs for IP-2007. Calcia also manufactures other products.

A product similar to IP-2007 that Argone could use as a substitute is available in the United States for $75 per unit.

Required

1. What is the minimum and maximum transfer price that would be acceptable to Argone and Calcia for IP-2007, and why?
2. What transfer price would minimize income taxes for Gemini Corporation as a whole? Would Calcia and Argone want to be evaluated on operating income using this transfer price?
3. Suppose Gemini uses the transfer price from requirement 2, and each division is evaluated on its own after-tax division operating income. Now suppose Calcia has an opportunity to sell 8,000 units of IP-2007 to an outside customer for $68 each. Calcia will not incur shipping costs because the customer is nearby and offers to pay for shipping. Assume that if Calcia accepts the special order, Argone will have to buy 8,000 units of the substitute product in the United States at $75 per unit.
   a. Will accepting the special order maximize after-tax operating income for Gemini Corporation as a whole?
   b. Will Argone want Calcia to accept this special order? Why or why not?
   c. Will Calcia want to accept this special order? Explain.
   d. Suppose Gemini Corporation wants to operate in a decentralized manner. What transfer price should Gemini set for IP-2007 so that each division acting in its own best interest takes actions with respect to the special order that are in the best interests of Gemini Corporation as a whole?

22-34 Transfer pricing, goal congruence. The Bosh Corporation makes and sells 20,000 multisystem music players each year. Its assembly division purchases components from other divisions of Bosh or from external suppliers and assembles the multisystem music players. In particular, the assembly division can purchase the CD player from the compact disc division of Bosh or from Hawei Corporation. Hawei agrees to meet all of Bosh's quality requirements and is currently negotiating with the assembly division to supply 20,000 CD players at a price between $44 and $52 per CD player.

A critical component of the CD player is the head mechanism that reads the disc. To ensure the quality of its multisystem music players, Bosh requires that if Hawei wins the contract to supply CD players, it must purchase the head mechanism from Bosh's compact disc division for $24 each.

The compact disc division can manufacture at most 22,000 CD players annually. It also manufactures as many additional head mechanisms as can be sold. The incremental cost of manufacturing the head mechanism is $18 per unit. The incremental cost of manufacturing a CD player (including the cost of the head mechanism) is $30 per unit, and any number of CD players can be sold for $45 each in the external market.

Required

1. What are the incremental costs minus revenues from sale to external buyers for the company as a whole if the compact disc division transfers 20,000 CD players to the assembly division and sells the remaining 2,000 CD players on the external market?
2. What are the incremental costs minus revenues from sales to external buyers for the company as a whole if the compact disc division sells 22,000 CD players on the external market and the assembly division accepts Hawei's offer at (a) $44 per CD player or (b) $52 per CD player?
3. What is the minimum transfer price per CD player at which the compact disc division would be willing to transfer 20,000 CD players to the assembly division?
4. Suppose that the transfer price is set to the minimum computed in requirement 3 plus $2, and the division managers at Bosh are free to make their own profit-maximizing sourcing and selling decisions. Now, Hawei offers 20,000 CD players for $52 each.
   a. What decisions will the managers of the compact disc division and assembly division make?
   b. Are these decisions optimal for Bosh as a whole?
   c. Based on this exercise, at what price would you recommend the transfer price be set?

22-35 Transfer pricing, goal congruence, ethics. Jeremiah Industries manufactures high-grade aluminum luggage made from recycled metal. The company operates two divisions: metal recycling and luggage fabrication. Each division operates as a decentralized entity. The metal recycling division is free to sell sheet aluminum to outside buyers, and the luggage fabrication division is free to purchase recycled sheet aluminum from other sources. Currently, however, the recycling division sells all of its output to the fabrication division, and the fabrication division does not purchase materials from any outside suppliers.

Aluminum is transferred from the recycling division to the fabrication division at 110% of full cost. The recycling division purchases recyclable aluminum for $0.50 per pound. The division's other variable costs equal $2.80 per pound, and fixed costs at a monthly production level of 50,000 pounds are $1.50 per pound.

During the most recent month, 50,000 pounds of aluminum were transferred between the two divisions. The recycling division's capacity is 70,000 pounds.

Due to increased demand, the fabrication division expects to use 60,000 pounds of aluminum next month. Metalife Corporation has offered to sell 10,000 pounds of recycled aluminum next month to the fabrication division for $5.00 per pound.

Required

1. Calculate the transfer price per pound of recycled aluminum. Assuming that each division is considered a profit center, would the fabrication manager choose to purchase 10,000 pounds next month from Metalife?

2. Is the purchase in the best interest of Jeremiah Industries? Show your calculations. What is the cause of this goal incongruence?

3. The fabrication division manager suggests that $5.00 is now the market price for recycled sheet aluminum, and that this should be the new transfer price. Jeremiah's corporate management tends to agree. The metal recycling manager is suspicious. Metalife's prices have always been considerably higher than $5.00 per pound. Why the sudden price cut? After further investigation by the recycling division manager, it is revealed that the $5.00 per pound price was a one-time-only offer made to the fabrication division due to excess inventory at Metalife. Future orders would be priced at $5.50 per pound. Comment on the validity of the $5.00 per pound market price and the ethics of the fabrication manager. Would changing the transfer price to $5.00 matter to Jeremiah Industries?

Collaborative Learning Problem

22-36 Transfer pricing, utilization of capacity. (J. Patell, adapted) The California Instrument Company (CIC) consists of the semiconductor division and the process-control division, each of which operates as an independent profit center. The semiconductor division employs craftsmen who produce two different electronic components: the new high-performance Super-chip and an older product called Okay-chip. These two products have the following cost characteristics:

	Super-chip	Okay-chip
Direct materials	$ 5	$ 2
Direct manufacturing labor, 3 hours × $20; 1 hour × $20	60	20

Due to the high skill level necessary for the craftsmen, the semiconductor division's capacity is set at 45,000 hours per year.

Maximum demand for the Super-chip is 15,000 units annually, at a price of $80 per chip. There is unlimited demand for the Okay-chip at $26 per chip.

The process-control division produces only one product, a process-control unit, with the following cost structure:

- Direct materials (circuit board): $70
- Direct manufacturing labor (3 hours × $15): $45

The current market price for the control unit is $132 per unit.

A joint research project has just revealed that a single Super-chip could be substituted for the circuit board currently used to make the process-control unit. Direct labor cost of the process-control unit would be unchanged. The improved process-control unit could be sold for $145.

Required

1. Calculate the contribution margin per direct-labor hour of selling Super-chip and Okay-chip. If no transfers of Super-chip are made to the process-control division, how many Super-chips and Okay-chips should the semiconductor division manufacture and sell? What would be the division's annual contribution margin? Show your computations.

2. The process-control division expects to sell 5,000 process-control units this year. From the viewpoint of California Instruments as a whole, should 5,000 Super-chips be transferred to the process-control division to replace circuit boards? Show your computations.

3. What transfer price, or range of prices, would ensure goal congruence among the division managers? Show your calculations.

4. If labor capacity in the semiconductor division were 60,000 hours instead of 45,000, would your answer to requirement 3 differ? Show your calculations.

Performance Measurement, Compensation, and Multinational Considerations

From Chapter 23 of *Cost Accounting: A Managerial Emphasis*, 14/e. Charles T. Horngren. Srikant M. Datar. Madhav Rajan.

Performance Measurement, Compensation, and Multinational Considerations

At the end of this school term, you're going to receive a grade that represents a measure of your performance in this course.

Your grade will likely consist of four elements—homework, quizzes, exams, and class participation. Do some of these elements better reflect your knowledge of the material than others? Would the relative weights placed on the various elements when determining your final grade influence how much effort you expend to improve performance on the different elements? Would it be fair if you received a good grade regardless of your performance? The following article about former AIG chief executive Martin Sullivan examines that very situation in a corporate context. Sullivan continued to receive performance bonuses despite pushing AIG to the brink of bankruptcy. By failing to link pay to performance, the AIG board of directors rewarded behavior that led to a government takeover of the firm.

Misalignment Between CEO Compensation and Performance at AIG[1]

After the September 2008 collapse of AIG, many shareholders and observers focused on the company's executive compensation. Many believed that the incentive structures for executives helped fuel the real estate bubble. Though people were placing long-term bets on mortgage-backed securities, much of their compensation was in the form of short-term bonuses. This encouraged excessive risk without the fear of significant repercussions.

Executive compensation at AIG had been under fire for many years. The Corporate Library, an independent research firm specializing in corporate governance, called the company "a serial offender in the category of outrageous CEO compensation."

Judging solely by company financial measures, AIG's 2007 results were a failure. Driven by the write-down of $11.1 billion in fixed income guarantees, the company's revenue was down 56% from 2006 results. AIG also reported $5 billion in losses in the final quarter of 2007 and warned of possible future losses due to ill-advised investments. Despite this, AIG chief executive Martin Sullivan earned $14.3 million in salary, bonus, stock options, and other long-term

---

[1] *Source:* Blair, Nathan. 2009. AIG – Blame for the bailout. Stanford Graduate School of Business No. A-203, Stanford, CA: Stanford Graduate School of Business; Son, Hugh. 2008. AIG chief Sullivan's compensation fell 32 percent. *Bloomberg.com*, April 4; Son, Hugh and Erik Holm. 2008. AIG's former chief Sullivan gets $47 million package. *Bloomberg.com*, July 1.

incentives. Sullivan's compensation was in the 90th percentile for CEOs of S&P 500 firms for 2007.

On June 15, 2008, AIG replaced Sullivan as CEO. By then, AIG reported cumulative losses totaling $20 billion. During Sullivan's three-year tenure at the helm, AIG lost 46% of its market value. At the time of his dismissal, the AIG board of directors agreed to give the ousted CEO about $47 million in severance pay, bonus, and long-term compensation.

Two months later, on the verge of bankruptcy, the U.S. government nationalized AIG. At a Congressional hearing in the aftermath of AIG's failure, one witness testified on Sullivan's compensation stating, "I think it is fair to say by any standard of measurement that this pay plan is as uncorrelated to performance as it is possible to be."

Companies measure reward and performance to motivate managers to achieve company strategies and goals. As the AIG example illustrates, however, if the measures are inappropriate or not connected to sustained performance, managers may improve their performance evaluations and increase compensation without achieving company goals. This chapter discusses the general design, implementation, and uses of performance measures, part of the final step in the decision-making process.

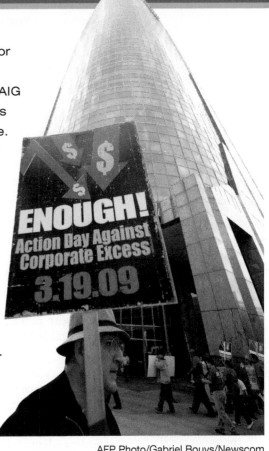

AFP Photo/Gabriel Bouys/Newscom

Financial and Nonfinancial Performance Measures

Many organizations are increasingly presenting financial and nonfinancial performance measures for their subunits in a single report called the *balanced scorecard*. Different organizations stress different measures in their scorecards, but the measures are always derived from a company's strategy. Consider the case of Hospitality Inns, a chain of hotels. Hospitality Inns' strategy is to provide excellent customer service and to charge a higher room rate than its competitors. Hospitality Inns uses the following measures in its balanced scorecard:

1. **Financial perspective**—stock price, net income, return on sales, return on investment, and economic value added
2. **Customer perspective**—market share in different geographic locations, customer satisfaction, and average number of repeat visits
3. **Internal-business-process perspective**—customer-service time for making reservations, for check-in, and in restaurants; cleanliness of hotel and room, quality of room service; time taken to clean rooms; quality of restaurant experience; number of new services provided to customers (fax, wireless Internet, video games); time taken to plan and build new hotels

4. **Learning-and-growth perspective**—employee education and skill levels, employee satisfaction, employee turnover, hours of employee training, and information-system availability

As in all balanced scorecard implementations, the goal is to make improvements in the learning-and-growth perspective that will lead to improvements in the internal-business-process perspective that, in turn, will result in improvements in the customer and financial perspectives. Hospitality Inns also uses balanced scorecard measures to evaluate and reward the performance of its managers.

Some performance measures, such as the time it takes to plan and build new hotels, have a long time horizon. Other measures, such as time taken to check in or quality of room service, have a short time horizon. In this chapter, we focus on *organization subunits'* most widely used performance measures that cover an intermediate-to-long time horizon. These are internal financial measures based on accounting numbers routinely reported by organizations. In later sections, we describe why companies use both financial and nonfinancial measures to evaluate performance.

Designing accounting-based performance measures requires several steps:

Step 1: Choose Performance Measures That Align with Top Management's Financial Goals. For example, is operating income, net income, return on assets, or revenues the best measure of a subunit's financial performance?

Step 2: Choose the Details of Each Performance Measure in Step 1. Once a firm has chosen a specific performance measure, it must make a variety of decisions about the precise way in which various components of the measure are to be calculated. For example, if the chosen performance measure is return on assets, should it be calculated for one year or for a multiyear period? Should assets be defined as total assets or net assets (total assets minus total liabilities)? Should assets be measured at historical cost or current cost?

Step 3: Choose a Target Level of Performance and Feedback Mechanism for Each Performance Measure in Step 1. For example, should all subunits have identical targets, such as the same required rate of return on assets? Should performance reports be sent to top management daily, weekly, or monthly?

These steps need not be done sequentially. The issues considered in each step are interdependent, and top management will often proceed through these steps several times before deciding on one or more accounting-based performance measures. The answers to the questions raised at each step depend on top management's beliefs about how well each alternative measure fulfills behavioral criteria such as: promoting goal congruence, motivating management effort, evaluating subunit performance, and preserving subunit autonomy.

Decision Point ▶

What financial and nonfinancial performance measures do companies use in their balanced scorecards?

Examine accounting-based measures for evaluating business unit performance, including return on investment (ROI),

... return on sales times investment turnover

residual income (RI),

... income minus a dollar amount for required return on investment

and economic value added (EVA®)

... a variation of residual income

Accounting-Based Measures for Business Units

Companies commonly use four measures to evaluate the economic performance of their subunits. We illustrate these measures for Hospitality Inns.

Hospitality Inns owns and operates three hotels: one each in San Francisco, Chicago, and New Orleans. Exhibit 1 summarizes data for each hotel for 2012. At present, Hospitality Inns does not allocate the total long-term debt of the company to the three separate hotels. The exhibit indicates that the New Orleans hotel generates the highest operating income, $510,000, compared with Chicago's $300,000 and San Francisco's $240,000. But does this comparison mean the New Orleans hotel is the most "successful"? The main weakness of comparing operating incomes alone is that differences in *the size of the investment* in each hotel are ignored. **Investment** refers to the resources or assets used to generate income. It is not sufficient to compare operating incomes alone. The real question is whether a division generates sufficient operating income relative to the investment made to earn it.

Three of the approaches to measuring performance include a measure of investment: return on investment, residual income, and economic value added. A fourth approach, return on sales, does not measure investment.

Exhibit 1

Financial Data for Hospitality Inns for 2012 (in thousands)

		San Francisco Hotel	Chicago Hotel	New Orleans Hotel	Total
	A	B	C	D	E
2	Hotel revenues	$1,200,000	$1,400,000	$3,185,000	$5,785,000
3	Hotel variable costs	310,000	375,000	995,000	1,680,000
4	Hotel fixed costs	650,000	725,000	1,680,000	3,055,000
5	Hotel operating income	$ 240,000	$ 300,000	$ 510,000	1,050,000
6	Interest costs on long-term debt at 10%				450,000
7	Income before income taxes				600,000
8	Income taxes at 30%				180,000
9	Net income				$ 420,000
10	Net book value at the end of 2012:				
11	Current assets	$ 400,000	$ 500,000	$ 660,000	$1,560,000
12	Long-term assets	600,000	1,500,000	2,340,000	4,440,000
13	Total assets	$1,000,000	$2,000,000	$3,000,000	$6,000,000
14	Current liabilities	$ 50,000	$ 150,000	$ 300,000	$ 500,000
15	Long-term debt				4,500,000
16	Stockholders' equity				1,000,000
17	Total liabilities and stockholders' equity				$6,000,000
18					

Return on Investment

Return on investment (ROI) is an accounting measure of income divided by an accounting measure of investment.

$$\text{Return on investment} = \frac{\text{Income}}{\text{Investment}}$$

Return on investment is the most popular approach to measure performance. ROI is popular for two reasons: it blends all the ingredients of profitability—revenues, costs, and investment—into a single percentage; and it can be compared with the rate of return on opportunities elsewhere, inside or outside the company. Like any single performance measure, however, ROI should be used cautiously and in conjunction with other measures.

ROI is also called the *accounting rate of return* or the *accrual accounting rate of return*. Managers usually use the term "ROI" when evaluating the performance of an organization's subunit and the term "accrual accounting rate of return" when using an ROI measure to evaluate a project. Companies vary in the way they define income in the numerator and investment in the denominator of the ROI calculation. Some companies use operating income for the numerator; others prefer to calculate ROI on an after-tax basis and use net income. Some companies use total assets in the denominator; others prefer to focus on only those assets financed by long-term debt and stockholders' equity and use total assets minus current liabilities.

Consider the ROIs of each of the three Hospitality hotels in Exhibit 1. For our calculations, we use the operating income of each hotel for the numerator and total assets of each hotel for the denominator.

Using these ROI figures, the San Francisco hotel appears to make the best use of its total assets.

Hotel	Operating Income	÷	Total Assets	=	ROI
San Francisco	$240,000	÷	$1,000,000	=	24%
Chicago	$300,000	÷	$2,000,000	=	15%
New Orleans	$510,000	÷	$3,000,000	=	17%

Each hotel manager can increase ROI by increasing revenues or decreasing costs (each of which increases the numerator), or by decreasing investment (which decreases the denominator). A hotel manager can increase ROI even when operating income decreases by reducing total assets by a greater percentage. Suppose, for example, that operating income of the Chicago hotel decreases by 4% from $300,000 to $288,000 [$300,000 × (1 − 0.04)] and total assets decrease by 10% from $2,000,000 to $1,800,000 [$2,000,000 × (1 − 0.10)]. The ROI of the Chicago hotel would then increase from 15% to 16% ($288,000 ÷ $1,800,000).

ROI can provide more insight into performance when it is represented as two components:

$$\frac{\text{Income}}{\text{Investment}} = \frac{\text{Income}}{\text{Revenues}} \times \frac{\text{Revenues}}{\text{Investment}}$$

which is also written as,

$$ROI = \text{Return on sales} \times \text{Investment turnover}$$

This approach is known as the *DuPont method of profitability analysis*. The DuPont method recognizes the two basic ingredients in profit-making: increasing income per dollar of revenues and using assets to generate more revenues. An improvement in either ingredient without changing the other increases ROI.

Assume that top management at Hospitality Inns adopts a 30% target ROI for the San Francisco hotel. How can this return be attained? We illustrate the DuPont method for the San Francisco hotel and show how this method can be used to describe three alternative ways in which the San Francisco hotel can increase its ROI from 24% to 30%.

	Operating Income (1)	Revenues (2)	Total Assets (3)	Operating Income / Revenues (4) = (1) ÷ (2)	×	Revenues / Total Assets (5) = (2) ÷ (3)	=	Operating Income / Total Assets (6) = (4) × (5)
Current ROI	$240,000	$1,200,000	$1,000,000	20%	×	1.2	=	24%
Alternatives								
A. Decrease assets (such as receivables), keeping revenues and operating income per dollar of revenue constant	$240,000	$1,200,000	$800,000	20%	×	1.5	=	30%
B. Increase revenues (via higher occupancy rate), keeping assets and operating income per dollar of revenue constant	$300,000	$1,500,000	$1,000,000	20%	×	1.5	=	30%
C. Decrease costs (via, say, efficient maintenance) to increase operating income per dollar of revenue, keeping revenue and assets constant	$300,000	$1,200,000	$1,000,000	25%	×	1.2	=	30%

Other alternatives, such as increasing the selling price per room, could increase both the revenues per dollar of total assets and the operating income per dollar of revenues. ROI makes clear the benefits managers can obtain by reducing their investment in current or long-term assets. Some managers know the need to boost revenues or to control costs, but they pay less attention to reducing their investment base. Reducing the investment base involves decreasing idle cash, managing credit judiciously, determining proper inventory levels, and spending carefully on long-term assets.

Residual Income

Residual income (RI) is an accounting measure of income minus a dollar amount for required return on an accounting measure of investment.

$$\text{Residual income } (RI) = \text{Income} - (\text{Required rate of return} \times \text{Investment})$$

Required rate of return multiplied by the investment is the *imputed cost of the investment*. The **imputed cost** of the investment is a cost recognized in particular situations but not recorded in financial accounting systems because it is an opportunity cost. In this situation, the imputed cost refers to the return Hospitality Inns could have obtained by making an alternative investment with similar risk characteristics.

Assume each hotel faces similar risks, and that Hospitality Inns has a required rate of return of 12%. The RI for each hotel is calculated as the operating income minus the required rate of return of 12% of total assets:

Hotel	Operating Income	−	Required Rate of Return	×	Investment	=	Residual Income
San Francisco	$240,000	−	(12%	×	$1,000,000)	=	$120,000
Chicago	$300,000	−	(12%	×	$2,000,000)	=	$ 60,000
New Orleans	$510,000	−	(12%	×	$3,000,000)	=	$150,000

Note that the New Orleans hotel has the best RI.

Some companies favor the RI measure because managers will concentrate on maximizing an absolute amount, such as dollars of RI, rather than a percentage, such as ROI. The objective of maximizing RI means that as long as a subunit earns a return in excess of the required return for investments, that subunit should continue to invest.

The objective of maximizing ROI may induce managers of highly profitable subunits to reject projects that, from the viewpoint of the company as a whole, should be accepted. Suppose Hospitality Inns is considering upgrading room features and furnishings at the San Francisco hotel. The upgrade will increase operating income of the San Francisco hotel by $70,000 and increase its total assets by $400,000. The ROI for the expansion is 17.5% ($70,000 ÷ $400,000), which is attractive to Hospitality Inns because it exceeds the required rate of return of 12%. By making this expansion, however, the San Francisco hotel's ROI will decrease:

$$\text{Pre-upgrade } ROI = \frac{\$240,000}{\$1,000,000} = 0.24, \text{ or } 24\%$$

$$\text{Post-upgrade } ROI = \frac{\$240,000 + \$70,000}{\$1,000,000 + \$400,000} = \frac{\$310,000}{\$1,400,000} = 0.221, \text{ or } 22.1\%$$

The annual bonus paid to the San Francisco manager may decrease if ROI affects the bonus calculation and the upgrading option is selected. Consequently, the manager may shun the expansion. In contrast, if the annual bonus is a function of RI, the San Francisco manager will favor the expansion:

$$\text{Pre-upgrade } RI = \$240,000 - (0.12 \times \$1,000,000) = \$120,000$$

$$\text{Post-upgrade } RI = \$310,000 - (0.12 \times \$1,400,000) = \$142,000$$

Goal congruence (ensuring that subunit managers work toward achieving the company's goals) is thus more likely using RI rather than ROI as a measure of the subunit manager's performance.

To see that this is a general result, observe that the post-upgrade ROI is a weighted average of the pre-upgrade ROI and the ROI of the project under consideration. Therefore, whenever a new project has a return higher than the required rate of return (12% in our example) but below the current ROI of the division (24% in our example), the division manager is tempted to reject it even though it is a project the shareholders would like to pursue.[2] On the other hand, RI is a measure that aggregates linearly. Therefore, the post-upgrade RI always equals the pre-upgrade RI plus the RI of the project under consideration (in the preceding example, the project's RI is $70,000 – 12% × $400,000 = $22,000, which is the difference between the post-upgrade and pre-upgrade RI amounts). As a result, a manager who is evaluated on residual income will choose a new project if and only if it has a positive RI. But this is exactly the criterion shareholders want the manager to employ; in other words, RI achieves goal congruence.

---

[2] Analogously, the manager of an underperforming division with an ROI of 7%, say, may wish to accept projects with returns between 7% and 12% even though these opportunities do not meet the shareholders' required rate of return.

Economic Value Added[3]

Economic value added is a specific type of RI calculation that is used by many companies. **Economic value added (EVA®)** equals after-tax operating income *minus* the (after-tax) weighted-average cost of capital *multiplied* by total assets minus current liabilities.

$$\begin{array}{l} \text{Economic value} \\ \text{added (EVA)} \end{array} = \begin{array}{l} \text{After-tax} \\ \text{operating income} \end{array} - \left[\begin{array}{l} \text{Weighted-} \\ \text{average} \\ \text{cost of capital} \end{array} \times \left(\begin{array}{l} \text{Total} \\ \text{assets} \end{array} - \begin{array}{l} \text{Current} \\ \text{liabilities} \end{array} \right) \right]$$

EVA substitutes the following numbers in the RI calculations: (1) income equal to after-tax operating income, (2) required rate of return equal to the (after-tax) weighted-average cost of capital, and (3) investment equal to total assets minus current liabilities.[4]

We use the Hospitality Inns data in Exhibit 1 to illustrate the basic EVA calculations. The weighted-average cost of capital (WACC) equals the *after-tax* average cost of all the long-term funds used by Hospitality Inns. The company has two sources of long-term funds: (a) long-term debt with a market value and book value of $4.5 million issued at an interest rate of 10%, and (b) equity capital that also has a market value of $4.5 million (but a book value of $1 million).[5] Because interest costs are tax-deductible and the income tax rate is 30%, the after-tax cost of debt financing is $0.10 \times (1 - \text{Tax rate}) = 0.10 \times (1 - 0.30) = 0.10 \times 0.70 = 0.07$, or 7%. The cost of equity capital is the opportunity cost to investors of not investing their capital in another investment that is similar in risk to Hospitality Inns. Hospitality Inns' cost of equity capital is 14%.[6] The WACC computation, which uses market values of debt and equity, is as follows:

$$WACC = \frac{(7\% \times \text{Market value of debt}) + (14\% \times \text{Market value of equity})}{\text{Market value of debt} + \text{Market value of equity}}$$

$$= \frac{(0.07 \times \$4,500,000) + (0.14 \times \$4,500,000)}{\$4,500,000 + \$4,500,000}$$

$$= \frac{\$945,000}{\$9,000,000} = 0.105, \text{ or } 10.5\%$$

The company applies the same WACC to all its hotels because each hotel faces similar risks.

Total assets minus current liabilities (see Exhibit 1) can also be computed as follows:

$$\text{Total assets} - \text{Current liabilities} = \text{Long-term assets} + \text{Current assets} - \text{Current liabilities}$$

$$= \text{Long-term assets} + \text{Working capital}$$

where

$$\text{Working capital} = \text{Current assets} - \text{Current liabilities}$$

After-tax hotel operating income is:

$$\begin{array}{l} \text{Hotel operating} \\ \text{income} \end{array} \times (1 - \text{Tax rate}) = \begin{array}{l} \text{Hotel operating} \\ \text{income} \end{array} \times (1 - 0.30) = \begin{array}{l} \text{Hotel operating} \\ \text{income} \end{array} \times 0.70$$

---

[3] S. O'Byrne and D. Young, *EVA and Value-Based Management: A Practical Guide to Implementation* (New York: McGraw-Hill, 2000); J. Stein, J. Shiely, and I. Ross, *The EVA Challenge: Implementing Value Added Change in an Organization* (New York: John Wiley and Sons, 2001).

[4] When implementing EVA, companies make several adjustments to the operating income and asset numbers reported under generally accepted accounting principles (GAAP). For example, when calculating EVA, costs such as R&D, restructuring costs, and leases that have long-run benefits are recorded as assets (which are then amortized), rather than as current operating costs. The goal of these adjustments is to obtain a better representation of the economic assets, particularly intangible assets, used to earn income. Of course, the specific adjustments applicable to a company will depend on its individual circumstances.

[5] The market value of Hospitality Inns' equity exceeds book value because book value, based on historical cost, does not measure the current value of the company's assets and because various intangible assets, such as the company's brand name, are not shown at current value in the balance sheet under GAAP.

[6] In practice, the most common method of calculating the cost of equity capital is by applying the capital asset pricing model (CAPM). For details, see J. Berk and P. DeMarzo, *Corporate Finance*, 2nd ed. (Upper Saddle River, NJ: Prentice Hall, 2010).

EVA calculations for Hospitality Inns are as follows:

Hotel	After-Tax Operating Income	−	[WACC ×	(Total Assets − Current Liabilities)]	=	EVA
San Francisco	$240,000 × 0.70	−	[10.50% ×	($1,000,000 − $ 50,000)]	=	$68,250
Chicago	$300,000 × 0.70	−	[10.50% ×	($2,000,000 − $150,000)]	=	$15,750
New Orleans	$510,000 × 0.70	−	[10.50% ×	($3,000,000 − $300,000)]	=	$73,500

The New Orleans hotel has the highest EVA. Economic value added, like residual income, charges managers for the cost of their investments in long-term assets and working capital. Value is created only if after-tax operating income exceeds the cost of investing the capital. To improve EVA, managers can, for example, (a) earn more after-tax operating income with the same capital, (b) use less capital to earn the same after-tax operating income, or (c) invest capital in high-return projects.[7]

Managers in companies such as Briggs and Stratton, Coca-Cola, CSX, Equifax, and FMC use the estimated impact on EVA to guide their decisions. Division managers find EVA helpful because it allows them to incorporate the cost of capital, which is generally only available at the company-wide level, into decisions at the division level. Comparing the actual EVA achieved to the estimated EVA is useful for evaluating performance and providing feedback to managers about performance. CSX, a railroad company, credits EVA for decisions such as to run trains with three locomotives instead of four and to schedule arrivals just in time for unloading rather than having trains arrive at their destination several hours in advance. The result? Higher income because of lower fuel costs and lower capital investments in locomotives.

Return on Sales

The income-to-revenues ratio (or sales ratio), often called *return on sales (ROS)*, is a frequently used financial performance measure. As we have seen, ROS is one component of ROI in the DuPont method of profitability analysis. To calculate ROS for each of Hospitality's hotels, we divide operating income by revenues:

Hotel	Operating Income	÷	Revenues (Sales)	=	ROS
San Francisco	$240,000	÷	$1,200,000	=	20.0%
Chicago	$300,000	÷	$1,400,000	=	21.4%
New Orleans	$510,000	÷	$3,185,000	=	16.0%

The Chicago hotel has the highest ROS, but its performance is rated worse than the other hotels using measures such as ROI, RI, and EVA.

Comparing Performance Measures

The following table summarizes the performance of each hotel and ranks it (in parentheses) under each of the four performance measures:

Hotel	ROI	RI	EVA	ROS
San Francisco	24% (1)	$120,000 (2)	$68,250 (2)	20.0% (2)
Chicago	15% (3)	$ 60,000 (3)	$15,750 (3)	21.4% (1)
New Orleans	17% (2)	$150,000 (1)	$73,500 (1)	16.0% (3)

The RI and EVA rankings are the same. They differ from the ROI and ROS rankings. Consider the ROI and RI rankings for the San Francisco and New Orleans hotels. The New Orleans hotel has a smaller ROI. Although its operating income is only slightly more than

---

[7] Observe that the sum of the divisional after-tax operating incomes used in the EVA calculation, ($240,000 + $300,000 + $510,000) × 0.7 = $735,000, exceeds the firm's net income of $420,000. The difference is due to the firm's after-tax interest expense on its long-term debt, which amounts to $450,000 × 0.7 = $315,000. Because the EVA measure includes a charge for the weighted average cost of capital, which includes the after-tax cost of debt, the income figure used in computing EVA should reflect the after-tax profit before interest payments on debt are considered. After-tax operating income (often referred to in practice as NOPAT, or net operating profit after taxes) is thus the relevant measure of divisional profit for EVA calculations.

twice the operating income of the San Francisco hotel—$510,000 versus $240,000—its total assets are three times as large—$3 million versus $1 million. The New Orleans hotel has a higher RI because it earns a higher income after covering the required rate of return on investment of 12%. The high ROI of the San Francisco hotel indicates that its assets are being used efficiently. Even though each dollar invested in the New Orleans hotel does not give the same return as the San Francisco hotel, this large investment creates considerable value because its return exceeds the required rate of return. The Chicago hotel has the highest ROS but the lowest ROI. The high ROS indicates that the Chicago hotel has the lowest cost structure per dollar of revenues of all of Hospitality Inns' hotels. The reason for Chicago's low ROI is that it generates very low revenues per dollar of assets invested. Is any method better than the others for measuring performance? No, because each evaluates a different aspect of performance.

ROS measures how effectively costs are managed. To evaluate overall aggregate performance, ROI, RI, or EVA measures are more appropriate than ROS because they consider both income and investment. ROI indicates which investment yields the highest return. RI and EVA measures overcome some of the goal-congruence problems of ROI. Some managers favor EVA because of the accounting adjustments related to the capitalization of investments in intangibles. Other managers favor RI because it is easier to calculate and because, in most cases, it leads to the same conclusions as EVA. Generally, companies use multiple financial measures to evaluate performance.

Decision Point ▶

What are the relative merits of return on investment (ROI), residual income (RI), and economic value added (EVA) as performance measures for subunit managers?

Choosing the Details of the Performance Measures

It is not sufficient for a company to identify the set of performance measures it wishes to use. The company has to make several choices regarding the specific details of how the measures are computed. These range from decisions regarding the time frame over which the measures are computed, to the definition of key terms such as "investment" and the calculation of particular components of each performance measure.

Alternative Time Horizons

Learning Objective 3

Analyze the key measurement choices in the design of each performance measure

. . . choice of time horizon, alternative definitions, and measurement of assets

An important element in designing accounting-based performance measures is choosing the time horizon of the performance measures. The ROI, RI, EVA, and ROS calculations represent the results for a single period, one year in our example. Managers could take actions that cause short-run increases in these measures but that conflict with the long-run interest of the company. For example, managers may curtail R&D and plant maintenance in the last three months of a fiscal year to achieve a target level of annual operating income. For this reason, many companies evaluate subunits on the basis of ROI, RI, EVA, and ROS over multiple years.

Another reason to evaluate subunits over multiple years is that the benefits of actions taken in the current period may not show up in short-run performance measures, such as the current year's ROI or RI. For example, an investment in a new hotel may adversely affect ROI and RI in the short run but benefit ROI and RI in the long run.

A multiyear analysis highlights another advantage of the RI measure: Net present value of all cash flows over the life of an investment equals net present value of the RIs.[8]

---

[8] This equivalence, often referred to as the "Conservation Property" of residual income, was originally articulated by Gabriel Preinreich in 1938. To see the equivalence, suppose the $400,000 investment in the San Francisco hotel increases operating income by $70,000 per year as follows: Increase in operating cash flows of $150,000 each year for 5 years minus depreciation of $80,000 ($400,000 ÷ 5) per year, assuming straight-line depreciation and $0 terminal disposal value. Depreciation reduces the investment amount by $80,000 each year. Assuming a required rate of return of 12%, net present values of cash flows and residual incomes are as follows:

Year	0	1	2	3	4	5	Net Present Value
(1) Cash flow	−$400,000	$150,000	$150,000	$150,000	$150,000	$150,000	
(2) Present value of $1 discounted at 12%	1	0.89286	0.79719	0.71178	0.63552	0.56743	
(3) Present value: (1) × (2)	−$400,000	$133,929	$119,578	$106,767	$ 95,328	$ 85,114	$140,716
(4) Operating income		$ 70,000	$ 70,000	$ 70,000	$ 70,000	$ 70,000	
(5) Assets at start of year		$400,000	$320,000	$240,000	$160,000	$ 80,000	
(6) Capital charge: (5) × 12%		$ 48,000	$ 38,400	$ 28,800	$ 19,200	$ 9,600	
(7) Residual income: (4) − (6)		$ 22,000	$ 31,600	$ 41,200	$ 50,800	$ 60,400	
(8) Present value of RI: (7) × (2)		$ 19,643	$ 25,191	$ 29,325	$ 32,284	$ 34,273	$140,716

This characteristic means that if managers use the net present value method to make investment decisions, then using multiyear RI to evaluate managers' performances achieves goal congruence.

Another way to motivate managers to take a long-run perspective is by compensating them on the basis of changes in the market price of the company's stock, because stock prices incorporate the expected future effects of current decisions.

Alternative Definitions of Investment

Companies use a variety of definitions for measuring investment in divisions. Four common alternative definitions used in the construction of accounting-based performance measures are as follows:

1. **Total assets available**—includes all assets, regardless of their intended purpose.

2. **Total assets employed**—total assets available minus the sum of idle assets and assets purchased for future expansion. For example, if the New Orleans hotel in Exhibit 1 has unused land set aside for potential expansion, total assets employed by the hotel would exclude the cost of that land.

3. **Total assets employed minus current liabilities**—total assets employed, excluding assets financed by short-term creditors. One negative feature of defining investment in this way is that it may encourage subunit managers to use an excessive amount of short-term debt because short-term debt reduces the amount of investment.

4. **Stockholders' equity**—calculated by assigning liabilities among subunits and deducting these amounts from the total assets of each subunit. One drawback of this method is that it combines operating decisions made by hotel managers with financing decisions made by top management.

Companies that use ROI or RI generally define investment as the total assets available. When top management directs a subunit manager to carry extra or idle assets, total assets employed can be more informative than total assets available. Companies that adopt EVA define investment as total assets employed minus current liabilities. The most common rationale for using total assets employed minus current liabilities is that the subunit manager often influences decisions on current liabilities of the subunit.

Alternative Asset Measurements

To design accounting-based performance measures, we must consider different ways to measure assets included in the investment calculations. Should assets be measured at historical cost or current cost? Should gross book value (that is, original cost) or net book value (original cost minus accumulated depreciation) be used for depreciable assets?

Current Cost

Current cost is the cost of purchasing an asset today identical to the one currently held, or the cost of purchasing an asset that provides services like the one currently held if an identical asset cannot be purchased. Of course, measuring assets at current costs will result in different ROIs than the ROIs calculated on the basis of historical costs.

We illustrate the current-cost ROI calculations using the data for Hospitality Inns (Exhibit 1) and then compare current-cost-based ROIs and historical-cost-based ROIs. Assume the following information about the long-term assets of each hotel:

	San Francisco	Chicago	New Orleans
Age of facility in years (at end of 2012)	8	4	2
Gross book value (original cost)	$1,400,000	$2,100,000	$2,730,000
Accumulated depreciation	$ 800,000	$ 600,000	$ 390,000
Net book value (at end of 2012)	$ 600,000	$1,500,000	$2,340,000
Depreciation for 2012	$ 100,000	$ 150,000	$ 195,000

Hospitality Inns assumes a 14-year estimated useful life, zero terminal disposal value for the physical facilities, and straight-line depreciation.

An index of construction costs indicating how the cost of construction has changed over the eight-year period that Hospitality Inns has been operating (2004 year-end = 100) is as follows:

Year	2005	2006	2007	2008	2009	2010	2011	2012
Construction cost index	110	122	136	144	152	160	174	180

Earlier in this chapter, we computed an ROI of 24% for San Francisco, 15% for Chicago, and 17% for New Orleans. One possible explanation of the high ROI for the San Francisco hotel is that its long-term assets are expressed in 2004 construction-price levels—prices that prevailed eight years ago—and the long-term assets for the Chicago and New Orleans hotels are expressed in terms of higher, more-recent construction-price levels, which depress ROIs for these two hotels.

Exhibit 2 illustrates a step-by-step approach for incorporating current-cost estimates of long-term assets and depreciation expense into the ROI calculation. We make these calculations to approximate what it would cost today to obtain assets that would produce the same expected operating income that the subunits currently earn. (Similar adjustments to represent the current costs of capital employed and depreciation expense can also be made in the RI and EVA calculations.) The current-cost adjustment reduces the ROI of the San Francisco hotel by more than half.

	Historical-Cost ROI	Current-Cost ROI
San Francisco	24%	10.8%
Chicago	15%	11.1%
New Orleans	17%	14.7%

Adjusting assets to recognize current costs negates differences in the investment base caused solely by differences in construction-price levels. Compared with historical-cost ROI, current-cost ROI better measures the current economic returns from the investment. If Hospitality Inns were to invest in a new hotel today, investing in one like the New Orleans hotel offers the best ROI.

Current cost estimates may be difficult to obtain for some assets. Why? Because the estimate requires a company to consider, in addition to increases in price levels, technological advances and processes that could reduce the current cost of assets needed to earn today's operating income.

Long-Term Assets: Gross or Net Book Value?

Historical cost of assets is often used to calculate ROI. There has been much discussion about whether gross book value or net book value of assets should be used. Using the data in Exhibit 1, we calculate ROI using net and gross book values of plant and equipment as follows:

	Operating Income (from Exhibit 1) (1)	Net Book Value of Total Assets (from Exhibit 1) (2)	Accumulated Depreciation (3)	Gross Book Value of Total Assets (4) = (2) + (3)	2012 ROI Using Net Book Value of Total Assets (calculated earlier) (5) = (1) ÷ (2)	2012 ROI Using Gross Book Value of Total Assets (6) = (1) ÷ (4)
San Francisco	$240,000	$1,000,000	$800,000	$1,800,000	24%	13.3%
Chicago	$300,000	$2,000,000	$600,000	$2,600,000	15%	11.5%
New Orleans	$510,000	$3,000,000	$390,000	$3,390,000	17%	15.0%

Using gross book value, the 13.3% ROI of the older San Francisco hotel is lower than the 15.0% ROI of the newer New Orleans hotel. Those who favor using gross book value claim it enables more accurate comparisons of ROI across subunits. For example, using

Exhibit 2   ROI for Hospitality Inns: Computed Using Current-Cost Estimates as of the End of 2012 for Depreciation Expense and Long-Term Assets

	A	B	C	D	E	F	G	H	I	J
1	**Step 1:** Restate long-term assets from gross book value at historical cost to gross book value at current cost as of the end of 2012.									
2		**Gross book value of long-term assets at historical cost**	×	**Construction cost index in 2012**	÷	**Construction cost index in year of construction**	=	**Gross book value of long-term assets at current cost at end of 2012**		
3	San Francisco	$1,400,000	×	(180	÷	100)	=	$2,520,000		
4	Chicago	$2,100,000	×	(180	÷	144)	=	$2,625,000		
5	New Orleans	$2,730,000	×	(180	÷	160)	=	$3,071,250		
6										
7	**Step 2:** Derive net book value of long-term assets at current cost as of the end of 2012. (Assume estimated useful life of each hotel is 14 years.)									
8		**Gross book value of long-term assets at current cost at end of 2012**	×	**Estimated remaining useful life**	÷	**Estimated total useful life**	=	**Net book value of long-term assets at current cost at end of 2012**		
9	San Francisco	$2,520,000	×	(6	÷	14)	=	$1,080,000		
10	Chicago	$2,625,000	×	(10	÷	14)	=	$1,875,000		
11	New Orleans	$3,071,250	×	(12	÷	14)	=	$2,632,500		
12										
13	**Step 3:** Compute current cost of total assets in 2012. (Assume current assets of each hotel are expressed in 2012 dollars.)									
14		**Current assets at end of 2012 (from Exhibit 1)**	+	**Long-term assets from Step 2**	=	**Current cost of total assets at end of 2012**				
15	San Francisco	$400,000	+	$1,080,000	=	$1,480,000				
16	Chicago	$500,000	+	$1,875,000	=	$2,375,000				
17	New Orleans	$660,000	+	$2,632,500	=	$3,292,500				
18										
19	**Step 4:** Compute current-cost depreciation expense in 2012 dollars.									
20		**Gross book value of long-term assets at current cost at end of 2012 (from Step 1)**	÷	**Estimated total useful life**	=	**Current-cost depreciation expense in 2012 dollars**				
21	San Francisco	$2,520,000	÷	14	=	$180,000				
22	Chicago	$2,625,000	÷	14	=	$187,500				
23	New Orleans	$3,071,250	÷	14	=	$219,375				
24										
25	**Step 5:** Compute 2012 operating income using 2012 current-cost depreciation expense.									
26		**Historical-cost operating income**	−	**Current-cost depreciation expense in 2012 dollars (from Step 4)**	−	**Historical-cost depreciation expense**	=	**Operating income for 2012 using current-cost depreciation expense in 2012 dollars**		
27	San Francisco	$240,000	−	($180,000	−	$100,000)	=	$160,000		
28	Chicago	$300,000	−	($187,500	−	$150,000)	=	$262,500		
29	New Orleans	$510,000	−	($219,375	−	$195,000)	=	$485,625		
30										
31	**Step 6:** Compute ROI using current-cost estimates for long-term assets and depreciation expense.									
32		**Operating income for 2012 using current-cost depreciation expense in 2012 dollars (from Step 5)**	÷	**Current cost of total assets at end of 2012 (from Step 3)**	=	**ROI using current-cost estimate**				
33	San Francisco	$160,000	÷	$1,480,000	=	10.8%				
34	Chicago	$262,500	÷	$2,375,000	=	11.1%				
35	New Orleans	$485,625	÷	$3,292,500	=	14.7%				

Decision Point ▶

Over what time frame should companies measure performance, and what are the alternative choices for calculating the components of each performance measure?

gross-book-value calculations, the return on the original plant-and-equipment investment is higher for the newer New Orleans hotel than for the older San Francisco hotel. This difference probably reflects the decline in earning power of the San Francisco hotel. Using the net book value masks this decline in earning power because the constantly decreasing investment base results in a higher ROI for the San Francisco hotel—24% in this example. This higher rate may mislead decision makers into thinking that the earning power of the San Francisco hotel has not decreased.

The proponents of using net book value as an investment base maintain that it is less confusing because (1) it is consistent with the amount of total assets shown in the conventional balance sheet, and (2) it is consistent with income computations that include deductions for depreciation expense. Surveys report net book value to be the dominant measure of assets used by companies for internal performance evaluation.

Target Levels of Performance and Feedback

Now that we have covered the different types of measures and how to choose them, let us turn our attention to how mangers set and measure target levels of performance.

Choosing Target Levels of Performance

Learning Objective 4

Study the choice of performance targets and design of feedback mechanisms

. . . carefully crafted budgets and sufficient feedback for timely corrective action

We next consider target-setting for accounting-based measures of performance against which actual performance can be compared. Historical-cost-based accounting measures are usually inadequate for evaluating economic returns on new investments, and in some cases, they create disincentives for expansion. Despite these problems, historical-cost ROIs can be used to evaluate current performance by establishing *target* ROIs. For Hospitality Inns, we need to recognize that the hotels were built in different years, which means they were built at different construction-price levels. Top management could adjust the target historical-cost-based ROIs accordingly, say, by setting San Francisco's ROI at 26%, Chicago's at 18%, and New Orleans' at 19%.

This useful alternative of comparing actual results with target or budgeted performance is frequently overlooked. The budget should be carefully negotiated with full knowledge of historical-cost accounting pitfalls. *Companies should tailor a budget to a particular subunit, a particular accounting system, and a particular performance measure.* For example, many problems of asset valuation and income measurement can be resolved if top management can get subunit managers to focus on what is attainable in the forthcoming budget period—whether ROI, RI, or EVA is used and whether the financial measures are based on historical cost or some other measure, such as current cost.

A popular way to establish targets is to set continuous improvement targets. If a company is using EVA as a performance measure, top management can evaluate operations on year-to-year changes in EVA, rather than on absolute measures of EVA. Evaluating performance on the basis of *improvements* in EVA makes the initial method of calculating EVA less important.

In establishing targets for financial performance measures, companies using the balanced scorecard simultaneously determine targets in the customer, internal-business-process, and learning-and-growth perspectives. For example, Hospitality Inns will establish targets for employee training and employee satisfaction, customer-service time for reservations and check-in, quality of room service, and customer satisfaction that each hotel must reach to achieve its ROI and EVA targets.

Choosing the Timing of Feedback

A final critical step in designing accounting-based performance measures is the timing of feedback. Timing of feedback depends largely on (a) how critical the information is for the success of the organization, (b) the specific level of management receiving the feedback, and (c) the sophistication of the organization's information technology. For example, hotel managers responsible for room sales want information on the number of rooms sold (rented) on a daily or weekly basis, because a large percentage of hotel costs are fixed costs. Achieving high room sales and taking quick action to reverse any declining sales trends are critical to the financial success of each hotel. Supplying managers with daily information about room sales is much easier if Hospitality Inns has a computerized room-reservation and check-in system. Top management, however, may look at information about daily room sales only on a monthly basis. In some instances, for example, because of concern about the low sales-to-total-assets ratio of the Chicago hotel, management may want the information weekly.

The timing of feedback for measures in the balanced scorecard varies. For example, human resources managers at each hotel measure employee satisfaction annually because satisfaction is best measured over a longer horizon. However, housekeeping department managers measure the quality of room service over much shorter time horizons, such as a week, because poor levels of performance in these areas for even a short period of time can harm a hotel's reputation for a long period. Moreover, housekeeping problems can be detected and resolved over a short time period.

Decision Point

What targets should companies use and when should they give feedback to managers regarding their performance relative to these targets?

Performance Measurement in Multinational Companies

Our discussion so far has focused on performance evaluation of different divisions of a company operating within a single country. We next discuss the additional difficulties created when the performance of divisions of a company operating in different countries is compared. Several issues arise.[9]

■ The economic, legal, political, social, and cultural environments differ significantly across countries.

■ Governments in some countries may limit selling prices of, and impose controls on, a company's products. For example, some countries in Asia, Latin America, and Eastern Europe impose tariffs and custom duties to restrict imports of certain goods.

■ Availability of materials and skilled labor, as well as costs of materials, labor, and infrastructure (power, transportation, and communication), may also differ significantly across countries.

■ Divisions operating in different countries account for their performance in different currencies. Issues of inflation and fluctuations in foreign-currency exchange rates affect performance measures.

As a result of these differences, adjustments need to be made to compare performance measures across countries.

Learning Objective 5

Indicate the difficulties that occur when the performance of divisions operating in different countries is compared

. . . adjustments needed for differences in inflation rates and changes in exchange rates

Calculating the Foreign Division's ROI in the Foreign Currency

Suppose Hospitality Inns invests in a hotel in Mexico City. The investment consists mainly of the costs of buildings and furnishings. Also assume the following:

■ The exchange rate at the time of Hospitality's investment on December 31, 2011, is 10 pesos = $1.

■ During 2012, the Mexican peso suffers a steady decline in its value. The exchange rate on December 31, 2012, is 15 pesos = $1.

■ The average exchange rate during 2012 is [(10 + 15) ÷ 2] = 12.5 pesos = $1.

■ The investment (total assets) in the Mexico City hotel is 30,000,000 pesos.

■ The operating income of the Mexico City hotel in 2012 is 6,000,000 pesos.

What is the historical-cost-based ROI for the Mexico City hotel in 2012?

To answer this question, Hospitality Inns' managers first have to determine if they should calculate the ROI in pesos or in dollars. If they calculate the ROI in dollars, what exchange rate should they use? The managers may also be interested in how the

---

[9] See M. Z. Iqbal, *International Accounting—A Global Perspective* (Cincinnati: South-Western College Publishing, 2002).

ROI of Hospitality Inns Mexico City (HIMC) compares with the ROI of Hospitality Inns New Orleans (HINO), which is also a relatively new hotel of approximately the same size. The answers to these questions yield information that will be helpful when making future investment decisions.

$$\text{HIMC's } ROI \text{ (calculated using pesos)} = \frac{\text{Operating income}}{\text{Total assets}} = \frac{6{,}000{,}000 \text{ pesos}}{30{,}000{,}000 \text{ pesos}} = 0.20, \text{ or } 20\%$$

HIMC's ROI of 20% is higher than HINO's ROI of 17%. Does this mean that HIMC outperformed HINO based on the ROI criterion? Not necessarily. That's because HIMC operates in a very different economic environment than HINO.

The peso has declined in value relative to the dollar in 2012. This decline has led to higher inflation in Mexico than in the United States. As a result of the higher inflation in Mexico, HIMC will charge higher prices for its hotel rooms, which will increase HIMC's operating income and lead to a higher ROI. Inflation clouds the real economic returns on an asset and makes historical-cost-based ROI higher. Differences in inflation rates between the two countries make a direct comparison of HIMC's peso-denominated ROI with HINO's dollar-denominated ROI misleading.

Calculating the Foreign Division's ROI in U.S. Dollars

One way to make a comparison of historical-cost-based ROIs more meaningful is to restate HIMC's performance in U.S. dollars. But what exchange rate should be used to make the comparison meaningful? Assume operating income was earned evenly throughout 2012. Hospitality Inns' managers should use the average exchange rate of 12.5 pesos = $1 to convert operating income from pesos to dollars: 6,000,000 pesos ÷ 12.5 pesos per dollar = $480,000. The effect of dividing the operating income in pesos by the higher pesos-to-dollar exchange rate prevailing during 2012, rather than the 10 pesos = $1 exchange rate prevailing on December 31, 2011, is that any increase in operating income in pesos as a result of inflation during 2012 is eliminated when converting back to dollars.

At what rate should HIMC's total assets of 30,000,000 pesos be converted? The 10 pesos = $1 exchange rate prevailing when the assets were acquired on December 31, 2011, because HIMC's assets are recorded in pesos at the December 31, 2011, cost, and they are not revalued as a result of inflation in Mexico in 2012. Because the cost of assets in HIMC's financial accounting records is unaffected by subsequent inflation, the exchange rate prevailing when the assets were acquired should be used to convert the assets into dollars. Using exchange rates after December 31, 2011, would be incorrect because these exchange rates incorporate the higher inflation in Mexico in 2012. Total assets are converted to 30,000,000 pesos ÷ 10 pesos per dollar = $3,000,000.

Then,

$$\text{HIMC's } ROI \text{ (calculated using dollars)} = \frac{\text{Operating income}}{\text{Total assets}} = \frac{\$480{,}000}{\$3{,}000{,}000} = 0.16, \text{ or } 16\%$$

As we have discussed, these adjustments make the historical-cost-based ROIs of the Mexico City and New Orleans hotels comparable because they negate the effects of any differences in inflation rates between the two countries. HIMC's ROI of 16% is less than HINO's ROI of 17%.

Residual income calculated in pesos suffers from the same problems as ROI calculated using pesos. Calculating HIMC's RI in dollars adjusts for changes in exchange rates and makes for more-meaningful comparisons with Hospitality's other hotels:

$$\text{HIMC's } RI = \$480{,}000 - (0.12 \times \$3{,}000{,}000)$$

$$= \$480{,}000 - \$360{,}000 = \$120{,}000$$

which is also less than HINO's RI of $150,000. In interpreting HIMC's and HINO's ROI and RI, keep in mind that they are historical-cost-based calculations. They do, however, pertain to relatively new hotels.

Decision Point

How can companies compare the performance of divisions operating in different countries?

Distinction Between Managers and Organization Units[10]

Our focus has been on how to evaluate the performance of a subunit of a company, such as a division. However, is evaluating the performance of a subunit manager the same as evaluating the performance of the subunit? If the subunit performed well, does it mean the manager performed well? In this section, we argue that the performance evaluation of a *manager* should be distinguished from the performance evaluation of that manager's *subunit*. For example, companies often put the most skillful division manager in charge of the division producing the poorest economic return in an attempt to improve it. The division may take years to show improvement. Furthermore, the manager's efforts may result merely in bringing the division up to a minimum acceptable ROI. The division may continue to be a poor performer in comparison with other divisions, but it would be a mistake to conclude from the poor performance of the division that the manager is performing poorly. The division's performance may be adversely affected by economic conditions over which the manager has no control.

As another example, consider again the Hospitality Inns Mexico City (HIMC) hotel. Suppose, despite the high inflation in Mexico, HIMC could not increase room prices because of price-control regulations imposed by the government. HIMC's performance in dollar terms would be very poor because of the decline in the value of the peso. But should top management conclude from HIMC's poor performance that the HIMC manager performed poorly? Probably not. Most likely, the poor performance of HIMC is largely the result of regulatory factors beyond the manager's control.

In the following sections, we show the basic principles for evaluating the performance of an individual subunit manager. These principles apply to managers at all organization levels. Later sections consider examples at the individual-worker level and the top-management level. We illustrate these principles using the RI performance measure.

Learning Objective 6

Understand the roles of salaries and incentives when rewarding managers

. . . balancing risk and performance-based rewards

The Basic Trade-Off: Creating Incentives Versus Imposing Risk

How the performance of managers and other employees is measured and evaluated affects their rewards. Compensation arrangements range from a flat salary with no direct performance-based incentive (or bonus), as in the case of many government employees, to rewards based on only performance, as in the case of real estate agents who are compensated only via commissions paid on the properties they sell. Most managers' total compensation includes some combination of salary and performance-based incentive. In designing compensation arrangements, we need to consider the *trade-off between creating incentives and imposing risk*. We illustrate this trade-off in the context of our Hospitality Inns example.

Sally Fonda owns the Hospitality Inns chain of hotels. Roger Brett manages the Hospitality Inns San Francisco (HISF) hotel. Assume Fonda uses RI to measure performance. To improve RI, Fonda would like Brett to increase sales, control costs, provide prompt and courteous customer service, and reduce working capital. But even if Brett did all those things, high RI is not guaranteed. HISF's RI is affected by many factors beyond Fonda's and Brett's control, such as a recession in the San Francisco economy, an earthquake that might negatively affect HISF, or even road construction near competing hotels which would drive customers to HISF. Uncontrollable factors make HISF's profitability uncertain and, therefore, risky.

As an entrepreneur, Fonda expects to bear risk. But Brett does not like being subject to risk. One way of "insuring" Brett against risk is to pay Brett a flat salary, regardless of the actual amount of RI earned. All the risk would then be borne by Fonda. This arrangement creates a problem, however, because Brett's effort is difficult to monitor. The absence of performance-based compensation means that Brett has no direct incentive to work harder or to undertake extra physical and mental effort beyond what is necessary to retain his job or to uphold his own personal values.

---

[10]The presentations here draw (in part) from teaching notes prepared by S. Huddart, N. Melumad, and S. Reichelstein.

Moral hazard describes a situation in which an employee prefers to exert less effort (or to report distorted information) compared with the effort (or accurate information) desired by the owner, because the employee's effort (or validity of the reported information) cannot be accurately monitored and enforced.[11] In some repetitive jobs, such as in electronic assembly, a supervisor can monitor the workers' actions, and the moral-hazard problem may not arise. However, a manager's job is to gather and interpret information and to exercise judgment on the basis of the information obtained. Monitoring a manager's effort is more difficult.

Paying no salary and rewarding Brett *only* on the basis of some performance measure—RI in our example—raises different concerns. In this case, Brett would be motivated to strive to increase RI because his rewards would increase with increases in RI. But compensating Brett on RI also subjects him to risk, because HISF's RI depends not only on Brett's effort, but also on factors such as local economic conditions over which Brett has no control.

Brett does not like being subject to risk. To compensate Brett for taking risk, Fonda must pay him extra compensation. That is, using performance-based bonuses will cost Fonda more money, *on average*, than paying Brett a flat salary. Why "on average"? Because Fonda's compensation payment to Brett will vary with RI outcomes. When averaged over these outcomes, the RI-based compensation will cost Fonda more than paying Brett a flat salary. The motivation for having some salary and some performance-based bonus in compensation arrangements is to balance the benefit of incentives against the extra cost of imposing risk on the manager.

Intensity of Incentives and Financial and Nonfinancial Measurements

What affects the intensity of incentives? That is, how large should the incentive component of a manager's compensation be relative to the salary component? To answer these questions, we need to understand how much the performance measure is affected by actions the manager takes to further the owner's objectives.

Preferred performance measures are those that are sensitive to or that change significantly with the manager's performance. They do not change much with changes in factors that are beyond the manager's control. Sensitive performance measures motivate the manager as well as limit the manager's exposure to risk, reducing the cost of providing incentives. Less-sensitive performance measures are not affected by the manager's performance and fail to induce the manager to improve. The more that owners have sensitive performance measures available to them, the more they can rely on incentive compensation for their managers.

The salary component of compensation dominates when performance measures that are sensitive to managers' actions are not available. This is the case, for example, for some corporate staff and government employees. A high salary component, however, does not mean incentives are completely absent. Promotions and salary increases do depend on some overall measure of performance, but the incentives are less direct. The incentive component of compensation is high when sensitive performance measures are available and when monitoring the employee's effort is difficult, such as in real estate agencies.

In evaluating Brett, Fonda uses measures from multiple perspectives of the balanced scorecard because nonfinancial measures on the balanced scorecard—employee satisfaction and the time taken for check-in, cleaning rooms, and providing room service—are more sensitive to Brett's actions. Financial measures such as RI are less sensitive to Brett's actions because they are affected by external factors such as local economic conditions beyond Brett's control. Residual income may be a very good measure of the economic viability of the hotel, but it is only a partial measure of Brett's performance.

Another reason for using nonfinancial measures in the balanced scorecard is that these measures follow Hospitality Inns' strategy and are drivers of future performance. Evaluating managers on these nonfinancial measures motivates them to take actions that will sustain long-run performance. Therefore, evaluating performance in all four perspectives of the balanced scorecard promotes both short- and long-run actions.

---

[11] The term *moral hazard* originated in insurance contracts to represent situations in which insurance coverage caused insured parties to take less care of their properties than they might otherwise. One response to moral hazard in insurance contracts is the system of deductibles (that is, the insured parties pay for damages below a specified amount).

Benchmarks and Relative Performance Evaluation

Owners often use financial and nonfinancial benchmarks to evaluate performance. Benchmarks representing "best practice" may be available inside or outside an organization. For HISF, benchmarks could be from similar hotels, either within or outside the Hospitality Inns chain. Suppose Brett has responsibility for revenues, costs, and investments. In evaluating Brett's performance, Fonda would want to use as a benchmark a hotel of a similar size influenced by the same uncontrollable factors, such as location, demographic trends, or economic conditions, that affect HISF. If all these factors were the same, *differences* in performances of the two hotels would occur only because of differences in the two managers' performances. Benchmarking, which is also called *relative performance evaluation*, filters out the effects of the common uncontrollable factors.

Can the performance of two managers responsible for running similar operations within a company be benchmarked against each other? Yes, but this approach could create a problem: The use of these benchmarks may reduce incentives for these managers to help one another, because a manager's performance-evaluation measure improves either by doing a better job or as a result of the other manager doing poorly. When managers do not cooperate, the company suffers. In this case, using internal benchmarks for performance evaluation may not lead to goal congruence.

Performance Measures at the Individual Activity Level

There are two issues when evaluating performance at the individual-activity level:

1. Designing performance measures for activities that require multiple tasks
2. Designing performance measures for activities done in teams

Performing Multiple Tasks

Most employees perform more than one task as part of their jobs. Marketing representatives sell products, provide customer support, and gather market information. Manufacturing workers are responsible for both the quantity and quality of their output. Employers want employees to allocate their time and effort intelligently among various tasks or aspects of their jobs.

Consider mechanics at an auto repair shop. Their jobs have two distinct aspects: repair work—performing more repair work generates more revenues for the shop—and customer satisfaction—the higher the quality of the job, the more likely the customer will be pleased. If the employer wants an employee to focus on both aspects, then the employer must measure and compensate performance on both aspects.

Suppose that the employer can easily measure the quantity, but not the quality, of auto repairs. If the employer rewards workers on a by-the-job rate, which pays workers only on the basis of the number of repairs actually performed, mechanics will likely increase the number of repairs they make and quality will likely suffer. Sears experienced this problem when it introduced by-the-job rates for its mechanics. To resolve the problem, Sears' managers took three steps to motivate workers to balance both quantity and quality: (1) They dropped the by-the-job rate system and paid mechanics an hourly salary, a step that deemphasized the quantity of repairs. Management determined mechanics' bonuses, promotions, and pay increases on the basis of an assessment of each mechanic's overall performance regarding quantity and quality of repairs. (2) Sears evaluated employees, in part, using data such as customer-satisfaction surveys, the number of dissatisfied customers, and the number of customer complaints. (3) Finally, Sears used staff from an independent outside agency to randomly monitor whether the repairs performed were of high quality.

Team-Based Compensation Arrangements

Many manufacturing, marketing, and design problems can be resolved when employees with multiple skills, knowledge, experiences, and perceptions pool their talents. A team achieves better results than individual employees acting alone.[12] Companies reward

---

[12] *Teams That Click: The Results-Driven Manager Series* (Boston: Harvard Business School Press, 2004).

individuals on a team based on team performance. Such team-based incentives encourage individuals to help one another as they strive toward a common goal.

The specific forms of team-based compensation vary across companies. Colgate-Palmolive rewards teams on the basis of each team's performance. Novartis, the Swiss pharmaceutical company, rewards teams on company-wide performance; a certain amount of team-based bonuses are paid only if the company reaches certain goals. To encourage the development of team skills, Eastman Chemical Company rewards team members using a checklist of team skills, such as communication and willingness to help one another. Whether team-based compensation is desirable depends, to a large extent, on the culture and management style of a particular organization. For example, one criticism of team-based compensation, especially in the United States, is that incentives for individual employees to excel are diminished, harming overall performance. Another problem is how to manage team members who are not productive contributors to the team's success but who, nevertheless, share in the team's rewards.

Executive Performance Measures and Compensation

The principles of performance evaluation described in the previous sections also apply to executive compensation plans. These plans are based on both financial and nonfinancial performance measures and consist of a mix of (1) base salary; (2) annual incentives, such as a cash bonus based on achieving a target annual RI; (3) long-run incentives, such as stock options (described later in this section) based on stock performance over, say, a five-year period; and (4) other benefits, such as medical benefits, pensions plans, and life insurance.

Well-designed plans use a compensation mix that balances risk (the effect of uncontrollable factors on the performance measure and hence compensation) with short-run and long-run incentives to achieve the organization's goals. For example, evaluating performance on the basis of annual EVA sharpens an executive's short-run focus. And using EVA and stock option plans over, say, five years motivates the executive to take a long-run view as well.

Stock options give executives the right to buy company stock at a specified price (called the exercise price) within a specified period. Suppose that on September 16, 2011, Hospitality Inns gave its CEO the option to buy 200,000 shares of the company's stock at any time before June 30, 2019, at the September 16, 2011, market price of $49 per share. Let's say Hospitality Inns' stock price rises to $69 per share on March 24, 2017, and the CEO exercises his options on all 200,000 shares. The CEO would earn $20 ($69 − $49) per share on 200,000 shares, or $4 million. If Hospitality Inns' stock price stays below $49 during the entire period, the CEO will simply forgo his right to buy the shares. By linking CEO compensation to increases in the company's stock price, the stock option plan motivates the CEO to improve the company's long-run performance and stock price. (See also the Concepts in Action feature.)[13]

The Securities and Exchange Commission (SEC) requires detailed disclosures of the compensation arrangements of top-level executives. In complying with these rules in 2010, Starwood Hotels and Resorts, for example, disclosed a compensation table showing the salaries, bonuses, stock options, other stock awards, and other compensation earned by its top five executives during the 2007, 2008, and 2009 fiscal years. Starwood, whose brands include Sheraton, Westin, and the W Hotels, also disclosed the peer companies that it uses to set executive pay and conduct performance comparisons. These include competitors in the hotel and hospitality industry (such as Host, Marriott, and Wyndham), as well as companies with similar revenues in other industries relevant to key talent recruitment needs (including Colgate-Palmolive, Nike, and Starbucks). Investors use this information to evaluate the relationship between compensation and performance across companies generally, and across companies operating in similar industries.

---

[13] Although stock options can improve incentives by linking CEO pay to improvements in stock price, they have been criticized for promoting improper or illegal activities by CEOs to increase the options' value. See J. Fox, "Sleazy CEOs Have Even More Options Tricks," www.money.cnn.com/2006/11/13/magazines/fortune/options_scandals.fortune/index.htm (accessed September 5, 2007).

Concepts in Action

Government Bailouts, Record Profits, and the 2009 Wall Street Compensation Dilemma

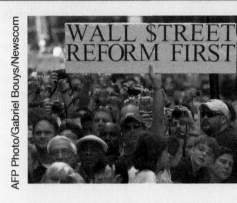

Wall Street firms paid out near-record bonuses to their employees for 2009 and many in the public were furious, given Wall Street's role in triggering the recent economic crisis. After losing $42.8 billion in 2008 and requiring a government bailout, Wall Street firms recorded $55 billion in 2009 profits, a sum nearly three times greater than the previous record. These results begged a serious question for managers at Goldman Sachs, Morgan Stanley, JPMorgan Chase, and leading financial institutions: After requiring public support just a year earlier, just how big should bankers' paydays be?

Highly paid executives on Wall Street are virtually always investment bankers or the top executives of the firms that employ them. Wall Street firms traditionally paid their investment bankers a share of the total revenue garnered by their unit. While this system worked in previous years, many argued it led to bankers taking the excessive risks that pushed the U.S. financial system to the brink of collapse.

Moreover, 2008 Wall Street bonuses infuriated the public. Just months after government intervention totaling $700 billion, the largest Wall Street banks paid out $56.9 billion in bonuses, or 45.4% of their 2008 revenues. As a result, President Barack Obama laid out strict new regulations on compensation for the 100 highest-paid employees at firms that the government deemed "exceptional assistance recipients" (i.e., firms receiving the largest bailouts). Further, there is little question that without the government intervening to save the financial sector in late 2008, the investment banks would have had a much worse year in 2009. This created a difficult situation for the banks. As one observer noted, "It is fair to say that some of the pay schemes promoted bad behavior and led to excessive risk, but you still need some sort of short-term incentive" for good performance, which Wall Street produced in 2009.

Wall Street firms tried to find some middle ground in 2009 by reducing bonus pools, or the amount of revenues allocated to bonuses, and introducing more long-term compensation into the bonus mix. At Goldman Sachs, for example, top executives received no cash bonuses in 2009, and instead received shares in the company that must be held for five years. For investment bankers and other employees, the company reduced its bonus pool to 36% of company revenue (down from 44% in 2008) and increased the stock-to-cash compensation ratio. Despite these changes, the average Wall Street bonus jumped 25% in 2009 to $123,850. At Goldman Sachs, where profits hit an all-time high, employees made an average of $500,000 each in 2009, including salary and bonus.

While many observers lauded the movement towards having a higher-percentage of bonuses be deferred, the size of 2009 Wall Street bonuses outraged others and ensured that investment banker compensation will remain a hot-button issue on Wall Street, Main Street, and in Washington, DC, for many years to come.

Source: Corkery, Michael. 2009. Goldman bows to pressure, makes changes to compensation. *Wall Street Journal* "Deal Journal," blog December 10; Elliott, Douglas J. 2010. *Wall Street Pay: A Primer.* Washington, DC: The Brookings Institution; Gandel, Stephen. 2009. Wall Street, meet Ken Feinberg, the pay czar. *Time,* November 2; Phillips, Matt. 2010. Goldman: Employees don't mind record low pay ratios. *Wall Street Journal.* "MarketBeat," blog February 3; Shell, Adam. 2010. Despite recession, average Wall Street bonus leaps 25%. *USA,* February 24; *Wall Street Journal.* 2010. The easy guide to Wall Street pay and bonuses. January 20; Weisman, Jonathan and Joanna S. Lublin. 2009. Obama lays out limits on executive pay. *Wall Street Journal,* February 5.

The SEC rules also require companies to disclose the principles underlying their executive compensation plans and the performance criteria—such as profitability, revenue growth, and market share—used in determining compensation. In its financial statements, Starwood described some of these principles as promoting the company's competitive position, providing a balanced approach to incentivizing and retaining employees, and aligning senior management's interests with those of shareholders. Starwood uses earnings per share and EBITDA as performance criteria to determine annual incentives for all of its executives. In addition, each executive has an individual scorecard of financial and nonfinancial performance measures. The company's board of directors creates the overall strategic direction of the company. Individual and strategic goals for executives are then established to support the overall company goals but are tailored to each executive's area of control.

Decision Point

Why are managers compensated based on a mix of salary and incentives?

Strategy and Levers of Control[14]

Given the management accounting focus of this book, this chapter has emphasized the role of quantitative financial and nonfinancial performance-evaluation measures that companies use to implement their strategies. These measures, such as ROI, RI, EVA, customer satisfaction, and employee satisfaction, monitor critical performance variables that help managers track progress toward achieving a company's strategic goals. Because these measures help diagnose whether a company is performing to expectations, they are collectively called **diagnostic control systems**. Companies motivate managers to achieve goals by holding them accountable for and by rewarding them for meeting these goals. The concern, however, is that the pressure to perform may cause managers to cut corners and misreport numbers to make their performance look better than it is, as happened at companies such as Enron, WorldCom, Tyco, and Health South. To prevent unethical and outright fraudulent behavior, companies need to balance the push for performance resulting from diagnostic control systems, the first of four levers of control, with three other levers: *boundary systems*, *belief systems*, and *interactive control systems*.

Boundary Systems

Boundary systems describe standards of behavior and codes of conduct expected of all employees, especially actions that are off-limits. Ethical behavior on the part of managers is paramount. In particular, numbers that subunit managers report should not be tainted by "cooking the books." They should be free of, for example, overstated assets, understated liabilities, fictitious revenues, and understated costs.

Codes of business conduct signal appropriate and inappropriate individual behaviors. The following are excerpts from Caterpillar's "Worldwide Code of Conduct":

> *While we conduct our business within the framework of applicable laws and regulations, for us, mere compliance with the law is not enough. We strive for more than that. . . . We must not engage in activities that create, or even appear to create, conflict between our personal interests and the interests of the company.*

Division managers often cite enormous pressure from top management "to make the budget" as excuses or rationalizations for not adhering to legal or ethical accounting policies and procedures. A healthy amount of motivational pressure is desirable, as long as the "tone from the top" and the code of conduct simultaneously communicate the absolute need for all managers to behave ethically at all times. Managers should train employees to behave ethically. They should promptly and severely reprimand unethical conduct, regardless of the benefits that might accrue to the company from unethical actions. Some companies, such as Lockheed-Martin, emphasize ethical behavior by routinely evaluating employees against a business code of ethics.

Many organizations also set explicit boundaries precluding actions that harm the environment. Environmental violations (such as water and air pollution) carry heavy fines and prison terms under the laws of the United States and other countries. But in many companies, environmental responsibilities extend beyond legal requirements.

Socially responsible companies set aggressive environmental goals and measure and report their performance against them. German, Swiss, Dutch, and Scandinavian companies report on environmental performance as part of a larger set of social responsibility disclosures (such as employee welfare and community development activities). Some companies, such as DuPont, make environmental performance a line item on every employee's salary appraisal report. Duke Power Company appraises employees on their performance in reducing solid waste, cutting emissions and discharges, and implementing environmental plans. The result? Duke Power has met all of its environmental goals.

---

[14]For a more-detailed discussion see R. Simons, *Levers of Control: How Managers Use Innovative Control Systems to Drive Strategic Renewal* (Boston: Harvard Business School Press, 1995).

Belief Systems

Belief systems articulate the mission, purpose, and core values of a company. They describe the accepted norms and patterns of behavior expected of all managers and other employees with respect to one another, shareholders, customers, and communities. For example, Johnson & Johnson describes its values and norms in a credo statement that is intended to inspire all managers and other employees to do their best.[15] Belief systems play to employees' *intrinsic motivation*, the desire to achieve self-satisfaction from good performance regardless of external rewards such as bonuses or promotion. Intrinsic motivation comes from being given greater responsibility, doing interesting and creative work, having pride in doing that work, establishing commitment to the organization, and developing personal bonds with coworkers. High intrinsic motivation enhances performance because managers and workers have a sense of achievement in doing something important, feel satisfied with their jobs, and see opportunities for personal growth.

Interactive Control Systems

Interactive control systems are formal information systems that managers use to focus the company's attention and learning on key strategic issues. Managers use interactive control systems to create an ongoing dialogue around these key issues and to personally involve themselves in subordinates' decision-making activities. An excessive focus on diagnostic control systems and critical performance variables can cause an organization to ignore emerging threats and opportunities—changes in technology, customer preferences, regulations, and industry competition that can undercut a business. Interactive control systems help prevent this problem by highlighting and tracking strategic uncertainties that businesses face, such as the emergence of digital imaging in the case of Kodak and Fujifilm, airline deregulation in the case of American Airlines, and the shift in customer preferences for mini- and microcomputers in the case of IBM. The key to this control lever is frequent face-to-face communications regarding these critical uncertainties. The result is ongoing discussion and debate about assumptions and action plans. New strategies emerge from the dialogue and debate surrounding the interactive process. Interactive control systems force busy managers to step back from the actions needed to manage the business today and to shift their focus forward to positioning the organization for the opportunities and threats of tomorrow.

Measuring and rewarding managers for achieving critical performance variables is an important driver of corporate performance. But these diagnostic control systems must be counterbalanced by the other levers of control, boundary systems, belief systems, and interactive control systems, to ensure that proper business ethics, inspirational values, and attention to future threats and opportunities are not sacrificed while achieving business results.

◀ **Decision Point**

What are the four levers of control, and why does a company need to implement them?

Problems for Self-Study

The baseball division of Home Run Sports manufactures and sells baseballs. Assume production equals sales. Budgeted data for February 2011 are as follows:

Current assets	$ 400,000
Long-term assets	600,000
Total assets	$1,000,000
Production output	200,000 baseballs per month
Target ROI (Operating income ÷ Total assets)	30%
Fixed costs	$400,000 per month
Variable cost	$4 per baseball

1. Compute the minimum selling price per baseball necessary to achieve the target ROI of 30%. **Required**

---

[15]A full statement of the credo can be accessed at www.jnj.com/connect/about-jnj/jnj-credo/.

2. Using the selling price from requirement 1, separate the target ROI into its two components using the DuPont method.

3. Compute the RI of the baseball division for February 2011, using the selling price from requirement 1. Home Run Sports uses a required rate of return of 12% on total division assets when computing division RI.

4. In addition to her salary, Pamela Stephenson, the division manager, receives 3% of the monthly RI of the baseball division as a bonus. Compute Stephenson's bonus. Why do you think Stephenson is rewarded using both salary and a performance-based bonus? Stephenson does not like bearing risk.

Solution

1.

$$\text{Target operating income} = 30\% \text{ of } \$1,000,000 \text{ of total assets}$$
$$= \$300,000$$
$$\text{Let } P = \text{Selling price}$$
$$\text{Revenues} - \text{Variable costs} - \text{Fixed costs} = \text{Operating income}$$
$$200,000P - (200,000 \times \$4) - \$400,000 = \$300,000$$
$$200,000P = \$300,000 + \$800,000 + \$400,000$$
$$= \$1,500,000$$
$$P = \$7.50 \text{ per baseball}$$

Proof:		
Revenues, 200,000 baseballs $\times$ \$7.50/baseball		\$1,500,000
Variable costs, 200,000 baseballs $\times$ \$4/baseball		800,000
Contribution margin		700,000
Fixed costs		400,000
Operating income		\$ 300,000

2. The DuPont method describes ROI as the product of two components: return on sales (income ÷ revenues) and investment turnover (revenues ÷ investment).

$$\frac{\text{Income}}{\text{Revenues}} \times \frac{\text{Revenues}}{\text{Investment}} = \frac{\text{Income}}{\text{Investment}}$$

$$\frac{\$300,000}{\$1,500,000} \times \frac{\$1,500,000}{\$1,000,000} = \frac{\$300,000}{\$1,000,000}$$

$$0.2 \times 1.5 = 0.30, \text{ or } 30\%$$

3. $RI = \text{Operating income} - \text{Required return on investment}$
   $= \$300,000 - (0.12 \times \$1,000,000)$
   $= \$300,000 - \$120,000$
   $= \$180,000$

4. Stephensons bonus $= 3\%$ of RI
   $= 0.03 \times \$180,000 = \$5,400$

The baseball division's RI is affected by many factors, such as general economic conditions, beyond Stephenson's control. These uncontrollable factors make the baseball division's profitability uncertain and risky. Because Stephenson does not like bearing risk, paying her a flat salary, regardless of RI, would shield her from this risk. But there is a moral-hazard problem with this compensation arrangement. Because Stephenson's effort is difficult to monitor, the absence of performance-based compensation will provide her with no incentive to undertake extra physical and mental effort beyond what is necessary to retain her job or to uphold her personal values.

Paying no salary and rewarding Stephenson only on the basis of RI provides her with incentives to work hard but also subjects her to excessive risk because of uncontrollable factors that will affect RI and hence Stephenson's compensation. A compensation arrangement based only on RI would be more costly for Home Run Sports because it would have to compensate Stephenson for taking on uncontrollable risk. A compensation arrangement that consists of both a salary and an RI-based performance bonus balances the benefits of incentives against the extra costs of imposing uncontrollable risk

Decision Points

The following question-and-answer format summarizes the chapter's learning objectives. Each decision presents a key question related to a learning objective. The guidelines are the answer to that question.

Decision	Guidelines
1. What financial and nonfinancial performance measures do companies use in their balanced scorecards?	Financial measures such as return on investment and residual income measure aspects of both manager performance and organization-subunit performance. In many cases, financial measures are supplemented with nonfinancial measures of performance from the customer, internal-business-process, and learning-and-growth perspectives of the balanced scorecard—for example, customer-satisfaction, quality of products and services, and employee satisfaction.
2. What are the relative merits of return on investment (ROI), residual income (RI), and economic-value added (EVA) as performance measures for subunit managers?	Return on investment (ROI) is the product of two components: income divided by revenues (return on sales) and revenues divided by investment (investment turnover). Managers can increase ROI by increasing revenues, decreasing costs, and decreasing investment. But, ROI may induce managers of highly profitable divisions to reject projects that are in the firm's best interest because accepting the project reduces divisional ROI.
	Residual income (RI) is income minus a dollar amount of required return on investment. RI is more likely than ROI to promote goal congruence. Evaluating managers on RI is also consistent with the use of discounted cash flow to choose long-term projects.
	Economic value added (EVA) is a variation of the RI calculation. It equals after-tax operating income minus the product of (after-tax) weighted-average cost of capital and total assets minus current liabilities.
3. Over what timeframe should companies measure performance, and what are the alternative choices for calculating the components of each performance measure?	A multiyear perspective induces managers to consider the long-term consequences of their actions and prevents a myopic focus on short-run profits. When constructing accounting-based performance measures, firms must first decide on a definition of investment. They must also choose whether assets included in the investment calculations are measured at historical cost or current cost, and whether depreciable assets are calculated at gross or net book value.
4. What targets should companies use and when should they give feedback to managers regarding their performance relative to these targets?	Companies should tailor a budget to a particular subunit, a particular accounting system, and a particular performance measure. In general, problems of asset valuation and income measurement in a performance measure can be overcome by emphasizing budgets and targets that stress continuous improvement. Timely feedback is critical to enable managers to implement actions that correct deviations from target performance.
5. How can companies compare the performance of divisions operating in different countries?	Comparing the performance of divisions operating in different countries is difficult because of legal, political, social, economic, and currency differences. ROI and RI calculations for subunits operating in different countries need to be adjusted for differences in inflation between the two countries and changes in exchange rates.
6. Why are managers compensated based on a mix of salary and incentives?	Companies create incentives by rewarding managers on the basis of performance. But managers face risks because factors beyond their control may also affect their performance. Owners choose a mix of salary and incentive compensation to trade off the incentive benefit against the cost of imposing risk.
7. What are the four levers of control, and why does a company need to implement them?	The four levers of control are diagnostic control systems, boundary systems, belief systems, and interactive control systems. Implementing the four levers of control helps a company simultaneously strive for performance, behave ethically, inspire employees, and respond to strategic threats and opportunities.

Terms to Learn

This chapter contains definitions of the following important terms:

belief systems

boundary systems

current cost

diagnostic control systems

economic value added (EVA®)

imputed cost

interactive control systems

investment

moral hazard

residual income (RI)

return on investment (ROI)

Assignment Material

MyAccountingLab

Questions

23-1 Give examples of financial and nonfinancial performance measures that can be found in each of the four perspectives of the balanced scorecard.

23-2 What are the three steps in designing accounting-based performance measures?

23-3 What factors affecting ROI does the DuPont method of profitability analysis highlight?

23-4 "RI is not identical to ROI, although both measures incorporate income and investment into their computations." Do you agree? Explain.

23-5 Describe EVA.

23-6 Give three definitions of investment used in practice when computing ROI.

23-7 Distinguish between measuring assets based on current cost and historical cost.

23-8 What special problems arise when evaluating performance in multinational companies?

23-9 Why is it important to distinguish between the performance of a manager and the performance of the organization subunit for which the manager is responsible? Give an example.

23-10 Describe moral hazard.

23-11 "Managers should be rewarded only on the basis of their performance measures. They should be paid no salary." Do you agree? Explain.

23-12 Explain the role of benchmarking in evaluating managers.

23-13 Explain the incentive problems that can arise when employees must perform multiple tasks as part of their jobs.

23-14 Describe two disclosures required by the SEC with respect to executive compensation.

23-15 Describe the four levers of control.

MyAccountingLab

Exercises

23-16 ROI, comparisons of three companies. (CMA, adapted) Return on investment (ROI) is often expressed as follows:

$$\frac{\text{Income}}{\text{Investment}} = \frac{\text{Income}}{\text{Revenues}} \times \frac{\text{Revenues}}{\text{Investment}}$$

Required

1. What advantages are there in the breakdown of the computation into two separate components?
2. Fill in the following blanks:

	Companies in Same Industry		
	A	B	C
Revenues	$1,000,000	$500,000	?
Income	$ 100,000	$ 50,000	?
Investment	$ 500,000	?	$5,000,000
Income as a percentage of revenues	?	?	0.5%
Investment turnover	?	?	2
ROI	?	1%	?

After filling in the blanks, comment on the relative performance of these companies as thoroughly as the data permit.

23-17 Analysis of return on invested assets, comparison of two divisions, DuPont method. Global Data, Inc., has two divisions: Test Preparation and Language Arts. Results (in millions) for the past three years are partially displayed here:

	A	B	C	D	E	F	G
		Operating Income	Operating Revenues	Total Assets	Operating Income/ Operating Revenues	Operating Income/ Revenues/ Total Assets	Operating Income/ Total Assets
1							
2	Test Preparation Division						
3	2011	$ 720	$ 9,000	$1,800	?	?	?
4	2012	920	?	?	11.5%	?	46%
5	2013	1,140	?	?	9.5%	6	?
6	Language Arts Division						
7	2011	$ 660	$ 3,000	$2,000	?	?	?
8	2012	?	3,525	2,350	20%	?	?
9	2013	?	?	2,900	?	1.6	20%
10	Global Data, Inc.						
11	2011	$1,380	$12,000	$3,800	?	?	?
12	2012	?	?	?	?	?	?
13	2013	?	?	?	?	?	?

1. Complete the table by filling in the blanks.
2. Use the DuPont method of profitability analysis to explain changes in the operating-income-to-total-assets ratios over the 2011–2013 period for each division and for Global Data as a whole. Comment on the results.

23-18 ROI and RI. (D. Kleespie, adapted) The Outdoor Sports Company produces a wide variety of outdoor sports equipment. Its newest division, Golf Technology, manufactures and sells a single product—AccuDriver, a golf club that uses global positioning satellite technology to improve the accuracy of golfers' shots. The demand for AccuDriver is relatively insensitive to price changes. The following data are available for Golf Technology, which is an investment center for Outdoor Sports:

Total annual fixed costs	$30,000,000
Variable cost per AccuDriver	$ 500
Number of AccuDrivers sold each year	150,000
Average operating assets invested in the division	$48,000,000

1. Compute Golf Technology's ROI if the selling price of AccuDrivers is $720 per club.
2. If management requires an ROI of at least 25% from the division, what is the minimum selling price that the Golf Technology Division should charge per AccuDriver club?
3. Assume that Outdoor Sports judges the performance of its investment centers on the basis of RI rather than ROI. What is the minimum selling price that Golf Technology should charge per AccuDriver if the company's required rate of return is 20%?

23-19 ROI and RI with manufacturing costs. Superior Motor Company makes electric cars and has only two products, the Simplegreen and the Superiorgreen. To produce the Simplegreen, Superior Motor employed assets of $13,500,000 at the beginning of the period, and $13,400,000 of assets at the end of the period. Other costs to manufacture the Simplegreen include the following:

Direct materials	$3,000 per unit
Setup	$1,300 per setup-hour
Production	$415 per machine-hour

General administration and selling costs total $7,340,000 for the period. In the current period, Superior Motor produced 10,000 Simplegreen cars using 6,000 setup-hours and 175,200 machine-hours. Superior Motor sold these cars for $12,000 each.

1. Assuming that Superior Motor defines investment as average assets during the period, what is the return on investment for the Simplegreen division?
2. Calculate the residual income for the Simplegreen if Superior Motor has a required rate of return of 12% on investments.

23-20 Financial and nonfinancial performance measures, goal congruencé. (CMA, adapted) Summit Equipment specializes in the manufacture of medical equipment, a field that has become increasingly competitive. Approximately two years ago, Ben Harrington, president of Summit, decided to revise the bonus plan (based, at the time, entirely on operating income) to encourage division managers to focus on areas that were important to customers and that added value without increasing cost. In addition to a profitability incentive, the revised plan includes incentives for reduced rework costs, reduced sales returns, and on-time deliveries. Bonuses are calculated and awarded semiannually on the following basis: A base bonus is calculated at 2% of operating income; this amount is then adjusted as follows:

a. (i) Reduced by excess of rework costs over and above 2% of operating income
   (ii) No adjustment if rework costs are less than or equal to 2% of operating income
b. (i) Increased by $5,000 if more than 98% of deliveries are on time, and by $2,000 if 96% to 98% of deliveries are on time
   (ii) No adjustment if on-time deliveries are below 96%
c. (i) Increased by $3,000 if sales returns are less than or equal to 1.5% of sales
   (ii) Decreased by 50% of excess of sales returns over 1.5% of sales

Note: If the calculation of the bonus results in a negative amount for a particular period, the manager simply receives no bonus, and the negative amount is not carried forward to the next period.

Results for Summit's Charter division and Mesa division for 2012, the first year under the new bonus plan, follow. In 2011, under the old bonus plan, the Charter division manager earned a bonus of $27,060 and the Mesa division manager, a bonus of $22,440.

	Charter Division		Mesa Division	
	January 1, 2012, to June 30, 2012	July 1, 2012, to Dec. 31, 2012	January 1, 2012, to June 30, 2012	July 1, 2012, to Dec. 31, 2012
Revenues	$4,200,000	$4,400,000	$2,850,000	$2,900,000
Operating income	$462,000	$440,000	$342,000	$406,000
On-time delivery	95.4%	97.3%	98.2%	94.6%
Rework costs	$11,500	$11,000	$6,000	$8,000
Sales returns	$84,000	$70,000	$44,750	$42,500

Required

1. Why did Harrington need to introduce these new performance measures? That is, why does Harrington need to use these performance measures in addition to the operating-income numbers for the period?
2. Calculate the bonus earned by each manager for each six-month period and for 2012.
3. What effect did the change in the bonus plan have on each manager's behavior? Did the new bonus plan achieve what Harrington desired? What changes, if any, would you make to the new bonus plan?

23-21 Goal incongruence and ROI. Bleefl Corporation manufactures furniture in several divisions, including the patio furniture division. The manager of the patio furniture division plans to retire in two years. The manager receives a bonus based on the division's ROI, which is currently 11%.

One of the machines that the patio furniture division uses to manufacture the furniture is rather old, and the manager must decide whether to replace it. The new machine would cost $30,000 and would last 10 years. It would have no salvage value. The old machine is fully depreciated and has no trade-in value. Bleefl uses straight-line depreciation for all assets. The new machine, being new and more efficient, would save the company $5,000 per year in cash operating costs. The only difference between cash flow and net income is depreciation. The internal rate of return of the project is approximately 11%. Bleefl Corporation's weighted average cost of capital is 6%. Bleefl is not subject to any income taxes.

Required

1. Should Bleefl Corporation replace the machine? Why or why not?
2. Assume that "investment" is defined as average net long-term assets after depreciation. Compute the project's ROI for each of its first five years. If the patio furniture manager is interested in maximizing his or her bonus, would the manager replace the machine before he or she retires? Why or why not?
3. What can Bleefl do to entice the manager to replace the machine before retiring?

23-22 ROI, RI, EVA. Performance Auto Company operates a new car division (that sells high performance sports cars) and a performance parts division (that sells performance improvement parts for family cars). Some division financial measures for 2011 are as follows:

	Home	Insert	Page Layout	Formulas	Data
		A	B	C	
1			New Car Division	Performance Parts Division	
2	Total assets		$33,000,000	$28,500,000	
3	Current liabilities		$ 6,600,000	$ 8,400,000	
4	Operating income		$ 2,475,000	$ 2,565,000	
5	Required rate of return		12%	12%	

1. Calculate return on investment (ROI) for each division using operating income as a measure of income and total assets as a measure of investment. Required
2. Calculate residual income (RI) for each division using operating income as a measure of income and total assets minus current liabilities as a measure of investment.
3. William Abraham, the New Car Division manager, argues that the performance parts division has "loaded up on a lot of short-term debt" to boost its RI. Calculate an alternative RI for each division that is not sensitive to the amount of short-term debt taken on by the performance parts division. Comment on the result.
4. Performance Auto Company, whose tax rate is 40%, has two sources of funds: long-term debt with a market value of $18,000,000 at an interest rate of 10%, and equity capital with a market value of $12,000,000 and a cost of equity of 15%. Applying the same weighted-average cost of capital (WACC) to each division, calculate EVA for each division.
5. Use your preceding calculations to comment on the relative performance of each division.

23-23 ROI, RI, measurement of assets. (CMA, adapted) Carter Corporation recently announced a bonus plan to be awarded to the manager of the most profitable division. The three division managers are to choose whether ROI or RI will be used to measure profitability. In addition, they must decide whether investment will be measured using gross book value or net book value of assets. Carter defines income as operating income and investment as total assets. The following information is available for the year just ended:

Division	Gross Book Value of Assets	Accumulated Depreciation	Operating Income
Radnor	$1,200,000	$645,000	$142,050
Easttown	1,140,000	615,000	137,550
Marion	750,000	420,000	92,100

Carter uses a required rate of return of 10% on investment to calculate RI.

Each division manager has selected a method of bonus calculation that ranks his or her division number one. Identify the method for calculating profitability that each manager selected, supporting your answer with appropriate calculations. Comment on the strengths and weaknesses of the methods chosen by each manager. Required

23-24 Multinational performance measurement, ROI, RI. The Seaside Corporation manufactures similar products in the United States and Norway. The U.S. and Norwegian operations are organized as decentralized divisions. The following information is available for 2012; ROI is calculated as operating income divided by total assets:

	U.S. Division	Norwegian Division
Operating income	?	6,840,000 kroner
Total assets	$7,500,000	72,000,000 kroner
ROI	9.3%	?

Both investments were made on December 31, 2011. The exchange rate at the time of Seaside's investment in Norway on December 31, 2011, was 9 kroner = $1. During 2012, the Norwegian kroner decreased steadily in value so that the exchange rate on December 31, 2012, is 10 kroner = $1. The average exchange rate during 2012 is [(9 + 10) ÷ 2] = 9.5 kroner = $1.

1a. Calculate the U.S. division's operating income for 2012. Required
 b. Calculate the Norwegian division's ROI for 2012 in kroner.
2. Top management wants to know which division earned a better ROI in 2012. What would you tell them? Explain your answer.
3. Which division do you think had the better RI performance? Explain your answer. The required rate of return on investment (calculated in U.S. dollars) is 8%.

23-25 ROI, RI, EVA and Performance Evaluation. Eva Manufacturing makes fashion products and competes on the basis of quality and leading-edge designs. The company has $3,000,000 invested in assets in its clothing manufacturing division. After-tax operating income from sales of clothing this year is $600,000. The cosmetics division has $10,000,000 invested in assets and an after-tax operating income this year of $1,600,000. Income for the clothing division has grown steadily over the last few years. The weighted-average cost of capital for Eva is 10% and the previous period's after-tax return on investment for each division was 15%. The CEO of Eva has told the manager of each division that the division that "performs best" this year will get a bonus.

1. Calculate the ROI and residual income for each division of Eva Manufacturing, and briefly explain which manager will get the bonus. What are the advantages and disadvantages of each measure? Required
2. The CEO of Eva Manufacturing has recently heard of another measure similar to residual income called EVA. The CEO has the accountant calculate EVA adjusted incomes of clothing and cosmetics, and finds that the adjusted after-tax operating incomes are $720,000 and $1,430,000, respectively. Also, the clothing division

has $400,000 of current liabilities, while the cosmetics division has only $200,000 of current liabilities. Using the preceding information, calculate EVA, and discuss which division manager will get the bonus.

3. What nonfinancial measures could Eva use to evaluate divisional performances?

23-26 Risk sharing, incentives, benchmarking, multiple tasks. The Dexter division of AMCO sells car batteries. AMCO's corporate management gives Dexter management considerable operating and investment autonomy in running the division. AMCO is considering how it should compensate Jim Marks, the general manager of the Dexter division. Proposal 1 calls for paying Marks a fixed salary. Proposal 2 calls for paying Marks no salary and compensating him only on the basis of the division's ROI, calculated based on operating income before any bonus payments. Proposal 3 calls for paying Marks some salary and some bonus based on ROI. Assume that Marks does not like bearing risk.

Required
1. Evaluate the three proposals, specifying the advantages and disadvantages of each.
2. Suppose that AMCO competes against Tiara Industries in the car battery business. Tiara is approximately the same size as the Dexter division and operates in a business environment that is similar to Dexter's. The top management of AMCO is considering evaluating Marks on the basis of Dexter's ROI minus Tiara's ROI. Marks complains that this approach is unfair because the performance of another company, over which he has no control, is included in his performance-evaluation measure. Is Marks' complaint valid? Why or why not?
3. Now suppose that Marks has no authority for making capital-investment decisions. Corporate management makes these decisions. Is ROI a good performance measure to use to evaluate Marks? Is ROI a good measure to evaluate the economic viability of the Dexter division? Explain.
4. Dexter's salespersons are responsible for selling and providing customer service and support. Sales are easy to measure. Although customer service is important to Dexter in the long run, it has not yet implemented customer-service measures. Marks wants to compensate his sales force only on the basis of sales commissions paid for each unit of product sold. He cites two advantages to this plan: (a) It creates strong incentives for the sales force to work hard, and (b) the company pays salespersons only when the company itself is earning revenues. Do you like his plan? Why or why not?

MyAccountingLab

Problems

23-27 Residual Income and EVA; timing issues. Doorchime Company makes doorbells. It has a weighted average cost of capital of 9%, and total assets of $5,550,000. Doorchime has current liabilities of $800,000. Its operating income for the year was $630,000. Doorchime does not have to pay any income taxes. One of the expenses for accounting purposes was a $90,000 advertising campaign. The entire amount was deducted this year, although the Doorchime CEO believes the beneficial effects of this advertising will last four years.

Required
1. Calculate residual income, assuming Doorchime defines investment as total assets.
2. Calculate EVA for the year. Adjust both the assets and operating income for advertising assuming that for the purposes of economic value added the advertising is capitalized and amortized on a straight-line basis over four years.
3. Discuss the difference between the outcomes of requirements 1 and 2 and which measure is preferred.

23-28 ROI performance measures based on historical cost and current cost. Nature's Elixir Corporation operates three divisions that process and bottle natural fruit juices. The historical-cost accounting system reports the following information for 2011:

	Passion Fruit Division	Kiwi Fruit Division	Mango Fruit Division
Revenues	$1,000,000	$1,400,000	$2,200,000
Operating costs			
(excluding plant depreciation)	600,000	760,000	1,200,000
Plant depreciation	140,000	200,000	240,000
Operating income	$ 260,000	$ 440,000	$ 760,000
Current assets	$ 400,000	$ 500,000	$ 600,000
Long-term assets—plant	280,000	1,800,000	2,640,000
Total assets	$ 680,000	$2,300,000	$3,240,000

Nature's Elixir estimates the useful life of each plant to be 12 years, with no terminal disposal value. The straight-line depreciation method is used. At the end of 2011, the passion fruit plant is 10 years old, the kiwi fruit plant is 3 years old, and the mango fruit plant is 1 year old. An index of construction costs over the 10-year period that Nature's Elixir has been operating (2001 year-end = 100) is as follows:

2001	2008	2010	2011
100	136	160	170

Given the high turnover of current assets, management believes that the historical-cost and current-cost measures of current assets are approximately the same.

1. Compute the ROI ratio (operating income to total assets) of each division using historical-cost measures. Comment on the results.
2. Use the approach in Exhibit 2 to compute the ROI of each division, incorporating current-cost estimates as of 2011 for depreciation expense and long-term assets. Comment on the results.
3. What advantages might arise from using current-cost asset measures as compared with historical-cost measures for evaluating the performance of the managers of the three divisions?

23-29 ROI, measurement alternatives for performance measures P. F. Skidaddle's operates casual dining restaurants in three regions: Denver, Seattle, and Sacramento. Each geographic market is considered a separate division. The Denver division is made up of four restaurants, each built in early 2002. The Seattle division is made up of three restaurants, each built in January 2006. The Sacramento division is the newest, consisting of three restaurants built four years ago. Division managers at P. F. Skidaddle's are evaluated on the basis of ROI. The following information refers to the three divisions at the end of 2012:

	Home Insert Page Layout Formulas Data Review View				
	A	B	C	D	E
1		Denver	Seattle	Sacramento	Total
2	Division revenues	$8,365,000	$6,025,000	$5,445,000	$20,138,000
3	Division expenses	7,945,000	5,521,000	4,979,000	18,445,000
4	Division operating income	723,000	504,000	466,000	1,693,000
5	Gross book value of long-term assets	4,750,000	3,750,000	4,050,000	12,300,000
6	Accumulated depreciation	3,300,000	1,750,000	1,080,000	6,130,000
7	Current assets	999,800	768,200	824,600	2,592,600
8	Depreciation expense	300,000	250,000	270,000	820,000
9	Construction cost index for year of construction	100	110	118	

Required

1. Calculate ROI for each division using net book value of total assets.
2. Using the technique in Exhibit 2, compute ROI using current-cost estimates for long-term assets and depreciation expense. Construction cost index for 2012 is 122. Estimated useful life of operational assets is 15 years.
3. How does the choice of long-term asset valuation affect management decisions regarding new capital investments? Why might this be more significant to the Denver division manager than to the Sacramento division manager?

23-30 ROI, RI, and Multinational Firms. Konekopf Corporation has a division in the United States, and another in France. The investment in the French assets was made when the exchange rate was $1.30 per euro. The average exchange rate for the year was $1.40 per euro. The exchange rate at the end of the fiscal year was $1.45 per euro. Income and investment for the two divisions are as follows:

	United States	France
Investment in assets	$5,450,000	3,800,000 euro
Income for current year	$ 681,250	486,400 euro

Required

1. The required return for Konekopf is 12%. Calculate ROI and RI for the two divisions. For the French division, calculate these measures using both dollars and euro. Which division is doing better?
2. What are the advantages and disadvantages of translating the French division information from euro to dollars?

23-31 Multinational firms, differing risk, comparison of profit, ROI and RI. Zynga Multinational, Inc., has divisions in the United States, Germany, and New Zealand. The U.S. division is the oldest and most established of the three, and has a cost of capital of 8%. The German division was started three years ago when the exchange rate for euro was 1 euro = $1.25. It is a large and powerful division of Zynga, Inc., with a cost of capital of 12%. The New Zealand division was started this year, when the exchange rate was 1 New Zealand Dollar (NZD) = $0.60. Its cost of capital is 14%. Average exchange rates for the current year are 1 euro = $1.40 and 1 NZD = $0.64. Other information for the three divisions includes the following:

	United States	Germany	New Zealand
Long term assets	$23,246,112	11,939,200 euro	9,400,000 NZD
Operating revenues	$13,362,940	5,250,000 euros	4,718,750 NZD
Operating expenses	$ 8,520,000	3,200,000 euros	3,250,000 NZD
Income tax rate	40%	35%	25%

Required

1. Translate the German and New Zealand information into dollars to make the divisions comparable. Find the after-tax operating income for each division and compare the profits.
2. Calculate ROI using after-tax operating income. Compare among divisions.
3. Use after-tax operating income and the individual cost of capital of each division to calculate residual income and compare.
4. Redo requirement 2 using pretax operating income instead of net income. Why is there a big difference, and what does it mean for performance evaluation?

23-32 ROI, RI, DuPont method, investment decisions, balanced scorecard. Global Event Group has two major divisions: print and Internet. Summary financial data (in millions) for 2011 and 2012 are as follows:

	Home	Insert	Page Layout	Formulas	Data	Review	View		
	A	B	C	D	E	F	G	H	I
1		Operating Income			Revenues			Total Assets	
2		2011	2012		2011	2012		2011	2012
3	Print	$3,740	$6,120		$18,300	$20,400		$18,650	$24,000
4	Internet	565	780		25,900	30,000		11,200	12,000

The two division managers' annual bonuses are based on division ROI (defined as operating income divided by total assets). If a division reports an increase in ROI from the previous year, its management is automatically eligible for a bonus; however, the management of a division reporting a decline in ROI has to present an explanation to the Global Event Group board and is unlikely to get any bonus.

Carol Mays, manager of the print division, is considering a proposal to invest $960 million in a new computerized news reporting and printing system. It is estimated that the new system's state-of-the-art graphics and ability to quickly incorporate late-breaking news into papers will increase 2013 division operating income by $144 million. Global Event Group uses a 12% required rate of return on investment for each division.

Required

1. Use the DuPont method of profitability analysis to explain differences in 2012 ROIs between the two divisions. Use 2012 total assets as the investment base.
2. Why might Mays be less than enthusiastic about accepting the investment proposal for the new system, despite her belief in the benefits of the new technology?
3. Chris Moreno, CEO of Global Event Group, is considering a proposal to base division executive compensation on division RI.
   a. Compute the 2012 RI of each division.
   b. Would adoption of an RI measure reduce Mays' reluctance to adopt the new computerized system investment proposal?
4. Moreno is concerned that the focus on annual ROI could have an adverse long-run effect on Global Event Group's customers. What other measurements, if any, do you recommend that Moreno use? Explain briefly.

23-33 Division managers' compensation, levers of control (continuation of 23-32). Chris Moreno seeks your advice on revising the existing bonus plan for division managers of Global Event Group. Assume division managers do not like bearing risk. Moreno is considering three ideas:

- Make each division manager's compensation depend on division RI.
- Make each division manager's compensation depend on company-wide RI.
- Use benchmarking, and compensate division managers on the basis of their division's RI minus the RI of the other division.

Required

1. Evaluate the three ideas Moreno has put forth using performance-evaluation concepts described in this chapter. Indicate the positive and negative features of each proposal.
2. Moreno is concerned that the pressure for short-run performance may cause managers to cut corners. What systems might Moreno introduce to avoid this problem? Explain briefly.

3. Moreno is also concerned that the pressure for short-run performance might cause managers to ignore emerging threats and opportunities. What system might Moreno introduce to prevent this problem? Explain briefly.

23-34 Executive compensation, balanced scorecard. Community Bank recently introduced a new bonus plan for its business unit executives. The company believes that current profitability and customer satisfaction levels are equally important to the bank's long-term success. As a result, the new plan awards a bonus equal to 1% of salary for each 1% increase in business unit net income or 1% increase in the business unit's customer satisfaction index. For example, increasing net income from $3 million to $3.3 million (or 10% from its initial value) leads to a bonus of 10% of salary, while increasing the business unit's customer satisfaction index from 70 to 73.5 (or 5% from its initial value) leads to a bonus of 5% of salary. There is no bonus penalty when net income or customer satisfaction declines. In 2011 and 2012, Community Bank's three business units reported the following performance results:

	Retail Banking		Business Banking		Credit Cards	
	2011	2012	2011	2012	2011	2012
Net income	$2,600,000	$2,912,000	$2,800,000	$2,940,000	$2,550,000	$2,499,000
Customer satisfaction	74	75.48	69	75.9	68	78.88

Required

1. Compute the bonus as a percent of salary earned by each business unit executive in 2012.
2. What factors might explain the differences between improvement rates for net income and those for customer satisfaction in the three units? Are increases in customer satisfaction likely to result in increased net income right away?
3. Community Bank's board of directors is concerned that the 2012 bonus awards may not actually reflect the executives' overall performance. In particular, it is concerned that executives can earn large bonuses by doing well on one performance dimension but underperforming on the other. What changes can it make to the bonus plan to prevent this from happening in the future? Explain briefly.

23-35 Ethics, manager's performance evaluation. (A. Spero, adapted) Hamilton Semiconductors manufactures specialized chips that sell for $25 each. Hamilton's manufacturing costs consist of variable cost of $3 per chip and fixed costs of $8,000,000. Hamilton also incurs $900,000 in fixed marketing costs each year.

Hamilton calculates operating income using absorption costing—that is, Hamilton calculates manufacturing cost per unit by dividing total manufacturing costs by actual production. Hamilton costs all units in inventory at this rate and expenses the costs in the income statement at the time when the units in inventory are sold. Next year, 2012, appears to be a difficult year for Hamilton. It expects to sell only 400,000 units. The demand for these chips fluctuates considerably, so Hamilton usually holds minimal inventory.

Required

1. Calculate Hamilton's operating income in 2012 (a) if Hamilton manufactures 400,000 units and (b) if Hamilton manufactures 500,000 units.
2. Would it be unethical for Randy Jones, the general manager of Hamilton Semiconductors, to produce more units than can be sold in order to show better operating results? Jones' compensation has a bonus component based on operating income. Explain your answer.
3. Would it be unethical for Jones to ask distributors to buy more product than they need? Hamilton follows the industry practice of booking sales when products are shipped to distributors. Explain your answer.

23-36 Ethics, levers of control. Monroe Moulding is a large manufacturer of wood picture frame moulding. The company operates distribution centers in Dallas and Philadelphia. The distribution centers cut frames to size (called "chops") and ship them to custom picture framers. Because of the exacting standards and natural flaws of wood picture frame moulding, the company typically produces a large amount of waste in cutting chops. In recent years, the company's average yield has been 76% of length moulding. The remaining 24% is sent to a wood recycler. Monroe's performance-evaluation system pays its distribution center managers substantial bonuses if the company achieves annual budgeted profit numbers. In the last quarter of 2010, Frank Jessup, Monroe's controller, noted a significant increase in yield percentage of the Dallas distribution center, from 74% to 85%. This increase resulted in a 5% increase in the center's profits.

During a recent trip to the Dallas center, Jessup wandered into the moulding warehouse. He noticed that much of the scrap moulding was being returned to the inventory bins rather than being placed in the discard pile. Upon further inspection, he determined that the moulding was in fact unusable. When he asked one of the workers, he was told that the center's manager had directed workers to stop scrapping all but the very shortest pieces. This practice resulted in the center over-reporting both yield and ending inventory. The overstatement of Dallas inventory will have a significant impact on Monroe's financial statements.

1. What should Jessup do? You may want to refer to the *IMA Statement of Ethical Professional Practice*.
2. Which lever of control is Monroe emphasizing? What changes, if any, should be made?

Collaborative Learning Problem

23-37 RI, EVA, Measurement alternatives, Goal congruence. Renewal Resorts, Inc., operates health spas in Ft. Meyers, Florida, Scottsdale, Arizona, and Monterey, California. The Ft. Meyers spa was the company's first, opened in 1986. The Scottsdale spa opened in 1999, and the Monterey spa opened in 2008. Renewal Resorts has previously evaluated divisions based on residual income (RI), but the company is considering changing to an economic value added (EVA) approach. All spas are assumed to face similar risks. Data for 2012 follow:

	A	B	C	D	E
		Ft. Meyers Spa	Scottsdale Spa	Monterey Spa	Total
2	Revenues	$4,100,000	$4,380,000	$3,230,000	$11,710,000
3	Variable costs	1,600,000	1,630,000	955,000	4,185,000
4	Fixed costs	1,280,000	1,560,000	980,000	3,820,000
5	Operating income	1,220,000	1,190,000	1,295,000	3,705,000
6	Interest costs on long-term debt at 8%	368,000	416,000	440,000	1,224,000
5	Income before taxes at 35%	852,000	774,000	855,000	2,481,000
6	Net income	553,800	503,100	555,750	1,612,650
7					
8	Net book value at 2012 year-end:				
9	Current assets	$1,280,000	$ 850,000	$ 600,000	$ 2,730,000
10	Long-term assets	4,875,000	5,462,000	6,835,000	17,172,000
11	Total assets	6,155,000	6,312,000	7,435,000	19,902,000
12	Current liabilities	330,000	265,000	84,000	679,000
13	Long-term debt	4,600,000	5,200,000	5,500,000	15,300,000
14	Stockholders' equity	1,225,000	847,000	1,851,000	3,923,000
15	Total liabilities and stockholders' equity	6,155,000	6,312,000	7,435,000	19,902,000
16					
17	Market value of debt	$4,600,000	$5,200,000	$5,500,000	$15,300,000
18	Market value of equity	2,400,000	2,660,000	2,590,000	7,650,000
19	Cost of equity capital				17%
20	Required rate of return				11%
21	Accumulated depreciation on long-term assets	2,200,000	1,510,000	220,000	

Required

1. Calculate RI for each of the spas based on operating income and using total assets as the measure of investment. Suppose that the Ft. Meyers spa is considering adding a new group of saunas from Finland that will cost $225,000. The saunas are expected to bring in operating income of $22,000. What effect would this project have on the RI of the Ft. Meyers spa? Based on RI, would the Ft. Meyers manager accept or reject this project? Why? Without resorting to calculations, would the other managers accept or reject the project? Why?
2. Why might Renewal Resorts want to use EVA instead of RI for evaluating the performance of the three spas?
3. Refer back to the original data. Calculate the WACC for Renewal Resorts.
4. Refer back to the original data. Calculate EVA for each of the spas, using net book value of long-term assets. Calculate EVA again, this time using gross book value of long-term assets. Comment on the differences between the two methods.
5. How is goal congruence affected by the selection of asset measurement method?

Index

Page references followed by "f" indicate illustrated figures or photographs; followed by "t" indicates a table.